McQuail's Mass Communication Theory

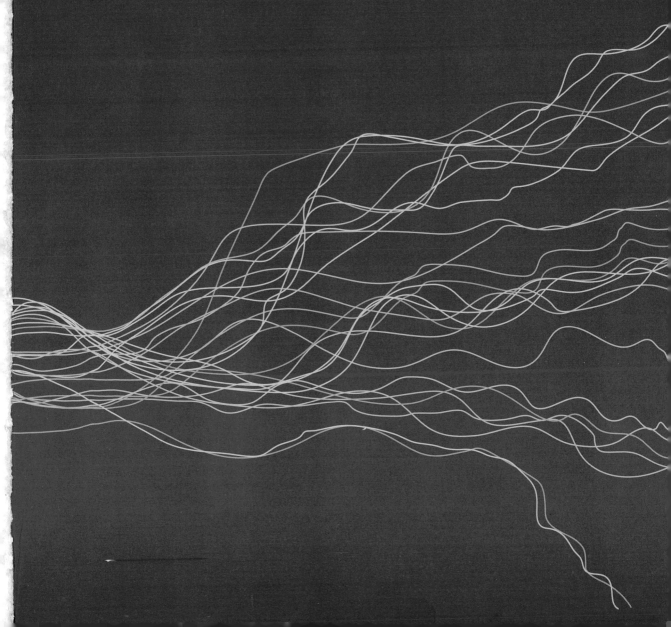

Dedicated to the future media audiences, especially:

Laurence, Alexander, William, Noah, Chaia, Alice, Miranda, Anarosa, and Ava, grand children all.

McQuail's Mass Communication Theory

WITHDRAWN

6th edition

Denis McQuail

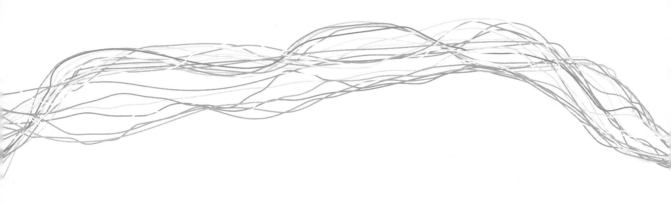

Los Angeles | London | New Delhi
Singapore | Washington DC

© Denis McQuail 1983, 1987, 1994, 2000, 2005, 2010

First edition published 1983
Second edition published 1987
Third edition published 1994
Fourth edition published 2000. Reprinted 2001, 2002, 2003, 2005
Fifth edition published 2005. Reprinted 2006, 2007, 2008, 2009
This sixth edition published 2010. Reprinted 2011

Apart from any fair dealing for the purposes of research or private
study, or criticism or review, as permitted under the Copyright,
Designs and Patents Act, 1988, this publication may be reproduced,
stored or transmitted in any form, or by any means, only with the prior
permission in writing of the publishers, or in the case of reprographic
reproduction, in accordance with the terms of licences issued by the
Copyright Licensing Agency. Enquiries concerning reproduction
outside those terms should be sent to the publishers.

SAGE Publications Ltd
1 Oliver's Yard
55 City Road
London EC1Y 1SP

SAGE Publications Inc.
2455 Teller Road
Thousand Oaks, California 91320

SAGE Publications India Pvt Ltd
B 1/I 1 Mohan Cooperative Industrial Area
Mathura Road
New Delhi 110 044

SAGE Publications Asia-Pacific Pte Ltd
3 Church Street
#10-04 Samsung Hub
Singapore 049483

Library of Congress Control Number: 2009932171

British Library Cataloguing in Publication data

A catalogue record for this book is available from
the British Library

ISBN 978-1-84920-291-6
ISBN 978-1-84920-292-3   (pbk)

Typeset by C&M Digitals (P) Ltd, Chennai, India
Printed and bound in Great Britain by Ashford Colour Press Ltd

Contents

Preface

This version is an updating and consolidation of the last edition, building with more confidence on the proposition that mass communication is evolving and becoming more complex rather than withering away. The earlier expectation of demise was based on the belief that the 'new media' of public communication that were appearing in the latter part of the 20th century would ultimately prove to be superior in all respects to the relatively crude forms of traditional 'mass media' (especially newspaper and television broadcasting). This supposition was itself out of step with the lessons of media history that has already demonstrated the power of different media forms to adapt and survive in new environments. It is now the turn of the traditional mass media to adapt to new technology under changing social, economic and cultural conditions. The persistence of mass communication as a process and the continued relevance of much of the accumulated theory and research stem, even so, from continuity in the kind and direction of dominant social forces, especially those that fall under the headings of globalization and modernization/development. In the same way that media of all kinds are converging, so also are theories of the new and old media converging.

Despite the expectation that mass communication will evolve and survive, the changes taking place to, and within, the spectrum of public communication media are fundamental, accelerating and open for all to see. They outpace the capacity of a book of this kind to keep pace with what is happening on the ground. But the purpose, as before, is not to chart media change, but to provide some relatively firm theoretical islands or platforms from which to observe and understand what is happening around us. The evidence for all this comes primarily from the continuing stream of findings of academic research in media and communication, which is itself always anchored in and directed by theory, but also rather slow to appear. The main changes made in this edition have been motivated by the aims of testing the continued relevance of old theory and of adding, where possible, to the stock of theory. Often it is reports about the effects and significance of new media that are most fruitful for the second purpose.

A process of revision of this kind depends not only on scanning and evaluating newly published theory and new empirical evidence. It also calls for continuing contact with others engaged in more active ways with the field of inquiry. I have been fortunate in having continued opportunities for exchange of ideas and for learning new things from colleagues, friends and students. I cannot repay all debts, but I would like to mention here some of the people, places and events that have been of particular help on the journey. I have been much helped, thanks to Karin Raeymackers, by ready access to the communication library of the University of Ghent, with its now rare collection of current and recent international journals. I have also appreciated regular contact with my co-editors and others associated with the *European Journal of Communication*, especially Els de Bens, Peter Golding and Liesbet van Zoonen. The periodic seminars organized by the *EJC* have been an important learning experience. A continuing link with the *Euromedia Research Group,* by participation in meetings and publication, has been another source of stimulation (too many names to name). Another recurring source of stimulation has been the chance to participate in the annual doctoral Summer School organized by the European Communication Research Association (ECREA) and held for the last five years at the University of Tartu, Estonia. I have benefited also from invitations to teach or give lectures at a number universities. Particular thanks are due in this respect to Prof. Takesato Watanabe at Doshisha University, Kyoto. I have similar debts to Helena Sousa, at the University of Minho, Potugal; Josef Trappel at the University of Zurich, Elena Vartanova at Moscow University Faculty of Journalism; Miquel de Moragas Spá at the Autonomous University of Barcelona; Miroljub Radoikovich, University of Belgrade; Konca Yumlu at Ege University, Izmir; Vita Zelče and Inta Brikše at the University of Latvia. Naming names is always a bit invidious and I have to omit many, but I will just mention my appreciation of renewed contact with my comrade-colleague of old, Jay Blumler, and last but not least my association with the self styled Soul Brothers, Cliff Christians, Ted Glasser, Bob White and Kaarle Nordenstreng, especially as our 'eternal' book on normative media theory has at last appeared. It is more than mere convention to say that the present book would not have appeared without the initiative, persistence and enthusiasm of Mila Steele, of Sage Publications. I hope it lives up to her high hopes. It is probably the last edition of this book, at my hand at least, but if mass communication endures so also will mass communication theory.

This Preface was written during a visit from young grandchildren who are already forming the future audience for mass media. For this reason I have dedicated the book to them all, borrowing an idea from Hanno Hardt. My last words of thanks are to my wife, Rosemary, for making so much possible.

Eastleigh, Hampshire, UK, November 2009

How to Use this Book

The text can best be used by readers as a resource for learning about a particular topic. There are several ways this can be approached. The table of contents provide an initial orientation, or map, to the book, and each chapter begins with a list of the main headings to help you orient yourself in the book. The subject index at the end of the book includes all key words and topics and can also be used for an initial search.

Each chapter contains boxes to help you explore the background, relevance and research on the themes and theories discussed in the book. Symbols beside the boxes help you navigate so you can quickly find summaries; review; name-check; and take it further with key quotes and additional information.

Theories: These boxes give a bullet-point outline to key theoretical propositions, helping consolidate your understanding of the essential themes and theories.

Information: These boxes supplement the discussion with essential addition information. Tables and lists give you extra information to help ground theory with empirical data.

Summaries: Use these as an easy reference to summarize many key themes and principles as you go along.

Quotations: Quotes from major thinkers and texts clarify and emphasize important principles and will help familiarize you with the some of the research literature on mass communication theory.

Questions: Key questions reflect in summary form the main divisions and points of debate in major issues of theory.

Research: Research examples will help you understand some of the ways in which theoretical questions can be answered empirically.

Further readings: An important aim of the book is to provide a guide to follow-up study. Each chapter ends with an annotated list of further readings to where the ground covered can be explored in more detail.

Online readings: all readings marked with a mouse can be accessed for free on the companion website (www.sagepub.co.uk/mcquail6). These articles examine issues and theories in detail and provide valuable links to other relevant sources.

Glossary: At the end of the book you will find a detailed glossary of all the key concepts defined in the book. Glossary terms are indicated in **bold** and with a star in the margin to help quick cross-referencing.

Part 1
Preliminaries

1

Introduction to the Book

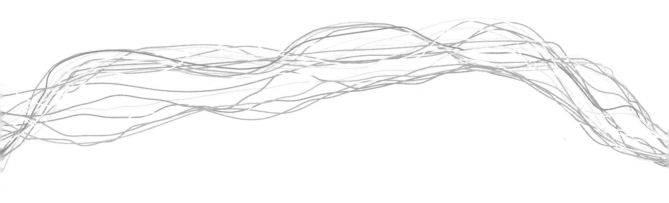

Our Object of Study

The term 'mass communication' was coined, along with that of 'mass media', early in the twentieth century to describe what was then a new social phenomenon and a key feature of the emerging modern world that was being built on the foundations of industrialism and popular democracy. It was an age of migration into cities and across frontiers and also of struggle between forces of change and repression and of conflict between empires and nation states. The mass media (a plural form) refer to the organized means of communicating openly, at a distance, and to many in a short space of time. They were born into the context and conflicts of this age of transition and have continued to be deeply implicated in the trends and changes of society and culture, as experienced at the personal level as well as that of society and the 'world system'.

The early mass media (newspapers, magazines, phonogram, cinema and radio) developed rapidly to reach formats that are still largely recognizable today, with changes mainly of scale and diversification as well as the addition of television in the mid-twentieth century. Similarly, what were regarded as the key features of mass communication seventy or more years ago are still foremost in our minds today: their capacity to reach the entire population rapidly and with much the same information, opinions and entertainment; the universal fascination they hold; their stimulation of hopes and fears in equal measure; the presumed relation to sources of power in society; the assumption of great impact and influence. There are, of course, many and continuing changes in the spectrum of available media and in many aspects of their content and form, and one purpose of this book is to chart and assess these changes.

At the outset, we need to recognize that mass communication as described is no longer the only means of society-wide (and global) communication. New technologies have been developed and taken up that constitute an alternative potential network of communication. Mass communication, in the sense of a large-scale, one-way flow of public content, continues unabated, but it is no longer carried only by the 'traditional' mass media. These have been supplemented by new media (especially the Internet and mobile technology) and new types of content and flow are carried at the same time. These differ mainly in being more extensive, less structured, often interactive as well as private and individualized.

Whatever changes are under way there is no doubting the continuing significance of mass media in contemporary society, in the spheres of politics, culture, everyday social life and economics. In respect of politics, the mass media provide an arena of debate and a set of channels for making policies, candidates, relevant facts and ideas more widely known as well as providing politicians, interest groups and agents of government with a means of publicity and influence. In the realm of culture, the mass media are for most people the main channel of cultural representation and expression, and the primary source of images of social reality and materials for forming and maintaining social identity. Everyday social life is strongly patterned by the routines of media use and infused by its contents through the way leisure time is spent, lifestyles are influenced, conversation is given its topics and models of behaviour are offered for all contingencies. Gradually, the media have grown in economic value, with ever larger and more international media corporations dominating the media market, with influence extending through sport, travel, leisure, food and clothing industries, and with interconnections with telecommunications and all information-based economic sectors.

For the reasons given, our focus on mass communication is not confined to the mass media, but relates to any aspect of that original process, irrespective of the technology or network involved, thus to all types and processes of communication that are extensive, public and technically mediated. Here the word 'public' means not only open to all receivers and to a recognized set of senders, but also relating to matters of information and culture that are of wide interest and concern in a society, without being addressed to any particular individual. There is no absolute line between what is private and public, but a broad distinction can usually be made. This book is designed to contribute to public scrutiny and understanding of mass communication in all its forms and to provide an overview of ideas and research, guided by the themes and issues summarized below.

The Structure of the Book

The contents are divided into twenty chapters, grouped according to eight headings. The first substantive part, 'Theories' (II), provides a grounding in the most basic and also the most general ideas about mass communication, with particular reference to the many relations that exist between media and social and cultural life. It starts with a brief historical review of the rise of mass media and follows with an explanation of alternative approaches to the study of mass media and society. The differences stem from varying perspectives on the media, the diversity of topics addressed, and the different ways of defining the issues and problems depending on the values of the observer. A subject of this kind cannot simply be studied 'objectively' by a single set of methods.

There are different kinds of theory, as explained later in this chapter, but most basically a theory is a general proposition, itself based on observation and logical argument, that states the relationship between observed phenomena and seeks either to explain or to predict the relation, in so far as this is possible. The main purpose of theory is to make sense of an observed reality and guide the collection and evaluation of evidence. A concept (see Chapter 3) is a core term in a theory that summarizes an important aspect of the problem under study and can be used in collecting and interpreting evidence. It requires careful definition. A model is a selective representation in verbal or diagrammatic form of some aspect of the dynamic process of mass communication. It can also describe the spatial and temporal relation between elements in a process.

The 'Theories' part deals separately with 'society' and 'culture', although the separation is artificial since one cannot exist without the other. But by convention, 'society' refers primarily to social relationships of all kinds, ranging from those of power and authority (government) to friendship and family relations as well as all material aspects of life. 'Culture' refers to ideas, beliefs, identity, symbolic expression of all kinds, including language, art, information and entertainment, plus customs and rituals. There are two other components. One relates to the norms and values that apply to the conduct of media organizations. Here theory deals with what media ought to be doing or not doing, rather than simply with why they do what they do. Not surprisingly, there are divergent views on this matter, especially given the strong claims that media make to freedom from regulation and control in the name of free speech and artistic expression and the strong public feelings that also exist about their responsibilities.

Secondly, this part deals with the consequences of media change for theory, especially because of the rise of new, interactive media, such as the Internet, that are 'mass media' in the sense of their availability, but are not really engaged in 'mass communication' as it has been earlier defined. Here the issue faced is whether 'new media' require new and different theory from that applying to 'mass communication' and whether mass communication is in decline.

The part entitled 'Structures' (III) deals with three main topics. First, it deals with the overall media system and the way it is typically organized at a national level. The central concept is that of a media 'institution' which applies to media both as a branch of industry subject to economic laws, and as a social institution meeting needs in society and subject to some requirements of law and regulation, guided in some degree by public policy. The media are unusual in being a business 'invested with a public interest' and yet free, for the most part, from any positive obligations. The second topic dealt with is a detailed inquiry into the normative expectations from media on the part of the public, government and audiences, with particular references to the principles and standards of their performance. What are the standards that should apply, how can media performance be assessed, and by what means can the media be made accountable? Thirdly, this part looks at the growing phenomenon of global media and the 'world system' of media that has its origins both in the new computer-based technologies of production and transmission and in larger globalizing trends of society.

The part headed 'Organizations' (IV) focuses on the locus of media production, whether a firm or a department within a larger firm, and deals with the numerous influences that shape production. These include pressures and demands from outside the boundaries of the organization, the requirements of routine 'mass production' of news and culture, and the personal and professional tendencies of the 'mass communicators'. There are several theories and models that seek to explain observed regularities in the process of selection and internal shaping of 'content' before it is transmitted.

The 'Content' part (V) is divided into two chapters, the first of which deals primarily with approaches to, and methods for, the analysis of content. Aside from simple description of media output according to internally given labels, it is not at all easy to describe content in a more illuminating manner, since there is no agreement on where the 'true meaning' is to be found, as between its producers, its recipients and the text of the 'message' itself. Secondly, theory and evidence are assembled to account for some of the observed regularities in content, with particular reference to the news genre.

In the next part, 'Audiences' (VI), the 'audience' refers to all the many sets of readers, listeners and viewers that receive media content or are the targets for media transmission. Without the audience there would be no mass communication, and it plays a dynamic role in shaping the flow and effects of media. Again, audience analysis has numerous tasks and can be carried out for many different purposes. It is far more than audience 'measurement' on behalf of the media industry and it has evolved along several theoretically distinct paths. Audience theory deals not only with the 'why' of media use, but also with its determinants and correlates in social and cultural life. Media 'use' has become so intertwined with other activities that we can no longer treat it in isolation from other factors of our experience. A key question to be answered is whether the media have evolved so far beyond the stage of mass communication that a concept based on the image of a passive recipient is still adequate.

Questions of media 'Effects' (Part VII) stand at the start and at the conclusion of the book and are at the centre of social and cultural concern about mass media. They continue to give rise to different theories and much disagreement. Alternative paths towards the goal of assessing effects are outlined. Differences of type of effect are explained, especially the difference between intended and unintended effect and between short-term impact on individuals and longer-term influence on culture and society. The main areas of media effects theory and research still tend to focus, on the one hand, on the potentially harmful social and cultural effects of the most popular forms of content, especially those that involve representations of sex and violence, and on the other hand, on media influence on public knowledge and opinion. The chapters are organized accordingly.

Themes and Issues in Mass Communication

The contents of the book are cross-cut by a number of general themes that recur in discussions of the social origins, significance and effects of communication, whether at the personal level or that of a whole society. At this point we can identify the main themes as follows:

- *Time*. Communication takes place in time and it matters when it occurs and how long it takes. Communication technology has steadily increased the speed at which a given volume of information can be transmitted from point to point. It also stores information for recovery at a later point in historic time. Mass media content in particular serves as a store of memory for a society and for groups within it, and this can be selectively recovered or lost.
- *Place*. Communication is produced in a given location and reflects features of that context. It serves to define a place for its inhabitants and to establish an identity. It connects places, reducing the distance that separates individuals, countries and cultures. Major trends in mass communication are said to have a delocalizing effect, or to establish a new global 'place', which increasingly people recognize as familiar.
- *Power*. Social relationships are structured and driven by power, where the will of one party is imposed on another, whether legitimately or not, or by influence, where the

wishes of another are sought out or followed. Communication as such has no power of compulsion but it is an invariable component and a frequent means of the exercise of power, whether effectively or not. Despite the voluntary character of attention to mass media, the question of their power over audiences is never far away.

- *Social reality*. The assumption behind much theory of mass communication is that we inhabit a 'real' world of material circumstances and events that can be known. The media provide us with reports or reflections of this reality, with varying degrees of accuracy, completeness or dependability. The notion of 'truth' is often applied as a standard to the contents of news and fiction, however difficult to define and assess.
- *Meaning*. A related theme that continually arises concerns the interpretation of the 'message', or content, of mass media. Most theories of mass media depend on some assumption being made about the meaning of what they carry, whether viewed from the point of view of the sender, the receiver or the neutral observer. As noted above, there is no unique source of meaning and no way of saying for certain what is meant, providing an endless potential for dispute and uncertainty.
- *Causation and determinism*. It is in the nature of theory to try to solve questions of cause and effect, whether by proposing some overall explanation that links observations or by directing inquiry to determine whether one factor caused another. Questions of cause arise not only in relation to the consequences of media messages on individuals, but also in relation to historical questions of the rise of media institutions in the first place and the reasons why they have certain typical characteristics of content and appeal. Do the media cause effects in society, or are they themselves more the outcome and reflection of prior and deeper social forces?
- *Mediation*. As an alternative to the idea of cause and effect, we can consider the media to provide occasions, links, channels, arenas and platforms for information and ideas to circulate. By way of the media, meanings are formed and social and cultural forces operate freely according to various logics and with no predictable outcome. The process of mediation inevitably influences or changes the meaning received and there is an increasing tendency for 'reality' to be adapted to demands of media presentation rather than vice versa.
- *Identity*. This refers to a shared sense of belonging to a culture, society, place or social grouping and involves many factors, including nationality, language, work, ethnicity, religion, belief, lifestyle, etc. The mass media are associated with many different aspects of identity formation, maintenance and dissolution. They can drive as well as reflect social change and lead to either more or less integration.
- *Cultural difference*. At almost every turn, the study of media-related issues reminds us how much the working of mass communications and media institutions, despite their apparent similarities across the globe, are affected by differences of culture at the level of individual, subgroup, nation, etc. The production and use of mass media are cultural practices that resist the universalizing tendencies of the technology and the mass-produced content.
- *Governance*. This refers to all the means by which the various media are regulated and controlled by laws, rules, customs and codes as well as by market management. There is a continuing evolution in these matters in response to changes in technology and society.

When we speak of the issues that will be dealt with in the book, we are referring to more specific matters that are problematic or in dispute in the public arena. They relate to questions on which public opinion often forms, on which governments may be expected to have policies for prevention or improvement, or on which the media themselves might have some responsibility. Not all issues are problematic in the negative sense, but they involve questions of current and future trends that are significant for good or ill. No list of issues can be complete, but the following comprise the main headings that come to mind, most of them already familiar to the reader. They serve not only as a foretaste of the content of the book but as a reminder of the significance of the topic of media in society and the potential relevance of theory to handling such questions. The issues are divided according to the terrain they occupy.

Relations with politics and the state

- Political campaigns and propaganda.
- Citizen participation and democracy.
- Media role in relation to war and terrorism.
- Influence on the making of foreign policy.
- Serving or resisting sources of power.

Cultural issues

- Globalization of content and flow.
- Promoting the quality of cultural life and cultural production.
- Effects on cultural and social identity.

Social concerns

- The definition of reality and mediation of social experience.
- Links to crime, violence, pornography and deviance.
- Relation to social order and disorder.
- Promotion of an information society.
- The use and quality of leisure time.
- Social and cultural inequality.

Normative questions

- Freedom of speech and expression.
- Social and cultural inequality: class, ethnicity, gender and sexuality.
- Media norms, ethics and professionalism.
- Media accountability and social responsibility.

Economic concerns

- Degree of concentration.
- Commercialization of content.
- Global imperialism and dependency.

Manner of Treatment

The book has been written as a continuous narrative, following a certain logic. It begins with a brief history of the media, followed by a general overview of the main concepts and theories that deal with the relation between mass communication on the one hand and society and culture on the other. Subsequently, the sequence of content follows a line from the 'source', in the form of mass media organizations, to the content they produce and disseminate, to reception by audiences and to a range of possible effects. This does seem to imply in advance a view of how we should approach the subject, although that is not the intention.

Because of the wide-ranging character of the issues outlined above and the complexity of many of them, it is only possible to give quite brief accounts. Each chapter begins with an introduction giving an overview of the main topics to be covered. Within chapters, the substance of the book is dealt with in headed sections. The topics are not defined according to the themes and issues just outlined, but they reflect the varying focus of theory and the research that has been carried out to test theories. In general, the reader will find a definition of relevant concepts, an explanation of the topic, a short review of relevant evidence from research and an overall assessment of matters of dispute. Each chapter ends with a brief overview of what has been concluded. Key points are summarized in the text in 'boxes' to provide a focus and to aid recall.

Limitations of Coverage and Perspective

Although the book is wide-ranging in its coverage and is intended to have an application to the mass communication phenomenon in general, rather than to any particular country, the viability of this aim is limited in various ways. First, the author has a location, a nationality and a cultural background that shape his experience, knowledge and outlook. There is much scope for subjective judgement and it is impossible to avoid it, even when trying to be objective. Secondly, the 'mass communication phenomenon' is itself not independent of the cultural context in which it is observed, despite similarities of technology and tendencies to uniformity of media organizational form and conduct as well as content. Although some histories of the mass media institution portray it as a 'western invention' that has been diffused as part of a process of 'modernization' from America and Europe to the rest of the world, there are alternative histories and the diffusion is far from a one-way or deterministic process. In short, this account of theory has an inevitable 'western' bias. Its body of theory derives to a large extent from western sources, especially in Europe and North America and written in English, and the research reported to test the ideas is mainly from the same locations. This does not mean it is invalid for other settings, but it means that conclusions are provisional and that alternative ideas may need to be formulated and tested.

The nature of the relation between media and society depends on circumstances of time and place. As noted above, this book largely deals with mass media and mass communication in modern, 'developed' nation states, mainly elective democracies with free-market (or mixed) economies which are integrated into a wider international set of economic and political relations of exchange, competition and also domination or conflict. It is most probable that mass media are experienced differently in societies with 'non-western' characteristics, especially those that are less individualistic and more communal in character, less secular and more religious. There are other traditions of media theory and media practice, even if western media theory has become part of the hegemonic global media project. The differences are not just a matter of more or less economic development, since profound differences of culture and long historical experience are involved. The problem goes deeper than an inevitable element of authorial ethnocentrism, since it also lies in the mainstream social scientific tradition that has its roots in western thought. The alternatives to social science offered by cultural studies are in other ways no less western in character.

Although the aim is to provide as 'objective' an account as possible of theory and evidence, the study of mass communication cannot avoid dealing with questions of values and of political and social conflict. All societies have latent or open tensions and contradictions that often extend to the international arena. The media are inevitably involved in these disputed areas as producers and disseminators of meaning about the events and contexts of social life, private as well as public. It follows from these remarks that we cannot expect the study of mass communication to provide theoretically neutral, scientifically verified information about the 'effects' or the significance of something that is an immensely complex as well as intersubjective set of processes. For the same reasons, it is often difficult to formulate theories about mass communication in ways that are open to empirical testing.

Not surprisingly, the field of media theory is also characterized by widely divergent perspectives. A difference of approach between left (progressive or liberal) and right (conservative) tendencies can sometimes be discerned. Leftist theory is, for instance, critical of the power exercised by media in the hands of the state or large global corporations, while conservative theorists point to the 'liberal bias' of the news or the damage done by media to traditional values. There has also been a difference between a critical and a more applied approach to theory that does not necessarily correspond to the political axis. Lazarsfeld (1941) referred to this as a critical versus administrative orientation. Critical theory seeks to expose underlying problems and faults of media practice and to relate them in a comprehensive way to social issues, guided by certain values. Applied theory aims to harness an understanding of communication processes to solving practical problems of using mass communication more effectively (Windahl and Signitzer, 2007). However, we can also distinguish two other axes of theoretical variation.

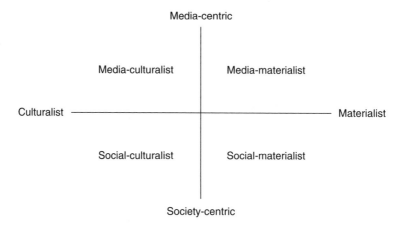

Figure 1.1 Dimensions and types of media theory. Four main approaches can be identified according to two dimensions: media-centric versus society-centric; and culturalist versus materialist

One of these separates 'media-centric' from 'society-centric' (or 'socio-centric') approaches. The former approach attributes much more autonomy and influence to communication and concentrates on the media's own sphere of activity. Media-centric theory sees mass media as a primary mover in social change, driven forward by irresistible developments in communication technology. It also pays much more attention to the specific content of media and the potential consequences of the different kinds of media (print, audiovisual, interactive, etc.). Socio-centric theory mainly views the media as a reflection of political and economic forces. Theory for the media is a special application of broader social theory (Golding and Murdock, 1978). Whether or not society is driven by the media, it is certainly true that mass communication theory itself is so driven, tending to respond to each major shift of media technology and structure.

The second, horizontal, dividing line is between those theorists whose interest (and conviction) lies in the realm of culture and ideas and those who emphasize material forces and factors. This divide corresponds approximately with certain other dimensions: humanistic versus scientific; qualitative versus quantitative; and subjective versus objective. While these differences partly reflect the necessity for some division of labour in a wide territory and the multidisciplinary character of media study, they also often involve competing and contradictory ideas about how to pose questions, conduct research and provide explanations. These two alternatives are independent of each other, and between them they identify four different perspectives on media and society (Figure 1.1).

The four types of perspective can be summarized as follows:

1. *A media-culturalist perspective.* This approach takes the perspective of the audience member in relation to some specific genre or example of media culture (e.g. reality TV or social networking) and explores the subjective meaning of the experience in a given context.
2. *A media-materialist approach.* Research in this tradition emphasizes the shaping of media content and therefore of potential effects, by the nature of the medium in respect of the technology and the social relations of reception and production that are implicated by this. It also attributes influence to the specific organizational contexts and dynamics or production.
3. *A social-culturalist perspective.* Essentially this view subordinates media and media experience to deeper and more powerful forces affecting society and individuals. Social and cultural issues also predominate over political and economic ones.
4. *A social-materialist perspective.* This approach has usually been linked to a critical view of media ownership and control, that ultimately are held to shape the dominant ideology transmitted or endorsed by the media.

While these differences of approach can still be discerned in the structure of the field of inquiry, there has been a trend to convergence between the different schools. Even so, the various topics and approaches outlined involve important differences of philosophy and methodology and cannot simply be ignored.

Different Kinds of Theory

If theory is understood not only as a system of law-like propositions, but as any systematic set of ideas that can help make sense of a phenomenon, guide action or predict a consequence, then one can distinguish at least five kinds of theory which are relevant to mass communication. These can be described as: social scientific, cultural, normative, operational and everyday theory.

Social scientific theory offers general statements about the nature, working and effects of mass communication, based on systematic and objective observation of media and other relevant sources, which can in turn be put to the test and validated or rejected by similar methods. There is now a large body of such theory and it provides much of the content of this book. However, it is loosely organized and not very clearly formulated or even very consistent. It also covers a very wide spectrum, from broad questions of society to detailed aspects of individual information sending and receiving. It also derives from different disciplines, especially sociology, psychology and politics. Some 'scientific' theory is concerned with understanding what is going on, some with developing a critique and some with practical applications in processes of public information or persuasion.

Cultural theory is much more diverse in character. In some forms it is evaluative, seeking to differentiate cultural artefacts according to some criteria of quality. Sometimes its goal is almost the opposite, seeking to challenge hierarchical classification as irrelevant to the true significance of culture. Different spheres of cultural production have generated their corpus of cultural theory, sometimes along aesthetic or ethical lines, sometimes with a social-critical purpose. This applies to film, literature, television, graphic art and many other media forms. While cultural theory demands clear argument and articulation, coherence and consistency, its core component is often itself imaginative and ideational. It resists the demand for testing or validation by observation. Nevertheless, there are opportunities for combined cultural and scientific approaches and the many problematics of the media call for both.

A third kind of theory can be described as normative since it is concerned with examining or prescribing how media ought to operate if certain social values are to be observed or attained. Such theory usually stems from the broader social philosophy or ideology of a given society. This kind of theory is important because it plays a part in shaping and legitimating media institutions and has considerable influence on the expectations concerning the media that are held by other social agencies and by the media's own audiences. A good deal of research into mass media has been stimulated by the wish to apply norms of social and cultural performance. A society's normative theories concerning its own media are usually to be found in laws, regulations, media policies, codes of ethics and the substance of public debate. While normative media theory is not in itself 'objective', it can be studied by the 'objective' methods of the social sciences (McQuail, 1992).

A fourth kind of knowledge about the media can best be described as operational theory since it refers to the practical ideas assembled and applied by media practitioners in the conduct of their own media work. Similar bodies of accumulated practical wisdom are to be found in most organizational and professional settings. In the case of the media, operational theory serves to guide solutions to fundamental tasks, including how to select news, please audiences, design effective advertising, keep within the limits of what society permits, and relate effectively to sources and society. At some points it may overlap with normative theory, for instance in matters of journalistic ethics and codes of practice.

Such knowledge merits the name of theory because it is usually patterned and persistent, even if rarely codified, and it is influential in respect of behaviour. It comes to light in the study of communicators and their organizations (e.g. Elliott, 1972; Tuchman, 1978; Tunstall, 1993). Katz (1977) compared the role of the researcher in relation to media production to that of the theorist of music or philosopher of science who can see regularities which a musician or scientist does not even need to be aware of.

Finally, there is everyday or common-sense theory of media use, referring to the knowledge we all have from our own personal experience with media. This enables us to make sense of what is going on, allows us to fit a medium into our daily lives, to understand how its content is intended to be 'read' as well as how we like to read it, to know what the differences are between different media and media genres, and much more. On the basis of such 'theory' is grounded the ability to make consistent choices, develop patterns of taste, construct lifestyles and identities as media consumers. It also supports the ability to make critical judgements. All this, in turn, shapes what the media actually offer to their audiences and sets both directions and limits to media influence. For instance, it enables us to distinguish between 'reality' and 'fiction', to 'read between the lines' or to see through the persuasive aims and techniques of advertising and other kinds of propaganda, to resist many of the potentially harmful impulses that the media are said to provoke. The working of common-sense theory can be seen in the norms for use of media which many people recognize and follow (see Chapter 16). The social definitions that mass media acquire are not established by media theorists or legislators, or even the media producers themselves, but emerge from the experience and practices of audiences over time. The history of media and their future prospects depends more on this very uncertain branch of theory than on anything else.

Communication Science and the Study of Mass Communication

Mass communication is one topic among many for the social sciences and only one part of a wider field of enquiry into human communication. Under the name 'communication science', the field has been defined by Berger and Chaffee (1987: 17) as a science which 'seeks to understand the production, processing and effects of symbol and signal systems by developing testable theories, containing lawful generalizations, that explain phenomena associated with production, processing and effects'. While this was presented as a 'mainstream' definition to apply to most communication research, in fact it is very much biased towards one model of enquiry – the quantitative study of communicative behaviour and its causes and effects. It is especially inadequate to deal with the nature of 'symbol systems' and signification, the process by which meaning is given and taken in varied social and cultural contexts. The main alternative approaches to the study of mass communication are outlined in the conclusion to this chapter.

Difficulties in defining the field have also arisen because of developments of technology that have blurred the line between public and private communication and between mass and interpersonal communication. It is now impossible to find any single agreed definition of a 'science of communication', for a number of circumstantial reasons, but most fundamentally because there has never been an agreed definition of the central concept of 'communication'. The term can refer to very diverse things, especially: the act or process of information transmission; the giving or taking of meaning; the sharing of information, ideas, impressions or emotions; the process of reception, perception and response; the exertion of influence; any form of interaction. To complicate matters further, communication can be either intentional or involuntary and the variety of potential channels and content is unlimited.

In addition, no 'science of communication' can be independent and self-sufficient, given the origins of the study of communication in many disciplines and the wide-ranging nature of the issues that arise, including matters of economics, law, politics and ethics as well as culture. The study of communication has to be interdisciplinary and must adopt varied approaches and methods (see McQuail, 2003b).

A less problematic way of locating the topic of mass communication in a wider field of communication inquiry is according to the different levels of social organization at which communication takes place. According to this criterion, mass communication can then be seen as one of several society-wide communication processes, at the apex of a pyramidal distribution of other communication networks according to this criterion (Figure 1.2). A communication network refers to any set of interconnected points (persons or places) that enable the transmission and exchange of information between them. For the most part, mass communication is a network that connects very many receivers to one source, while new media technologies usually provide interactive connections of several different kinds.

At each descending level of the pyramid indicated there is an increasing number of cases to be found, and each level presents its own particular set of problems for research and theorizing. In an integrated modern society there will often be one large public communication network, usually depending on the mass media, which can reach and involve all citizens to varying degrees, although the media system is also itself often fragmented according to regional and other social or demographic factors.

Mass media are not the only possible basis for an effective communication network that extends throughout a society. Alternative (non-mass-media) technologies for supporting society-wide networks do now exist (especially the network of physical transportation, the telecommunications infrastructure and the postal system), but these usually lack the society-wide social elements and public roles which mass communication has. In the past (and in some places still today) society-wide public networks were provided by the church or state or by political organizations, based on shared beliefs and usually a hierarchical chain of contact. This extended from the 'top' to the 'base' and employed diverse means of communication, ranging from formal publications to personal contacts.

Alternative communication networks can be activated under unusual circumstances to replace mass media, for instance in the case of a natural disaster, major accident or outbreak of war, or other emergency. In the past, direct word of mouth was the only possibility, while today mobile telephones and the Internet can be effectively employed for interconnecting a large population. In fact the original motive for designing the Internet in the USA in the 1970s was precisely to provide an alternative communication system in the event of a nuclear attack.

At a level below that of the whole society, there are several different kinds of communication network. One type duplicates the social relations of larger society at the level of region, city or town and may have a corresponding media system of its own (local press, radio, etc.). Another is represented by the firm, work organization or profession, which may not have a single location but is usually very integrated within its own organizational boundaries, within which much communication flow takes place. A third type is that represented by the 'institution' – for instance, that of government, or education, or justice, or religion, or social security. The activities of a social institution are always diverse and also require correlation and much communication, following patterned routes and forms. The networks involved in this case are limited to achieving certain limited ends (e.g. education, maintaining order, circulating economic information, etc.) and they are not open to participation by all.

Below this level, there are even more and more varied types of communication network, based on some shared feature of daily life: an environment (such as a neighbourhood), an interest (such as music), a need (such as the care of small children) or an activity (such as sport). At this level, the key questions concern attachment and identity, co-operation and norm formation. At the intragroup (e.g. family) and interpersonal levels, attention has usually been given to forms of conversation and patterns of interaction, influence, affiliation (degrees of attachment) and normative control. At the intrapersonal level, communication research concentrates on the processing of information (e.g. attention, perception, attitude formation, comprehension, recall and learning), the giving of meaning and possible effects (e.g. on knowledge, opinion, self-identity and attitude).

This seemingly neat pattern has been complicated by the growing 'globalization' of social life, in which mass communication has played some part. There is a yet higher 'level' of communication and exchange to consider – that crossing and even ignoring national frontiers, in relation to an increasing range of activities (economic, political, scientific, publicity, sport, entertainment, etc). Organizations and institutions are less confined within national frontiers, and individuals can also satisfy communication needs outside their own society and their immediate social environments. The once strong correspondence between patterns of personal social interaction in shared space and time on the one hand, and systems of communication on the other, has been much weakened, and our cultural and informational choices have become much wider.

This is one reason why the idea of an emerging 'network society' has been advanced (see Castells, 1996; van Dijk, 1999; also Chapter 6 in this book). Such developments also mean that networks are to an increasing degree not confined to any one 'level' of society, as implied by Figure 1.2. New hybrid (both public and private) means of communication allow communication networks to form more easily without the usual 'cement' of shared space or personal acquaintance. In the past, it was possible to match a particular communication technology approximately with a given 'level' of social organization as described, with television at the highest level, the press and radio at the regional or city level, internal systems, telephone and mail at the institutional level, and so forth. Advances in communication technology and their widespread adoption mean that this is no longer possible. The Internet, for instance, now supports communication at virtually all levels. It also sustains chains or networks that connect the social 'top' with the 'base' and are vertical (in both directions) or diagonal, not just horizontal. For instance, a political website can provide access to political leaders and elites as well as to citizens at grass-roots level, allowing a wide range of patterns of flow. For the time being, however, the society-wide communicative function of the 'traditional' core mass media of newspapers, television and radio has not greatly changed in itself, although their near monopoly of public communication is increasingly being challenged.

Despite the growing complexity of the network society, each level indicates a range of similar questions for communication theory and research. These are posed in Box 1.1.

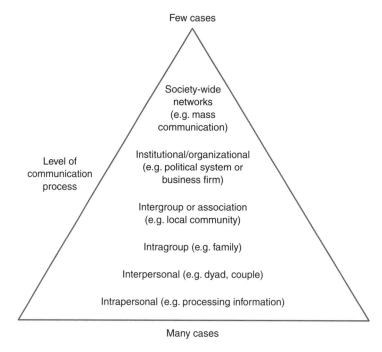

Figure 1.2 The pyramid of communication networks: mass communication is one amongst several processes of social communication

1.1 Questions for theory and research about communication networks and processes

- Who is connected to whom in a given network and for what purpose?
- What is the pattern and direction of flow?
- How does communication take place? (channels, languages, codes)
- What types of content are observed?
- What are the outcomes of communication, intended or unintended?

Alternative Traditions of Analysis: Structural, Behavioural and Cultural

While the questions raised at different levels are similar in very general terms, in practice very different concepts are involved, and the reality of communication differs greatly from level to level. (For instance, a conversation between two family members takes place according to different 'rules' from those governing a news broadcast to a large audience, a television quiz show or a chain of command in a work organization.) For this reason, among others, any 'communication science' has, necessarily, to be constructed from several different bodies of theory and evidence, drawn from several of the traditional 'disciplines' (especially sociology and psychology in the earlier days, but now also economics, history and literary and film studies and more besides). In this respect, the deepest and most enduring divisions separate interpersonal from mass communication, cultural from behavioural concerns, and institutional and historical perspectives from those that are cultural or behavioural. Putting the matter simply, there are essentially three main alternative approaches: the structural, the behavioural and the cultural.

The *structural* approach derives mainly from sociology but includes perspectives from history, politics, law and economics. Its starting point is 'socio-centric' rather than 'media-centric' (as shown in Figure 1.1), and its primary object of attention is likely to be media systems and organizations and their relationship to the wider society. In so far as questions of media content arise, the focus is likely to be on the effect of social structure and media systems on patterns of news and entertainment. For instance, commercial media systems tend to concentrate more on entertainment, while public service media provide relatively more information and traditional culture. In so far as questions of media use and effect are concerned, the approach emphasizes the consequences of mass communication for other social institutions. This includes, for instance, the influence of political marketing on the conduct of elections or the role of news management and PR in government policy. The fundamental dynamics of media phenomena are located in the exercise of power, in the economy and the socially organized application of technology. The structural approach to media analysis is more linked to the needs of management and also of media policy formation.

The *behavioural* approach has its principal roots in psychology and social psychology but it also has a sociological variant. In general, the primary object of interest is individual human behaviour, especially in matters to do with choosing, processing and responding to communication messages. Mass media use is generally treated as a form of rational, motivated action that has a certain function or use for the individual and also some objective consequences. Psychological approaches are more likely to use experimental methods of research based on individual subjects. The sociological variant focuses on the behaviour of members of socially defined populations and favours the multivariate analysis of representative survey data collected in natural conditions. Individuals are classified according to relevant variables of social position, disposition and behaviour, and the variables can be statistically manipulated. In the study of organizations, participant observation is commonly adopted. This approach is mainly found in relation to the study of persuasion, propaganda and advertising. Communication is primarily understood in the sense of transmission.

The *cultural* approach has its roots in the humanities, in anthropology and in linguistics. While very broad in potential, it has been mainly applied to questions of meaning and language, to the minutiae of particular social contexts and cultural experiences. The study of media is part of a wider field of cultural studies. It is more likely to be 'media-centric' (although not exclusively), sensitive to differences between media and settings of media transmission and reception, more interested in the in-depth understanding of particular contents and situations than in generalization. Its methods favour the qualitative and in-depth analysis of social and human signifying practices and the analysis and interpretation of 'texts'. The cultural approach draws on a much wider range of theory, including feminist, philosophical, semiotic, psychoanalytic, film and literary theories. Typically, there is no direct application for the cultural approach, although it can yield many important insights for media producers and planners. It helps in a fuller understanding of the audience and in accounting for success and failure in qualitative ways.

Conclusion

This chapter has been intended to provide a brief sketch of the overall field of inquiry within which the humanistic and social scientific study of mass communication is located. It should be clear that the boundaries around the various topics are not clearly fixed, but change according to shifts of technology and society. Nevertheless there is a community of scholarship that shares a set of concerns, concepts and tools of analysis that will be explored in the chapters that follow.

Further Reading

Devereux, E. (2007) *Media Studies: Key Issues and Debates*. London: Sage.
A wide-ranging set of original chapters on important topics in the field, with supplementary teaching materials and references.

Grossberg, L., Wartella, E. and Whitney, D.C. (1998) *Media Making*. Thousand Oaks, CA: Sage.
A comprehensive presentation of the field of study of mass media from different perspectives – sociological, cultural and media industrial.

McQuail, D. (ed.) (2002) *Reader in Mass Communication Theory*. London: Sage.
A set of key readings, classic and modern, organized in sections that correspond to the main divisions of the present book and chosen to support the same range of content as this edition.

Silverstone, R. (1999) *Why Study the Media?* London: Sage.
A concise and clearly argued personal statement of the significance of the media in society. Still valid, despite changes in the last decade.

Online Readings

Castells, M. (2007) 'Communicative power and counter power in the network society', *International Journal of Communication*, 1: 238–66.
Sreberny, A. (2004) 'Society, culture and media: thinking comparatively', in J.D.H. Downing, D. McQuail, P. Schlesinger and E. Wartella (eds), *The Sage Handbook of Media Studies*, pp. 83–103. Thousand Oaks, CA: Sage.

2
The Rise of Mass Media

The aim of this chapter is to set out the approximate sequence of development of the present-day set of mass media. It is also to indicate major turning points and to tell briefly something of the circumstances of time and place in which different media acquired their public definitions in the sense of their perceived utility for audiences and their role in society. These definitions have tended to form early in the history of any given medium and to have been subsequently adapted in the light of newer media and changed conditions. This is a continuing process. The chapter concludes with some reflections on the two main dimensions of variation between media: one relates to the degree of freedom and the other to the conditions of use.

From the Beginning to Mass Media

We have distinguished already between a *process* of mass communication and the actual *media* that make it possible. The occurrence of human communication over time and at a distance is much older than are the mass media now in use. This process was integral to the organization of early societies, which persisted for long periods and extended over large areas. Even the element of large-scale (mass) dissemination of ideas was present at an early point in time, in the propagation of political and religious awareness and obligations. By the early Middle Ages, the church in Europe had elaborate and effective means in place to ensure transmission to everyone without exception. This could be called mass communication, although it was largely independent of any 'media' in the contemporary sense, aside from the sacred texts. When independent media arrived in the form of printing, authorities of church and state reacted with alarm at the potential loss of control that this represented and at the opportunities opened up for disseminating new and deviant ideas. The bitter propaganda struggles of the religious wars during the sixteenth century are evidence enough. It was the historical moment when a technology for mass communication – the printing press – irrevocably acquired a particular social and cultural definition.

In telling the history of mass media, we deal with four main elements that are of significance in the wider life of society. These are:

- certain communicative purposes, needs, or uses;
- technologies for communicating publicly to many at a distance;
- forms of social organization that provide the skills and frameworks for organizing production and distribution;
- forms of regulation and control.

These elements do not have a fixed relationship to each other and depend very much on the circumstances of time and place. Sometimes a technology of communication is applied to a pre-existing need or use, as when printing replaced copying by hand or the telegraph replaced the physical transport of key messages. But sometimes a technology, such as film or broadcast radio, precedes any clear evidence of need. The combinations of the above elements that actually occur are usually dependent both on material factors and on features of the social and cultural climate that are not easy to pin down. Even so, it seems probable that a certain degree of freedom of thought, expression and action has been the single most necessary condition for the development of print and other media, although not for the initial invention. The techniques of printing and even the use of movable type were known and applied in China and Korea long before Gutenberg, who is credited as the (European) inventor in the mid-fifteenth century (Gunaratne, 2001).

In general, the more open the society, the more inclination there has been to develop communication technology to its fullest potential, especially in the sense of being universally available and widely used. More closed or repressive regimes either limit development or set strict boundaries to the ways in which technology can be used. Printing was not introduced into Russia until the early seventeenth century and not in the Ottoman Empire until 1726. In the following summary of the history and characteristics of different media, a 'western' perspective and set of values are being applied, since the institutional frameworks of mass media were initially mainly western (European or North American) and most other parts of the world have taken up and applied the same technologies in a similar way. Even so, there is no reason why mass media need follow only one path in the future, always converging on the western model. There are diverse possibilities, and it is quite possible that cultural differences will trump technological imperatives. The history of media already shows up certain important differences between societies, for instance the large variation in the readership of books and newspapers or in the rates and pace of Internet diffusion.

In the following pages, each of the main mass media is identified in respect of its technology and material form, typical formats and genres, perceived uses and institutional setting.

Print Media: the Book

The history of modern media begins with the printed book – certainly a kind of revolution, yet initially only a technical device for reproducing a range of texts the same as, or similar to, what was already being extensively copied by hand. Only gradually does printing lead to a change in content – more secular, practical and popular works (especially in the vernacular languages) as well as political and religious pamphlets and tracts – which played a part in the transformation of the medieval world. At an early date, laws and proclamations were also printed by royal and other authorities. Thus, there occurred a revolution of society in which printing played an inseparable part (Eisenstein, 1978).

The antecedents of the book lie in classical times when there were numerous established authors and when works of many kinds, both fictional and non-fictional, were copied and circulated for reading or verbal transmission. In the west, at least, the culture of the book largely disappeared after the end of the Roman Empire until revived by monastic activities, although some key texts were preserved for reasons of learning or religion.

In the early medieval period, the book was not regarded primarily as a means of communication. Rather, it was a store or repository of wisdom, and especially of sacred writings and religious texts that had to be kept in uncorrupted form. Around the central core of religious and philosophical texts there accumulated also works of science and practical information. The main material form of the book at this time was of bound volumes of separate pages within strong covers (known as the *codex*), reflecting the requirements for safe storage and reading aloud from a lectern plus the demands of travel and transportation. Books were meant both to last and to be disseminated within limited circles. The modern book is a direct descendant of this model, and similar uses are embedded within it. The alternative form of rolls of paper or parchment was discontinued, especially when the printing press replaced writing by hand and required the pressing of flat sheets. This ensured the triumph of the medieval manuscript book format, even when miniaturized.

Another important element of continuity between writing and printing is the library, a store or collection of books. This remained similar in concept and physical arrangement, at least until the advent of digital libraries. It also reflected and confirmed the idea of a book as a record or permanent work of reference. The character of the library did not change much with printing, although printing stimulated the acquisition of private libraries. The later development of the library has given it some claim to be considered not only as a medium but even as a mass medium. It is certainly often organized as a means of public information and was envisaged from the mid-nineteenth century onwards as an important tool of mass enlightenment.

The successful application of print technology to the reproduction of texts in place of handwriting, about the mid-fifteenth century, was only the first step in the emergence of what we now call a 'media institution' (see p. 59) – an organized set of interrelated activities and roles, directed towards certain goals and governed by a set of rules and procedures. Printing gradually became a new craft and a significant branch of commerce (Febvre and Martin, 1984). Printers were later transformed from tradespeople into publishers, and the two functions gradually became distinct. Equally important was the emergence of the idea and role of the 'author' since earlier manuscript texts were not typically authored by living individuals.

A natural further development was the role of professional author, as early as the late sixteenth century, typically supported by wealthy patrons. Each of these developments reflects the emergence of a market and the transformation of the book into a commodity. Although print runs were small by modern standards, cumulative sales over time could be large. Febvre and Martin (1984) estimate that by 1,500 up to 15,000 titles had been published, and during the sixteenth century more than a million copies of Luther's translation of the Bible had been printed. There was a thriving book trade, with much export and import between those countries with printing industries, especially France, England, the German states and Italy. In fact many of the basic features of modern media are already embodied in book publishing by the end of the sixteenth century, including the earliest form of reading public. There was the beginning of copyright in the form of privileges granted to printers in respect of certain texts. Various forms of monopoly practice were appearing, for instance the Stationers' Company in London, which was convenient for purposes of censorship, but also offered some protection to authors and maintained standards (Johns, 1998).

The later history of the book is one of steady expansion in volume and range of content and also of struggle for freedom of the press and the rights of authors. Nearly everywhere from the early sixteenth century onwards, government and church authorities applied advance censorship to printed matter, even if not with the effectiveness of a modern totalitarian state. The most famous early and eloquent claim for freedom from government licensing was made by the English poet John Milton in a tract published in 1644 (*Areopagitica*). Freedom of the press went hand in hand with democratic political freedoms and the former was only achieved where democracy had triumphed. This close association remains.

The key features of the book both as a medium and as an institution are summarized in Box 2.1. These typical features are interrelated in the idea of the book as it has been known since the sixteenth century. The 'medium' features relate to technology, form and manner of use and the wider institution of production and distribution.

The book as a medium and institution: key features 2.1

Medium aspects
- Technology of movable type
- Bound pages, *codex* form
- Multiple copies
- For personal reading
- Individual authorship

Institutional aspects
- Commodity form
- Market distribution
- Diversity of content and form
- Claim to freedom of publication
- Subject to some legal limits

Print Media: the Newspaper

It was almost two hundred years after the invention of printing before what we now recognize as a prototypical newspaper could be distinguished from the handbills, pamphlets and newsletters of the late sixteenth and early seventeenth centuries. Its chief precursor seems, in fact, to have been the letter rather than the book – newsletters circulating via the rudimentary postal service, concerned especially with transmitting news of events relevant to international trade and commerce (Raymond, 1999). It was thus an extension into the public domain of an activity that had long taken place for governmental, diplomatic or commercial as well as for private purposes. The early newspaper was marked by its regular appearance, commercial basis (openly for sale) and public character. Thus, it was used for information, record, advertising, diversion and gossip.

The seventeenth-century commercial newspaper was not identified with any single source but was a compilation made by a printer-publisher. The official variety (as published by Crown or government) showed some of the same characteristics but was also a voice of authority and an instrument of state. The commercial newspaper was the form which has given most shape to the newspaper institution, and its development can be seen in retrospect as a major turning point in communication history – offering first of all a service to its anonymous readers rather than an instrument to propagandists or authorities.

In a sense the newspaper was more of an innovation than the printed book – the invention of a new literary, social and cultural form – even if it might not have been so perceived at the time. Its distinctiveness, compared with other forms of cultural communication, lies in its orientation to the individual reader and to reality, its utility and disposability, and its secularity and suitability for the needs of a new class: town-based business and professional people. Its novelty consisted not in its technology or manner of distribution, but in its functions for a distinct class in a changing and more liberal social-political climate.

The later history of the newspaper can be told either as a series of struggles, advances and reverses in the cause of liberty or as a more continuous history of economic and technological progress. The most important phases in press history that enter into the modern definition of the newspaper are described in the following paragraphs. While separate national histories differ too much to tell a single story, the elements mentioned, often intermingling and interacting, have all played a part in the development of the press institution. The principal features of the newspaper are summarized in Box 2.2.

2.2 The newspaper as medium and institution: key features

Medium aspects

- Regular and frequent appearance
- Print technology
- Topicality of contents and reference
- Individual or group reading

Institutional aspects

- Urban, secular audience
- Relative freedom, but self-censored
- In public domain
- Commodity form
- Commercial basis

From its early days, the newspaper was an actual or potential adversary of established power, especially in its own self-perception. Potent images in press history refer to violence done to printers, editors and journalists. The struggle for freedom to publish, often within a broader movement for freedom, democracy and citizen rights, is emphasized in journalism's own mythology. The part played by underground presses under foreign occupation or dictatorial rule has also been celebrated. Established authority has often confirmed this self-perception of the press by finding it irritating and inconvenient (although also often malleable and, in the last resort, very vulnerable to power). However, early newspapers did not generally seek to offend authorities and were sometimes produced on their behalf (Schroeder, 2001). Then, as now, the newspaper was likely to identify most with its intended readers.

There has been a steady progression towards more press freedom, despite major setbacks from time to time. This progress has sometimes taken the form of greater sophistication in the means of control applied to the press. Legal restraint replaced violence, then fiscal burdens were imposed (and later reversed). Now institutionalization of the press within a market system serves as a form of control, and the modern newspaper, as a large business enterprise, is vulnerable to more kinds of pressure or intervention than its simpler forerunners were. The newspaper did not really become a true 'mass' medium until the twentieth century, in the sense of directly reaching a majority of the population on a regular basis, and there are still quite large inter-country differences in the extent of newspaper reading (see Box 2.3). There has been a gradual worldwide decline in newspaper reading over the last decade, despite the increase in literacy, with the rise of the Internet probably playing some part (Küng et al., 2008). It has been customary and it is still useful to distinguish between certain types or genres of newspaper (and of journalism), although there is no single typology to suit all epochs and countries. The following passages describe the main variants.

Percentage of non-readers in the adult population of some European countries (2004/5) (Elvestad and Blekesaune, 2008: 432)   **2.3**

Norway	4	Poland	30
Switzerland	9	France	39
Estonia	17	Spain	49
Germany	19	Greece	66
United Kingdom	26		

The party-political press

One common early form of the newspaper was the party-political paper dedicated to the task of activation, information and organization. The party newspaper (published by or for the party) has lost ground to commercial press forms, both as an idea and as a viable business enterprise. The idea of a party press, even so, still has its place as a component in democratic politics. Where it does survive in Europe (and there are examples elsewhere), it is typically independent from the state (though possibly subsidized), professionally produced, serious and opinion-forming in purpose. Its uniqueness lies in the attachment of its readers by way of shared party allegiance, its sectionalism and its mobilizing function for party objectives. Examples include the 'vanguard press' of the Russian revolutionary movement, the party-political newspapers (especially social democratic) of several Scandinavian countries and the official party press of former communist regimes.

The prestige press

The late-nineteenth-century bourgeois newspaper was a high point in press history and contributed much to our modern understanding of what a newspaper is or should be. The 'high-bourgeois' phase of press history, from about 1850 to the turn of the century, was the product of several events and circumstances. These included: the triumph of liberalism and the absence or ending of direct censorship or fiscal constraint; the forging of a business-professional establishment; plus many social and technological changes favouring the rise of a national or regional press of high information quality.

The new prestige or 'elite' press was independent from the state and from vested interests and was often recognized as a major institution of political and social life (especially as a self-appointed former of opinion and voice of the 'national interest'). It tended to show a highly developed sense of social and ethical responsibility (in practice fundamentally conformist) and it fostered the rise of a journalistic profession dedicated to the objective reporting of events. Many countries still have one or more newspapers that try to maintain this tradition. By wide consensus, the newspapers still recognized as having an 'elite' status are likely to include the *New York Times*, *The Times* (London), *Le Monde, El Pais, NRC Handelsblad* (The Netherlands). Current expectations about what is a 'quality' newspaper still reflect the professional ideals of the prestige press and provide the basis for criticisms of newspapers which deviate from the ideal by being either too partisan or too 'sensational', or just too 'commercial'. The prestige press currently seems better placed than most to survive the current pressure on newspapers, by virtue of their importance to a political and economic elite, although to do so it may need to accelerate its transition to online forms.

The popular press

The last main type of newspaper has been with us for a century or so without much change of essential character. This is the truly 'mass' newspaper that was created for sale to the urban industrial masses and designed to be read by almost everyone. It was a fundamentally commercial enterprise (rather than a political or professional project) and was made possible by advances in technologies of scale, concentrations of population, the spread of literacy, low cost to the reader and large amounts of advertising revenue. In general, the popular press has always specialized in 'human interest' stories (Hughes, 1940), in dramatic and sensational styles of reporting and presentation, in the coverage of crime, disasters, crises, scandals, war and celebrities. Although not primarily interested in politics, it has often played a political role at key moments in national societies. Because of its typical smaller page format, the term 'tabloid' has been widely applied to this type of newspaper and its contents, as in the term 'tabloidization' (Connell, 1998). This means a process of becoming more sensational, trivial and irresponsible.

The local and regional press

In many countries, the most important newspaper sectors have been and remain the local and regional press. The forms are too varied to be described as a single type. They can be serious or popular, daily or weekly, urban or rural, with large as well as small circulations. The main features they have in common are: a set of news values relevant to a local readership; a typically consensual and bipartisan approach (although there are exceptions); and a dependence on support from local advertisers. Some local papers are free, others are paid for and they have generally been most threatened by online news and advertising. The status as newspapers or free sheets, often largely devoted to advertising, and now a rapidly rising category, is questionable, although they are regarded as such by readers and some may define themselves as such.

Other Print Media

The printing press gave rise to other forms of publication than book and newspaper. These include plays, songs, tracts, serial stories, poems, pamphlets, comics, reports, prospectuses, maps, posters, music, handbills, wall newspapers and much more. The single most significant is probably the periodical (weekly or monthly) magazine that appeared in great diversity and with wide circulations from the early eighteenth century onwards. Initially aimed at the domestic and cultural interests of the gentry, it eventually developed into a mass market of high commercial value and enormous breadth of coverage. The periodical magazine still belongs largely to the domestic and personal sphere and supports a wide range of interests, activities and markets. In the early twentieth century it was more like a mass medium than it is today, and its diffuseness and uncertain impact have led to a general neglect by communication research.

These comments apply to the commercial periodical. In many countries there has been and remains a significant opinion-forming or political periodical press, often with an influence beyond its circulation size. At key moments in some societies particular magazines have played important social, cultural or political roles. In conditions of political oppression or commercial domination, the 'alternative' periodical has often been an essential instrument of resistance and expression for minority movements (see Downing, 2000; Huesca, 2003; Gumucio-Dagron, 2004).

Film as a Mass Medium

Film began at the end of the nineteenth century as a technological novelty, but what it offered was scarcely new in content or function. It transferred to a new means of presentation and distribution of an older tradition of entertainment, offering stories, spectacles, music, drama, humour and technical tricks for popular consumption. It was also almost instantly a true mass medium in the sense that it quite quickly reached a very large proportion of populations, even in rural areas. As a mass medium, film was partly a response to the 'invention' of leisure – time out of work – and an answer to the demand for affordable and (usually) respectable ways of enjoying free time for the whole family. Thus it provided for the working class some of the cultural benefits already enjoyed by their social 'betters'. To judge from its phenomenal growth, the latent demand met by film was enormous. Of the main formative elements named above, it would not be the technology or the social climate but the needs met by the film for individuals that mattered most. The most apparent are those for escape from humdrum reality into a more glamorous world, the wish for strong narratives to be caught up in, the search for role models and heroes, the need to fill leisure time in safe, affordable and sociable ways. In these respects, not much has changed.

The characterization of the film as 'show business' in a new form for an expanded market is not the whole story. There have been three other significant strands in film history. First, the use of film for propaganda is noteworthy, especially when applied to national or societal purposes, based on its great reach, supposed realism, emotional impact and popularity. The two other strands in film history were the emergence of several schools of film art (Huaco, 1963) and the rise of the social documentary film movement. These were different from the mainstream in having either a minority appeal or a strong element of realism (or both). Both have a link, partly fortuitous, with film as propaganda in that both tended to develop at times of *social crisis*.

There continue to be thinly concealed ideological and implicitly propagandist elements in many popular entertainment films, even in politically 'free' societies. This reflects a mixture of forces: deliberate attempts at social control; unthinking adoption of populist or conservative values; various marketing and PR infiltrations into entertainment; and the pursuit of mass appeal. Despite the dominance of the entertainment function in film history, films have often displayed didactic, propagandistic tendencies. Film is certainly more vulnerable than other media to outside interference and may be more subject to conformist pressures because so much capital is at risk. It is a reflection of this situation that, in the aftermath of the 9/11 attack on the Twin Towers, US government leaders sought a meeting with leaders of the film industry to discuss ways in which film could make a contribution to the newly announced 'war on terror'.

The main turning points in film history have been: the 'Americanization' of the film industry and film culture in the years after the First World War (Tunstall, 1977); the coming of television and the separation of film from the cinema. The relative decline of nascent, but flourishing, European film industries at that time (hastened by the Second World War) probably contributed to a homogenization of film culture and a convergence of ideas about the definition of film as a medium, with Hollywood as a dominant model. Television took away a large part of the film-viewing public, especially the general family audience, leaving a much smaller and younger film audience. It also took away or diverted the social documentary stream of film development and gave it a more congenial home in television, where it appeared in journalistic magazines, special reports and 'public affairs' programming. However, it did not have similar effects on the art film or for film aesthetics, although the art film may have benefited from the 'demassification' and greater specialization of the film/cinema medium. For the first two generations of filmgoers, the film experience was inseparable from having an evening out, usually with friends and usually in venues that were far grander than the home. In addition, the darkened cinema offered a mixture of privacy and sociability that gave another dimension to the experience. Just as with television later, 'going to the pictures' was as important as seeing any particular film.

The 'separation of film and cinema' refers to the many ways in which films can be seen, after initial showing in a film theatre. These include television broadcasting, cable transmission, videotape and DVD sale or hire, satellite TV and now digital broadband Internet and mobile phone reception. These developments have several potential consequences. They make film less typically a shared public experience and more a private one. They reduce the initial 'impact' of mass exposure to a given film. They shift control of selection in the direction of the audience and allow new patterns of repeat viewing and collection. They make it possible to serve many specialist markets and easier to cater for the demand for violent, horrific or pornographic content. They also prolong the life of films. Despite the liberation entailed in becoming a less 'mass' medium, the film has not been able to claim full rights to political and artistic self-expression, and most countries retain an apparatus of licensing, censorship and powers of control.

Although the film/cinema medium has been subordinated to television in many respects, it has also become more integrated with other media, especially book publishing, popular music and television itself. It has acquired a greater centrality (Jowett and Linton, 1980), despite the reduction of its immediate audience, as a showcase for other media and as a cultural source, out of which come books, strip cartoons, songs, and television 'stars' and series. Thus, film is as much as ever a mass culture creator. Even the decline of the cinema audience has been more than compensated by a new domestic film audience reached by television, digital recordings, cable and satellite channels. Key features are summarized in Box 2.4.

2.4 The film medium and institution: key features

Medium aspects

- Audiovisual channels of reception
- Private experience of public content
- Extensive (universal) appeal
- Predominantly narrative fiction
- International in genre and format

Institutional aspects

- Subjection to social control
- Complex organization of and distribution
- High cost of production
- Multiple platforms of distribution

Broadcasting

Radio and television have, respectively, a ninety and a sixty-plus-year history as mass media, and both grew out of pre-existing technologies – telephone, telegraph, moving and still photography, and sound recording. Despite their obvious differences in content and use, radio and television can be treated together in terms of their history. Radio seems to have been a technology looking for a use, rather than a response to a demand for a new kind of service or content, and much the same is true of television. According to Williams (1975: 25), 'Unlike all previous communications technologies, radio and television were systems primarily designed for transmission and reception as abstract processes, with little or no definition of preceding content.' Both came to borrow from existing media, and most of the popular content forms of both are derivative from film, music, stories, theatre, news and sport.

A distinctive feature of radio and television has been their high degree of regulation, control or licensing by public authority – initially out of technical necessity, later from a mixture of democratic choice, state self-interest, economic convenience and sheer institutional custom. A second and related feature of radio and television media has been their centralized pattern of distribution, with supply radiating out from metropolitan centres, with little or no return flow. Perhaps because of their closeness to power, radio and television have hardly anywhere acquired, as of right, the same freedom that the press enjoys, to express views and act with political independence. Broadcasting was thought too powerful as an influence to fall into the hands of any single interest without clear limitations to protect the public from potential harm or manipulation.

Television has been continuously evolving, and it would be risky to try to summarize its features in terms of communicative purposes and effects. Initially, the main genre innovation of television stemmed from its capacity to transmit many pictures and sound live, and thus act as a 'window on the world' in real time. Even studio productions were live broadcasts before the days of efficient video recording. This capacity of simultaneity has been retained for some kinds of content, including sporting events, some newscasting, and certain kinds of entertainment show. What Dayan and Katz (1992) characterize as 'media events' (such as state visits, the Olympic Games, coronations, large political demonstrations) are often likely to have significant live coverage. Most TV content is not live, although it often aims to create an illusion of ongoing reality. A second important feature of television is the sense of intimacy and personal involvement that it seems able to cultivate between the spectator and presenter or the actors and participants on screen.

The status of television as the most 'massive' of the media in terms of reach, time spent and popularity has barely changed over thirty years and it adds all the time to its global audience. Even so, there is now some evidence of gradual decline in total audiences, although significant inter-country differences in its dominance of free time remain, as indicated in a summary way in Box 2.5.

Differences in time spent with television, 2000 and 2007 2.5

Country	Viewing minutes per day	
	2000	2007
United States	299	297
United Kingdom	234	233
Italy	238	239
France	219	214
Netherlands	166	194
Norway	163	154
Czech Republic	19	194
Germany	233	203
Ireland	185	185

(*Source*: International Television Expert Group, www.ip-network.com)

Despite the fact that television has been largely denied an autonomous political role and is primarily considered a medium of entertainment, it plays a vital role in modern politics. It is considered to be the main source of news and information for most people and the main channel of communication between politicians and citizens, especially at election times. In this informally allocated role of public informer, television has generally remained credible and trusted. Another role is that of educator – for children at school and adults at home. It is also the largest single channel of advertising in nearly all countries, and this has helped to confirm its mass entertainment functions. In terms of its distribution, broadcast television has fragmented in most countries into many separate channels. Even so, the typical pattern that remains is one in which a few (national) channels are very dominant in audience and financial terms. An enduring feature of the appeal of television seems to lie in the very fact that it is a medium that brings people together to share the same experiences in an otherwise fragmented and individuated society and not only in the circle of the family.

The main features of broadcast television and radio are summarized in Box 2.6.

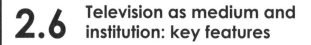

2.6 Television as medium and institution: key features

Medium aspects

- Very diverse types of content
- Audiovisual channels
- Close, personal and domestic association
- Low intensity and involvement experience

Institutional aspects

- Complex technology and organization
- Subject to legal and social control
- National *and* international character
- High public visibility

Radio notably refused to die in the face of the rise of television and it has prospered on the basis of several distinctive features. Competition with television led to a degree of deliberate differentiation. The close supervision of national radio systems relaxed after the rise of television and there was a 'pirate' phase, in which amateurs and independent entrepreneurs set up competing illegal stations. Radio ceased to be a highly regulated national 'voice' and became more free to experiment and to express new, minority and even deviant sounds in voice and music. As a medium, it has much more channel capacity and therefore much greater and more diverse access. It is much cheaper and more flexible in production than television and also cheap and flexible in use for its audience. There are no longer limitations on the place where radio can be listened to or the time of reception, since listening can be combined with other routine activities. It has possibilities for interaction with its audience by way of the telephone and can accommodate many different genres. In fact, radio has flourished since the coming of television, even if it can no longer claim the mass audience of its glory days in the 1940s. The main features discussed are outlined in Box 2.7.

Radio as medium and institution: key features 2.7 ▬

Medium aspects

- Sound appeal only
- Portable and flexible in use
- Multiple types of content, but more music
- Participative (two-way) potential
- Individual and intimate in use

Institutional aspects

- Relative freedom
- Local and decentralized
- Economical to produce

Recorded Music

Relatively little attention has been given to music as a mass medium in theory and research, perhaps because the implications for society have never been clear, and neither have there been sharp discontinuities in the possibilities offered by successive technologies of recording and reproduction/transmission. Recorded and replayed music has not even enjoyed a convenient label to describe its numerous media manifestations, although the generic term 'phonogram' has been suggested (Burnett, 1990, 1996) to cover music accessed via record players, tape players, compact disc players, VCRs (video cassette recorders), broadcasting and cable, etc.

The recording and replaying of music began around 1880 and records were quite rapidly diffused, on the basis of the wide appeal of popular songs and melodies. Their popularity and diffusion were closely related to the already established place of the piano (and other instruments) in the home. Much radio content since the early days has consisted of music, even more so since the rise of television. While there may have been a gradual tendency for the 'phonogram' to replace private music-making, there has never been a large gap between mass-mediated music and personal and direct audience enjoyment of musical performance (concerts, choirs, bands, dances, etc). The phonogram makes music of all kinds more accessible at all times in more places to more people, but it is hard to discern a fundamental discontinuity in the general character of popular musical experience, despite changes of genre and fashion.

Even so, there have been big changes in the broad character of the phonogram since its beginnings. The first change was the addition of radio broadcast music to phonogram records, which greatly increased the range and amount of music available and extended it to many more people than had access to gramophones or jukeboxes. The transition of radio from a family to an individual medium in the post-war 'transistor' revolution was a second major change, which opened up a relatively new market of young people for what became a burgeoning record industry. Each development since then – portable tape players, the Sony Walkman, the compact disc, music video and ipod – has given the spiral another twist, still based on a predominantly young audience. The result has been a mass media industry which is very interrelated, concentrated in ownership and internationalized (Negus, 1992). Despite this, music media have significant radical and creative strands which have developed despite increased commercialization (Frith, 1981). The growth of music downloading and sharing via the Internet has added to the distribution traffic and seriously challenged the power of music rights holders.

While the cultural significance of music has received sporadic attention, its relationship to social and political events has been recognized and occasionally celebrated or feared. Since the rise of the youth-based industry in the 1960s, mass-mediated popular music has been linked to youthful idealism and political concern, to supposed degeneration and hedonism, to drug-taking, violence and antisocial attitudes. Music has also played a part in various nationalist independence movements. For instance, songs of protest and nationalism were a potent element in the pursuit of independence of Ireland from Britain. More recently, the end of Soviet control of Estonia was described as the 'singing revolution' because music enabled people to come together and express their aspirations for restoration of autonomy and the suppressed national culture. While the content of music has never been easy to regulate, its distribution has predominantly been in the hands of established institutions, and its perceived deviant tendencies have been subject to some sanctions. In any case, most popular music expresses and responds to rather enduring conventional values and personal needs, with no subversive aim or potential. These points about music are summarized in Box 2.8.

2.8   Recorded music (phonogram) as medium and institution: key features

Medium aspects

- Sound experience only
- Personal and emotional satisfactions
- Main appeal to youth
- Mobile, flexible individual in use

Institutional aspects

- Low degree of regulation
- High degree of internationalization
- Multiple technologies and platforms
- Links to major media industry
- Organizational fragmentation
- Central to youth culture

The Communications Revolution: New Media versus Old

The expression 'new media' has been in use since the 1960s and has had to encompass an expanding and diversifying set of applied communication technologies. The editors of the *Handbook of New Media* (Lievrouw and Livingstone, 2006) point to the difficulties of saying just what the 'new media' comprise. They choose to define them in a composite way, linking information communication technologies (ICT) with their associated social contexts, bringing together three elements: technological artefacts and devices; activities, practices and uses; and social arrangements and organizations that form around the devices and practices. As noted above, much the same definition applies to 'old media', although the artefacts, uses and arrangements are different. As far as the essential features of 'new media' are concerned, the main ones seem to be their interconnectedness, their accessibility to individual users as senders and/or receivers, their interactivity, their multiplicity of use and open-ended character, and their ubiquity and 'delocatedness' (see also Chapter 6).

Our primary concern in this book is with mass communication, which is closely related to the old media and seems thus to be rendered obsolete by new media. However, as noted already, mass communication is not a process that is limited to mass media nor has it necessarily declined. The new media technologies also carry mass communication activities. Lüders (2008) argues that distinctions between mass media and personal media have not been abolished but have become unstable. Even so, the rise of new media is seen by some as a revolt against mass communication, an idea that has a long history in critical theory (see Enzensberger, 1970). The two main driving forces of change were initially satellite communication and the harnessing of the computer. The key to the immense power of the computer as a communication machine lies in the process of digitalization that allows information of all kinds in all formats to be carried with the same efficiency and also intermingled. In principle, there is no longer any need for the various different media that have been described, since all could be subsumed in the same computerized communication network and reception centre (in the home, for instance). So far this has not happened, and it is bound to be a gradual process if and when it does. But we already see many signs of newspaper moving to a life online. Alongside computer-based technologies there are other innovations that have in some degree changed some aspects of mass communication (Carey, 2003). New means of transmission by cable, satellite and radio have immensely increased the capacity to transmit. New means of storage and retrieval, including the personal video recorder, CD-ROM, compact disc, DVD, ipod, etc., have also expanded the range of possibilities, and even the remote control device has played a part. While not directly supporting mass communication, the many new possibilities for private 'media-making' (camcorders, PCs, printers, cameras, mobile phones, etc.) have expanded the world of media and forged bridges between public and private communication and between the spheres of professional and amateur. Finally, we should note the new kinds of 'quasi-media', including computer games and virtual reality devices, that overlap with the media in their culture and in the satisfactions of use.

The implications of all this for mass media are still far from clear, although it is certain that the 'traditional' media have also benefited greatly from new media innovations as well as acquiring new competitors. Secondly, we can already conclude that the communications revolution has generally shifted the 'balance of power' from the media to the audience in so far as there are more options to choose from and more active uses of media available. Traditional mass communication was essentially one-directional, while the new forms of communication are essentially *interactive*. Mass communication has in several respects become less massive and less centralized.

The Internet

Beyond that, it is useful to distinguish between the implications of enhanced transmission and the emergence of any new medium as such. The former means more speed, capacity and efficiency, while the latter opens up new possibilities for content, use and effects. The foremost claim to status as a new medium and maybe also a mass medium is the Internet. Even so, mass features are not its primary characteristic. The Internet began primarily as a non-commercial means of intercommunication and data exchange between professionals, but its more recent rapid advance has been fuelled by its potential as a purveyor of goods and many profitable services and as an alternative to other means of personal and interpersonal communication (Castells, 2001). The medium is not yet mature or clearly defined, in line with Lievrouw's (2004: 12) still valid assessment that there is 'no overarching killer application of online interaction'. Nevertheless, there is a case for seeing both search engines and social networking sites as dominant and unique applications. Initially, diffusion proceeded most rapidly in North America and Northern Europe. In the USA, it appeared to reach a ceiling of diffusion in 2001, at around 60% to 70% of the population (Rainie and Bell, 2004), but with much continuing flux. More recent figures indicate even higher household penetration in other countries (Küng et al., 2008). Actual use varies considerably in amount and type and overlap with the use of other media (e.g. music, film, radio). Some applications of the Internet, such as online news, are clearly extensions of newspaper journalism, although online news itself is also evolving in new directions, with new capabilities of content and new forms (as where a member of the public adopts the role of journalist).

The Internet's claim to full medium status is based in part on its having a distinctive technology, manner of use, range of content and services, and a distinct image of its own. However, the Internet has no clear institutional status and is not owned, controlled or organized by any single body, but is simply a network of internationally interconnected computers operating according to agreed protocols. Numerous organizations, but especially service providers and telecommunication bodies, contribute to its operation (Braman and Roberts, 2003). The Internet as such does not exist anywhere as a legal entity and is not subject to any single set of national laws or regulations (Lessig, 1999). Klotz (2004) said that no new legal paradigm for cyberspace has been realized, although it is at too early a stage of development to conclude that there never will be legal framework. At the time of writing, in 2009, this is still the position.

However, those who use the Internet can be accountable to the laws and regulations of the country in which they reside as well as to international law (Gringras, 1997). We return to the question of the Internet in Chapter 6 and elsewhere, but for the moment we can record its chief characteristics as a (mass) medium. Essential features of the Internet are summarized in Box 2.9, without distinguishing between 'medium' and 'institutional' aspects, since the former are so multiple and the latter so undeveloped.

The Internet as a medium: essential features **2.9**

- Computer-based technologies
- Hybrid, non-dedicated, flexible character
- Interactive potential
- Private and public functions
- Low degree of regulation
- Interconnectedness
- Ubiquity and de-locatedness
- Accessible to individuals as communicators
- A medium of both mass and personal communication

Differences between Media

It is much less easy to distinguish these various media from each other than it used to be. This is partly because some media forms are now distributed across different types of transmission channel, reducing the original uniqueness of form and experience in use. Secondly, the increasing convergence of technology, based on digitalization, can only reinforce this tendency. Newspapers are already widely accessible as text on the Internet, and the telephone system is also delivering media content, especially by way of the Internet. The clear lines of regulatory regime between the media are already blurred, both recognizing and encouraging greater similarity between different media. Thirdly, *globalizing* tendencies are reducing the distinctiveness of any particular national variant of media content and institution. Fourthly, the continuing trends towards integration of national and global media corporations have led to the housing of different media under the same roof, encouraging convergence by another route.

Nevertheless, on certain dimensions, clear differences do remain. There are some obvious differences in terms of typical content. There is also evidence that media are perceived differently in terms of physical and psychosocial characteristics (see Box 6.4, Chapter 6). Media vary a good deal in terms of perceived trust and credibility, although findings vary from country to country. Here we look only at two enduring questions. First, how *free* is a medium in relation to the wider society? Secondly, what is a medium good for and what are its perceived *uses*, from the point of view of an individual audience member?

Dimension of freedom versus control

Relations between media and society have a material, a political and a normative or social-cultural dimension. Central to the political dimension is the question of freedom and control. The main normative issue concerns how media ought to use the freedom they have. As noted above, near-total freedom was claimed and eventually gained for the *book*, for a mixture of reasons, in which the claims of politics, religion, science and art all played some part. This situation remains unchallenged in free societies, although the book has lost some of its once subversive potential as a result of its relative marginalization (book reading is a minority or minor form of media use). The influence of books remains considerable, but has to a large extent to be mediated through other more popular media or other institutions (education, politics, etc.).

The *newspaper* press bases its historical claim to freedom of operation much more directly on its political functions of expressing opinion and circulating political and economic information. But the newspaper is also a significant business enterprise for which freedom to produce and supply its primary product (information) is a necessary condition of successful operation in the marketplace. Broadcast television and radio are still generally licensed and have limited political freedom in practice, partly because of their privileged access to scarce spectrum space (despite the proclaimed 'end of scarcity') and partly because of their believed impact and power to persuade. But they are also often expected to use their informative capacity to support the democratic process and serve the public good in other ways. Even so, the current trend is for market forces to have a greater influence on the conduct of broadcasting than either political control or voluntary social responsibility.

The various *new media*, using cable, satellite or telecommunications networks for distribution, still await clear definitions of their appropriate degree of political freedom. The key new medium in this respect is the Internet. Freedom from control may be claimed on the grounds of privacy or the fact that these are not media of indiscriminate mass distribution but are directed to specific users. They are so-called 'common carriers' that generally escape control over their content because they are open to all on equal terms and primarily for personal or business rather than public matters. They also increasingly share the same communicative tasks as media with established editorial autonomy. The unclear status of most new media in respect of freedom is still a matter of dispute, since they are *de facto* very free, but also give rise to widespread fears of misuse.

The intermedia differences relating to *political* control (freedom means few regulations and little supervisory apparatus) follow a general pattern. In practice this means that the nearer any medium gets to operating as a *mass medium*, the more it can expect the attentions of governments and politicians, since it affects the exercise of power. In general, activities in the sphere of fiction, fantasy or entertainment are more likely to escape attention than are activities that touch directly on the ongoing reality of events and circumstances.

Virtually all media of public communication have a radical potential, in the sense of being potentially subversive of reigning systems of social control. They can provide access for new voices and perspectives on the existing order; new forms of organization and protest are made available for the subordinate or disenchanted. Even so, the institutional development of successful media has usually resulted in the elimination of the early radical potential, partly as a side-effect of commercialization, partly because authorities fear disturbance to society (Winston, 1986). According to Beniger (1986), the driving logic of new communication technology has always been towards increased control. This generalization is now being tested with reference to the Internet and looks like being validated.

The *normative* dimension of control operates according to the same general principles, although sometimes with different consequences for particular media. For instance, film, which has generally escaped direct political control, has often been subject to self-censorship and to monitoring of its content, on grounds of its potential moral impact on the young and impressionable (especially in matters of violence, crime or sex). The widespread restrictions applied to television in matters of culture and morals stem from the same tacit assumptions. These are that media that are very popular and have a potentially strong emotional impact on many people need to be supervised in 'the public interest'.

However, the more communication activities can be defined as either educational or 'serious' in purpose or, alternatively, as artistic and creative, the more freedom from normative restrictions can usually be claimed. There are complex reasons for this, but it is also a fact that 'art' and content of higher moral seriousness do not usually reach large numbers and are seen as marginal to power relations.

The degree of control of media by state or society depends partly on the feasibility of applying it. The most regulated media have typically been those whose distribution is most easily supervised, such as centralized national radio or television broadcasting or local cinema distribution. Books and print media generally are much less easy to monitor or to suppress. The same applies to local radio, while desktop publishing and photocopying and all manner of ways of reproducing sound and images have made direct censorship a very blunt and ineffective instrument.

The difficulty of policing national frontiers to keep out unwanted foreign communication is another consequence of new technology that promotes more freedom. While new technology in general seems to increase the promise of freedom of communication, the continued strength of institutional controls, including those of the market, over actual flow and reception should not be underestimated. It is also becoming clearer that the Internet is not impossible to control, as once believed, since all traffic can be monitored and traced and some countries have effectively blocked websites and content they dislike and can punish users. There is also extensive self-censorship by service providers in the face of threats or legal uncertainty.

The main issues raised in this section are summarized in Box 2.10 dealing with social control, with particular reference to two aspects: means or types of control and motives.

2.10 Social control of media

Types of control

- Censorship of content
- Legal restrictions
- Control of infrastructures
- Economic means
- Self-regulation or self-censorship

Motives for control

- Fear of political subversion
- For moral or cultural reasons
- Combat cyber-crime
- National security

Dimensions of use and reception

The increasing difficulty of typifying or distinguishing media channels in terms of content and function has undermined once stable social definitions of media. The newspaper, for instance, may now be as much an entertainment medium, or a consumers' guide, as it is a source of information about political and social events. Cable and satellite television systems are no longer confined to offering general programming for all. Even so, a few dominant images and definitions of what media 'are best for' do appear to survive, the outcome of tradition, social forces and the 'bias' of certain technologies.

For instance, television, despite the many changes and extensions relating to production, transmission and reception, remains primarily a medium of family entertainment, even if the family is less likely to be viewing together (see Chapter 16). It is still a focus of public interest and a shared experience in most societies. It has both a domestic and a collective character that seem to endure. The traditional conditions of family living (shared space, time and conditions) may account for this, despite the technological trend to individuation of use and specialization of content. The expected diffusion of digital radio and television might tend to reinforce the latter trend, along with demographic trends to more one-person households, more divorce and fewer children.

2.11 Dimensions of media use: questions arising

- Inside or outside the home?
- Individual or shared experience?
- Public or private in use?
- Interactive or not?

The questions about media use in Box 2.11 indicate three dimensions of media reception that mainly apply to traditional media: whether within or outside the home; whether an individual or a shared experience; and whether more public or more private. Television is typically shared, domestic and public. The newspaper, despite its changing content, conforms to a different type. It is certainly public in character, but is less purely domestic and is individual in use. Radio is now many things but often rather private, not exclusively domestic and more individual in use than television. Both the book and the music phonogram also largely follow this pattern. In general, the distinctions indicated have become less sharp as a result of changes of technology in the direction of proliferation and convergence of reception possibilities.

The newer digital media have added to the uncertainty about which medium is good for what purpose, but they have also added a fourth dimension by which media can be distinguished: that of degree of interactivity. The more interactive media are those that allow continual motivated choice and response by users. While the video game, CD-ROM, Internet and telephone chatline are clear examples where interaction is the norm, it is also the case that multi-channel cable or satellite television has an increased interactive potential, as do the recording and replay facilities of the domestic VCR. Interactivity has developed from a simple reaction possibility to the creation and supply of content, as with some social networking sites.

Conclusion

This chapter has offered a commentary on the evolution of mass media from the early days of printing in the late Middle Ages to the present age of information communication technology and the information society. It has told the story not as a narrative with dates and descriptions of events, but in terms of brief sketches of the mass media and their main forms, in chronological order. It has highlighted their main characteristics in terms of capacity to communicate, uses for an audience and regard by the larger society. Although the primary distinction is according to a type of technology, equal importance attaches to social, cultural and political factors. Certain technologies survived the evolutionary struggle, so to speak, and some others (not described here) did not make it. The same applies to the various uses to which the media have been put. There is no determining logic at work. Notable is the fact that all the media described are still with us and, in their own way, flourishing, despite recurrent predictions that one master medium would drive out weaker competitors. They have all found a means of adapting to changed conditions and new competitors.

Further Reading

Briggs, A. and Burke, P. (2005) *A Social History of the Media: from Gutenberg to the Internet*, 2nd edn. Oxford: Polity Press.
A comprehensive overview of the key developments in society and media during the modern era, written by two historians.

McLuhan, M. (1962) *The Gutenberg Galaxy*. Toronto: University of Toronto Press.
A seminal book about the revolutionary part played by the printing press in changing European culture and society. With high literary quality and many imaginative insights and examples.

Williams, R. (1975) *Television, Technology and Cultural Form*. London: Fontana.
An original analysis by a leading British critical scholar of the cultural consequences of technology, with particular reference to television. It still merits its seminal status.

Online Readings

Flichy, P. (2006) 'New media history', in L. Lievrouw and S. Livingstone (eds), *The Handbook of New Media*, pp. 187–204. London: Sage.

Gunaratne, S.A. (2001) 'Paper, printing and the printing press', *Gazette*, 63 (6): 459–79.

Lehman-Wilzig, S. and Cohen-Avigdor, N. (2004) 'The natural life cycle of new media evolution', *New Media and Society*, 6 (6): 707–30.

Rössler, P. (2001) 'Between online heaven and cyber hell: the framing of "the internet" by traditional media coverage in Germany', *New Media and Society*, 2 (1): 7–28.

Stober, S. (2004) 'What media evolution is: a theoretical approach to the history of new media', *European Journal of Communication*, 19 (4): 483–505.

Part 2
Theories

3

Concepts and Models for Mass Communication

❋   This chapter is concerned with defining basic concepts for the study of **mass communication** and explaining their origin in terms of the way the relationship between mass media and society has developed over the last century. Although new media have arisen and social and economic circumstances are very different, there are many continuities and many of the issues that faced the early media theorists and researchers are still with us, sometimes in more acute form. This overview of concepts provides a framework that can be applied to the issues listed in Chapter 1 (p. 9). In the second part of the chapter attention focuses on the main alternative perspectives and methods that have been adopted, with particular reference to the difference between critical and applied research and between quantitative, cause-and-effect methods and qualitative, cultural approaches.

❋   Lastly, the chapter outlines four models that have been developed for **framing** and studying the mass communication process, each with its own bias, but also with distinctive advantages. They are not so much alternative as complementary.

Early Perspectives on Media and Society

The twentieth century can plausibly be described as the 'first age of mass media'. It was also marked by alternating wonder and alarm at the influence of the mass media. Despite the enormous changes in media institutions and technology, and in society itself, and also the rise of a 'science of communication', the terms of public debate about the potential social significance of 'the media' seem to have changed remarkably little. A description of the issues which emerged during the first two or three decades of the twentieth century is of more than just historical interest, and early thinking provides a point of reference for understanding the present. Three sets of ideas were of particular importance from the outset. One concerned the question of

❋   the *power* of the new means of communication; a second, the question of social *integration* or disintegration that they might cause; and the third, the question of public *enlightenment*, which they might either promote or diminish. These themes are dealt with in depth in Chapter 4.

The power of mass media

❋   A belief in the power of mass media was initially based on the observation of their great reach and apparent impact, especially in relation to the new popular **newspaper**
❋   press. According to DeFleur and Ball-Rokeach (1989), newspaper circulation in the USA peaked in 1910, although it happened a good deal later in Europe and other parts of the
❋   world. The popular press was mainly funded by commercial **advertising** its content was characterized by sensational **news** stories, and its control was often concentrated in the hands of powerful press 'barons'. The First World War saw the mobilization of press and film in most of Europe and the United States for the national war aims of contending states. The results seemed to leave little doubt of the potency of media influence on the 'masses', when effectively managed and directed.

This impression was yet further reinforced by what happened in the Soviet Union and later in Nazi Germany, where the media were pressed into the service of **propaganda** on behalf of ruling party elites. The co-option of news and **entertainment** media by the allies in the Second World War removed any doubts about their propagandist value. Before the century was half way on its course, there was already a strongly held and soundly based view that mass publicity was effective in shaping opinion and influencing behaviour. It could also have effects on international relations and alliances. More recent events, including the fall of communism, the Balkan wars, two Gulf wars and the 'war on terror', have confirmed the media as an essential and volatile component in any international power struggle, where **public opinion** is also a factor. The conditions for effective media power have generally included a national media industry capable of reaching most of the population, a degree of consensus in the message disseminated (whatever its direction) and some measure of credibility and trust in the media on the part of audiences.

While by now, there is much more knowledge and also scepticism about the direct 'power' of mass communication, there is no less reliance on mass media in the spheres of advertising, **public relations** and political **campaigning**. Politics is routinely conducted (and also reported) on the assumption that skilful media presentation is absolutely vital to success in all normal circumstances.

Communication and social integration

Social theorists in the late nineteenth and early twentieth centuries were very conscious of the 'great transformation' which was taking place, as slower, traditional and communal ways gave way to fast-paced, secular, urban living and to a great expansion in the scale of social activities. Many of the themes of European and North American sociology at this time reflect this collective self-consciousness of the problems of change from small-scale to large-scale and from rural to urban societies. The social theory of the time posited a need for new forms of integration in the face of the problems caused by industrialization and urbanization. Crime, prostitution, poverty and dependency were associated with the increasing anonymity, isolation and uncertainty of modern life.

While the fundamental changes were social and economic, it was possible to point to newspapers, film and other forms of popular **culture** (music, books, magazines, comics) as potential contributors both to individual crime and declining morality and also to rootlessness, impersonality and lack of attachment or **community**. In the United States, large-scale immigration from Europe in the first two decades of the twentieth century highlighted questions of social cohesion and integration. This is exemplified in the work of the Chicago School of Sociology and the writings of Robert Park, G.H. Mead, Thomas Dewey and others (Rogers, 1993). Hanno Hardt (1979, 1991) has reconstructed the main lines of early theory concerning communication and social integration, both in Europe and in North America.

The links between popular mass media and social integration were easy to perceive in terms both negative (more crime and immorality) and individualistic (loneliness, loss of collective beliefs), but a positive contribution to cohesion and community was also expected from modern communications. Mass media were a potential force for a new kind of cohesion, able to connect scattered individuals in a shared national, city and local experience. They could also be supportive of the new democratic politics and of social reform movements. Not least in importance was the contribution of mass media, especially the cinema, to making hard lives more bearable.

How the influence of media came to be interpreted was often a matter of an observer's personal **attitude** to modern society and the degree of optimism or pessimism in their social outlook. The early part of the twentieth century, as well as (or perhaps because of) being a high point of nationalism, revolution and social conflict, was also a time of progressive thinking, democratic advance and scientific and technological progress.

In our time, circumstances have changed, although the underlying theme remains the same. There is still concern about the weakness of the ties that bind individuals together and to their society, the lack of shared values, the lack of social and civic participation, and the decline in what has been called 'social capital' (Putnam, 2000). The ties of trade unions, politics, religion and family all seem to have grown steadily weaker. Problems of integration arise in relation to new ethnic groups and migrants that have arrived in industrialized countries from rural and culturally distant societies. There are new demands for communications media to provide for the **identity** and expressive needs of old and new minorities within larger societies as well as to contribute to social harmony. The individuating effects of the **Internet** have been contrasted with the positive cohesive effect of the traditional newspaper press and broadcast television (Sunstein, 2006).

Mass communication as mass educator

The spirit of the early twentieth century (modern and forward-looking) supported a third set of ideas about mass communication – that the media could be a potent force for public enlightenment, supplementing and continuing the new institutions of universal schooling, public libraries and popular education. Political and social reformers saw a positive potential in the media, taken as a whole, and the media also saw themselves as, on balance, making a contribution to progress by spreading **information** and ideas, exposing political corruption and also providing much harmless enjoyment for ordinary people. In many countries, journalists were becoming more professional and adopting **codes** of ethics and good practice.

The democratic task of the press in informing the newly enfranchised masses was widely recognized. The newly established radio institutions of the 1920s and 1930s, especially in Europe, were often given a public cultural, educational and informative mission as well as the task of promoting national identity and unity. Each new mass medium has been hailed for its educational and cultural benefits and has been feared for its disturbing influence. The potential for communication technology to promote enlightenment has been invoked once again in respect of the latest communication technologies – those based on the computer and telecommunications (e.g. Neuman, 1991). More fears than hopes are now being voiced about the enlightenment role of the major mass media, as they increasingly seek to make profits in a highly competitive marketplace where entertainment has more market value than education or art. Public **broadcasting** is again being defended against market forces on the grounds of its contribution to public knowledge and societal solidarity. Arguments are heard for a similar public service presence in **cyberspace**.

✱

✱

The media as problem or scapegoat

Despite hopeful as well as fearful scenarios, the passing of decades does not seem to have changed the tendency of public opinion both to blame the media (see Drotner, 1992) and to demand that they do more to solve society's ills. There are successive instances of alarm relating to the media, whenever an insoluble or inexplicable social problem arises. The most constant element has been a negative perception of the media – especially the inclination to link media portrayals of crime, sex and violence with the seeming increase in social and moral disorder. These waves of alarm have been called '**moral panics**', partly because they are based on little evidence either of media cause or actual effect.

✱

New ills have also been found to lay at the door of the media, especially such phenomena as violent political protest and demonstration, xenophobia, and even the supposed decline of democracy and rise of political apathy and cynicism. Individual harms now include references to depression, acquisitiveness, obesity (or its opposite) and lassitude. The most recent object of such waves of alarm has been the Internet, suspected of encouraging paedophilia, **pornography**, violence and hate as well as aiding terrorist organizations and international crime. Paradoxically or not, it has usually been the media themselves that have highlighted and amplified many of these alarmist views, perhaps because they seem to confirm the power of the media, but more likely because they are already popularly believed and also newsworthy.

✱

The 'Mass' Concept

This mixture of popular **prejudice** and social theorizing about the media has formed the background against which research has been commissioned, hypotheses have been formulated and tested, and more precise theories about mass communication have been developed. And while the interpretations of the direction (positive or negative) of mass media influence show much divergence, the most persistent element in public estimation of the media has been a simple agreement on their strong influence. In turn, this perception owes much to various meanings of the term 'mass'. Although the concept of '**mass society**' was not fully developed until after the Second World War, the essential ideas were circulating before the end of the nineteenth century. The key term 'mass' in fact unites a number of concepts which are important for understanding how the process of mass communication has usually been understood, right up to the present.

✱

✱

Early uses of the term usually carried negative associations. It referred initially to the multitude or the 'common people', usually seen as uneducated, ignorant and potentially irrational, unruly and even violent (as when the mass turned into a mob of rioters) (Bramson, 1961). It could also be used in a positive sense, however, especially in the socialist tradition, where it connoted the strength and solidarity of ordinary working people when organized for collective purposes or when having to bear oppression. The terms 'mass support', 'mass movement' and 'mass action' are examples whereby large numbers of people acting together can be seen in a positive light. As Raymond Williams (1961: 289) commented: 'There are no masses, only ways of seeing people as masses.'

Aside from its political references, the word 'mass', when applied to a set of people, has unflattering implications. It suggests an amorphous collection of individuals without much individuality. One standard dictionary definition defines the word as an 'aggregate in which individuality is lost' (*Shorter Oxford English Dictionary*). This is close to the meaning which early sociologists sometimes gave to the media **audience.** It was the large and seemingly undifferentiated audiences for the popular media that provided the clearest examples of the concept. The main features attributed to the mass are given in Box 3.1. These include both objective and also subjective or perceived features.

3.1 The concept of mass: theoretical features

- Composed of a large aggregate of people
- Undifferentiated composition
- Mainly negative perception
- Lacking internal order or structure
- Reflective of a wider mass society

The Mass Communication Process

The term 'mass communication' came into use in the late 1930s, but its essential features were already well known and have not really changed since, even if the media themselves have in some ways become less massive. Early mass media were quite diverse in their scale and conditions of operation. For instance, popular films could be seen in village tents as well as metropolitan picture palaces. The newspaper press ranged from popular city dailies to small local weeklies. Even so, we can discern the typical form of mass communication according to certain general characteristics, which have already been introduced in Chapter 1.

The most obvious feature of the mass media is that they are designed to reach the *many*. Potential audiences are viewed as large aggregates of more or less anonymous consumers, and the relationship between sender and receiver is affected accordingly. The 'sender' is often the organization itself or a professional communicator (journalist, presenter, producer, entertainer, etc.) whom it employs. If not this, it is another voice of society given or sold access to media channels (advertiser, politician, preacher, advocate of a cause, etc.). The relationship is inevitably one-directional, one-sided and impersonal, and there is a social as well as a physical distance between sender and receiver. The former usually has more authority, prestige or expertise than the latter. The relationship is not only asymmetrical, it is often calculative or manipulative in intention. It is essentially non-moral, based on a service promised or asked for in some unwritten contract with no mutual obligation.

The symbolic content or message of mass communication is typically 'manufactured' in standardized ways (mass production) and is reused and repeated in identical forms. Its flow is overwhelmingly one-directional. It has generally lost its uniqueness and originality through reproduction and overuse. The media message is a product of work with an exchange value in the media market and a use value for its receiver, the media consumer. It is essentially a commodity and differs in this respect from the symbolic content of other types of human communication.

One early definition (Janowitz, 1968) reads as follows: 'Mass communications comprise the institutions and techniques by which specialized groups employ technological devices (press, radio, films, etc.) to disseminate symbolic content to large, heterogeneous and widely dispersed audiences.' In this and similar definitions, the word 'communication' is really equated with 'transmission', as viewed by the sender, rather than the fuller meaning of the term which includes the notions of response, sharing and interaction. This definition is also limited by its equating the *process* of mass communication with the *means* of transmission. However, the two are not synonymous. In particular, we can now see that new media can serve both for mass communication and for personalized, individual communication.

We can also see that the true mass media also had uses that cannot be counted as mass communication (e.g. as a means passing time, companionship, etc.). There are other common uses of the same technologies and other kinds of relationships mediated through the same **networks**. For instance, the basic forms and technologies of 'mass' communication are the same as those used for very local newspapers or radio and they might also be used in education. Mass media can also be used for individual, private or organizational purposes. The same media that carry public messages to large publics for public purposes can also carry personal notices, advocacy messages, charitable appeals, situations-vacant advertisements and many varied kinds of information and culture. This point is especially relevant at a time of **convergence** of communication technologies, when the boundaries between public and private and large-scale and individual communication networks are increasingly blurred.

Mass communication was, from the beginning, more of an idea than a reality. The term stands for a condition and a process that is theoretically possible but rarely found in any pure form. Where it does seem to occur, it often turns out to be less massive, and less technologically determined, than it appears on the surface. The defining characteristics of the concept are set out in Box 3.2. All of these have an objective basis, but the concept as a whole is often used in a subjective and imprecise way.

3.2   The mass communication process: theoretical features

- Large-scale distribution and reception of content
- One-directional flow
- Asymmetrical relation between sender and receiver
- Impersonal and anonymous relationship with audience
- Calculative or market relationship with audience
- Standardization and commodification of content

The Mass Audience

Herbert Blumer (1939) was the first to define the mass formally as a new type of social formation in modern society, by contrasting it with other formations, especially the *group*, *crowd* and **public**. In a small group, all its members know each other, are aware of their common membership, share the same values, have a certain structure of relationships which is stable over time, and interact to achieve some purpose. The crowd is larger but still restricted within observable boundaries in a particular space. It is, however, temporary and rarely re-forms with the same composition. It may possess a high degree of identity and share the same 'mood', but there is usually no structure or order to its moral and social composition. It can act, but its actions are often seen to have an affective and emotional, often irrational, character.

The third collectivity named by Blumer, the public, is likely to be relatively large, widely dispersed and enduring. It tends to form around an issue or cause in public life, and its primary purpose is to advance an interest or opinion and to achieve political change. It is an essential element in democratic politics, based on the ideal of rational discourse within an open political system and often comprising the better-informed section of the population. The rise of the public is characteristic of modern liberal democracies and related to the rise of the 'bourgeois' or party newspapers described earlier.

The term 'mass' captured several features of the new audiences for cinema and radio (and to some extent the popular press) that were not covered by any of these three concepts. The new audience was typically much larger than any group, crowd or public. It was very widely dispersed, and its members were usually unknown to each other or to whoever brought the audience into existence. It lacked self-awareness and self-identity and was incapable of acting together in an organized way to secure objectives. It was marked by a shifting composition within changing boundaries. It did not act for itself but was, rather, 'acted upon' (and thus an object of manipulation). It was heterogeneous in consisting of large numbers from all social strata and demographic groups, but also homogeneous in its choice of some particular object of interest and according to the perception of those who would like to manipulate it. The main features attributed to the mass audience are summarized in Box 3.3.

> ### The mass audience:
> ### main theoretical features
>
> # 3.3
>
> - Large numbers of readers, viewers, etc.
> - Widely dispersed
> - Non-interactive and anonymous relation to each other
> - Heterogeneous composition
> - Not organized or self-acting
> - An object of management or manipulation by the media

The audience for mass media is not the only social formation that can be characterized in this way, since the word 'mass' is sometimes applied to consumers in the expression 'mass market' or to large bodies of voters (the 'mass electorate'). It is significant, however, that such entities also often correspond with media audiences and that mass media are used to direct or control both consumer and political behaviour.

Within the conceptual framework sketched, media use was represented as a form of 'mass behaviour', which in turn encouraged the application of methods of 'mass research' – especially large-scale surveys and other methods for recording the reach and response of audiences to what was offered. A commercial and organizational logic for 'audience research' was furnished with theoretical underpinnings. It seemed to make sense, as well as being practical, to discuss media audiences in purely *quantitative* terms. In fact, the methods of research tended only to reinforce a **biased** conceptual perspective ✳ (treating the audience as a mass market). Research into ratings and the reach of press and broadcasting reinforced a view of the audiences as a mass market of consumers.

The Mass Media as an Institution of Society

Despite changing technology, mass communication persists within the whole framework of the mass media institution. This refers broadly to the set of media organizations and activities, together with their own formal or informal rules of operation and sometimes legal and policy requirements set by the society. These reflect the expectations of the public as a whole and of other social institutions (such as politics, governments, law, religion and the economy). Media institutions have gradually developed around the key activities of **publication** and dissemination. They also overlap with other ✳ institutions, especially as these expand their public communication activities. They are internally segmented according to type of technology (print, film, television, etc.) and often within each type (such as national versus local press or broadcasting). They also change over time and differ from one country to another (see Chapter 9). Even so, there are several typical defining features, additional to the central activity of producing and distributing 'knowledge' (information, ideas, culture) on behalf of those who want to communicate and in response to individual and collective demand.

While it is quite common to find the entire set of mass media referred to as an institution in such expressions as the 'effects of the media' or 'responsibilities of media in society', in free societies there is no formal institution of the media in the way that there is in respect of health, education, justice or the military. Nevertheless, the media separately or together do tend to develop institutional forms that are embedded in and recognized by, the wider society. The 'press' is a good example of this. There are no formal definitions or boundaries, but it typically describes all newspapers and magazines, journalists, editors and media owners. There is no formal external regulation, but there are voluntary codes of conduct and ethics. The press accepts some public responsibilities and receives some rights and privileges in return, especially a guarantee of freedom. Other media, such as broadcasting, develop their own institutional identity. There is enough in common between all media to justify a reference to a single 'media institution', the main conceptual features of which are shown in Box 3.4.

3.4 The mass media institution: main theoretical features

- The core activity is the production and distribution of information and culture
- Media acquire functions and responsibilities in the 'public sphere' that are overseen by the institution
- Control is mainly by self-regulation, with limits set by society
- Boundaries of membership are uncertain
- Media are free and in principle independent of political and economic power

Mass Culture and Popular Culture

The typical *content* which flowed through the newly created channels to the new mass audience was from the start a very diverse mixture of stories, images, information, ideas, entertainment and spectacles. Even so, the single concept of '**mass culture**' was commonly used to refer to all this (see Rosenberg and White, 1957). Mass culture had a wider reference to the tastes, preferences, manners and styles of the mass (or just the majority) of people. It also once had a generally negative connotation, mainly because of its associations with the assumed cultural preferences of 'uncultivated', non-discriminating or just lower-class audiences.

The term is now quite dated, partly because class differences are less sharply drawn or clearly acknowledged and they no longer separate an educated professional minority from a large, poor and ill-educated working-class majority. It is also the case that the former hierarchy of 'cultural taste' is no longer widely accepted.

Even when in fashion, the idea of mass culture as an exclusively 'lower-class' phenomenon was not empirically justified, since it referred to the normal cultural experience of almost everyone to some degree (Wilensky, 1964). The expression 'popular culture' is now generally preferred because it simply denotes what many or even most people like. It may also have some connotation of what is popular with the young in particular. More recent developments in media and **cultural studies** (as well as in society) have led to a positive valuation of popular culture. For some media theorists (e.g. Fiske, 1987), the very fact of popularity is a token of value in political as well as cultural terms.

＊

Definitions and contrasts

Attempts to define mass culture often contrasted it (unfavourably) with more traditional forms of (symbolic) culture. Wilensky, for instance, compared it with the notion of 'high culture', which will refer to two characteristics of the product:

> (1) it is created by, or under the supervision of, a cultural elite operating within some aesthetic, literary, or scientific tradition … (2) critical standards independent of the consumer of their product are systematically applied to it … 'Mass culture' will refer to cultural *products manufactured solely for the mass market*. Associated characteristics, not intrinsic to the definition, are *standardization* of product and *mass behaviour* in its use. (1964: 176, original emphasis)

Mass culture was also differentiated from an earlier cultural form – that of folk culture or a traditional culture which more evidently comes from the people and usually predates (or is independent of) mass media and the mass production of culture. Original folk culture (especially expressed in dress, customs, song, stories, dance, etc.) was being widely rediscovered in Europe during the nineteenth century. Often, this was for reasons connected with the rise of nationalism, otherwise as part of the 'arts and crafts' movement and the romantic reaction against industrialism. The rediscovery (by the middle classes) was taking place at the very time that it was rapidly disappearing among worker and peasant classes because of social change. Folk culture was originally made unselfconsciously, using traditional forms, themes, materials and means of expression, and had usually been incorporated into everyday life. Critics of mass culture often regretted the loss of the integrity and simplicity of folk art, and the issue is still alive in parts of the world where mass-produced culture has not completely triumphed. The new urban industrial working class of Western Europe and North America were the first consumers of the new mass culture after being cut off from the roots of folk culture. No doubt the mass media drew on some popular cultural streams and adapted others to the conditions of urban life to fill the cultural void created by industrialization, but intellectual critics could usually see only a cultural loss. The main features of mass culture are summarized in Box 3.5.

3.5 The idea of mass culture: main features

- Non-traditional form and content
- Intended for mass consumption
- Mass produced and formulaic
- Pejorative image
- Commercial
- Homogenized

Other views of mass culture

The rise of mass culture was open to more than one interpretation. Bauman (1972), for instance, took issue with the idea that mass communication media *caused* mass culture, arguing that they were more a tool to shape something that was happening in any case as a result of the increasing cultural homogeneity of national societies. In his view, what is often referred to as 'mass culture' is more properly just a more universal or standardized culture. Several features of mass communication have contributed to the process of standardization, especially dependence on the market, the supremacy of large-scale organization and the application of new technology to cultural production. This more objective approach helps to defuse some of the conflict that has characterized the debate about mass culture. In some measure, the 'problem of mass culture' reflected the need to come to terms with new technological possibilities for symbolic reproduction (Benjamin, 1977) which challenged established notions of art. The issue of mass culture was fought out in social and political terms, without being resolved in aesthetic terms.

Despite the search for a seemingly value-free conception of mass culture, the issue remains conceptually and ideologically troublesome. As Bourdieu (1986) and others have clearly demonstrated, different conceptions of cultural merit are strongly connected with social class differences. Possession of economic capital has usually gone hand in hand with possession of 'cultural capital', which in class societies can also be 'encashed' for material advantages. Class-based value systems once strongly maintained the superiority of 'high' and traditional culture against much of the typical popular culture of the mass media. The support for such value systems (though maybe not for the class system) has weakened, although the issue of differential cultural quality remains alive as an aspect of a continuing cultural and media policy debate.

Lastly, we can keep in mind that, as noted above, 'popular culture' has been widely 'revalued' by social and cultural theorists and largely deproblematized. It is no longer viewed as lacking in originality, creativity or merit and is often celebrated for its meanings, cultural significance and expressive value (see pp. 117–18).

Reassessing the concept of mass

The idea of a mass or a mass society was always an abstract notion, expressing a critical view of contemporary cultural trends. Today, it probably seems even more theoretical and less relevant. Nevertheless, some of the ills and discontents that it once referred to are still with us, sometimes under new names. These include: experience of loneliness and feelings of isolation; feelings of powerlessness in the face of economic, political and environmental forces outside our control; the sense of impersonality in much of modern life, sometimes made worse by information technology; a decline in togetherness; and a loss of security.

What is probably clearer now is that mass media can be as much a part of the solution as of the problem. Depending on who and where we are, they offer ways of coping with the difficulties of large-scale society, making sense of our predicament and mediating our relations with larger forces. The media are now probably less 'massive', one-directional and distant, and more responsive and participant.

But they are not always benign in their working. They can exert power without accountability and destroy individual lives by aggressive intrusion into privacy, by **stereotyping** and stigmatizing and by systematic misinformation. When they agree on some issue there is little tolerance of deviance, and when they decide to support the authorities there is no court of appeal. They can undermine as well as support the democratic political process. They have in fact some of the characteristics of benevolent despots – by turns endearing, capricious, ferocious or irrational. For these reasons, it is necessary to keep a long memory even for what seem old-fashioned notions.

The Rise of a Dominant Paradigm for Theory and Research

The ideas about media and society, and the various subconcepts of 'mass' that have been described, have helped to shape a framework of research into mass communication which has been described as 'dominant' in more than one sense. The 'dominant paradigm' combines a view of powerful mass media in a mass society with the typical research practices of the emerging social sciences, especially social surveys, social-psychological experiments and statistical analysis. The underlying view of society in the dominant paradigm is essentially normative. It presumes a certain kind of normally functioning 'good society' which would be democratic (elections, universal suffrage, representation), liberal (secular, free-market conditions, individualistic, freedom of speech), pluralistic (institutionalized competition between parties and interests), consensual and orderly (peaceful, socially integrated, fair, legitimate), and also well informed. The liberal-pluralist perspective does not view social inequality as essentially problematic or even unjust, as long as tensions and conflicts can be resolved by existing institutional means.

The potential or actual good or harm to be expected from mass media has largely been judged according to this model, which coincides with an idealized view of western society. The contradictions within this view of society and its distance from social reality are often ignored. Most early research concerning media in developing or Third World countries was guided by the assumption that these societies would gradually converge on the same (more advanced and progressive) western model. Early communication research was also influenced by the notion that the model of a liberal, pluralist and just society was threatened by an alternative, totalitarian form (communism), where the mass media were distorted into tools for suppressing democracy. The awareness of this alternative helped to identify and even reinforce the norm described. The media often saw themselves as playing a key role in supporting and expressing the values of the 'western way of life'. Since the virtual extinction of communism, other enemies have emerged, notably international terrorism, sometimes linked (by the media and authorities) with religious fundamentalism or other 'extremist' or revolutionary movements.

Origins in functionalism and information science

The theoretical elements of the dominant paradigm were not invented for the case of the mass media but were largely taken over from sociology, psychology and an applied version of information science. This took place especially in the decade after the Second World War, when there was a largely unchallenged North American **hegemony** over both the social sciences and the mass media (Tunstall, 1977). Sociology, as it matured theoretically, offered a functionalist framework of analysis for the media as for other institutions. Lasswell (1948) was the first to formulate a clear statement of the 'functions' of communication in society – meaning essential tasks performed for its maintenance (see Chapter 4). The general assumption is that communication works towards the integration, continuity and order of society, although mass communication also has potentially dysfunctional (disruptive or harmful) consequences. Despite a much reduced intellectual appeal, the language of functions has proved difficult to escape from in discussions of media and society.

The second theoretical element influential in the dominant paradigm guiding media research stemmed from information theory, as developed by Shannon and Weaver (1949), which was concerned with the technical efficiency of communication channels for carrying information. They developed a model for analysing information transmission that visualized communication as a sequential process. This process begins with a *source* that selects a *message*, which is then *transmitted*, in the form of a *signal*, over a *communication channel*, to a *receiver*, who transforms the signal back into a message for a *destination*. The model was designed to account for differences between messages as sent and messages as received, these differences being considered to result from *noise* or *interference* affecting the channels. This 'transmission' model was not directly concerned with *mass* communication, but it was popularized as a versatile way of conceiving many human communication processes, with particular reference to the effects of message transmission.

A third pillar of the paradigm is to be found in the methodological developments of the mid-century period. A combination of advances in 'mental measurement' (especially applied to individual attitudes and other attributes) and in statistical analysis appeared to offer new and powerful tools for achieving generalized and reliable knowledge of previously hidden processes and states. The methods seemed able to answer questions about the influence of mass media and about their effectiveness in persuasion and attitude change. An additional contribution to the paradigm was the high status of 'behaviourism' in psychology and of the experimental method in particular, often based on one version or another of **stimulus–response** theory (see pp. 470–71). These developments were very much in line with the requirements of the transmission model.

Bias of the paradigm towards studying media effects and social problems

According to Rogers (1986: 7), the transmission model 'was the single most important turning point in the history of communication science' and it 'led communication scientists into a linear, effects-oriented approach to human communication in the decades following 1949'. Rogers also notes that the result was to lead communication scientists into 'the intellectual cul-de-sac of focusing mainly upon the *effects* of communication, especially mass communication' (1986: 88). Rogers and others have long recognized the blind spot in this model, and more recent thinking about communication research has often taken the form of a debate with the model. Even so, the linear causal approach was what many wanted, and still do want, from communication research, especially those who see communication primarily as an efficient device for getting a message to many people, whether as advertising, political propaganda or public information.

The fact that communication does not usually look that way from the point of view of receivers, nor works as envisaged, has taken a long time to register. The theoretical materials for a very different model of (mass) communication were actually in place relatively early – based on previous thinking by several (North American) social scientists, especially G.H. Mead, C.H. Cooley and Robert Park. Such a 'model' would have represented communication as essentially social and interactive, concerned with sharing of meaning, not impact (see Hardt, 1991).

Against this background, the path taken by 'mainstream' mass media research is clear enough. Research has mostly been concerned with the measurement of the effects of mass media, whether intended or unintended. The main aims of research in the dominant paradigm have been the improvement of the effectiveness of communication for legitimate ends (such as advertising or public information) or the assessment of whether mass media are a cause of social problems (such as crime, violence or other kinds of delinquency, but also social unrest). Traces of the linear causal model are widely found in research and even the findings that have accumulated around its 'failure' have been paradoxically supportive. The main reason for the failure to find effects was thought to be the mediating role of social group and personal relationships. According to Gitlin (1978), out of 'failed' (read: no measured effect) research comes a positive message of health for the checks and balances of the status quo and also a vindication of the empirical research tradition.

Box 3.6 summarizes the ideas presented in the preceding section. The elements of the paradigm bring together several features of the case: the kind of society in which it might apply; some ideas about the typical purposes and character of mass communication; assumptions about media effects; plus a justification of the role of research.

3.6 The dominant paradigm of communication research: main assumptions

- A liberal-pluralist ideal of society
- The media have certain functions in society
- Media effects on audiences are direct and linear
- Group relations and individual differences modify effects of media
- Quantitative research and variable analysis
- Media viewed either as a potential social problem or a means of persuasion
- Behaviourist and quantitative methods have primacy

An Alternative, Critical Paradigm

The critique of the dominant paradigm also has several elements, and what follows is a composite picture woven from different voices that are not always in accord. In particular, there is a theoretical and methodological line of criticism that is distinct from normative objections. From a pragmatic point of view, the simple transmission model does not work for a number of reasons: signals simply do not reach receivers, or not those intended; messages are not understood as they are sent; and there is always much 'noise' in the channels that distorts the message. Moreover, little communication is actually unmediated; what evades the mass media is typically filtered through other channels or by way of personal contacts (see the discussion of 'personal influence' and the 'two-step flow' on pp. 472–3). All this undermines the notion of powerful media. Early notions of the media as a hypodermic syringe or 'magic bullet' that would always have the intended effect were swiftly shown to be quite inadequate (Chaffee and Hochheimer, 1982; DeFleur and Ball-Rokeach, 1989). It has been clear for several decades that mass media simply do not have the direct effects once attributed to them (Klapper, 1960). In fact, it has always been difficult to prove any substantial effect.

A different view of society and the media

Most broadly, the 'alternative paradigm' rests on a different view of society, one which does not accept the prevailing liberal-capitalist order as just or inevitable or the best one can hope for in the fallen state of humankind. Nor does it accept the rational-calculative, utilitarian model of social life as at all adequate or desirable, or the commercial model as the only or best way to run media. There is an alternative, idealist and sometimes utopian **ideology**, but nowhere a worked-out model of an ideal social system. Nevertheless, there is a sufficient common basis for rejecting the hidden ideology of pluralism and of conservative functionalism.

    There has been no shortage of vocal critics of the media themselves, from the early years of the twentieth century, especially in relation to their commercialism, low standards of truth and decency, control by unscrupulous monopolists and much more. The original ideological inspiration for a well-grounded alternative has been socialism or **Marxism** in one variant or another. The first significant impulse was given by the *émigrés* from the **Frankfurt School** who went to the USA in the 1930s and helped to promote an alternative view of the dominant commercial mass culture (Jay, 1973; Hardt, 1991; see Chapter 5, pp. 115–16). Their contribution was to provide a strong intellectual base for seeing the process of mass communication as manipulative and ultimately oppressive (see Chapter 5). Their critique was both political and cultural. The ideas of C. Wright Mills concerning a mass society (see p. 94) articulated a clear alternative view of the media, drawing on a native North American radical tradition, eloquently exposing the liberal fallacy of pluralist control.

    It was during the 1960s and 1970s that the alternative paradigm really took shape, under the influence of the 'ideas of 1968', combining anti-war and liberation movements of various kinds as well as neo-Marxism. The causes at issue included student democracy, feminism and anti-imperialism. The main components of, and supports for, an alternative paradigm are as follows. The first is a much more sophisticated notion of ideology in media content which has allowed researchers to 'decode' the ideological messages of mass-mediated entertainment and news (which tend towards legitimating established power structures and defusing opposition). The notion of fixed meanings embedded in media content and leading to predictable and measurable impact was rejected. Instead, we have to view meaning as constructed and messages as decoded according to the social situation and the interests of those in the receiving audience.

    Secondly, the economic and political character of mass media organizations and structures nationally and internationally has been re-examined. These institutions are no longer taken at face value but can be assessed in terms of their operational strategies, which are far from neutral or non-ideological. As the critical paradigm has developed, it has moved from an exclusive concern with working-class subordination to a wider view of other kinds of domination, especially in relation to youth, alternative subcultures, gender and ethnicity.

    Thirdly, these changes have been matched by a turn to more 'qualitative' research, whether into culture, discourse or the ethnography of mass media use. This is sometimes referred to as a 'linguistic' turn since it reflected the renewed interest in studying the relation between language and society (sociolinguistics) and a conviction that the symbolic mediation of reality is actually more influential and open to study than reality itself. It is linked to the interest in exposing concealed ideological meanings as noted above. This has provided alternative routes to knowledge and forged a link back to the neglected pathways of the sociological theories of symbolic interactionism and phenomenology that emphasized the role of individuals in expressing and constructing their own personal environment (see Jensen and Jankowski, 1991). This is part of a more general development of cultural studies, within which mass communication can be viewed in a new light. According to Dahlgren (1995), the cultural studies tradition 'confronts the scientistic self-delusion' of the dominant paradigm, but there is an inevitable tension between textual and socio-institutional analysis.

The communication relations between the First World and the Third World, especially in the light of changing technology, have also encouraged new ways of thinking about mass communication. For instance, the relationship is no longer seen as a matter of the enlightened transfer of development and democracy to 'backward' lands. It is at least as plausibly seen as economic and cultural domination. Lastly, although theory does not necessarily lead in a *critical* direction, the 'new media' have forced a re-evaluation of earlier thinking about media effects, if only because the model of one-directional mass communication can no longer be sustained. The main points of the perspective are summarized in Box 3.7.

3.7 The alternative paradigm: main features

- Critical view of society and rejection of value neutrality
- Rejection of the transmission model of communication
- Non-deterministic view of media technology and messages
- Adoption of an interpretative and constructionist perspective
- Qualitative methodology
- Preference for cultural or political-economic theories
- Wide concern with inequality and sources of opposition in society

Paradigms compared

The alternative perspective is not just a mirror image of the dominant paradigm or a statement of opposition to the mechanistic and applied view of communication. It is based on a more complete view of communication as sharing and ritual rather than as just 'transmission' (see p. 70). It is complementary as well as being an alternative. It offers its own viable avenues of inquiry, but following a different agenda. The paradigm has been especially valuable in extending the range of methods and approaches to popular culture in all its aspects. The interaction and engagement between media experiences and social-cultural experiences are central to all this.

While this discussion has presented two main versions, it is arguable that both the 'alternative' and the 'dominant' approach each bring together two distinct elements – one 'critical' (motivated by strong value judgements of the media), the other 'interpretative' or 'qualitative' (more concerned with understanding). Potter et al. (1993) proposed a threefold division of the main paradigms for communication science: a 'social science' approach in which empirical questions about media were investigated by means of quantitative methods; an interpretative approach, employing qualitative methods and emphasizing the meaning-giving potential of media; and a 'critical analysis' approach based on critical social theory, especially from a leftist or political economic perspective. Fink and Gantz (1996) found this scheme to work well in a **content analysis** of published communication research. Meyrowitz (2008) ✳ has suggested that there are root narratives about the influence of media and that underlie these and similar differences of approach that have been sketched. He names the narratives as, respectively, narratives of 'power', 'pleasure' and 'pattern'. The first relates to ideas about power and resistance to power and primarily to the dominant paradigm. The second narrative ('pleasure') points to cultural factors and personal choice as related more to influence. The third ('pattern') looks more to an explanation of influence to media structure and type, thus in part to **'medium theory'**, described ✳ later in the book (pp. 142–3).

Leaving aside these issues of classification, it is clear that the alternative paradigm continues to evolve under the dual influence of changing theory (and fashion) and also the changing concerns of society in relation to the media. Although value-relativist postmodernist theory (see pp. 128–30) has tended to demote concerns about ideological manipulation, commercialism and social problems, new issues have arisen. These relate, among others, to the environment, personal and collective identity, health and risk, trust and authenticity. Meanwhile, older issues, such as racism, war propaganda and inequality, have refused to go away.

The differences of approach between dominant and alternative paradigms are deep-rooted, and their existence underlines the difficulty of having any unified 'science of communication'. The differences stem also from the very nature of (mass) communication, which has to deal in ideology, values and ideas and cannot escape from being interpreted within ideological frameworks. While the reader of this book is not obliged to make a choice between the two main paradigms, knowing about them will help to make sense of the **diversity** of theories and of disagreements about ✳ the supposed 'facts' concerning mass media.

Four Models of Communication

The original definition of mass communication as a process (see p. 56) depended on objective features of mass production, reproduction and distribution which were shared by several different media. It was very much a technologically- and organizationally-based definition, subordinating human considerations. Its validity has long been called into question, especially as a result of the conflicting views just discussed and, more recently, by the fact that the original mass production technology and the factory-like forms of organization have themselves been made obsolescent by social and technological change. We have to consider alternative, though not necessarily inconsistent, models (representations) of the process of public communication. At least four such models can be distinguished, aside from the question of how the 'new media' should be conceptualized.

A transmission model

At the core of the dominant paradigm can be found (see pp. 163–4) a particular view of communication as a process of *transmission* of a fixed quantity of information – the *message* as determined by the sender or source. Simple definitions of mass communication often follow Lasswell's (1948) observation that the study of mass communication is an attempt to answer the question, 'Who says what to whom, through what channel and with what effect?' This represents the linear sequence already mentioned, which is largely built into standard definitions of the nature of predominant forms of mass communication. A good deal of early theorizing about mass communication (see, for example, McQuail and Windahl, 1993) was an attempt to extend and to improve on this simplistic version of the process. Perhaps the most complete early version of a model of mass communication, in line with the defining features noted above and consistent with the dominant paradigm, was offered by Westley and MacLean (1957).

Their achievement was to recognize that mass communication involves the interpolation of a new 'communicator role' (such as that of the professional journalist in a formal media organization) between 'society' and 'audience'. The sequence is thus not simply (1) sender, (2) message, (3) channel, (4) many potential receivers, but rather (1) events and 'voices' in society, (2) channel/communicator role, (3) messages, (4) receiver. This revised version takes account of the fact that mass communicators do not usually originate 'messages' or communication. Rather they *relay* to a potential audience their own account (news) of a selection of the events occurring in the environment, or they give **access** to the views and voices of some of those (such as advocates of opinions, advertisers, performers and writers) who want to reach a wider public. There are three important features of the complete model as drawn by Westley and MacLean: one is the emphasis on the *selecting* role of mass communicators; the second is the fact that selection is undertaken according to an assessment of what the audience will find interesting; and the third is that communication is not purposive, beyond this last goal. The media themselves typically do not aim to persuade or educate or even to inform.

According to this model, mass communication is a self-regulating process that is guided by the interests and demands of an audience that is known only by its selections and responses to what is offered. Such a process can no longer be viewed as linear, since it is strongly shaped by 'feedback' from the audience both to the media and to the advocates and original communicators. This view of the mass media sees them as relatively open and neutral service organizations in a secular society, contributing to the work of other social institutions. It also substitutes the satisfaction of the audience as a measure of efficient performance for that of information transfer. It is not accidental that this model was based on the American system of free-market media. It would not very accurately fit a state-run media system or even a European public broadcasting institution. It is also innocent of the idea that the free market might not necessarily reflect the interests of audiences or might also conduct its own form of purposeful propaganda.

A ritual or expressive model

The transmission model remains a useful representation of the rationale and general operation of some media in some of their functions (especially general news media and advertising). It is, however, incomplete and misleading as a representation of many other media activities and of the diversity of communication processes that are at work. One reason for its weakness is the limitation of communication to the matter of 'transmission'. This version of communication, according to James Carey (1975: 3),

> is the commonest in our culture and is defined by terms such as sending, transmitting or giving information to others. It is formed off a metaphor of geography or transportation ... The centre of this idea of communication is the transmission of signals or messages over time for the purpose of control.

It implies instrumentality, cause-and-effect relations and one-directional flow. Carey pointed to the alternative view of communication as 'ritual', according to which

> communication is linked to such terms as sharing, participation, association, fellowship and the possession of a common faith ... A ritual view is not directed towards the extension of messages in space, but the maintenance of society in time; not the act of imparting information but the representation of shared beliefs. (1975: 8)

This alternative can equally be called an 'expressive' model of communication, since its emphasis is also on the intrinsic satisfaction of the sender (or receiver) rather than on some instrumental purpose. Ritual or expressive communication depends on shared understandings and emotions. It is celebratory, consummatory (an end in itself) and decorative rather than utilitarian in aim and it often requires some element of 'performance' for communication to be realized. Communication is engaged in for the pleasures of reception as much as for any useful purpose. The message of ritual communication is usually latent and ambiguous, depending on associations and symbols that are not chosen by the participants but made available in the culture. Medium and message are usually hard to separate. Ritual communication is also relatively timeless and unchanging.

Although, in natural conditions, ritual communication is not instrumental, it can be said to have consequences for society (such as more integration) or for social relationships. In some planned communication campaigns – for instance, in politics or advertising – the principles of ritual communication are sometimes taken over and exploited (use of potent symbols, latent appeals to cultural values, togetherness, myths, tradition, etc.). Ritual plays a part in unifying and in mobilizing sentiment and action. Examples of the model can be found in the spheres of art, religion and public ceremonials and festivals.

Communication as display and attention: a publicity model

Besides the transmission and ritual models, there is a third perspective that captures another important aspect of mass communication. This can be summarily labelled a *publicity model*. Often the primary aim of mass media is neither to transmit particular information nor to unite a public in some expression of culture, belief or values, but simply to catch and hold visual or aural attention. In doing so, the media attain one direct economic goal, which is to gain audience revenue (since attention equals consumption, for most practical purposes), and an indirect one, which is to sell (the probability of) audience attention to advertisers. As Elliott (1972: 164) has pointed out (implicitly adopting the transmission model as the norm), 'mass communication is liable not to be communication at all', in the sense of the 'ordered transfer of meaning'. It is more likely to be 'spectatorship', and the media audience is more often a set of spectators rather than participants or information receivers. The *fact* of attention often matters more than the *quality* of attention (which can rarely be adequately measured).

While those who use mass media for their own purposes do hope for some effect (such as persuasion or selling) beyond attention and publicity, gaining the latter remains the immediate goal and is often treated as a measure of success or failure. The publicity strategies of multi-media conglomerates are typically directed at getting maximum attention for their current products in as many media as possible and in multiple forms (interviews, news events, photos, guest appearances, social media sites, etc.). The goal is described as seeking to 'achieve a good share of mind' (Turow, 2009: 201). A good deal of research into media effect has been concerned with questions of image and awareness. The fact of being known is often more important than the content of what is known and is the only necessary condition for **celebrity**. Similarly, the supposed power of the media to set political and other 'agendas' is an example of the attention-gaining process. Much effort in media production is devoted to devices for gaining and keeping attention by catching the eye, arousing emotion, stimulating interest. This is one aspect of what has been described as '**media logic**' (see p. 330–31), with the *substance* of a message often subordinated to the devices for presentation (Altheide and Snow, 1979, 1991).

The attention-seeking goal also corresponds with one important perception of the media by their audiences, who use the mass media for diversion and passing time. They seek to spend time 'with the media', to escape everyday reality. The relationship between sender and receiver according to the display–attention model is not necessarily passive or uninvolved, but it is morally neutral and does not, in itself, imply a transfer or creation of meaning.

Going with the notion of communication as a process of display and attention are several additional features that do not apply to the transmission or ritual models:

- Attention-gaining is a zero-sum process. The time spent attending to one media display by one person cannot be given to another, and available audience time is finite, although time can be stretched and attention diluted. By contrast, there is no quantifiable limit to the amount of 'meaning' that can be sent and acquired or to the satisfactions that can be gained from participating in ritual communication processes.

- Communication in the display–attention mode exists only in the present. There is no past that matters, and the future matters only as a continuation or amplification of the present. Questions of cause and effect relating to the receiver do not arise.
- Attention-gaining is an end in itself and in the short term is value-neutral and essentially empty of meaning. Form and technique take precedence over message content.

These three features can be seen as underlying, respectively, the *competitiveness*, the *actuality/transience* and the *objectivity/detachment* which are pronounced features of mass communication, especially within commercial media institutions.

Encoding and decoding of media discourse: a reception model

There is yet another version of the mass communication process, which involves an even more radical departure from the transmission model than the two variants just discussed. This depends very much on the adoption of the critical perspective described above, but it can also be understood as the view of mass communication from the position of many different receivers who do not perceive or understand the message 'as sent' or 'as expressed'. This model has its origins in **critical theory, semiology** and **discourse analysis**. It is located more in the domain of the cultural rather than the social sciences. It is strongly linked to the rise of '**reception analysis**' (see Holub, 1984; Jensen and Rosengren, 1990). It challenges the predominant methodologies of empirical social scientific audience research and also the humanistic studies of content because both fail to take account of the 'power of the audience' in giving meaning to messages.

    The essence of the 'reception approach' is to locate the attribution and construction of meaning (derived from media) with the receiver. Media messages are always open and 'polysemic' (having multiple meanings) and are interpreted according to the context and the culture of receivers. Among the forerunners of reception analysis was a persuasive variant of critical theory formulated by Stuart Hall (1974/1980) which emphasized the stages of transformation through which any media message passes on the way from its origins to its reception and interpretation. Hall accepted the premise that intended meaning is built into (encoded) symbolic content in both open and concealed ways that are hard to resist, but recognized the possibilities for rejecting or re-interpreting the intended message.

    It is true that communicators choose to encode messages for ideological and institutional purposes and to manipulate language and media for those ends (media messages are given a 'preferred reading', or what might now be called 'spin'). Secondly, receivers ('decoders') are not obliged to accept messages as sent but can and do resist ideological influence by applying variant or oppositional readings, according to their own experience and outlook. This is described as 'differential decoding'.

    In Hall's model of the process of **encoding** and decoding, he portrays the television programme (or any equivalent media text) as a *meaningful discourse*. This is encoded according to the *meaning structure* of the mass media production organization and its main supports, but decoded according to the different meaning structures and frameworks of knowledge of differently situated audiences. The path followed through the stages of the model is simple in principle. Communication originates within media institutions whose typical frameworks of meaning are likely to conform to dominant power structures. Specific messages are 'encoded', often in the form of established content **genres** (such as 'news', 'pop music', 'sport reports', '**soap operas**', 'police/detective series') which have a face-value meaning and inbuilt guidelines for interpretation by an audience. The media are approached by their audiences in terms of 'meaning structures', which have their origin in the ideas and experience of the audience.

*

While the general implication is that meaning as decoded does not necessarily (or often) correspond with meaning as encoded (despite the mediation of conventional genres and shared language systems), the most significant point is that decoding can take a different course from that intended. Receivers can read between the lines and even reverse the intended direction of the message. It is clear that this model and the associated theory embody several key principles: the multiplicity of meanings of media content; the existence of varied 'interpretative' communities; and the primacy of the receiver in determining meaning. While early effect research recognized the fact of selective perception, this was seen as a limitation on, or a condition of, the transmission model, rather than part of a quite different perspective.

Comparisons

The discussion of these different models shows the inadequacy of any single concept or definition of mass communication that relies too heavily on what seem to be intrinsic characteristics or biases of the *technology* of multiple reproduction and dissemination. The human uses of technology are much more diverse and more determinant than was once assumed. Of the four models, summarized in comparative terms in Figure 3.1, the transmission model is largely taken from older institutional contexts – education, religion, government – and is really appropriate only to media activities which are instructional, informational or propagandist in purpose. The expressive

| Model | Orientation of | |
	Sender	Receiver
Transmission model	Transfer of meaning	Cognitive processing
Expressive or ritual model	Performance	Consummation/shared experience
Publicity model	Competitive display	Attention-giving spectatorship
Reception model	Preferential encoding	Differential decoding/ construction of meaning

Figure 3.1   Four models of the mass communication process compared: each model involves differences of orientation on the part of sender and receiver

or ritual model is better able to capture elements which have to do with art, drama, entertainment and the many symbolic uses of communication. It also applies to the many new audience participant and 'reality' television formats. The publicity or display–attention model reflects the central media goals of attracting audiences (high ratings and wide reach) for purposes of prestige or income. It covers that large sector of media activity that is engaged in advertising or public relations, directly or indirectly. It also applies to activities of news management and media 'spin' carried out by governments in their own self-interest. The reception model reminds us that the seeming power of the media to mould, express or capture is partly illusory since the audience in the end disposes.

Conclusion

The basic concepts and models for the study of mass communication that have been outlined in this chapter were developed on the basis of the special features indicated (scale, simultaneity, one-directionality, etc.) and under conditions of transition to the highly organized and centralized industrial society of the twentieth century. Not everything has changed, but we are now faced with new technological possibilities for communication that are not massive or one-directional, and there is a shift away from the earlier massification and centralization of society. These matters are taken up again in Chapter 6.

These changes are already recognized in mass communication theory, although the shift is still cautious and much of the conceptual framework erected for mass communication remains relevant. We still have mass politics, mass markets and mass consumption. The media have extended their scale on a global dimension. The beliefs vested in the power of publicity, public relations and propaganda by other names are still widely held by those with economic and political power. The 'dominant paradigm' that emerged in early communication research is still with us because it fits many of the conditions of contemporary media operation and it meets the needs of media industries, advertisers and publicists. Media propagandists remain convinced of the manipulative capacity of the media and the malleability of the 'masses'. The notion of information transfer or transportation is still alive and well.

As far as a choice of model is concerned, we cannot simply choose one and ignore the others. They are relevant for different purposes. The transmission and attention models are still the preferred perspectives of media industries and would-be persuaders, while the ritual and decoding models are deployed as part of the resistance to media domination as well as shedding light on the underlying process. Neither party to this underlying conflict of purpose and outlook can afford to discount the way mass communication looks to the other side since all four models reflect some aspects of the communication process.

The four models are compared in Figure 3.1, which summarizes points made in the text and highlights the fact that each model posits a distinctive type of relationship between sender and receiver that involves a mutually agreed perception of its central character and purpose.

Further Reading

Dervin, B., Grossberg, L., O'Keefe, B.J. and Wartella, E. (eds) (1989) *Rethinking Communication. Vol. 1: Paradigm Issues.* Newbury Park, CA: Sage. Contains a set of important position statements by leading theorists.

McQuail, D. and Windahl, S. (1993) *Communication Models for the Study of Mass Communication.* London: Longman.
A handy account and evaluation of the principal models that either guided or have been derived from mass media research, during earlier decades.

Meyrowitz, J. (2008) 'Power, pleasure and patterns: intersecting narratives of media influence', *Journal of Communication*, 58 (4): 641–63.
A fresh way of classifying and comparing the main alternative approaches to the study of communication.

Online Readings

Ball-Rokeach, S.J. (1985) 'The origins of individual media-system dependency', *Communication Research*, 12 (4): 485–510.
Fenton, N. (2007) 'Bridging the mythical divide: political economy and cultural studies approaches to the analysis of media', in E. Devereux (ed.), *Media Studies*, pp. 7–31. London: Sage.
Jankowski, N.W. (2006) 'Creating community with media: history, theories and scientific investigations', in L. Lievrouw and S. Livingstone (eds), *Handbook of New Media*, pp. 55–74. London: Sage.

4

Theory of Media and Society

In this chapter, we look more closely at ideas about the relation between mass media and society, reserving the cultural implications for Chapter 5, even though society and culture are inseparable and the one cannot exist without the other. Treating society first also implies a primacy for society that is questionable, since the media and what they produce can also be considered as part of 'culture'. In fact most media theory relates to both 'society' and 'culture' together and has to be explained in relation to both. For present purposes, the domain of 'society' refers to the material base (economic and political resources and power), to social relationships (in national societies, communities, families, etc.) and to social roles and occupations that are socially regulated (formally or informally). The domain of 'culture' refers primarily to other essential aspects of social life, especially to *symbolic expression*, *meanings* and *practices* (social customs, institutional ways of doing things and also personal habits).

Most of the chapter is concerned with explaining the main theories or theoretical perspectives that have been developed for understanding the way media work and accounting for the typical cultural production that they engage in. Most of these theories do make the assumption that material and social circumstances are a primary determinant, but there is also scope for recognizing the independent influence that ideas and culture can have in their turn on material conditions. Before the theories of media and society are considered, the main issues or broad themes that have framed inquiry into mass communication are described. A general frame of reference for looking at the connections between media and society is also proposed. First of all, we return in more detail to the conundrum of the relation between culture and society.

Media, Society and Culture: Connections and Conflicts

Mass communication can be considered as both a 'societal' and a 'cultural' phenomenon. The mass media institution is part of the structure of society, and its technological infrastructure is part of the economic and power base, while the ideas, images and information disseminated by the media are evidently an important aspect of our culture (in the sense defined above).

In discussing this problem, Rosengren (1981b) offered a simple typology which cross-tabulates two opposed propositions: 'social structure influences culture'; and its reverse, 'culture influences social structure'. This yields four main options that are available for describing the relation between mass media and society, as shown in Figure 4.1.

If we consider mass media as an aspect of society (base or structure), then the option of *materialism* is presented. There is a considerable body of theory that views culture as dependent on the economic and power structure of a society. It is assumed that whoever owns or controls the media can choose, or set limits to, what they do. This is the essence of the Marxist position.

If we consider the media primarily in the light of their contents (thus more as culture), then the option of *idealism* is indicated. The media are assumed to have a

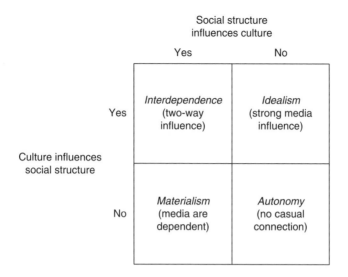

Figure 4.1   Four types of relation between culture (media content) and society

potential for significant influence, but it is the particular ideas and values conveyed by the media (in their content) which are seen as the primary causes of social change, irrespective of who owns and controls. The influence is thought to work through individual motivations and actions. This view leads to a strong belief in various potential media effects for good or ill. Examples include the promotion by the media of peace and international understanding (or having the opposite effect), of pro- or antisocial values and behaviour, and of enlightenment or the secularization and modernization of traditional societies. A form of idealism or 'mentalism' concerning media also lies behind the view that changes in media forms and technology can change our way of gaining experience in essential ways and even our relations with others (as in the theories of McLuhan 1962, 1964).

The two options remaining – of interdependence and of autonomy – have found less distinctive theoretical development, although there is a good deal of support in common sense and in evidence for both. *Interdependence* implies that mass media and society are continually interacting and influencing each other (as are society and culture). The media (as cultural industries) respond to the demand from society for information and entertainment and, at the same time, stimulate innovation and contribute to a changing social-cultural climate, which sets off new demands for communication. The French sociologist Gabriel Tarde, writing about 1900, envisaged a constant interweaving of influences: 'technological developments made newspapers possible, newspapers promote the formation of broader publics, and they, by broadening the loyalties of their members, create an extensive network of overlapping and shifting groupings' (Clark, 1969). Today, the various influences are so bound together that neither mass communication nor modern society is conceivable without the other, and each is a necessary, though not a sufficient, condition for the other. From this point of view we have to conclude that the media may equally be considered to mould or to mirror society and social changes.

The option of *autonomy* in the relations between culture and society is not necessarily inconsistent with this view, unless interpreted very literally. It is at least very likely that society and mass media can be independent of each other up to a point. Societies that are culturally very similar can sometimes have very different media systems. The autonomy position also supports those who are sceptical about the power of the media to influence ideas, values and behaviour – for instance, in allegedly promoting conformity, stimulating 'modernity' or damaging the cultural identity of poorer or less powerful countries. There are different views about how much autonomy in relation to society the media can have. The debate is especially relevant to the central thesis of 'internationalization' or **'globalization'**, which implies a convergence and homogenization of a worldwide culture, as a result of the media. The autonomy position would suggest that imported media culture is superficial and need not significantly touch the local culture. It follows that **cultural imperialism** is not likely to happen simply by chance or against the will of the culturally 'colonized' (see Chapter 10).

An inconclusive outcome

As with many of the issues to be discussed, there are more theories than there is solid evidence, and the questions raised by this discussion are much too broad to be settled by empirical research. According to Rosengren (1981b: 254), surveying what scattered evidence he could find, research gives only 'inconclusive, partly even contradictory, evidence about the relationship between social structure, societal values as mediated by the media, and opinions among the public'. This assessment is just as valid thirty years later, suggesting that no single theory holds under all circumstances.

It seems that the media can serve to repress as well as to liberate, to unite as well as to fragment society, to promote as well as to hold back change. What is also striking in the theories to be discussed is the ambiguity of the role assigned to the media. They are as often presented in a 'progressive' as in a 'reactionary' light, according to whether the dominant (pluralist) or alternative (critical, radical) perspective is adopted. Despite the uncertainty, there can be little doubt that the media, whether moulders or mirrors of society, are the main messengers *about* society, and it is around this observation that the alternative theoretical perspectives can best be organized.

Mass Communication as a Society-wide Process: the Mediation of Social Relations and Experience

A central presupposition, relating to questions both of society and of culture, is that the media institution is essentially concerned with the production and distribution of *knowledge* in the widest sense of the word. Such knowledge enables us to make some sense of our experience of the social world, even if the 'taking of meaning' occurs in relatively autonomous and varied ways. The information, images and ideas made available by the media may, for most people, be the main source of an awareness of a shared past time (history) and of a present social location. They are also a store of memories and a map of where we are and who we are (identity) and may also provide the materials for orientation to the future. As noted at the outset, the media to a large extent serve to constitute our perceptions and definitions of social reality and normality for the purposes of a public, shared social life, and are a key source of standards, models and norms.

The main thing to emphasize is the degree to which the different media have come to be interposed between ourselves and any experience of the world beyond our immediate personal environment and our direct sensory observation. They also provide most of us with the main point of contact with the institutions of the society in which we live. In a secular society, in matters of values and ideas, the mass media tend to 'take over' from the early influences of school, parents, religion, siblings and companions. We are consequently very dependent on the media for a large part of our wider 'symbolic environment' (the 'pictures in our heads'), however much we may be able to shape our own personal version. It is the media which are likely to forge the elements which are held in common with others, since we now tend to share much the same media sources and 'media culture'. Without some degree of shared perception of reality, whatever its origin, there cannot really be an organized social life. Hjarvard (2008) sketches a theory of social and cultural change in which the media gradually develop historically until they emerge in the nineteenth century as an independent social institution. More recently this has developed further to become a means of integrating other social institutions.

The mediation concept

These comments can be summed up in terms of the concept of mediation of contact with social reality. Mediation involves several different processes. As noted already, it refers to the relaying of second-hand (or third-party) versions of events and conditions which we cannot directly observe for ourselves. Secondly, it refers to the efforts of other actors and institutions in society to contact us for their own purposes (or our own supposed good). This applies to politicians and governments, advertisers, educators, experts and authorities of all kinds. It refers to the indirect way in which we form our perceptions of groups and cultures to which we do not belong. An essential element in mediation as defined here is the involvement of some technological device between our senses and things external to us.

Mediation also implies some form of *relationship*. Relationships that are mediated through mass media are likely to be more distant, more impersonal and weaker than direct personal ties. The mass media do not monopolize the flow of information we receive, nor do they intervene in all our wider social relations, but their presence is inevitably very pervasive. Early versions of the idea of 'mediation of reality' were inclined to assume a division between a public terrain in which a widely shared view of reality was constructed by way of mass media messages, and a personal sphere where individuals could communicate freely and directly. More recent developments of technology have undermined this simple division, since a much larger share of communication and thus of our contact with others and our environmental reality is mediated via technology (telephone, computer, fax, e-mail, etc.), although on an individual and a private basis. The implications of this change are still unclear and subject to diverse interpretations.

Thompson (1993, 1995) has suggested a typology of interaction to clarify the consequences of the new communication technologies that have detached social interaction and symbolic exchange from the sharing of a common locale. He notes (1993: 35) that 'it has become possible for more and more individuals to acquire information and symbolic content through mediated forms of interaction'. He distinguished two types of interaction alongside face-to-face interaction. One of these, which he calls 'mediated interaction', involves some technical medium such as paper, electrical wires, and so on, which enables information or symbolic content to be transmitted between individuals who are distant in space or time or both. The partners to mediated interaction need to find contextual information as well having fewer ones than in face-to-face contact.

The other type is called 'mediated quasi-interaction' and refers to relations established by the media of mass communication. There are two main distinguishing features. First, in this case, participants are not oriented towards other specific individuals (whether as sender or receiver), and symbolic forms (media content) are produced for an indefinite range of potential recipients. Secondly, mediated quasi-interaction is monological (rather than dialogical), in the sense that the flow of communication is one-way rather than two-way. There is also no direct or immediate response expected from the receiver. Thompson argues that the 'media have created a new kind of **public sphere** which is despatialized and non-dialogical in character' (1993: 42) and is potentially global in scope.

Mediation metaphors

In general, the notion of mediation in the sense of media intervening between ourselves and 'reality' is no more than a metaphor, although it does point to several of the roles played by the media in connecting us to other experience. The terms that are often used to describe this role reflect different attributions of purposefulness, **interactivity** and effectiveness. Mediation can mean different things, ranging from neutrally informing, through negotiation, to attempts at manipulation and control. The variations can be captured by a number of communication images, which express different ideas about how the media may connect us with reality. These are presented in Box 4.1.

> # i
>
> # 4.1   Metaphors for media roles
>
> - As a *window* on events and experience, which extends our vision, enabling us to see for ourselves what is going on, without interference from others.
> - As a *mirror* of events in society and the world, implying a faithful reflection (albeit with inversion and possible distortion of the image), although the angle and direction of the mirror are decided by others, and we are less free to see what we want.

- As a *filter*, *gatekeeper* or *portal*, acting to select parts of experience for special attention and closing off other views and voices, whether deliberately or not.
- As a *signpost*, *guide* or *interpreter*, pointing the way and making sense of what is otherwise puzzling or fragmentary.
- As a *forum* or *platform* for the presentation of information and ideas to an audience, often with possibilities for response and feedback.
- As a *disseminator* who passes on and makes information not available to all.
- As an *interlocutor* or informed partner in conversation who responds to questions in a quasi-interactive way.

Some of these images are to be found in the media's own self-definition – especially in the more positive implications of extending our view of the world, providing integration and continuity and connecting people with each other. Even the notion of filtering is often accepted in its positive sense of selecting and interpreting what would otherwise be an unmanageable and chaotic supply of information and impressions. These versions of the mediating process reflect differences of interpretation of the role of the media in social processes. In particular, the media can extend our view of the world in an open-ended way or they can limit or control our impressions. Secondly, they may choose between a neutral, passive role and one that is active and participant. They can vary on two main dimensions: one of openness versus control, another of neutrality versus being actively participant. The various images discussed do not refer to the truly interactive possibilities of newer media, in which the 'receiver' can become a 'sender' and make use of the media in interaction with the environment. However, it is now clear that new online media can fulfil most of the roles indicated as well as additional ones, as outlined in Chapter 6 (p. 139), with reference to Internet **portals**.

✳

A Frame of Reference for Connecting Media with Society

The general notion that mass communication interposes in some way between 'reality' and our perceptions and knowledge of it refers to a number of specific processes at different levels of analysis. The Westley and MacLean (1957) model (see p. 86) indicates some of the additional elements needed for a more detailed frame of reference. Most significant is the idea that the media are sought out by institutional advocates as channels for reaching the general public (or chosen groups) and for conveying their chosen perspective on events and conditions. This is broadly true of competing politicians and governments, advertisers, religious leaders, some thinkers, writers and artists, and so on. We are reminded that experience has always been mediated by the institutions of society (including the family), and what has happened is that a new mediator (mass communication) has been added which can extend, compete with, replace or even run counter to the efforts of other social institutions.

The simple picture of a 'two-step' (or multiple) process of mediated contact with reality is complicated by the fact that mass media are not completely free agents in relation to the rest of society. They are subject to formal and informal control by the very institutions (including their own) that have an interest in shaping public perceptions of reality. Their objectives do not necessarily coincide with the aim of relaying some objective 'truth' about reality. An abstract view of the 'mediation of reality', based on Westley and MacLean but also reflecting these points, is sketched in Figure 4.2. The media provide their audience with a supply of information, images, stories and impressions, sometimes according to anticipated needs, sometimes guided by their own purposes (e.g. gaining revenue or influence), and sometimes following the motives of other social institutions (e.g. advertising, making propaganda, projecting favourable images, sending information). Given this diversity of underlying motivation in the *selection* and *flow* of the 'images of reality', we can see that mediation is unlikely to be a purely neutral process. The 'reality' will always be to some extent selected and constructed and there will be certain consistent biases. These will reflect especially the differential opportunities available for gaining media access and also the influence of 'media logic' in constituting reality (see pp. 330–31).

Figure 4.2 also represents the fact that experience is neither completely nor always mediated by the mass media. There are still certain direct channels of contact with social institutions (e.g. political parties, work organizations, churches). There is also some possibility of direct personal experience of some of the more distant events reported in media (e.g. crime, poverty, illness, war and conflict). The potentially diverse sources of information (including personal contact with others, and via the Internet) may not be completely independent from each other, but they provide some checks on the adequacy and reliability of 'quasi-mediated interaction'.

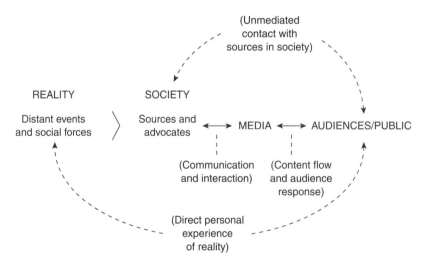

Figure 4.2 A frame of reference for theory formation about media and society: media interpose between personal experience and more distant events and social forces (based on Westley and MacLean, 1957)

Main themes of media-society theory

The main themes and issues to be dealt with in this book have already been introduced in Chapter 1 and also in Chapter 3 under the heading 'Early perspectives on media and society'. Here we return in more depth to these matters. The theories available to us are fragmentary and selective, sometimes overlapping or inconsistent, often guided by conflicting ideologies and assumptions about society. Theory formation does not follow a systematic and logical pattern but responds to real-life problems and historical circumstances. Before describing some of the theories that have been formulated, it is useful to look at the main themes that have shaped debate during the 'first age of mass communication', especially relating to power, integration, social change and space/time.

Theme I: Power and Inequality

The media are invariably related in some way to the prevailing structure of political and economic power. It is evident, first of all, that media have an economic cost and value, are an object of competition for control and access. Secondly, they are subject to political, economic and legal regulation. Thirdly, mass media are very commonly regarded as effective instruments of power, with the potential capacity to exert influence in various ways. Fourthly, the power of mass media is not equally available to all groups or interests. Box 4.2 introduces the theme of media power by naming the main kinds of effects, whether intended or not, that have been attributed to the mass media.

Hypothetical aims or effects of mass media power **4.2**

- Attracting and directing public attention
- Persuasion in matters of opinion and belief
- Influencing behaviour
- Providing definitions of reality
- Conferring status and legitimacy
- Informing quickly and extensively

In discussions of media power, two models are usually opposed to each other: one a model of dominant media, the other of pluralist media (see Figure 4.3). The first of these sees media as exercising power on behalf of other powerful institutions. Media organizations, in this view, are likely to be owned or controlled by a small number of powerful interests and to be similar in type and purpose. They disseminate a limited and undifferentiated view of the world shaped by the perspectives of ruling interests.

	Dominance	Pluralism
Societal source	Ruling class or dominant elite	Competing political, social, cultural interests and groups
Media	Under concentrated ownership and of uniform type	Many and independent of each other
Production	Standardized, routinized	Creative, free, original Controlled
Content and world view	Selective and decided from 'above'	Diverse and competing views, responsive to audience demand
Audience	Dependent, passive, organized on large scale	Fragmented, selective, reactive and active
Effects	Strong and confirmative of established social order	Numerous, without consistency or predictability of direction, but often no effect

Figure 4.3 Two opposing models of media power (mixed versions are more likely to be encountered)

Audiences are constrained or conditioned to accept the view of the world offered, with little critical response. The result is to reinforce and legitimate the prevailing structure of power and to head off change by filtering out alternative voices.

The pluralist model is, in nearly every respect, the opposite, allowing for much diversity and unpredictability. There is no unified and dominant elite, and change and democratic control are both possible. Differentiated audiences initiate demand and are able to resist persuasion and react to what the media offer. In general, the 'dominance' model corresponds to the outlook both of conservatives pessimistic about the 'rise of the masses' and also of critics of the capitalist system disappointed by the failure of the revolution to happen. It is consistent with a view of the media as an instrument of 'cultural imperialism' or a tool of political propaganda. The pluralist view is an idealized version of what liberalism and the free market will lead to. While the models are described as total opposites, it is possible to envisage mixed versions, in which tendencies towards mass domination or economic monopoly are subject to limits and counter-forces and are 'resisted' by their audiences. In any free society, minorities and opposition groups should be able to develop and maintain their own alternative media.

The question is whether media exercises power in their own right and interest. However, this possibility exists and is to be found in fictional as well as factual portrayals of media moguls and empires. There are cases of media owners using their position to advance some political or financial goal or to enhance their own status. There is prima facie evidence of effects on public opinion and actions. More often, the independent power the media is said to cause unintended harmful effects. These relate, for example, to the undermining of democratic politics, cultural and moral debasement, and the causing of personal harm and distress, mainly in the pursuit of profit. Essentially they are said to exert power without responsibility and use the shield of **freedom of the press** to avoid accountability. This discussion of media effects gives rise to a number of questions which are posed in Box 4.3.

The power of mass media: questions arising **4.3**

- Are the media under control?
- If so, who controls the media and in whose interest?
- Whose version of the world (social reality) is presented?
- How effective are the media in achieving chosen ends?
- Do mass media promote more or less equality in society?
- How is access to media allocated or obtained?
- How do the media use their power to influence?
- Do the media have power of their own?

Theme II: Social Integration and Identity

A dual perspective on media

Theorists of mass communication have often shared with sociologists an interest in how social order is maintained and in the attachment of people to various kinds of social unit. The media were early associated with the problems of rapid urbanization, social mobility and the decline of traditional communities. They have continued to be linked with social dislocation and a supposed increase in individual immorality, crime and disorder. A good deal of early media theory and research focused on questions of integration. For instance, Hanno Hardt (2003) has described the concerns of nineteenth- and early-twentieth-century German theorists with the integrative role of the press in society. The principal functions of the press he discerned are set out in Box 4.4.

The perceived social functions of the early press **4.4**

- Binding society together
- Giving leadership to the public
- Helping to establish the 'public sphere'
- Providing for the exchange of ideas between leaders and masses
- Satisfying needs for information
- Providing society with a mirror of itself
- Acting as the conscience of society

Mass communication as a process has often been typified as predominantly individualistic, impersonal and isolating, and thus leading to lower levels of social solidarity and sense of community. Addiction to television has been linked to non-participation and declining 'social capital' in the sense of participating in social activities and having a sense of belonging (Putnam, 2000). The media have brought messages of what is new and fashionable in terms of goods, ideas, techniques and values from city to country and from the social top to the base. They have also portrayed alternative value systems, potentially weakening the hold of traditional values.

An alternative view of the relation between mass media and social integration has also been in circulation, based on other features of mass communication. It has a capacity to unite scattered individuals within the same large audience, or to integrate newcomers into urban communities and immigrants into a new country by providing a common set of values, ideas and information and helping to form identities (Janowitz, 1952; Clark, 1969; Stamm, 1985; Rogers, 1993). This process can help to bind together a large-scale, differentiated modern society more effectively than would have been possible through older mechanisms of religious, family or group control. In other words, mass media seem in principle capable both of supporting and of subverting social cohesion. The positions seem far apart, one stressing centrifugal and the other centripetal tendencies, although in fact in complex and changing societies both forces are normally at work at the same time, one compensating to some extent for the other.

Ambivalence about social integration

The main questions that arise for theory and research can thus (much as in the case of power) be mapped out on two criss-crossing dimensions. One refers to the direction of effect: either *centrifugal* or *centripetal*. The first refers to the stimulus towards social change, freedom, individualism and **fragmentation**. The second refers to effects in the form of more social unity, order, cohesion and integration. Both social integration and dispersal can be valued differently, depending on preference and perspective. One person's desirable social control is another person's limitation of freedom; one person's individualism is another person's non-conformity or isolation. So the second dimension can be described as normative, especially in the assessment of these two opposite tendencies of the working of mass media. The question it represents is whether the effect at issue should be viewed with *optimism* or *pessimism* (McCormack, 1961; Carey, 1969). While early critics of mass communication (e.g. C.W. Mills) emphasized the dangers of over-integration and social conformity, the individualizing effects of newer media have come to be viewed by social critics as socially corrosive (e.g. Sunstein, 2006).

In order to make sense of this complicated situation, it helps to think of the two versions of media theory – centrifugal and centripetal – each with its own position on a dimension of evaluation, so that there are, in effect, four different theoretical positions relating to social integration (see Figure 4.4). These can be named as follows:

1   *Freedom, diversity*. This is the optimistic version of the tendency for media to have a fragmenting effect on society that can also be liberating. The media spread new ideas and information and encourage mobility, change and modernization.
2   *Integration, solidarity*. This optimistic version of the reverse effect of mass communication as a unifier of society stresses the needs for a sense of identity, belonging and citizenship, especially under conditions of social change.

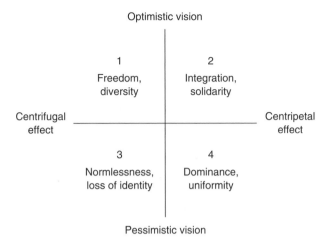

Figure 4.4   Four versions of the consequences of mass communication for social integration

3   *Normlessness, loss of identity.* The pessimistic alternative view of greater freedom points to detachment, loss of belief, rootlessness and a society lacking in social cohesion and social capital.
4   *Dominance, uniformity.* Society can be over-integrated and over-regulated, leading to central control and conformity, with the mass media as instruments of control.

This version of the integrating effects of mass communication leaves us with a number of questions (Box 4.5) that have to be answered for different societies at different points in time and no general answer is possible.

Questions about media and integration 4.5

- Do mass media increase or decrease the level of social control and conformity?
- Do media strengthen or weaken intervening social institutions, such as family, political party, local community, church, trade union?
- Do media help or hinder the formation of diverse groups and identities based on subculture, opinion, social experience, social action, and so on?
- Do mass media promote individual freedom and choice of identity?
- Do online media have a bias against integration?

Theme III: Social Change and Development

A key question that follows on from the preceding discussion is whether or not mass communication should be viewed primarily as a cause or as an effect of social change.

Wherever the media exert influence they also cause change; the options of social centralization or dispersal are two main kinds of change that have been discussed. As we have seen, no simple answer can be expected, and different theories offer alternative versions of the relationship. At issue are the alternative ways of relating three basic elements: (1) the technology of communication and the form and content of media; (2) changes in society (social structure and institutional arrangements); and (3) the distribution among a population of opinion, beliefs, values and practices. All consequences of mass media are potentially questions about social change, but most relevant for theory have been the issues of 'technological determinism' and the potential to apply mass media to the process of development. The first refers to the effect on society of changing communications media. The second refers to the more practical question of whether or not (and how) mass media might be applied to economic and social development (as an 'engine of change' or 'multiplier of modernity'). Questions about change and development are set out in Box 4.6.

4.6 Questions about change and development

- What part do or can media play in major social change?
- Are the media typically progressive or conservative in their working?
- Can media be applied as an 'engine of change' in the context of development?
- How much of media-induced change is due to technology rather than to typical content?
- Do the media diffuse innovations effectively?

The story of the rise of the media, as told in Chapter 2, certainly tends to depict media as a generally progressive force, especially because of the link between democracy and freedom of expression and between media and the opening of markets and liberalization of trade. However, there are other narratives to consider. For instance, critical theory has typically viewed the media in modern times as conformist and even reactionary. In the early twentieth century, as in Nazi Germany and Soviet Russia, the media were employed as a tool of change, even if with mixed success.

The case of 'modernization' and development in Third World countries received much attention in the early post-Second World Word War years, when mass communication was seen, especially in the USA, as a powerful means of spreading American ideals throughout the world and at the same time helping to resist communism. But it was also promoted as an effective instrument of social and economic development, consistent with the spirit of free enterprise. Several effects were predicted to follow on from the voluntary import of US mass media content. These included: consumer aspirations, values and practices of democracy, ideas of liberty, literacy (see Lerner, 1958). Subsequently, there was a large investment in communication projects designed to diffuse many technical and social innovations (Rogers and Shoemaker, 1973). The results were hard to evaluate and the efforts described gradually became redundant or impossible to pursue in a changed world.

In more recent years, the biggest change associated with mass media has probably been the transition from communism in Europe after 1985. The role of the media in these events is still a matter of debate, although the process of *glasnost* did give the media a part to play in internal change within the Soviet Union, and once started they seemed to amplify it.

Theme IV: Space and Time

Communication has often been said to have space and time dimensions and also to 'build bridges' over discontinuities in our experience created by distance and time. There are numerous aspects to each proposition. Communication makes possible an extension of human activity and perception across distance in several ways. Most obviously, in the form of transportation we are taken from place to place and our contacts, experiences and horizons are extended. Symbolic communication can achieve something of the same effect without our having to move physically. We are also provided with maps and guides to places and routes to points in real space. The location of our activity is defined by webs of communication, by shared forms of discourse and by much that is expressed in language and other forms of expression. Virtually all forms of symbolic communication (books, art, music, newspapers, cinema, etc.) are identified with a particular location and have a varying 'transmission' range that can be specified geographically. Processes of mass communication are typically described and registered in spatial terms, with reference to particular media markets, circulation or reception areas, audience 'reach', and so on. At the same time, the end of cost and capacity constraints on electronic transmission means that communication is no longer tied to any one territory and is, in principle, delocalized.

Political and social units are territorial and use communications of many kinds to signal this fact. Communication is always initiated at one point and received at one or many other points. Bridges are built and physical distance seems to be reduced by ease of communication and reception. The Internet has created various kinds of 'virtual space' and new maps to go with it, especially those that show the web of interconnections. New technologies have made it possible for messages sent to materialize at distant points. The account could be continued, but the richness of the theme of space can be appreciated.

Much the same could be said in relation to time. The multiplication and acceleration of channels for transmission and exchange of communication have made instantaneous contact with other sources and destinations an everyday possibility. We no longer have to wait for news or wait to send it, from whatever place. There is effectively no time restriction on the amount of information that can be sent. There is increasingly no time restriction on when we can receive what we want to receive. Technologies of storage and access allow us to disregard the constraint of time on much communication behaviour. All that is lacking is more time to do all this. Paradoxically, although new technologies make it possible and easy to store our memories and all the information we want, information and culture seem to be subject to faster obsolescence and decay. The limits are increasingly set by human capacity to process any more any faster. The long-heralded problem of information overload has arrived in daily experience. Whatever the costs and benefits, it is hard to deny the revolutionary character of recent changes. For key propositions, see Box 4.7.

> # 4.7 Media effects relating to space and time: key propositions
>
> - Media have abolished distance
> - Virtual space becomes an extension of real space
> - Media serve as collective memory
> - The gap between technical transmission and human reception capacity widens exponentially
> - Media lead to delocalization and detemporalization

Media–Society Theory I: the Mass Society

In this and the following sections, several distinctive theoretical approaches to these themes are discussed. They are presented more or less in chronological order of their formulation and they span the range from optimistic to pessimistic, from critical to neutral. The first to be dealt with, mass society theory, is built around the concept of 'mass' which has already been discussed in Chapter 3. The theory emphasizes the interdependence of institutions that exercise power and thus the integration of the media into the sources of social power and authority. Content is likely to serve the interests of political and economic power holders. The media cannot be expected to offer a critical or an alternative definition of the world, and their tendency will be to assist in the accommodation of the dependent public to their fate.

The 'dominant media' model sketched above reflects the mass society view. Mass society theory gives a primacy to the media as a causal factor. It rests very much on the idea that the media offer a view of the world, a substitute or pseudo-environment, which is a potent means of manipulation of people but also an aid to their psychic survival under difficult conditions. According to C. Wright Mills (1951: 333), 'Between consciousness and existence stand communications, which influence such consciousness as men have of their existence.'

Mass society is, paradoxically, both 'atomized' and centrally controlled. The media are seen as significantly contributing to this control in societies characterized by largeness of scale, remoteness of institutions, isolation of individuals and lack of strong local or group integration. Mills (1951, 1956) also pointed to the decline of the genuine public of classic democratic theory and its replacement by shifting aggregates of people who cannot formulate or realize their own aims in political action. This regret has been echoed more recently by arguments about the decline of a 'public sphere' of democratic debate and politics, in which large-scale, commercialized mass media have been implicated (Dahlgren, 1995, 2005).

Although the expression 'mass society' is no longer much in vogue, the idea that we live in a mass society persists in a variety of loosely related components. These include a nostalgia (or hope) for a more 'communitarian' alternative to the present individualistic age as well as a critical attitude towards the supposed emptiness, loneliness, stress and consumerism of life in a contemporary free-market society. The seemingly widespread public indifference towards democratic politics and lack of participation in it are also often attributed to the cynical and manipulative use of mass media by politicians and parties.

The actual abundance and diversity of many old and new forms of media seem, however, to undermine the validity of mass society theory in its portrayal of the media as one of the foundation stones of the mass society. In particular, the new electronic media have given rise to an optimistic vision of what society can become that runs counter to the central mass society thesis. The relative monopoly control typical of the rise of the original mass media is now challenged by the rise of online media that are much more accessible to many groups, movements and also individuals. This challenges not just the economic power of old media but also their guaranteed access to large national audiences at the time of their own choosing. There is a darker side to this vision, however, since the Internet also opens up new means of control and **surveillance** of the online population and is not immune to control by media conglomerates. The central ideas are stated in Box 4.8.

Mass society theory of media: main propositions **4.8**

- Society is organized centrally and on a large scale
- The public becomes atomized
- Media are centralized, with one-way transmission
- People come to depend on media for their identity
- Media are used for manipulation and control

Media–Society Theory II: Marxism and Political Economy

While Karl Marx only knew the press before it was a true mass medium, the tradition of Marxist analysis of the media in capitalist society is still of some relevance. There have been several variants of Marxist-inspired analysis of modern media, merging into the present-day 'critical **political economy**' (Murdock and Golding, 2005).

The question of power is central to Marxist interpretations of mass media. While varied, these have always emphasized the fact that ultimately they are instruments of control by and for a ruling class. The founding text is Marx's *German Ideology*, where he states:

The class that has the means of material production has control at the same time over the means of mental production so that, thereby, generally speaking, the ideas of those who lack the means of mental production are subject to it. (cited in Murdock and Golding, 1977: 15)

Marxist theory posits a direct link between economic ownership and the dissemination of messages that affirm the legitimacy and the value of a class society. These views are supported in modern times by evidence of tendencies to great concentration of media ownership by capitalist entrepreneurs (e.g. Bagdikian, 1988; McChesney, 2000) and by much correlative evidence of conservative tendencies in content of media so organized (e.g. Herman and Chomsky, 1988).

Revisionist versions of Marxist media theory in the twentieth century concentrated more on ideas than on material structures. They emphasized the ideological **effects of media** in the interests of a ruling class, in 'reproducing' the essentially exploitative relationships and manipulation, and in legitimating the dominance of capitalism and the subordination of the working class. Louis Althusser (1971) conceived this process to work by way of what he called 'ideological state apparatuses' (all means of **socialization**, in effect), which, by comparison with 'repressive state apparatuses' (such as the army and police), enable the capitalist state to survive without recourse to direct violence. Gramsci's (1971) concept of *hegemony* relates to this tendency. Marcuse (1964) interpreted the media, along with other elements of mass production systems, as engaged in 'selling' or imposing a whole social system which is at the same time both desirable and repressive.

All in all, the message of Marxist theory is plain, but questions remain unanswered. How might the power of the media be countered or resisted? What is the position of forms of media that are not clearly in capitalist ownership or in the power of the state (such as independent newspapers or public broadcasting)? Critics of mass media in the Marxist tradition either rely on the weapon of exposure of propaganda and manipulation (e.g. Herman and Chomsky, 1988; Herman, 2000) or pin their hopes on some form of collective ownership or alternative media as a counter to the media power of the capitalist class. The main contemporary heir to Marxist theory is to be found in political economy theory.

Political-economic theory is a socially critical approach that focuses primarily on the relation between the economic structure and dynamics of media industries and the ideological content of media. From this point of view, the media institution has to be considered as part of the economic system, with close links to the political system. The consequences are to be observed in the reduction of independent media sources, concentration on the largest markets, avoidance of risks, and reduced investment in less profitable media tasks (such as investigative reporting and documentary filmmaking). We also find neglect of smaller and poorer sectors of the potential audience and often a politically unbalanced range of news media.

The main strength of the approach lies in its capacity for making empirically testable propositions about market determinations, although the latter are so numerous and complex that empirical demonstration is not easy. While the approach centres on media activity as an economic process leading to the commodity (the media product or content), there is a variant of the political-economic approach that suggests that the primary product of the media is really *audience*. This refers to the fact that they deliver audience attention to advertisers and shape the behaviour of media publics in certain distinctive ways (Smythe, 1977). What commercial media sell to their clients is a certain more or less guaranteed number of potential customers according to a market-relevant profile. This perspective is more difficult to apply to online advertising and in particular to the **search engine** as a major vehicle of advertising (Bermejo, 2009; and see below, p. 402).

The political economy approach is now being applied to the case of the Internet. Fuchs (2009) builds on Smythe's ideas in suggesting that the key to the Internet economy lies especially in the **commodification** of the users of free access platforms which deliver targets for advertisers and publicists as well as often providing the content at no cost to networks providers and site-owners. In the case of very popular websites such as *Myspace* and *YouTube*, the distinction from mass communication is not very clear.

The relevance of political-economic theory has been greatly increased by several trends in media business and technology (perhaps also enhanced by the fall from grace of a strictly Marxist analysis). First, there has been a growth in **media concentration** worldwide, with more and more power of ownership being concentrated in fewer hands and with tendencies for mergers between electronic hardware and software industries (Murdock, 1990; McChesney, 2000; Wasko, 2004). Secondly, there has been a growing global 'information economy' (Melody, 1990; Sussman, 1997), involving an increasing convergence between telecommunication and broadcasting. Thirdly, there has been a decline in the public sector of mass media and in direct public control of telecommunication (especially in Western Europe), under the banner of 'deregulation', 'privatization' or 'liberalization' (McQuail and Siune, 1998; van Cuilenburg and McQuail, 2003). Fourthly, there is a growing rather than diminishing problem of information inequality. The expression **'digital divide'** refers to the inequality in access to and use of advanced communication facilities (Norris, 2002), but there are also differences in the quality of potential use. The essential propositions of political-economic theory (see Box 4.9) have not changed since earlier times, but the scope for application is much wider (Mansell, 2004).

Critical political-economic theory: main propositions **4.9**

- Economic control and logic are determinant
- Media structure always tends towards monopoly
- Global integration of media ownership develops
- Contents and audiences are commodified
- Real diversity decreases
- Opposition and alternative voices are marginalized
- Public interest in communication is subordinated to private interests
- Access to the benefits of communication are unequally distributed

Media–Society Theory III: Functionalism

Functionalist theory explains social practices and institutions in terms of the 'needs' of the society and of individuals (Merton, 1957). Society is viewed as an ongoing system of linked working parts or subsystems, each making an essential contribution to continuity and order. The media can be seen as one of these systems. Organized social life is said to require the continued maintenance of a more or less accurate, consistent, supportive and complete picture of the working of society and of the social environment. It is by responding to the demands of individuals and institutions in consistent ways that the media achieve unintended benefits for the society as a whole.

The theory depicts media as essentially self-directing and self-correcting. While apolitical in formulation, it suits pluralist and voluntarist conceptions of the fundamental mechanisms of social life and has a conservative bias to the extent that the media are more likely to be seen as a means of maintaining society as it is rather than as a source of major change.

Although functionalism in its early versions has been largely discarded in sociology, it survives as an approach to the media in new forms (e.g. Luhmann, 2000) and it still plays a part in framing and answering research questions about the media. It remains useful for some purposes of description and it offers a language for discussing the relations between mass media and society and a set of concepts that have proved hard to replace. This terminology has the advantage of being to a large extent shared by mass communicators themselves and by their audiences and of being widely understood.

Specifying the social functions of media

The main functions of communication in society, according to Lasswell (1948), were surveillance of the environment, correlation of the parts of the society in responding to its environment, and the transmission of the cultural heritage. Wright (1960) developed this basic scheme to describe many of the effects of the media and added entertainment as a fourth key media function. This may be part of the transmitted culture but it has another aspect – that of providing individual reward, relaxation and reduction of tension, which makes it easier for people to cope with real-life problems and for societies to avoid breakdown (Mendelsohn, 1966). With the addition of a fifth item, mobilization – designed to reflect the widespread application of mass communication to political and commercial propaganda – we can name the following set of basic ideas about media tasks (functions) in society:

Information

- Providing information about events and conditions in society and the world.
- Indicating relations of power.
- Facilitating innovation, adaptation and progress.

Correlation

- Explaining, interpreting and commenting on the meaning of events and information.
- Providing support for established authority and norms.
- Socializing.
- Co-ordinating separate activities.
- Consensus building.
- Setting orders of priority and signalling relative status.

Continuity

- Expressing the dominant culture and recognizing subcultures and new cultural developments.
- Forging and maintaining commonality of values.

Entertainment

- Providing amusement, diversion and the means of relaxation.
- Reducing social tension.

Mobilization

- Campaigning for societal objectives in the sphere of politics, war, economic development, work and sometimes religion.

We cannot give any general rank order to these items, or say anything about their relative frequency of occurrence. The correspondence between function (or purpose) and precise content of media is not exact, since one function overlaps with another, and the same content can serve different functions. The set of statements refers to functions for society and needs to be reformulated in order to take account of the perspectives either of the media themselves (their own view of their tasks) or of the individual user of mass media, as in **'uses and gratifications'** theory and research (see Chapter 16).   ✱ Media function can thus refer both to more or less objective tasks of the media (such as news or editorializing) and to motives or benefits as perceived by a media user (such as being informed or entertained).

Among the general 'functions for society', most agreement seems to have been achieved on the idea of the media as a force for social integration (as noted already). Studies of media content have also often found that mainstream mass media tend to be conformist and supportive rather than critical of dominant values. This support takes several forms, including the avoidance of fundamental criticism of key institutions, such as business, the justice system and democratic politics; giving differential access to the 'social top'; and symbolically rewarding those who succeed according to the approved paths of virtue and hard work, while symbolically punishing those who fail or deviate (see Chapter 18). Dayan and Katz (1992) argue that major social occasions portrayed on television (public or state ceremonies, major sporting events) and often drawing huge audiences worldwide help to provide otherwise missing social cement. One of the effects of what they call **'media events'**   ✱

is to confer status on leading figures and issues in society. Another is on social relations: 'With almost every event, we have seen *communitas and camaraderie* emerge from normally atomized – and sometimes deeply divided – societies' (1992: 214).

In the light of these observations, it is not so surprising that research on effects has failed to lend much support to the proposition that mass media, for all their attention to crime, sensation, violence and deviant happenings, are a significant cause of social, or even individual, crime and disorganization. The more one holds to a functionalist theory of media, the less logical it is to expect socially disintegrative effects. Even so, this theoretical approach can be applied in cases of apparent harm. All social systems are at risk of failure or error and the term 'dysfunction' was coined to label effects that seem to have a negative character. The media, lacking clear purpose and direction in society, are more prone to dysfunctions than other institutions and are less easy to correct. However, what is functional or not is nearly always disputable on subjective grounds. For instance, media critical of authorities are performing a useful watchdog role, but from another point of view they are undermining authority and national unity. This is the fundamental and irremediable weakness of functionalism. Key propositions of the theory are found in Box 4.10.

4.10 Functionalist theory of media: main propositions

- Media are an institution of society
- They perform the necessary tasks of order, control and cohesion
- They are also necessary for adaptation and change
- Functions are recognizable in the effects of the media
- Management of tension
- There are also unintended harmful effects which can be classified as dysfunctions

---

Media–Society Theory IV: Social Constructionism

Social **constructionism** is an abstract term for a very broad and influential tendency in the social sciences, sparked off especially by the publication of Berger and Luckman's book *The Social Construction of Reality* (1967). In fact the intellectual roots are a good deal deeper, for instance in the symbolic interactionism of Blumer (1969) and the phenomenological sociology of Alfred Schutz (1972). In this work, the notion of society as an objective reality pressing on individuals is countered with the alternative (and more liberating) view that the structures, forces and ideas of society are created by human beings, continually recreated or reproduced and also open to challenge and change. There is a general emphasis on the possibilities for action and also for choices in the understanding of 'reality'. Social reality has to be made and given meaning (interpreted) by human actors. These general ideas have been formulated in many different ways, according to other theoretical ideas, and represent a major paradigm change in the human sciences in the later twentieth century.

They have also had a particular appeal to students of mass communication and are at the centre of thinking about processes of media influence as well as being a matter of debate. The general idea that mass media influence what most people believe to be reality is of course an old one and is embedded in theories of propaganda and ideology (for instance, the role of the media as producing a 'false consciousness'). The unthinking, but unceasing, promotion by media of nationalism, patriotism, social conformity and belief systems could all be interpreted as examples of social construction. Later critical theory argued for the possibility of such ideological impositions being contested and resisted, emphasizing the possibilities for reinterpreting the hegemonic message. Even so, the emphasis in critical theory is on the media as a very effective *reproducer* of a selective and biased view of reality.

Aside from the question of ideology, there has been much attention to social construction at work in relation to mass media news, entertainment and popular culture and in the formation of public opinion. In respect of news, there is now more or less a consensus among media scholars that the picture of 'reality' that news claims to provide cannot help but be a selective construct made up of fragments of factual information and observation that are bound together and given meaning by a particular frame, angle of vision or perspective. The genre requirements of news and the routines of news processing are also at work. Social construction refers to the processes by which events, persons, values and ideas are first defined or interpreted in a certain way and given value and priority, largely by mass media, leading to the (personal) construction of larger pictures of reality. Here, the ideas of 'framing' and **'schemata'**
play their part (see Chapter 14). Central propositions are in Box 4.11.

Social constructionism: main propositions **4.11**

- Society is a construct rather than a fixed reality
- Media provide the materials for reality construction
- Meanings are offered by media, but can be negotiated or rejected
- Media selectively reproduce certain meanings
- Media cannot give an objective account of social reality (all facts are interpretations)

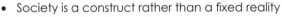

Media–Society Theory V: Communication Technology Determinism

There is a long and still active tradition of searching for links between the dominant communication technology of an age and key features of society, bearing on all the themes outlined above. To label this body of thinking 'determinist' does not do justice to the many differences and nuances, but there is a common element of 'media-centredness' (see p. 12). There is also a tendency to concentrate on the potential for (or bias towards) social change of a particular communication technology and to subordinate other variables. Otherwise, there may be little in common between the theories.

Any history of communication (as of other) technologies testifies to the accelerating pace of invention and of material and other consequences, and some theorists are inclined to identify distinct phases. Rogers (1986), for instance, locates turning points at the invention of writing, the beginning of printing in the fifteenth century, the mid-nineteenth-century start to the telecommunication era, and the age of interactive communication beginning in 1946 with the invention of the mainframe computer. Schement and Curtis (1995) provide us with a detailed 'timeline', extending from pre-history to modern times, of communication technology inventions, which they classify according to their being either 'conceptual/institutional' (such as writing) or 'devices for acquisition and storage' (such as paper and printing), or being related to processing and distribution (such as computers and satellites). History shows several apparent trends but especially a shift over time in the direction of more speed, greater dispersion, wider reach and greater flexibility. They underline the capacity for communication more readily to cross barriers of time and space. These matters are discussed in more detail in Chapter 5 (pp. 125–7) with reference to the cultural and social factors shaping the evolution of media technologies.

The Toronto School

The first significant theorist in this tradition seems to have been the Canadian economic historian H.M. Innis, who founded the '**Toronto School**' of thinking about the media in the period after the Second World War. Innis (1950, 1951) attributed the characteristic features of successive ancient civilizations to the prevailing and dominant modes of communication, each of which will have its own 'bias' in terms of societal form. For example, he regarded the change from stone to papyrus as causing a shift from royal to priestly power. In ancient Greece, an oral tradition and a flexible alphabet favoured inventiveness and diversity and prevented the emergence of a priesthood with a monopoly over education. The foundation and endurance of the Roman Empire was assisted by a culture of writing and documents on which legal-bureaucratic institutions, capable of administering distant provinces, could be based. Printing, in its turn, challenged the bureaucratic monopoly of power and encouraged both individualism and nationalism.

There are two main organizing principles in Innis's work. First, as in the economic sphere, communication leads over time to monopolization by a group or a class of the means of production and distribution of knowledge. In turn, this produces a disequilibrium that either impedes changes or leads to the competitive emergence of other forms of communication, which tend to restore equilibrium. This can also be taken to mean that new communication technologies undermine old bases of social power. Secondly, the most important dimensions of empire are *space* and *time*, and some means of communication are more suitable for one than for the other (this is the main so-called bias of communication). Thus, empires can persist either through time (such as ancient Egypt) or extensively in space (such as Rome), depending on the dominant form of communication.

McLuhan's (1962) developments of the theory offered new insights into the consequences of the rise of print media (see also Eisenstein, 1978), although his main purpose of explaining the significance of electronic media for human experience has not really been fulfilled (McLuhan, 1964) (see also Chapter 5). Of printing, McLuhan wrote: 'the typographic extension of man brought in nationalism, industrialism and mass markets, and universal literacy and education'.

Gouldner (1976) interpreted key changes in modern political history in terms of communication technology. He connects the rise of 'ideology', defined as a special form of rational discourse, to printing and the newspaper, on the grounds that (in the eighteenth and nineteenth centuries) these stimulated a supply of interpretation and ideas (ideology). He then portrays the later media of radio, film and television as having led to a decline of ideology because of the shift from 'conceptual to iconic symbolism', revealing a split between the 'cultural apparatus' (the intelligentsia), which produces ideology, and the 'consciousness industry', which controls the new mass public. This anticipates a continuing 'decline in ideology' as a result of the new computer-based networks of information. The main propositions of media technological determinism are presented in Box 4.12.

Media technological determinism: main propositions 4.12

- Communication technology is fundamental to society
- Each technology has a bias to particular communication forms, contents and uses
- The sequence of invention and application of communication technology influences the direction and pace of social change
- Communication revolutions lead to social revolutions

Moving away from media determinism

Most informed observers are now wary of single-factor explanations of social change and do not really believe in direct mechanistic effects from new technology. Effects occur only when inventions are taken up, developed and applied, usually to existing uses at first, then with a great extension and change of use according to the capacity of the technology and the needs of a society. Development is always shaped by the social and cultural context (Lehmann-Wilzig and Cohen-Avigdor, 2004; Stober, 2004). It no longer makes sense to think in terms of a single dominant medium with some unique properties. This may have been justifiable in the case of the book or, in some respects, at a later stage the telegraph and telephone. At present, very many different new media forms coexist with many of the 'old' media, none of which has disappeared. At the same time, the argument that media are converging and linking to comprise an all-encompassing network has considerable force and implications (Neuman, 1991). It may also be true that new media forms can have a particular social or cultural 'bias' (see Chapter 6) which makes certain effects more likely. These possibilities are discussed in the following section.

Media–Society Theory VI: the Information Society

The assumption of a revolutionary social transition as a result of new communication technology has been with us for quite some time, although it is not without its critics (e.g. Leiss, 1989; Ferguson, 1992; Webster, 1995, 2002). Ferguson (1986) treated this 'neo-technological determinism' as a *belief system* which was tending to operate as a self-fulfilling prophecy. The term 'communications revolution', along with the term **'information society'**, has now almost come to be accepted as an objective description of our time and of the type of society that is emerging.

    The term 'information society' seems to have originated in Japan in the 1960s (Ito, 1981), although its genealogy is usually traced to the concept of 'post-industrial' society first proposed by the sociologist Daniel Bell (1973). Another source was the idea of an 'information economy' developed by the economists Machlup (1962) and Porat (1977) (see Schement and Curtis, 1995). Bell's work belonged to the tradition that relates types of society to succeeding stages of economic and social development. The main characteristics of the post-industrial society were found in the rise in the service sector of the economy relative to manufacture or agriculture and thus the predominance of 'information-based' work. Theoretical knowledge (scientific, expert, data-based) was becoming the key factor in the economy, outstripping physical plant and land as bases of wealth. Correlatively, a 'new class' was emerging based on the possession of knowledge and personal relations skills. Most of the observed post-industrial trends were seen to accelerate in the last quarter of the twentieth century. The production and distribution of information of all kinds, especially using computer-based technology, have themselves become a major sector of the economy.

    Aside from the accumulating evidence of the significance of information in contemporary economy and society, there has not been much agreement or clarity about the *concept* of 'information society'. Melody (1990: 26–7) describes information societies simply as those that have become 'dependent upon complex electronic information networks and which allocate a major portion of their resources to information and communication activities'. Van Cuilenburg (1987) put the chief characteristic as the exponential increase in production and flow of information of all kinds, largely as a consequence of reduced costs following miniaturization and computerization. However, he also called attention to our relative incapacity to process, use or even receive much more of the increasing supply of information. Since then, this imbalance has become much greater. Reductions in costs of transmission have continued to fuel the process of exponential growth. There is a continually decreasing sensitivity to distance as well as to cost and a continually increasing speed, volume and interactivity of possibilities for communication.

Despite the importance of the trends under way, it has not really been established that any revolutionary transformation in society has yet occurred, as opposed to a further step in the development of capitalism (Schement and Curtis, 1995: 26). What is still missing is evidence of a transformation in social relationships (Webster, 1995). Several commentators have emphasized the increased 'interconnectedness' of society as a result of 'information society' trends extending to a global level. According to Neuman (1991: 12), this is the underlying 'logic behind the cascade of new technologies'.

Some writers (e.g. van Dijk, 1993; Castells, 1996) choose to use the term 'network society' instead of 'information society'. Van Dijk (1999) suggests that modern society is in a process of becoming a network society: 'a form of society increasingly organizing its relationships in media networks which are gradually replacing or complementing the social networks of face to face communication'. A network structure of society is contrasted with a centre–periphery and hierarchical mass society, or one that largely conforms to the traditional bureaucratic model of organization that was typical of industrial society in the nineteenth and twentieth centuries. It exhibits numerous overlapping circles of communication that can have both a vertical and a horizontal range. Such networks can serve to exclude as well as connect. Traditional mass media exhibited a similar structure and were inclusive of all.

The idea of interconnectedness relates to another aspect of contemporary society that has attracted comment, and that is the high degree of *dependence* on others. This is hardly a new idea since it was the basis of Durkheim's century-old social theory concerning the division of labour. But there is arguably a qualitative change in our era, resulting from the continued excursions of information technology into every aspect of life, especially where intelligent machines replace human agency. One aspect that has been emphasized by Giddens (1991) is the degree to which we have to put our trust in expert systems of all kinds for maintaining normal conditions of life. We also live with increased awareness of risks of many kinds (health, environmental, economic, military) that are both derived from the public circulation of information and also managed by reference to information. Elsewhere Giddens refers to the globalized world as one 'out of control – a runaway world' (1999: 2). In addition, it would seem that the 'culture' of contemporary society, in the traditional sense of mental and symbolic pursuits and customary ways of passing time free from essential obligations, is largely dominated by a vast array of informational services in addition to the mass media.

A notable, although intangible, dimension of the concept of 'information society' is the fact that it has come to form part of contemporary self-consciousness, and in some versions it is almost a new world view. For instance, de Mue (1999) compares the transition taking place to the development of mechanics in the seventeenth and eighteenth centuries. He writes:

> While the mechanistic world view is characterized by the postulates of analysability, lawfulness and controllability, the informationistic world view is characterized by the postulates of synthesizability, programmability and manipulability ... it fundamentally alters human experience and the evaluation of and association with reality.

For others, informatization connotes a new vision of progress for all and a future with unlimited horizons, more or less in continuation of the model we already have. Established mass media have played a key part in publicizing a 'euphoric' and utopian view of new media potential (see Rössler, 2001). This perspective carries some ideological baggage, tending to legitimate some trends of the time (e.g. faith in science and high technology as solutions to problems) and to delegitimate others (especially ideological politics about class and inequality). By emphasizing the means and processes of communication and the quantitative dimensions of change, it de-emphasizes the precise content and purpose of it all. In this respect, a connection with **postmodernism** can also be made. It is at least apparent that very divergent interpretations are possible.

Despite scattered insights of this kind, the information society concept has been dominated by economic, sociological, geographical and technological considerations. The *cultural* dimension has been relatively neglected, aside from recognition of the great volume of information and symbolic production, and unless we view postmodernist thinking as filling this gap. The rise of an 'information culture' that extends into all aspects of everyday life may be easier to demonstrate than the reality of an information society.

It is clear that the 'information economy' is much larger than the mass media on their own, and the primary information technologies involved are not those of mass production and distribution of print material for the general public or mass dissemination by broadcasting or electronic recordings. It could be argued that the birth of the 'information age', although presaged by mass communication, marks a new and separate historical path. Certainly, the mass media were well established before the supposed information 'revolution' and may be better considered as part of the industrial age rather than of its successor. There were early voices that foretold the death of mass media precisely because of the rise of new information technologies that are said to render them obsolete (e.g. Maisel, 1973).

The information society concept has not been universally accepted as helpful for analysis, for reasons that have in part been explained. A central problem is the lack of an overt political dimension, since it seems to have no core of political purpose, simply an (attributed) inevitable technocratic logic of its own (van Dijk, 1999). In this it may at least match the predominant spirit of the times in both popular and intellectual 'western' circles. It is quite clear that in several contexts, the information society idea has been harnessed for public policies with technocratic goals for nation states or regions (Mattelart, 2003). The general consensus about the significance of changes occurring in communication technology is not accompanied by unanimity about the social consequences. Hassan (2008) believes that the information society idea is essentially ideological and supportive of the neo-liberal economic project that benefits most from global interconnectivity. Some of these issues are returned to in Chapter 6, which deals with new media developments. However, certain main theoretical points are summarized in Box 4.13.

> ## Information society theory: main propositions **4.13**
>
> - Information work replaces industrial work
> - Production and flow of information accelerates
> - Society is characterized by increasing interconnectivity
> - Disparate activities converge and integrate
> - There is increasing dependency on complex systems
> - Trends to globalization accelerate
> - Constraints on time and space are much reduced
> - Consequences are open to alternative interpretations, both positive and negative
> - There are increased risks of loss of control
> - Information society theory is an ideology more than a theory

Conclusion

These theoretical perspectives on the relation between media and society are diverse in several respects, emphasizing different causes and types of change and pointing to different paths into the future. They cannot all be reconciled, since they represent alternative philosophical positions and opposed methodological preferences. Nevertheless, we can make some sense of them in terms of the main dimensions of approach, each of which offers a choice of perspective and/or method. First, there is a contrast between a critical and a more or less positive view of the developments at issue. Although scientific inquiry seeks a degree of **objectivity** and neutrality, this does not prevent one either approving or disapproving of a tendency indicated by a theory. In respect of Marxism, political economy theory and mass society theory, there is an inbuilt critical component. In contrast, functionalism leans in a positive direction as far as the working of media is concerned. Information society theory is open to critical and positive views, while social constructionism and technology determinism are open ended.

    Secondly, there is a difference between a more socio-centric and a more media-centric view. We can view media either as dependent on society and mirroring its contours or as primary movers and moulders. The main media-centric theories are those relating to communication technology and the information society. There are of course other variables to consider, especially those relating to approach and method of inquiry. Humanistic, qualitative and speculative methods can be chosen instead of traditional objective methods of 'scientific' research (see Rosengren, 1983).

This account is really incomplete without some of the theory relating to culture that will be discussed in Chapter 5, but it gives some idea of the general structure of thinking about mass media and society.

Further Reading

Curran, J. and Gurevitch, M. (2005) *Mass Media and Society*, 4th edn. London: Hodder Arnold.
An authoritative and periodically updated volume of twenty chapters on varied aspects of the media–society relationship. Theoretically strong and broadly critical in approach. Key chapters are by Livingstone, Murdock and Golding, Curran, Hesmondhalgh and Garnham.

Hassan, R. (2008) *The Information Society*. Cambridge: Polity Press.
This thoughtful study rescues a somewhat tired and battered concept and restores it to some value as a means of understanding the ongoing effects of digitization.

Online Readings

Corner, J. (2007) 'Media, power and culture', in E. Devereux (ed.), *Media Studies*, pp. 211–30. London: Sage.
Hermes, J. (2007) 'Media representation of social structure: gender', in E. Devereux (ed.), *Media Studies*, pp. 191–210. London: Sage.
Klaehn, J. (2002) 'A critical review and assessment of Herman and Chomsky's propaganda model', *European Journal of Communication*, 17 (2): 147–83.
Webster, F. (2002) 'The information society revisited', in L. Lievrouw and S. Livingstone (eds), *The Handbook of New Media*, pp. 443–57. London: Sage.

5

Mass Communication and Culture

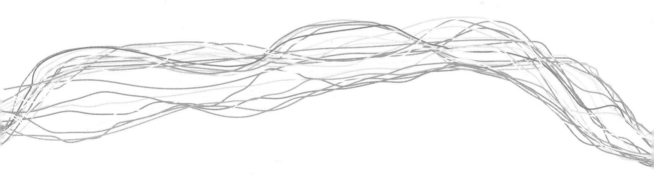

This chapter sets out to explore the more 'cultural' dimensions of the theories already discussed in Chapter 4 and to introduce some additional perspectives. The general framework of 'mediation' (see pp. 83–4) remains relevant, but here the emphasis shifts to *what* is mediated (the particular meanings) and to the process by which meaning is given and taken (sometimes referred to as 'signification'). Since the earlier days of mass communication research, a distinctive 'culturalist' perspective on mass media has been developing, especially under the influence of the humanities (literature, linguistics, philosophy), as distinct from the more social scientific emphasis of 'mainstream' communication science. At some points, or on some issues, the two traditions have merged, although there remain substantial differences of thinking and method. This book, and this chapter, are written primarily from a social scientific perspective, but aim also to benefit from some of the insights and ideas of the 'culturalists'.

The culturalist approach takes in all aspects of the production, forms and reception of texts in this sense and the discourses that surround them. While mass media necessarily fall within the range of cultural studies, the latter has a much wider range of reference, and there is only a limited overlap of issues and theory. As will be shown, the culture cannot only be defined in terms of texts, but relates just as much to patterns of life and thought and potentially all human activity. To put it briefly, 'media-cultural' theory is concerned not only with the content of mass media, but also with the context of production and reception and with all the surrounding practices.

Communication and Culture

James Carey (1975) proposed an alternative to the dominant view of communication as *transmission* in the form of a 'ritual' model (see p. 71), and he has also advocated an approach to communication and society in which culture is allotted a more central place. 'Social life is more than power and trade ... it also includes the sharing of aesthetic experience, religious ideas, personal values and sentiments, and intellectual notions – a ritual order' (Carey, 1988: 34). Accordingly, he defined communication as 'a symbolic process whereby reality is produced, maintained, repaired and transformed' (1988: 23).

In order to take further the question of the relation between *mass* communication and culture in this sense, we need to be more precise about what presents itself as an object of study. This is made difficult by the many senses in which the term 'culture' is used, itself a reflection of the complexity of the phenomenon. Culture is defined by Carey as a *process*, but it can also refer to some *shared attribute* of a human group (such as their physical environment, tools, religion, customs and practices, or their whole way of life). Culture also can refer to *texts* and *symbolic artefacts* (e.g. works of art and architecture) that are encoded with particular meanings by and for people with particular cultural identifications.

Towards defining culture

It is not possible to give a precise definition of culture because the term covers so many things and is variously used, but if we extract essential points from these different usages, it seems that culture must have all of the following attributes. It is something collective and shared with others (there is no purely individual culture). It must have some symbolic form of expression, whether intended as such or not. It has some pattern, order or regularity, and therefore some evaluative dimensions (if only a degree of conformity to a culturally prescribed pattern). There is (or has been) a dynamic continuity over time (culture lives and changes, has a history and potentially a future). Perhaps the most general and essential attribute of culture is communication, since cultures could not develop, survive, extend and generally succeed without communication. Finally, in order to study culture we need to be able to recognize and locate it, and essentially there are three places to look: in people, in things (texts, artefacts) and in human practices (socially patterned behaviours). These main features are summarized in Box 5.1.

There are some obvious implications for the study of mass communication since every aspect of the production and use of mass media has a cultural dimension. We can focus on *people* as producers of culturally meaningful media texts, or as 'readers of texts' from which they take cultural meanings, with implications for the rest of social life. We can focus on the *texts* and *artefacts* themselves (films, books, newspaper articles) and on their symbolic forms and possible meanings. We may want to study the *practices* of *makers* of media products or of *users* of the media. Media audience composition and behaviour (practices around the choice and use of media) are always culturally patterned, before, after and during the media experience.

The main properties of culture **5.1**

- Collectively formed and held
- Open to symbolic expression
- Ordered and differentially valued
- Systematically patterned
- Dynamic and changing
- Spatially located
- Communicable over time and space

Themes of media-cultural theory

This broad terrain can be narrowed down by identifying the main questions and theoretical issues. As outlined in the following paragraphs.

1. *The quality of mass culture.* The first 'cultural' question on the agenda of media theory was that of the quality of the new mass culture made possible by mass communication. This topic has already been discussed (pp. 60–2) and, as we saw, the initial tendency was to view mass culture in a negative light. It nearly always involved a view of people as a mass – the new form of social collectivity, which was otherwise often perceived as without any other culture of its own.

2. *The nature of popular culture.* The rise of a distinctive 'media culture' has also stimulated a rethinking about the nature of 'popular culture', which has now to be seen not just as a cheap alternative, mass produced for mass consumption, but as a vital new branch of cultural creativity and enjoyment (Schudson, 1991; McGuigan, 1992). The issue of mass culture also stimulated the rise of critical cultural theory, which, among other things, has been extended to consider issues of gender and of subculture in relation to mass communication. Embedded in the debate about mass culture is the eternal question of 'quality' and how it can be defined or recognized.

3. *The impact of technology.* A third key theme relates to the potential consequences of the new technologies themselves for the experience of meaning in the emerging modern world. Communication technology has many implications for the way we may come to know our own social world and our place in it. Before the invention of audiovisual media, cultural experience was mediated by personal contact, religious ceremonies, public performance or printed texts (for the small minority). Mediated cultural experience is accessible to virtually all in a great variety of forms that may alter its meaning and salience.

4. *Political economy and culture.* There are political-economic aspects of the organized production of culture represented by mass media industries. We have come to think of the media as a 'consciousness industry', driven by economic logic as well as by cultural changes. An important aspect is the 'commodification' of culture in the form of the 'software' produced by and for the communication 'hardware', both of which are sold and exchanged in enlarging markets.

5. *Globalization.* Along with technological change and 'marketization' has come a steady increase in the internationalization of cultural production and distribution (this has sometimes been referred to as 'Americanization'). The theme of 'globalization' captures a range of debates about the costs and benefits, or just the consequences, for pre-existing cultural content and forms. Does globalization lead to homogenization, diversification or **hybridization**? Can minority forms survive and new ones develop?

6. *Identity.* This is linked to another theme of media-cultural theory, relating to cultural identity, which can be defined at various levels, from the national or ethnic to the local and linguistic. The typical culture (in the sense of media texts) produced by the major media industries is often globalized in form, even when it appears in local or national variants and languages. Communication is necessary for identity, and mass media (including the Internet) can be both harmful as well as beneficial for identity. In some parts of the world there has been a search for some means through public policy to secure valued forms of cultural diversity.

7. *Gender.* Issues of cultural identity arise for minorities defined in ways other than shared location, religion or ethnicity. Subcultures based on gender or sexual orientation provide examples, but there are numerous potential bases for cultural identity formation.

8. *Ideology.* Last but not least is the question of how ideology of many different kinds is embodied in cultural production and how it can be 'read' in media texts and find some effect on an audience. Particular attention is paid to covert or unconscious meanings that stem from the cultural context or the language or coding system employed. These points are summarized in Box 5.2.

Themes of media-cultural theory 5.2

- Mass culture quality and basis for popular appeal
- Communication technology effects
- Commodification and marketization of culture
- Globalization
- Cultural diversity and identity
- Cultural identity
- Gender and subculture
- Ideology and hegemony embedded in cultural forms

The Beginnings: the Frankfurt School and Critical Cultural Theory

A socially based critical concern with the rise of mass culture goes back at least to the mid-nineteenth century, and in the mid-twentieth century was represented in England by the rise of more radical (and populist) critical theory as expressed in the work of Richard Hoggart, Raymond Williams and Stuart Hall. The initial thrust of these critics was to attack the commercial roots of cultural 'debasement' and to speak up for the working-class consumer of mass culture as the victim (and not only that) rather than the villain of the story. The aim was to redeem the people on whose supposedly 'low tastes' the presumed low quality of mass culture was often blamed. In North America at about the same time or earlier, a similar debate was raging (see Rosenberg and White, 1957), with an eloquent denunciation of the banality of mass culture. Since then, 'mass culture' itself has largely been rescued from the stigma of low quality, although in the course of this the original concept of mass culture has been largely abandoned.

For the wider development of ideas about mass communication and the character of 'media culture', within an international framework, the various national debates about cultural quality have probably been less influential than a set of ideas, owing much to neo-Marxist thinking, which developed and diffused in the post-war years. The term 'critical theory' refers to this long and diverse tradition, which owes its origins to the work of a group of post-1933 *émigré* scholars from the Marxist School of Applied Social Research in Frankfurt. The most important members of the group were Max Horkheimer and Theodor Adorno, but others, including Leo Lowenthal, Herbert Marcuse and Walter Benjamin, played an important role (see Jay, 1973; Hardt, 1991).

The School had been established originally to examine the apparent failure of revolutionary social change as predicted by Marx. In explanation of this failure they looked to the capacity of the 'superstructure' (especially ideas and ideology represented in the mass media) to subvert the material and historical forces of economic change (and also the promise of the Enlightenment). History (as interpreted by Marx) seemed to have 'gone wrong' because ideologies of the dominant class had come to condition the economic base, especially by promoting a 'false consciousness' among the working masses. The *commodity* is the main instrument of this process. The theory of commodification originates in Marx's *Grundrisse*, in which he noted that objects are commodified by acquiring an exchange value, instead of having merely an intrinsic use value. In the same way, cultural products (in the form of images, ideas and symbols) are produced and sold in media markets as commodities. These can be exchanged by consumers for psychic satisfactions, amusement and illusory notions of our place in the world, often resulting in the obscuration of the real structure of society and our subordination in it (false consciousness).

Marcuse (1964) gave the description 'one-dimensional' to the mass consumption society founded on commerce, advertising and spurious egalitarianism. The media and the 'culture industry' as a whole were deeply implicated in this critique. Many of these ideas were launched during the 1940s by Adorno and Horkheimer (1972, in translation), which contained a sharp and pessimistic attack on mass culture. This was criticized for its uniformity, worship of technique, monotony, escapism and production of false needs, its reduction of individuals to customers and its removal of all ideological choice (see Hardt, 1991: 140). According to Shils (1957), the very jaundiced Frankfurt School view of mass culture was not only anti-capitalist but also anti-American, and mainly reflected the first impact of modern mass media on a group of displaced European intellectuals. In several respects, the critique of mass culture outlined is very close to that found in different versions of the then contemporary mass society theory.

Ideology and resistance

Critical cultural theory has now extended well beyond its early concerns with ideological domination, although in one way or another the study of ideology in media culture remains central. So does the significance of media culture for the experience of particular groups in society, such as youth, the working class, ethnic minorities and other marginal categories. Research and theory on these topics were pioneered at the Centre for Contemporary Cultural Studies at the University of Birmingham during the 1970s. The person most associated with the work of this school, Stuart Hall, has written that the cultural studies approach:

> is opposed to the base–superstructure way of formulating the relationship between ideal and material forces, especially where the base is defined by the determination by the 'economic' in any simple sense. ... It defines 'culture' as both the means and values which arise amongst distinctive social groups and classes, on the basis of their given historical conditions and relationship, through which they 'handle' and respond to the conditions of existence. (quoted in Gurevitch et al., 1982: 267)

The critical approach associated with the **Birmingham School** was also responsible for an important shift from the question of ideology embedded in media texts to the question of how this ideology might be 'read' by its audience. Stuart Hall (1974/1980) proposed a model of *encoding–decoding* media discourse, which represented the media text as located between its producers, who framed meaning in a certain way, and its audience, who 'decoded' the meaning according to their rather different social situations and frames of interpretation (see pp. 73–4).

These ideas proved a considerable stimulus to rethinking the theory of ideology and of false consciousness. They led to research on the potential for 'differential decoding' (e.g. Morley, 1980), with a view, especially, to finding evidence of working-class resistance to dominant media messages. The direct results were meagre in this respect, but indirectly the theory was very effective in 're-empowering' the audience and returning some optimism to the study of media and culture. It also led to a wider view of the social and cultural influences which mediate the experience of the media, especially ethnicity, gender and 'everyday life' (Morley, 1986, 1992). The main tenets of critical cultural theory are listed in Box 5.3.

Critical cultural theory points: main propositions **5.3**

- Mass culture is a debased form in capitalist society
- Mass culture produces false consciousness
- Commodification is the central process
- Mass culture embodies a hegemonic ideology
- Ideology can be decoded differentially and even reversed
- Popular culture can be distinguished from mass culture

The Redemption of the Popular

The mass media are largely responsible for what we call either 'mass culture' or 'popular culture', and they have 'colonized' other cultural forms in the process. The most widely disseminated and enjoyed symbolic culture of our time (if it makes any sense to refer to it in the singular) is what flows in abundance by way of the media of films, television, newspapers, **phonogram**, video, and so on. It makes little sense to suppose that this flood can in some way be dammed, turned back or purified, or to view the predominant culture of our time simply as a deformed offspring of commerce from a once pure stock.

There is even little possibility of distinguishing an elite from a mass taste, since nearly everyone is attracted to some of the diverse elements of popular media culture. Tastes will always differ, and varying criteria of assessment can be applied, but we should at least accept the media culture of our time as an accomplished fact and treat it on its own terms. The term 'mass culture' is likely to remain in circulation, but the alternative form 'popular culture' (meaning essentially 'culture which is popular' – much enjoyed by many people) seems preferable and no longer carries a pejorative association. Popular culture in this sense is a hybrid product of numerous and never-ending efforts for expression in a contemporary idiom aimed at reaching people and capturing a market, and an equally active demand by people for what Fiske (1987) would call 'meanings and pleasures'.

The (semiotic) power of the people

The so-called 'redemption of the popular' depends a good deal on the decoding theory of Hall outlined above (pp. 73–4). According to this, the same cultural product can be 'read' in different ways, even if a certain dominant meaning may seem to be built in. Fiske (1987) defines a media text as the *outcome* of its reading and enjoyment by an audience. He defines the plurality of meanings of a text as its 'polysemy'. The associated term **'intertextuality'** refers partly to the interconnectedness of meanings across different media contents (blurring any line between elite and popular culture), but also to the interconnectedness of meanings across media and other cultural experiences. An example of both terms is provided by the fact that a cultural phenomenon, like the pop singer Madonna, could appeal to, yet have quite different meanings for, both young girls and ageing male readers of *Playboy* magazine (Schwichtenberg, 1992).

There are entirely different readings of much popular media content in different subcultures, opening a way of escape from potential social control. Fiske (1987: 126) writes:

> The preferred meanings in television are generally those that serve the interests of the dominant classes; other meanings are structured in relations of dominance–subordination ... the semiotic power of the subordinate to make their own meanings is the equivalent of their ability to evade, oppose, or negotiate with this social power.

For Fiske, the primary virtue of popular culture is precisely that it is popular, both literally 'of the people' and dependent on 'people power'. He writes: 'Popularity is here a measure of a cultural form's ability to serve the desires of its customers ... For a cultural commodity to become popular it must be able to meet the various interests of the people amongst whom it is popular as well as the interests of its producers' (1987: 310). Popular culture must be relevant and responsive to needs or it will fail, and success (in the market) may be the best test that culture is both (in practice the criterion of success supersedes any notion of intrinsic quality). Fiske rejects the argument that lines of division of cultural capital follow the lines of division of economic capital (Bourdieu, 1986). Instead he argues that there are two economies, with relative autonomy, one cultural and the other social. Even if most people in a class society are subordinated, they have a degree of *semiotic power* in the cultural economy – that is, the power to shape meanings to their own desires.

Unanswered questions

Despite the re-evaluation of popular culture that has occurred and the rise of postmodernism (discussed below), several charges of the kind made by Frankfurt School critics remain on the table. Much of the content offered by media that is both popular and commercially successful is still open to much the same objections as in more elitist and less enlightened times. Media culture often displays one or more of the following limitations. It is, variously, repetitive, undemanding, thematically limited and conformist. Many examples can be found of popular content that are ideologically tendentious, nasty and positively anti-intellectual. Its production is governed by a predominantly commercial logic since most popular culture is produced by large corporations with an overriding concern for their own profits, rather than for enriching the cultural lives of the people. Audiences are viewed as consumer markets to be manipulated and managed. Popular formulas and products tend to be used until threadbare, then discarded when they cease to be profitable, whatever the audience might demand in the 'cultural economy'. There is not much empirical support for the theory that media texts are decoded in oppositional ways (Morley, 1997: 124).

The new 'cultural populism' has, not surprisingly, produced its own backlash (McGuigan, 1992; Ferguson and Golding, 1997). Gitlin (1997) sees the new cultural studies as a populist project that has simply inverted the old hierarchy of cultural values, without overthrowing it. In his view, it has become anti-political, which was not its avowed intention. Instead of being against capitalism, it has come to 'echo the logic of capitalism' (1997: 32).

The 'redemption' arguments largely ignore the continuing semiotic inequality whereby a more educated and better-off minority has access both to popular culture *and* to 'unpopular' culture (such as classical music, great literature and modern and avant-garde art). The majority are still limited to popular forms alone and totally dependent on the commercial media market (Gripsrud, 1989).

There is a risk in the backlash against polemical and overstated claims for popular culture and not much light has been generated by the debate. One way out of the impasse, without going back to the past, is to make use of the concept of **lifestyle**, in recognition of the flux and diversity of contemporary social life, especially as cultural capital is more widely and evenly distributed by way of the educational system. For example, Andersson and Jansson (1998), in a study of Swedish media use, identify the phenomenon of a 'progressive cultural lifestyle', which combines an interest in both popular and traditional culture. The social group concerned combines high cultural capital with limited economic resources. This lifestyle is identified both by preferences and by styles of media use. It is eclectic, fragmented and relaxed in style. We do not know how far these observations can be generalized but they suggest that new times produce new cultural paradigms.

∗

The idea of 'quality' of mass media cultural provision nevertheless remains on the agenda of applied media theory, even if its meaning has shifted, because there are still relevant policy issues and also public concerns about quality. Quality no longer refers exclusively to the degree of conformity to a traditional cultural canon, but may be defined in terms of creativity, originality, diversity of cultural identity and various ethical or moral principles (Schrøder, 1992), depending on whose perspective is chosen. Of course, as advocates of popular culture also argue, quality has also to be measured by the pleasures and satisfactions it provides and these can be indicated, albeit crudely, by success in the market. It can certainly no longer be assumed that what has most appeal has less 'quality', but the material economic dynamic of cultural production cannot be so easily distinguished from the 'semiotic' cultural economy. It is also clear from inquiries into the meaning and measurement of 'cultural quality' that there is no single source of objective definition and that quite different criteria are applied by, for instance, professional media producers, audiences, social or cultural critics and media managers (Ishikawa, 1996) (see Chapter 14). There is no agreed theory of popular culture but relevant points of debate are listed as propositions in Box 5.4.

5.4 The debate about popular culture: main points of debate

- Popular culture represents the power of the people
- Popularity is a quality in itself
- Popular culture has universal appeal
- Popular culture is important to many subgroup identities
- Popular culture is commodified culture

Gender and the Mass Media

Hermes (2007: 191) argues that we need to understand how the media represent gender because 'constructions of femininity and masculinity are part of a dominant ideology'. Beyond this, she points out that the media still offer guides and examples of general behaviour and we need to be able to decode these messages. One area where the theory of differential cultural reading of media texts has made important advances, in collaboration with feminist research, is in relation to gender. While communication studies, even of the radical critical tendency, have long seemed to be largely 'gender-blind' (perhaps more a matter of unwillingness to see), one can now justifiably speak of a 'cultural feminist media studies project' (van Zoonen, 1994; Gallagher, 2003). This goes far deeper and wider than the original limited agenda of matters such as the under-representation of women in the media and the stereotyping and sex-role socialization which was and still is a feature of much media content. Current concerns also go beyond issues of pornographic media content which matter to feminists (and others) not only because they are offensive and symbolically degrading, but because they might be a stimulus to rape and violence.

The amount of gender-related media research is now very large and, although in part it follows lines of theory pioneered with reference to social class and race, it has several other dimensions. These include an attention to Freudian psychoanalytic theory following the ideas of Jacques Lacan and Nancy Chodorow. Their focus was primarily on the role of gender in 'positioning' the spectator in relation to images (film, television, photographic) of male and female. Another line of research focused on the part played by the media in transmitting a patriarchal ideology concerning the place of women in society. There are now many connections with the wider field of feminist studies (Long, 1991; Kaplan, 1992).

According to van Zoonen (1994), most of the earlier gender-relevant media research, including psychoanalytic theory, implicitly at least, followed the transmission model of effect, based on the direct reaction of a receiver to a message stimulus. She suggests that there has now emerged a new paradigm, essentially culturalist in character, which offers a better way of understanding how the media are related to gender. At the core of the new approach is the idea of 'gender as discourse, a set of overlapping and sometimes contradictory cultural descriptions and prescriptions referring to sexual difference' (1994: 40). The second key basis is an emphasis on the active *construction* of meanings and identities by 'readers' of media texts. In general, the new perspective for feminist media research addresses the following main questions: how are discourses of gender encoded in media texts? How do audiences use and interpret gendered media texts? How does audience reception contribute to the construction of gender at the level of individual identity?

The question of gender touches almost every aspect of the media–culture relationship. Most central is probably the question of gender definition. Van Zoonen (1991: 45) writes that the meaning of gender 'is never given but varies according to specific cultural and historical settings ... and is subject to ongoing discursive struggle and negotiation'. Partly at issue is how gender differences and distinctiveness are signified (see Goffman, 1976; Hermes, 2007). Another general aspect of the struggle is over the differential value in society attaching to masculinity and to femininity.

The gendering of content may also be studied at the point of production since most media selection and production work is carried out by men. In this matter, attention has also been directed to 'the news', which was for long largely a male preserve and in its dominant forms and contents (politics, economics, sport) was oriented more to male readers (see Chapter 11, pp. 300–301). A continuing theme of feminist media critique has been the relative invisibility of women in news and their ghettoization to certain topics. Gallagher (2003) cites a large-scale and international study (by Media Watch, 1995) showing that only 17% of news subjects were women, with much lower percentages in relation to politics and business.

This has been changing, and one of the components of contemporary critiques of the 'decline' of the news media has been the alleged trivialization, personalization and **sensationalism** which are (whether correctly or not, but in line with dominant stereotypes) often synonymous with 'feminization'. News media, both television and the press, are certainly actively seeking to interest female readers and are also engaging in extreme competition for the elusive mass audience.

Studies of media audiences and the reception of media content have shown that there are relatively large differences according to gender in the manner of use of media and the meanings attached to the activity. Certain genres are clearly gendered in their appeal. A good deal of the evidence can be accounted for by patterned differences in social roles, by the typical everyday experience and concerns of men and women, and by the way gender shapes the availability and use of time. It also relates to power roles within the family and the general nature of the relationships between women and male partners or of women in the wider family (Morley, 1986).

Different kinds of media content (and their production and use) are also associated with expressions of common identity based on gender (Ferguson, 1983; Radway, 1984) and with the different pleasures and meanings acquired (Ang, 1985). There may also be deep roots in psychological differences between male and female (Williamson, 1978). In considering these matters, however, it is especially important to take note of van Zoonen's warning that the context is continually changing and that 'the codes that confer meaning onto the signs of femininity are culturally and historically specific and will never be completely unambiguous or consistent' (1994: 149).

A gender-based approach also raises the question of whether media choice and interpretation can provide some lever of change or element of resistance for women in a social situation still generally structured by inequality. The potential for oppositional reading and resistance has been invoked both to explain why women seem attracted to media content with overtly patriarchal messages (such as romance fiction) and to help re-evaluate the surface meaning of this attraction (Radway, 1984). One can say, in summary, that differently gendered media culture, whatever the causes and the forms taken, evokes different responses, and that differences of gender lead to alternative modes of taking meaning from media.

Feminism is a political as well as a cultural project and feminist media studies have inevitably been caught up in wider debate within cultural media studies about the political significance or not of popular culture. This stems in part from the great attention that has been paid to popular genres like soap operas and talk shows that are oriented to female audiences. For instance, van Zoonen (2004) cites evidence to show that the communities of interest that form around popular soap operas can also play a significant part in actively connecting the majority of people to public issues of the day. It was clear where early researchers stood on this issue, especially where popular content (romances, children's stories, women's magazines) was seen as stereotyped and carrying a predominantly patriarchal and conservative ideology or pandering to male sexuality. Things have changed in the media, with much more content by women and for women, with no inhibitions about female sexuality (e.g. McRobbie, 1996). They have also changed in media research through the 'redemption' of popular genres (e.g. Radway, 1984; Ang, 1991).

However, there remains a tension over the direction to be taken by feminist theory and research in respect of the political goals of the movement. Not all are convinced about the relevance of the changes in the media and new popular cultural theory. Van Zoonen, for instance, emphasizes the need to distinguish between news and entertainment. As to the former, she says it is 'completely justified to expect a decent, ethical and more or less accurate representation of feminist politics and politicians in news media' (1994: 152). She does not apply the same criteria to popular culture, which belongs to the realm of 'collective dreams, fantasies and fears'. Without necessarily disagreeing, Hermes (1997) takes a more positive view of the potential role of popular culture, arguing for a concept of 'cultural citizenship'. She writes (1997: 86):

The lynch-pin of theories of the public sphere is reason ... popular culture research (guided by postmodernist and feminist theory) has argued that emotion and feeling are just as important to our everyday lives. If democracy can be said to be about deliberation among the many about how to attain the best life possible for as many as possible, then it makes no sense to set such exclusive store by reasoned argument in our theorization of it. We need to rethink citizenship as cultural citizenship and accept that those who inhabit mass democracies use many different logics to shape their lives.

The various points discussed are reviewed in Box 5.5 in terms of a set of propositions about media and gender.

Gender and media: propositions   **5.5**

- Media have marginalized women in the public sphere
- Media purvey stereotypes of femininity and masculinity
- Production and content of media are gendered
- Reception of media is gendered
- Female perspective offers alternative criteria of quality
- The personal is political
- Media offer positive and supportive as well as negative role models

---

Commercialization

Embedded in the early critique of mass culture, and still alive at the fringes of the discussion (certainly in the context of media policy), is the notion of 'commercialism' (the condition) or '**commercialization**' (the process). Although it sounds somewhat outdated, in an era dominated by commercial criteria, it expresses some ideas that are still relevant to current media industry dynamics and to media-cultural change, and it is closely related to the critique of commodification (see p. 116). The critique of commercialization is particularly difficult to reconcile with the redemption of the popular since popularity is usually a necessary condition of commercial success and to dislike one implies a dislike of the other.

While at one level the term 'commercialism' may refer objectively to particular free-market arrangements, it has also come to imply consequences for the type of media content which is mass produced and 'marketed' as a commodity, and for the relations between the suppliers and the consumers of media. The term 'commercial', applied as an adjective to some types of media provision, identifies correlates of the competitive pursuit of large markets (Bogart, 1995). Aside from an abundance of advertising matter (commercial propaganda), commercial content is likely, from this perspective, to be more oriented to amusement and entertainment (escapism), more superficial, undemanding and conformist, more derivative and standardized. Picard

(2004) links the commercializing trends of newspapers with a decline in quality (see Box 5.6). Evidence in support of his view can be found in McManus (1994).

5.6 Newspaper commercialization: key quotation

The primary content of newspapers today is commercialized news and designed to appeal to broad audiences, to entertain, to be cost effective and whose attention can be sold to advertisers. The result is that stories that may offend are ignored in favor of those more acceptable and entertaining to a larger number of readers, that stories that are costly to cover are downplayed or ignored and that stories creating financial risks are ignored. This leads to the homogenization of newspaper content, to coverage of safe issues and to a diminution of the range of opinion and ideas expressed. (Picard, 2004: 61)

There has been much comment on the '**tabloidization**' of newspapers as they compete for readers. The equivalent process in television has led to many new forms of 'reality' television, which deal in all kinds of '**human interest**' and dramatic topics in a variety of formats. The term 'tabloidization' comes from the smaller format of the more popular (or boulevard) newspapers in some countries. Generally, as Langer (2003) shows, it is a question of access (who gets in the news) and of representation (how they are depicted). Connell (1998) discusses the British variants, taking the term to mean that 'sensationalist' news discourses have displaced 'rationalist' discourses, with a strong emphasis on narrative. Bird (1998) looked at the 'tabloidization' of American television news and concludes from her audience study that there has been a real trend towards *personalization* and *dramatization* which does make news more accessible to the many, but has also led to a trivialization of what people actually learn from news. The term '**infotainment**' has been widely used in this connection (Brants, 1998).

While it is true that essentially the same market arrangements can just as easily support the supply and consumption of greatly varied and high-quality cultural products, the critique of commerce has another dimension. It can be argued that commercial relationships in communication are intrinsically distancing and potentially exploitative. The commercial variant of a communicative relationship does not support the formation of ties of mutual attachment or lead to shared identity or community. It is calculative and utilitarian on both sides, reflecting essential features of the 'transmission' or 'publicity' rather than the 'ritual' model of communication in society (see pp. 70–73). The fundamental problem is that profit becomes the overwhelming motive.

It makes little sense to argue that the free-market arrangements that have sustained print media for five hundred years and audiovisual cultural production for one hundred years are intrinsically 'harmful' to culture. A narrower concept of 'commercial' as a critical expression is called for and the components of this have been indicated. The key components of the still contested concept of commercialization are reviewed in Box 5.7 in the form of a set of propositions advanced by critics.

Critique of commercialization: propositions **5.7**

- Leads to trivialization and tabloidization
- Causes content decisions to be market-driven
- Involves exploitation of 'weaker' consumers
- Promotes consumerist attitudes to culture and life
- Commodifies culture and relations with the audience
- Reduces cultural integrity of media content
- Leads to over-reliance on advertising and loss of independence

---

Communication Technology and Culture

McLuhan's (1964) advance on Innis (see pp. 102–103) was to look at the process by which we experience the world through different media of communication and not just at the relation between communication and social power structures. He proclaimed that all media (by which he meant anything which embodies cultural meaning and can be 'read' as such) are 'extensions of man', thus extensions of our senses. Like others, he drew attention to the implications of a shift from a purely *oral* communication to one based on a written language (by about 5000 BC). Much of cultural experience remained predominantly oral until comparatively recent times. McLuhan also focused on *how* we experience the world, not on *what* we experience (thus not on the content). Each new medium transcends the boundaries of experience reached by earlier media and contributes to further change. McLuhan correctly saw different media working together, while perhaps less plausibly he predicted the attainment of a 'global village' in which information and experience would be freely available for all to share. More recently, Meyrowitz (1985) proposed a theory of mass media and social change that owes something to Marshall McLuhan (with help from Irving Goffman). Meyrowitz's (1985) thesis is that the all-pervasiveness of electronic media has fundamentally changed social experience by breaking down the compartmentalization between social spaces that was typical of earlier times. Human experience, in his view, has traditionally been segmented by role and social situation and sharply divided between private ('backstage') and public ('onstage') domains. **Segmentation** was by age, gender and social status, and the 'walls' between zones of experience were high. Television appears to put all aspects of social experience on show to all, without distinction. There are no longer any secrets, for instance, about adulthood, sex, death or power.

A general proposition was that, as more of our senses are engaged in the process of taking meaning (as media become increasingly 'cool', or frictionless, as against single-sense or 'hot' media), the more involving and participatory the experience is. According to this view, experiencing the world by reading printed text is isolating and non-involving (encouraging the rational, individual attitude). Television viewing is involving, although not very informing, and also conducive of a less rational and calculative attitude. No proof (or disproof) has ever been offered, and the ideas were described by McLuhan himself only as perceptions or 'probes'. As he wished, they stimulated much speculation in an era in which audiovisual media have seemed in many respects to take over from print media.

The Toronto School (see Chapter 4, pp. 102–103) was the primary impulse towards a new branch of theory described as 'medium theory'. In this context, a medium is any vehicle for carrying meaning, with some distinctive characteristics in respect of technology, form, manner of use, means of encoding or social definition. This covers a wide range, starting with drawing and continuing through printing to all the current electronic media. There is a 'soft' form of determination at work, in which a medium is attributed a certain bias towards particular kinds of content, uses and effects. This approach has proved more fruitful than 'hard' determination in identifying the more subtle influences of the way in which media are used, for instance in political communication and in seeing the differences between new and old media.

Most other relevant theory of communication technology has focused on possible influences on the form or content of given media messages and thus on the meanings they make available. Even so, no technology–culture effect can be established because the technologies themselves are also cultural artefacts, and there is no way of breaking into the circle. Such theory as we have is little more than a description of observable patterns in the cultural meanings offered via mass media, which may be influenced by various characteristics, not only technological, of a given medium. A general view of the process by which changing technology can influence media culture is given in Figure 5.1. Perhaps the most important point that it illustrates is that technologies are unlikely to have a direct impact on cultural practices; their effects are mediated through a relevant institution, in this case the mass media. Stober (2004) provides us with an evolutionary historical theory of the process of invention and diffusion of new communication technologies, based on the necessity for institutionalization, but emphasizing that change depends on the invention of improvements on old media. A somewhat similar analysis of change relating to the Internet has been developed by Lehmann-Wilzig and Cohen-Avigdor (2004), identifying a number of stages through which evolution passes.

In trying to account for technological influence on (media) culture, we may extend the notion of *bias* introduced by Innis and recognize several tendencies that follow from the characteristics of a particular media technology (and its institutional development). We can name five types of media bias as follows, without exhausting the possibilities. There is a bias of *sense experience*, following McLuhan, so that we may experience the world in more or less visual imagery (see Hartley, 1992) or in more or less of an involving and participant way. Secondly, there is a bias of *form* and representation, with 'messages' strongly coded (as in print) or essentially uncoded, as in photographs (Barthes, 1967). Thirdly, there is the bias of message *content*, for instance in terms of more or less realism or polysemy, more open or closed formats (other dimensions are possible). Fourthly, there is a bias of *context of use*, with some media lending themselves to private and individualized reception, others being more collective and shared. Fifthly, there is a bias of *relationship*, contrasting one-way with interactive media.

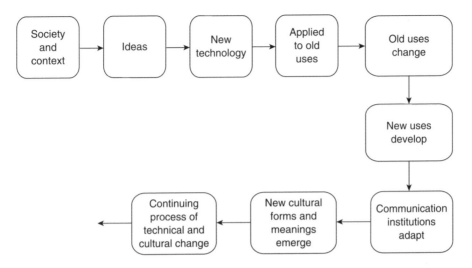

Figure 5.1   Interactive sequence of communication and technological and cultural change: technologies arise from society and have effects on society depending on the form of application

Bias does not mean determinism, but it contains a predeliction towards certain kinds of experience and ways of mediation. Ellis's (1982) comparison of broadcast television with cinema film provides an instructive illustration of how the (unintended) bias of a medium can work in subtle but systematic and multiple ways, affecting content and probable ways of perception and reception. The comparison is shown in summary terms in Box 5.8. The differences shown are not only or even primarily due to technology, but to many other factors. While many things have changed in the succeeding decades, the comparison is still largely valid.

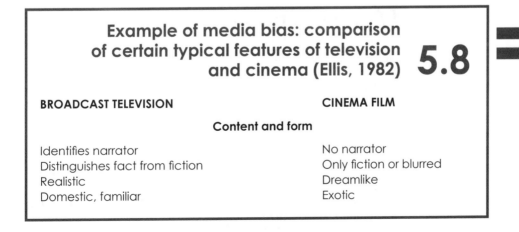

Example of media bias: comparison of certain typical features of television and cinema (Ellis, 1982) **5.8**

BROADCAST TELEVISION	CINEMA FILM
Content and form	
Identifies narrator	No narrator
Distinguishes fact from fiction	Only fiction or blurred
Realistic	Dreamlike
Domestic, familiar	Exotic

> *(Continued)*
>
> | | |
> |---|---|
> | Open-ended | Logical, sequential |
> | Impression of being live | Not live, historic present |
> | Neutral attitude | Takes sides |
> | Tone of normality and safety | Tension and anxiety |
>
> **Audience aspects**
>
> | | |
> |---|---|
> | Permanent audience | Occasional one-off audience |
> | Low engagement | Rapt attention, self-loss |
> | Intimacy | Detachment, voyeurism |

One of the few effects of new communication technology on which there is wide agreement is the trend towards internationalization of mass communication. The question of potential cultural effects flowing from this trend has been much debated. The movement towards a global media culture has several sources, most notably the greatly increased capacity to transmit sounds and (moving) images at low cost across frontiers and around the world, overcoming limits of time and space. Equally potent as a cause is the rise of global media businesses (and global markets for media products), which provides the organizational framework and driving force for globalization. Neither of these conditions has arrived suddenly, nor is the idea of transnational culture itself novel (it long predates the very idea of the national), but what may be new is the increased transcultural communicative potential of pictures and music. The relevant changes in the structure of media industries and global media flow, especially in relation to television, have been extensively studied, but the cultural consequences are much less open to observation and have led to great speculation and more sound than light. The process of cultural 'transnationalization' that is assumed to be taking place has a variety of meanings and is discussed in more detail in Chapter 10.

Mass Media and Postmodern Culture

The notion of a 'postmodern condition' (Harvey, 1989) captured the imagination of many social and cultural theorists, and it seemed very much a theory for the information society (see Chapter 4). Despite its wide currency, it is a complex and obscure concept that involves several ideas that are relevant to the mass media. Its political implication is that the 'Enlightenment project' has reached its historic conclusion, especially the emphasis on material progress, egalitarianism, social reform and the application of bureaucratic means to achieving socially planned objectives. It is also now commonplace to refer to our era as 'postmodern' in the literal sense of being a late stage of the 'modern' period that was characterized by rapid social change, industrialization and the factory system, capitalism, bureaucratic forms of organization and mass political movements.

In this aspect, the term implies a clear chronological and conceptual distinction from 'modernism'. As Morley (1996) points out, this in itself raises some difficulties since the term 'modern' originated in the fifth century AD (in its Latin form) and has taken on different meanings in different epochs since then. In its current meaning it usually refers to typical features of society and culture of the nineteenth and early twentieth centuries, without any clear indication of any dividing line. The principal theorist of 'modernization' (without explicitly making the claim), writing a century ago, can probably be considered to be the German sociologist Max Weber, whose key concept in the analysis of social change was 'rationalization'. In this respect, we can also plausibly regard modernism as originally a specifically western (European) notion.

As a social-cultural philosophy, postmodernism undermines the traditional notion of culture as something fixed and hierarchical. It favours forms of culture that are transient, of the moment, superficially pleasing and appealing to sense rather than reason. Postmodern culture is volatile, illogical, kaleidoscopic and hedonistic. It favours emotion over reason. Mass media culture has the advantage of appealing to many senses as well as being associated with novelty and transience. Many features of (commercial) popular media culture reflect postmodernist elements. Music video on television was hailed as the first postmodern television service (Kaplan, 1987; Grossberg, 1989; Lewis, 1992). Old ideas of quality of art and serious messages cannot be sustained, except by reference to authority, and are seen as inescapably 'bourgeois'.

This is a potent set of ideas that goes much further than providing a defence for the once much maligned and patronized 'culture of the masses'. It is an entirely new representation of the situation that has turned some of the weapons of cultural critics against themselves (for instance, their claim to speak on behalf of the masses). It gains strength both from a real shift of social values and from a re-evaluation of popular culture and the probability that there has also been a real cultural revolution within the mass media, leading towards a new aesthetic. Television and popular music have become the dominant arts of the time and have shown enormous inventiveness and power to change.

The idea of postmodernism has been easier to characterize in cultural than in social terms since the features of 'modern' society mentioned are still in evidence, maybe even reinforced if one thinks of how much the world is ruled by global financial markets that operate with inexorable and uniform logic. The term 'postmodern' refers more to the dominant ethos or spirit of the times and to certain aesthetic and cultural trends. Docherty (1993) interprets postmodern cultural and social philosophy as a response to the post-1968 reappraisal of revolutionary aspirations, which had, in their turn, been based on the premise of an end to capitalism and the birth of a new utopia. This dream had been originally founded on the ideas of material progress, reason and enlightenment that were embedded in the very idea of modern society.

Viewed like this, postmodernism stands for a retreat from political ideology, a certain loss of faith in the gods of reason and science. This shapes the contemporary *Zeitgeist* (spirit of the age) in the sense that we no longer share any fixed belief or commitment and there is a tendency to hedonism, individualism and living in the present moment. This is in accord with another widely cited characterization of postmodernism by Lyotard (1986), to the effect that there is no longer any *grand narrative*, no organizing or explanatory framework or central project for humanity. The cultural aesthetics of postmodernism involve a rejection of tradition and a search for novelty, invention, momentary enjoyment, nostalgia, playfulness, pastiche and inconsistency. Jameson (1984) refers to postmodernism as the 'cultural logic of late capitalism', even though there is no logic to be found. Gitlin (1989) suggests that postmodernism is specifically North American, capturing many features of American culture.

Grossberg et al. (1998) associate it especially with the process of commercialization of everything. Certainly the postmodern ethos is much more favourable to commerce than were earlier cultural perspectives since opposition to capitalism is undermined and commerce can be seen as responding to consumer wants or as actively promoting changes in fashion, style and products. However, there is scope for social and cultural optimism as well as pessimism within the range of postmodern thought. Ien Ang has also underlined the need to distinguish between conservative and critical post-modernism as intellectual attitudes. She writes: 'the former does indeed succumb to an "anything goes" attitude ... [but] the latter, critical postmodernism is motivated by a deep understanding of the limits and failures of what Habermas calls the "unfinished project of modernity"' (1998: 78).

The forms of contemporary advertising, especially on television, seem to exhibit most of the cultural features mentioned above. The work of Jean Baudrillard (1983) helps us to understand the essence of postmodern culture, especially his concept of *simulacrum*, which refers to the fact that the difference between an image and the reality is no longer important. The mass media provide an inexhaustible supply of images of a pseudo-reality that serves instead of experience and becomes for many hard to distinguish from reality itself. The idea is well exemplified by the film *The Truman Show* (1997) where the whole plot turns on the situation of a real person whose life has been lived within the plot of a long-running soap opera dealing with an imaginary community. These notions of convergence of image and reality are also expressed in virtual reality devices that substitute simulated for real experience. The concept has gained increased currency from the rise of new forms and uses of the Internet and mobile telephony. Poster (2006: 138) argues that we should use the concept of postmodernity for the cultural study of new media although 'in a manner that makes it suitable for analysis without either a celebratory fanfare or sarcastic smiles'.

The appeal of the postmodern concept is based on its helping to link many perceived tendencies in the media (including new media) and in its summing up of the essence of the media's own logic. It also seems useful as a word to connect diverse social changes (for instance, the fragmentation of the class structure, the decline in political ideology, and globalization). But apart from that it has little substance of its own, no analytic purchase to speak of and no intrinsic fixed meaning. Put like this, it sounds like a caricature of itself. Postmodernism is not a logical body of theory, but some propositions can be derived from it, as shown in Box 5.9.

Postmodernism: some propositions **5.9**

- The rational-linear modern era is passing
- There are no longer any reliable large organizing ideas about culture and society
- There are no fixed cultural values
- Experience and reality are illusory and ephemeral
- The new qualities in culture are novelty itself, pastiche, humour and shock
- Commercial culture is postmodern culture

Conclusion

This chapter has summarized a broad range of cultural issues in which the mass media are implicated. Indeed, it is impossible now to distinguish between a sphere of 'culture' and that of media, as once could have been done. This applies to all the senses in which the term 'culture' has been used, including symbolic reproduction, the artefacts we employ, everyday social life and all the rituals of society. Media are the centre of the whole complex and the central task for theory has had to be redefined. In the earliest period of self-consciousness about the media (the first half of the twentieth century) it was possible to debate the 'effects' of radio, television, film, and so on, on something that was called 'culture', usually referring to a valued set of objects, practices, relations and ideas. This formulation is now largely outmoded, although there is some opportunity for observing cultural shifts at moments of development in technology, as with the so-called 'new media'. The elimination of the 'causal model' does not, however, lessen the number of questions that can be addressed, or prevent answers being provided by alternative routes and methods and from new perspectives. There is still an axis of critical thinking that can be applied to what we observe. There are still many new problematic (as well as positive) features of culture in the media age to be studied and debated.

Further Reading

Carey, J.W. (1975/2002) 'A cultural approach to communication'. Reprinted in D. McQuail (ed.), *Reader in Mass Communication Theory*, pp. 36–45. London: Sage.
A clear and eloquent statement of an alternative view of communication to the dominant model of information transfer that guided early mass communication research.

Fiske, J. (1987) *Television Culture*. London: Routledge.
An influential and popular early text applying the cultural study perspective, with many clear definitions and illustrations that are still of value.

Hardt, H. (1993) *Critical Communication Studies*. London: Routledge.
Charts the rise of critical theory in the United States under the influence especially of *émigré* members of the Frankfurt School.

Online Readings

Hermes, J. (2007) 'Media representations of social structure: gender', in E. Devereux (ed.), *Media Studies*, pp. 191–210. London: Sage.
Kellner, D. (1997) 'Overcoming the divide: cultural studies and political economy', in M. Ferguson and P. Golding (eds), *Cultural Studies in Question*, pp. 102–20. London: Sage.
McGuigan, J. (1997) 'Cultural populism revisited', in M. Ferguson and P. Golding (eds), *Cultural Studies in Question*, pp. 138–54. London: Sage.
Vyncke, P. (2002) 'Lifestyle segmentation', *European Journal of Communication*, 17 (4): 445–64.

6

New Media – New Theory?

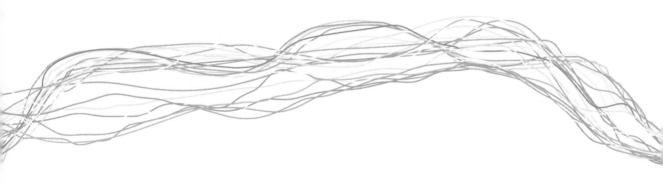

Theory relating to mass communication has to be continually reassessed in the light of new technologies and their applications. In Chapter 2, we recognized the arrival of new types of media that extend and change the entire spectrum of socio-technological possibilities for public communication. No complete transformation has yet taken place, and it is too early to predict how far and fast the process of change will go. The underlying assumption in this chapter is that a medium is not just an applied technology for transmitting certain symbolic content or linking participants in some exchange. It also embodies a set of social relations that interact with features of the new technology. New theory is only likely to be required if there is a fundamental change in the forms of social organization of media technologies, in the social relations that are promoted, or in what Carey (1998) terms the 'dominant structures of taste and feeling'.

New Media and Mass Communication

The mass media have already changed very much, certainly from the early-twentieth-century days of one-way, one-directional and undifferentiated flow to an undifferentiated mass. There are social and economic as well as technological reasons for this shift, but it is real enough. Secondly, information society theory, as outlined in Chapter 4, also indicates the rise of a new kind of society, quite distinct from mass society, one characterized by complex interactive networks of communication. In the circumstances, we need to reassess the main thrust of media social-cultural theory.

The 'new media' discussed here are in fact a disparate set of communication technologies that share certain features, apart from being new, made possible by digitalization and being widely available for personal use as communication devices. As we have seen (p. 39), 'new media' are very diverse and not easy to define, but we are particularly interested in those new media and applications that on various grounds enter the sphere of mass communication or directly or indirectly have consequences for the 'traditional' mass media. Attention focuses mainly on the collective ensemble of activities that fall under the heading 'Internet', especially on the more public uses, including online news, advertising, broadcasting applications (including downloading of music, etc.), forums and discussion activities, the World Wide Web (WWW), information searches and certain community-forming potentials. We are less concerned with private e-mail, game-playing and many other more or less private services provided by way of the Internet.

Generally, new media have been greeted (not least by the old media) with intense interest, positive and even euphoric expectations and predictions, and a general overestimation of their significance (Rössler, 2001). We are still in this phase, although gradually more sober voices are being heard and there is alarm as well as optimism about their wider consequences, especially in the absence of any developed framework of regulation or control. Ideas about the impact of new media went far ahead of the reality and, even now, research in this area is still occupied with scaling down expectations. The main aim of the chapter is to make a preliminary estimate of the current status of the issues that have been raised and to assess theory and actual impact. Of particular interest is the impact on other mass media and on the nature of mass communication itself.

As a preliminary orientation to the topic, it is helpful to look at the relationship between personal media and mass media, as conceptualized by Marika Lüders (2008)

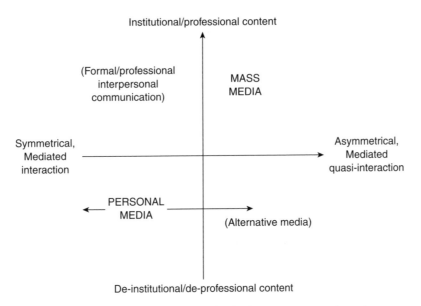

Figure 6.1 Two-axes model of relationship between personal and mass media (Lüders, 2008)

and displayed in Figure 6.1. The underlying assumption is that the distinction between mass and personal communication is no longer clear since the same technologies can be and are used for both purposes. The differences can only be understood by introducing a social dimension, relating to the type of activity and social relations involved. Instead of the concept 'medium', Luders prefers the term 'media forms', which refers to specific applications of the technology of the Internet, such as online news, social networking, etc. She writes (2008: 691):

> Distinctions between personal media and mass media may be outlined as differences in the type of involvement required from users. Personal media are more symmetrical and require users to perform actively as both receivers and producers of messages.

The second main relevant dimension is that of the presence or not of an institutional or professional context that is typical of mass media production. Between them, the two dimensions of symmetricality and institutionalism locate the different types of relation between personal and mass media. An additional element is the distinction made by Thompson (1993) between (technically) mediated and quasi-mediated communication, as outlined above in Chapter 4, p. 84.

What is New about the New Media?

The most fundamental aspect of information and communication technology (ICT) is probably the fact of *digitalization*, the process by which all texts (symbolic meaning in all encoded and recorded forms) can be reduced to a binary code and can share the same process of production, distribution and storage. The most widely noted potential consequence for the media institution is the *convergence* between all existing media forms in terms of their organization, distribution, reception and regulation. As we have seen, many different forms of mass media have so far survived, retained their separate identity and even flourished. The general institution of mass media has also survived as a distinct element of public social life, perhaps even strengthened because of its central position for politics and commerce. The 'new electronic media' can be viewed initially as an addition to the existing spectrum rather than as a replacement. On the other hand, we have to consider that digitalization and convergence might have much more revolutionary consequences.

If we consider the main features of the media institution, as outlined in Box 3.4 (p. 60), it seems that the Internet in particular already deviates from that typification on three of the six points named. First, the Internet is not only or even mainly concerned with the production and distribution of messages, but is at least equally concerned with processing, exchange and storage. Secondly, the new media are as much an institution of private as of public communication and are regulated (or not) accordingly. Thirdly, their operation is not typically professional or bureaucratically organized to the same degree as mass media. These are quite significant differences that underscore the fact that the new media correspond with mass media primarily in being widely diffused, in principle available to all for communication, and at least as free from control.

Attempts to characterize the new media, especially as embodied in the Internet, have been hindered by their very diversity of uses and **governance** as well as by uncertainty about their future development. The computer, as applied to communication, has produced many variant possibilities, no one of which is dominant. Postmes et al. (1998) describe the computer as a 'uniquely undedicated' communication technology. In a similar vein, Poster (1999) describes the essence of the Internet as its very *undetermination*, not only because of its diversity and uncertainty in the future, but also because of its essentially postmodernistic character. He also points to key differences with broadcasting and print, as shown in Box 6.1.

6.1 New media differences from old: key quotation

The Internet incorporates radio, film and television and distributes them through 'push' technology:

It transgresses the limits of the print and broadcasting models by (1) enabling many-to-many conversations; (2) enabling the simultaneous reception, alteration and redistribution of cultural objects; (3) dislocating communicative action from the posts of the nation, from the territorialized spatial relations of modernity; (4) providing instantaneous global contact; and (5) inserting the modern/late modern subject into a machine apparatus that is networked. (Poster, 1999: 15)

More succinctly, Livingstone (1999: 65) writes: 'What's new about the internet may be the combination of interactivity with those features which were innovative for mass communication – the unlimited range of content, the scope of audience reach, the global nature of communication.' This view suggests extension rather than replacement. An assessment made five years after this by Lievrouw (2004) underlines a general view that the 'new media' have gradually been 'mainstreamed', routinized and even 'banalized'. Research on political communication speaks of the 'normalization' of the Internet, meaning its adaptation to the needs of the established forms of campaigning (Vaccari, 2008b). It is certainly true that applications and uses have not lived up to the euphoria and **hype** of early claims and visions for society or expectations for profitability, but it is too early to make an assessment.

Several key innovatory features of the Internet have not yet been properly studied in their own right. One of these is the new concept and reality of the web portal. Kalyanaraman and Sundar (2008: 239) point out that 'One of the unique features of the World Wide Web as a mass medium lies in the fact that message sources are indistinct from message receivers'. One result of this is the popularity of 'portals' that help to sift and sort the vast amounts of information available. However, the concept is both abstract and under-theorized. These authors propose a preliminary classification of portals based on the idea of metaphors, much as used above in Chapter 4, p. 81 (Box 4.1). They propose five metaphors that cover the main functions of the Web for its sources and receivers/users. These are summarily set out in Box 6.2. The purpose is to achieve clarification of the meaning and function of the portal by further empirical investigation of the viability of this frame.

Metaphors for Internet portals: main features (based on Kalyanaraman and Sundar, 2008) **6.2**

Gateway: Door to access information on the Web or to access the Web itself.
Billboard: Help to increase awareness of – and confidence in – other sites in the portal as well as external websites.
Network: Places that cater to users with commonality of interests and showcase one's own interests.
Niche: Fulfils a specific role for general or targeted users or groups.
Brand: One-stop online source that offers several or a specific set of transactional functions.

In general, differences between new and old media can be appreciated in more detail if we consider the main roles and relationships that are found within the traditional media institutions, especially those concerned with authorship (and performance), publication, production and distribution, and reception. In brief, the main implications are as follows.

For *authors*, there are increased opportunities, if posting on the Internet, desktop publishing, 'blogging' and similar autonomous acts count as publication. However, the status and rewards of the author, as understood until now, have depended on the significance and location of publication and on the degree and kind of public attention received. Writing a private letter or a poem, or taking photographs, is not true authorship. The conditions of public recognition and esteem have not really changed with the new technology, and the condition of having a large audience and widespread fame may even have become more difficult to achieve. It is not easy to become famous on the Internet, without the co-operation of the traditional mass media. There are also increasing difficulties in maintaining **copyright** as well as those arising from competition with the supply of 'free content'.

For *publishers*, the role continues but has become more ambiguous for the same reasons that apply to authors. Until now a publisher was typically a business firm or a non-profit public institution. The new media open up alternative forms of publication and present opportunities and challenges for traditional publishing. The traditional publication functions of *gatekeeping*, editorial intervention and validation of authorship will be found in some types of Internet publication, but not in others.

As to the *audience* role, there are large possibilities for change, especially in the direction of greater autonomy and equality in relation to sources and suppliers. The audience member is no longer really part of a mass, but is either a member of a self-chosen network or special public or an individual. In addition, the balance of audience activity shifts from reception to searching, consulting and interacting more personally. As a result, the term 'audience' is in need of supplementation with the overlapping term of 'user', with quite different connotations (see pp. 447–8). Despite this, there is evidence of continuity in the mass audience (see Chapter 16) and there is still a demand by the audience for gatekeeping and editorial guidance. Rice (1999: 29) remarks on the paradox of the extended range of choices facing the audience: 'Now individuals must makes more choices, must have more prior knowledge, and must put forth more effort to integrate and make sense of the communication. Interactivity and choice are not universal benefits; many people do not have the energy, desire, need or training to engage in such processes.'

These comments are incomplete without reference to the changed roles in relation to the economics of media. For the most part, mass media were financed by selling their products to audiences and being paid by client advertisers for the chance of audience attention to their messages. The Internet introduces many complications and changes, with new types of relation and forms of commodification. These are discussed elsewhere, especially in Chapter 9.

As far as the relations between different roles are concerned, we can posit a general loosening and more independence, especially affecting authors and audiences. Rice (1999: 29) has noted that 'the boundaries between publisher, producer, distributor, consumer and reviewer of content are blurring'. This casts doubt on the continued appropriateness of the idea of an *institution* in the sense of some more or less unified social organization with some core practices and shared norms. In the general meltdown it is likely that we will recognize the emergence of separate, more specialized institutional complexes of media activity. These will be based either on technologies or on certain uses and content (for example, relating to news **journalism**, entertainment films, business, sport, pornography, tourism, education, **professions**, etc.), with no shared institutional identity. In that sense, the mass media will have withered away. Box 6.3 lists the main hypothetical effects of the new media.

Main changes linked to the rise of new media **6.3**

- Digitalization and convergence of all aspects of media
- Increased interactivity and network connectivity
- Mobility and delocation of sending and receiving
- Adaptation of publication and audience roles
- Appearance of diverse new forms of media 'gateway'
- Fragmentation and blurring of the 'media institution'

The Main Themes of New Media Theory

In Chapter 4, mass media were looked at in the light of four very broad concerns: to do with *power and inequality*, *social integration and identity*, *social change and development*, and *space and time.* Up to a point, theoretical perspectives on the new media can still be discussed in relation to the same themes. However, it also soon becomes clear that on certain issues the terms of earlier theory do not fit the new media situation very well. In respect of *power*, for instance, it is much more difficult to locate the new media in relation to the possession and exercise of power. They are not as clearly identified in terms of ownership, nor is access monopolized in such a way that the content and flow of information can be easily controlled. Communication does not flow in a predominantly vertical or centralized pattern from the 'top' or the 'centre' of society. Government and law do not control or regulate the Internet in a hierarchical way as they do the 'old media' (Collins, 2008). There are also reasons for supposing that as the Internet becomes successful, it will fall more and more into the hands of large media conglomerates, negating some of its freedom (Dahlberg, 2004). There are also reasons for considering new media as contributing to the controlling power of central authority, especially via the surveillance of users.

There is now greater equality of access available as sender, receiver, spectator or participant in some exchange or network. It is no longer possible to characterize the dominant 'direction' or bias of influence of information flows (as with press and television news and comment), although the issue of the degree of freedom available to the new 'channels' is far from settled. Breen (2007) reports fears that the Internet might develop beyond its open and democratic early phase to become a multi-tier service with more privileged access to those who can pay more to produce and provide content or pay more to receive higher value content.

In relation to *integration and identity*, the conceptual terrain is much the same as that dealt with earlier. The same broad issue is still whether the new media are a force for fragmentation or cohesion in society. The basic configuration of the Internet, however, and the nature of its use point to predominantly fragmenting social effects

(Sunstein, 2006). On the other hand, it opens up the way for new and diverse vicarious relationships and networks that are integrating in different ways and may be more binding (Slevin, 2000). Older concerns about mass media took as their basis the central case of the nation state, usually coinciding with the territory served by a mass medium. Alternatively, it might be a region, city or other political-administrative zone. Identity and cohesion were largely defined in geographical terms. The key questions are no longer confined to pre-existing social relationships and identities.

Rasmussen (2000) argued that new media have qualitatively different effects on social integration in a modern network society, drawing on Giddens' (1991) theories of modernization. The essential contribution is to bridge the widening gap that is said to be opening up between the private and public worlds, the 'lifeworld' and the world of systems and organizations. This gap may also be increasing as a result of the new electronic highways. In contrast to television, the new media can play a direct role in individual life projects. They also promote a diversity of uses and wider participation. In short, the new media help to re-embed the individual after the 'disembedding' effects of modernization.

In respect of potential for *social change*, the potential for new communications as an agent of planned economic or social change requires reassessment. At first sight, there is a big difference between mass media that can be systematically applied to goals of planned development by way of mass information and persuasion (as in health, population, technical innovation campaigns) and the open-ended, non-purposive uses that are typical of new technology. The loss of direction and control over content by the sender seems to be crucial.

However, it may be that more participatory media are equally or better suited to producing change because they are more involving as well as more flexible and richer in information. This would be consistent with the more advanced models of the change process. Some of the new media are also less dependent on infrastructure. The problem, however, lies not in the nature of the technology, but in the continuing material barriers to access. The process of 'development' may still have to precede the deployment of new media, just as old media had to have an audience in order to have some effect.

Much has been written about the new media overcoming barriers of *space and time*. In fact, 'old media' were good at bridging space, although perhaps less good in relation to cultural divisions. They were much faster than the physical travel and transportation that preceded them. But their capacity was limited and transmission technology required fixed plant and great expense to overcome distance. Sending and receiving were both very much physically located (in production plants, offices, homes, etc.). New technology has freed us from many constraints, although there are other continuing social and cultural reasons why much communication activity still has a fixed location. The Internet, despite its apparent lack of frontiers, is still largely structured according to territory, especially national and linguistic boundaries (Halavais, 2000), although there are also new factors in its geography (Castells, 2001). Communication is concentrated in the USA and Europe, and cross-border traffic tends to use English. How far time has been conquered is more uncertain, except in respect of greater speed of transmission, the escape from fixed time schedules, and the ability to send a message to anyone anywhere at any time (but without guarantee of reception or response). We still have no better access to the past or the future, or more time for communication, and the time saved by new flexibility is quickly spent on new demands of intercommunication.

Applying Medium Theory to the New Media

As Rice et al. (1983: 18) observed some time ago, the 'notion that the channel of communication might be as important a variable in the communication process as source, message, receiver and feedback, may have been overlooked'. Referring to the work of the Toronto School (see Chapter 4, pp. 102–3), they add that 'One need not be a technological determinist to agree that the medium may be a fundamental variable in the communication process.' Nevertheless, it is still very difficult to pin down the 'essential' characteristics of any given medium, and the ground for distinguishing between 'new' and 'old' media is not very solid.

The main problem lies in the fact that in actual experience it is hard to distinguish the channel or medium from the typical *content* that it carries or the typical *use* that is made of it or the *context of use* (for instance, home, work or public place). Precisely the same problem has bedevilled earlier research into the relative advantages and capacities of different 'traditional' media as channels of communication. However, this does not mean that there is no important difference or emerging discontinuity between old and new. At the moment we can do little more than make plausible suggestions. Quortrup (2006) concluded that 'medium theory' cannot deal with the case of new digital media because they have an unlimited number of features and not certain fixed ones. He treats this as the most essential feature of 'new media'. They are characterized by complexity and their basic function is to manage social complexity. Thus we can understand the new media best in terms of 'complexity theory', which lies somewhere between order (system theory) and chaos theory.

Rice (1999) has argued that it is not very profitable to try to characterize each medium according to its specific attributes. Instead, we should study the attributes of media in general and see how new media 'perform' in these terms. Contrasts and comparisons of media tend to 'idealize' certain features of a medium (for example, face-to-face communication or the virtues of the traditional book), ignoring paradoxes of positive and negative consequences. The diversity of the category 'new media' and their continually changing nature set an obvious limit to theory forming about their 'consequences'. The technological forms are multiplying but are also often temporary. Nevertheless, we can identify five main categories of 'new media' which share certain channel similarities and are approximately differentiated by types of use, content and context, as follows:

- *Interpersonal communication media*. These include the telephone (increasingly mobile) and e-mail (primarily for work, but becoming more personal). In general, content is private and perishable and the relationship established and reinforced may be more important than the information conveyed.
- *Interactive play media*. These are mainly computer-based and video games, plus virtual reality devices. The main innovation lies in the interactivity and perhaps the dominance of 'process' over 'use' gratifications (see p. 426).
- *Information search media*. This is a wide category, but the Internet/WWW is the most significant example, viewed as a library and data source of unprecedented size, actuality and accessibility. The search engine has risen to a commanding position as a tool for users as well as a source of income for the Internet. Besides the Internet, the (mobile)

telephone is also increasingly a channel for information retrieval, as are broadcast teletext and radio data services.

- *Collective participatory media*. The category includes especially the uses of the Internet for sharing and exchanging information, ideas and experience and developing active (computer-mediated) personal relationships. Social networking sites belong under this heading. Uses range from the purely instrumental to affective and emotional (Baym, 2002).
- *Substitution of broadcast media*. The main reference is to uses of media to receive or download content that in the past was typically broadcast or distributed by other similar methods. Watching films and television programmes, listening to radio and music, etc. are the main activities.

The diversity indicated by this typology makes it hard to draw up any useful summary of *medium* characteristics that are unique to the new media or applicable to all five categories. Fortunati (2005) emphasized the parallel tendencies of **'mediatization'** of the Internet and 'Internetization' of the mass media as a way of understanding the process of mutual convergence (see also Luders, 2008). The subjective perception of new media characteristics shows wide variations between people. In one study of perceived difference from face-to-face communication, for example, Peter and Valkenburg (2006) looked at differences in the factors of controllability, reciprocity, breadth and depth, but found no clear consensus on the image of the Internet. A different set of criteria are relevant for comparison with mass communication. Box 6.4 indicates certain dimensions or variables that have been thought to help in differentiating new from old media, as seen from the perspective of an individual 'user'.

6.4 Key characteristics differentiating new from old media, from the user perspective

- *Interactivity*: as indicated by the ratio of response or initiative on the part of the user to the 'offer' of the source/sender
- *Social presence* (or *sociability*): experienced by the user, meaning the sense of personal contact with others that can be engendered by using a medium (Short et al., 1976; Rice, 1993)
- *Media richness*: the extent to which media can bridge different frames of reference, reduce ambiguity, provide more cues, involve more senses and be more personal
- *Autonomy*: the degree to which a user feels in control of content and use, independent of the source
- *Playfulness*: uses for entertainment and enjoyment, as against utility and instrumentality
- *Privacy*: associated with the use of a medium and/or its typical or chosen content
- *Personalization*: the degree to which content and uses are personalized and unique

The meaning and measurement of interactivity

Although interactivity is most frequently mentioned as the defining feature of new media, it can mean different things and there is already an extensive litera-ture on the topic (Kiousis, 2002). Kiousis arrived at an 'operational definition' of interactvity by reference to four indicators: proximity (social nearness to others); sensory activation; perceived speed; and telepresence. In this definition, more depends on the perception of the user than on any intrinsic or objective medium quality. Downes and McMillan (2000) name five dimensions of interactivity, as follows:

- the direction of communication;
- flexibility about time and roles in the exchange;
- having a sense of place in the communication environment;
- level of control (of the communication environment);
- perceived purpose (oriented to exchange or persuasion).

It is clear from this that conditions of interactivity depend on much more than just the technology employed.

An early attempt to conceptualize the Internet as a mass medium by Morris and Ogan (1996) approached it from the point of view of the audience. They placed the concepts of uses and gratifications, degree and type of involvement and degree of social presence on the agenda, but were unable to reach any firm conclusion about the essential characteristics of the Internet as a medium. Lindlof and Schatzer (1998) offered a view of the Internet derived from audience ethnography, commenting on the diversity of its forms that include news groups, mailing lists, simulation spaces, websites, and so on. In their view, **computer-mediated communication** is different from other media use because it is transient, multimodal, with few codes of conduct governing use, and allowing for a high degree of 'end-user manipulation of content'. They note that the condition of irrelevance of location of source 'offers new possibili-ties for civic life, shared learning and intercultural contact free of geographical limits, but also opens spaces for explicit sexual content, hate speech, rumor propagation, alcohol advertisements aimed at children'.

Although we can characterize new media according to their potential, this is not the same as empirical verification (see the discussion of community on pp. 148–9). A case in point is the potential for sociability and interactivity. While it is true that the computer machine does connect people with other people, at the point of use it involves solitary behaviour, individualistic choices and responses and frequent ano-nymity (see Turner et al., 2001; Baym, 2002). The relationships established or medi-ated by the new communicating machines are often transient, shallow and without commitment. They may be regarded less as an antidote to the individualism, root-lessness and loneliness associated with modern life than as a logical development towards forms of social interaction that can be achieved to order, as it were.

New Patterns of Information Traffic

Another useful way of considering the implications of the changes under discussion is to think in terms of alternative types of *information traffic* and the balance between them. Two Dutch telecommunication experts, Bordewijk and van Kaam (1986), have developed a model which helps to make clear and to investigate the changes under way. They describe four basic communication patterns and show how they are related to each other. The patterns are labelled 'allocution', 'conversation', 'consultation' and 'registration'.

Allocution

With allocution (a word derived from the Latin for the address by a Roman general to assembled troops), information is distributed from a centre simultaneously to many peripheral receivers, with limited opportunity for feedback. This pattern applies to several familiar communication situations, ranging from a lecture, church service or concert (where listeners or spectators are physically present in an auditorium) to the situation of broadcasting, where radio or television messages are received at the same moment by large numbers of scattered individuals. Another characteristic is that time and place of communication are determined by the sender or at the 'centre'. Although the concept is useful for comparing alternative models, the gap between personal address to many and impersonal mass communication is a very large one and is not really bridgeable by a single concept. The case of an 'assembled audience' is quite different from that of a 'dispersed audience'.

Conversation and exchange

With conversation, individuals (in a potential communication network) interact directly with each other, bypassing a centre or intermediary and choosing their own partners as well as the time, place and topic of communication. This pattern applies in a wide range of situations where interactivity is possible, including the exchange of personal letters or electronic mail. The electronically mediated conversation does, however, usually require a centre or intermediary (such as the telephone exchange or service provider), even if this plays no active or initiatory role in the communication event.

Characteristic of the conversational pattern is the fact that parties are *equal* in the exchange. In principle, more than two can take part (for example, a small meeting, a telephone conference or a computer-mediated discussion group). However, at some point, increased scale of participation leads to a merger with the allocutive situation.

Consultation

Consultation refers to a range of different communication situations in which an individual (at the periphery) looks for information at a central store of information – data bank, library, reference work, computer disc, and so on. Such possibilities are increasing in volume and diversifying in type. In principle, this pattern can also apply to the use of a traditional print-based newspaper (otherwise considered an allocutive mass medium), since the time and place of consultation and also the topic are determined by the receiver at the periphery and not by the centre.

Registration

The pattern of information traffic termed 'registration' is, in effect, the consultation pattern in reverse, in that a centre 'requests' and receives information from a participant at the periphery. This applies wherever central records are kept of individuals in a system and to all systems of surveillance. It relates, for instance, to the automatic recording at a central exchange of telephone calls, to electronic alarm systems and to automatic registration of television set usage in 'people-meter' audience research or for purposes of charging consumers. It also refers to the collation of personal particulars of e-commerce customers, for purposes of advertising and targeting. The accumulation of information at a centre often takes place without reference to, or knowledge of, the individual. While the pattern is not historically new, the possibilities for registration have increased enormously because of computerization and extended telecommunication connections. Typically, in this pattern, the centre has more control than the individual at the periphery to determine the content and occurrence of communication traffic.

An integrated typology

These four patterns complement and border upon (or overlap with) each other. The authors of the model have shown how they can be related in terms of two main variables: of central versus individual control of information; and of central versus individual control of time and choice of subject (see Figure 6.2). The allocation pattern stands here for the typical 'old media' of mass communication and conforms largely to the transmission model – especially broadcasting, where a limited supply of content is made available to a mass audience. The consultation pattern has been able to grow, not only because of the telephone and new telematic media, but because of the diffusion of video- and sound-recording equipment and the sheer increase in the number of channels as a result of cable and satellite. The new media have also differentially increased the potential for 'conversational' or interactive communication between widely separated individuals. As noted, 'registration' becomes both more practicable

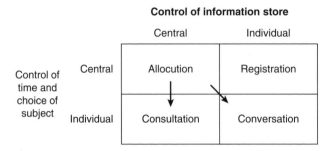

Figure 6.2   A typology of information traffic. Communication relationships are differentiated according to the capacity to control the supply and the choice of content; the trend is from allocutory to consultative or conversational modes (Bordewijk and van Kaam, 1986)

and more likely to occur, although it is not a substitute for other types of communication traffic. It can be viewed as extending the powers of surveillance in the electronic age.

The arrows inserted in Figure 6.2 reflect the redistribution of information traffic from allocutory to conversational and consultative patterns. In general, this implies a broad shift of balance of communicative power from sender to receiver, although this may be counterbalanced by the growth of registration and a further development of the reach and appeal of mass media. Allocutory patterns have not necessarily diminished in volume, but they have taken new forms, with more small-scale provision for segmented audiences based on interest or information need ('narrowcasting'). Finally, we can conclude from this figure that patterns of information flow are not as sharply differentiated as they might appear, but are subject to overlap and convergence, for technological as well as social reasons. The same technology (for example, the telecommunications infrastructure) can provide a household with facilities for each of the four patterns described.

This way of portraying the changes under way invites us to consider again the relevance of the current body of media theory concerning 'effects'. It seems that much of this only applies to the allocutory mode, where a transmission model may still be valid. For other situations we need an interactive, ritual or user-determined model. Even so, at present we do not have very adequate theory or research for investigating possible changes in the way new media are experienced.

Computer-mediated Community Formation

The idea of 'community' has long held an important position in social theory, especially as a tool for assessing the impact of social change and as a counterpoise to the idea of a mass. In earlier thinking, a community referred to a set of people sharing a place (or some other bounded space), an identity and certain norms, values and cultural practices, and usually small enough to know or interact with each other. A community of this kind usually shows some features of differentiation by status among its members and thus an informal hierarchy and form of organization.

The traditional mass media were viewed ambivalently in their relation to the typical (local) community. On the one hand, their largeness of scale and importation of outside values and culture were viewed as undermining local communities based on personal interaction. On the other hand, the media in adapted localized forms could serve and reinforce community under the best conditions. Although it is another use of the term 'community', it was also observed that mass-distributed, small-scale media (specialist publications or local radio) could help sustain 'communities of interest'. The general estimation was that the larger the scale of distribution, the more inimical to community and local social life, but even this judgement was challenged by evidence of continued localized interpersonal behaviour. Not least relevant was the fact that mass media often provide topics of conversation for discussion and thus help to lubricate social life in families, workplaces and even among strangers.

Against this background, there has been a continuing debate about the consequences of each succeeding media innovation. In the 1960s and 1970s, the introduction of cable television was hailed not only as a way of escaping from the limitations and drawbacks of mass broadcast television but as a positive means of community creation. Local cable systems could link up homes in a neighbourhood to each other and to a local centre. Programming could be chosen and made by local residents (Jankowski, 2002). Many extra services of information and help could be added on at low cost. In particular, access could be given to a wide variety of groups and even individual voices, with limited expense. The restricted bandwidth of broadcast television ceased to be a major practical constraint, and television by cable promised to approach the abundance of print media, at least in theory.

The notions of a 'wired community' and a 'wired city' became popular (see Dutton et al., 1986) and experiments were conducted in many countries to test the potential of cable television. This was the first 'new medium' to be treated seriously as an alternative to 'old-style' mass media. In the end, the experiments were largely discontinued and failed to live up to expectations, giving rise to the expression 'the cable fable'. The more utopian hopes were based on false foundations, especially the assumption that such community-based miniature versions of large-scale professional media were really wanted enough by the people they were meant to serve. Problems of financing and organization were often unsurmountable. Cable distribution became not an alternative to mass media, but predominantly just another means of mass distribution, albeit with some space for local access in some places. What was distinctive about these cable visions was the fact that a physical 'community' already existed but with unfulfilled potential that better intercommunication was supposed to realize.

Virtual community

A new set of expectations concerning community has developed around computer-mediated communication (CMC). The core idea is that of a **'virtual community'** that

✻

can be formed by any number of individuals by way of the Internet at their own choice or in response to some stimulus (Rheingold, 1994). Lindlof and Schatzer (1998) define a virtual community as one 'founded intentionally by people who share a set of similar interests, often revolving around certain texts or tropes imported from non-CMC venues, such as soap operas and their characters'.

Some features of real communities can be attained, including interaction, a common purpose, a sense of identity and belonging, various norms and unwritten rules ('netiquette', for instance), with possibilities for exclusion or rejection. There are also rites, rituals and forms of expression. Such online communities have the added advantage of being, in principle, open and accessible, while real communities are often hard to enter. Although the traditional notion of community is useful as a starting point for theory about the consequences of new media, the forms of association made possible by new media are likely to be of a different type. They will probably be uncertain, fluid and cosmopolitan rather than local (Slevin, 2000).

There have been numerous empirical studies of online 'communities', usually based on some common interest, for instance **fandom** for a music group, or on some shared characteristic, such as sexual orientation or a particular social or health situation (see Jones, 1997, 1998; Lindlof and Schatzer, 1998). The typical conditions for the formation of a virtual community seem to include minority status, physical dispersal of members and a degree of intensity of interest. It can be appreciated that CMC offers possibilities for motivated and interactive communication that are not available from mass media or from the immediate physical environment. Turner et al.'s (2001) study of online health support communities indicates that face-to-face and online contacts are not exclusive and have a mutual interaction.

Proponents of the online community idea are usually aware that the term is a metaphor (Watson, 1997) rather than the real thing. On the other hand, the 'real thing' is itself often rather elusive and sometimes mythical. Jones (1997: 17) cites Benedict Anderson's (1983) view that 'Communities are to be distinguished not by their falseness/genuineness, but by the style in which they are imagined.' Jones writes: 'The Internet's communities are imagined in two ways inimical to human communities.' One is their frequent lack of significance, and another the fact that there is an aimless and coincidental kind of connectedness about the experience. The term 'pseudo-community', taken from Beniger (1987), is used to express doubts about the genuineness of the virtual community.

The very fact of mediation by a machine tends to reduce the awareness of being in touch with other people. Even the advocates of virtual community, such as Rheingold (1994), recognize that online identities are often not genuine or revealed. They are adopted 'personae' often designed to conceal aspects of identity, for instance age or gender (Jones, 1997: 107). Participation in many online discussions and interactions is thus essentially anonymous, and this may sometimes be part of the attraction. Baym (2002) comments on the lack of information about participants as much as the misinformation. A feature of dubious value is the attendance of 'lurkers', who are not declared as participants at all.

The claim to the term 'community' in its established meaning is undermined by the lack of transparency and authenticity of the group formed by way of computer-mediated communication. Not least important is the lack of commitment of 'members'. Postman (1993) has criticized the adoption of the community metaphor because there is a lack of the essential element of accountability and mutual obligation. Although computer-mediated communication does offer new opportunities to cross social and cultural boundaries, it can also indirectly reinforce the same boundaries. Those who want to belong to a community in cyberspace have to conform to its norms and rules in order to be recognized and accepted.

Political Participation, New Media and Democracy

The earlier mass media of press and broadcasting were widely seen as beneficial (even necessary) for the conduct of democratic politics. The benefit stemmed from the flow of information about public events to all citizens and the exposure of politicians and governments to the public gaze and critique. However, negative effects were also perceived because of the dominance of channels by a few voices, the predominance of a 'vertical flow', and the heightened commercialism of the media market, leading to neglect of democratic communication roles. The typical organization and forms of mass communication limit access and discourage active participation and dialogue.

The new electronic media have been widely hailed as a potential way of escape from the oppressive 'top-down' politics of mass democracies in which tightly organized political parties make policy unilaterally and mobilize support behind them with minimal negotiation and grass-roots input. They provide the means for highly differentiated provision of political information and ideas, almost unlimited access in theory for all voices, and much feedback and negotiation between leaders and followers. They promise new forums for the development of interest groups and formation of opinion. They allow dialogue to take place between politicians and active citizens, without the inevitable intervention of a party machine. Not least important, as Coleman (1999) points out, is the 'role of new media in the subversive service of free expression under conditions of authoritarian control of the means of communication'. It is certainly not easy for governments to control access to and the use of the Internet by dissident citizens, but also not impossible.

Even 'old politics', it is said, might work better (and more democratically) with the aid of instant electronic polling and new tools of campaigning. The ideas concerning the public sphere and **civil society** discussed elsewhere (see pp. 179–81) have stimulated the notion that new media are ideally suited to occupy the space of civil society between the private domain and that of state activity. The ideal of a public sphere as an open arena for public conversation, debate and exchange of ideas seems open to fulfilment by way of forms of communication (the Internet, in particular) that allow citizens to express their views and communicate with each other and their political leaders without leaving their homes.

The arguments for welcoming a 'new politics' based on new media are quite diverse and different perspectives are involved. Dahlberg (2001) describes three basic camps or models. First, there is the model of 'cyber-libertarianism' that wants an approach to politics based on the model of the consumer market. Surveys, plebiscites and televoting fit this outlook, replacing older processes. Secondly, there is a 'communitarian' view that expects the benefits to come from greater grass-roots participation and input and the strengthening of local political communities. Thirdly, there is a perceived benefit to 'deliberative democracy' made possible by improved technology for interaction and for exchange of ideas in the public sphere (Coleman, 2001).

Bentivegna (2002) has summarized the potential benefits of the Internet to politics in terms of six main attributes, as shown in Box 6.5. She also describes the main limitations and the obstacles which have so far prevented any democratic transformation. In her view 'the gap between the political realm and citizens has apparently not been reduced, participation in political life has remained ... stable' (2002: 56). The reasons cited include: the 'glut of information' that limits the effective use that can be made of it; the fact that the Internet creates private 'lifestyle' alternatives to public and political life in the form of the virtual communities discussed above; the cacophony of voices that impedes serious discussion; the difficulties for many in using the Internet. In addition, there is the now much demonstrated fact that the new media tend to be used mainly by the small minority that is already politically interested and involved (Davis, 1999; Norris, 2000). If anything, new media possibilities may widen the gap between active participants and the rest.

6.5 Theoretical benefits of the Internet for democratic politics

- Scope for interactivity as well as one-way flow
- Co-presence of vertical and horizontal communication, promoting equality
- Disintermediation, meaning a reduced role for journalism to mediate the relationship between citizen and politicians
- Low costs for senders and receivers
- Immediacy of contact on both sides
- Absence of boundaries and limits to contacts

There has been a growing tendency to downplay the probable benefits for the public sphere, in the light of experience (Downey and Fenton, 2003). Scheufele and Nisbet's (2002) inquiry into the Internet and citizenship concluded that there was a 'very limited role for the Internet in promoting feelings of efficacy, knowledge and participation'. There is also evidence that the existing political party organizations have generally failed to make use of the potential of the Internet, but rather turned it into yet another branch of the propaganda machine. Vaccari (2008a) speaks of a process of 'normalization', after high expectations. Stromer-Galley (2000) had already found, for instance, that campaign managers did not really want interaction which is risky, problematic and burdensome. They used the Internet mainly as a vehicle for 'infomercials'. This, of course, applies beyond the case of politics. Crogan (2008) has pointed out that the Internet promotes ways of seeing the world as 'targets', offering much improved accuracy and effectiveness, compared to older mass media. In doing so, they are actually reinforcing the 'transportation model' so much associated with early mass media.

Technologies of Freedom?

The heading to this section forms the title of a seminal work by Ithiel de Sola Pool (1983) that celebrated electronic means of communication because of the escape they offered from what he regarded as the illegitimate imposition of **censorship** and regulation on broadcast radio and television. The essence of his argument was that the only logical (though disputed) case for state control of media was spectrum short-age and the need to allocate access opportunity in semi-monopoly conditions. The emerging new era could grant the freedom enjoyed by print media and common car-riers (telephone, mails, cable) to all public media. Distribution by cable, telephone line, new radio waves and satellite was rapidly removing the claim for regulation aris-ing out of scarcity. Moreover, the growing 'convergence of modes' of communication made it increasingly impossible as well as illogical to regulate one type of medium and not others.

The freedom that has been claimed as a feature of the new media (especially the Internet) is not precisely the same freedom as Pool was claiming for media in general. Essentially, Pool wanted the freedom of the market and the 'negative freedom' (no government intervention) of the US **First Amendment** to apply to all media. The image of freedom attaching to the Internet has had more to do with its vast capacity and with the lack of structure, organization and management that characterized its early years when it was a freely accessible playground for all comers, with much use subsidized by academic institutions or other public bod-ies. Castells (2001: 200) writes that 'the kind of communication that thrives on the Internet is that related to free expression in all its forms … It is open source, free-posting, decentralized broadcasting, serendipitous interaction … that find their expression on the Internet.' This view is in line with the aspirations of its founders. The system was there for all to use, even if the original motives for its creation were strategic and military, while the motives for its subsequent promo-tion and expansion were mainly economic and in the interests of telecommunica-tion operators.

The system had and retains an inbuilt resistance to attempts to control or man-age it. It appeared not to be owned or managed by anyone in particular, to belong to no territory or jurisdiction. In practice its 'content' and the uses made of it were not easy to control or sanction, even where jurisdiction could be established. In this it shared many features of common carrier media, such as mails and telephone. Contrary to Pool's vision of freedom and unlike, for instance, the early experiments with videotex, there was no charge for access as sender and receiver.

Relative to most other media, the Internet does remain free and unregulated. However, there have been clear tendencies, as it has grown in success and use, for its freedom to be limited (for instance, in the US 1996 Communications Act and then the

Patriot Act of 2001; Gromback, 2006). As it has become more like a mass medium, with high penetration and a potential for reaching an important segment of the consumer market, there is a higher stake in forms of regulation and management. As Lessig (1999: 19) has pointed out: 'The architecture of cyberspace makes regulating behaviour difficult, because those you're trying to control could be located in any place ... on the Net'. However, the means are available by way of control of the architecture and of the code that governs the architecture. It is increasingly a medium for commerce (selling goods as well as information services), so that financial security has to be achieved. It has also become big business. Hamelink (2000: 141) remarks that although no one owns the Net and there is no central regulatory body, 'it is possible for some industrial players to own all the technical means that are required to access and use the Net'. He anticipates a near future when 'governance and access to cyberspace will be in the hands of a few gatekeepers ... controlled by a small group of market leaders' (2000: 153). Ten years later, this prediction is well on the way to being confirmed.

As the Internet penetrates more homes, with ordinary families, rather than offices and universities, the demands for applying criteria of 'decency' and also for means of enforcement have also grown, despite jurisdictional difficulties. As with earlier media, once a claim to great social impact is made, the demand for control grows and the practical obstacles to control turn out not to be so insurmountable. More and more of the normal legitimate accountability claims against public media are arising (for example, about intellectual property, **libel**, privacy). The seeming anarchy of many service providers and content organizers is giving way to a more structured market situation. Successful pressure is being put on service providers to take some responsibility for what appears on their services, even if the control is haphazard and often has a 'chilling' effect. There will be less 'free' content of any market value. The management of the system will also have to be more transparent as well as more efficient.

A new means of control?

Police and intelligence services are paying more attention to the need for surveillance and control, especially in respect of potential transborder crime, child pornography, terrorism, domestic disaffection, plus many new kinds of cyber-crime. Ten years into the twenty-first century, there is an ever-growing list of exceptions to the freedoms of the Internet, varying from one national jurisdiction to another and correlated with the general level of freedom (or its absence) in each state. The situation after the declaration of a 'war on terror' since 2001 has made it easier for governments and authorities to implement restrictions on the liberty of the Net, as in most other spheres (Foerstal, 2001; Braman, 2004). Taken together, the tendencies described lead to a severe modification of the Internet's anarchic and open image, although this may simply reflect the onset of 'normalization' that has been exhibited before in respect of other media. The situation is too early and too unsettled to make an assessment, but not too early to say that even the most free *means* of communication cannot escape the operation of various 'laws' of social life. These include those of communication itself (which bind participants together in some mutual obligations or expectations), and especially those of economics and social pressure.

The more apocalyptic visions of the future indicate a potential for social control through electronic means that far outstrips those available in the industrial age, except where brute force could be used. The monitoring and tracking of informational traffic and interpersonal contacts are increasing, based essentially on the 'registration' pattern of computerized information traffic indicated above. Jansen (1988: 23–4) wrote of the new potential for systematically eroding the privacy of the home and of interpersonal relations: 'Once the wires are in place, the Electronic Panopticon (referring to Jeremy Bentham's model prison with wings radiating from a central observation point) works automatically. Only the minimal supervision from the Tower is required'.

Rheingold (1994: 15) wrote: 'the Net can also be an enormous invisible cage. Virtual communities are a hyper-realistic illusion of technical advance as a refuge from the destruction of human communities.' These visions of the future are based on real possibilities. However, they are not universally shared, nor have they yet been realized. Green (1999), for instance, regards these fears as technologically deterministic and one-sided. He points to the potential for new media, as noted above, to reverse the direction of surveillance and to express democratic impulses by way of access to centres of power.

Still missing in the case of the Internet is a nuanced understanding of what 'freedom' means in this context (Chalaby, 2001). The freedom from surveillance and 'right to privacy' are a different kind of freedom, protecting anonymity, not publication. Both these (and other) kinds of freedom are important, but the potential and actual uses of the Internet are too diverse for all forms of freedom to be claimed. Freedom of speech and expression, as established for other media, recognizes some limits on the rights of others, the necessities of society and the realities of social pressure. It is unrealistic to expect the Internet to enjoy freedoms that have been restricted for other media on grounds accepted as legitimate.

In most sober assessments of the development of communication technology, it is dystopians who seem more convincing than utopians, at least in rejecting the possibility of a quick fix. Beniger's (1986) interpretative history of communication innovations since the early nineteenth century finds that they fit within a pattern not of increasing liberation, but of increasing possibilities for management and control. He uses the term 'control revolution' to describe the communications revolution. Whatever the potential, the needs of commerce, industry, military and bureaucracy have done most to promote development and determine how innovations are actually applied.

Another chronicler of communication innovation (Winston, 1986) recognized that most new technologies have innovative potential, but the actual implementation always depends on two factors. One is the operation of 'supervening social necessity' that dictates the degree and form of development of inventions. The second is the 'law of the suppression of radical potential', which acts as a brake on innovation to protect the social or corporate status quo. In general, he argues for theories of 'cultural' rather than technological determination. Carey (1998) took a similar position about the 'new media', arguing that 'globalization, the Internet and computer communications are all *underdetermined* by technology and history. The final determination of these new forms is one prepared by politics.'

New Equalizer or Divider?

✱
The **rhetoric** surrounding new media has often embodied a claim that electronic media help to produce a more equal as well as a more liberated society. The big advantage is the ready access for all who want to speak, unmediated by the powerful interests that control the content of print media and the channels of broadcasting. You do not need to be rich and powerful to have a presence on the World Wide Web. The potential of new media to bypass established institutional channels does also seem to improve the chances for the many and reduce their dependence on the various monopolistic sources of information and influence. If all homes have the technology and the trend of expansion goes in that direction, then universal access to cultural and informational goods in a coming 'videotopia' seems to follow. The political voices that have urged us to develop the 'electronic highway' into homes, libraries, schools and workplaces see this as an emancipatory programme of action as well as a necessity for economic progress (Mattelart, 2003).

The critics have not been silent on this prospect. The school of political economy sees little reason to change a view of the world according to which the chief beneficiaries of 'electronic highways' will continue to be large electronic and telecommunication firms (Sussman, 1997; McChesney, 2000; Wasko, 2004). The new media are no different from the old media in terms of the social stratification of ownership and access. It is the better-off that first acquire and then upgrade the technology and are always ahead of the poor. They are differentially empowered and, if anything, move further ahead. Social and information gaps widen rather than narrow and there emerges an 'information underclass' as well as a social underclass. Much is made of the 'digital divide' as a successor to the 'information gap' (see pp. 489–91) that was once predicted as a result of the coming of television (Norris, 2000; Castells, 2001; Hargittai, 2004). Historic conditions play a part in shaping the impact of new technology, not only in the developing world but in former communist countries such as Russia (Rantanen, 2001; Vartanova, 2002). As Selwyn (2004) points out, access to channels is not the same as actual use. Even use is structured according to the availability of skills that are not evenly distributed, leading to a second-level 'digital divide' that cannot be overcome by technology and has not been measured.

There has also been controversy in relation to gender. Despite the general advantage that women seem to have gained in employment terms from informatization of work, there has been a persistent claim that computers have a male bias. Some theorists of feminism (e.g. Ang and Hermes, 1991) resist any idea that there is an essential difference between men and women in relation to being comfortable with computer technology. However, according to Turkle (1988), the problem is not that computers have a male bias, but that 'the computer is socially constructed as male'. A similar discussion has accompanied the diffusion of the Internet. Van Zoonen (2002) has sketched a discourse in which the Internet has been variously seen as constructed as more female or more male or even, by 'cyberfeminists', as open to mixed and new gender definitions. Her own research indicates that both gender and technology are too multidimensional as concepts for any single assessment to be made. In so far as use of the Internet is concerned, the initial imbalance of female users has fallen, even if some difference remains (Singh, 2001; Rainie and Bell, 2004).

It is true that the networks, circles and connections between users of new technology based on telecommunications and computers do not have to follow the lines of national frontiers in the same way as old mass media almost invariably have done. It may therefore be less appropriate to apply the centre–periphery model of mass communication which reflects the varying degrees of dependency in poorer and smaller countries and regions on a few 'primary producers' of news and entertainment. The possession of the right technology does open doorways to new possibilities for information and intercommunication, irrespective of the 'level of development' of one's own home place. Some of the gaps and obstacles to development may be leap-frogged.

Nevertheless, the great imbalance of communication capacity still exists, and exceptions apply only to a small minority for certain purposes. The basic research has not been done to show the nature and extent of global imbalance. But there are enough data and indications to suppose that the informational 'content' made available by new technology and the rates of participation in consulting and exchanging information strongly favour the 'have' regions and nations (and especially the 'Anglo-Saxon' parts). The costs of technology and its use continue to favour the same already privileged beneficiaries, as does the investment in infrastructure and management systems. The more new media become economically more interesting, the more this trend is likely to be accentuated.

In the early days of mass media, there was also a belief that the communicative reach and power of radio and television could help bridge the gaps in social and economic development. The reality proved to be different, and mass media, in their transnational forms at least, were likely to do more for their originating societies and cultures than for their supposed beneficiaries in the 'Third World'. The same tendency to see technology as a changer of the world is still present (Waisbord, 1998). It is hard to see how the situation is different, despite the greater potential for the 'users' and receivers of new media to claim access and to take over the means of cultural oppression. The way new communications technology has developed seems to favour specifically western values and cultural forms, including their individualism and personal freedom.

Conclusion

This excursion into theory for new media has been somewhat inconclusive, although recognizing a strong case for revision of theory. Even so, public communication continues much as before. The central values of liberalism, democracy, work, human rights and even communication ethics are evolving rather than collapsing at the start of the twenty-first century. Even the old problems addressed by such values are still in place, including war, injustice, inequality, crime and want. The more specific and central question addressed by this chapter is whether or not the ideas and frameworks that were developed to pose and test questions about mass communication are still serviceable.

There are some reasons for supposing that they might not be. There is a definite trend towards 'demassification' of old media as the proliferation of channels and platforms for transmission eats into the 'mass audience' and replaces it with innumerable small and more 'specialized' audiences. The new media and the Internet in particular have made the idea of the 'personal newspaper' (the so-called *Daily Me*), in which content is assembled according to individual taste and interest, a realistic possibility (even if not much in demand). The more this happens, and it could apply to radio and television as well, the less the mass media will provide a common basis in knowledge and outlook or serve as the 'cement of society'. This has been widely regretted as a loss to the larger enterprise of a democratic and socially just society (Sunstein, 2006). Some evidence on online news does point to a localizing trend, but there is also a globalizing potential being opened up. At the same time there is accumulating evidence (discussed on pp. 509–10) to show that, in the case of news at least, there is still a perceived need for reliability in news, and the trust that some news sources and commentators (in conventional media) have earned cannot be dispensed with or easily substituted. The same applies to politicians and parties. Apart from fringe activities, it is hard to find much evidence of any increase in alternative politics or politicians. Much the same reasons apply. There may well be a decline in attachment to politics, but there seems no reason either for attributing this to the new media or for seeing them as an antidote.

It is arguable that there is no 'media institution' any more, but many different loosely connected elements. There are new forces at work and new trends that may not be open to capture by familiar concepts and formulas. Nevertheless, the basic features of the role of media in public and private life seem to persist. The new media have gradually come to be accepted as mass media for the good reason that their uses exhibit many of the features of old media, especially when treated by their owners as mass advertisers and as 'platforms' for media content, such as music and films. As Webster and Lin (2002) report, there are striking regularities in web-use behaviour that conform to familiar mass media patterns, such as concentration on a small number of very popular sites by very large numbers of users.

The evidence so far does not support the view that new technology is having a strongly deterministic effect towards change in the short or even medium term; it is neither producing any very reliable explosion of freedom nor (as yet) seriously diminishing what **freedom of communication** exists already. Nevertheless, there are areas with a potential for change that require monitoring. One is the redrawing of social (and cultural) boundaries that the formation of new networks of interconnected individuals encourages. Another is the potential transformation of political communication (really of politics) in the widest sense as the old 'allocutive' means seem to perform less well. Finally, there remains the issue of potentially increasing divisions in the benefits of new media as a result of underlying social and economic inequalities.

Further Reading

Castells, M. (2001) *The Internet Galaxy*. Oxford: Oxford University Press.
The leading exponent of theory of network society sets out to do for the Internet what McLuhan did for print media and television, with a result that it is still a good guide to enquiry and issues arising.

Havalais, A. (2009) *Search Engine Society*. Cambridge: Polity Press.
An informative and thoughtful examination of a neglected phenomenon of great significance lying at the heart of the Internet.

Lessig, L. (1999) *Code and other Laws of Cyberspace*. New York: Basic Books.
A comprehensive and fundamental assessment of the nature of the Internet mainly from a socio-legal perspective, with many insights into its similarities with and differences from other media. A cautionary rather than a visoionary tale that has not dated or been superceded.

Morris, M. and Ogan, C. (1994) 'The Internet as a mass medium', *Journal of Communication*, 46 (1): 39–50.
Perhaps the first attempt to make a coherent assessment of the consequences of the Internet for mass communication at a very early stage of development, and still relevant.

Online Readings

Baym, N. (2006) 'Interpersonal life online', in L. Lievrouw and S. Livingstone (eds), *The Handbook of New Media*, pp. 35–54. London: Sage.
Bentivegna, S. (2006) 'Rethinking politics in the age of ICTs', *European Journal of Communication*, 21 (3): 331–44.
Fortunati, L. (2005) 'Mediatizing the net and intermediatizing the media', *The International Communication Gazette*, 67 (6): 29–44.
Koolstra, C.M. and Bos, M.J.W. (2009) 'The development of an instrument to determine different levels of interactivity', *The International Communication Gazette*, 71 (5): 373–91.
Lüders, M. (2008) 'Conceptualising personal media', *New Media and Society*, 10 (5): 683–702.

7

Normative Theory of Media and Society

The mass media are presumed not only to have certain objective effects on society, but also to serve a social purpose. This means that some of the effects that have been observed are both intended and positively valued. These include the effects of disseminating information, expressing different voices and views, helping public opinion to form on issues and facilitating debate. The many entertainment and cultural activities of the media can also count as approved purposes. Where effects are intended we can usually identify who is behind them, in this case primarily those who own or direct the media and work in them as well as those for whom the media provide channels of communication, including governments, authorities and individual communicators. Not surprisingly, there are many different opinions (public, private and institutional) about just what the media ought or ought not to be doing and on how well they are performing, but there is no doubt that much is expected. When we speak of **normative theory** we refer to the ideas of right and responsibility that underlie these expectations of benefit from the media to individuals and society.

In this chapter we examine ideas of how the media *ought* or *are* expected to be organized and to behave in the wider **public interest** or for the good of society as a whole. The positive aims of media activity are not always or even often clearly stated and sometimes have to be inferred from statements of what they ought not to do, so we begin with the question of sources.

Sources of Normative Obligation

These points are clear enough, but what is less clear is the problems that they conceal. The central difficulty is that 'the media' in a free society do not, for the most part, have any obligation to carry out many of the positively valued purposes that have been referred to and that are taken for granted. They are not run by the government, nor do they work on behalf of society. Their formal responsibilities are largely the same as those of other citizens and organizations within a society and thus mainly defined in negative terms. They are required to do no harm. Beyond that, the media are free to choose, or avoid, various positive ends. They tend collectively to resent any attempt to prescribe their role in society, whether on the part of governments, special interests, individuals or even media theorists. Despite this, there is much in the history, constitution and conduct of the media institution which recognizes certain unwritten obligations that for various reasons are often respected in practice. There are also several sources of external pressure that cannot be ignored. Normative theory of media covers both internally chosen purposes and the claims from outside about how they should conduct themselves.

Among the sources of normative expectation, the most fundamental are probably those that stem from the historical context that has shaped the role of the media institution. In most democracies this has meant a close link between democratic political institutions and the role of the media as carrier of news and former of opinion. This link is not usually constitutionally established (although Germany is an exception) and cannot be enforced, but neither is it really optional. Extensive reference can be found in social and political theory. Related to this is the much broader orientation of journalism to the public life of the national society and international community. This is also deeply embedded in custom and convention as well as in the expression of professional claims and aspirations.

Secondly, there are claims laid on the media as a whole by the general public and expressed either as public opinion or, more inescapably, by the public as an audience of a particular media publication. In this case, the view of the public about what the media ought to be doing, if it is clearly expressed, has a more binding character. This reflects the fact that media are tied into a nexus of market relations with their customers and clients, the latter (e.g. as advertisers) also having some influence on media conduct. There remain two other sources of influence, with variable power. One of these is the state and agents of government. Circumstances determine how independent media can be of the views of government, which always has some capacity to reward or punish. It is unusual to find large and well-established media that do not see some self-interest in respecting the legitimate wishes and interests of the state (for instance, in matters of public order or national emergency), even if the right to criticize is preserved.

The other source of influence is more diffuse but often effective. It stems from the many interests, especially economic but also cultural and social, that are affected by the mass media, particularly in respect of news and information. Powerful individuals and organizations can be hurt by the news and may also need it to further their ends. For this reason they keep a close eye on media conduct for their own protection or seek to influence it. All in all this adds up to an environment of expectation and scrutiny that has considerable cumulative influence. Box 7.1 provides a summary of the main sources of normative expectation on media conduct and performance.

Sources of normative expectations from media   **7.1**

- Social and political theory on the press
- Professional theory and practice of journalism
- The public as citizens (public opinion)
- The public as audience
- The media market
- The state and its agencies
- Interested parties in the society affected by media

The Media and the Public Interest

One way of summarizing the situation arising from the many pressures on media to deliver certain benefits is to say that there is a 'public interest' in how the media conduct themselves. This concept is both simple and also very contested in social and political theory. The idea of a public interest has deep historical roots in identifying those matters that needed some collective public control and direction for the good of the society or nation, for instance the building and maintenance of roads and waterways, the regulation of weights, measure and currency, the provision of policing and defence. In more modern times the phrase was used to apply to the management and ownership of public utilities such as water, gas, electricity and telephones. These were matters that could not easily be left to private individuals or the working of the market (Held, 1970; Napoli, 2001).

As applied to the mass media, its simple meaning is that the media carry out a number of important, even essential, tasks in a contemporary society and it is in the general interest that these are performed and performed well. It also implies that we should have a media system that is operated according to the same basic principles governing the rest of society, especially in relation to justice, fairness, democracy and reigning notions of desirable social and cultural values. It is clearly in the public interest that the media do not cause social problems or extreme offence. But the idea of a public interest also involves positive expectations, as in the original fields of application.

This simple notion does not take us very far in practice. The first problem encountered is that public control, even in the supposed public interest, of all media is inconsistent with freedom of expression, as usually understood. Moreover, media are usually established not to serve the public interest as such, but to follow some goal of their own choosing. The goal is sometimes defined in cultural, professional or political terms but more often it is the goal of making profit as a business. Sometimes it is both at the same time. This points to the key problem of determining just what the public interest might be and of who should decide it. There are always diverse and conflicting versions of what is good for a society as a whole, and there is even support for the view that it is better for the media not to pursue any normative goal at all. Rather, the many different media should be left free to do what they want, within the limits of the law. Where media are run on a commercial basis, as they mainly are, the media's view of what is the public interest tends to equate it with what interests the public. This shifts the responsibility for norms, ethics and values to the society.

The difficulties of handling the public interest concept are inextricably connected with its high significance. In this respect, Blumler (1998: 54–5) makes three key points. First, just as in the case of government, there are questions of authority as well as of power: 'In communications, the media are similarly placed. The justification for their freedoms, their wide-ranging roles in society, politics and culture, and their place in regulatory orders depends ultimately on the public interests presumed to be served thereby.' In short, the power of the media, like that of government, has to be used in a *legitimate* way, which is not far removed from the notion of *responsibility*. Secondly, Blumler argues that 'a certain transcendent quality attaches to the notion of the public interest. It is different from and, in policy terms, superior to particular interests. This entails a longer-term perspective, in which the claims of successor generations and the future of society are included as well as people's immediate needs.' Thirdly, 'notions of the public interest must work in an imperfect and impure world'. This means inevitable tension, compromise and improvisation according to circumstances.

Held (1970) has described two of the main versions of what constitutes the public interest and how its content might be established. One is a 'majoritarian' view, according to which the issue should be settled by reference to the popular vote. In the case of media this would tend to equate the public interest with 'giving the public what it wants', pleasing the majority of consumers in the media market. There is another way of interpreting the majoritarian position. For instance, Morrison and Svennevig (2007) looked for an empirical verification of the idea of public interest by way of an inquiry into its meaning for the British public. They discovered a widespread consensus that some matters are of 'social importance' for media to cover and they related this to an underlying conception of social solidarity. The opposing view is called 'unitarian' or 'absolutist' since the public interest would be decided by reference to some single dominant value or ideology. This would lead at best to a paternalistic system in which decisions about what is good are decided by guardians or experts. Between the free-market version of the public interest and the paternalistic model, there are alternatives, but none offers clear guidance. The other main way is an approach that involves debate and democratic decision-making on the one hand and, on the other, *ad hoc* judicial determinations of what is or is not in the public interest in a given case. As we will see later, there are a number of different ways in which the accountability of media to society in terms of the public good can be achieved or at least pursued (see pp. 210–13).

Whatever the arguments about the concept of public interest, it is quite obvious that the mass media have everywhere been subject to extensive control and regulation by law and other formal or informal means with a view to getting them to do what 'society' wants, or to prevent them from doing what it doesn't. The actual means and content of control vary a good deal from one national media 'system' to another, influenced by the usual political, cultural and economic determinants. They vary also from one medium to another and are rarely internally coherent or consistent.

Leaving theory aside, in the practice of media politics, law and regulation, there seems to have been quite a lot of agreement on the main components of the public interest in respect of mass media, going well beyond the minimum requirement of causing no harm. To judge from many cases where public interest has had to be specified, the main requirements from the media are as listed in Box 7.2. These points summarize the main normative expectations relating, respectively, to the structure and content of media in western-type democracies.

Main public interest criteria for media 7.2

Structure

- Freedom of publication
- Plurality of ownership
- Extensive (near-universal) reach
- Diversity of channels and forms

Content

- Diversity of information, opinion and culture
- Supportive of public order and the law
- High quality of information and culture
- Supportive of the democratic political system (public sphere)
- Respectful of international obligations and human rights
- Avoiding harm to society and individuals

Main Issues for Social Theory of the Media

Here we concentrate on the main types of problem that have surfaced in debates concerning the relation between media and society. The terrain of normative theory can be mapped out in terms of the issues that have arisen concerning media structure, conduct or performance. On the whole, the issues correspond to the entries in Box 7.2 and can be explained briefly in the following terms. First, there are issues that relate primarily to how a media system is structured and the conditions of its operation:

- *Freedom of publication.* It is widely agreed that media should be free from control by government or other powerful interests, sufficient to allow them to report and express freely and independently and to meet the needs of their audiences. Freedom consists essentially in the absence of advance censorship or licensing, or of punishment after the event for publication that is not otherwise unlawful. People need also to be free to receive the media of their choice.
- *Plurality of ownership.* Here the prevailing norm opposes concentration of ownership and monopoly of control, whether on the part of the state or the private media industry. The guiding principle is that the media system should not be dominated by a few controlling interests.
- *Universality of provision.* As in the public utility model, the communication network of a society should reach all citizens at equal cost to consumers, the obligation to provide coverage falling on the state. A main aim of public broadcasting systems is to meet this criterion.
- *Diversity of channels and forms.* Ideally, media structure will also have many different types of media and separate channels to maximize the chance of meeting a wide range of public communication needs. Citizens should have access as senders and receivers to media that reflect their ideas and meet their interests and needs. Different types of media (e.g. press and broadcasting) should be under different control.
- *Diversity of information, opinion and cultural content.* It is desirable that the media system overall should exhibit a range of output that reflects the diversity of the society, especially in the key dimensions of region, politics, religion, ethnicity, culture, and so on. Media channels should be open to new movements and ideas and give reasonable access to small minorities.

A second set of issues relates to the kind of service (content provision) that might be expected if the 'public interest' is to be served. Key elements include:

- *Support for maintaining public order and the security of the state.* While the media are not normally required to do the work of the police or other authorities, on whom they should keep a critical eye, there is a widely held view in democracies that there are some legitimate limits to media freedom and some matters on which they do have a duty to assist authority. The circumstances envisaged where this issue arises are usually extreme ones involving grave external threats, actual war, disasters, extreme internal conflict or violent terrorist acts. The claim on media to support the public order can, however, extend to ordinary crime. The obligations mentioned may well also apply to any citizen.

- *Quality of cultural provision*. The issues that fall in to this category are diverse, ranging from questions of morals and decency to matters of culture and aesthetic taste. In general, the media are expected to respect, if not support, the dominant values and moral standards of their own society and to give expression, though less strongly, to the traditional valued culture, and the arts and language of their own national society or region. Quality in media culture may be assessed according to different standards and perspectives. It includes support for original and creative production, and the opportunity for minority arts and culture to be expressed.
- *Support for the democratic process*. This heading refers to a wide range of positive expectations about the essential (also normal) contribution of mass media to the working of political and other social institutions. This contribution is made through publishing full, fair and reliable information on public matters, assisting in the expression of diverse points of view, giving access to many voices in society, facilitating the participation of citizens in social and political life, and so on.
- *Meeting international human rights obligations*. While media are typically national institutions, they can have an international range of coverage and they have an effect on membership of the wider international community. A broad range of potential issues arises, including the quality of reporting about other countries, the possible incitement to hatred of foreigners, or engaging in propaganda for war. On the positive side, there are some grounds for expecting media to report constructively on matters to do with development, foreign disasters and emergencies and on global issues of health and the environment.

There is a third category of issues of a proscriptive kind, where the media are required to avoid various kinds of harm, usually unintended. The main additional requirements are as follows:

- *Respecting the rights of individuals*. The media often impinge negatively on individual rights, even where these are protected either in law or in popular opinion. The most frequently occurring issues concern personal reputation (libel and slander), rights to privacy and personal dignity, property rights (e.g. copyright), and rights to anonymity by those accused. There is inevitably a disputed frontier zone where it can be claimed that violation of private rights is justified by a larger public interest. This arises, for instance, in the case of political scandals, or some criminal matters (e.g. exposing paedophiles), or where a public celebrity is involved. However, much media conduct can claim no justification and serves no public interest. The media also often shock or offend particular individuals and groups, causing distress and indirect harm.
- *Harm to society*. Fears are often expressed about the general and long-term effects on society as a result of media publication, even where no harm is intended. The welfare of children or other vulnerable groups may be involved, or encouragement may be given to crime, violence and other behaviour considered antisocial, such as drinking, drug-taking or promiscuity.
- *Harm to individuals*. A separate entry is reserved for specific instances of harm to individuals caused by the provocation of harmful acts by others or the person concerned. There have been well-documented cases of the media playing an apparently stimulating role in crimes or suicide and there is a sustainable argument that certain

kinds of representations, for instance violent pornography, can lead to imitation or have corrupting effects. Cases of imitation of terrorist acts fall within this category.

There are, of course, numerous other issues on which content may be subject to praise or complaint on public interest grounds. The latter include some health or safety issues (e.g. tobacco advertising), judicial matters (e.g. contempt of court), effects on the working of the political system (publication of opinion poll results), and the causing of offence to public mores by displays that are violent, blasphemous or pornographic. These examples are sufficient to underline the point that the media, perhaps more than any other social institution, operate in the full glare of publicity and are as much watched by the rest of society as they watch society. How and with what results this public scrutiny of the public watchdog takes place are discussed later.

Early Approaches to Theory: the Press as 'Fourth Estate'

The first media were print media, and the most significant freedoms are those gained and still claimed by and for print media. For this reason, the term 'press theory' is often used to relate to news and journalism generally. In an important sense, in the times and places covered by this discussion (mostly twentieth-century western-type democracies), the only fully respected theory of the press has been the theory of *press freedom*. Everything else is a qualification or a limitation designed for some end of the common good.

In the light of this, we can say that the 'original' theory of the press was concerned with the role of journalism in the political process, as propounded by a variety of liberal thinkers, including Thomas Paine, John Stuart Mill, Alexis de Tocqueville and many others. The term **'fourth estate'** was reputedly coined by Edmund Burke in late-eighteenth-century England to refer to the political power possessed by the press, on a par with the other three 'estates' of power in the British realm: Lords, Church and Commons. The power of the press arose from its ability to give or withhold publicity and from its informative capacity. The first key freedom was to report and comment on the deliberations, assemblies and acts of governments. This freedom was the cornerstone of representative democracy and of progress. All the revolutionary and reformist movements from the eighteenth century onwards inscribed liberty of the press on their banners and made use of it in practice to advance their causes (Hardt, 2003).

In this particular, mainly Anglo-American, tradition of thought, freedom of the press was closely linked with the idea of freedom of the individual and with liberal and utilitarian political philosophy. Philosophical support for press freedom was found essentially in arguments against censorship and suppression of opinion. John Stuart Mill's famous argument for the liberty of the press, dating from 1859, is quoted in Box 7.3.

John Stuart Mill (1859) on the liberty of the press: key quotation **7.3**

The peculiar evil of silencing the expression of an opinion is, that it is robbing the human race, posterity as well as the existing generation, those who dissent from the opinion even more than those who hold it. If the opinion is right, they are deprived of the opportunity of exchanging error for truth; if wrong, they lose what is almost as great a benefit, the clearer perception and livelier impression of truth, produced by its collision with error. (Mill, 1991/1859).

These ideas were later worked into the notion of a 'self-righting' mechanism by which the freely expressed truth will surely triumph over error when both are published freely. The core idea goes back to John Milton's pamphlet, *Areopagitica* (1644) against licensing of the press in England. Another popular way of expressing the same idea is in terms of 'the free marketplace of ideas', first used in 1918 by an American judge. Although used metaphorically, this phrase has had the unfortunate effect of linking freedom of the press very closely with the idea of a literal free market.

The historical context of the struggle for press freedom was almost invariably one of antagonism between publication and some authority, first church and later government, in many aspects. It is not surprising that press freedom came to be defined primarily as freedom from restriction. This was the meaning it had been given in legal terms in the United States, in the words of the First Amendment to the US Constitution (1791), to the effect that 'Congress shall make no law ... abridging the freedom of speech or of the press.' By contrast, reformed constitutions in many other countries have referred to a right guaranteed to citizens. For example, Article 7 of the 1848 Constitution of The Netherlands says: 'No one needs advance permission in order to make public through the printing press any thoughts or feelings, aside from everyone's responsibility in law.'

By the early twentieth century it was clear to many reformers that press freedom in the economic sense and expressed in the purely negative terms of rejecting government interference was failing to give voice to the full meaning of freedom of expression, which includes some notion of a realistic opportunity of access to the channels of publication. Instead of being a vehicle for advancing freedom and democracy, the press was becoming (especially in the Anglo-American homeland of such ideas) more and more a means of making money and propaganda for the new and powerful capitalist classes, and especially the 'press barons'.

At the start of the twenty-first century the threats to freedom from increasing media monopoly have not gone away (McChesney, 2000; Baker, 2007), despite expansion of media content and channels. The liberating promise of the Internet has not yet been fulfilled and it is looking vulnerable in the face of colonization by large media firms of the most successful websites and clear evidence that governments are intolerant of many of the new freedoms.

The 1947 Commission on Freedom of the Press and the Theory of Social Responsibility

In response to widespread criticism of the American newspaper press, especially because of its sensationalism and commercialism, but also its political imbalance and monopoly tendencies, a private commission of inquiry was set up in 1942 and reported in 1947 (Hutchins, 1947). The founder was the publisher Henry Luce and it was conducted under the high-minded chairmanship of Robert Hutchins, Chancellor of Chicago University (Blanchard, 1977). The aim of the commission was 'to examine areas and circumstances under which the press of the United States is succeeding or failing; to discover where free expression is or is not limited, whether by government censorship pressure from readers or advertisers or the unwisdom of its proprietors or the timidity of its management'.

The commission forms an important milestone in the present story for several reasons. It was the first of many such inquiries and reports, often initiated by governments to look into the failure of the media to meet the needs of society and the possibilities for reform. In the United States there has since been no equivalent public inquiry into the press, but several commissions have looked at specific problems arising from the activities of the media, especially in relation to violence, pornography and civil unrest.

Secondly, the 1947 commission was perhaps the first occasion since freedom of the press was attained when the need for intervention by government to put right the ills of the press was contemplated, and this in the heartland of capitalism. Thirdly, it served as an influential example to other countries, especially in the period of reform and reconstruction that followed the Second World War. Fourthly, the findings of the report contributed something of substance to subsequent theorizing and to the practice of accountability, although there is no real evidence that it actually improved the press of the time.

The findings of the commission (Hutchins, 1947) were critical of the press for its frequent failings and for being so limited in the access it gave to voices outside the circle of a privileged and powerful minority. The report coined the notion of **social responsibility** and named the key journalistic standards that the press should seek to maintain. A responsible press should 'provide a full, truthful, comprehensive and intelligent account of the day's events in a context which gives them meaning'. It should 'serve as a forum for the exchange of comment and criticism' and be a 'common carrier of the public expression'. Thirdly, the press should give a 'representative picture of constituent groups in society' and also present and clarify the 'goals and values of society'. The report criticized the sensationalism of the press and the mixing of news with editorial opinion.

In general the commission supported the concept of a diverse, objective, informative and independent press institution which would avoid causing offence or encouraging crime, violence or disorder. Social responsibility should be reached by self-control, not government intervention. However, the latter was not ruled out. Siebert et al.'s (1956) subsequent interpretation of social responsibility locates it under a concept of positive liberty – 'freedom for' rather than 'freedom from'. They wrote (1956: 95): 'Social responsibility theory holds that the government must not merely allow freedom; it must actively promote it ... When necessary, therefore, the government should act to protect the freedom of its citizens.' The acts of government mentioned include legislation to forbid 'flagrant abuses', and it may also 'enter the field of communication to supplement existing media'.

The 'theory of social responsibility' involved a view of media ownership as a form of public trust or stewardship, rather than as an unlimited private franchise. One of the members of the commission, William Hocking (1947: 169), wrote: 'Inseparable from the right of the press to be free has been the right of the people to have a free press. But the public interest has advanced beyond that point; it is now the right of the people to have *an adequate press*.' And of the two rights, he added: 'it is the right of the public that now takes precedence'. This is one fundamental basis for the demand for responsibility. The other basis derives from the fact that the ownership of modern mass communications (then newspapers and broadcasting especially) was already highly concentrated, giving great power to a small number of people. This power carried with it a responsibility to exercise it with great caution and respect for others. It has been an influential idea, not only in the press but also in the legitimation of the government regulation of broadcasting, especially in the United States. Until the deregulatory moves of the 1980s, the US Federal Communication Commission (FCC) often acted on the assumption that broadcasting was a public trust, subject to review and even revocation. The main principles of the theory are set out in Box 7.4.

Social responsibility theory: main propositions 7.4

- The media have obligations to society, and media ownership is a public trust
- News media should be truthful, accurate, fair, objective and relevant
- The media should be free, but self-regulated
- The media should follow agreed codes of ethics and professional conduct
- Under some circumstances, government may need to intervene to safeguard the public interest

---

The social responsibility tradition that received its philosophical basis in the American commission of 1947 was actually put into practice with much more determination and effects in countries other than the United States, especially in Western Europe in the two or three decades following the Second World War. The impulse was threefold: the wish to make a new beginning after the war, the general rise of more 'progressive' politics, and the experience of a wave of press concentration that revived fears of private media monopoly.

Picard (1985) coined the term 'democratic-socialist theory of the press' to describe the European 'social welfare' model of mass media in this period. In a number of countries (especially Britain and Sweden), searching public enquiries were undertaken into the state of the media (see, for instance, Royal Commission on the Press, 1977). These looked at press diversity and concentration, and in some cases subsidies were introduced to maintain a range of competing newspapers and especially to support ailing and minority publications. The guiding objective was certainly the health of democracy. The public interest was interpreted as justifying various forms of intervention by the state in what had been a free market, although actual intervention was kept to a minimum. The European Union has to some extent inherited the mantle of the nation state: it has conducted enquiries into the level of media diversity and concentration of ownership and has at least contemplated the need for concerted measures to protect these important democratic values, although no action has been taken. The political will to enforce social responsibility against the claims of the market and the power of the established media is not strong enough.

Professionalism and Media Ethics

*

Another significant response to the perceived failings of the mass newspaper press, especially its commercialism but also its lack of political independence, was the development of professionalism in journalism. This took various forms, including the organization into associations, the formation of **press councils** and the drawing up of principles of good practice in the form of codes of practice and ethics. The historical development of journalism and the institutional forms taken are outside the scope of this discussion, but are nevertheless of great importance for the content and implementation of normative theory. Press councils are typically voluntary, or at least non-governmental, bodies that mediate between the public and the mass media (see Sonninen and Laitila, 1995; Bertrand, 2003). Their main function is to adjudicate on complaints from any party affected by the media, but especially the printed press (broadcasting has its own separate forms). This function implies the need to have some codes of standards or principles to which reference can be made, and in general press councils are instruments of self-regulation for the press that acknowledge a responsibility to the public.

A journalistic code of ethics refers to a set of principles of professional conduct that are adopted and controlled by journalists themselves. The movement towards codifying journalistic practice had already started in the USA before the 1947 Hutchins Committee Report, and one of the first canons of journalism was published by the American Society of Newspaper Editors in 1923. Codes of conduct were being introduced in Europe at around the same time, notably in France, Sweden and Finland, and eventually in nearly all countries (Laitila, 1995).

The phenomenon reflects the general process of professionalization of journalism, but also the wish of the media industry to protect itself from criticism, and especially from the threat of external intervention and reduced autonomy. The study of codes on their own can give a misleading impression of what journalism is really about, but their content provides a good idea of what it was felt that journalism *ought* to be doing. At least they reveal the values that journalists publicly proclaim as guidelines for their work. To that extent they constitute a form of normative theory. Nevertheless, the codes are often little more than collections of disparate and practical prescriptions that do not express any single organizing idea about the nature of society or the overall social purpose of the institution. To discover this requires some interpretation.

The many different codes reflect differences in the conventions and traditions of the country concerned and in the relative influence of different interested parties – publishers, editors, journalists or an external regulatory body. Most codes concentrate on the provision of reliable information and on avoiding distortion, suppression, bias, sensationalism and the invasion of privacy (Harris, 1992). But some codes go further in expressing some view of the larger role of journalism in society.

A comparative study of journalistic codes in 31 European countries carried out by Laitila (1995) shows there to be a very large number of different principles, although she classified them in terms of six types of accountability. These were: to the public; to the sources and referents; to the state; to the employer; for professional integrity; for protection of the status and unity of the profession. Laitila found quite a high level of agreement on certain general principles. Six in particular, all with some degree of relevance to the wider society, were found in nearly all of the 31 codes examined. These are summarized in Box 7.5.

Most frequently found principles in journalistic codes **7.5**

- Truthfulness of information
- Clarity of information
- Defence of the public's rights
- Responsibilities in forming public opinion
- Standards of gathering and presenting information
- Respecting the integrity of the sources

(*Source:* Laitila, 1995)

Certain specific provisions that were common (present in more than 70% of codes) included: the prohibition of discrimination on the basis of race, ethnicity, religion, and so on; respect for privacy; and prohibition of bribes or any other benefits.

Codes are nearly always national in formulation, but there has been some movement to recognize the broader significance of news in world affairs. Under the auspices of Unesco, a set of 'international principles of professional ethics in journalism' was drawn up (Traber and Nordenstreng, 1993) that drew attention to additional matters. These included the idea of a 'right to information' and the need to respect universal values and the diversity of cultures. There was also emphasis on the need for journalism to promote human rights, peace, national liberation, social progress and democracy (see Nordenstreng, 1998).

Although the content of codes of journalism mainly reflects 'western' value systems, some key elements do translate to other cultural contexts. Hafez (2002) has compared European codes of journalism with those in North Africa, the Middle East and Muslim Asia. He concludes that 'there is a broad international consensus that standards of truth and objectivity should be central values of journalism'. He notes that in Muslim countries there is less emphasis on freedom of expression and more on privacy. There is a continuing search for internationally valid standards of journalistic practice (Herrscher, 2002; Perkins, 2002). Although international human rights treaties, such as that of the United Nations and also the European Convention on Human Rights, concentrate on affirming rights to free expression, they also have a potential for outlawing abuses of media freedom when the media advocate discrimination, hatred and violence, as they did in the former Yugoslavia and in Rwanda.

On the face of it, it does look as if there is quite a lot of common ground in what journalists in different countries formally accept as the appropriate standards. In that sense, there is something like a shared body of normative theory to apply to daily practice. There is much less attention to be found in most codes, if at all, to the larger purposes of journalism in society. The predominant emphasis nearly everywhere is on the standards of objective (neutral), independent and informative (factually correct) journalism.

Mancini (1996) has commented on the disjunction between the widely diffused and proclaimed adherence to this liberal theory of journalism and the actual practice in many countries. The 'gap' between theory and practice is found on two main points. One relates to the investigative, critical and advocacy role of the journalist, which gets little notice in any code. Another relates to the supposed independence and neutrality of journalism, when in practice most journalism operates in rather close symbiosis with government, political parties, powerful economic interests and other authorities. These observations lead at least to the conclusion that journalistic codes are inadequate and incomplete as theory, and perhaps also to the view that they should better be regarded as a particular ideology with a particular purpose.

Quite a few media organizations, especially in television broadcasting, maintain internal codes of practice (sometimes published, sometimes not) dealing with the same and other issues to provide guidelines for editors and producers. These are somewhat different from the professional codes because they mainly assist internal control and accountability. Sometimes they are designed to cope with the special circumstances of audiovisual media, with their greater potential for impact. They also play a part in responding to external content regulations that apply not only to journalism, but also to fiction and dramatic representations. In those circumstances, different specific problems arise, although in the end they usually derive from the same basic principles, which include truth, fairness, openness, respect for others, decency and the need to avoid harmful public consequences.

Beyond the area of news journalism, there is extensive evidence of media self-regulation in the form of voluntary codes designed mainly to protect the public from some possible harm or the industry from outside pressure. Advertising is nearly everywhere subject to various self-imposed restrictions and guidelines. Motion pictures have from early on been subject to forms of censorship at the point of production, and continue in many countries to be subject to public supervision or self-regulation. Broadcast television has been even more restricted. These types of codification do little more than reveal a fear of the influence of the media and a fear of public disapproval.

A new source of concern has been opened by the rapid and widespread growth of weblog journalism (blogging) by individuals both within and also outside the walls of existing media. There is a good deal of uncertainty about the line between old and new journalistic forms (Matheson, 2004; Singer, 2005). A particular problem concerns the normative standards that can be expected from the new news blogging activity, which is not subject to any form of accountability. A new code of ethics for blogging has been proposed to supplement the traditional commitments to objectivity with norms of transparency, freedom and interactivity (Kuhn, 2007). However, some institutional structure is usually required to back up codes and most bloggers reject control of this kind. This matter is dealt with again in Chapter 11.

Four Theories of the Press and Beyond

A significant moment in the development of theorizing about the media (again really the newspaper press) occurred through the publication of a small textbook by three American authors (Siebert et al., 1956). This set out to describe the then current alternative 'theories of the press', concerning the relation between press and society. The book has been widely sold, translated, used in education and debated ever since (Nordenstreng, 1997), perhaps because of the striking claim of its title and the gap it fills in the literature on mass media. It has also been subject to extensive review, criticism and effective refutation, especially as one of the 'four theories' – that of Soviet communism – has disappeared (Nerone, 1995). An important aspect of the whole project was the proposition that the 'press always takes on the form and coloration of the social and political structures within which it operates. Especially, it reflects the system of social control' (Siebert et al., 1956: 1).

Aside from Soviet theory, the three other 'theories' presented are labelled 'authoritarian', 'libertarian' and 'social responsibility' (described on p. 171), respectively. What is called 'authoritarian theory' is really a description of two or more centuries of control of the press by various (mostly European) repressive regimes, a situation from which the USA happily escaped by freeing itself from Britain. Authoritarianism is mostly empty of theoretical content, although its fundamental guiding principle is summarized by Dr Samuel Johnson, the eighteenth-century English writer, in the words: 'Every society has a right to preserve public peace and order, and therefore has a good right to prohibit the propagation of opinions which have a dangerous tendency' (quoted in Siebert et al., 1956: 36). According to Johnson, it is not the magistrate who has such a right but society, and he adds that the restraint of opinion may be morally wrong but is 'politically right'. Libertarian theory (in modern terms, free press theory) has been outlined earlier in this chapter.

The book was published at a critical moment in the Cold War when the two sides were pitted in a battle for the hearts and minds of the still uncommitted world and the freedom and unfreedom of the media was a central issue. The USA was actively trying to export its own ideology of liberalism and free enterprise, and its model of press freedom was especially important in this (Blanchard, 1986). At the very least it can be said that the 'four theories' fitted this programme. According to Nerone (1995), the authors 'uncritically accepted the very ideological mystification the media owners propound to explain their own existence. The myth of the free press in the service of society exists because it is in the interests of media owners to perpetuate it'.

As Nerone (1995) shows, libertarian theory identifies press freedom very closely with property rights – the ownership of the means of publication – neglecting the economic barriers to access and the abuse of monopolistic publishing power. Secondly, the liberty of the press is too much framed as a negative concept – freedom *from* government. An alternative, more positive or affirmative version would endow the concept with ideas of purposes and positive benefits, which might need some social intervention. As Glasser (1986: 93) writes:

> From the perspective of a negative concept of freedom, the press is under no obligation to extend its liberty or to accommodate the liberty of others ... From the perspective of an affirmative understanding ... in contrast, freedom and responsibility stand side by side ... [and] an individual's ability to gain the benefits of liberty must be included among the conditions definitive of liberty.

Thirdly, as we have noted, libertarian theory does not seem to apply very well to media other than to the printed press or to many media functions other than journalism. It has much reference to opinion and belief, but much less to say about information and many of the issues of freedom that arise in the newer conditions of an information society, including access, confidentiality, privacy, property rights, and so on, except to suppose that the market will provide. Fourthly, the theory is vague about who has or benefits from the right to freedom. If it is the newspaper proprietor who has the right, what of the rights of editors, journalists and even the public? There are many points of detailed dispute, including the question of where the limits to freedom may be set. At what point can the state legitimately intervene to protect 'essential' interests? Historical example has shown that states usually adopt the authoritarian perspective when they think they need to and can get away with it, following Dr Johnson's notion of a political right (see above). Critics of the 1991 US Patriot Act (Gronbeck, 2004) have alleged that it significantly limits the traditional constitutional freedom of American journalism.

Despite these and other limitations, the *Four Theories* book has promoted not only counterattack and debate, but also many attempts to rewrite or extend the four 'theories' (Nordenstreng, 1997). Several commentators, including McQuail (1983), Altschull (1984) and Hachten (1981), have suggested that we need to have a category for 'development theory' alongside the liberal and Marxist variants. This would recognize the fact that societies undergoing a transition from underdevelopment and colonialism to independence often lack the money, infrastructure, skills and audiences to sustain an extensive free-market media system. A more positive version of media theory is needed which focuses on national and developmental goals as well as the need for autonomy and solidarity with other nations in a similar situation. In the circumstances, it may be legitimate for government to allocate resources selectively and to restrict journalistic freedom in some ways. Social responsibility comes before media rights and freedoms. In practice, many media systems in the developing world still qualify for the 'authoritarian' label. De Smaele (1999) has tested the applicability of the four theories to another case of development, that of the post-Soviet media democratization.

While attempts are still made to improve the original typification of press theories (e.g. Ostini and Fung, 2002), the goal of formulating consistent and coherent 'theories of the press' in this way is bound to break down sooner or later. One major reason is the distinctively western character and historical location of the original model, which several writers have challenged, offering alternatives for non-western cultures (e.g. Gunaratne, 2005; Yin, 2008). Another is because the theories formulated are more about societies than the media. Experience of societal change (e.g. when repressive regimes have collapsed) shows that media rapidly adapt to new circumstances (Gunther and Mugham, 2000). It also partly stems from the complexity and incoherence of media systems and thus the impossibility of matching a press theory with a type of society. The approach has been unable to cope with the diversity of media and changing technology and times. It has little to say about music, the cinema, or most of television, which is concerned with entertainment, fiction, sport and games. In most countries today, the media do not constitute a single system with a distinctive philosophy or rationale. What the media are likely to share, if anything, is an attachment to their own distinctive 'media logic', which has to do with communication rather than content, purpose or effects. This does not invalidate the quest for normative theory, but it needs to follow a different path. A move away from normative models of the media has been made by Hallin and Mancini (2004), who propose instead a new typology of relations between media and politics based on comparative analysis of systems (see Chapter 9, pp. 240–42). However, a more sympathetic assessment by Christians et al. (2009) aims to rescue the general project of normative press theory by relating it more openly to the needs of society and the requirements of democratic politics. The work of journalism in this view is inescapably normative and the implications of this have to be faced up to, especially in efforts to promote the positive role of journalism, in accordance with public expectations and professional ideals.

The Public Service Broadcasting Alternative

As we have noted, libertarian theory has found it difficult to cope with broadcasting in general and with the public broadcasting model in particular, even in its very limited American manifestation. This is because it gives primacy to the needs of society or the collective needs of citizens rather than to individual rights, consumer freedom or market forces. The initial rationale for government intervention in broadcasting, as early as the 1920s, was based primarily on the need to regulate the use of limited transmission wavelengths, in the interests of both the industry and consumers. In America, a system of licensing of private operators was adopted, involving regulation by the FCC not only of technical matters but also of some social and political matters. These included the need to provide (locally) relevant information, balance and fairness on controversial and political issues and, in general, diversity. Significant vestiges of these policies still remain. However, the term 'public broadcasting' in the

United States generally refers to the minority network mainly financed by viewers and listeners voluntarily and choosing to pursue certain cultural goals.

In many other countries, **public service broadcasting** refers to a system that is set up by law and generally financed by public funds (often a compulsory licence paid by households) and given a large degree of editorial and operating independence. The general rationale for such systems is that they should serve the public interest by meeting the important communication needs of society and its citizens, as decided and reviewed by way of the democratic political system.

There has never been a generally accepted 'theory' of public service broadcasting, and different national variants have somewhat different versions of the rationale and logic of operation. The general developments of audiovisual media in recent years and the expansion of the scope of media markets, globally as well as nationally, have created a crisis for institutions that have operated in a largely consensual way for decades. There has been much rethinking of aims and forms (see Blumler, 1992; Hoffmann-Riem, 1996; Atkinson and Raboy, 1997; Bardoel and d'Haenens, 2008; Enli, 2008). A key unresolved issue is the extent to which public service media should be encouraged or permitted to extend their operations online (Trappel, 2008). In practice, they have done so and have helped to provide more public open space in cyberspace and offer an alternative to ubiquitous and growing commercialization. The objections come mainly from commercial rivals claiming unfair competition.

If there is a common theory it consists of certain goals that it is presumed can only be adequately achieved by a public form of ownership and/or regulation. The goals that recur in different systems are listed in Box 7.6. In general, these goals are ways of achieving compliance with expectations of serving a 'public interest', as outlined above (pp. 164–5).

7.6   Main goals of public service broadcasting

- Universality of geographic coverage (reception as well as transmission)
- Diversity in providing for all main tastes, interests and needs as well as matching the full range of opinions and beliefs
- Providing for special minorities
- Having concern for the national culture, language and identity
- Serving the needs of the political system
- Providing balanced and impartial information on issues of conflict
- Having a specific concern for 'quality', as defined in different ways
- Putting public interest before financial objectives

Public broadcasting theory also relates to the kind of organization that would be needed in order to achieve the goals indicated. In particular, the theory involves the view that the free market, left to itself, would fail to satisfy the criteria indicated because it might not be profitable to do so. The theory consequently also holds that an effective system for serving the public interest has to meet certain structural conditions. A public broadcasting system should have:

- a founding charter or mission;
- public financing to some degree;
- independence from government;
- mechanisms of accountability to the society and general public;
- mechanisms of accountability to the audience.

The main weakness of public broadcasting 'theory' lies in two sources of tension. One is between the necessary independence and the necessary accountability for finance received and goals achieved or missed. The other is between achieving the goals set by 'society' in the public interest and meeting the demands of the audience as a set of consumers in the wider media (and audience) market. Without public interest goals there is no rationale for continuing, but without audiences, public service goals cannot really be achieved. In effect, there is a third source of tension. Intense competition in globalized markets and the increasing reliance on the market to provide for all public services have weakened the position of public broadcasting in the face of predatory enemies and reduced its capacity to compete on equal terms. Public broadcasting is also still recognized as one of the few defences against the failings of media markets, as a guarantee of media diversity and also as an instrument of public cultural and information policy. Despite limitations, it seems to deliver promised results (Curran et al., 2009). Gripsrud (2007: 483) concludes that 'in Europe broadcast television has been one of if not *the* most important institution in the national public spheres (outside parliaments) for the last fifty years or so, delivering essential information and a broad cultural repertoire to citizens and also providing central, common forums for entire nation-states'. Whatever the weakness of the theory, the practical consequences are real enough.

Mass Media, Civil Society and the Public Sphere

Especially since the translation into English in 1989 of Jürgen Habermas's book, *The Structural Transformation of the Public Sphere* (1962), there has been much reference to the concept of a *public sphere* in speaking of the role of the mass media in political life. In general, the public sphere refers to a notional 'space' which provides a more or less autonomous and open arena or forum for public debate. Access to the space is free, and freedoms of assembly, association and expression are guaranteed. The 'space' lies between the 'basis' and the 'top' of society, and mediation takes place between the two. The basis can also be considered to be the private sphere of the life of individual citizens, while the political institutions at the centre or top are part of the public life.

A condition of civil society is one of openness and plurality, where there are many more or less autonomous and voluntary agencies between citizen and state that provide security for the individual. There is also adequate democratic political process, provision for justice and protection of human rights. Walzer (1992: 89) writes of an essential 'space of uncoerced human association and also the set of relational networks – formed for the sake of family, faith, interest and ideology – that fill this space'. The idea of the civil society stands opposed to the 'mass society' analysed by Mills (1956) (see pp. 94–5) and it is also at odds with various totalitarian systems. The media, when organized in an appropriate way, especially when open, free and diverse, can be considered one of the most important intermediary institutions of the civil society.

In Habermas's account of the rise of democracy, historically, the first version of the public sphere or space was represented mainly by the eighteenth-century coffee house or debating society, where active participants in political life met, discussed and formed political projects. An important role was to keep a check on government by way of an informed and influential public opinion. The principal means of communication were direct private conversation, public assemblies and small-scale print media. The formation of this public sphere owed much to the conditions of capitalism and economic freedom and individualism, and the first form of public space was described as a 'bourgeois' public sphere, reflecting its class basis. Subsequent developments have included the rise of new corporate interests and the general substitution of mass communication for the interpersonal discussion among elites. Habermas is generally somewhat pessimistic about the consequences for democracy in modern times since the public was more likely to be manipulated by the media than helped to form opinions in a rational way. This view is encapsulated in a quotation given in Box 7.7.

7.7   Habermas on the public sphere: key quotation

With regard to the colonization of the public sphere by market imperatives, what I have in mind here is [that] … [u]nder the pressure of shareholders who thirst for higher revenues, it is the intrusion of the functional imperatives of the market economy into the 'internal logic' of the production and presentation of messages that leads to the covert displacement of one category of communication by another: issues of political discourse become assimilated into and absorbed by the modes and contents of entertainment. Besides personalization, the dramatization of events, the simplification of complex matters, and the vivid polarization of conflicts promote civic privatism and a mood of antipolitics. (Habermas, 2006: 422)

Despite much criticism by other scholars of the idealizing of a bygone and elitist form of political life (e.g. Curran, 1990), the idea of a public sphere has been found to have value under conditions of mature capitalism (see Dahlgren, 1995, 2001).

Positive expectations concerning the role of the media in the public sphere have often been expressed in relation to new media. Dahlgren (2005) names the different ways in which the Internet can help: improving direct relations between government and citizens; giving platforms and channels for advocates and activists; hosting civic forums for debate and discussion; adding a new and more diverse branch of journalism. Rasmussen (2008) describes the differentiation with the political public sphere and, in particular, distinguishes between 'media of focus' that allow elites to present their ideas to the society at large and 'media of diversity' that represent what is going on at all levels of the public sphere. The former are mainly older mass media, the latter are Internet-based. In addition, numerous critiques of the decline of journalistic standards draw on and reinforce traditional standards of informativeness, responsibility and defence of the public interest (e.g. Patterson, 1994; Fallows, 1996; Blumler and Kavanagh, 1999). Some of these expectations are reviewed in the light of evidence in Chapter 19. In this context, we can place the notion of the press as an institution in society, as re-interpreted by Cook (2006). By this he meant that there are fully worked out patterns of behaviour and norms for relating the news media to government, certainly in western democratic society. The underlying rules and norms are often informal but exert great force by custom and application. According to this view, the whole procedure of making laws and governing is intimately dependent on the news media, with one side influencing and constraining the other, with mutual negotiation. The depth and strength of the institution means that the newer news media are more likely to adapt to the institution than vice versa.

In Europe, where there has been a political project over several decades to establish a viable set of cross-national democratic institutions, including a Parliament and Court of Justice, the goal of a supportive public sphere extending across national frontiers has been pursued by theorists and policy-makers (Lauristin, 2007). The key is often seen to lie in the hands of the mass media, as with national public spheres. There are many obstacles, not least the fact that there are no specifically European media to speak of and virtually all media are national in orientation and in the main have pressing objectives that are not met by serving this project (*European Journal of Communication*, 2007). Box 7.8 summarizes the contribution that media are expected to make to the democratic public sphere.

Ways in which media support the public sphere   **7.8**

- Enlarging the space for debate
- Circulating information and ideas as a basis for public opinion
- Interconnecting citizens and governments
- Providing mobilizing information
- Challenging the monopoly of government over politics
- Extending freedom and the diversity of publication

Response to the Discontents of the Public Sphere

Aside from the potential of the new media, one of the solutions to current ills that has been proposed has come from the (American) journalist community itself, under the name of 'civic' or **'public' journalism** (Glasser and Craft, 1997; Schudson, 1998;

Glasser, 1999; Haas and Steiner, 2006). A basic premise of the public journalism movement is that journalism has a *purpose*, that it ought to try to improve the quality of civic life by fostering participation and debate. Schudson describes it as based on a 'trustee model' rather than a market or advocacy model. He writes (1998: 136): 'in the Trustee Model, journalists should provide news according to what they, as a professional group, believe citizens should know'. From this we can see a basis of legitimation in the professionalism of the journalist, rather than in some more all-embracing political theory.

In Schudson's words, 'The journalists are professionals who hold citizenship in trust for us.' According to Glasser and Craft, public journalism calls for a shift from a 'journalism of information' to a 'journalism of conversation'. The public needs not only information but also engagement in the day's news that invites discussion and debate. It should be clear that public journalism parts company with the tradition of neutrality and objective reporting, but it is not a return to politicized or advocacy journalism. The means for achieving the goals of the new 'movement' remain somewhat in dispute since the media themselves are structurally unchanged and it is in doubt whether this version of the professional task can really transcend the constraints of a competitive media market system and counter the fundamental causes of political apathy and cynicism. Assessments of what has actually been achieved by public journalism are not very encouraging. Massey and Haas (2002) survey evaluative research on the topic and conclude that there has been little practical impact, even if the idea remains in favour with some. However, it has also been criticized for undermining the essential autonomy of journalism (McDevitt, 2003) and libertarian theorists are strongly opposed. The public journalism movement does not seem to have found much of a following in Europe. Attention has focused more on the need to strengthen existing public service media and other non-commercial media and also on the potential for harnessing new media to improve democratic participation (van Dijk, 1996; Brants and Siune, 1998).

Alternative Visions

Dissatisfaction with established media has also found expression in the celebration of completely different forms, free from the established systems. There are several strands of alternative theory that are in one way or another disconnected from 'mainstream' press theory as it has been described, but note should be taken of two somewhat different theoretical perspectives on the role of the media, one under the heading of 'emancipatory theory', the other of 'communitarianism'.

Emancipatory media theory

One branch of critical theory came to espouse the promise of the first 'new media', especially because of the potential for small-scale, grass-roots communication in channels independent from dominant mass media. The 'countercultural' ideas of the 1960s, anarchistic and individualistic rather than communistic, supported such a move; and the then new technologies of interactive cable, CCTV, copying, recording and replay seemed to put the potential for communication liberation in the hands of the people and out of the hands of the publishing monopolies (Enzensberger, 1970). The guiding principles uniting the loose coalition of ideas referred to here are participation, interaction, smallness of scale, locatedness, cultural autonomy and variety, emancipation and self-help. The emphasis is often on the *process* of communicating rather than the content, which is for individuals to determine.

These ideas about new and small-scale media typically apply to rich, media-abundant and supposedly democratic societies. Much of the world is not like this. There is still room for theory that addresses the condition of struggle for basic rights. John Downing (2000) coins the term 'rebellious communication' to refer to media that operate in a positive way for political ends in situations of oppression. Such media operate in a positive way in the critical tradition. They include those serving a political cause, ranging from female emancipation to the overthrow of oppressive or bourgeois regimes, and include manifestations of 'alternative' publication such as *samizdat* in the Soviet Union, and grass-roots micro-media in developing countries or in situations of authoritarian rule or foreign occupation. According to Downing (2000: xi), they 'generally serve two overriding purposes: (a) to express opposition vertically from subordinate quarters directly at the power structure and its behavior; (b) to build support, solidarity and networking laterally against policies'. They are often stimulated by and help to generate 'new social movements' and in general have in common that 'they break someone's rules, although rarely all of them in every respect'. Much of the early theorizing surrounding the significance of the Internet has extended essentially the same line of emancipatory thinking.

Communitarian theory and the media

A relatively new development is expressed in terms of 'communitarianism', which re-emphasizes the social ties connecting people, in contrast to modern libertarian individualism (MacIntyre, 1981; Sandel, 1982; Rorty, 1989; Taylor, 1989). It stresses duties owed to society as well as rights to be claimed. In respect of media, relations between media and audience take on a more mutual character, especially where they share a social identity and a place (an actual community). One exponent of communitarian thinking stresses the ethical imperative of the media to engage in dialogue with the public it serves (Christians, 1993). In some respects the call is to return to a more organic social form, in which the press plays an integrative, expressive and articulating role. Not self-interest but partnership is seen as the way forward.

'In the communitarian model', according to Nerone (1995: 70–1):

> the goal of reporting is not intelligence but civic transformation. The press has bigger fish to fry than merely improving technology and streamlining performance ... The question is its vocational norm ... In a communitarian world-view, the news media should seek to engender a like-minded philosophy among the public. A revitalized citizenship shaped by community norms becomes the press's aim. News would be an agent of community formation.

Communitarian theory of the press is in some respects quite radical. In some other respects it is reactionary and anti-libertarian, although its spirit is voluntaristic. The impression of conservatism stems from its strong emphasis on an ethical imperative and the need to forge active ties with others. It is probably fair to say that communitarianism is more at home in the American radical tradition than in Europe or in the different forms of communal society in Asia and Africa. Like public journalism, it does not seem to have travelled very far from its context of origin.

Normative Media Theory: Four Models

It is impossible to find any agreed and economical framework for containing the many varieties of theory described in this chapter, but we can propose four different normative theory models that cover the terrain. The term 'model' is rather loosely used here to refer to an interrelated set of typical features (both ideas and arrangements) of a media system that has a single underlying normative principle. They inevitably overlap, but they each have their own internal logic. They can be summarized as follows:

- *A liberal-pluralist or market model.* This is based on the original free press (libertarian) theory as presented above, which identifies press freedom with the freedom to own and operate the means of publication without permission or interference from the state. It emphasizes the individual and his or her needs, and defines the public interest as what interests the public. The public sphere will be served by the operation of a 'free marketplace of ideas'. Accountability to society and to other individuals is also achieved by way of the media market and some forms of minimal self-regulation, with a minimal role for the state.
- *A social responsibility or public interest model.* Here, the right to freedom of publication is accompanied by obligations to the wider society that go beyond self-interest. A 'positive' notion of freedom, involving some social purpose, is envisaged. Responsible media will maintain high standards by self-regulation but government intervention is not excluded. Mechanisms of accountability to society and public will be in place. Public service broadcasting can be located within this model.
- *A professional model.* The choice of roles for society and the guardianship of standards belong in the model to the 'press' itself and to the journalistic profession. They are the inheritors of the fruits of struggles for freedom and democracy in past times and are still the best guarantors of the interest of the public since their primary concern is serving the public's need for information and comment and providing the platforms for expression of diverse views. The institutional and professional autonomy of journalism is also the best guarantee of an adequate watch being kept on those in power.
- *An alternative media model.* This represents a range of non-mainstream media, with different aims and origins. Nevertheless there are some shared values, especially the emphasis on smallness of scale and grass-roots organization, participation and community, shared goals between producers and audiences, plus opposition (in some cases) to the powers of state and industry. The model rejects a universal rationality as well as ideals of bureaucratic-professional competence and efficiency. It emphasizes the rights of subcultures with their particularistic values and promotes intersubjective understanding and a real sense of community.

Conclusion

The purpose of this chapter has been to outline the main theoretical ideas that have been expressed relating to what the media *ought* to do in society, rather than about what they actually do. They are called normative theories because they state certain norms and standards (criteria of what is good or bad) and apply these to the actions of the media, and especially to defining various *expectations* concerning the structure, conduct and performance of the media. Such expectations are usually expressed already by those who have dealings with the media and by public opinion. Theories are ways of framing these ideas more clearly.

Of its nature, normative theory is subjective and there is only limited agreement between the different perspectives outlined. Agreement is most likely on certain things the media ought not to be doing, such as spreading misinformation or inciting crime and violence. Normative theory includes perspectives from inside as well as outside the media, although mainly the latter. The media generally do not like to be told what they ought to be doing and are not very sympathetic to this kind of theory.

Further Reading

Christians, C.G., Glasser, T.L., McQuail, D., Nordenstreng, K. and White, R.A. (2009) *Normative Theories of the Media: Journalism in Democratic Societies.* Urbana, IL: University of Illinois Press.
The authors seek to explicate the role of journalism in democratic societies by exploring the philosophical underpinnings and political realities that shape a normative approach, one concerned with what journalism *ought* to be doing in and for society. The starting point is a revised view of the classic work *Four Theories of the Press*, now long dated.

Habermas, J. (2006) 'Political communication in media society', *Communication Theory*, 16 (4): 411–26.
A concise and up-to-date statement of the core ideas of theory of the public sphere as they relate to mass communication, by the principal author of such ideas.

Hallin, D.C. and Mancini, P. (2004) *Comparing Media Systems: Three Models of Media and Politics.* Cambridge: Cambridge University Press.
The authors take an alternative approach to normative theory of media–society linkages by examining in detail the arrangements made in practice between political actors and the media for supporting democratic politics, in a number of western democracies. This leads to three basic models or types, to which the countries examined can be assigned. This work has been much discussed and tested in research.

Nerone, J.C. (ed.) (1995) *Last Rights: Revisiting Four Theories of the Press.* Urbana, IL: University of Illinois Press.

Several leading authors critically examine this standard introduction to normative theory, from varied perspectives, explaining its origins and context, but also exposing weaknesses and gaps. Basic principles of normative theory for today are also put forward.

Online Readings

Bardoel, J. and d'Haenens, L. (2008) 'Re-inventing public service broadcasting: promises and problems', *Media, Culture and Society*, 30 (3): 295–317.

Christians, C. (2004) 'Ethical and normative perspectives', in J.D.H. Downing, D. McQuail, P. Schlesinger and E. Wartella (eds), *The Sage Handbook of Media Studies*, pp. 19–40. Thousand Oaks, CA: Sage.

Gunaratne, S.A. (2002) 'Freedom of the press: a world system perspective', *Gazette*, 64 (4): 342–69.

Laitila, T. (1995) 'Journalistic codes of ethics in Europe', *Journal of Communication*, 10 (4): 513–26.

Part 3
Structures

8

Media Structure and Performance: Principles and Accountability

This chapter is about the standards and criteria of quality that are applied to the operation of the mass media, for the most part from the point of view of the outside society and the 'public interest' as outlined above. The normative theory described in the last chapter has developed over time and in different places and its application depends on time, place and circumstances. There is no unique set of criteria for serving the public interest. However, the same criteria are sometimes applied by the public as audience and by professionals within the media institution itself. Market criteria, especially those to do with value for money, consumer choice and profitability, often overlap with social-normative criteria, for instance the audience for news typically values alternative sources and reliable, unbiased information.

Despite the diversity of normative theory, there are a small number of basic values that are usually highly regarded where public communication is concerned, and these values provide the framework for the presentation in the first part of the chapter. These can be summarized under the following headings: *freedom, equality, diversity, truth and information quality* and *social order and solidarity*.

The main aim here is to say briefly why each of these values is important and what each means in terms of what the media typically do. We need to be able to define the values in terms of more or less concrete or observable 'outputs' if we are to assess media quality, engage in debate on the issues outlined in Chapter 7 (see pp. 166–8), or hold media accountable for their actions. The task is complicated by the fact that the values apply at different levels of media operation. For present purposes, we can distinguish between three levels: structure, conduct and performance. *Structure* refers to all matters relating to the media system, including its form of organization and finance, ownership, form of regulation, infrastructure, distribution facilities, and so on. *Conduct* refers to the manner of operation at the organizational level, including the methods of selecting and producing content, editorial decision-making, market policy, relations established with other agencies, procedures for accountability, and so on. *Performance* essentially refers to content: to what is actually transmitted to an audience. The main values outlined have a different reference at each level, and for the most part we concentrate on structure and performance rather than conduct.

Media Freedom as a Principle

Freedom has an obvious claim to be considered as the basic principle of any theory of public communication, from which other benefits should flow. As we have seen, the pursuit of freedom of expression and publication has been the central theme in the history of the press and is intimately connected with democracy. Nevertheless, there are different versions and aspects of freedom, and the word does not speak for itself, as we have seen. Freedom is a condition, rather than a criterion, of performance, and thus applies primarily to media structure. Once a right to freedom exists, we cannot easily distinguish between one freely chosen use of freedom of expression and another, within limits set by law, although we evaluate these uses according to other values.

We have to make a distinction between freedom of the media (or the press, as it is sometimes called) and freedom of expression, although sometimes the same thing is meant. Freedom of expression is a much wider right. It refers to the substance or content of what is communicated (opinion, ideas, information, art, etc.) while the press refers to one main 'container', vehicle or means for enabling publication. Zeno-Zencovich (2008) compares this to the difference between wine (the contents) and the bottle. The important point is that in law and regulation, the safeguarding of freedom tends to have been transferred from the substance to the means. According to Zeno-Zencovich (2008: 7), 'the sense of freedom of expression as a political freedom enjoyed by individuals and the groups in which they associate has been lost and has become attached to persons who can at best be considered marginal to the diffusion of thought'. This is an implicit attack on the right of owners of media to claim all rights of freedom on the grounds of possession of the means of publication.

The various potential benefits to individuals and society that freedom can provide, in addition to the intrinsic value of the right to free expression, help to indicate other relevant criteria of assessment that can be applied. These benefits are outlined in Box 8.1.

Main public benefits of media freedom **8.1**

- Systematic and independent public scrutiny of those in power and an adequate supply of reliable information about their activities (this refers to the 'watchdog' or critical role of the press)
- Stimulation of an active and informed democratic system and social life
- Opportunities to express ideas, beliefs and views about the world
- Continued renewal and change of culture and society
- Increase in the amount and variety of freedom available

Freedom at the level of structure

Freedom of communication has a dual aspect: offering a wide range of voices and responding to a wide-ranging demand or need. For the benefits of freedom of expression and publication to be realized, certain conditions are called for. There must be access to channels of expression and also opportunities to receive diverse kinds of information. The main structural conditions for effective media freedom are as follows:

- absence of censorship, licensing or other controls by government so that there is an unhindered right to publish and disseminate news and opinions and no obligation to publish what one does not wish to;
- the equal right and possibility for citizens to have access to channels of expression and publication as well as access as receivers ('right to communicate');
- real independence from excessive control and interference by owners and outside political or economic interests;
- competitiveness of the system, with limits to media concentration and cross-ownership;
- freedom for news media to obtain information from relevant sources.

These conditions of structure leave many issues unresolved. There are several potential conflicts and inconsistencies embedded in these requirements. First, freedom of public communication can never be absolute but has to recognize limits sometimes set by the private interests of others or by the higher collective good of a society. In practice, a 'higher good' is usually defined by the state or other power holders, especially in time of war or crisis. Secondly, there is a potential conflict of interest between owners or controllers of media channels and those who might want access to the channels but have no power (or legal right) to secure it (either as senders or as receivers). Thirdly, the conditions as stated place control of freedom in the hands of those who own the media of publication and do not recognize the rights to freedom of publication of those who work in the media (e.g. journalists, producers, etc.). Fourthly, there may be an imbalance between what communicators want to say and what others want to hear: the freedom of one to send may not coincide with the freedom of another to choose. Finally, it may be necessary for government or public power to intervene in the media structure to secure some freedoms that are not, in practice, delivered by the unfettered system (for instance, by setting up public broadcasting or regulating ownership). A number of the problems indicated are dealt with by adopting rules of conduct and conventions that are not matters of obligation or right.

There have been numerous attempts to measure the degree of press freedom in national media systems, usually for the ostensible purpose of promoting democracy and protecting the interests of journalists. Becker et al. (2007) provide an overview and assessment of the main indicators that are used as well as of typical results. The earliest measurement was made by the US Freedom House and it defined freedom as 'the legal environment of the media, political processes that influence reporting and economic factors that affect access to information'. Ratings are typically based on both legal protection for media independence and also on the application of law and the actual experience of journalists. The two often do not match. Such measurements are mainly of use in showing trends over time and in providing comparisons between actual media systems.

Freedom at the level of performance

As noted, it is not easy to assess the freedom of the content of media since freedom of communication can be used in many different ways, or even misused, as long as it does not actually do harm. Nevertheless, the expected benefits of freedom of publication, as summarized in Box 8.1, do give some indication of additional criteria and expectations. For instance, in respect of news and information (journalism), the media are expected to make use of their freedom to follow an active and critical editorial policy and to provide reliable and relevant information. Free media should not be unduly conformist and should be marked by diversity of opinion and information. They should carry out an investigative and watchdog role on behalf of the public (see Waisbord, 2000). This does not prevent them taking sides or engaging in advocacy, but they should not be simply instruments of propaganda. A free media system is characterized by

FREEDOM PRINCIPLE

Structural conditions:

INDEPENDENCE OF
CHANNELS

ACCESS TO
CHANNELS

DIVERSITY OF
CONTENTS

Leading to performance values of:

RELIABILITY; CRITICAL STANCE;
ORIGINALITY

CHOICE; CHANGE;
RELEVANCE

Figure 8.1   Criteria of freedom in media structure and performance

innovation and independence. Similar criteria apply in the area of culture and entertainment. Conditions of freedom should lead to originality, creativity and great diversity. Free media will be prepared, when necessary, to offend the powerful, express
controversial views and deviate from convention and from the commonplace. The
more that the qualities of content mentioned are missing, the more we may suspect
that the structural conditions of media freedom are not being met or that the media
are not making use of their freedom as envisaged by the original proponents of liberty
of the press.

The main elements discussed can now be expressed as logically related components, as summarized in Figure 8.1. Some of the elements appear again in respect of
other values, especially that of diversity.

Media Equality as a Principle

The principle of equality is valued in democratic societies, although it has to be translated into more specific meanings when it is applied to the mass media. As a principle, it
underlies several of the normative expectations that have already been referred to.

Equality at the level of structure

In relation to communication and political power, equality at the level of structure
should lead to different or opposed interests in society having more or less the same
mass media access opportunities to send and receive. In practice, this is most unlikely
to be realized, although steps may be taken by public policy to put right some of the
inequalities. The institution of public broadcasting is one means in this direction. Public
policy can also limit media monopoly and provide some support for competing media.
Equality supports policies of universal provision in broadcasting and telecommunication and of sharing out the costs of basic services. Equality also implies that the normal
principles of the free market should operate freely, fairly and transparently.

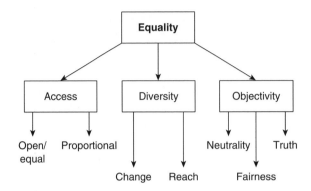

Figure 8.2   Equality as a media performance principle, together with related concepts

Equality at the level of performance

Equality requires that no special favour be given by the media to power holders and that access to media should be given to contenders for office and, in general, to oppositional or deviant opinions, perspectives or claims as well as established positions. In relation to business clients of the media, equality requires that all legitimate advertisers be treated on the same basis (the same rates and conditions). Equality will support the expectation of fair access, on equivalent terms, for alternative voices (the diversity principle in another form) that meet relevant criteria. In short, equality calls for an absence of discrimination or bias in the amount and kind of access available to senders or receivers, as far as is practicable. Considerations of equality take us into the area of objectivity, discussed in more detail below (pp. 200–203), as well as into the topic of diversity (to follow). The real chances of media equality are likely to depend on the level of social and economic development of a society and the capacity of its media system. There will have to be enough space on different and mutually independent channels for any degree of equality to be realized in practice. Even so, neither high economic welfare nor an extensive system is a sufficient condition of equality. The United States, for instance, meets both conditions, but does not seem to have communication equality of actual media use or of outcomes in an equally informed society (Entman, 2005; Curran et al., 2009). The reason may lie in the fact that the society values freedom of opportunity over both actual economic and social equality. The main sub-principles related to the value of equality can be expressed as in Figure 8.2.

Media Diversity as a Principle

The principle of diversity (also identified as a major benefit of freedom and linked with the concepts of access and equality) is especially important because it underpins the normal processes of progressive change in society. This includes the periodic replacement of ruling elites, the circulation of power and office, and the countervailing power of different interests which pluralistic forms of democracy are supposed to deliver. Diversity stands very close to freedom as a key concept in any discussion of media theory (Glasser, 1984). It presupposes, most generally, that the more, and more different, channels of public communication there are, carrying the maximum variety of (changing) content to the greatest variety of audiences, the better. Put like this, diversity seems rather empty of any value direction or prescription about *what* should actually be communicated. Indeed, this is a correct interpretation since diversity, like freedom, is neutral as to content. It is a valuation of variety, choice and change in themselves. Even so, it is up to society to decide which values should be upheld by a media system, e.g. ethnicity, political or religious, etc. Diversity in what the media have to offer is also clearly a direct benefit to audiences and can be a reflection of a wide range of access to channels of publication. Despite the general valuation of diversity, there can be too much of a good thing, leading to a fragmented and divided society, as Sunstein (2001, 2006) warns us, with reference to the Internet.

The main expected benefits of diversity for society are outlined in Box 8.2.

Main public benefits expected from diversity 8.2

- Opening the way for social and cultural change, especially where it takes the form of giving access to new, powerless or marginal voices
- Providing a check on the misuse of freedom (for instance, where the free market leads to concentration of ownership)
- Enabling minorities to maintain their separate existence in a larger society
- Limiting social conflicts by increasing the chances of understanding between potentially opposed groups and interests
- Adding generally to the richness and variety of cultural and social life
- Maximizing the benefits of the 'free marketplace of ideas'

Diversity at the level of structure

The main structural requirements for the diversity of a media system are much the same as for equality. There should be many (or sufficiently) different and independent media firms or producers to match the requirements of the society. In accounting for diversity of *provision*, the extent to which real alternatives are on offer can be registered according to several alternative yardsticks. The media system should consist of different types of media (such as press, radio or television). It should reflect geographical diversity, with media for national, regional or local populations. Media should also reflect the structure of the society, where relevant according to language, ethnic or cultural identity, politics, religion or belief. There is evidence, however, that enlarging the number of channels and choices (as happened in Europe after the deregulation of television) does not necessarily enlarge the diversity of content, rather there is simply much more of the same mixture (van der Wurf, 2004).

Two basic variants of the 'diversity as equal treatment' principle have been identified. According to one version, a literal equality should be on offer: everyone receives the same level of provision and has the same chances for access as the senders. This applies, for instance, where contending parties receive equal time in an election, or in those countries (such as Canada, Switzerland or Belgium) where separate language groups receive an equivalent separate media service. An alternative and more usual version means only a 'fair', or appropriate, allocation of access and treatment. Fairness is generally assessed according to the principle of proportional representation. Media provision thus should proportionately reflect the actual distribution of whatever is relevant (social groups, political beliefs, etc.) in the society, or reflect the varying distribution of audience demand or interest. Another basic variable of structure is whether diversity is achieved by having separate channels (e.g. newspaper titles) for different interests (so-called external diversity) or having different voices represented within the same channel (internal diversity).

The inadequacy of formal structural provision in fully commercial media system has been demonstrated by Glasser et al. (2008). He contrasts the diversity supported by liberal pluralism (essentially the market), handed down from above and reflecting an existing unequal distribution of power and social position, with the kind that is really needed in a multicultural society. This calls for media to be effectively in the hands of the more powerless and disadvantaged, with equalization of chances to communicate on their own behalf.

Diversity at the level of performance

The differentiation of media provision (content) should approximately correspond to the differences at source or to those at the receiving end. Essentially, the content provided by the media system should match overall the information, communication and cultural needs of the society. In fact, diversity of performance is most likely to be assessed in terms of the output of particular media organizations – newspaper titles, television stations, and so on. The question of diversity of media content can be assessed according to numerous dimensions. These include: genre, taste, style or format in culture and entertainment; news and informational topics covered; political viewpoints, and so on. The possibilities for assessment are unlimited, but most questions of diversity turn on one or more of the following criteria: reflection of social and cultural differences; equal access to all voices; and a wide choice for consumers. The main criteria for measuring diversity are summarized in Box 8.3.

> ## Main requirements of the diversity norm for structure and performance **8.3**
>
> - Media should reflect in their structure and content the various social, economic and cultural realities of the societies (and communities) in which they operate, in a more or less proportional way
> - Media should offer more or less equal chances of access to the voices of various social and cultural minorities that make up the society
> - Media should serve as a platform for different interests and points of view in a society or community
> - Media should offer relevant choices of content at one point in time and also variety over time of a kind that corresponds to the needs and interests of their audiences

As with freedom of expression, complete diversity is an unattainable ideal. There are also certain inconsistencies and problems in these normative requirements. The degree of diversity that is possible is limited by media channel capacity and by editorial selections that have to be made. The more that media are *proportionally* reflective of society, the more likely it is that small, or even quite large, minorities will be effectively excluded from mass media since a small proportion of access will be divided between many claimants, with unequal social and economic resources. Similarly, catering properly for dominant groups and for consistent expectations and tastes in mass media limits the chance to offer a very wide choice or much change. However, the full range of many different minority media in a society can help to compensate for the limitations of 'traditional' mass media. Thus, diversity of structure can compensate for lack of diversity in dominant channels. It looks as if the Internet has contributed to diversity in this respect, although the alleged 'ghettoization of minorities' is not an ideal solution. As a footnote to this discussion, it is important to keep in mind that diversity in itself is not necessarily of value, unless it relates to some criterion or dimension that is significant. Karppingen (2007) criticizes 'naïve pluralism' in media politics diversity'. Too much diversity can even be dysfunctional for the public sphere, when it leads to social fragmentation.

Truth and Information Quality

The historic claims for freedom of communication were strongly related to the value of *truth* in one or other of its senses. Most important in the early days of public communication (by print) were: religious truth as guarded by the established church; personal religious truth according to the individual conscience; scientific truth; legal truth; and historical truth (social and economic reality), especially as it affected government and business. Although the meaning of truth and its value vary according to the context and topic mentioned, there was and remains a broadly shared interest (sometimes a necessity) in having access to 'knowledge' (information) that can be depended on (reliability) from trusted sources, that matches the reality of experience, and that is relevant and useful in various applications. While the expectation that media should provide information of acceptable quality has a more practical than philosophical or normative foundation, it is hardly less important in modern thinking about media standards than the principles of freedom, equality or diversity.

The benefits stemming from a supply of trustworthy knowledge hardly need stating, especially when one considers what the opposite would be: lies, misinformation, propaganda, slander, superstition or ignorance. But it is worth noting the main arguments for having media structures that will help to produce high information quality (and truth), as in Box 8.4.

8.4 The benefits of information quality (media truth)

- Contributing to an informed society and a skilled workforce
- Providing the basis for democratic decision-making (an informed and critical electorate)
- Guarding against propaganda and irrational appeals
- Warning against risks
- Meeting everyday needs of the public for information

The objectivity concept

The most central concept in media theory relating to information quality has probably been that of objectivity, especially as applied to news information. Objectivity is a particular form of media *practice* (as described below) and also a particular attitude to the task of information collection, processing and dissemination. It should not be confused with the broader notion of truth, although it is one version of it. One main feature is the adoption of a position of detachment and neutrality towards the object of reporting. Secondly, there is an effort to avoid partisanship: not taking sides in matters of dispute or showing bias. Thirdly, objectivity requires strict attachment to accuracy and other truth criteria (such as relevance and completeness). It also presumes a lack of ulterior motive or service to a third party. The process of observing and reporting should thus not be contaminated by subjectivity, nor should it interfere with the reality being reported on. In some respects it has an affinity, in theory at least, with the ideal of rational, 'undistorted' communication advocated by Habermas (1962/1989).

This version of an ideal standard of reporting practice has become the dominant ideal for the role of the professional journalist (Weaver and Wilhoit, 1986). It has links with the principle of *freedom* since independence is a necessary condition of detachment and truthfulness. Under some conditions (such as political oppression, crisis, war and police action), the freedom to report can only be obtained in return for a guarantee of objectivity. On the other hand, freedom also includes the right to be biased or partisan.

The link with *equality* is also strong: objectivity requires a fair and non-discriminatory attitude to sources and to objects of news reporting, all of which should be treated on equal terms. Additionally, different points of view on matters where the facts are in dispute should be treated as of equal standing and relevance, other things being equal.

In the relationships that develop in the operating environments of media, objectivity may be crucial. Agencies of the state and advocates of various interests are able to speak directly to their chosen audiences by way of the media, without undue distortion or intervention by the gatekeepers and without compromising the independence of channels. Because of the established conventions of objectivity, media channels can distance their editorial content from the advertising matter that they carry, and advertisers can do likewise in respect of editorial content. Editorial opinion can also be distinguished from news.

In general, media audiences appear to understand the principle of objective performance well enough, and its practice helps to increase public credence and trust both in the information and also in the opinions which the media offer. The media themselves find that objectivity gives their own news product a higher and wider market value. Finally, because the objectivity standard has such a wide currency, it is often invoked in claims and settlements concerning bias or unequal treatment. Most modern news media set a lot of store by their claim to objectivity in its several meanings. Policies for broadcasting in many countries impose, by various means, a requirement of objectivity on their public broadcasting systems, sometimes as a condition of their independence from government.

A framework for objectivity research and theory

One version of its components has been set out by Westerstahl (1983) in the context of research into the degree of objectivity shown by the Swedish broadcasting system. This version (Figure 8.3) recognizes that objectivity has to deal with *values* as well as with facts and that facts also have evaluative implications.

In this scheme 'factuality' refers, first, to a form of reporting which deals in events and statements that can be checked against sources and are presented free from comment, or at least clearly separated from any comment. Factuality involves several other 'truth criteria': completeness of an account, accuracy, and an intention not to mislead or suppress what is relevant (good faith). The second main aspect of factuality is 'relevance'. This is more difficult both to define and to achieve in an objective way. It relates to the process of *selection* rather than to the form of presentation and requires that selection takes place according to clear and coherent principles of what is significant for the intended receiver and/or the society (Nordenstreng, 1974). In general, what affects most people most immediately and most strongly is likely to be considered most relevant (though there may be a gap between what the public perceives as of interest and what experts say is significant).

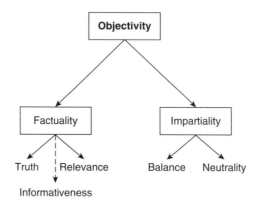

Figure 8.3   Component criteria of objectivity (Westerstahl, 1983)

According to Westerstahl's scheme, impartiality presupposes a 'neutral attitude' and has to be achieved through a combination of balance (equal or proportional time/space/emphasis) as between opposing interpretations, points of view or versions of events, and neutrality in presentation.

The scheme in Figure 8.3 has been given an extra element, that of 'informativeness', which is important to the fuller meaning of objectivity. The reference is to qualities of informational content which are likely to improve the chances of actually getting information across to an audience: being noticed, understood, remembered, and so on. This is the pragmatic side of information, which is often undervalued or neglected in normative theory but is essential to the fuller notion of good informational performance.

The main information quality requirements are as follows:

- Mass media should provide a comprehensive supply of relevant news and background information about events in the society and the world around.
- Information should be objective in the sense of being factual in form, accurate, honest, sufficiently complete and true to reality, and reliable in the sense of being checkable and separating fact from opinion.
- Information should be balanced and fair (impartial), reporting alternative perspectives and interpretations in a non-sensational, unbiased way, as far as possible.

Limits of objectivity

Several potential difficulties are embedded in these norms, especially because of uncertainty about what constitutes an adequate or relevant supply of information and about the very nature of 'objectivity' (Hemánus, 1976; Westerstahl, 1983; Hackett, 1984; Ryan, 2001). It has often been argued that following the rules of objectivity leads to new and less obvious forms of bias (see Chapter 14). It can give advantages to well-organized and well-financed or otherwise dominant parties to matters of dispute, regardless of the intrinsic value of the position taken. Few would argue for impartiality towards evil deeds, but the concept does not help to find any line to draw. There are also possible inconsistencies with claims of media freedom (which does not distinguish between 'true' and 'false' expression) and of diversity (which emphasizes the multiplicity and inconsistency of reality). We can also note that such criteria are more appropriate to the *totality* of media information in a society, rather than to any particular channel or sector. Not all media are equally expected by their own audiences to provide full and objective information on 'serious' topics.

Objectivity (and related standards of factuality and so on) is not unanimously regarded as either necessary, virtuous or even possible to achieve. But there is a good deal of force in Lichtenberg's (1991: 230) argument that 'in so far as we aim to understand the world we cannot get along without assuming both the possibility and value of objectivity'. Ryan (2001) reviewed and responded to critics of objectivity, partly on the basis of a definition of objectivity that recognizes conflicts of fact and opinion and problems of verification and interpretation. Later (Ryan, 2006) he suggested that criticism of the objective approach had so weakened its appeal to journalists that it contributed to the failure of US news media coverage of the Iraq war, by opening the door to pro-war news and editorializing. The problems associated with objectivity, and especially the impossibility of avoiding all bias in news, are discussed later in relation to the concept of 'news' (pp. 355–8).

The debate about appropriate standards of information has given rise to a divide between those who press for maximum information quality (the 'full news standard') and those who argue in favour of a more realistic minimum standard (the 'burglar alarm' version, essentially headlines and short items). This last would alert citizens only to essential matters and relevant issues and dangers of the moment. An upholder of the full news standard, Bennett (2003) has criticized the minimal view on the grounds that it is an alarm that often does not ring. An alternative view is that the amount and weight of news is less important than its diversity, giving citizens a real chance of understanding events and evaluating alternative courses of action (Porto, 2007).

Social Order and Solidarity

The normative criteria which belong under this heading are those which relate to the integration and harmony of society, as viewed from different (even opposed) perspectives. On the one hand, there is a rather consistent tendency on the part of those in authority to look to public communication media for at least tacit support in the task of maintaining order. On the other hand, pluralistic societies cannot be conceived as having one single dominant order which has to be maintained, and mass media have mixed and divided responsibilities, especially with reference to alternative social groups and subcultures and to the expression of the conflicts and inequalities of most societies. Problems also arise over how far the media can go in their support for opposition or potential subversion (as it may seem from 'the top'). The relevant principles concerning the media are mixed and not mutually compatible but can be expressed in something like the following way.

Perspective

	From 'above'	From 'below'
Social	Control/compliances	Solidarity/attachment
Cultural	Conformity/hierarchy	Autonomy/identity

Domain

Figure 8.4   Ideas concerning mass media and order depend on whose order and what kind of order is involved

The concept of order is used here in a rather elastic way, to apply to symbolic (cultural) systems such as religion, art and customs, as well as to forms of social order (community, society and established structures of relations). This broad distinction is also cut across by a distinction of perspective – from 'above' and 'below', as it were. This distinction is essentially that between established authority of society on the one hand, and individuals and minority groups on the other. It also corresponds approximately to the distinction between order in the sense of control and order in the sense of solidarity and cohesion – the one 'imposed', the other voluntary and self-chosen. These ideas about order can be arranged as shown in Figure 8.4.

Any complex and viable social system will exhibit all the sub-aspects of order shown here. There will be mechanisms of social control as well as voluntary attachments, often by way of membership of component groups in society. There will be a sharing of common meanings and definitions of experience as well as much divergence of identity and actual experience. Shared culture and solidaristic experience tend to be mutually reinforcing. The relationship between mass communication and these different concepts has been handled in theories of media and society in divergent, though not logically inconsistent, ways (see Chapter 4). Functionalist theory attributes to mass media a latent purpose of securing the continuity and integration of a social order (Wright, 1960) by promoting co-operation and a consensus of social and cultural values.

Critical theory has usually interpreted mass media as agents of a dominant, controlling class of power holders who seek to impose their own definitions of situations and their values and to marginalize or delegitimize opposition. The media are often seen as serving conflicting goals and interests and as offering alternative versions of an actual or desirable social order. The question '*Whose* order?' has first to be settled. Relevant normative theory cannot be concerned only with the disruption of order (such as with conflict, crime or deviance), but should also relate to the failings of the established order as perceived by more marginal, or minority, social and cultural groups.

Expectations and norms relating to order

From the perspective of social control, the relevant norms are often applied to condemn positive portrayals of violence, disorder and deviance or to support privileged access and positive symbolic support for established 'order' institutions and authorities – the law, church, school, police, military, and so on. The second subprinciple (that of solidarity) involves the recognition that society is composed of many subgroups, different bases of identity and different interests. From this perspective, a viable normative expectation from mass media is that they should sympathetically recognize the alternatives and provide access and symbolic support for relevant minority groups and views. In general, this (normative) theoretical position will encompass an outward-looking and empathic orientation to social groups and situations that are marginal, distant or deviant from the point of view of a dominant national society.

To summarize a very mixed set of normative perspectives concerning social order:

- In respect of the relevant public which they serve (at national or local level, or as defined by group and interest), the media should provide channels of intercommunication and support.
- The media may contribute to social integration by paying concerned attention to socially disadvantaged or injured individuals and groups.
- The media should not undermine the forces of law and order by encouraging or symbolically rewarding crime or social disorder.
- In matters of national security (such as war, threat of war, foreign subversion or terrorism), the freedom of action of media may be limited by considerations of national interest.
- On questions of morals, decency and taste (especially in matters of the portrayal of sex and violence and the use of bad language), the media should to some degree observe the reigning norms of what is broadly publicly acceptable and avoid causing grave public offence.

Cultural Order

The domain of the 'cultural' is not easy to keep separate from that of the 'social' or to define, but here it mainly refers to symbolic content transmitted. Normative media theory has typically been concerned either with matters of cultural 'quality' (of media content) or with 'authenticity' in respect of real-life experience. The subdivision of the sphere of the cultural for present purposes of representation in a normative framework follows a similar line to that applied in the social domain: between a 'dominant', official or established culture and a set of possible alternatives or subcultures. In practice, the former implies a hierarchical view of culture, according to which cultural values and artefacts which have been 'certified' by established cultural institutions will be relatively privileged compared with 'alternative' cultural values and forms.

Cultural quality norms

Normative theory, often expressed in wider cultural policies, can support different kinds of cultural quality in the mass media. First, it often protects the 'official' cultural heritage of a nation or society, especially in education and science, art and literature. Secondly, it supports distinctive regional, local or minority group variants of cultural expression, on grounds of authenticity, identity and for political reasons. Thirdly, some theory (see p. 118) recognizes the equal rights of all cultural expressions and tastes, including 'popular culture'.

Although there have been many heated discussions about the possible cultural responsibilities of mass media, there is little agreement on what to do about them, and less action. Principles of cultural quality are likely to be advanced as desirable but are rarely enforceable. There is rarely enough consensus on what criteria of cultural quality mean for action to be taken. Even so, we can identify the most commonly invoked principles as follows:

- Media content should reflect and express the language and contemporary culture (artefacts and way of life) of the people which the media serve (nationally, regionally and locally); it should be relevant to current and typical social experience.
- Some priority should be given to the educational role of the media and to the expression and continuity of the best in the cultural heritage of a country.
- Media should encourage cultural creativity and originality and the production of work of high quality (according to aesthetic, moral, intellectual and occupational criteria).
- Cultural provision should be diverse, reflecting demand, including demand for 'popular culture' and entertainment.

The Meaning of Accountability

It is not easy to define 'accountability' in its full sense (see McQuail, 2003a). Feintuck (1999: 120) offers a legal definition in two parts. One of these is 'a requirement to give an account of one's actions, either directly to the public, or via public authorities'. Secondly, it means 'being liable to sanction if found in breach of some requirement or expectation attaching to the exercise of power'. This is useful, but the intention here is to widen the scope of application, given that much media activity does not fall within the legitimate scope of public power. Often the term 'accountability' is used interchangeably with 'answerability', especially where the latter means to have to explain or justify one's actions. But there are several different ways in which this can take place. Pritchard (2000: 3) writes that the essence of accountability lies in a process of naming, blaming and claiming. Essentially this means to identify a problem, name the media outlet responsible and claim some apology or compensation. The core reference is to a process of public scrutiny whereby the public activities of the media (acts of publication) are confronted with the legitimate expectations of society. The latter have been reviewed already and can be expressed in terms of the criteria that have just been outlined. We define **media accountability** in a provisional way here as follows:

> Media accountability is all the voluntary or involuntary processes by which the media answer directly or indirectly to the society and those immediately affected for the quality and/or consequences of publication.

Because of the complexity and sensitivity of the issues that arise, it is clear that we are not dealing with a simple or single mechanism of social control or regulation. The various elements that contribute to accountability are part of the normal operation of the media in any open society. In keeping with central tenets of normative theory, media accountability processes should meet four general criteria:

- They should respect rights to free publication.
- They should prevent or limit harm arising from publication to individuals as well as to society.
- They should promote positive aspects of publication rather than merely being restrictive.
- They should be public and transparent.

The first of these four criteria reflects the primacy of the requirement of free expression in democracies. The second implies that obligations to 'society' are in the first instance obligations to individual human beings with rights, needs and interests. The third puts the emphasis on dialogue and interaction between media and other institutions of society. The fourth implies that internal control by the media is not sufficient. The fundamental difficulty of meeting these four criteria lies in the inescapable tension between freedom and accountability since total freedom recognizes no obligations to answer for actions to others, within the normal limits of the law. Typically, constitutional law in democracies rules out any constraint on the 'freedom of the press', so the legitimate scope for avoiding accountability is very wide (see Dennis et al., 1989).

This presentation of the case here is based on the assumption that there is such a thing as a 'public interest', as discussed above. Secondly, it assumes that the media are important enough to society to justify holding them to account and that effective accountability is not necessarily inconsistent with basic freedom. Freedom involves some elements of responsibility to others and is limited according to the rights of others.

It is useful here to make a distinction between the concepts of accountability and responsibility. The latter refers to the obligations and expectations that are directed at the media. Accountability, on the other hand, refers primarily to the processes by which media are called to account. As Hodges (1986) puts it:

> The issue of responsibility is the following: to what social needs should we expect journalists to respond? The issue of accountability is: how might society call on journalists to account for performance of the responsibilities given to them? Responsibility has to do with defining proper conduct, accountability with compelling it.

In considering processes of accountability, it is useful to distinguish between responsibilities in terms of the degree of compulsion involved. Some are entirely voluntary and self-chosen, some are contracted between media and audiences or clients, and others are required by law. The pressure to be accountable can thus be moral or social rather than legal. In general, the more voluntary, the softer or more optional are the mechanisms of accountability, the less conflict with freedom is involved. A softer mode of accountability is one that does not involve a financial or other penalty, but instead usually involves a verbal process of inquiry, explanation or apology. The media prefer to avoid external adjudication and penalties, for obvious reasons: hence the prevalence of self-regulatory mechanisms of

Answerability		Liability
Moral/social basis	*v*	*Legal basis*
Voluntary	*v*	*Imposed*
Verbal forms	*v*	*Formal adjudication*
Co-operative	*v*	*Adversarial*
Non-material penalty	*v*	*Material penalty*
Reference to quality	*v*	*Reference to harm*

Figure 8.5   Two accountability models compared (McQuail, 2003a: 205)

accountability. These may also be more appropriate to issues of communication, where there is usually no physical or material damage.

Two Alternative Modes of Accountability

For accountability to take place there has to be some response to what the media do (publication), and the media have to listen. Accountability means answering to *some-one* for *something* according to some *criterion* and with varying degrees of obligation on the part of the media. Combining some of these ideas, it becomes possible to sketch two alternative models of accountability: one that can be called a liability mode, another an answerability mode.

The *liability model* puts the emphasis on potential harm and danger that might arise from media publication, whether harm to individuals or to society (for instance, danger to morals or public order). The measures taken in line with this model will involve material penalties imposed by private or public law.

In contrast, the *answerability model* (or mode) is non-confrontational and emphasizes debate, negotiation, voluntariness and dialogue as the best means to bridge differences that arise between media and their critics or those affected. The means of accounting will be predominantly verbal rather than formal adjudications, and any penalties will also be verbal (e.g. publication of apologies, corrections or replies) rather than material.

It is always difficult to weigh up the balance between private (individual) harm (e.g. to the reputation of a public figure) and possible public benefit (e.g. exposure of some scandal or abuse). In practice, there are also likely to be 'chilling' effects on publication where severe material penalties might follow after the event of publication. The greatest danger is to small publishers, giving greater advantage to rich media corporations who can afford to risk financial losses in the pursuit of audiences. The 'answerability' model is generally most consistent with ideas of participant democracy and most likely to encourage diversity, independence and creativity of expression. The main features of the two 'modes' are summarized in Figure 8.5.

Lines and Relations of Accountability

By definition, accountability involves a relationship between media and some other parties. We can recognize two separate *stages* of accountability: one *internal* and the other *external*. The former involves a chain of control within the media, such that specific acts of publication (e.g. news items or television programmes) can be made the responsibility of the media organization and its owners. Important issues do arise in this respect concerning the degree of autonomy or freedom of expression of those who work in the media (e.g. journalists, writers, editors, producers). There is a tension between freedom and responsibility 'within the walls' of the media, so to speak, which is too often resolved in favour of media owners. In any case, we cannot rely on internal control or management to satisfy the wider social need for accountability. Internal control may either be too strict (protecting the organization from claims) and thus a form of self-censorship, or too much directed at serving the interests of the media organization rather than society.

Here we are concerned with the 'external' relationships between media and those affected by, or with an interest in, publication. These are varied and overlapping, as we can appreciate from a simple enumeration of the main potential partners, as shown in Figure 8.6. Accountability relations routinely arise between media and:

- their own audiences;
- their clients, such as advertisers, sponsors or backers;
- those who supply content, including news sources and producers of entertainment, sports and cultural production;
- those who are the subject of reporting, whether as individuals or as groups (here called 'referents');
- owners and shareholders of media firms;
- government regulators and law-makers as guardians of the public interest;
- social institutions that are affected by media or depend on media for their normal operation;
- public opinion, standing here for 'society as a whole';
- various pressure and interest groups that are affected by publication.

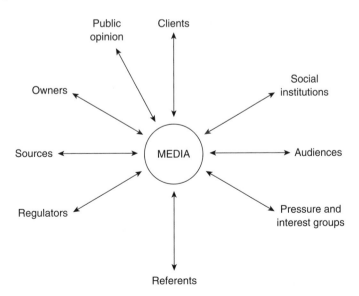

Figure 8.6   Lines of accountability between media and external agents in relation to publication

Frames of Accountability

Given the variety of issues and potential claimants, it is not surprising that there are numerous types of process. In addition, different media are subject to different 'regimes', or even none at all (Chapter 9). The entire mass production process involves a routine and continuous accounting, both internally in anticipation of problems and externally after publication by many interested parties. Most of this activity falls within the scope of the 'answerability' model outlined above. However, more problematic issues and stronger claims do arise and media are likely to resist them. In this case, more coercive procedures may become involved. Typically, an accountability process in such cases requires some formal procedures and a machinery of external third-party adjudication. Here too there is much room for diversity since forms of adjudication can range from the justice system, where legal offence is alleged (e.g. libel), to voluntary systems instituted by the media themselves.

Because of this diversity, it is useful to think in terms of a small number of basic 'frames of accountability', each representing an alternative, although not mutually exclusive, approach to accountability, and each having its own typical discourse, logic, forms and procedures. A frame in this sense involves several common elements: there must be a relationship between a media 'agent' and some external 'claimant', often with a third party as an adjudicator; there are some criteria or principles of good conduct; and there are rules, procedures and forms of account. We can define a frame of accountability as follows:

> A frame of accountability is a frame of reference within which expectations concerning conduct and responsibility arise and claims are expressed. A frame also indicates or governs the ways in which such claims should be handled.

Following in part the example of Dennis et al. (1989), the four most generally prevalent accountability frames in this sense can be identified respectively under the headings: *law and regulation*, *financial/market*, *public responsibility* and *professional responsibility*. We can briefly describe them by reference to the typical instruments and procedures; the issues they are most suited to dealing with; the degree of compulsion involved; and the relative advantages and disadvantages they have.

The frame of law and regulation

The first of these frames refers to all public policies, laws and regulations that affect media structure and operation. The main purpose should be to create and maintain the conditions for free and extensive intercommunication in society and to advance the public good as well as to limit potential harm to legitimate private and public interests.

The main *mechanisms and procedures* normally comprise regulatory documents concerning what media may and may not do, together with formal rules and procedures for implementing the provisions of any regulation. The main issues dealt with under this heading relate either to alleged harm to individuals or to other matters on which media (especially electronic media) can be regulated and called to account.

As to the *advantages* of this approach to accountability, the first is that there is ultimately some power to enforce claims. There is also democratic control, by way of the political system, over ends and means as a check on abuse of powers of compulsion. Any limits to freedom, as well as to the scope of any regulation, are clearly established. The *disadvantages* and limitations are quite severe, most importantly because of the potential conflict between the aim of protecting freedom of publication and making the media accountable. The fear of penalties can work in much the same way as (pre-publication) censorship, even where this is not legitimate. Law and regulation are easier to apply to structures (e.g. questions of ownership) than to content, where freedom of expression arises and where definitions are difficult. In general, law and regulation give more advantage to those with power and money, even when the intention is to protect the interests of all. Finally, it has been observed that laws and regulations are often ineffective, hard to enforce, unpredictable in their wider and long-term effects and hard to change or remove when they become out of date. They can also become part of a system of vested interests (e.g. in matters of subsidy or licensing).

The market frame

The market has not always been seen as a significant mechanism of public accountability, but in practice it is an important means for balancing the interests of media organizations and producers and those of their clients and audiences (consumers). The *mechanisms* are the normal processes of demand and supply in a free (and therefore competitive) market that should in theory encourage 'good' and discourage 'bad' performance. Various kinds of audience and market research provide evidence, additional to sales, about the public response to what is offered by the media.

In principle, a wide range of issues is covered by market accountability, although the main focus is on aspects of communication 'quality' as seen by the consumer. Quality relates not only to content, but also to technical quality. The market should encourage improvement by way of competition. There is no *compulsion* involved in control through market forces, which is one of the *advantages* of the approach. The laws of supply and demand should ensure that the interests of producers and consumers are kept in balance. The system is self-regulating and self-correcting, with no need for outside regulation or control.

The *limitations* of the market have probably received more attention than have the advantages. From one critical perspective the main problem of the media is that they are too 'commercialized', meaning organized for ends of profit rather than communication and lacking any true standard of quality. From this point of view, the market cannot serve as a check on itself. Without taking this principled standpoint, there are other arguments against the market as a means of accounting. One is the fact that markets are rarely perfect and the theoretical advantages of competition are not realized. Where private monopoly develops, there is no effective counterweight to media practices that seek only to maximize short-term gain. Market thinking tends to define freedom and quality of media in terms of freedom and welfare of media owners.

The frame of public responsibility

This refers to the fact that the media organizations are also social institutions that fulfil, with varying degrees of voluntariness and explicit commitment, certain important public tasks that go beyond their immediate goals of making profits and giving employment. Dennis et al. (1989) use the term 'fiduciary' model to refer to a similar idea of media being held in trust on behalf of the public. Others have written of a 'trustee model' of media, based on a similar notion, but usually with reference to public broadcasting (Hoffmann-Riem, 1996; Feintuck, 1999). Whether they acknowledge this or not, public opinion in open societies generally expects the media (taken as a whole) to serve the public interest in matters of information, publicity and culture. Where media are seen to be failing, they may be called to account by public opinion or other guardians of the public interest, including politicians.

The *mechanisms and procedures* mainly consist of the activities of pressure groups, including media consumer organizations and the public opinion surveys by which general public opinion is expressed. In a number of countries, there are various forms of press or broadcasting councils and procedures for public complaint that are adopted voluntarily by the media industry as a means of meeting claims from society. Governments have sometimes instituted commissions and inquiries to assess performance. Some media are operated as public trusts on a non-profit basis to serve some public informational or social purpose. The very large volume of public debate, review and criticism, often carried by the media (or some of them), is an important means of informal control.

The main *advantages* of a developed public responsibility frame include the fact that the needs of society can be expressed in a direct way – by claims made, on the media, to provide for these needs. In addition, intrinsic to this frame is the idea of a continuous interactive relationship between media and society. The public can answer back to the media in their roles as citizens or members of some interest group or minority (not just as consumers or as individuals with legal rights), and the media are under pressure to respond and have the means to do so. This mode of accountability is very open and democratic by definition as well as being voluntary and therefore protective of freedom.

There are also *limitations*. An obvious weakness is the very voluntary character mentioned. Some media reject the trustee status and will use their freedom not to be responsible. There is not necessarily any real 'system' of accountability here, except in relation to public broadcasting, and it works better in some countries and traditions than in others. Trends towards globalization (multinational control of media) and media concentration undermine this model.

The frame of professional responsibility

This refers to accountability that arises out of the self-respect and ethical development of professionals working in the media (e.g. journalists, advertisers, public relations), who set their own standards of good performance. It can also apply to associations of owners, editors, producers, and so on, that aim to protect the interests of the industry by self-regulation.

The *mechanisms and procedures* generally consist of a published set of principles or code of conduct that is adopted by members of a media professional group, together with some procedures for hearing and judging complaints and claims against particular media actions. The *issues* can be any matter dealt with in the code of ethics or conduct, but normally relating to some harm or offence caused to an individual or group. The development of professionalism in the media is often supported by government and other public institutions and assisted by improved education and training.

The *advantages* are that the system of accountability (in so far as there is one) is generally likely to work because it is both voluntary and in the self-interest of the media and professionals. It has the benefit of being non-coercive and it encourages voluntary self-improvement as well as self-control. In practice, there are also considerable *limitations*. It is narrow in its application and does not usually exert strong pressure on powerful media. It is not sufficiently independent of the media themselves and is also very fragmentary in its coverage (Fengler, 2003). In general, professionalism is not very strongly developed within the media and employees have relatively little autonomy in relation to management and owners.

Comparative assessment

It is clear that in an open society there are likely to be many overlapping processes of accountability but no complete system, and no single one of the 'frames' described is sufficient for the task on its own or uniquely superior to the others. There are many gaps (performance issues are not dealt with adequately), and some media accept no responsibility except what is imposed by market forces.

The diversity of forms and means of accountability can be considered a positive feature in itself, even if the overall result is not satisfactory. In general, according to the principle of openness, we should prefer forms of accountability that are transparent, voluntary and based on active relationships and dialogue and debate. The alternatives of external control, legal compulsion and threats of punishment may be more effective in the short term and sometimes the only way to achieve some goals, but in the long term they run counter to the spirit of the open society.

Conclusion

In this chapter, the main normative principles that apply to the working of media, the standards they are widely expected to adhere to, have been described. These have their origins and first expression in the body of political and social theory reviewed in Chapter 7. They are also often backed up by market forces, public opinion, pressure groups, law and government. The processes of accountability that have been briefly outlined, although they improve the chances of implementation of the standards outlined, are not to be confused with means of control by government or anyone else. They are not incompatible with media freedom, but are inescapable components of the normal operating environment of media in an open society.

The continuing changes in the media have not yet fundamentally altered the *content* of the norms described, but they have affected their relative force and the priorities among them. The increasing number of alternative media channels, in particular, has reduced the pressure on seemingly 'dominant' media (for instance, the national newspaper press or broadcast television) to fulfil some perceived public roles. There is probably less fear of media monopoly, despite concentration tendencies, because the potential for competition is greater. More media channels also seem to promise more diversity, although the quality of that diversity is far from assured. The new medium of the Internet certainly delivers great diversity as well as many new types of communication service. It also seems to have escaped the pressure to conform to several of the norms outlined, although it does exemplify the values of freedom and equality as well as diversity. Where it has increasingly been judged wanting is in relation to social and cultural issues and its uncertain reliability as an information source. It also lies largely outside any mechanism of control and in practice escapes most of the forms of accountability described apart from that of the marketplace. This does not mean that it will always be 'ungovernable' (Lessig, 1999) or be able to escape accountability indefinitely.

Despite the lack of any clear regulatory framework nationally or internationally, there are many instances of the Internet being 'called to account' on a wide range of issues, even if not very effectively. Public opinion creates a pressure for response to complaints that works in part through the market for Internet services. Many of those who use the Internet to send messages and other content (including established media) apply their own standards and methods of self-regulation. Individual bloggers are also open to self-correction. But this points to one of the problems in the way of developing more systematic accountability which is the enormous multiplicity of agencies involved (Verhulst, 2006: 340). Apart from this, of course, too much systematic accountability would run counter to the promise of freedom and diversity that is a main benefit of the Internet.

Further Reading

Bertrand, J.C. (2003) *An Arsenal for Democracy*. Creskill, NJ: Hampton Press.
A systematic and explanatory catalogue of the numerous and varied formal and informal arrangements and instruments by which societies hold their media systems to account. A much-cited, cross-cultural resource book.

Feintuck, M. and Varley, M. (2006) *Media Regulation, Public Interest and the Law*, 2nd edn. Edinburgh: Edinburgh University Press.
A thorough and original exploration of the numerous socio-legal issues raised by the operation of mass media. Although largely based on UK experience, it has much wider potential application because of attention to fundamental principles.

Napoli, P. (2001) *Foundations of Communications Policy*. Creskill, NJ: Hampton Press.
A systematic and informative exploration of fundamental principles of media policy, this time based on the situation in the United States, but with wide relevance to all democratic communication systems.

Online Readings

Bar, F. and Sandvig, C. (2008) 'US communication policy after convergence', *Media, Culture and Society*, 30 (4): 531–50.

McDonald, D.G. and Dimmick, J. (2003) 'The conceptualization and measurement of diversity', *Communication Research*, 30 (1): 60–79.

McQuail, D. (1992) *Media Performance: Mass Communication and the Public Interest*, pp. 237–73. London: Sage. (Part VII on mass media, order and social control).

Puppis, M. (2008) 'National media regulation in an era of free trade', *European Journal of Communication*, 23 (4): 405–24.

van Cuilenburg, J.J. and McQuail, D. (2003) 'Media policy paradigm shifts', *European Journal of Communication*, 18 (2): 181–207.

Verhulst, S. (2006) 'The regulation of digital content', in L. Lievrouw and S. Livingstone (eds), *The Handbook of New Media*, pp. 329–49. London: Sage.

9

Media Economics and Governance

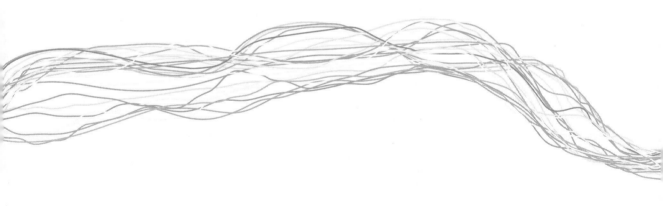

So far, mass media have been discussed as if they were an institution of society rather than an industry. They have become increasingly more of the latter without necessarily becoming less of the former, and an understanding of the main principles of the structure and dynamics of the media calls for an economic as well as a political and a social-cultural analysis. Although the media have grown up in response to the social and cultural needs of individuals and societies, they are largely run as business enterprises. A trend in this direction has accelerated in recent years for several reasons, especially because of the increasing industrial and economic significance of the entire information and communication sector. Associated with this is the widespread privatization of state telecommunication enterprises and an extension of their activities nationally and internationally. The shift to free-market economies in former communist states has been an additional factor. Even where media are run as public bodies, they are more subject to financial discipline and operate in competitive environments.

A book about mass communication theory is not the place for a thorough treatment of these matters, but it is impossible to understand the social and cultural implications of mass media without at least a sketch of the wider political and economic forces at work shaping media institutions. The public regulation, control and economics of media embody certain general principles that belong to the sphere of theory, and the aim of this chapter is to explain these principles, avoiding detail of local and temporary circumstances.

Media 'Not Just Any Other Business'

The key to the unusual character of the media institution is that its activities are inextricably both economic and political as well as being very dependent on continually changing technologies. These activities involve the production of goods and services which are often both private (consumption for individual personal satisfaction) and public (viewed as necessary for the working of society as a whole and also in the public domain). The public character of the media derives mainly from the political function of the media in a democracy, but also from the fact that information, culture and ideas are considered as the collective property of all. Nor, as with other public goods, such as air and daylight, does their use diminish their availability for others.

More specifically, mass media have grown up historically with a strong and widely shared image as having an important part to play in public life and being essentially within the public domain. Certainly, this was and remains true of the newspaper, but it applies in different ways to most of the newer mass media. What media do or do not do has mattered to societies, and this has been reflected in complex systems of ideas about what they should or should not be doing (see Chapters 7 and 8). It is also reflected in varied mechanisms to encourage, protect or limit them on behalf of a supposed 'public interest'. Despite this, the media generally have to operate wholly or partly according to the dictates of market economics. Even in this aspect, they may attract the attention of governments for the same reasons that other private businesses are subject to various forms of legal and economic regulation.

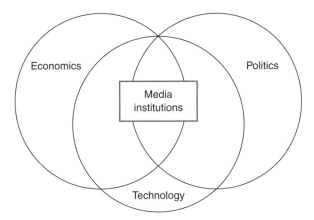

Figure 9.1   The media are at the centre of three overlapping kinds of influence

Alternative theoretical perspectives

Not surprisingly, there is no agreed objective description of the media institution that can be separated from the varying national/societal circumstances in which media operate. One option is to apply an *economic/industrial* perspective (see Tunstall, 1991), looking at the distinctive and varying characteristics of the media as economic enterprises, as between different media and different contexts. An alternative perspective is that offered by critical *political-economic* theory (as introduced on pp. 96–7). This provides concepts derived especially from the critique of capitalism, with reference to processes of concentration and commercialization. A third main possibility is to examine media structures according to a *public interest* or policy perspective and in the light of normative criteria of conduct and performance that have been discussed in the last two chapters. There is a fourth possibility: to look at the media institution from an *internal* or *media professional* point of view. Each of these perspectives will be drawn on for some purposes in the following pages.

We can represent the unique position of media as at the centre of three main forces – political, economic and technological – and thereby requiring alternative modes of analysis (Figure 9.1).

The main questions for theory to answer

A theoretical analysis is only possible if certain general issues or problems are first identified. At a descriptive level, we focus mainly on the question of *differences*. How do media differ from each other in economic and policy terms? How and why are the economics and regulation of media untypical both of normal business and of normal public services? How and why do national media institutions vary in structure and control? This last aspect of the comparison is important precisely because media are not only businesses, responding to economic forces, but also deeply rooted (usually nationally based) social and cultural institutions.

There is also relevant theory concerning the current *dynamics* of media industries, especially the trends towards expansion, diversification and convergence of media, mainly on the basis of new technology and new economic opportunities. There are trends towards concentration, integration and internationalization of media activity. Four main questions arise here. First, what are the likely consequences of media concentration and can the trends indicated be managed on behalf of the public interest? Secondly, what are the consequences of media internationalization for media and society? Thirdly, how far is media change being driven by technology and how far by economics or politics and social forces? Fourthly, the expansion of media-based communication by way of telecommunications, especially mobile phones and the Internet, has raised new regulatory issues as well as creating pressure for regulation that did not exist before. In particular, the telecommunications system is increasingly a vehicle for distributing content that was originally broadcast, such as films, music and television. This is one example of the convergence of technology, with all media digitalized and, in principle, interconnected.

The main questions for theory are posed in Box 9.1.

9.1 Questions for theory arising from economy and governance

- How do particular media differ in economic and political terms?
- How and why do national media systems differ in structure and control?
- How and why are the economics of media different from those of other industries?
- What are the causes and consequences of media concentration?
- What are the causes and consequences of internationalization?
- What is the relative weight of technology convergence as a force for media change?
- How is the performance of media affected by the source of finance?

The Basics of Media Structure and Levels of Analysis

The scene can be set by a reminder of the main features of economically developed media systems. The term 'media system' refers to the actual set of mass media in a given national society, despite the fact that there may be no formal connection between the elements. Most media systems, in this sense, are the chance result of historical growth, with one new technology after another being developed and leading to the adaptation of existing media. Sometimes a media system is linked by a shared political-economic logic, as with the free-enterprise media of the United States or the state-run media of China. Many countries have 'mixed' systems, with private and public elements, and these may well be organized according to a set of national media policy principles, leading to a degree of integration. Occasionally, there may be a single ministry of communications, or communications regulatory body, which has some responsibilities across a range of different media, private or public, which adds another 'systemic' component (Robillard, 1995). The media may also be treated as a coherent system by their audiences or by advertisers, and certainly the term 'the media' is often used in this collective sense.

Within the media system, specific different types are to be found based on different medium technologies: print, television, radio, recorded music, the Internet, telecommunications, and so on. However, these are often subdivided into different 'media forms', for instance print media into books, magazines, newspapers. The resulting groupings may also be described as media 'sectors', especially in policy discourse or for purposes of economic analysis, but the divisions are often arbitrary and *ad hoc*, so that the unity of such 'sectors' is often as illusory as is that of the whole system. There are many differentiating as well as integrating factors (especially through separate or shared distribution systems). For instance, the medium of film can refer to the cinema, video and DVD hire or sale, broadcast or subscription television, and so on. These are different means of distribution, often different businesses and organizations, although there is usually some form of vertical integration. We need to distinguish another unit of analysis: that of the firm or enterprise, which may constitute a significant part of a sector or have holdings which cut across boundaries of media type or geography (the multimedia, and often multinational, firm). Some media products can be regarded as belonging to specific 'genres' (e.g. international news, romantic fiction, etc.) and finally as particular products (as a film, book title, song, etc.) for purposes of analysis, independent of the medium or sector. The main (approximate) media system components are shown in Box 9.2. A new and somewhat different element has been added in the form of the Internet portal, especially the ones that have many users and many types of customized content. Major examples include Yahoo, Google, AOL and the BBC. As the term implies, portals are gateways into a larger territory and have the usual functions of selection and control (Kalyanaraman and Sundar, 2008).

Media structure and levels of analysis **9.2** i

- International media
- Media system (all national media)
- Multimedia firm (with major holdings in several media)
- Media sector (newspapers, books, television, film, music, etc.)
- Circulation/distribution area (nation, region, city, locality)
- Unit medium channel (newspaper title, television station, etc.)
- Particular genre
- Unit media product (book, film, song, etc.)
- Internet portal

Some Economic Principles of Media Structure

Different media markets and sources of income

According to Picard (1989: 17), 'A market consists of sellers that provide the same good or service, or closely substitutable goods or services, to the same group of consumers.' In general, markets can be defined according to place, people, type of revenue and the nature of the product or service. The mainstream media of newspapers, radio and television can be classified according to a fundamental line of economic division between the *consumer market* for media products and services and the *advertising market*, in which a service is sold to advertisers in the form of access to the audience, although there was often no distinction between the two, since newspapers, for example, provided both types of market at the same time. One can note that within the consumer market there is another division: between the market for 'one-off' products like books, tapes, videos and newspapers sold directly to consumers, and that for continuous media services like cable or broadcast television or online media. In fact, there are other sources of income besides the two mentioned. They include sponsorship, product placement and public relations as well as public money and support from private backers, non-profit trusts, and not forgetting direct support from an audience, as in the case of the German newspaper *Tageszeitung*.

The Internet has added further complication since new sources of revenue are available, including the costs of being online, payments for websites, producer subventions. It has also undermined the economics of older media by making most content available without charge or open to piracy. The first victim of advertising on the Internet seems to be the newspaper in both local and national variants. This impact seems irreversible as far as the 'mass audience' for news is concerned. The share of all advertising taken by online media has grown steadily since the turn of the century and within that category are several different types, especially display, search and classified advertising. This has presented several practical and theoretical problems. The most pressing practical problem has been to obtain some measure of value of 'audience' use in order to charge advertisers. Bermejo (2009) has charted the story of different efforts to measure the audience, ending up with the concept of a 'visit' or 'click' as an indicator of frequency of use. However, this gives no indication of the time spent on a particular site and other means of pricing have to be found to charge those who want to place advertisements or messages in other locations, especially search engines, that have become a focus of intense interest because of their high popularity and profitability (Machill et al., 2008). The theoretical problems mentioned relate especially to the implications for the 'commodification' of content and relations with the audience (Bermejo, 2009).

Advertising versus consumer revenue: implications

The difference between the two main sources of revenue – direct product sales and advertising – is still a useful tool for comparative analysis and for explaining media features and trends. The distinction cuts across the difference between media types, although some media are rather unsuitable for advertising, while others can operate equally in both markets (especially television, radio, newspapers, magazines and the Internet). There are some 'advertising revenue only' media, with no consumer revenue – for instance, free newspapers, promotional magazines and quite a lot of television.

The distinction also has a non-economic significance. In particular, it is usually thought (from the critical or public interest and professional perspectives) that the higher the dependence on advertising as a source of revenue, the less independent the content from the interests of the advertisers and business generally. Picard (2004) notes that the American newspaper industry received more than 80% of its income from advertising and that advertising accounts for an average of 60% of content. This does not necessarily mean less independence, but it may imply less credibility as an information source, if the content of news relates to what is advertised, and less creative autonomy. In the extreme case of media that are totally financed or sponsored by advertising, the ostensible content is hard to distinguish from advertising itself, propaganda or public relations. The question of advertiser influence on media organizations is discussed again in Chapter 11. There is little doubt about certain general kinds of influence, such as the bias towards youth and higher-income groups and the preference for neutral rather than politicized media (Tunstall and Machin, 1999).

From the economic perspective, operation in the different markets raises other considerations. One is the question of financing since the costs of advertising-supported media are usually covered in advance of production, while in the consumer market the income has to follow the outlay. Secondly, there are different criteria and methods for assessing market performance. Advertising-based media are assessed according to the number and type of consumers (who they are, where they live) reached by particular messages (for example, circulation, readership and reach/ratings). These measures are necessary for attracting would-be advertising clients and for establishing the rates that can be charged. The market performance of media content that is paid for directly by consumers is assessed by the income received from sales and subscriptions to services. Ratings of (qualitative) satisfaction and popularity may be relevant to both markets, but they count for relatively more in the consumer income market.

Performance in one market can affect performance in another, where a medium operates in both. For instance, an increase in newspaper sales (producing more consumer revenue) can lead to higher advertising rates, provided that the increase does not lead to a lower than average level of social-economic composition, with a reverse effect on unit advertising rates. It is also clear that the difference of revenue base can lead to different kinds of opportunity or vulnerability to wider economic circumstances. Media that are heavily dependent on advertising are likely to be more sensitive to the negative impact of general economic downturns than media that sell (usually low-cost) products to individual consumers. The latter may also be in a better position to cut costs in the face of falls in demand (but this depends on the cost structure of production).

Media market reach and diversity

The difference between the two revenue markets interacts with other features of the media market. As noted above, the social composition of the audience reached (and 'sold' to advertisers) is important because of differences in purchasing power and in type of goods advertised. There is a logic in the advertising-based mass media which favours a convergence of media tastes and consumption patterns (less diversity). This is because homogeneous audiences are often more cost-effective for advertisers than heterogeneous and dispersed markets (unless they are very large mass markets for mass products). This is one reason for the viability of the free newspaper that provides complete coverage of a particular area with relatively high homogeneity (Bakker, 2002). However, on occasion there can be a premium on diversity, when a medium can accurately deliver small but profitable niche markets. This is one of the potentials of the Internet and of other specialist (non-mass) channels.

The relationship between the pursuit of mass markets and homogeneity of audience is much less clear in the case of the Internet, since the enormous capacity of the latter enables it to reach a great variety of audiences with a great variety of content due to favourable economics. This does not necessarily mean the start of a new era of diverse and unstratified media provision, since the economic model of online media is still in an experimental stage. It is possible, even likely, that there will be a trend for paid-for premium sources, as with cable and satellite broadcasting. A major innovation of the Internet as an advertising medium is its capacity to accurately identify and reach many dispersed markets for particular products and services, based on data obtained from online.

Competition for revenue

In line with this, it has been argued more generally that 'competition for a single revenue source results in imitative uniformity' (Tunstall, 1991: 182). Tunstall suggests that this is the reason for the perceived 'low-taste' quality (or just 'imitative uniformity') of North American network television, which is financed almost entirely from mass *consumer* advertising (see DeFleur and Ball-Rokeach, 1989). The same applies to the alleged low standards of the British tabloid newspapers which compete for much the same mass (down-) market. Tunstall also argues that this kind of large undifferentiated market maximizes the power of the powerful (for instance, by the threat of advertising withdrawals, or simply pressure). Certainly, one of the benefits argued for a public sector in European television has been that it avoids the situation where all broadcasting competes for the same revenue sources (e.g. Peacock, 1986). However, it is also the case that advertising itself is increasingly diversified, allowing support for a wide range of media contents. The competition of different media for the same advertising income can encourage diversity. The degree and kind of competition are important modifying variables. Reliance on advertising as such need not lead to uniformity of provision.

In the early twenty-first century, the largest question mark in this territory still stands against the possibilities for advertising on the Internet. There has been a rapid growth in use of this new medium for advertising, although it is not yet clear that the revenue produced is sufficient to make many media operations on the Internet profitable. Nevertheless, some predictions point to alarming impacts on established media, especially newspapers, that depend on the type of advertising that looks most suited to the new media – especially classified, personal, property, specialized, and jobs. This threat to the future of the newspaper may be more immediate than the luring away of readers to electronic competitors.

Media cost structure

The issue of media cost structure was noted earlier as a variable in the economic fortunes of media. One of the peculiarities of traditional mass media as compared with some other economic enterprises is the potential imbalance between the 'fixed costs' and the 'variable costs' of production. The former refer to such things as land, physical plant, equipment and distribution network. The variable costs refer to materials, 'software' and (sometimes) labour. The higher the ratio of fixed to variable costs, the more vulnerable a business is to a changing market environment, and traditional mass media typically have a high ratio, with heavy capital investments which have to be recouped later by sales and advertising revenue.

It is in the nature of the typical media product that it has a very high 'first-copy' cost. A single daily newspaper or the first print of a film carries all the burden of the fixed costs, while the marginal cost of additional copies rapidly declines. This makes traditional media such as newspapers vulnerable to fluctuations in demand and in advertising revenue and puts a premium on economies of scale and exerts a pressure towards agglomeration. It also exerts pressure towards the separation of production from distribution since the latter often involves high fixed costs (for instance, cinemas, cable networks, satellites and transmitters). High fixed costs also erect a high barrier to would-be new entrants into the media business. Under authoritarian regimes, the economic vulnerability of newspapers has made it easier for governments to threaten them with very costly interruptions of supply or distribution.

In this matter also, the new 'weightless' media open up new uncertainties for the established media. In general, it looks as if fixed costs can be much lower than with traditional media, with much lower entry costs and therefore greater ease of entering the market. Nevertheless, the production costs of high value content that competes for high popularity in international markets such as films and games will continue to be under upward pressure. New factors have also been introduced into the media market with the appearance of new formats and websites, such as social networking, or e-Bay and the general appearance of user-produced content. The division between fixed and variable costs is less relevant to new developments. In summary, Box 9.3 lists the main conclusions that have been drawn from the study of media markets.

9.3 Economic principles of media markets

- Media still differ according to whether they have fixed or variable cost structures
- Media markets have an increasingly multiple income character, especially on the Internet platform
- Media based on advertising revenue are more vulnerable to unwanted external influence on content
- Media based on consumer revenue are vulnerable to shortage of finance
- Different sources of revenue require different measures of market performance
- Where a multiple market applies, performance in one market can affect performance in another
- Advertising in specialist media can promote diversity of supply
- Certain kinds of advertising benefit from concentration of the audience market
- Competition for the same revenue sources leads to uniformity

Ownership and Control

Fundamental to an understanding of media structure is the question of ownership and how the powers of ownership are exercised. The belief that ownership ultimately determines the nature of media is not just a Marxist theory but virtually a common-sense axiom summed up in Altschull's (1984) 'second law of journalism': 'the contents of the media always reflect the interests of those who finance them'. Not surprisingly, there are several different forms of ownership of different media, and the powers of ownership can be exercised in different ways.

As implied by Altschull's remark, it is not just ownership that counts, it is a wider question of who actually pays for the media product. Although there are media whose owners do personally pay for the privilege of influencing content, most owners just want profit, and most media are financed from different sources. These include a range of private investors (among them other media companies), advertisers, consumers, various public or private subsidy givers, and governments. It follows that the line of influence from ownership is often indirect and complex – and it is rarely the only line of influence.

Most media belong to one of three categories of ownership: commercial companies, private non-profit bodies and the public sector. However, within each of these there are significant divisions. For media ownership it will be relevant whether a company is public or private, a large media chain or conglomerate or a small independent. It may also matter whether or not a media enterprise is owned by a so-called 'media tycoon' or 'mogul', typified as wanting to take a personal interest in editorial policy (Tunstall and Palmer, 1991). Non-profit bodies can be neutral trusts, designed to safeguard independence of operations (as with the *Guardian* newspaper), or bodies with a special cultural or social task, such as political parties, churches, and so on. Public ownership also comes in many different forms, ranging from direct state administration to elaborate and diversified constructions designed to maximize independence of decision-making about content.

The effects of ownership

For mass communication theory, it is nearly always the ultimate publication decision that matters most. Liberal theory rests on the assumption that ownership can be effectively separated from control of editorial decisions. Larger (allocative) decisions about resources, business strategy, and the like, are taken by owners or boards of owners, while editors and other decision-makers are left free to take the professional decisions about content which is their special expertise. In some situations and countries there are intermediary institutional arrangements (such as editorial statutes) designed to safeguard the integrity of editorial policy and the freedom of journalists. Otherwise, professionalism, codes of conduct, public reputation (since media are always in the public eye) and common (business) sense are supposed to take care of the seeming problem of undue owner influence (this is discussed in Chapter 11).

The existence of checks and balances cannot, however, obscure several facts of life for media operation. One is that, ultimately, commercial media have to make profits to survive, and this often involves taking decisions which directly influence content (such as cutting costs, closing down, shedding staff, investing or not, and merging operations). Publicly owned media do not escape an equivalent economic logic. It is also a fact that most private media have a vested interest in the capitalist system and are inclined to give support to its most obvious defenders – conservative political parties. The overwhelming endorsement by US newspaper editorials of Republican presidential candidates over the years (Gaziano, 1989), and similar phenomena in some European countries, are not likely to be the result of either chance or the natural wisdom of editors.

There are many less obvious ways in which a similar tendency operates, not least potential pressure from advertisers. Public ownership is thought to neutralize or balance these particular pressures, although that too means following a certain editorial line (albeit one of neutrality). The conventional wisdom of liberal theory suggests that the best or only solution to such problems lies in multiplicity of private ownership. The ideal situation would be one in which many small or medium companies compete with each other for the interest of the public by offering a wide range of ideas, information and types of culture. The power which goes with ownership is not necessarily bad in itself but only becomes so when concentrated or used selectively to limit or deny access. This position underestimates the fundamental tension between market criteria of size and profit and social-cultural criteria of quality and influence. They may simply not be reconcilable (Baker, 2007). The issue of concentration lies at the heart of the theoretical debate. Key propositions about ownership and control are presented in Box 9.4.

9.4 Media ownership and control

- Freedom of the press supports the rights of owners to decide on content
- Form of ownership inevitably has an influence on content
- Multiplicity of ownership and free competition are the best defence against misuse of powers of ownership
- There are usually checks and balances in the system to limit undesirable owner influence

Competition and Concentration

In the theory of media structure, much attention has been paid to the question of uniformity and diversity. Most social theory concerned with the 'public interest' places a value on diversity, and there is also an economic dimension involved: that of monopoly versus competition. Free competition, as noted, should lead to variety and to change of media structure, although critics point to a reverse effect: that it leads to monopoly, or at least oligopoly (undesirable on economic as well as social grounds) (Lacy and Martin, 2004). As far as media economics are concerned, there are three main aspects to the question: *intermedia* competition, *intramedium* competition and *interfirm* competition. Intermedia competition depends chiefly on whether products can be substituted for one another (such as news on the Internet for news on television or in the newspaper) and on whether advertising can be substituted from one medium to another. Both substitutions are possible but they occur only up to a certain point. There always appears to be some 'niche' in which a particular medium has an advantage (Dimmick and Rothenbuhler, 1984). All media types also seem to be able to offer some distinctive advantages to advertisers: of form of message, timing, type of audience, context of reception, and so on (Picard, 1989). The rise of the Internet is challenging all media on several points at once (see Küng et al., 2008).

Horizontal versus vertical concentration

In general, because units of the *same* medium sector are more readily substitutable than those *between* media, the focus of attention is often directed at intramedium competition (such as of one newspaper with another in the same market, geographically or otherwise defined). This is where concentration has most tended to develop – within the same medium sector (this may also in part be the result of public policies to limit cross-media monopoly). In general, media concentration has been distinguished according to whether it is 'horizontal' or 'vertical'. Vertical concentration refers to a pattern of ownership which extends through different stages of production and distribution (for instance, a film studio owning a cinema chain) or geographically (a national concern buying city or local newspapers, say).

While the tendency to vertical concentration continues, there is also a trend towards 'disaggregation' of media activities, especially the separation of production activity from distribution. This has been accelerated by the Internet because there are many competing portals and there is virtually no production capacity. The old style hierarchy of control of large media firms has given way to a more unstructured network model in which market arrangements drive the relations between parts of the organization rather than direct 'command and control' (Collins, 2008). This applies with particular force to the Internet.

Horizontal concentration refers to mergers within the same market (for example, of two competing city or national newspaper organizations or of a telephone and a cable network). Both of these processes have happened on a large scale in a number of countries, although the effects may have been modified by continuing intermedia choice and the rise of new media. Diversity is often protected by public policies against 'cross-media ownership' (different media being owned and operated by the same firm, especially in the same geographical market). The media can also become involved in horizontal concentration through the merging of firms in different industries, so that a newspaper or television channel can be owned by a non-media business (see Murdock, 1990). This does not directly reduce media diversity but can add to the power of mass media and have wider implications for advertising.

Other types of concentration effect

Another relevant set of distinctions by type of concentration (de Ridder, 1984) relates to the *level* at which it occurs. De Ridder distinguished between publisher/concern (ownership), editorial and audience levels. The first refers to increased powers of owners (for instance, the growth of large chains of separate newspapers, as in the USA and Canada) or of television stations (as in Italy after deregulation). The units making up such media enterprises *can* remain editorially independent (as far as content decisions are concerned), although rationalization of business and organization often leads to the sharing of certain services and reduces the difference between them. In any case, there is a separate question as to whether editorial concentration, as measured by the number of independent titles, rises or falls in line with publisher concentration. The degree of editorial independence is often hard to assess. The impact of the Internet on these two types of concentration cannot yet be adequately assessed. There is clearly a *de facto* increase in the number of portals and owners, but there are also evident tendencies for empire-building by large and successful operators such as Google and AOL–Time Warner.

The third issue – that of audience concentration – refers to the concentration of audience market share, which also needs to be separately assessed. A relatively minor change of ownership can greatly increase audience concentration (in terms of the proportion 'controlled' by a publishing group). A large number of independent newspaper titles does not in itself set limits to media power or ensure much real choice if most of the audience is concentrated on one or two titles, or is served by one or two firms. The condition of the system is certainly not very diverse in that case. The reasons for concern about concentration turn on these two points. There seems little doubt that the Internet has increased audience diversity by adding so many small new niche audiences, but there is also an interest in being able to reach large user groups.

Audience concentration can be achieved without ownership. Large media conglomerates seek outlets for products across boundaries of media and ownership. The aim is to maximize the reach among defined target groups. Media executives call this 'achieving a good share of mind' (Turow, 2009: 201). All forms of exposure count towards this goal, including informal mentions or appearances in social media sites such as *YouTube*, often in return for payments.

Degrees of concentration

The degree of media concentration is usually measured by the extent to which the largest companies control production, employment, distribution and audience. Although there is no ceiling beyond which one can say that the degree is undesirable, according to Picard (1989: 334) a rule of thumb threshold of acceptability is one where the top four firms in an industry control more than 50%, or the top eight firms more than 70%. There are several media instances where such thresholds are exceeded or approached, such as the daily newspaper press in the USA, the national daily press in Britain, Japan and France, television in Italy and the international phonogram industry. Concentration in the (large) search engine market is still unregulated, but far exceeds the level in the press, with Google dominating usage and advertising revenue (Machill et al., 2008).

The situation of concentration can vary from one of perfect competition to one of complete monopoly, with varying degrees in between. Different media occupy different places on this continuum, for a variety of reasons. Perfect competition is rare, but a relatively high level of competition is shown in many countries by book and magazine publishing. Television and national newspapers are generally oligopolistic markets, while true monopoly is now very rare. It was once to be found in the unusual case of 'natural' monopoly – for instance, in cable and telecommunication. A 'natural monopoly' is one where the consumer is best served, on grounds of cost and efficiency, by there being a single supplier (it is usually accompanied by measures to protect the consumer). Most of such monopolies have been abolished in a wave of privatization and deregulation of telecommunications.

The reasons for increasing media concentration and integration of activities are the same as for other branches of business, especially the search for economies of scale and greater market power. In the case of the media it has something to do with the advantages of a vertically integrated operation since larger profits may be made from distribution than from production. There is also an incentive for media companies to acquire media with a stable cash flow of the kind provided by conventional television channels and daily newspapers (Tunstall, 1991). Control of software production and distribution can be very helpful for electronic companies, which need to make heavy investments in product innovations (such as forms of recording) that depend for their takeoff on a good supply of software.

There are also increasing advantages in sharing services and being able to link different distribution systems and different markets. This is generally known as 'synergy'.

As Murdock (1990: 8) remarks: 'In a cultural system built around "synergy" more does not mean different; it means the same basic commodity appearing in different markets and in a variety of packages.' In this kind of environment, an upward spiral to concentration is continually being applied because the only way to survive is by growth. The unification of the Single European Market since 1993 has played a part in this spiralling effect. Often, national restrictions on growth within a single country (because of anti-monopoly or cross-media ownership regulations) have stimulated cross-national monopoly forming (Tunstall, 1991). The setting up of the World Trade Organization (WTO) in 1994 to implement the General Agreement on Tariffs and Trade (GATT) has marked a new phase in media transnationalization. The media are primarily defined as businesses and it is now much harder to justify public intervention in the national media (Pauwels and Loisen, 2003). In general, it is clear that globalization and the drive for 'free markets' have been mutually reinforcing, primarily driven by economic and commercial motives.

Policy issues arising

The trend towards greater media concentration, nationally and internationally, gives rise to three main kinds of public policy issues. One relates to pricing, another to the product and a third to the position of competitors. The main pricing issue has to do with consumer protection: the more monopoly there is, the greater the power of the provider to set prices. The main product issue has to do with the content of a monopoly-supplied media service, especially questions of adequate quality and choice, both for the consumer and for would-be providers of content. The third issue, concerning competitors, refers to the driving out of competitors as a result of economies of scale or advantages in the advertising market of a high density of coverage or the use of financial power to engage in 'ruinous competition'.

For all the reasons given, there has been much research directed at the consequences of concentration (whether good or bad) – especially for the newspaper sector, where concentration has been greatest (see Picard et al., 1988). The results of research have been generally inconclusive, partly because of the complexity whereby the fact of concentration is usually only one aspect of a dynamic market situation. Baker (2007) has warned of the limited value and relevance of many empirical studies of effects of concentration, especially the statistical studies common in the late 1980s. Typically, the time frame is too short to be revealing and the key events that reveal misuse of power are too sporadic to be captured. In addition, the risk of abuse cannot be measured precisely, but requires an evaluative assessment. Most attention has focused on the consequences for content, with particular reference to the adequacy of *local news and information*, the performance of the *political and opinion-forming* functions of media, the degree of *access* to different voices and the degree and kind of *choice and diversity*. While, by definition, media concentration always reduces choice in some respects, it is possible that the profits of monopoly can be returned to the consumer or community in the form of better media, however defined (also a value judgement) (Lacy and Martin, 2004). More likely is that the profits from concentration will be channelled to shareholders, which is, after all, the primary purpose behind concentration (Squires, 1992; McManus, 1994).

The main points made about media competition and concentration in this section are summarized in Box 9.5.

9.5   Concentration and competition

- Concentration can be found at three levels: intermedia, intramedium (within a sector) and interfirm
- Concentration can be either horizontal or vertical
- Concentration can be observed within an organization at three levels: publisher/owner, editorial and audience
- Degree of concentration can be measured in terms of: market value share, audience share and share of channels
- The effects of concentration are difficult to assess beyond an increase in market power and reduction of diversity
- Concentration is reckoned to be excessive where three or four firms control more than 50% of the market
- Concentration is driven by excessive competition, the search for synergy and very high profit
- Some kinds and degree of concentration can benefit consumers
- Undesirable effects of excessive concentration are: loss of diversity, higher prices and restricted access to media
- Concentration can be combated by regulation and by encouraging new entrants to the market

Mass Media Governance

The manner in which the media are controlled in democratic societies reflects both their indispensability (taken as a whole) for business, politics and everyday social and cultural life, and also their relative immunity to government regulation. Some controls, limitations and prescriptions are necessary, but principles of freedom (of speech and markets) require a cautious, even minimal, approach to regulatory control. It makes sense to use the term 'governance' in this context to describe the overall set of laws, regulations, rules and conventions which serve the purposes of control in the general interest, including that of media industries. Governance refers to a process in which a range of different actors co-operate for different purposes, with actors drawn from market and civil society institutions as well as from government. It thus refers not only to formal and binding rules, but also to numerous informal mechanisms, internal and external to the media, by which they are 'steered' towards multiple (and often inconsistent) objectives. Despite the 'bias against control', there is an extensive array of actual or potential forms of control on media. Because of the diversity of the terrain covered, it is inappropriate to speak of a 'system' of governance, although there are some general principles and regularities to be found in much the same form in many countries. Essentially, governance entails some set of standards or goals, coupled with some procedures of varying strictness for enforcing or policing them. Generally speaking, governance implies a less hierarchical approach, usually with strong elements of self-regulation. According to Collins (2006), the drift away from hierarchy is driven largely by the increasing complexity of the systems in question. It applies particularly to the Internet because of the general absence of direct state control, unclear legal framework and mixture of private and public uses.

Purposes and forms of governance

The variety of forms of governance that apply to the mass media reflects the diversity of purposes of control for different actors. These include:

- the protection of the essential interests of the state and of public order, including the prevention of public harm;
- the safeguarding of individual rights and interests;
- meeting the needs of the media industry for a stable and supportive operating environment;
- the promotion of freedom and other communication and cultural values;
- the encouragement of technological innovation and economic enterprise;
- the setting of technical and infrastructural standards;
- the meeting of international obligations, including observance of human rights;
- the encouragement of media accountability.

It is clear that such wide-ranging goals call for a diverse set of mechanisms and procedures, given the limited scope for direct governmental action. The outline in Chapter 8 of four frameworks for media accountability (law, market, public responsibility and professionalism) has given an overview already of the main alternatives available. The complex terrain can be mapped out according to two main dimensions: *external* versus *internal*, and *formal* versus *informal*, as sketched in Figure 9.2. The main forms of governance are classified in this way into four types, each with appropriate mechanisms for implementation.

Governance applies at various levels. First, we can distinguish between the international, national, regional and local levels, according to the way a media system is organized. In practice, international regulation has been limited mainly to technical and organizational matters, but the scope of control has been growing, especially as media are becoming more international (see Chapter 10, pp. 267–9). Matters of human rights and potential public harm claim increasing attention. The potential of media propaganda for fomenting inter-ethnic and international hatred has been forced on world attention by calamitous events in the Balkans, the Middle East, Africa and elsewhere as well as the difficult task of reconstructing media after conflict (see Price and Thompson, 2002). Most forms of governance operate at the national level, but some countries with a federalized or regional structure devolve responsibility for media matters from the centre.

	Formal	*Informal*
External	Law and regulation applied via courts and public regulatory bodies	Market forces; Lobby groups; Public opinion; Review and criticism
Internal	Management; Self-regulation by firm or industry; Organizational culture	Professionalism; Codes of ethics and conduct

Figure 9.2   The main forms of media governance

More relevant to note here is the distinction between *structure, conduct* and *performance* that has already been introduced (p. 192), and where regulation can apply respectively to a media system, a particular firm or organization, or some aspect of content. As a general rule, control can be applied more readily the further away the point of application is from content because there is less chance of infringing essential freedoms of expression. Here structure relates mainly to conditions of ownership, competition, infrastructure, universal service or other carriage obligations. It includes the major matter of public broadcasting. Conduct relates to such matters as editorial independence, relations with sources and government, matters to do with the justice system, formal self-regulation and accountability. The level of performance covers all matters to do with content and services to audiences, often with particular reference to alleged harm or offence. The main propositions relating to media governance in relatively free media systems are given in Box 9.6.

9.6 Media governance: main propositions

- Different media need different forms of governance
- Control is more justifiable for mass media than for small-scale media because of the scale of possible effects
- Control can be applied more legitimately to structure than to content
- Neither prepublication censorship nor punishment for publication alone are consistent with freedom and democracy
- Self-regulation is generally preferable to external or hierarchical control

The Regulation of Mass Media: Alternative Models

For historical and other reasons, different media have been subject to different types and degrees of regulation. The differences are related to four main factors: first, the strength of a medium's claim to freedom, especially in the light of its typical content and uses; secondly, the degree to which a potential harm to society is perceived; thirdly, for reasons of equitable allocation; and finally, the relative practicability of effective regulation. Three models in particular have been identified (Pool, 1983) and are outlined below. These still help to explain the main differences in the degree to which governments can intervene, although they are becoming less distinct, especially because of deregulation and technological convergence. The essential features of each model are compared in Figure 9.3.

The free press model

The basic model for the press is one of freedom from any government regulation and control that would imply censorship or limits on freedom of publication. Press freedom is often enshrined as a principle in national constitutions and in international charters, such as the European Convention on Human Rights (ECHR, Article 10) or the United Nations Charter (Article 19). However, the press freedom model is often modified or extended by public policy in order to guarantee the expected public interest benefits of a free and independent press. Prominent among the reasons for public policy attention to newspapers has been the trend towards concentration which, although the result of free economic competition, effectively reduces access to press channels and choice for citizens.

Because of this, the press often receives some legal protection as well as some economic benefits. Both imply some element of public scrutiny and supervision, however benevolent. Economic benefits can range from postal and tax concessions to loan and subsidy arrangements. There may also be anti-concentration laws and rules against foreign ownership. The state has played a particularly active role in the evolution of newspaper media in recent times in several European Mediterranean countries, within the framework of a Free Press (Aguado et al., 2009). It is interesting to see how this relates to the 'Mediterranean model' of press–politics relations, mentioned below (p. 241). The press freedom model applies in much the same way to book publishing (where it originates) and to most other print media. By default, it also applies to music, although without any special privileges. Legal action can still be taken against the press for certain offences, such as defamation.

The broadcasting model

By contrast, radio and television broadcasting and, less directly, many newer means of audiovisual delivery have been subject from their beginning to high levels of restriction

	Print	Broadcasting	Common carrier
Regulation of infrastructure	None	High	High
Regulation of content	None	High	None
Sender access	Open	Restricted	Open
Receiver access	Open	Open	Restricted

Figure 9.3   Three regulatory models compared

and direction, often involving direct public ownership. The initial reasons for regulation of broadcasting were mainly technical or to ensure the fair allocation of scarce spectrum and control of monopoly. However, regulation became deeply institutionalized, at least until the 1980s when new technologies and a new climate of opinion reversed the trend.

The general concept of public service lies at the core of the broadcasting model, although there are several variants as well as weaker forms (as in the USA) or stronger forms (as in Europe) (see pp. 178–9). Public service broadcasting in a fully developed form (such as in Britain) generally has several main features, supported by policy and regulation. The broadcasting model can involve many different kinds of regulation. Usually, there are specific media laws to regulate the industry and often some form of public service bureaucracy to implement the law. Quite often, the services of production and distribution may be undertaken by private enterprise concerns, operating concessions from the government and following some legally enforceable supervisory guidelines.

The decline in strength of the broadcasting model has been marked by increasing tendencies towards 'privatization' and 'commercialization' of broadcasting, especially in Europe (see McQuail and Siune, 1998; Steemers, 2001; Bardoel and d'Haenens, 2008; Enli, 2008). This has involved, most notably, the transfer of media channels and operation from public to private ownership, increased levels of financing from advertising, and the franchising of new commercial competitors for public broadcasting channels. New restrictions on activities (e.g. online) have been imposed for reasons of protecting other media from unfair competition from subsidized media. A test of public interest has to be met for any such extension. Despite its relative decline, the broadcasting model shows no sign of being abandoned. It has generally performed well in the audience market (aided by its financial security) but its value to civil society has also been increasingly recognized. Not least in its advantages is its guarantee of adequate and fair access to all political parties in the democratic process and its tendency to privilege access for 'national' interests.

The common carrier model

The third main model of regulation predates broadcasting and is usually called the common carrier model because it relates primarily to communication services such as mail, telephone and telegraph, which are purely for distribution and intended to be open to all as universal services. The main motive for regulation has been for efficient implementation and management of what are (or were) 'natural monopolies' in the interests of efficiency and the consumer. In general, common carrier media have involved heavy regulation of the infrastructure and of economic exploitation, but only very marginal regulation of content. This is in sharp contrast to broadcasting, which is characterized by a high degree of content regulation, even where infrastructure is increasingly in private hands.

While the three models are still useful for describing and making sense of the different patterns of media regulation, the retention of these separate regimes is increasingly called into question. The main challenge comes from the technological 'convergence' between modes of communication which makes the regulatory separation between print, broadcasting and telecommunication increasingly artificial and arbitrary (Iosifides, 2002). The same means of distribution, especially satellites and telecommunication, can be used to deliver all three kinds of media (and others). Cable systems are now often legally permitted to offer telephone services, broadcasting can deliver newspapers, and the telephone network can provide television and other media services. For the moment, a political and regulatory logic survives, but it will not endure.

The hybrid status of the Internet

The Internet has developed in a spirit of *de facto* freedom from any control (Castells, 2001) and in its early days was considered as a 'common carrier' medium, using the telecommunications system for the transmission and exchange of messages and information. It is still very free in practice, more so even than the press since it offers open access to all would-be senders. Even so, its freedom lacks formal protection in law and looks increasingly vulnerable. This follows from its growing commercial functions, fears about its uses and effects as well as its adaptation to other functions, including broadcasting. It is still unclear what its status is in relation to the three models outlined.

One of the distinctive features of the Internet is that it is not regulated specifically at national level and does not fall neatly into any jurisdictional zone. It is also especially hard to regulate because of its transnational character, diversity of functions and unsubstantial character (Akdeniz et al., 2000; Verhulst, 2002). There is a variety of international and national self-regulatory and steering bodies, but their responsibilities and powers are limited (Hamelink, 2000; Slevin, 2000). Much of the burden of what control there is falls on the shoulders of Internet service providers whose rights and legal obligations are also poorly defined (Braman and Roberts, 2003). Uncertainty can sometimes protect freedom, but it also holds back development and opens the way for outside control.

There is an increasing likelihood that the Internet will simply be too important to be left in its semi-regulated condition. Collins (2008) argues against three myths of Internet governance: first, that the market can take care of most decisions; secondly, that self-governance is pervasive and effective; and thirdly, that its governance is essentially different from that of older media. He points to many examples of emerging elements of external control nationally and internationally. In particular, that the Internet is not a single medium and will not call for

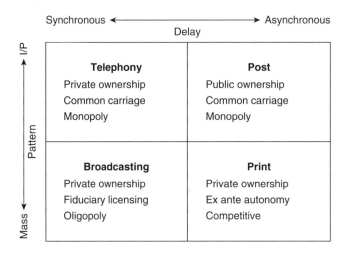

Figure 9.4   Policy regimes governing past communication platforms
Source: Bar and Sandvig (2008: 535)

a single regulatory regime. Further, he writes that 'governance of the Internet and of legacy media [press broadcasting, etc.] is converging as legacy media echo the Internet's disaggregated structure, as they move from the historical vertically integrated structure' (Collins, 2008: 355). This refers especially to such things as the separation of production from transmission and the outsourcing of many aspects of the production and marketing process.

The different 'regimes' of regulation, as summarized in Figure 9.3, have some relationship with the typology of information traffic described earlier in Chapter 6 (pp. 146–8). The broadcasting model corresponds to allocution (direct address), the newspaper model more to consultation and the common carrier model to the Internet (plus telephony). An alternative path towards explaining the differences between regimes governing the four main traditional communication media has been suggested by Bar and Sandvig (2008), which also helps to explain the special position of the Internet. This is outlined in Figure 9.4 and is based on the situation of US media.

Figure 9.4 summarizes the key differences between media on two key dimensions – mass versus interpersonal pattern and instant versus delayed or mediated contact – that are of significance for public regulatory policy. The principles of structure and policy summarized under each of the four media types are those that have applied in the United States, but they are also now widely the same in other parts of the world as a result of privatization and deregulation. The main exception relates to broadcasting, which often has an element of public ownership and control. A most important point to note is that the Internet can appear in all four quadrants, depending on the use in question and how it is classified. It can be a broadcasting, exchange, consultation or personal medium. Since it has no fixed classification, no single regime will serve the purposes of regulation and policy has to take the goals of communication into account, regardless of the technology. The difference between public and private uses remains of primary importance.

Media Policy Paradigm Shifts

The trend towards convergence of regulatory models for different media is part of a larger pattern of change in approaches to media policy. Some elements of this have already been noted, including the early attempts to make the mass media more accountable to society and, more recently, the influence of globalization and the trends to 'deregulation' and privatization of media. Following van Cuilenburg and McQuail (2003), over the longer term of a century of communication development we can detect three main phases of communication policy in different parts of the world.

The first can be described as a phase of *emerging communication industry policy* lasting from the later nineteenth century until the Second World War. There was no coherent policy goal beyond those of protecting the strategic interests of governments and nations and promoting the industrial and economic development of new communication systems (telephony, cable, wireless telegraphy, radio, etc.).

The second main phase can be described as one of *public service*. It begins with the recognition of a need to legislate for broadcasting, but this time with a new awareness of the social significance of the medium for political, social and cultural life. Communications were seen as much more than technologies. New ideas of 'communication welfare' were introduced which went much further than the requirement of controlled allocation of scarce frequencies. Policy was positive in promoting certain cultural and social goals as well as negative in the sense of forbidding certain kinds of harm to 'society'. For the first time, the press came within the scope of public policy in order to limit the power of monopoly owners and maintain 'standards' in the face of commercial pressures. This phase reached its apex in Europe in the 1970s and has been in relative decline ever since, although important elements remain.

A third phase of policy has now developed as a result of many of the trends that have already been discussed, but especially the trends of internationalization, digitalization and convergence. The key event has been the move to centre stage of telecommunications (Winseck, 2002). The period into which we have moved is one of intense innovation, growth and competition on a global scale. Policy still exists, but the *new paradigm* is based on new or adapted goals and values. Policy is still guided ultimately by political, social and economic goals, but they have been reinterpreted and reordered. Economic goals take precedence over the social and political. The content of each value sphere has also been redefined, as shown in Figure 9.5. The key principles summing up public communications policy are freedom, universal service and access, plus accountability, mainly defined in terms of media self-regulation with light outside control (Burgelman, 2000; Napoli, 2001; Verhulst, 2006). Some years further on, this revised paradigm seems a valid interpretation of the course of events, but the rise of the Internet is not well accounted for, with new kinds of problems as well as communication benefits and a lack of effective means of securing the public good, or preventing alarm, except by essentially restrictive and retrogressive actions.

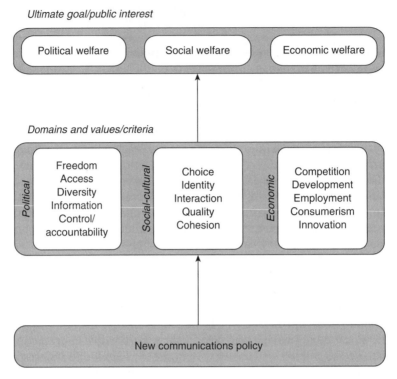

Ultimate goal/public interest

Political welfare   Social welfare   Economic welfare

Domains and values/criteria

Political
Freedom
Access
Diversity
Information
Control/
accountability

Social-cultural
Choice
Identity
Interaction
Quality
Cohesion

Economic
Competition
Development
Employment
Consumerism
Innovation

New communications policy

Figure 9.5   The new communications policy paradigm (van Cuilenberg and McQuail, 2003: 202)

Media Systems and Political Systems

Much of the foregoing discussion of media policy and regulation, as well as earlier chapters on normative theories of the media, leaves little doubt about the complex and powerful links between mass media and the national political system (and even the state itself) even where there is formally little or no connection. This is not to argue that the media are necessarily subordinate to politicians or government. The links between the two are as often characterized by conflict and suspicion.

The links between political and media systems do show large intercultural differences (Gunther and Mugham, 2000). Nevertheless, in each case the connections are related to structure, conduct and performance. First, there is a body of law, regulation and policy in every country, which has been negotiated through the political system, and which guarantees rights and freedoms and sets obligations and limits even to the most free of media in the public sphere. In many countries there is a public sector of the media (usually broadcasting) over which governments have ultimate control, and there are diverse ways in which the management of these organizations is penetrated by political interests, even where they have some autonomy.

Owners of private media generally have financial and strategic interests that lead to efforts to influence political decision-making. Not infrequently they have open ideological positions and even political ambitions of their own. The endorsement of political parties by newspapers is more common than not and sometimes political parties control newspapers. For electoral reasons, politicians are often obliged to court the favour of powerful media so that the flow of influence can be two-way.

At the level of performance, the content of most daily media is still often dominated by politics, but not usually because it is so fascinating and newsworthy for the public. While citizens do need to be informed and advised in the longer term, they do not really need what they are offered every day. The reasons lie partly in the advantages for news media in terms of a free staple commodity and partly in the enormous efforts made by political interests (in the widest sense) to gain access to the public for their diverse ends. It also stems from long-standing links between media and political institutions that cannot easily be broken. Politics cannot do without the media, and the kind of (news) media we have would struggle without politics.

There have been numerous attempts to analyse the relationship. Siebert et al.'s book *Four Theories of the Press* (1956) (discussed in Chapter 7, pp. 175–7) still offers a founding principle that has guided most attempts. This is given in the form of a quotation in Box 9.7.

**The basic principle of
media–society relationships 9.7**

The press always takes on the form and coloration of the social and political structures within which it operates. Especially, it reflects the system of social control where the relations of individuals and institutions are adjusted. (Siebert et al., 1956: 1)

Hallin and Mancini (2004) distilled three fundamental models of the relationship between national media systems and political systems, based on a study of seventeen western democracies. The first model is labelled as 'liberal' or 'North Atlantic'; the second as 'democratic corporatist' or 'Northern European'; and the third as 'polarized pluralist' or 'Mediterranean'. The labels indicate the geographical setting of the models which in turn reflects the influence of a number of important cultural and economic factors with deep historical roots. In Box 9.8 a summary comparison is provided of some key aspects of each model, derived from some of the main variables studied. In this presentation, the term 'parallelism' means that media tend to be structured and aligned according to competing parties and ideologies in the country concerned. 'Clientilism' means that media are penetrated by outside interests and serve their ends voluntarily or for money, thus departing from legal-rational norms of conduct (Roudikova, 2008).

9.8 Three models of the media–political system relationship (Hallin and Mancini, 2004)

	Liberal	Democratic corporatist	Polarized pluralist
Role of state in media	Weak	Strong (welfare)	Strong
Consensus or polarization of politics	Mixed	More consensus	More Polarized
Professionalization of journalism	Low	High	Medium
Press–politics parallelism	Low	Medium	High
Presence of clientilism	Low	Low	High

A limitation of this proposal is the rather narrow base of also similar democratic systems on which it rests, although it has since been applied in research in many other countries and is open to adaptation and extension. It is also rather biased towards the newspaper press. Typically, any given case tends to deviate from any single one of the types to a greater or less degree, reducing the value of the typology. Even so, it has proved its value as an entry point for analysis. Although the study described did not look at the 'new democracies' that were added to Europe after the fall of communism around 1990, Jakubowicz (2007) has found it useful for explaining what happened. He concluded that this otherwise very disparate set of countries is closest to the Mediterranean model since most are characterized by late democratization, a weak rational legal authority, often dirigiste state, political parallelism and a tumultuous political life. Jacubowicz supposes that eventually these countries might advance to the democratic corporatist form but are unlikely to reach the condition of a liberal system.

The issue of media–state relations cannot be settled only by reference to general models. The question arises as to why in modern times the mainstream media in free democracies seem so inclined to reflect rather than challenge the policy directions of the government of the day. Why do they so readily carry out the role of 'social controller' signalled by Siebert et al., rather than the role of watchdog and critic celebrated in journalistic ideology? There are several kinds of answer, some of which are proposed in Chapter 11. Bennett (1990) has put forward a well-supported theory of relations between the state and government power on the one hand, and the press on the other, as things are in the USA. It holds that responsible journalists generally limit their understanding of their critical role in relation to the state, where issues of conflict arise, to representing or 'indexing' the range of views of government and other major institutional actors. They do not have an obligation to introduce minority or 'extreme' viewpoints, or to reflect an independent voice of 'public opinion'. The theory was supported by a study of the coverage by the *New York Times* of the US funding of the *contras* in Nicaragua. Subsequently, other cases have been studied, notably the Iraq war that started in

2003 (Bennett et al., 2007). A vivid illustration of the effects of indexation is given by Bennett et al. (2007) in the case of the publication of the Abu Ghraib torture photographs in 2004. The administration refused to use the word 'torture', preferring 'abuse' or 'mistreatment', and were overwhelmingly followed in this by the mainstream US media. 'Indexing' theory offers a convincing explanation of this phenomenon, as expressed by Bennett et al. in Box 9.9.

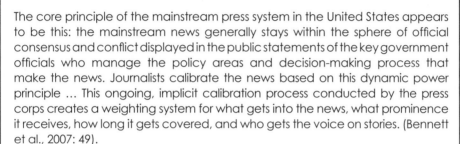

The central idea of indexation theory **9.9**

The core principle of the mainstream press system in the United States appears to be this: the mainstream news generally stays within the sphere of official consensus and conflict displayed in the public statements of the key government officials who manage the policy areas and decision-making process that make the news. Journalists calibrate the news based on this dynamic power principle ... This ongoing, implicit calibration process conducted by the press corps creates a weighting system for what gets into the news, what prominence it receives, how long it gets covered, and who gets the voice on stories. (Bennett et al., 2007: 49).

Although the rationale described in Box 9.9 is consistent with democratic principle, since journalists primarily reflect the perspective of elected representatives, it also allows the latter much power to define their own view of public opinion and act accordingly without much restraint from the press. What is missing seems to be a role for the media in speaking for the public or informing independently. The process described as 'indexing' is clearly present in other countries, partly because it is in some respects a consequence of the addiction of journalists to the practice of objectivity which requires both 'balance' and easy access to credible sources that leads generally to the authorities and established 'experts'. In countries with well-established public broadcasting systems, these tend to follow a version of the 'indexing' logic, although with scope for diversity. However, the precise situation depends on the prevailing political culture. In Japan, for instance, the public broadcaster takes care of impartial information, but the mainstream newspaper press, despite political diversity, operates a form of news cartel (the *kasha* press clubs) that maintains a cosy relationship with power and generally acts as a conduit for the information provided by government and other institutions (Gamble and Watanabe, 2004). In Russia, there is much evidence that the media are very dependent on government and commercial support, with an almost institutionalized clientelism infecting journalism (Stromback and Dimitrova, 2005; Roudikova, 2008). Becker (2005) supports a very pessimist view of media freedom under Putin, but also emphasizes the need to differentiate between the many more or less authoritarian regimes in the world, as between the self-proclaimed democracies.

Conclusion

This chapter has provided an overview of the main features of media economics and of the typical system of regulation (governance). Both show distinctive features compared with other industry sectors and other institutional areas. The key to differences in both cases is the dual character of media, being both a commercial enterprise and a key element in the political, cultural and social life of society. They cannot be left entirely to the marketplace or be closely regulated. Neither media firms nor governments have a free hand to implement policy. Although the trend is towards greater freedom, there will be limits to action.

As far as governance is concerned, the most typical and distinguishing features are as follows. Mass media can only be regulated in marginal or indirect ways by governments. The forms of governance are extremely varied, including internal as well as external, informal as well as formal means. The internal and informal are probably the more important. Different forms of regulation are applied to different technologies of distribution. Forms of governance are rooted in the history and political cultures of each national society.

Further Reading

Baker, E. (2007) *Media Concentration and Democracy*. Cambridge: Cambridge University Press.
The work of an established authority on crucial issues for democracy arising from the commercialization of the mass media. Based on US experience, but equally relevant for other market-based media systems.

Küng, L., Picard, G. and Towse, R. (eds) (2008) *The Internet and the Mass Media*, pp. 86–101. London: Sage.
A set of chapters by different authors on aspects of the impact of the Internet on the existing mass media, especially on media markets and industries, media organization and regulatory issues. Succint and empirically informed. Primary reference is to European circumstances.

Terzis, G. (2007) *European Media Governance: National and Regional Dimensions*. Bristol, UK: Intellect.
Multi-authored resource book with regional overview articles and chapters on media systems of thirty-two countries.

Turow, J. (2009) *Media Today: An Introduction to Mass Communication*, 3rd edn. New York: Routledge.
A great source of highly accessible information about contemporary media industries and processes. Although based on US conditions, it is of much relevance for understanding global media operations.

Online Readings

Albarran, A. (2004) 'Media economics', in J.D.H. Downing, D. McQuail, P. Schlesinger and E. Wartella (eds), *The Sage Handbook of Media Studies*, pp. 291–308. Thousand Oaks, CA: Sage.

Croteau, D. and Hoynes, W. (2007) 'The media industry: structure, strategy and debates', in E. Devereux (ed.), *Media Studies*, pp. 32–54. London: Sage.

Fengler, S. and Russ-Mohl, S. (2008) 'Journalists and the information-attention markets: towards an economic theory of journalism', *Journalism*, 9 (6): 667–90.

Fuchs, C. (2009) 'Information and communication technologies and society: a contribution to the critique of the political economy of the Internet', *European Journal of Communication*, 24 (1): 69–87.

Mansell, R. (2004) 'Political economy, power and the media', *New Media and Society*, 6 (1): 96–105.

10

Global Mass Communication

The pace of internationalization has accelerated because of advances in distribution technology and new economic imperatives. The mass media are affected, like everything else, by the general phenomenon of globalization. They are in a special position themselves as both an object and an agent of the globalizing process. They are also the means by which we become aware of it. Changes in distribution technology have been the most evident and immediate cause of change, but economics has also played a decisive part. We look at the internationalization of media ownership and of the content that flows through media channels.

There are several reasons for devoting a separate chapter to this aspect of mass communication. One is the fact that the global character of mass media became increasingly problematized after the Second World War. Problems arose from ideological struggles between the free-market West and communist East, economic and social imbalance between the developed and the developing world, plus the growth of global media concentration threatening freedom of communication. The issue of cultural and economic domination by the media of the developed world and the consequences for minority cultures everywhere needs special attention. We have reached a point where qualitative change might lead to more genuinely global media, involving independent media serving audiences across national frontiers. This means the emergence of international media as such, with their own audiences, and not just the internationalization of content and organization of media. The Internet takes a central position in scenarios for the future of international communication and also brings questions of governance of global media into sharper focus.

Origins of Globalization

Books and printing were international in their origins since they predated the era of nation states and served cultural, political and commercial worlds that extended throughout Europe and beyond. Many early printed books were in Latin or were translated from another language, and the earliest newspapers were often compiled from newsletters that circulated widely throughout Europe. The early-twentieth-century newspaper, film or radio station were recognizably the same from New York to New South Wales and Vladivostok to Valparaiso. Nevertheless, the newspaper as it developed became very much a national institution, and national boundaries largely delineated the circulation of print media in general. The national character of early mass media was reinforced by the exclusiveness of language as well as by cultural and political factors. When film was invented, it too was largely confined within national frontiers, at least until after the 1914–18 war. Its subsequent diffusion, especially in the form of the Hollywood film, is the first real example of a transnational *mass* medium (Olson, 1999). When radio was widely introduced during the 1920s, it was once more an essentially national medium, not only because of the spoken word in different languages, but also because transmission was generally only intended to serve the national territory.

By comparison, we are now being constantly reminded of how international the media have become and how the flow of news and culture encompasses the globe and draws us into a single 'global village', to use the words of McLuhan (1964). The major newspapers from the mid-nineteenth century onwards were well served by powerful and well-organized news agencies that made use of the international telegraph system, and foreign news was a staple commodity of many newspapers across the world. The predominant features of the geopolitical scene, especially nationalism itself and also imperialism, encouraged an interest in international events, especially where war and conflict provided good news copy (this predates the nineteenth century, e.g. Wilke, 1995). In the early part of the twentieth century, governments began to discover the advantages of the media for international as well as domestic propaganda purposes. Since the Second World War a good many countries have used radio to provide a worldwide service of information and culture designed to foster a positive national image, promote the national culture and maintain contact with expatriates.

Early recorded music also had a quasi-international character, first because of the classical repertoire and secondly because of the increasing diffusion of American popular songs, sometimes associated with musical films. There has always been a real or potential tension between the desire to maintain a national, cultural and political hegemony and the wish to share in cultural and technological innovations from elsewhere. National minorities have also sought to assert a cultural identity in the face of imperialist cultural domination in the literal sense (for instance, within the British, Austrian and Russian empires). The United States was a latecomer to the imperialist role. After the Second World War in particular, it pursued a policy of advancing US media penetration around the world, not least in the form of a belief system about the desirable structure of media in society – a combination of free markets, free expression and ostensible political neutrality, with inevitable contradictions.

Television is still probably the single most potent influence in the accelerating media globalization process, partly because, as with the cinema film, its visual character helps it to pass barriers of language. In its early days, the range of terrestrial transmission was limited to national frontiers in most countries. Now, cable, satellite and other means of transmission have largely overcome these limitations. Another new force for internationalization is the Internet, which does not have to observe national boundaries at all, even if language, culture and social relations do ensure that frontiers still structure the flow of content.

Driving Forces: Technology and Money

Technology has certainly given a powerful push to globalization. The arrival of television satellites in the late 1970s broke the principle of national sovereignty of broadcasting space and made it difficult and ultimately impossible to offer effective resistance to television transmission and reception from outside the national territory. But the extent to which satellites reach global audiences directly with content from abroad is often exaggerated and is still relatively small, even in regions such as Europe. There are other means of diffusion that work in the same direction – for instance by connecting cable systems and simply by physically transporting CDs or DVDs. But the main route is by exports of content channelled through nationally-based media.

While technology has been a necessary condition of extensive globalization, and the truly global medium of the Internet illustrates this most clearly, the most immediate and enduring driving forces behind globalization have been economic (and the brakes have been cultural). Television was established on the model of radio broadcasting, as a continuous service at least during the evening, then later during the day and ultimately on a 24-hour basis. The cost of filling broadcasting time with original or domestic material has always exceeded the capacity of production organizations, even in wealthy countries. It is virtually impossible to fill schedules without great repetition or extensive importing.

The expansion of television since the 1980s, made possible by new, efficient and low-cost transmission technologies, has been driven by commercial motives and has fuelled demand for imports. It has also stimulated new audiovisual production industries in many countries that look, in their turn, for new markets. The main beneficiary and the main exporter has been the United States, which has a large and surplus production of popular entertainment and an entrée into many markets secured by the cultural familiarity of its products, mainly as a result of decades of American films. The English language is an added advantage but is not decisive, since most TV exports have always been dubbed or subtitled when transmitted.

An important component of international mass communication is advertising, linked to the globalization of many product markets and reflecting the international character of many advertising agencies and the dominance of the market by a small number of firms. The same advertising messages appear in different countries, and there is also an indirect internationalizing effect on the media that carry the advertising. Last but not least of the forces promoting globalization has been the vast expansion and the privatization of telecommunications infrastructure and business (Hills, 2002). The main causes of media globalization are given in Box 10.1.

10.1 Causes of media globalization

- More powerful technologies for long-distance transmission
- Commercial enterprise
- Follow-on from trade and diplomatic relations
- Colonization and imperialism, past and present
- Economic dependency
- Geopolitical imbalances
- Advertising
- Expansion of telecommunications

Global Media Structure

As a background to this discussion, it is useful to have an overview of the 'global media system', in so far as this can be done, since there is no formal arrangement beyond national frontiers. The simplest way to begin is with the many separate sovereign states that interact and communicate with each other. The pathways of flow and exchange between nations follow some regular and predictable (although changing) patterns and this helps us to visualize a structure of a kind. The states involved vary a great deal and the factors of variation largely shape the overall 'structure'. The main factors are size (of territory and population), level of economic development, language, political system and culture. The size of a country affects all aspects of media, but population provides either an economic base for domestic production or a large target market for other countries' exports. Language and culture encourage certain flows between countries with a mutual affinity and also set limits to what is possible, as do political and ideological barriers. Economic muscle is the main determinant of dominance in the overall set of relationships. The world of the media is also in respects stratified by region. Tunstall (2007: 330) points to four levels. Below the global level are located the nation state, the national region and the locality. Even so, media are overwhelmingly still organized at a national level.

Much theory and research has explored the basic structure outlined, but a central organizing idea is that of a centre–peripheral pattern of relations between nations (Mowlana, 1985). Those with a core position have the most developed media, are wealthier and larger in population. The peripheral nations have the reverse characteristics. There are, of course, intermediary positions. Core nations are likely to have larger flows to other countries, which are not balanced by return flows. Mutual exchanges are likely to be greater between countries that are 'close' in terms of geography, culture or economic relations. Peripheral countries do not export media content, but their capacity to import is also limited by lack of development. This sometimes leads to a different kind of self-sufficiency than that enjoyed by rich core nations.

The underlying circumstances of global media structure set the scene for theorizing, debate and research about the reality and desirability of globalization. At the start, around the 1960s, thinking was dominated by the extreme dominance of the USA, especially in Hollywood entertainment and the global news agencies. The Soviet Union was a core counterplayer, along with China and the rest of the communist world. The Third World provided a large set of peripheral countries, although with much variation. With the near demise of communism and rapid development of much of Asia and Latin America, the world structure looks quite different. The USA still dominates as a producer of international entertainment, but a large part of the world's population now lives in the Indian subcontinent or China or a few other large countries, including Japan, Brazil, Indonesia, Nigeria and Mexico, that are largely self-sufficient in media. Tunstall (2007: 6) concludes that 'taking these ten countries together, probably not more than 10 percent of their entire audience time is spent with foreign media'. Today the largest media producers (not always exporters) are likely to be the USA, China, Mexico, Egypt, Brazil and India. Tunstall adds that the most globalized media countries, those that do most importing, 'fall into three categories: 1, small-population poorer countries; 2, small countries with a large neighbour and a shared language; and 3, the various rich but smaller European countries that import from diverse sources'. The main questions arising from the structure of the global media system are posed in Box 10.2.

10.2 Global media structure: main questions arising

- What is the pattern of dominance and imbalance of media flow?
- What are the causes of patterns observed?
- What are the consequences of the structure as observed?
- What are dynamics and directions of change?
- How should we evaluate media globalizing trends?

Multinational Media Ownership and Control

The recent phase of the 'communications revolution' has been marked by a new phenomenon of media concentration, both transnational and multimedia, leading to the world media industry being increasingly dominated by a small number of very large media firms (Chalaby, 2003). In some cases, these developments are the achievement of a fairly traditional breed of media 'mogul' (Tunstall and Palmer, 1991), though with new names. Despite the high visibility of larger-than-life media moguls, it is likely that the trend is rather towards more impersonal patterns of ownership and operation, as befits such large global enterprises. Media developments in emerging markets such as South America and India have given rise to their own national media moguls and multimedia firms, often with foreign investments (see Chadha and Kavoori, 2005).

Certain types of media content lend themselves to globalization of ownership and control of production and distribution. These include news, feature films, popular music recordings, television serials and books. Tunstall (1991) refers to these as 'one-off' media, by contrast with the 'cash-flow' media of newspapers and television stations, which have generally resisted multinational ownership. The 'one-off' product can be more easily designed for an international market and lends itself to more flexible marketing and distribution over a longer timespan. 'News' was the first product to be 'commodified' by way of the main international news agencies. These are, in effect, 'wholesale' suppliers of news as a commodity, and it is easy to see why national news media find it much more convenient and economical to 'buy in' news about the rest of the world than to collect it themselves.

The rise of the global news agencies of the twentieth century was made possible by technology (telegraph and radio telephony) and stimulated by war, trade, imperialism and industrial expansion (Boyd-Barrett, 1980, 2001; Boyd-Barrett and Rantanen, 1998). Government involvement was quite common. For these reasons, the main press agencies in the era after the Second World War were North American (UPI and Associated Press), British (Reuters), French (AFP) and Russian (Tass). Since then, the US predominance has declined in relative terms with the virtual demise of UPI, while other agencies have grown (such as the German DPA, Chinese Xinhua and the Japanese Kyodo). Tass has been replaced by Itar–Tass, still a state agency.

According to Tunstall (2007), despite general American media dominance, Europe had become the largest producer and consumer of foreign news. Paterson (1998: 79) writes that the three television news agencies that originate much of the international news used by the world's broadcasters are Reuters, World Television News (WTN) and Associated Press Television News (APTV). Tunstall and Machin (1999: 77) refer to a virtual 'world news duopoly' controlled by the US Associated Press and the British Reuters. The French AFP, German DPA and Spanish EFE are also big players. It is clear that predominance is shaped by the domestic strength of the media organizations concerned, in terms of market size, degree of concentration and economic resources. The English language confers an extra advantage.

The foremost example of internationalization of media ownership, production and distribution is that of the popular music industry (a development of the last fifty years), with a high proportion of several major markets being in the hands of 'big five' companies. Following the merger of Bertelsmann and Sony in 2004, there are four dominant companies: Sony, Warner, Universal and EMI. About a third of all worldwide recording sales are in American hands (Turow, 2009). Advertising provides another example of very high concentration and internationalization. According to Tunstall (2007), about six leading super-agencies have the lion's share of the world's advertising expenditure. Advertising agencies tend also to control market research, media buying and public relations companies. As Thussu (2009: 56) comments, 'a Western, and more specifically, Anglo-American stamp is visible on global advertising', with a trend towards global branding. Most attention tends to be paid to the US-based multimedia firms with global operations, such as AOL–Time Warner, Disney, NBC–Vivendi, Bertelsman, News Corporation, Sony, etc., but there are now quite a few multimedia conglomerates elsewhere in the world.

Globalization and concentration of large media companies tend also to lead to cartel-forming, and the very large firms co-operate in various ways as well as compete. Companies also co-operate by sharing revenue, co-production, co-purchasing of movies, and dividing up local outlets. Although the story becomes increasingly complicated by the rise of Japanese and European media enterprises, there is little doubt that the USA has benefited most from global expansion in media markets. According to Chan-Olmstead and Chang (2003), European media firms are less inclined to diversify internationally.

Varieties of Global Mass Media

Global mass communication is a multifaceted phenomenon that takes a variety of forms. These include:

- Direct transmission or distribution of media channels or complete publications from one country to audiences in other countries. This covers foreign sales of newspapers (sometimes in special editions) and books, certain satellite television channels, and officially sponsored international radio broadcast services.
- Certain specifically international media, such as MTV Europe, CNN International, BBC World, TVCinq, Televisora del Sur, Al-Jazeera, and so on, plus the international news agencies.
- Content items of many kinds (films, music, TV programmes, journalistic items, etc.) that are imported to make up part of domestic media output.

- Formats and genres of foreign origin that are adapted or remade to suit domestic audiences.
- International news items, whether about a foreign country or made in a foreign country, that appear in domestic media.
- Miscellaneous content such as sporting events, advertising and pictures that have a foreign reference or origin.
- The World Wide Web (last but not least) in many different forms, overlapping with some of the above.

It is clear from this inventory that there is no sharp dividing line between media content that is 'global' and that which is 'national' or local. Mass communication is almost by definition 'global' in potential, although most countries have a mainly domestic media supply. The United States is one such case, but American media culture does have many foreign cultural influences, through trade and immigration. It is also indirectly globalized by the orientation of much of its own production towards world markets.

Despite the many manifestations of media globalization, there are few media outlets (channels, publications, etc.) that actually address a significantly large foreign audience directly (even if the potential in terms of households reached is large, as shown by Chalaby (2003)). At most, certain successful products (e.g. a hit film or TV show, a music recording, a sporting event) will receive a worldwide audience in the end. This implies that 'exporting' countries still have a considerable capacity to influence the 'national' media experience of 'receiving' countries. We have to consider how far the 'foreign' content has been subject to 'gatekeeping' controls at the point of import (for instance, edited, screened and selected, dubbed or translated, given a familiar context). The main mechanism of 'control' is not usually policy or law, or even economics (which often encourages imports), but the audience demand for their 'own' media content in their own language. There are natural barriers of language and culture that resist globalization (Biltereyst, 1992). Economics can limit as well as stimulate imports. In general, the wealthier a country, even when small in population, the more chance it has to afford its media autonomy. The forms of globalization are diverse and the meaning of the term, elastic. Some of these meanings are shown in Box 10.3.

10.3 The meanings of media globalization

- Increasing ownership by global media firms
- Increasing similarity of media systems across the world
- The same or very similar news and entertainment products are found globally
- Audiences can choose media from other countries
- Trends of cultural homogenization and westernization
- Decontextualization of media experience in respect of location and culture
- Reduction in national communication sovereignty and more free flow of communication

International Media Dependency

According to dependency theorists, a necessary condition for throwing off the dependent relationship is to have some self-sufficiency in the realm of information, ideas and culture. Mowlana (1985) proposed a model in which two dimensions are the most important determinants of the degree of communication dependence or autonomy. The model represents a now familiar sequence from sender (1) to receiver (4), mediated by a technologically based production (2) and distribution (3) system. In international communication, contrary to the typical national media situation, the four stages of origination, production, distribution and reception can be (and often are) spatially, organizationally and culturally separated from each other. Media products from one country are typically imported and incorporated into a quite different distribution system and reach audiences for which they were not originally intended. Quite commonly, especially in respect of film and television, the entire origination and production of products occurs in one country and the distribution in another. This is how the 'North' is often related to the 'South' in media terms.

This typically extended and discontinuous process is dependent on two kinds of expertise (and also of property), one relating to hardware, the other to software. Production hardware includes cameras, studios, printing plants, computers, and so on. Production software includes not only actual content items but also performance rights, management, professional norms and routine operating practices of media organizations (know-how). Distribution hardware refers to transmitters, satellite links, transportation, home receivers, recorders, and so on. Distribution software includes publicity, management, marketing and research. Both production and distribution stages are affected by extramedia as well as intramedia variables – on the production side by circumstances of ownership and the cultural and social context, and on the distribution side by the economics of the particular media market.

The model thus describes conditions of multiple dependency in the flow of communication from more to less developed countries. The latter are often dependent in respect of all four main types of hardware and software, and each may be controlled by the originating country. Self-sufficiency in media terms is virtually impossible, but there can be extreme degrees of insufficiency, and it is never possible to truly 'catch up'. As Golding (1977) first pointed out, the potential influence that goes with media dependency is not confined to cultural or ideological messages in content; it is also embedded in professional standards and practices, including journalistic ethics and **news values**. These points can also be explained in terms of the centre–periphery pattern discussed above.

The gobal communication situation is one of increasing complexity as a result of new markets, new media and changes in economic fortunes and geopolitical realities, but some forms of dependency will persist, with different patterns for different media. However, overall, the framework explains less than formerly. In the emerging and still unclear 'system' of global communication flows, it is probable that the nation state will be less significant as a unit of analysis. It is more difficult to assign information and culture to a country of origin. Multinational production and marketing in the control of large corporations and multilateral media flows will establish their own patterns of dominance and dependency.

Cultural Imperialism and Beyond

In the era immediately following the Second World War, when communication research was largely an American monopoly, the mass media were commonly viewed as one of the most promising channels of modernization (i.e. westernization) and especially as a potent tool for overcoming traditional attitudes (Lerner, 1958). From this perspective, the flow of mass media from the developed or capitalist West to the less developed world was seen as both good for its recipients and also beneficial in combating the alternative model of modernization based on socialism, planning and government control. The kinds of media flow envisaged were not direct propaganda or instruction, but the ordinary entertainment (plus news and advertising) that was presumed to show a prosperous way of life and the social institutions of liberal democracy at work. The flood of American print, film, music and television provided the main example and testing of the theory.

This was undoubtedly a very ethnocentric way of looking at global communication flow and it eventually provoked a critical reaction from scholars and political activists and also from those at the receiving end. Before long the issue was inescapably caught up in Cold War polemics and left-wing resistance movements in semi-colonial situations (especially in Latin America). However, unlike the international propaganda efforts of previous times, the new 'media imperialism' seemed to be carried out at the willing request of the mass audience for popular culture and was thus much more likely to 'succeed'. Of course, it was not the audience making a direct choice, but domestic media firms choosing on their behalf, for economic rather than ideological reasons.

Most of the issues surrounding global mass communication have a direct or indirect connection with the thesis of 'cultural imperialism', or the more limited notion of 'media imperialism' (see below). Both concepts imply a deliberate attempt to dominate, invade or subvert the 'cultural space' of others and suggest a degree of coercion in the relationship. It is certainly a very unequal relationship in terms of power. It also implies some kind of overall cultural or ideological pattern in what is transmitted, which has often been interpreted in terms of 'western values', especially those of individualism, secularism and materialism.

It has a political as well as a cultural content, however, in the first case essentially a submission to the global project of American capitalism (Schiller, 1969). In the case of relations with Latin America noted already, the idea of an American 'imperialist' project for the hemisphere, certainly in the 1960s and 1970s, was not fanciful (Dorfman and Mattelart, 1975). Critical theorists have not always agreed on whether it was the economic aims of global market control or the cultural and political aims of 'westernization' and anti-communism that took precedence, although the two aspects are obviously connected. The (critical) political economy theorists emphasize the economic dynamics of global media markets that work blindly to shape the flows of media commodities. Not surprisingly, such dynamics favour the free-market model and in general promote western capitalism.

The critics of global media imperialism have generally been countered by a mixed set of supporters of the free market or just pragmatists who see the imbalance of flow as a normal feature of the media market. In their view, globalization has benefits for all and is not necessarily problematic (e.g. Pool, 1974; Hoskins and Mirus, 1988; Noam, 1991; Wildman, 1991). It may even be temporary or reversed under some circumstances. BBltereyst (1995) has described the situation in terms of two dominant and opposed paradigms under the headings of *dependency* and *free flow*. In his view, both paradigms rest on somewhat weak grounds empirically. The critical dependency model is based very largely on evidence of quantity of flow and some limited interpretation of ideological tendencies of content. There is little or no research on the posited effects. The free-flow theorists tend to assume minimal effects on the grounds that the audience is voluntary, and they make large and unfounded assumptions about the cultural neutrality and ideological innocence of the globally traded content. It is also quite possible to view the ongoing globalization of media as having no ultimate goal or purpose and no real effect (in line with the 'cultural autonomy' position signalled in Chapter 4, pp. 81–2). It is simply an unplanned outcome of current political, cultural and technological changes.

If the process of global mass communication is framed from the point of view of the national societies at the receiving end, according to the media imperialist thesis there are at least four propositions to consider. These are listed in Box 10.4 and will be discussed later in the chapter. However, there has been a shift in thinking about globalization that has moved on from the overwhelmingly negative perspective of media imperialism. It is not a return to the 'optimism' of the modernization phase, but more a reflection of postmodern ideas and new cultural theory that avoids the normative judgements of earlier theory.

Media imperialism: main propositions **10.4**

- Global media promote relations of dependency rather than economic growth
- The imbalance in the flow of mass media content undermines cultural autonomy or holds back its development
- The unequal relationship in the flow of news increases the relative global power of large and wealthy news-producing countries and hinders the growth of an appropriate national identity and self-image
- Global media flows give rise to a state of cultural homogenization or synchronization, leading to a dominant form of culture that has no specific connection with real experience for most people

---

Globalization re-evaluated

The cultural imperialism thesis has been largely abandoned in the more recent tendency to frame many of the same issues in terms of 'globalization' (Sreberny-Mohammadi, 1996; Golding and Harris, 1998). As we have seen, there has been a strong challenge to the critique of popular mass media and its general cultural pessimism. This has also affected thinking about the effects of global cultural exchange, although perhaps not about the global flow of news. Certainly, we quite often encounter positive, even celebratory views of the global inclusiveness brought about by mass media. The shared symbolic space can be extended, and the constraints of place and time that are associated with nationally compartmentalized media systems can be evaded. Globalization of culture can even look good compared with the ethnocentrism, nationalism and xenophobia that characterize some national media systems. The new era of international peace (the 'new world order') that was supposed to have been ushered in by the end of the Cold War was thought to require a significant presence of internationalist media (Ferguson, 1992). The consequences of the 'war on terror' have yet to be revealed but the initial indications from global entertainment as well as news make it likely to have a polarizing effect, a return to global divisions similar to those of the Cold War.

Most of the propositions arising from the media imperialism thesis tend to frame global mass communication as a process of cause and effect, as if the media were 'transmitting' ideas, meaning and cultural forms from place to place, sender to receiver. To that extent, the critics use much the same language as the original 'theorists of development'. There is a general consensus that this 'transportation' model of how media work is not very appropriate outside certain cases of planned communication. If nothing else, we need to take much more account of the active participation of the audience in shaping any 'meaning' that is taken from mass media (Liebes and Katz, 1990).

It is arguable that the media may even help in the process of cultural growth, diffusion, invention and creativity, and are not just undermining existing culture. Much modern theory and evidence supports the view that media-cultural 'invasion' can sometimes be *resisted* or redefined according to local culture and experience. Often the 'internationalization' involved is self-chosen and not the result of imperialism. Lull and Wallis (1992) use the term 'transculturation' to describe a process of 'mediated cultural interaction' in which Vietnamese music was crossed with North American strains to produce a new cultural *hybrid*. There are likely to be many examples of a similar process. Theorists tend to see globalization as accompanied by a process of 'glocalization', according to which international channels, such as CNN and MTV, adapt to the circumstances of regions served (Kraidy, 2001). The incorportation of different formats and performance standards into home production is another aspect of the process (Wasserman and Rao, 2008).

There is arguably a general and perhaps irresistible process of 'deterritorialization' of culture under way (Tomlinson, 1999). Secondly, alternative 'readings' of the same 'alien' content are, as we have seen, quite possible. 'Semiotic power' can also be exercised in this context, and media content can be decoded differentially according to the culture of receivers (Liebes and Katz, 1986). This is probably too optimistic a view to bear much weight, and the evidence is not yet very strong. Foreign cultural content may also be received with a different, more detached attitude (Biltereyst, 1991) than home-made media culture. Despite the attractions of global media culture, language differences still present a real barrier to cultural 'subversion' (Biltereyst, 1992). Evidence concerning the reception of foreign news (aside from its availability) is still very fragmentary, but there is elsewhere some evidence and good theory to support the view that foreign news events are framed by audiences not only in terms of possible relevance to the home country, but also according to personal circumstance. They are understood or 'decoded' according to more familiar social and cultural contexts (Jensen, 1998).

The 'problem' of potential cultural damage from transnationalized media may well be exaggerated. Globally, many distinct regional, national (and subnational) cultures within Europe and other regions are still strong and resistant. Audiences can probably tolerate several different and inconsistent worlds of cultural experience (such as local, national, subgroup and global) without one having to destroy the others. The media can extend cultural choices in a creative way, and internationalization can work creatively. This relativizing of the problem does not abolish it, and there are circumstances under which cultural loss does occur.

This revised and more positive perspective on globalization rests on the observation that the international flow of media generally responds to demand, and has to be understood in terms of the wants and needs of receivers and not just the actual or supposed motives of the suppliers. This fact does not in itself invalidate the media imperialist critique, given the constraints in the global media market. Many features of the world media situation attest to the even more powerful grip of the capitalist apparatus and ethos on media nearly everywhere, with no place left to hide.

The Media Transnationalization Process

Under this heading we look at the process by which content and audience experience are in some sense globalized. It is an effect process (if there is one) with two stages: first, transformation of content; and secondly, impact on audiences. In his analysis of the international flows of television, Sepstrup (1989) suggested that we differentiate *flows* in the following way:

- *national* – where foreign (not home-produced) content is distributed in the national television system;
- *bilateral* – where content originating in and intended for one country is received directly in a neighbouring country;
- *multilateral* – where content is produced or disseminated without a specific national audience in mind.

In the *national* case, all content is distributed by the home media, but some of the items will be of foreign origin (films, TV shows, news stories, etc.). The *bilateral* case refers mainly to direct cross-border transmission or reception, where audiences in a neighbouring country are reached on a regular basis. This is common, for example, in respect of the USA and Canada, Britain and Ireland, The Netherlands and Belgium. The *multilateral* type covers most examples of overtly international media channels (MTV, CNN, etc.). The first type of internationalization is by far the most important in terms of volume of flow and reach to audiences, yet at the same time, as we have noted, it is potentially open to national control.

The model of transnationalizing effects proposed by Sepstrup (1989) on the basis of this characterization is reproduced in Figure 10.1. This shows the relationship between three notional countries, in which X is a major producer and exporter of media content and Y and Z are importers. There are three main lines of

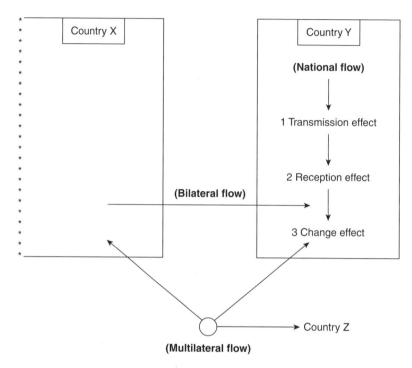

Figure 10.1   Internationalization of television: three types of flow (McQuail and Windahl, 1993: 225, based on theory in Sepstrup, 1989)

transnationalizing effect: national, bilateral and multilateral. The first of these operates on the basis of imports and is really a process by which a national media system is internationalized by way of borrowing content. The next step in the process, if there is one, is that the national system becomes the agent for influencing its audiences in an 'international' direction, for good or ill. For this to take place, the content not only has to be transmitted, but has to be received and responded to in a positive way. Only if this happens can we speak of a process of internationalization that affects the culture and the society.

Of the other two processes, the case of bilateral flow (direct cross-border transmission) most often occurs when neighbouring countries already have much in common in terms of culture, experience and usually language. The case of multilateral flow from one country direct to many others is growing in importance with the growth of the Internet, which facilitates multiple multilateral flows.

The more that content is filtered through the national media system, the more it is subject to selection and adapted, reframed and recontextualized to fit local tastes, attitudes and expectations. The chance of 'culture clash' is diminished. This transformation is greater where the receiving countries are well developed, culturally and economically. The transformation process (in the transmission) is likely to be least operative where there is already cultural affinity between the country of origin and the country of reception (and thus less room for cultural change). It is also limited where the receiving country is poor and undeveloped, the cultural distance is high and the opportunity to accept influence (in the form of new ideas or new kinds of behaviour) is low.

The direction of any transnationalizing effect seems very predictable from the structure of the world media system as outlined above, although the degree of effect from mass communication alone is very uncertain. The arrival and growth of the Internet does widen the possibility of access to global information and cultural resources. Access is now also possible without reliance on the various gatekeepers that always restrict and control the flow of content in more traditional media. These gatekeepers operate at both the sending and receiving ends of distribution channels. The Internet (and the World Wide Web) is a genuinely international medium and potentially opens a vast new resource to all. However, it remains another fact that Internet 'content' is dominated by 'western' (and English language) originators, how-ever diverse, and access is dependent on expensive equipment, significant costs for poor people, and language and other skills.

International News Flow

As noted earlier, the globalization of news really began in earnest with the rise of the international news agencies in the nineteenth century (see Boyd-Barrett and Rantanen, 1998), and news was the first media product to be effectively commodified for international trade. The reasons for this are not altogether clear, although the his-tory of mass media shows the early and perennial importance of a service of current information for attracting audiences. The 'news' has become a more or less standard-ized and universal genre as a component of print and electronic media, and along with it the 'news story'. The news story can have a value as useful information or can satisfy curiosity and human interest, regardless of where it is heard.

The televising of news has accelerated the cross-cultural appeal of news by telling the story in pictures to which can be added words in any language or with any 'angle'. Television news film agencies followed in the footsteps of the print news agencies. The picture may well tell a story but the words pin down the intended meaning. Television news film, like print news, has been based on the principle of journalistic 'objectivity' that is designed to guarantee the reliability and credibility of accounts of events. While earlier international 'foreign' news concentrated on poli-tics, war, diplomacy and trade, there has been an enormous expansion of the scope for international news, with particular reference to sport, the world of showbusi-ness, finance, tourism, celebrity **gossip**, fashion and much more.

A debate about the imbalance of news flow as between North and South raged during the 1970s and became highly politicized, caught up in Cold War polemics. An attempt was made by media-dependent countries to use Unesco as a means towards a new world information and communication order (NWICO) that would establish some normative guidelines for international reporting (see Hamelink, 1994; Carlsson, 2003). A claim was also made for some control over reporting on grounds of equity, sovereignty and fairness. These requests were strongly rejected by defenders of the 'free-flow' principle (essentially the free market), mainly western governments and western press interests (see Giffard, 1989). An international inquiry made recommendations for new guidelines (McBride et al., 1980) but it was largely ignored and the path via Unesco was also closed (see Hamelink, 1998). A new phase of accelerated liberalization of communication, nationally and internationally, and other geopolitical changes largely closed down the debate, even though the underlying circumstances were little changed.

Along the way, however, much light was shed by research and by the public debate on the actual structure of news flow and the underlying dynamics of the global news industry. It was repeatedly confirmed that news (whether press or TV) in more developed countries does not typically give a great deal of space to foreign news (except in specialist or elite publications). Foreign news is largely devoted to events in other countries that are large, nearby and rich, or connected by language and culture. It is also narrowly focused on the interests of the receiving country. Most foreign news can often be accounted for by attention to a small number of ongoing crises (e.g. conflict in the Middle East) of relevance to the developed world. Large areas of the physical world are found to be systematically absent or miniscule on the implied 'map' of the world represented by the universe of news event locations (e.g. Gerbner and Marvanyi, 1977; Womack, 1981; Rosengren, 2000). In particular, developing countries are only likely to enter the news frame of developed countries when some events there threaten the economic or strategic interests of the 'great powers'. Alternatively, news is made when problems and disasters reach a scale so as to interest audiences in distant and safer lands.

The reasons for the 'bias' of international news selection that still largely persists are not hard to find or to understand. In the first place they result from the organization of news flow by way of agencies and each news medium's own gatekeeping. The ultimate arbiter is the average news consumer, who is usually thought of as not very interested in distant events. Agencies collect news 'abroad' with a view to what will interest the ultimate 'home' audience, and the foreign news editors of home media apply an even more precise set of criteria of a similar kind. The result is to largely eliminate news of distant places that is not dramatic or directly relevant to the receiving nation.

There has been much research into the factors shaping the structure of foreign news. Most basic is the fact that the flow of news reflects patterns of economic and political relations as well as geographical closeness and cultural affinity (Rosengren, 1974; Ito and Koshevar, 1983; Wu, 2003). The flow of news is positively correlated with other forms of transaction between countries. We need or want to know about those parts of the world with which we trade or with whom we are friendly or unfriendly. The other main factor is power: we need to know about more powerful countries that can affect us. There are more detailed explanations of foreign news selection. Galtung and Ruge (1965) proposed that selection was the outcome of three sets of factors: *organizational*, dealing with the availability and distribution of news; *genre related*, dealing with what conventionally counts as of interest to news audiences; and *social-cultural* factors, mainly referring to the values by which topics are chosen.

Other analyses of patterns of attention in foreign news have largely confirmed the validity of these points. News will tend not to deal with distant and politically unimportant nations (except in some temporary crisis), with non-elites or with ideas, structures and institutions. Long-term processes (such as development or dependency) are not easy to turn into news, as normally understood. However, we should keep in mind that most studies of news have concentrated on 'serious' (i.e. political and economic) content and hard news. Less attention has been given to areas that may be quantitatively and in other ways more significant, in particular material about sport, music, entertainment, celebrity gossip and other human interest matters which may easily become 'news'. The news that most people enjoy is dominated by such topics and they are quite likely to be international in character, reflecting global media culture.

A recent study of international news relating to the events of 9/11 has cast some doubt on the persistence of some of the tendencies outlined. This study, by Arcetti (2008), of four countries (the USA, France, Pakistan and Italy) examined the sources drawn on in news reports of the events. It showed that each media channel had its own distinctive pattern of sources, the majority coming from its own national resources. Secondly, there is little evidence of the media agenda of a foreign country being imported, since news selections were made according to the domestic (own nation) perspective. Thirdly, weaker players in the news system, such as Pakistan, actually had a more diverse source pattern than the American media, making foreign news dominance unlikely. All in all, the study brings into question both globalizing and homogenizing effects.

Among expectations about the Internet was the hope that it would widen access to and enrich the flow of international news, simply by virtue of the seemingly unlimited capacity and the open availability from sources around the world. First indications of results are not so promising. For instance, one study looked at the determinants of news on the most visited US websites – CNN.com and nytimes.com – and where possible compared online with print versions (Wu, 2007). The results showed that online news followed almost the same patterns as traditional news outlets and the associated factors were the same, especially patterns of trade, news agencies, geographical and cultural proximity. The main explanation is that economic pressure leads most online news to depend heavily on news agencies.

Another study, by Chang et al. (2009), came to a consistent conclusion, this time based on a study of online news in fifteen countries. The main focus was on links between core and peripheral countries, as indicated by the location of hyperlinks in online news texts. This showed where editors looked for their sources. The results confirmed that core countries did have more incoming hyperlinks, especially the USA and the UK. It also showed that the core countries of the United States, the UK, Japan and Canada were well interconnected. The pattern is a familiar one but notable is the seeming failure of the USA to have any significant hyperlinks to any peripheral country in the study, except South Africa. In contrast, the UK stands out as having a clear pattern of linkage to nearly all the peripheral countries. British media, especially the BBC, are more inclined to send hyperlinks to websites in the countries reported in the news. This at least shows that the hope mentioned above is not entirely empty, if the will and economic resources are present.

A summary of the factors relevant to news flow is given in Box 10.5.

10.5 Factors affecting the selection and flow of international news

- Occurrence of events abroad with home relevance or interest
- Timing of events and news cycles
- Reporting and transmitting resources available
- Operation of international news agencies
- Journalistic news values
- Patterns of geography, trade and diplomacy
- Cultural affinity between countries

The Global Trade in Media Culture

There has been an enormous expansion of television production and transmission outside the United States since the 1970s, leaving the USA relatively less dominant in global media terms than it was thirty years ago. This means that more countries can satisfy more of their own needs from home production. Sreberny-Mohammadi (1996) cites findings that show unexpectedly high levels of local production. For instance, India and Korea produced about 92% of their televised programming, and 99% of Indian daily viewing was of home-produced content. But there are still high levels of penetration, especially in respect of American films and television drama, nearly everywhere and the adaptation of international, mainly US, formats to local circumstances. The phenomenon of 'Bollywood' captures this process very well. Sreberny-Mohammadi warns against over-interpretation of the evidence of 'indigenization', since much is produced by large corporations operating under exactly the same logic as the former villains of cultural imperialism.

In the background to the European case there is a long history of grumbling (usually by cultural elites) about the threat of 'Americanization' to cultural values and even civilization. In the aftermath of the Second World War, the dominance of American media was an accomplished fact, but impoverished countries still restricted film imports and supported nascent national film and television industries. In general, television services were developed on the basis of national public service models that gave some priority to promoting and protecting the national cultural identity.

More recent attitudes in Western Europe to importing audiovisual content have been shaped by three main factors, aside from expansion and privatization. One has been the political-cultural project of a more united Europe (see below). The second has been the goal of creating a large internal European market, in which European audiovisual industries should have their place in the sun. Thirdly, there was a wish to reduce the large trade deficit in media products. All goals were perceived to be undermined by the one-directional transatlantic flow of content. According to Tunstall and Machin (1999), the attempts to enlarge the market have mainly benefited American exporters by creating a single market and opening it up to competition.

The mixing of cultural and economic motives and arguments confused the issue considerably, but the EU accepts the principle of open markets. The resulting compromise has allowed principles of free trade and cultural sovereignty to survive, though without much practical effect on the course of events. The European Union retains some policies that give some protection to European television and film industries (especially its Directive on Television Without Frontiers, which privileges European production), but the trading deficit in such goods continues (Dupagne and Waterman, 1998).

Although media imports to Europe basically arise from the general attractiveness of the product to the media audience, it is also clear that, in any given country, the most popular television programmes (highest ratings) are nearly always home produced (even if based on international media formats). For example, in the UK, in April 2009 there was no single American production in the 100 top-rated network programmes on British TV. Leading American imports generally come second in order of preference, but there is also a large amount of imported content that is used to fill daytime or late-night schedules with small audiences or to stock new low-budget satellite and cable channels. The practice of bundling a set of contents together for sale that are not really wanted also leads to over-supply. The price of US exports is always adjusted to the particular market situation, and there is a 'cultural discount' factor in operation that relates the price to degree of cultural affinity between exporter and importer (the lower the affinity, the lower the price) (Hoskins and Mirus, 1988).

Imported content from the USA falls largely into the category of drama and fiction and reflects the high cost of own production on the part of other countries rather than the overwhelming appeal or superior quality of the product. The much heralded transnational (multilateral) satellite channels such as CNN and MTV have had limited success in reaching mass audiences in Europe and have been forced to regionalize content and transmission and adapt their content and format to cope with local requirements. The arrival of digital television has given some impetus to transnationalization, but the barriers are not primarily technological (Papathanossopolous, 2002). The story of MTV Europe, as told by Roe and de Meyer (2000), is indicative of what happened more generally over time to the transnational satellite television channels that spearheaded the 'invasion' of Europe in the 1980s and 1990s. MTV was initially very successful in gaining a new youth audience for mainly Anglo-American pop music. However, competing channels in Germany, The Netherlands and elsewhere forced MTV to respond with a policy of regionalization, employing the 'local' language but not changing the music significantly. This process has continued and the lesson does seem to be that, while the English language is an asset because it is the language of pop music, it is not in general an advantage for channel presentation.

Because this book is about mass media it largely ignores other forms of cultural globalization, although these are often connected with the media and vice versa. Rich countries have always borrowed cultural elements from colonies, dependencies and trading partners in the form of ideas, designs, fashions, cuisine, flora and much more. Immigrant groups have also taken their culture with them when they converge on the same rich countries. The diffusion of symbolic cultures now also takes place by way of the media, advertising and marketing, often via the search for new products to feed the lifestyle demands of consumers. This works in both directions (centre and periphery). Moorti (2003) describes the case of the import of Indian motifs into American fashion culture, especially the bindi (vermilion mark) and nose-ring. Such symbols are adopted by American women as a fashion statement and also a signifier of cosmopolitanism and exoticism, without anything changing in the hierarchical relationship between white and Asian women. Moorti calls this 'symbolic cannibalism' and a typical example of commodification rather than real multiculturalism. It is also an example of postmodern pastiche. Many similar examples can be found.

Towards a Global Media Culture?

A recurring theme of debate and research arising out of media globalization concerns cultural identity. Imported media culture is thought to hinder the development of the native culture of the receiving country, or even many local and regional cultures within a country. Often the perceived problems are associated with a smaller country being located in the shadow of a dominant nation, as in the case of Canada *vis-à-vis* the USA or Ireland and the UK.

Underlying the above issues is a strong 'belief system' holding that cultures are both valuable collective properties of nations and places, and also very vulnerable to alien influences. The value attributed to a national culture is rooted in ideas developed during the nineteenth and twentieth centuries, when national independence movements were often intimately connected with the rediscovery of distinctive national cultural traditions (for example, in Greece, Ireland and Finland). The frequent lack of correlation between newly established national boundaries (often invented) and 'natural' cultural divisions of peoples has done little to modify the rhetoric about the intrinsic value of national culture.

A similar situation arises in the case of national minorities trapped within a larger nation state and with limited autonomy. There is a good deal of confusion about the meaning of national or cultural identity although in a given case it is usually clear what is involved. Schlesinger (1987) suggests an approach by way of a general concept of 'collective identity'. A collective identity, in this sense, persists in *time* and is resistant to change, although survival also requires that it be consciously expressed, reinforced and transmitted. For this reason, having access to and support from relevant communications media is evidently important. Television, in particular, can play a significant part in supporting national identity, by way of language and representation. Castello (2007), drawing on Catalan experience, makes a convincing case for the view that a nation needs its own fiction and therefore a cultural policy that helps it to flourish.

One cultural consequence of media globalization may be overlooked because it is obvious: the rise of a globalized media culture as such (see Tomlinson, 1999). Media internationalization probably does lead to more homogenization or 'cultural synchronization'. According to Hamelink (1983: 22), this process 'implies that the decisions regarding the cultural development of a given country are made in accordance with the interests and needs of a powerful central nation. They are then imposed with subtle but devastating effectiveness without regard for the adaptive necessities of the dependent nation.' As a result, cultures are less distinctive and cohesive and also less exclusive.

There is no shortage of examples of cultural themes, styles, images and performances that are circulated and consumed on a global basis by way of mass communication (and new media). Global media culture is typified by its emphasis on novelty, fashion, celebrity in all fields, youth and sex. Often the particular stars of celebrity culture are truly global; sometimes they are local but the phenomenon is otherwise the same. Not by chance, the international media are given some credit (or blame) for promoting this type of culture. The trend is found as much in news as in entertainment. According to Thussu (2009), the globalization of television along the US market-driven model has led to the worldwide circulation of 'infotainment', with the same standards of newsworthiness and often the same news and the same sources, everywhere. The model of 24-hour news, in particular, has spread across the globe. While such a global media culture may appear value-free, in fact it embodies a good many of the values of western capitalism, including individualism and consumerism, hedonism and commercialism. It may add to the cultural options and open horizons for some, but it may also challenge and invade the cultural space of pre-existing local, indigenous, traditional and minority cultures. The main hypothesized effects of globalization are summarized in Box 10.6.

Cultural effects of globalization: potential effects 10.6

- Synchronization of culture
- Undermining national, regional and local cultures
- Commodification of cultural symbols
- Increased multiculturalism
- Hybridization and evolution of cultural forms
- Rise of a global 'media culture'
- Deterritorialization of culture

Global Media Governance

In the absence of global government, international communication is not subject to any central or consistent system of control. The forces of the free market and of national sovereignty combine to keep it this way. Nevertheless, there is quite an extensive set of international controls and regulations that do constrain nationally based media, typically as a result of voluntary co-operation for necessity or mutual advantage (Ó Siochrú et al., 2003). For the most part, such regulation is designed to facilitate global media in technical and trade matters, but some elements are concerned with normative matters, however non-binding.

The origins of global governance are to be found in agreements designed to facilitate the international postal service, by way of the Universal Postal Union in the mid-nineteenth century. At about the same time (1865), the International Telegraph Union was founded to help co-ordinate interconnections and establish agreement on tariffs, with a subsequent extension to responsibility for the radio spectrum. In both cases, for the moment, governments and state monopolies played a key role. After the Second World War, the United Nations provided an arena for debate on mass-media matters, with particular reference to freedom of expression (guaranteed by its charter), the free flow of communication between countries and issues of sovereignty. In 1978 an attempt was made in Unesco, at the behest of Third World countries, to introduce a media declaration stating a number of principles for the conduct of international media, especially in relation to propaganda for war and hostile reporting. Opposition by western countries and free-market media led to its failure, but it did place a number of new and contentious issues on the agenda of concern and debate and contributed to the recognition of certain communication rights and obligations. There are still international treaties, including the UN Declaration and both the European and the American Conventions on Human Rights, that offer some redress to those injured by misuse of communication.

The paradigm shift that occurred towards deregulation and privatization, coupled with the new 'communications revolution' based on computers and telecommunications, closed off the path towards greater international normative regulation. But the same shift increased the need for technical, administrative and economic co-operation on a range of issues. Most recently, the development of the Internet has stimulated calls for international regulation, but this time with some reference to content as well as structure.

The following bodies now play a variety of key roles in the emerging system of governance:

- The (renamed) International Telecommunication Union (ITU), governed by a council of delegates nominated by national governments, deals with telecommunication technical standards, spectrum allocation, satellite orbits and much besides.
- The World Trade Organization has immense power on economic matters and impinges more and more on the media, as they become bigger business and more commercialized. Central are issues of free trade and protection, with implications for limits to national sovereignty in relation to media policy. The policy of the EU for protecting broadcasting is especially vulnerable, as is public broadcasting generally (Puppis, 2008). Apart from the EU, other regional trade organizations, such as the North American Free Trade Association (NAFTA), can impinge on media issues.
- The United Nations Educational, Scientific and Cultural Organization (Unesco), a branch of the UN established in 1945, has wide competence on cultural and educational matters, but little power and no clearly specific media functions. However, it is active on questions of freedom of expression and the Internet.
- The World Intellectual Property Organization (WIPO), established in 1893, has a main aim of harmonizing relevant legislation and procedure and resolving disputes between owners of rights, authors and users.

- The International Corporation for Assigned Names and Numbers (ICANN) is the latest addition to the array of governance bodies. It is a voluntary private body that aims to represent the community of Internet users. It started in 1994 after privatization of the World Wide Web and its main function was to allocate addresses and domain names, plus some server management functions. It has little power to deal directly with the emerging social and other problems relating to the Internet. Formally, it is answerable to the US Department of Commerce, but efforts are being made to make its governance more genuinely international.

There are many other bodies with varying remits for issues relating to international media. Many represent various industry interests, including those of publishers, journalists and producers. There are also many non-governmental organizations (NGOs) speaking for interests in 'civil society'. For the reasons given, effective regulation is still largely confined to technical and economic matters rather than social and cultural issues, with the possible exception of freedom of communication. Nevertheless, there are many scattered signs of growing internationalism and, arguably, a need for a more suitable frame of analysis than is offered simply by an array of national states (see Gunaratne, 2002).

Conclusion

Global mass communication is a reality, and since the second half of the twentieth century there has almost certainly been a steady strengthening of the conditions of globalization. These are: the existence of a free market in media products; the existence of and respect for an effective 'right to information', and thus political freedom and freedom of speech; and the technologies that can offer fast, capacious and low-cost channels of transmission across borders and large distances. Nevertheless, the real chances for global sending or receiving and the probability of it taking place depend on more mundane matters, especially those relating to the national media system and its degree of connectedness to other systems.

Paradoxically, the country endowed with all three of the conditions mentioned, the USA, is one of the least likely to be a beneficiary by way of the mass media coming from outside its own frontiers. This does not apply to many sectors where the US imports 'culture' from around the world along with other products. The means are there but the will and motivation are missing. The countries most favoured by a real experience of international media are likely to be small and wealthy enough both to sustain a viable national culture and to enjoy the eclectic fruits of the global information society. There has to be an appreciation of these fruits, or some pressing need, for global mass communication to prosper, and the main hope for this now lies with the Internet and World Wide Web and the further extension of digitalization.

A condition for global communication to become a more significant component of public communication (as opposed to an important element of media markets) will be some movement towards a global political order and some form of international government.

Further Reading

Boyd-Barrett, O. and Rantanen, T. (eds) (1998) *The Globalization of News*. London: Sage.
Still a valuable guide to the fundamental facts and issues of the global flow of news, with particular reference to the operation of world news agencies.

Chadha, K. and Kavoori, A. (2005) 'Globalization and national media systems: mapping interactions in policies markets and formats', in J. Curran and M. Gurevitch (eds), *Mass Media and Society*, 4th edn, pp. 84–103. London: Hodder Arnold.
This provides a very clear account of the thesis that globalization and media are intimately and causally interrelated, supported by an extensive review of literature.

Ó Siochrú, S. and Girard, B., with Mahan, A. (2002) *Global Media Governance*. Lanham, MD: Rowman and Littlefield.
A concise overview and explantion of the various agencies with international media regulatory responsibilities.

Thussu, D. (2009) *News as Entertainment*. London: Sage.
A lively and well-informed account and evaluation of the culture and content of news-making across the globe, with particular reference to its rise as a form of popular entertainment (infotainment).

Tunstall, J. (2007) *The Media Were American*. Oxford: Oxford University Press.
The author returns to re-examine the thesis of his own earlier influential study of American global media hegemony. His work reports a significant decline in global media dominance, largely due to European success in news and the great success of emerging economies at supplying their own media needs. There are still large areas of US strength.

Online Readings

Arcetti, C. (2008) 'News coverage of 9/11 and the demise of the media flows, globalization and localization hypotheses', *The International Communication Gazette*, 70 (6): 463–85.
Bitereyst, D. (1991) 'Resisting American hegemony: a comparative analysis of the reception of domestic and US fiction', *European Journal of Communication*, 6 (4): 469–97.
Chang, T.-K., Himelboim, L. and Dong, D. (2009) 'Open global networks, closed international flows', *The International Communication Gazette*, 71 (3): 137–59.
Ferguson, M. (1992) 'The mythology about globalization', *European Journal of Communication*, 7 (1): 69–93.
Sinclair, J. (2004) 'Globalization, supranational institutions and media', in J.D.H. Downing, D. McQuail, P. Schlesinger and E. Wartella (eds), *The Sage Handbook of Media Studies*, pp. 65–82. Thousand Oaks, CA: Sage.

Part 4
Organizations

11

The Media Organization: Pressures and Demands

Theory about mass communication began with little awareness of the place where media messages originated, except for the vague designation of a 'mass communicator' as source. The originating organization was taken for granted and theory began with the message itself. Research on media production, after beginning with descriptions of media occupations, especially in film and journalism (Rosten, 1937, 1941), gradually widened its focus so as to take account of professional cultures and the occupational context of media work that could affec t what was produced. This chapter looks in turn at each of the main kinds of influence that are brought to bear during the production and processing phase of mass communication. These include external influences from society and the media market as well as from owners, advertisers and the audience. These are looked at primarily from the perspective of the 'communicators' themselves. Attention is also paid to relations internal to the media organization and to the conflict, tensions and problems encountered. The main tensions arise from recurring dilemmas that lie at the heart of media-making. These include the potential clash between profit on the one hand, and art or social purpose on the other, and the problem of reconciling creative and editorial freedom with the demands of routine and large-scale production.

The overriding aim of the chapter is to identify and assess the potential influence of various organizational and communicator factors on what is actually produced. Research into 'news-making', prompted initially by evidence of patterning and selective attention (sometimes called 'bias') in news content, showed the news product to be, in one sense or another, both a routine product of a 'news factory' (Bantz et al., 1980) and also a very predictable symbolic 'construction' of reality. It is here that the choice of critical perspective (and wider social theory) comes into play. Less attention has been paid to the production of non-journalistic content, especially drama, music and entertainment, but similar forces are at work.

Major changes in the structure of media industries, especially the processes of globalization, ownership conglomeration and organizational fragmentation, provide new theoretical challenges. New means of distribution (such as cable, satellite and the Internet) have also given rise to new kinds of media organization, although research and theory have still to catch up.

Research Methods and Perspectives

A very simple and general framework within which questions can be posed was introduced in Chapter 9. *Structural* features (for instance, size, forms of ownership and media-industrial functions) can be seen as having direct consequences for the *conduct* of particular media organizations. Conduct refers to all the systematic activities that in turn affect *performance*, in the sense of the type and amount of media content produced and offered to audiences. According to this model, we need to look not only at internal features of media organizations but also at their relations with other organizations and with the wider society.

Most of the research and theory discussed in the following pages are 'media-centric' rather than 'society-centric' (see pp. 12–13), taking or recording the view from within the media. This may lead to an over-estimation of the significance of organizational influences on content. From a 'society-centric' point of view, much of what media organizations do is determined by external social forces, including, of course, the requirements of media audiences. The question of 'paradigm choice' (see pp. 65–6) has not been very sharply posed in relation to research on media organizations since it calls for a mixture of both qualitative and quantitative methods and attracts critical as well as neutral perspectives.

The predominant method of research has been participant observation of media people at work or in-depth interviewing of involved informants. However, this method requires co-operation from the media organizations under study and this has been increasingly difficult to obtain. On some points, survey research has provided essential additional information (for instance, on questions of occupational role and social composition).

In general, the theory that has been formulated on the basis of research into media organizations, while fragmentary, has been fairly consistent. It supports the view that content is systematically more influenced by organizational routines, practices and goals than by personal or ideological factors. However, this proposition is itself open to alternative interpretations. It could be taken to mean that ownership and control influence content, thus supporting the social critical view. Or it could reflect the fact that any kind of standardized or mass production process involves some systematic influence on content. From the latter perspective, the 'bias' that has been observed in media content is more likely to be caused by work routines than by hidden ideology.

The Main Issues

Two overarching issues of structure and content can be identified:

- What degree of freedom does a media organization possess in relation to the wider society, and how much freedom is possible within the organization?
- How do media-organizational routines and procedures for selecting and processing content influence what is produced?

These two questions roughly correspond to the duality noted above of the structural effect on organizational conduct and the effect of the latter, in its turn, on content produced. Shoemaker and Reese (1991) name five main hypotheses concerning the influence of structural and organizational factors on content, as shown in Box 11.1.

Hypotheses about factors influencing content (Shoemaker and Reese, 1991) 11.1

- Content reflects social reality (mass media as mirror of society)
- Content is influenced by media workers' socialization and attitudes (a communicator-centred approach)
- Content is influenced by media-organizational routines
- Content is influenced by social institutions and forces outside the media
- Content is a function of ideological positions and maintains the status quo (the hegemonic approach)

The first of these hypotheses is not directly discussed in this chapter, although the kind and degree of 'reflection of reality' are certainly affected by a number of organizational factors. The most directly relevant of the five hypotheses are the second, third and fourth. The final hypothesis also largely lies outside the scope of this chapter because it is so broad. However, in general, it presumes that media organizations are not really autonomous, but are penetrated by other sources of power (especially political and economic). The more it appears that outside forces shape the operation of media, the more plausible this hypothesis becomes. Some light will be shed on this matter later.

Levels of Analysis

It is increasingly difficult to speak of a 'media organization' as if there were a single ideal-typical form. The original term was largely based on the model of an independent newspaper, within which all the principal activities of management, financial control, news collecting, editing and processing, plus printing and distribution, took place more or less under one roof. This model was always untypical of media in general, not applying, for instance, to the film, book publishing or music industries, and applying only variably to radio and television. It is virtually impossible to apply it to most of the so-called new media, which interrelate several separate and disparate organizational functions.

The diversity of organizational forms is matched by the diversity of occupational groups that might qualify as 'mass communicators'. These have been taken as including movie moguls and press tycoons, actors, television producers, film directors, scriptwriters, book authors, newspaper and broadcast journalists, songwriters, disc jockeys, musicians, literary agents, newspaper and magazine editors, website designers, advertisers and public relations people, campaign managers, and many more. Most of these categories can also be subdivided according to the type of medium, size or status of the work organization, employment status, and so on. An increasing amount of media work takes place on a freelance or entrepreneurial basis, and many media workers (notably writers and actors) belong to no single production organization, even if they may be members of professional or craft associations. As a result, the concepts of 'mass communicator' and of 'media profession' are almost as leaky as that of media organization.

The uncertainty on what counts as a media organization and what counts as a mass communicator has increased considerably as a result of the expansion and **digitization** of media and the rise of the Internet. Deuze (2007) sees this uncertainty as the main defining feature of media work in a world that is characterized by 'liquidity', mobility and lack of compartmentalization. The same content can appear on many media platforms. There is no professional or economic monopoly on the potential to reach a large audience by way of the Internet. Moreover, there is an increasing tendency for media to make, employ or encourage user-generated content in many different forms. The seemingly alternative social media sites are also being used by 'big media' and major communicators for advertising and publicity.

Despite this diversity, it still makes sense to try to place questions of media organization within a common framework. One useful step is to think in terms of levels

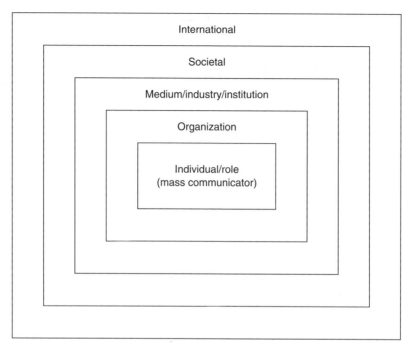

Figure 11.1   Mass media organizations: levels of analysis

of analysis, so that the different phases of media work and the significant relations between units of organizational activity and between media and the 'outside world' can be identified for study. Dimmick and Coit (1982), for instance, describe a hierarchy with nine different levels at which influence or power may be exercised. The main levels and associated sources of influence, in descending order of 'distance' from the point of production, are supranational, the society, media industry, supra-organizational (e.g. media conglomerates), the community, intra-organizational and individual.

For the purposes of this chapter, a similar but modified hierarchy is employed, as shown in Figure 11.1. There is no hierarchy in the sense that the 'higher-order' influence has primacy in terms of strength and direction, but it does serve to represent the society-centric perspective, according to which media are dependent on their society. It also corresponds to the most likely general balance of power in society. Even so, it is more appropriate to consider the relations between media communicators and their environment as, in principle, interactive and negotiable. It is also appropriate to emphasize that the media organization operates within and maintains its own 'boundaries' (however permeable) and has some degree of autonomy.

The arrangement of entries in Figure 11.1 recognizes the significance of the individual who carries out media work and is subject to the requirements of the organization, but also has some freedom to define his or her place in it. Most of the discussion which follows relates to the central area of the 'organizational level', but also takes account of the relations across the boundary between the work organization and other agents and agencies of the wider media institution and society.

It is clear from Chapter 7 that media organizations in their relations with the wider society are formally or informally regulated or influenced by normative expectations on either side. Such matters as the essential freedoms of publication and the ethical guidelines for many professional activities are laid down by the 'rules of the game' of the particular society. This implies, for instance, that the relations between media organizations and their operating environments are governed not solely by law, market forces or political power, but also by unwritten social and cultural guidelines and obligations.

The Media Organization in a Field of Social Forces

Any theoretical account of media organizations and occupations has to take note of a number of different relationships within and across the boundaries of the organization. These relationships are often active negotiations and exchanges and sometimes conflicts, latent or actual. The influential model of mass communication drawn by Westley and MacLean (1957), which has already been discussed (pp. 85–6), represents the communicator role as that of a broker between, on the one hand, would-be 'advocates' in society with messages to send and, on the other, the public seeking to satisfy its information and other communication needs and interests.

Gerbner (1969) portrayed mass communicators as operating under pressure from various external 'power roles', including clients (such as advertisers), competitors (other media in the main), authorities (especially legal and political), experts, other institutions and the audience. He wrote:

> While analytically distinct, obviously neither power roles nor types of leverage are in reality separate or isolated. On the contrary, they often combine, overlap and telescope ... the accumulation of power roles and possibilities of leverage gives certain institutions dominant positions in the mass communication of their societies.

Using these ideas and relying on the wide support for such a view in the research literature, we can portray the position of the media organization in general terms as follows. Those within it have to make decisions at the centre of a field of different constraints, demands or attempted uses of power and influence, as in Figure 11.2. The general hierarchy shown in Figure 11.1 has been converted into a view of more specific actors and agencies in the environment of a media organization. This representation is primarily derived from research on news media (especially newspapers), but the picture would be much the same for many similar 'self-contained' and multipurpose media, including broadcast television (see, for example, Wallis and Baran, 1990).

The pressures and demands illustrated in Figure 11.2 are not all necessarily *constraining* on media organizations. Some can be sources of liberation, for instance, by way of alternative sources of income, or government policy protection for their task. Some of the forces cancel or balance each other (such as audience support against advertiser pressure, or media institutional prestige against external institutional or source pressure). Lack of external pressure would probably indicate social marginality or insignificance.

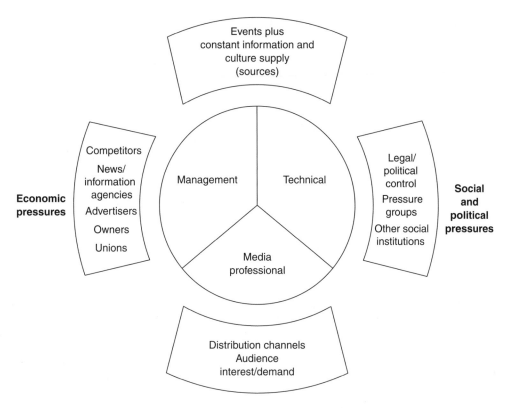

Figure 11.2   The media organization in a field of social forces

A further refinement of this scheme, based on the work of Engwall (1978), involves the internal division of the media organization into three dominant work cultures (management, technical and professional), indicating the main sources of tension and lines of demarcation which have been found to exist within media organizations. This presentation allows us to identify five main kinds of relationship – with society, with pressure groups, with owners, clients and sources, with audiences and also internally – which need to be examined in order to gain some understanding of the conditions affecting organizational activity and the mass communicator role. Each of the five types of relationship is discussed in the following pages.

Relations with Society

A good deal has already been said on this matter, especially in Chapters 7 and 9. The influence of society is ubiquitous and continuous, and arises in virtually all of the media's external relationships. In liberal-democratic societies, the media are free to operate within the limits of the law, but conflicts still occur in relations with government and with powerful social institutions. The media are also continually engaged, sometimes in an antagonistic way, with their main sources and with organized pressure groups. How these issues are defined and handled depends in part on the self-defined goals of the media organization.

The ambiguity of media organizational goals

Most organizations have mixed goals, and rarely are they all openly stated. Mass media are no exception, and they may even be particularly ambiguous in this respect. In organizational theory, a differentiation is often made between utilitarian and normative organizational goals (e.g. Etzioni, 1961). The utilitarian organization aims to produce or provide material goods or services for financial ends, while the normative organization aims to advance some value or achieve a valued condition, based on the voluntary commitment of its participants. The position of mass media organizations in respect of this typology is unclear since they often have a mixture of utilitarian and normative goals and forms of operation. Most media are run as businesses but often with some 'ideal' goals, and some media are run primarily for 'idealistic' social or cultural purposes, without seeking profit. For instance, public broadcasting organizations (in Europe especially) have generally had a bureaucratic form of organization but with non-profit social and cultural goals.

Another suggested basis for organizational classification distinguishes according to *type of beneficiary*. Blau and Scott (1963) ask: 'Is it the society as a whole, a particular set of clients, the owners, the audience, or the employees of the organization, whose welfare or good is being served?' Again, no single answer can be given for the media as a whole, and particular organizations often have several actual or potential beneficiaries. Nevertheless, there is some reason to hold that the general public (not always the direct audience) should be the chief beneficiary (see the discussion of public interest on pp. 163–4).

A common element in all the normative press theories discussed (in Chapter 7) is that the media should meet the needs and interests of their audience in the first instance and the interests of clients and the state only secondarily. Since media depend on the continuous voluntary choices of their audiences if they are to be either effective or profitable, this principle has a common-sense basis, and it accords with the media's own view.

Tunstall (1971) described the organizational goals of news journalism in economic terms, distinguishing between revenue goals and non-revenue goals. The latter refer to purposes without a direct financial aspect, such as gaining prestige, exercising influence or power in society, or achieving some normative end (for instance, serving the community). Revenue goals are of two main kinds: gaining income from direct sales to consumers and from selling space to advertisers. Different kinds of publication policy go with the variation of goals in these terms. While the audience appears to be subordinate in this typology, in practice the satisfaction of advertisers and the gaining of revenue from sales both depend on pleasing the audience, and non-revenue goals are often shaped by some conception of wider public interest. Furthermore,

Tunstall indicates that in the case of conflict of goals within a newspaper, the audience revenue goals (increasing the circulation by pleasing the audience) provide the 'coalition goal' on which most can agree (especially management and journalists).

Some media organizations (especially public service media and those with an opinion-forming or informational purpose) clearly do seek to play some part in society, but the nature of this role is also open to diverse interpretations. Certain kinds of publication, especially prestige or elite newspapers (such as *Le Monde*, the *Financial Times* or the *Washington Post*), have set out deliberately to be influential through the quality of their information or the authority of their opinion (Padioleau, 1985). There are several other options for the exercise of influence, and it is not the exclusive property of an internationally known elite press. Small-scale media can be influential in more restricted spheres, and influence can obviously be exercised by mass circulation newspapers and popular television. The various goals of media organizations are summarized in Box 11.2. These are not mutually exclusive, but typically one or other is given overriding priority.

Main goals of media organizations 11.2

- Profit
- Social influence and prestige
- Maximizing an audience
- Sectional goals (political, religious, cultural, etc.)
- Serving the public interest

The journalist's role: engagement or neutrality?

A broad choice has to be made between a more active and participant or a more neutral and societal role for the journalist. Cohen (1963: 191) distinguished two separate self-conceptions of the reporter's role as that of 'neutral reporter' or 'participant'. The first refers to ideas of the press as informer, interpreter and instrument of government (lending itself as channel or mirror), the second to the traditional 'fourth estate' notion, covering ideas of the press as representative of the public, critic of government, advocate of policy and general watchdog.

The weight of evidence is that the neutral, informative role is most preferred by journalists, and it goes with the importance attached by most journalists to objectivity as a core professional value (Janowitz, 1975; Johnstone et al., 1976; Schudson, 1978; Tuchman, 1978; Weaver and Wilhoit, 1996). Weaver (1998: 478) concluded from an overview of a 21-nation study of journalists that 'the single professional role most journalists agree on is the importance of getting information to the public quickly'. Strong political commitment (and active engagement) is by definition not easy to reconcile with even-handed neutral reporting, and many news organizations have guidelines designed to limit the influence of personal beliefs on reporting. The preference for 'objectivity' also accords with the commercial logic of media businesses, since partisanship tends to narrow the audience appeal. Journalists in popular tabloid media seem to adopt much the same view on this as do more heavyweight journalists for the elite press, even if the results are very different (Deuze, 2005).

The active or participant role has also received considerable support, depending on conditions of time and place and on how it is understood. Fjaestad and Holmlov (1976) identified two main kinds of purpose, each endorsed by over 70% of journalist respondents in Sweden: those of 'watchdog' on local government and of 'educator' or public informant. Johnstone et al. (1976) found that 76% of US journalists thought it extremely important that media should 'investigate claims and statements made by government'. This is in line with several elements in the North American journalistic tradition. These include the political philosophy of 'reformism' (Gans, 1979), the choice of an 'adversary role' *vis-à-vis* government (Rivers and Nyhan, 1973) and the idea that media should look out for the interests of their audience, whom they claim to represent. This is different from partisan advocacy of a particular point of view.

A survey of US journalists by Weaver and Wilhoit (1986) showed that in 1982–3 there had been some withdrawal from the critical perspective held by journalists in 1971, although they remained somewhat reformist in spirit and, on balance, politically more inclined to the left than to the right. Endorsement of the questionnaire item on the 'extreme importance' of media investigating claims and statements made by government had dropped from 76% to 66%, and there was more support for neutral-informative than for participant elements of the journalist's role. Nevertheless, there was also significant minority support for an 'adversary' role.

A similar enquiry in the early 1990s found approximately the same balance of views on journalists' roles (Weaver and Wilhoit, 1996: 133–41). Differences in choice of predominant role have been shown to correspond with different value priorities. Plaisance and Skewes (2003) found that opting for an adversary role was correlated with personally endorsing the values of courage, independence, justice and open-mindedness, while the 'disseminator' role went with values of 'minimizing harm', fairness and self-control. This suggests an element of personality determination.

In place of the simple 'neutral versus participant' dichotomy, Weaver and Wilhoit (1986) opted for a tripartite division of roles as interpreter, disseminator or adversary, in that order of prominence. The *interpreter* role was based on the items 'analysing and interpreting complex questions', 'investigating claims made by government' and 'discussing national policy as it happens'. The second type – that of *disseminator* – mainly relates to 'getting information to the public quickly' and 'concentrating on the largest possible audience'. The third, *adversary*, role (applying to both government and business) was much weaker but was still recognized to some degree by a majority of journalists. The resulting scheme of role perceptions is reproduced in Figure 11.3, showing the main overlap between them. The percentages in the three boxes show the choice by the whole sample of journalists for the roles indicated. The figures attached to the arrows show the percentage of the source box who also endorsed the role at the destination (for example, 45% of those choosing the adversary role also selected that of disseminator). This reveals something of the structure of attitudes, the 'bridge' position between the adversarial and informational positions. The picture was much the same in the early 1990s (Weaver and Wilhoit, 1996).

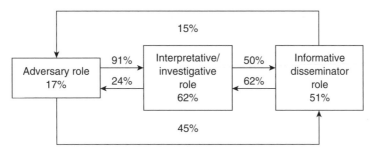

Figure 11.3   Journalists' role perceptions: interpretation and information come first, with opposition a clear but distinctive third option (Weaver and Wilhoit, 1986)

Public broadcasting institutions, such as the BBC, are under a particular obligation to be neutral and balanced, and the chief aim of BBC decision-makers in news and actuality has been described as 'holding the middle ground' (Kumar, 1975) – acting as a broker between disputants rather than being a participant. The question as to whether this lends itself to supporting the established social order has often been discussed. However, this does not prevent fundamental criticism being reported or carried. While times have changed, the forces at work are likely to be similarly balanced. The crisis experienced by the BBC in reporting controversial aspects of the Iraq war in 2003–4 showed how sensitive the relations with government can be. In general, public broadcasting organizations in continental Europe provide more open recognition of different political and ideological streams and also of government influence.

The *plurality* of role conceptions held by journalists is also stressed by Weaver and Wilhoit, who write (1986: 116): 'only about 2 percent of the respondents are exclusively one-role oriented'. They also remind us that, on such matters as role perception and journalistic ethics, there seem to be large cross-cultural differences. Patterson (1998) compared the journalistic cultures of five countries – the United States, Britain, Germany, Italy and Sweden – based on surveys with journalists in each country. One of the main differences stemmed from the wide variation in the degree of partisanship of media systems as a whole, according to journalists' own perceptions. In particular, the United States was exceptional in the degree to which its major news organizations were perceived as concentrated in the middle of the political spectrum. While objectivity as a norm was regarded as of some importance in each country, its meaning varied quite a lot. The predominant meaning ascribed by American journalists was as 'expressing fairly the position of each side in a political dispute'.

This is in line with 'indexing' theory, as discussed in Chapter 9 (pp. 242–3). However, international comparison suggests that journalists tend to follow the national consensus of their own country. For instance, the media in Germany were mainly critical of the military intervention in Iraq in 2003, but in doing so were also following the main policy line of the German government (Lehmann, 2005) and also German public opinion. British media were divided on the issue, torn between supporting the official interpretation of national interest and a mainly unfavourable public opinion. According to Patterson's study, journalists in Germany and Sweden attach much more weight to getting 'beyond the statements of the contending sides to the hard facts of a political dispute'. On the face of it, this is much more independent and interventionist, but the general principle that news journalism reflects the balance of power and opinion in society also seems to hold.

A new dimension to research has been added by the opportunity to compare role conceptions of journalists after the fall of communism in Europe. An example is Wu et al.'s (1996) survey of American and Russian journalists. On most points, especially in relation to information dissemination, objectivity and expressing public opinion, the two populations were similar, but Russian journalists opted for a more politically active role. Yet there is also a difference emerging between an older and a newer generation of Russian journalists (Voltmer, 2000; Pasti, 2005).

It looks as if role conceptions are both variable and quite strongly related to political culture and the degree to which democracy is firmly established (see Weaver, 1998: 477–8). For instance, in countries where democracy is weaker, there is less emphasis on the watchdog role. Weaver (1996: 87) remarks that 'political system similarities and differences are far more important than cultural similarities and differences, organizational constraints or individual characteristics in predicting the variance in perceptions of three roles (timely information, interpretation, and entertainment) by journalists in these countries'.

It is also useful to consider the concept of different 'national news cultures', as suggested by Deuze (2002). It looks as if Britain, Australia and the United States are differentially more attached to the watchdog, informational and investigative roles. Germany and The Netherlands do not share this strong attachment, but they are distinctive in giving attention to the role of 'standing up for the disadvantaged'. Deuze suggests this might reflect a 'pro-people' rather than 'anti-government' stance.

Journalism as a profession

The study of the journalistic role has been strongly influenced by the general notion of a profession, derived from the sociology of occupations. A profession is typically thought to have several key features, especially: a significant public role in society; a core body of expertise requiring long training; self-control of entry and regulation; clear codes of ethics and conduct. On balance, there seems to be stronger arguments for denying journalism the status of profession than otherwise. Knight et al. (2008) provide a catalogue of objections to the claim, especially the low public esteem for and trust in journalists and their susceptibility to propaganda from powerful sources or commercial interests.

Fengler and Russ-Mohl (2008) add a new dimension to the debate by proposing an 'economic theory of journalism', according to which most of the alleged tendencies and defects of journalistic behaviour can be explained by economic motives and calculations on the part of individual journalists or media firms. Support for this view can be found in Bourdieu's 'field theory of journalism', which focuses on the key issue of autonomy. In this theory the reference is to a 'field of forces' in which many external influences are at work. In the case of journalism, the pressures come mainly for the neighbouring fields of economics or politics, resulting in a lower degree of autonomy.

Benson and Neveu (2005: 11) emphasize the degree to which news has become a political institution in its own right. Treating journalism as a loosely interrelated set of activities, with unclear boundaries, does seem to accord with the increasingly diverse reality of 'news work'. In the end, it may not greatly matter to those outside whether or not the occupation is classed as a profession, although the degree to which relevant criteria of professionalism are met does matter. These criteria have to do with the quality of work done, the reliability of information published, the honesty of purpose and the benefits for society that are sought.

Several observers have emphasized the existence of an 'ideology of journalism', although there are different versions of what it contains, depending on the institutional setting and national location. In a thorough analysis of 'journalistic culture', Hanitsch (2007) lists the ideological elements of objectivism, empiricism and alternative ethical tendencies of either idealism or relativity. Fengler and Russ-Mohl (2008), in line with their economic theory, are dismissive of what they call a 'nirvana approach' that portrays journalism as an idealistic form of public service. Deuze (2005: 447) has given a fairly consensual view of the main components of journalistic ideology. These are as shown in Box 11.3. As Deuze notes, some of these elements are inconsistent or contradictory.

The occupational ideology of journalists: main elements (Deuze, 2005) 11.3

- Public service
- Objectivity
- Autonomy
- Immediacy
- Ethics

For members of most professions, the appropriate wider social role which they perform is usually 'taken care of' by the institution – as in medicine or teaching – leaving individuals to concentrate on the practice of their skills. To a certain extent this is true of mass communicators, but full professionalization has been held back by the internal diversity of media and the wide range of goals. There is also a continued uncertainty about what is actually the central and unique professional skill of the journalist (and this is even more in question for other media occupations). The sociologist Max Weber (1948) referred to the journalist as belonging to 'a sort of pariah caste' and, like the artist, lacking a fixed social classification. Schudson (1978) aptly characterized journalism as an 'uninsulated profession', because of the lack of clear boundaries.

According to Tuchman's (1978) study of news work, professionalism has largely come to be defined according to the needs of the news organization itself. The height of professional skill is the exercise of a practical craft, which delivers the required informational product, characterized by a high degree of *objectivity*, key marks of which are obsessive facticity and neutrality of attitude. The objectivity of news has become, in her view, the equivalent of a professional ideology. This analysis is consistent with other indications from media work that professionalism is a degree of accomplishment which cannot be measured by tests or examinations and can only be recognized by fellow professionals. A study of the BBC by Burns (1977) found that professionalism was understood not only in terms of the mission of the organization but as a dedication to the task and craft of making 'good television'. It was interpreted as the opposite of 'amateurism'.

The question of whether journalism should be considered as a profession remains in dispute, both within and without the media world. Windahl et al. (2007) conclude that the knowledge base of journalists does not command the same respect as that of occupational groups that are acknowledged to be professions. Kepplinger and Koecher (1990: 307) maintain that 'journalists cannot really be counted among the professional class', largely on the grounds that they behave very selectively with those they have to deal with and professionals should treat everyone equally. They write that journalists also deny a moral responsibility for unintentionally negative consequence of their reports, while applying a stronger standard to others. However, the same authors also observe that 'this selectivity is a basis for the reputation of journalism and a prerequisite for its success' (1990: 307). Olen (1988) makes a similar point by contending that journalism *should not* become a profession since it involves the exercise of a right to freedom of expression that cannot be monopolized by an institution (that of journalism).

It can also be argued that the critical role of the press may oblige it at times to act in an 'irresponsible' way, as defined by established institutions. Intended here are actions that break rules and conventions but also may serve the public interest. Such actions can range from exposing scandals in high places to revealing alleged national secrets. The publication of the secret 'Pentagon papers' by *The New York Times* in 1971, against strong government pressure, is a favourite example. The documents showed US policy in Vietnam in a very negative light and contributed to further decline in public support for the war, but was also argued to have cost American lives. In the UK, the publication in 2009 of stolen confidential details of expenses claimed by Members of Parliament was widely held to be justified by its results.

There is some evidence of a generally increased tolerance for 'unethical' practices. Some light is shed on this issue by Brodasson's (1994: 242) contention that journalism does at times at least have one important attribute of other professions – that of 'sacredness'. Journalists do have occasion to perform altruistic services. He writes that while journalism 'falls short on some traditional criteria ... it is evident that both its perceived functions as a vital service and its sacred aspect are present in at least some sectors of journalism'. He also comments that it is intimately connected with democracy, but paradoxically is most likely to display its altruism and sacredness under non-democratic conditions, when it requires dedication and bravery.

Online journalism

The rise of online journalism continues in a number of forms, partly as an extension of existing print journalism and partly as various types of news weblogs (or **blogs**). The latter began as more or less personal journals or commentaries but have developed as an alternative news space, earning the title of 'blogosphere' (Reese et al., 2007). There is a great deal and wide variety of independent news sources (Sundae and Ness, 2001), plus much that is unprofessional and idiosyncratic. This can be interpreted as both positive and negative. Boczkowski (2004) sees journalism becoming less journalist-centred and more user-centred, as well as losing its clear boundary as a professional activity. Deuze (2003) distinguished four main types of online journalistic site, as follows: mainstream, indexing and category, meta-journalism and comment, and share and discussion. Bardoel (2002) pointed to key features of online journalism as being interactivity, hypertextuality, multimodality and asynchronicity.

Domingo and Heinonen (2008) propose a typology of journalistic weblogs along a continuum from least to most institutionalized in relation to the established media. At one end are blogs produced by members of the public outside media control and at the other end those that are produced by professional staff journalists. In between are 'audience blogs' that are written by members of the public at the invitation of the media and also 'journalistic blogs' that are written by professional journalists on their own account, aside from their normal work. This last form is not always welcomed by media organizations and creates problems with respect to impartiality and editorial policy as well as issues of copyright. Even so, their existence gives support to the cause and claim of journalistic autonomy. In general, online news, in whatever form, seems to give more attention to the role of interpreter rather than of disseminator of information or adversary (Cassidy, 2005).

Normally, journalistic content online has potential advantages in terms of space available (few constraints) and the opportunity to call upon a range of sources, or to provide external links. While this does happen (see Arcetti, 2008), there are also indications that most online news follows established patterns of sourcing and does not stray far from the boundaries of the national media system. The mainstream media operate within a specific geographic market. A Canadian study (Gasher and Klein, 2007) of the websites of three different leading online news sites – *The Times* (UK), *Liberation* (France) and *Haretz* (Israel) – suggests that the same pattern applies online. The percentage of named places with a domestic location in each country was respectively 93%, 68% and 89%. Singer (2005) studied twenty weblogs in the mainstream media dealing with politics and civic affairs and found them to follow the same procedures as in mainstream news. There are many links, but mostly to other mainstream media sites. She speaks of journalists as 'normalizing' the weblog in terms of traditional journalistic norms and practices. Elsewhere, Singer (2007) writes of the claim of the 'popular' (i.e. non-professional) blog sector as adopting the self-appointed role of 'watchdog of the watchdogs'. The evidence of a fairly close relation in practice between traditional media and the more serious section of the blogosphere continues to grow. Messner et al. (2008) speak of a 'source cycle', with traditional media and blogs drawing on each other and certain blogs becoming legitimated as sources as a result. Reese et al. (2007) describe a complementary relationship between traditional media and citizen bloggers.

The Internet blog offers opportunities for improving relations with an audience but it also threatens the 'ownership' of the news by journalists. McCoy (2001), on the basis of a case study, underlined the tendency of the established press to affirm its authority as the definer of what is news in the face of the new media challenge. In another sense, it is a threat to ownership by virtue of the ease with which almost any provider can offer a basic news service, drawing on the main news agencies. Although online journalism has been welcomed for potentially increasing diversity and access, the reality is not always so promising. Cohen (2002) described it as on the whole even more 'market-driven' and commercial than established newspaper journalism, notwithstanding its claim to be more autonomous.

Relations with Pressure and Interest Groups

Relations between media and society are often mediated through a wide range of more or less informal, but often organized, pressure groups which seek to influence directly what the media do – especially by trying to set limits to what they publish. There are many examples of established bodies, such as religious, occupational or political bodies, complaining and lobbying on a range of issues, often to do with matters of morality, perceived political bias or minority representation (Shoemaker and Reese, 1991). In many countries there is legal and social pressure on the media to be positive towards minorities of all kinds, including ethnic groups, women, gays and lesbians, and more sensitive to the needs of vulnerable groups such as children, the poor, disabled and homeless people, and the mentally ill.

While the media are usually cautious in handling such pressures and are reluctant to yield their autonomy (the pressures often tend to cancel each other out), there is evidence of success by outside agencies in influencing content. Usually access depends on perceived legitimacy of the claim to be heard, but sometimes PR can influence this perception (Yoon, 2005). Access may also be given where a medium's commercial interests might be threatened by bad publicity. According to an extensive (US) study by Montgomery (1989: 217), the most effective advocacy groups 'were those whose goals were most compatible with the TV network system and whose strategies were fashioned with a keen sense of how that system functioned'. Success also depends on the degree of support among the general public for a particular advocacy position. The general effect is likely to show up in entertainment television as blandness, conformity and an avoidance of controversy. In general, the media are less open to external pressures of this kind in relation to 'hard' news.

It is usually impossible to distinguish unacceptable pressure (or the act of yielding to it) from the general tendency of the media to try to please as many of their audiences (and advertisers) as possible and to avoid hurting minorities or encouraging antisocial activities. The media are also wary of legal reprisal (Tuchman, 1978) and inclined to avoid unnecessary controversy or departures from verifiable facts which are in the public domain. Media avoidance behaviour in response to social or legal pressure has to be accepted as legitimate, within the rules of the media-institutional 'game', but the general result is to ensure a differentially more positive treatment for the better-organized and more socially central minorities and causes (Shoemaker, 1984). Weaker and more deviant groups get a worse press and exert little influence. Paletz and Entman (1981: 125) exemplified such marginal groups with little positive access to, or control over, media coverage as 'unofficial strikers, urban rioters, welfare mothers, student militants, radicals and impoverished reactionaries'. The composition of this category will vary, but the general principle remains the same. For instance, Lubbers et al. (1998) showed that Dutch press reports relating to minorities appeared to operate within an implicit hierarchy of favourability of treatment that ranged from the most established to the newest kinds of immigrant group.

Relations with Owners and Clients

The central issue which arises under this heading is the extent to which media organizations can claim to exercise autonomy in relation first to their owners, and secondly to other direct economic agencies in their environment, especially those which provide operating funds: investors, advertisers, sponsors. According to Altschull's (1984) dictum that 'The content of the news media always reflects the interests of those who finance the press', the answer is fairly clear and also consistent with the principles of free press theory in its 'market' version. Nevertheless, there is usually some scope for autonomy on the part of 'communicators'.

Proprietor influence

There is no doubt that owners in market-based media have ultimate power over content and can ask for what they want to be included or left out. There is plenty of circumstantial evidence to show that this power is used (Shoemaker and Reese, 1991; Curran and Seaton, 1997) (see also Chapter 9, pp. 227–9). Even so, there are quite strong conventions relating to journalism which protect the decision-making autonomy of editors on particular news stories. Meyer's (1987) survey evidence confirmed that US journalistic ethics frowned on owner intervention, although editors reported a fair degree of autonomy in practice. Similar evidence was obtained in Britain by the Royal Commission on the Press (1977). Schultz's (1998) study of Australian journalists showed strong support for the fourth estate role, but also a recognition that it was often compromised by commercial considerations and owner pressure. It is not too surprising that journalists should claim more autonomy, or that editors of established newspapers are reluctant to admit being told what to do by proprietors.

Nevertheless, there is an inevitable tendency for owners of news media to set broad lines of policy, which are likely to be followed by the editorial staff they employ. There may also be informal and indirect pressure on particular issues that matter to owners (for instance, relating to their other business interests) (Turow, 1994). Much credible, but often anecdotal, evidence supports this conclusion, and, in the end, the theory of economically free press legitimates this state of affairs. Newspaper owners are free to use their papers to make propaganda, if they wish to do so, provided they accept the risk of losing readers and credibility. The worldwide press condemnation of Unesco's efforts to improve international reporting, as reported by Giffard (1989), is a convincing example of the media industry protecting its own interests. There is an argument, though one difficult to substantiate, that media have simply become too big a business to be run by personal whim, and decisions have to be taken impersonally on grounds of managerial and market considerations.

The general effect of monopoly media ownership on content has proved difficult to pin down (see, for example, Picard et al., 1988), although there is little doubt that a condition of true monopoly would be harmful for freedom of expression and consumer choice. Shoemaker and Reese (1991) conclude that those who work for large chains are likely to have a lower attachment to and involvement in the community in which they work. For them, the (larger) media organization takes precedence over community influence. Correlatively, locally based media may gain strength and independence from ties with the community or city that they serve. The degree of freedom for journalists, producers, writers and entertainers in public broadcasting may be formally less than in market-based media (although this is not necessarily so), but the limits are normally clear and not subject to arbitrary breach or suspension.

The influence of advertisers

The consequences of advertising financing for media content are perennially discussed. On the one hand, it is obvious that the *structure* of much of the mass-media industry in most capitalist countries reflects the interests of advertisers – something that has developed historically along with other social and economic changes. It is no accident that media markets often coincide with other consumer divisions (see Chapter 9). Most free-market media are finely tuned to jointly maximizing the needs of advertisers and their own interests as a normal condition of operation. The 'normal' influence extends to the matching of media content patterns according to the consumption patterns of targeted audiences. Media design, layout, planning and scheduling often reflect advertiser interests. What is less easy to demonstrate is that particular advertisers can directly intervene to influence significant publication decisions in their own interests, beyond what is already provided for in the system.

As with proprietorial intervention in news, there is little doubt that it happens from time to time on a local or specific basis (e.g. Shoemaker and Reese, 1991). McManus (1994) describes a systematic pattern of commercial influence on reporting. Baker (1994: 99) observes that 'advertisers, not governments are the primary censors of media content in the United States today'. He cites evidence of advertisers using their market power to attempt to block particular communications that damage their interests and also of advertiser pressure that influences personnel as well as editorial decisions in the media. But influence comes in diverse forms that are often hard to detect and not necessarily illegitimate (for instance, providing information that has a promotional value, product placement, sponsoring, etc.). Bogart (1995: 93–4) summarizes the (in his view, considerable) influence of advertising on media content in terms of five key points, as shown in Box 11.4.

The influence of advertising (Bogart, 1995) **11.4**

- Advertisers rarely try to buy journalists to slant news in their favour; more often they try to suppress news they don't like
- They are sensitive about the environment for their messages and edgy about controversy
- When advertisers yield to vigilante pressure, media producers veer towards self-censorship
- Advertisers shape content when they sponsor broadcast programmes
- The virtual end of local press competition shows how advertisers determine the life and death of media

---

Advertiser influence is generally ethically disapproved, especially when it affects news (Meyer, 1987), and it may not even be in the interests either of media (especially news media) or of advertisers to be seen to be too close to each other. Both can lose credibility and effectiveness if a form of conspiracy against the media public is suspected. In general, it seems that economically strong and 'elite' media are best in a position to resist undue pressure (see Gans, 1979). But the same is true of media that are supported by varied balanced sources of revenue (that is, subscriber payments as well as advertisers, or, in Europe especially, broadcast licence revenue plus advertising income). Media organizations most likely to be influenced by advertiser pressure are those whose sole or overwhelming source of revenue is advertising, especially where the competition is heavy (Picard, 2004).

The main pressures and constraints on news arising from the media market have been summarized by McManus (1994) in terms of a 'market model'. This is derived from the principle that market forces require conduct that minimizes cost, protects the interests of owners and clients, and maximizes the income-producing audience. The model is expressed in the statement about news selection contained in Box 11.5.

Main predictions of the market model (McManus, 1994) **11.5**

The probability of an event/issue becoming news is:

- inversely proportional to the harm the information might cause to investors or sponsors;
- inversely proportional to the cost of covering it;
- directly proportional to the expected breadth of the appeal to audiences that advertisers are willing to pay for.

The main difference from a 'journalistic theory of news production' lies in the lack of any reference in such a theory to harm to owners or costs and a concentration on the significance of the story and the size of an interested audience. As McManus notes, the two theories do not lead to differences of selection in all cases and, under certain ideal conditions of rationality, perfect knowledge and diversity, the models might even converge. Cohen (2002) supposes that online media are especially likely to follow the market-driven model.

Relations with the Audience

Although the audience is, by conventional wisdom, the most important of the clients and influences in the environment of any media organization, research tends to show the audience as having a low salience for many actual communicators, however closely ratings and sales figures are followed by management. Media professionals display a high degree of 'autism' (Burns, 1969), consistent perhaps with the general attitude of professionals, whose very status depends on their knowing better than their clients what is good for them.

Hostility to the audience?

Altheide (1974: 59) comments that the pursuit of large audiences by the television stations which he studied 'led to a cynical view of the audience as stupid, incompetent and unappreciative'. Elliott (1972), Burns (1977) and Schlesinger (1978) found something of the same to be true of British television. Schlesinger (1978: 111) attributed this partly to the nature of professionalism: 'A tension is set up between the professionalism of the communicator, with its implied autonomy, and the meeting of apparent audience demands and desires, with their implication for limiting autonomy.' Ferguson (1983) also reported a somewhat arrogant attitude to the audience on the part of women's magazine editors. In her study of Australian journalists, Schultz (1998) uncovered some resentment at the need to please the audience, thus limiting autonomy. She associated this with a 'reduced capacity to understand public opinion' (1998: 157) and an unwillingness to accept accountability mechanisms. Gans (1979) reported that US TV journalists were appalled by the lack of audience recognition of what they found good. The situation stems partly from the fact that the dominant criterion applied by the organization is nearly always the ratings (i.e. the volume of sales of the product, the size of the audience sold to the advertiser). However, most media professionals, with some justification, do not recognize ratings as a very reliable measure of intrinsic quality.

It is possible that hostility towards the audience is somewhat exaggerated by media respondents themselves, since there is contrary evidence that some media people have a strong positive attitude to their audience in the abstract. Ferguson, again, noted that women's magazine editors showed a strong sense of responsibility to their audience and wanted to provide a helpful service (1983: 140). Weaver and Wilhoit (1986) found that the single most important factor contributing to work satisfaction of journalists was the possibility of helping people (endorsed by 61%). They also found that the single most frequent source of feedback to journalists was from individual members of the audience. The resistance to ratings and other audience statistics, which are largely a management tool with little to say about actual audiences (Ang, 1991), should not necessarily be equated with negative views of the audience. In the sphere of online media, direct feedback from the audience can sometimes be threatening to individual communicators, but there is also a new opportunity to turn contacts into a tool of management.

Insulation and uncertainty

On a day-to-day or item-by-item basis, most mass communicators in established media do not need to be concerned about the immediate response of the audience, and they have to take decisions about content in advance of any response. This, coupled with the intrinsic difficulty of 'knowing' a large and very disparate audience, contributes to the relative insulation described above. The most common institutional device for making contact with the audience, that of audience research, serves an essential management function and relates media to the surrounding financial and political system, but seems to convey little that is meaningful to the individual mass communicator (Burns, 1977; Gans, 1979). Attitudes to the audience tend to be guided and differentiated according to the role orientations set out above.

Among communicators, if one follows the line of Burns' findings, the 'pragmatic' are happy with the ratings which also satisfy the organization. The craft-oriented are content with the judgements of their fellow professionals. Those committed to the goals of the organization (for instance, carrying out a cultural mission, or political or commercial propaganda) are content with these goals as internally assessed. Those wishing to have influence in society look to their influential contacts in relevant social contexts. For everyone, there are friends, relatives and casual contacts who can provide feedback of a more comprehensible kind.

Images of the audience

There remains a continuing problem of uncertainty for those who do want to communicate, who do want to change or influence the general public and use media for this purpose, or who direct themselves at minorities or minority causes where impact matters (see Hagen, 1999). One readily available solution is the construction of an abstract image of the kind of people they would like to reach (Bauer, 1958; Pool and Shulman, 1959). According to Gans (1957: 318), 'The audience participates in the making of a movie through the audience image held by the creator.' Shoemaker and Reese (1991: 96) conclude that 'Journalists write primarily for themselves, for their editors, and for other journalists.' Nevertheless, communicating to a large and amorphous audience 'out there' is bound to remain problematic for those who care about 'getting a message across'. Audiences are mainly just spectators, who observe and applaud but do not interact with the senders and performers (Elliott, 1972).

Media organizations, as distinct from the individual 'communicators' within them, are to a large extent in the business of producing spectacles as a way of creating audiences and generating profit and employment (see the 'publicity model' on pp. 72–3). They need some firm basis on which to predict the interests and likely degree of attention of an audience. As Pekurny (1982) points out, feedback from ratings cannot tell you how to improve television programmes, and neither are they often available until long after a programme is made. Pekurny says that the 'real feedback system' is not the home viewing audience but the writers, producers, cast and network executives themselves. In addition, there is strong reliance on the 'track records' of particular producers and production companies and on reusing successful past formulas. This conclusion is supported by Ryan and Peterson (1982), who tell us that in popular music the most important factor guiding selection in the production process (see p. 332) is the search for a good 'product image'. This essentially means trying to match the characteristics of previously successful songs.

Aspects of Internal Structure and Dynamics

The analysis made so far, in line with the scheme in Figure 11.1, points to a degree of differentiation and division within the boundaries of the organization. There are several sources of division. One of the most obvious is the diversity of function (such as news, entertainment or advertising) of many media organizations, with different interests competing for status and finance. The personnel of media organizations come from different social backgrounds and vary according to age, gender, ethnicity, social background and other attributes. We have already noted the duality of purpose of many media (both material and ideal) and the endemic conflict between creative ends (which have no practical limits) and the need to organize, plan, finance and 'sell' media products. Most accounts of media-organizational goals point to differences of orientation and purpose that can be a source of latent conflict.

Internal diversity of purpose

The fact that mass media organizations have mixed goals is important for locating the media in their social context, understanding some of the pressures under which they operate and helping to differentiate the main occupational choices available to media workers. It is one essential aspect of a general ambiguity over social role that has already been discussed. Some further light on this question is shed by the characterization of the newspaper as a 'hybrid organization' (Engwall, 1978), in the sense that it cannot be clearly placed on either of two key organizational dimensions:

the manufacture–service dimension, and the dimension of variability of product technology and use. The newspaper organization is engaged in both making a product
and providing a service. It also uses a wide variety of production technology, from the
simple to the complex.

In varying degrees, this holds true for other mass media organizations, certainly in broadcasting. Engwall found that several different 'work cultures' flourish,
each justified according to a different goal or work task – namely, the news-oriented
culture, the politically oriented, the economically oriented and the technically oriented. The first two tend to go together and are expressed by the professional or
creative category noted above (also closer to the 'normative' type), while the second
two are essentially 'utilitarian', having much in common with their counterparts in
other business organizations. In so far as this situation can be generalized, it seems
that media organizations are likely to be as internally divided as to purpose as they
are different from each other. That this should happen without excessive conflict
suggests some fairly stable forms of accommodation to the attendant problems.
Such an accommodation may be essential in what Tunstall (1971) has characterized by the paradoxical term of 'non-routine bureaucracy'.

The Influence of Personal Characteristics of Mass Communicators

Many studies of media organizations or occupations include, as a matter of course,
an examination of the social background and outlook on society of the group of
respondents under study. This is sometimes because of an assumption that the
personal characteristics of those most directly responsible for media production
will influence content. It is a hypothesis that accords well with the ideology or
mythology of the media themselves and stands opposed to the notion of organizational or technological determinism. It is also a familiar idea among audiences
that the personality and values of the author, for instance of a novel or a film, will
give the work its primary meaning, despite its being processed in a media industry.
The expectation that media will 'reflect society' (the first hypothesis considered on
pp. 227–8) can be supported on the grounds either that it is what their audiences
want or that those who work in the media are a cross-section of society, at least in
their values and beliefs.

However, these views need to be modified to allow for the influence of organizational goals and settings. Most media products are the work not of a single author but
of teams, and ideas of personal authorship are not very relevant, despite the tendency
of media to promote individual stars and celebrities. Shoemaker and Reese (1991) suggest that lines of influence can follow one or other of the paths shown in Figure 11.4.
In essence, what is shown are two alternative paths – one in which organizational role
subordinates or conceals personal characteristics, and another in which having power or
status in an organization permits an individual communicator to express their personal
beliefs and values in public communication.

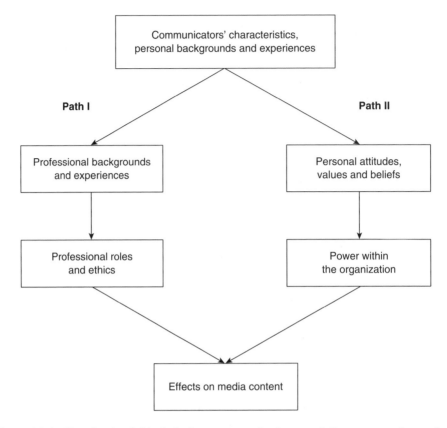

Figure 11.4 How factors intrinsic to the communicator may influence media content: institutional versus professional pathways (Shoemaker and Reese, 1991)

The first question to arise is whether there is any distinctive pattern of social experience or personal values to be found among media communicators. Inevitably, there are as many descriptions of social background as there are studies, and even though most concern journalists, there is no single pattern to report. However, there is a good deal of evidence, not surprisingly, to show that journalists in many countries are not marginal in income terms but belong on average to the middle category, and thus within the economically secure sector of society, without being rich.

There are evidently big variations between the stars of journalism and the ordinary salariat, as in other branches of media business. Lichter and Rothman (1986), for instance, painted a portrait of 240 personnel of elite US news media, showing them to be not only well off but demographically unrepresentative in being more white and more male than the country as a whole and less likely to hold a religious belief. One can probably assume that people who work for less elite media are also less of an elite themselves, although they may still be demographically unrepresentative (for instance, in terms of gender and ethnicity).

Weaver and Wilhoit (1986, 1992) found that, since 1971, the composition of the corps of US journalists had changed remarkably in one respect: a much greater representation of women (from 20% to 34%), although there were relatively fewer black and Hispanic journalists. A survey of American media personnel in 1996 showed only 11% to be of minority ethnic origin, a good deal below the general population figure. There seems little doubt about the general class position of the average media worker: it is a middle-class occupation, but less professionalized or well paid than other established professions (law, medicine, accountancy, etc.) and with a small elite of well-paid stars. Peters and Cantor's (1982) account of the movie acting profession stresses the extreme gap between the powerless and insecure many and the minority at the top.

The theoretical significance of such observations is less easy to establish. Johnstone et al. (1976) concluded that 'in any society those in charge of mass communication tend to come from the same social strata as those in control of the economic and political systems'. Gans (1979) also suggested that the middle-class position of the journalistic profession is a guarantee of their ultimate loyalty to the system. Therefore, they are free, in the US system, because they can be trusted to see and interpret the world in much the same way as the real holders of power, holding the same basic ideology and values. Gans found that news journalists generally held what are called 'motherhood' values, including support for the family and a nostalgia for small-town pastoralism. They also tended to be ethnocentric, pro-Democratic, individualistic and in favour of 'responsible capitalism', moderatism, social order and leadership.

Gans' interpretation is persuasive, more so than the alternative idea that they are not only an elite but a left-leaning one, according to Lichter and Rothman (1986), with subversive motives and a penchant for supporting deviance and extremist movements. This image of 'liberal' media has often been restated in the USA. Gans' view of journalists as 'safe' but not reactionary is also more convincing than the other notion that they are a conservative elite, mainly serving the interests of the state, the governing class and big business (as inferred by Herman and Chomsky, 1988).

More significant than evidence of the values held by journalists (but not inconsistent with it) may be the finding that media personnel owe most of their relevant attitudes and tendencies to socialization from the immediate work environment (e.g. Breed, 1955; Weaver and Wilhoit, 1986: 127–8). This thesis, while not discounting the influence of social background and personal belief, returns us to the greater probability of organizational, rather than individual and subjective, determination. We need also to keep in mind that journalists and others tend, where possible, to work for organizations with compatible values. The possibility for personal influence by mass communicators varies according to the genre and the type of organization. Non-news genres offer more scope for expressing personal beliefs, and there is probably more scope where commercial and financial pressures are less (Tunstall, 1993).

The review of evidence by Shoemaker and Reese (1991) relating to the influence of personal beliefs and values is inconclusive. Even so, to conclude that there is no influence would seem to rule out any real degree of personal autonomy and to overestimate the power of work socialization (see also Plaisance and Skewes, 2003). Shoemaker and Reese (1991: 72) see the relation as variable: 'it is possible that when communicators have more power over their messages and work under fewer constraints, their personal attitudes, values and beliefs have more opportunity to influence content' (see Figure 11.4). It is fairly evident, for instance, that individuals who reach high status in different media (journalism, film, television, music) do have and use opportunities for expressing personal opinions and beliefs. The 'logic of media', which favours personalization, often supports this tendency, as long as it does not also conflict with commercial logic.

Women in news organizations

The case of gender seems to promise a good test of the proposition that personal characteristics will influence content, since it has been a claim of part of the feminist movement that the media have been in various ways on the 'other side' in numerous campaigns throughout the gender war. As usual, it turns out not to be so easy to reach a conclusion. There is an empirical correlation between the relatively low numbers and lower occupational status of women in news media organizations (Gallagher, 1981; Thoveron, 1986; *Media Studies Journal*, 1993; European Commission, 1999) on the one hand, and the under-representation or stereotyping of women in the news (for instance, in terms of topic and context, as well as the more obvious use of female 'sex symbols') on the other. A European Commission report (1999) cites studies showing that in French news media only 17% of those cited or interviewed were women. Similar figures showed 22% for Finnish news and 13% in the United Kingdom. The same source concludes that women 'portrayed in the media are younger, more likely to be shown as married, less likely to be shown as in paid employment', compared with men (1999: 12). An extensive study of the way in which US electronic news media framed feminists and feminism showed both topics as making a rare appearance and, where they do, to be demonized and trivialized. Content implicitly differentiated between feminists and 'regular women' (Lind and Salo, 2002).

The issue is not confined to the question of news, but news is often singled out as of particular significance for the wider question of gender inequality and construction in society. The correlation between male domination (in power positions if not always numerically) of virtually all media organizations and male-oriented themes or patriarchal values offers prima facie support for the view that greater occupational equality in the media would make a difference to content (see Chapter 5). The evidence for this remains weak, however. Baehr (1996) says that decisions about content are much more influenced by financial necessity than by personal preference. The European Commission report cited above is also doubtful about any automatic connection between numbers of women employed in media (even in senior positions) and the way women are portrayed.

According to evidence from The Netherlands reported by van Zoonen (1994), the typical lesson learnt in journalism schools was that 'feminism – even moderately defined – and professional journalism were at odds with each other'. In other words, socialization worked to induce conformity in practice to traditional ways of making news, even though many young women journalists felt they had autonomy. One general conclusion to be drawn from this and other evidence is that gender always interacts with the organizational context. The results may be different from case to case. So far, evidence of the direct influence of gender in the newsroom is very limited (Armstrong, 2004; Craft and Wanta, 2004; Steiner, 2009).

Van Zoonen (1988, 1991) has also argued that a more fundamental approach to the construction of gender is needed. She points to basic inconsistencies in the assumption that having more women in the newsroom would change the news (for the better). For one thing, on closer inspection the available evidence does not give good empirical support for this assumption. There have been significant increases in female participation in the workforce (see, for example, Weaver and Wilhoit, 1986, 1996; *Media Studies Journal*, 1993) without any noticeable changes in the 'nature of news'. An American case study by Zoch and van Slyke Turk (1998) examined 1,000 news stories over ten years to see if female reporters were more likely to choose female sources. They found a small tendency in this direction, mainly due to the kinds of stories that women were still more likely to be asked to cover. The theory takes for granted that journalists have enough autonomy to have influence as individuals, whereas this has to be treated as problematic and variable.

There are also divergent views as to what constitutes 'change'. Should the news become 'feminized', or should 'femininity' itself be redefined (perhaps in the direction of masculinity)? The European Commission report cites French research by Erik Neveu that showed 'signs of a feminine tone or slant among women journalists in terms of a tendency to report on "ordinary lives", a less deferential attitude towards authorities, and the use of psychological approaches in the reporting of political lives' (1999: 11). However, this was not evidence of a 'feminine habitus' within journalism, but the result of a circular process following the allocation of certain topics to men or women.

There are two distinct issues here: that of journalistic autonomy versus determination (by external forces or the organizational hierarchy or 'media logic') and that of the desirability of change in the nature of news and the direction which it might take. None of this is an argument against the fact of there being gender differences, or against more equal employment for women, or against change, but the various issues are separate and cannot all be bundled together under the general heading of having more women in news organizations. If the central matter is the way gender is constructed, then a broader approach is needed. It is also the case that broad changes in media, including efforts to attract more female readers to the press and the differentially growing purchasing power of women, are leading to certain 'feminizing' trends, perhaps independent of the number of women employed or their degree of managerial responsibility. Even so, a necessary condition for more equitable treatment of women in news will be the gradual rise of women to positions of power within media organizations.

Role Conflicts and Dilemmas

Not surprisingly, most studies of media organizations reveal many different kinds of latent conflict, based on a variety of factors, although quite often reflecting a tension between the aspirations of 'lower-level' participants and those in control of media. The influence of proprietors on news has already been discussed (pp. 291–2). An early study by Breed (1955) detailed the (mainly informal) socializing mechanisms that helped to ensure the maintenance of policy. Young reporters would be expected to read the newspaper they worked on and to sit in on editorial conferences. Policy was also learned through informal gossip with colleagues. Deviations were discouraged by feelings of obligation to superiors, by the satisfactions of belonging to the in-group and sometimes by management sanctions and rewards in giving assignments. In general, according to Breed's research, what policy actually was remained covert. Research by Bantz (1985), however, led to the conclusion that the organizational culture of news organizations is intrinsically oriented towards conflict. The relevant factors include: distrust of external sources; the conflict between professional norms and both business and entertainment norms; competition over stories; and the premium in news on conflict.

Returning to the question of conflict based on hierarchy, Muriel Cantor's (1971) study of a group of producers employed in making films for major television networks indicated the existence of three main types. First, there were 'film-makers', mainly younger, well-educated people ambitious to become feature film directors and comparable to the 'professional' category of broadcasters which Burns (1977) singled out. Secondly, there was a group of writer-producers, whose chosen purpose was to make stories with a worthwhile message and to communicate with a wide public. Thirdly, there were older, less well-educated career producers, whose main orientation was to the network and their career within it.

Not surprisingly, the last-mentioned group was least likely to have conflicts with management, since their main aim of reaching the biggest possible audience was shared by the networks. The film-makers, for different reasons, were prepared to accept network goals because they wanted to practise their craft, accumulate money and move on to feature films. It was the writer-producers who came most into conflict with the networks (management) because of their different attitude to the content that they were required to produce. Management wanted a saleable, risk-free product, while the writers still retained some ideals of the craft and wanted to convey a worthwhile message. The chance to reach a large audience was essential to their purpose, but the price, in terms of conforming to commercial goals, was a high one to have to pay.

The lessons of other research on communicators (mainly journalists) seem to lead to a similar conclusion: that where conflict occurs between media organization and employee, it is likely to be where the political tendency or economic self-interest of the organization gets in the way of individual freedom of expression. Flegel and Chaffee (1971) support the view that a devotion to the craft and a 'technical orientation' towards a quality product, requiring co-operation, help to reduce conflict and promote a sense of autonomy. According to Sigelman (1973), the potential problem of conflict on grounds of belief is usually avoided by selective recruitment and self-selection by entrants into media organizations with compatible work environments. Perhaps most significant in news media is the fact that being able to handle the news according to the reigning policy becomes a skill and even a value in itself. The objective of getting the news overrides personal feelings. Presumably, similar processes occur in other media organizations.

Turow (1994) raises the possibility of an increasing potential for internal conflict and even a need for it as a result of more and more concentration of ownership.

In particular, conflicts of interest arise when news events actually concern media themselves (increasingly common) and the media in question happen to belong to the same overall corporation. Professional journalistic values call for freedom to report on controversies that might damage the commercial interests of the parent company, and editorial permission may be denied. Turow's evidence shows that this does happen and that there is already a tendency for 'silent bargains' to be made that encourage conformity and co-operation with overall company policy. A covert reward system exists that stresses caution and loyalty.

It is not clear how much the power of owners and chief editors to influence content is a source of conflict. Gans' (1979: 95) account of several US news media is somewhat ambiguous about the power of corporate executives over reporters. On the one hand, they do make 'policy', conduct frequent and regular briefings, look after the commercial and political interests of the firm, and 'suggest, select and veto news stories whenever they choose'. On the other hand, they do not use their power on a day-to-day basis, and there are countervailing powers that lie with television news producers and editors, if not with individual reporters. Survey evidence tends to support the view that journalists mainly regard themselves as having a reasonable degree of autonomy (e.g. Weaver and Wilhoit, 1986), even if the problem of pressure from 'policy' does arise (see Meyer, 1987; Schultz, 1998). The main kinds of role dilemma that have arisen are summarized in Box 11.6. However, there are indications that the appearance of alternative opportunities for established journalists to operate as independent reporters and commentators by way of the Internet and the resistance on the part of media firms which once had a virtual monopoly on employment is giving rise to a new dilemma. Loyalties to an established title or channel are divided or much weaker and there are new options for autonomy.

Media–occupational role dilemmas 11.6

- Active participatory versus neutral and informational
- Creative and independent versus bureaucratic and routine
- Communicative purpose versus meeting consumer demand
- Personal inclination versus job requirement
- Co-operation versus conflict

Conclusion

As we have seen, media occupations are weakly 'institutionalized' when compared, for instance, with law, medicine or accountancy, and professional success will often depend on the unaccountable ups and downs of public taste or on personal and unique qualities which cannot be imitated or transmitted. Apart from certain performance skills, it is hard to pin down an essential or 'core' media accomplishment. It may be that the freedom, creativity and critical approach that many media personnel still cherish, despite the bureaucratic setting of their work, are ultimately incompatible with full professionalization in the traditional sense. There are inevitable conflicts at the heart of media work, whether open or latent. Perhaps the most fundamental dilemma is one of freedom versus constraint in an institution whose own ideology places a value on originality and freedom, yet whose organizational setting requires relatively strict control.

Further Reading

Bennett, W.L., Lawrence, R.G. and Livingstone, S. (2007) *When the Press Fails*. Chicago: Chicago University Press.
The case in question is the relative failure of the US mainstream press to question the rationale and facts leading up to the invasion on Iraq in 2003. The explanation is found primarily in the position of neutrality adopted by the press in the face of a consensus in the public debate on the part of leading political actors and experts.

Benson, R. and Neveu, E. (eds) (2005) *Bourdieu and the Journalistic Field*. Cambridge: Polity Press.
Contains a key statement by Bourdieu on the concept of the 'journalistic field' and a set of commentaries by others, focusing especially on the question of journalistic autonomy in relation to political and economic pressures.

Ettema, J.S. and Whitney, D.C. (1982) *Individuals in Mass Organizations*. Beverly Hills, CA: Sage.
A wide-ranging set of studies of different media genres and industries focusing on the potential impact of organizational constraints and pressures on creativity and other quality indicators. Although now old, the same principles apply.

Shoemaker, P.J. and Reese, S.D. (1996) *Mediating the Message*, 2nd edn. New York: Longman.
The book provides a systematic framework of hypotheses about the effects of organizational factors on news production and assembles a large amount of relevant research evidence.

Online Readings

Aday, S., Slivington, M. and Herbert, M. (2005) 'Embedding the truth: a cross-cultural analysis of objectivity and TV coverage of the Iraq war', *Harvard International Journal of Press/Politics*, 10 (1): 3–21.
Carlson, M. (2007) 'Order versus access: news search engines and the challenge to traditional journalistic roles', *Media, Culture and Society*, 29 (6): 1014–30.
Deuze, M. (2005) 'Popular and professional ideology: tabloid reporters and editors speak out', *Media, Culture and Society*, 27 (6): 801–22.
Singer, J.B. (2007) 'Contested autonomy: professional and popular claims on journalism norms', *Journalism Studies*, 8 (1): 79–95.

12

The Production of Media Culture

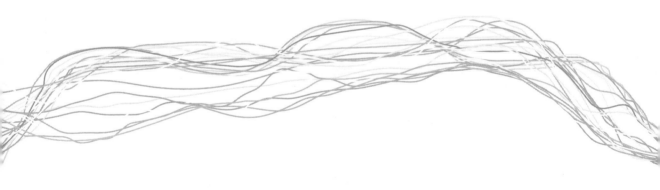

We have looked up to now at a range of more or less static or constant factors that shape the work of media organizations. These relate, in particular, to the composition and internal social structure of the media workforce and the relations that are maintained, under a variety of economic and social pressures, with the world outside the organization. The context of the media is never really static, but it may appear stable as a result of a balance achieved between outside forces and organizational goals. There is currently much change and destabilization. The most significant single cause of change is the process of convergence and the most significant actual change is probably the rise of network **connectivity** and new potential for bypassing older channels of mass communication.

In respect of production, convergence mainly shows itself in the inter-changeability of media platforms and the blurring of several long-standing boundaries between: professional and amateur; public and private; fixed and mobile. In the following sections we focus mainly on two interrelated aspects of organizational activity, which can be described respectively as 'selecting' and 'processing'. The first refers to the sequence of decisions which extends from the choice of 'raw material', as it were, to delivering the finished product. The second refers to the application of work routines and organizational criteria (including both professional and business aspects) that affect the nature of this product as it passes through the 'chain' of decision-making.

This way of describing media-organizational work originates primarily from research on news production, but it can apply more or less equally to a range of other media products and media settings (Hirsch, 1977). In the case of news, the chain extends from 'noticing' an event in the world, through writing about or filming it, to preparing a news item for transmission. In the case of a book, a movie, a television show or a piece of popular music, a similar chain extends from an idea in someone's head, through an editorial selection process and many phases of transformation, to the final product (Ryan and Peterson, 1982).

All phases of media production involve a large volume of work that becomes routinized as a matter of necessity. The regularities of behaviour and thinking that result from these routines give rise to empirical generalizations and to the possibility of theorizing about what is going on. The routines also reflect the 'operational' theories in the heads of media professionals (see p. 14).

Media-Organizational Activities: Gatekeeping and Selection

The term 'gatekeeping' has been widely used as a metaphor to describe the process by which selections are made in media work, especially decisions regarding whether or not to allow a particular news report to pass through the 'gates' of a news medium into the news channels (see White, 1950; Reese and Ballinger, 2001; Shoemaker et al., 2001). However, the idea of gatekeeping has a much wider potential application since it can apply to the work of literary agents and publishers, and to many kinds of editorial and production work in print and television. It applies to decisions about distribution and marketing of existing media products (e.g. films). In a wider sense it refers to the power to give or withhold access to different voices in society and is often a locus of conflict. One common tension in democratic societies is between governments (or politicians) and the media over the amount and kind of attention they receive in mass media. Another example relates to the kind of representation and amount of access given to minorities.

Despite its appeal and plausibility, the gatekeeping concept has a number of weaknesses and has been continuously revised since its first applications. Weak points are its implication of there being one (initial) gate area and one main set of selection criteria, its simple view of the 'supply' of news, and its tendency to individualize decision-making. In a comprehensive overview of the concept and related research, Shoemaker (1991) has extended the original model to take account of the wider social context and many factors at work. She draws attention to the role of advertisers, public relations, pressure groups, plus varied sources and 'news managers' in influencing decisions. In her model, gatekeeping usually involves multiple and successive acts of selection over the period of news production. Often group decision-making is involved. Reference is made not only to aspects of content but also to the kind of audience expected and to questions of cost. The main points of this model were largely confirmed in a case study of local television news by Berkowitz (1990). News selection can vary considerably in the degree of activity involved, and the concept as generally understood seems better suited to more passive kinds of 'news discovery' than the more enterprising variety (McManus, 1994).

More important is the extent to which gatekeeping is an autonomous journalistic action, rather than a choice mainly forced by economic pressures at the level of the news organization or by political pressures from outside. Both suggestions are supported by Bourdieu's field theory of journalism (Benson and Neveu, 2005) or Fengler and Russ-Mohl's (2008) economic theories discussed in Chapter 11. A more recent topic of debate concerns the Internet, especially in the form of search engines such as Yahoo and other portals that provide current information. It has been suggested that these alternatives bypass mass media news and make the original concept of gatekeeper obsolete (Quandt and Singer, 2009). Established journalism is no longer a privileged source of news. Nor is it able to selectively control the supply. Nevertheless, there is no reduction in the wish of interested actors to ensure that their particular message gets rapid, extensive and prominent public attention and for this it is still usually necessary to pass through the gates of the mass media.

Ideological versus organizational factors

In early studies of news gatekeeping (White, 1950; Gieber, 1956) most interest was focused on the large number of items that failed to gain entry and on the reasons for exclusion. In the nature of the early research, there was a tendency to emphasize the subjective character of news selection decisions and the autonomy of the news editor. Later, more attention was given to systematic influences on selection that can be considered as either 'organizational' or 'ideological'. The former refers primarily to bureaucratic routines, the latter to values and cultural influences which are not purely individual and personal but which stem also from the social (and national) setting of news activity. The necessity for normal processes of news selection to be strongly influenced by routine was recognized long ago by Walter Lippmann (1922: 123), when he wrote: 'without standardization, without stereotypes, without routine judgements, without a fairly ruthless disregard of subtlety, the editor would soon die of excitement'.

Subsequent research demonstrated that the content of news media tends consistently to follow a predictable pattern and that different organizations behave in a similar way when confronted by the same events and under equivalent conditions (Glasgow Media Group, 1976; McQuail, 1977; Shoemaker and Reese, 1991). There appears to be a stable perception on the part of news decision-makers about what is likely to interest an audience and a good deal of consensus within the same social-cultural settings (Hetherington, 1985). A condition for this generalization is one of limited diversity within the media system as a whole.

An alternative explanation to that of subjective individual judgement is to be found in the concept of *news value*, which is an attribute of a news event that transforms it into an interesting 'story' for an audience. However, news values are always relative, such that a current event of interest can be rapidly eclipsed by another that is more recent as well as more interesting. While the general idea of news values was already familiar, a study of foreign news in the Norwegian press by Galtung and Ruge (1965) led to the first clear statement of the news values (or 'news factors') that influence selection. They indicated three main types of factor that played a part: organizational, genre related and socio-cultural. The organizational factors are the most universal and least escapable, and they also have some ideological consequences. The collection of news has to be organized, and there is a bias towards events and news stories that fit the time-frame and the machinery of selection and retransmission. This favours recent events that occur near the reporting facilities (often in cosmopolitan centres with good communications) and with availability of creditable sources. Genre-related factors include a preference for news events that fit advance audience expectations (consonance with past news) and that can be readily placed within a familiar interpretative 'frame', for instance, frames of conflict or endemic crisis (see Harcup and O'Neill, 2001).

The social-cultural influences on foreign news selection stem from certain western values that focus on individuals and involve an interest in elite people and also negative, violent or dramatic happenings. The main factors predicted to influence news coverage are listed in Box 12.1. Most of the terms used are self-explanatory, but not all. Clarity of meaning mainly refers to lack of ambiguity of meaning for the audience. Consonance means that an event both fits into established frames of interpretation and also that there are no competing alternative frames.

> ### Foreign news event factors predictive of coverage (Galtung and Ruge, 1965) 12.1
>
> - Large scale of events
> - Occurrence close to home
> - Clarity of meaning
> - Short time scale of occurrence
> - Relevance to the audience
> - Consonance with past events
> - Potential for personification
> - Negativity
> - Larger significance and wider consequences
> - Drama and action in the narrative

Although the first gatekeeping studies presumed that news selection was guided by an expert assessment of what would interest audiences, there has been mixed support for this view. Research comparing audience interests in news topics and editorial judgements of the same matter has shown wide mismatching (e.g. Bogart, 1979; Robinson and Levy, 1986; Hargrove and Stempel, 2002). A comparison between editors and readers of 'top stories' as polled in the USA for 1995–9 showed 48% agreement and no correlation between audience interest in news and actual coverage (Tai and Chang, 2002). The study concluded that US editors did not give audiences what they wanted. However, there are different ways of explaining the findings, especially the fact that institutional forces and sources strongly influence the news agenda.

Influences on News Selection

The gatekeeping concept, as already noted, has a built-in limitation in its implication that news arrives in ready-made and unproblematic event-story form at the 'gates' of the media, where it is either admitted or excluded. This does apply to the large volume of news that arrives from news agencies, but does not account for the whole selection process. Manheim (1998) describes the 'myth structure of journalism', of which one component is the idea that news is a 'naturally occurring product' of the political environment and the visible content of events. Following this, he typifies journalistic news gathering according to two dominant and two subsidiary types. The main types are that of 'hunter-gathering', referring to the collection of surface phenomena as potential stories, and that of 'cultivation', referring to the 'beat' system for planned collection of news and clever use of familiar sources. This involves more positive activity. The other two types are relatively rare and refer to 'investigative' and 'enterprise' journalism, but these also share the assumption that news occurs naturally.

The gatekeeping framework is also largely based on the assumption that there is a given, finite, knowable reality of events in the 'real world', from which it is the task of the media to select according to appropriate criteria of reality reflection, significance or relevance. As Fishman (1980: 13) writes, 'most researchers assumed that news either reflects or distorts reality and that reality consists of facts and events out there which exist independently of how news workers think of them and treat them in the news production process'. For Fishman, the central concern should be the 'creation of news', and in this he has been followed by a number of other influential theorists.

It is clear that the eventual news content of the media arrives by several different routes and in different forms. It may have to be sought out or ordered in advance, or its 'discovery' may have to be systematically planned. At times it also has to be internally manufactured or constructed. Such a process of construction, like the selection of news, is not random and subjective. It takes place largely according to schemes of interpretation and of relevance which are those of the bureaucratic institutions that either are sources of news or process events (police departments, courts, welfare agencies, government committees, etc.). According to Fishman (1982), 'what is known and knowable by the media depends on the information-gathering and information-processing resources' of these agencies. The main factors that influence eventual choice can be considered under the headings of 'people', 'place' and 'time', usually in one combination or another. Alongside or built into these features, however, are questions of cost and of audience appeal.

People and selection

In general, 'western media' like news events that involve personal actions, even if this involves only making statements, and also like to 'personalize' abstract topics to make them more concrete and interesting to the audience. There is a general tendency to look for well-known people, especially leading politicians and celebrities, around which to construct news. The more prominent the person involved in any sphere, the more attention and privileged access as a source can be expected. News is often reports of what prominent people say about events rather than reports of the events themselves.

Probably the primary case of 'person as event' is still that of the US President, a power figure supported by a large and effective publicity machine. As one study (Grossman and Kumar, 1981) noted, in all the variety of possibilities for reporting the President there is one constant imperative: closeness to senior officials and, if possible, the President in person on as exclusive a basis as possible. Other kinds of celebrity figure that fit the same picture can readily be imagined. World events tend to be told as stories about heroes and villains, for instance heroes of the fall of communism such as Gorbachev and Walesa, or villains now threatening the west such as Osama bin Laden. A great deal of news gathering revolves around people, especially since people are more permanently available than events, and (unlike institutions) they can speak.

The significance of personal contacts with anyone close to those inside circles of power or celebrity has been underlined by research as well as by informal accounts of news producers. Reese et al.'s (1994) study of various 'sources' appearing or cited on American mainstream news media in the late 1980s showed a remarkable concentration on a relatively small number of interconnected individuals whose views were used to validate the news. Bennett et al. (2007) argue that the capacity of the US administration to manage the 'reality' in relation to the Iraq war was aided by the media habitually turning to a narrow range of sources it considers legitimate and credible. 'Of 414 stories on the buildup to and rationale for the war told by ABC, CBS and NBC from September 2002 through March 2003, only 34 originated outside the White House' (Bennett et al., 2007: 43).

What we see of the world through media eyes is sometimes the result of chance encounters or informal communication networks developed by people in the media, but more often it is the result of a deliberate search for access by sources with their own agenda. The power to make news that attaches to certain offices also helps to account for the differential influence of certain sources and the potential for 'pseudo-events' to be assembled around the activities of prominent people (Dayan and Katz, 1992). The relative status of people in the news is one of the elements of 'media logic' discussed below (pp. 331–2).

Location and selection

The nearer the location of news events is to the city, region or nation of the intended audience, the more likely it is to be noticed. Nearness may, however, be overridden as a factor by other considerations, such as power or the intrinsic character of events (for instance, their scale and negativity). Westerstahl and Johansson (1994) showed, from a large-scale cross-national study of foreign news selection, that two attributes of news account for a large amount of selection. These are the 'importance' of the event country and the 'proximity' to the home media. These authors trace the origin of this observation to a German author writing in 1695! The fact that recognition of events as news has to involve a specific location helps to explain the success with which authorities (especially in war situations) can manage news, by virtue of their control over physical access to the site of events. Israel's attack on Gaza at New Year 2009 demonstrated this power, with all foreign journalists excluded from the war zone. Aside from the simple need to be able to observe, the conventions of objective news require evidence of location and timing, and that which has no verifiable location is a 'non-event'.

The importance of location was emphasized by Walter Lippmann (1922) in his account of the routinization of news gathering. He wrote that news consists of events which 'obtrude' above what is normal, which can be anticipated by observation at those places where past newsworthy events have happened or been made public – such as courts, police stations, parliaments, airports and hospitals. News media are normally linked to a 'net' that covers the globe, its nodal points marked by the presence of an agency or a correspondent. The idea of a *news net* was developed by Tuchman (1978) as an image of a device designed to 'catch' news, like fish. Its capacity depends on the fineness of the mesh and the strength of its fibre. The finer strands of the net (for small fish) are provided by 'stringers', while reporters and the wire services provide the larger mesh. There is a hierarchy involved, with status in the news net determining whose information is more likely to be identified as news (preference goes to seniority and to own reporters rather than news agencies) (see Box 12.2).

12.2 The news net: key quote

The spatial anchoring of the news net at centralized institutions is one element of the frame delineating strips of everyday reality as news ... The news net imposes a frame upon occurrences through the co-operation of the complex bureaucracy associated with the dispersion of reporters ... Finally, the news net incorporates three assumptions about readers' interests: readers are interested in occurrences at specific localities; they are concerned with the activities of specific organizations; they are interested in specific topics. (Tuchman, 1978: 223, 225)

The news net has a very tight weave in places where power is concentrated, like the Washington–New York corridor or the Paris–Berlin–London triangle. The advance planning of news coverage in spatial terms thus involves a set of presuppositions about where news is likely to happen, which will have a certain self-fulfilling tendency. This tendency is witnessed by the great continuity of flow of news from regions like the Middle East, once these have been established as sites for events and as foci of political concern. The corollary of this is that news flow is less easily generated from locations where sudden and unexpected events take place.

The influence of location on reporting occurs initially through the assignment of reporters to places where 'news events' are likely to occur. The advance identification of such events depends partly on beliefs about what will interest the audience (an aspect of typification). Most news organizations have a structure of desks or departments which is partly based on location such as city news, crime news (courts and police) and politics. Traditionally, on local media at least, this was expressed in terms of a series of 'beats'.

The news beat, as explained by Fishman (1980), is not only *territorial* and *topical* (subject defined), but also a social setting, a network of social relations involving reporters and sources who frequent particular places. The news beat is established in order to facilitate the uncovering of 'news events', but it inevitably leads to the construction of events. What happens in a certain place (on the news beat) is much more likely to be defined as news just because it is observed (compared with a 'non-event', which is another event which is not observed).

Time dimension

News type		Pre-scheduled	Unexpected	Non-scheduled
	Hard	●	●	
	Soft			●
	Spot		●	
	Developing		●	
	Continuing	●	●	

Figure 12.1   Time and types of news (Tuchman, 1978)

Time and selection

Not surprisingly, since it is built into the definition of news, time has enormous influence as a consideration on selection. Timeliness is an essential ingredient of novelty and relevance, both of which are highly prized in news. It also depends on and amplifies one of the most significant properties of communication technology – its capacity to overcome barriers of time (as well as space). In addition to a net to capture space, there is also a frame for dealing with time since time underlies the typification of events as news. The news net is designed to maximize the chance of capturing news events when, as well as where, they are likely to occur. Typifying events according to their time scale, especially in relation to the news production cycle, increases the chance of actually reporting as news those events that fit the conventional definitions of news. News people implicitly operate with a time-based typology of news which helps in planning their work (see Figure 12.1).

The main types are 'hard news', dealing with immediate events, and 'soft news', mainly background or time-free news. In addition, there are three other categories: 'spot' (very new, immediate, just breaking) news, 'developing' news, and 'continuing' news. There is also a time dimension, according to which news can be classified as 'pre-scheduled', 'unscheduled' or 'unexpected', and 'non-scheduled'. The first refers to 'diary' events that are known about in advance and for which coverage can be planned. The second refers to news of events that happen unexpectedly and need to be disseminated immediately – the most difficult for routine handling, but not the largest category of news. The third relates to news (usually soft) that is not tied to any particular time and can be stored and released at the convenience of the news organization. The typification of events in this way narrows the range of uncertainty, but also encourages the tendency to rely on 'continuing' news and on pre-scheduled or non-scheduled event news, thus telling against uniqueness and novelty. The extraordinary influence of time in the news operation has been especially noticed in broadcasting. Schlesinger (1978: 105) refers to a 'stopwatch culture', which goes beyond what is needed for practical purposes: 'It is a form of fetishism in which to be obsessed about time is to be professional in a way which newsmen have made peculiarly their own.' Its consequence, in his view, is to do some violence to history and reduce the meaningfulness of news.

Although preplanned (diary) events make up a large part of the routine news coverage, there are occasions when planned events of a non-routine kind can take on a special significance. There may be occasions when either event organizers or the media themselves are in a position to influence the way news is reported by fulfilling their own wishes or expectations. There are various accounts of how the planning of expected event coverage strongly influences the eventual content of coverage. Following an idea from Lang and Lang (1953), Halloran et al. (1970) studied the sequence of events preceding a planned demonstration and protest march in London in 1968, directed against the US war in Vietnam. They showed how media stories in the weeks before the event predefined it as both significant and violent, fomented by foreigners and with potential threats to property and even the social order (it was supposedly a 'year of revolution'). One result of this 'prestructuring' of the meaning and course of the event was to shape the organizational and physical arrangements for event coverage as well as the interpretations of its significance.

In fact, the planned event was relatively peaceful, but the news apparatus was committed in advance to an alternative version and found it difficult to reconcile the reality with the established expectation. The result was distortion and unbalanced reporting. Similar phenomena have been noticed in relation to planned military events, like the 1982 British expedition to the Falklands, the Gulf War of 1991 and the initially peaceful US 'invasion' of Somalia in 1992. More commonly, the problem for the media organization is a reverse one of catching up with unplanned events in unexpected locations.

Molotch and Lester (1974) proposed a fourfold typology of events of which the largest category is that of 'routine events', the three others being 'accidents', 'scandals' and 'serendipity' (chance). Routine events, however, are divided into three types, as shown in Box 12.3.

---

i 12.3 A typology of routine events (Molotch and Lester, 1974)routine. Those where 'event promoters have habitual access to the news assemblers'

- Those where 'event promoters seek to disrupt the routine access of others in order to make events of their own'
- Those where 'the access is afforded by the fact that the promoter and news assemblers are identical'

The first category refers to normal situations, such as the reporting of national politics. The second refers to demonstrations and publicity-gaining acts by 'outsiders'.

The last category relates to 'media events' and 'pseudo-events', in which the media are closely implicated. This typology also has implications for the exercise of source power.

Sometimes events break through routines, and the really dramatic and unexpected dominates the news. This is captured by what Tuchman (1978) refers to as the news typification of 'What a story!' Events in this category are extremely diverse, united only by their unexpectedness, significance, and strain on the credibility of all concerned (see also Berkowitz, 1992). The fact of a news medium having a scoop on a story that is less than world-shattering can also make it 'What a story!' The main point is to remind us that the reporting of events is a dynamic process, while the 'news value' assessment approach may miss the dynamic.

An aspect of news work that is related to the 'What a story!' phenomenon is the notion of a *key event*. This refers to the kind of event that becomes a big news story not only because of its scale, unexpectedness and dramatic quality, but because of some unusual degree of public resonance and significance in symbolizing some deeper public crisis or anxiety. The original idea was provided by Fishman (1982), who referred to a particular account of a crime as triggering a wave of news coverage about crime. Other examples that have been mentioned include the Chernobyl disaster, the death of Princess Diana, and so on. Key events are real happenings and not at all the same as 'media events'.

Kepplinger and Habermeier (1995) investigated the hypothesis that key events can have a powerful effect on the representation of reality by triggering a wave of reporting that is quite disproportionate to the reality of the occurrence of events. An example close to home for them was the wave of reports about racial attacks on immigrants in Germany that occurred in 1992 and 1993. Their study of news reporting in Germany before and after certain significant events confirmed the hypothesis that key events do stimulate much enhanced attention to certain topics over a certain period, without there being any change in the reality of these topics. One way in which the media coped with the fact that there was no changed reality was to report about other similar events in the past. This is not the normal role of the newspaper. In general, the findings underline the risk of treating frequency or prominence of news as a reliable guide to the reality of events.

The term 'mediahype' has been coined (Vasterman, 2005: 515) to refer to 'a media generated, wall-to-wall news wave, triggered by one specific event and expanded by the self-reinforcing processes within the news production of the media'. Associated criteria of mediahype are its sudden and unexpected appearance and gradual fading away, the lack of correspondence with the frequency of actual events, and the tendency to provoke reactions from social actors that in turn generate more 'news'. Most countries have their own examples, but a global instance is offered by the 2009 worldwide alarm at the feared pandemic of swine flu, seemingly escalated and kept alive by media coverage, without a great deal of hard evidence to justify fears. Fengler and Russ-Mohl (2008) offer the mediahype as an example of media behaviour prompted by economic factors, since most of the actual news involved in such cases is a free public good that all media compete for and feast on to excess. There are many other kinds of 'free' news but usually it comes with some ulterior motive on the part of the source, as summarized in Box 12.4.

12.4 News selection factors

- Power, status or fame of individuals involved in events
- Personal contacts of reporters
- Location of events
- Location of power
- Predictability and routine
- Proximity to the audience of people and events in the news
- Recency and timeliness of events
- Timing in relation to the news cycle
- Exclusivity
- Economic benefits (from audience, sponsors, etc.)

The Struggle over Access between Media and Society

The question of access to the media (and thus to society itself as audience) by any one institutional element of the society has already been raised at several points. The initial frame of reference in Chapter 4 (Figure 4.2) represents the media as creating (or occupying) channels 'between' the institutions of society and its members. One of the main kinds of pressure on media organizations, as shown in Figure 11.2, is that for access by social and political interests. Much of the normative theory discussed in Chapter 7 turns in the end on the question of who in society should have access and on what terms.

The way the issue has been posed assumes that the mass media effectively control the flow of information between society and its members. However, this is called into question by the appearance of new media that produce not only content but also 'connectivity' of anyone with anyone else. This enables many new and uncontrolled channels to develop and for the roles of sender and receiver to converge (Deuze, 2007; Quandt and Singer, 2009). Nevertheless, the mediation of power in most societies still seem to be carried out by mass media, albeit in new, converged forms and society still seems intent on keeping as much control as possible of old channels and extending it to new networks.

Even in democratic societies, offering a high degree of freedom to their media, there are clear expectations, sometimes backed by considerable pressure, that mass media will make channels available for society-wide communication, especially 'downwards' from leaders or elites to the base of society. This may be achieved by legal provision, by purchase of time/space in a free market, or by the media voluntarily serving as an open means of public communication. It matters a good deal to the media how 'access for society' is achieved, since freedom of the press is generally held to include the right not to publish and thus to withhold access. In practice, the operation of normal news values and the dependence of media on influential sources generally ensure that access is available to the social 'top' at least. For similar reason, much the same applies to fiction that is usually over-populated by elites.

A continuum of media autonomy

The situation can be understood in terms of a continuum: at one extreme the media are totally 'penetrated' by, or assimilated to, outside interests, whether state or not; at the other end, the media are totally free to exclude or admit as they will. Under normal conditions neither extreme will be found. Pluralistic theory presupposes that the diversity of organizations and possibilities for access will ensure an adequate mix of opportunity for 'official' voices of society and for critical and alternative views.

'Access for society' means more, however, than giving a platform for opinions, information, and the like. It also relates to the *manner* in which media portray what passes for the reality of society. They may do this in ways that alter, distort or challenge it. In the end, the question of societal access involves a very complex set of conventions over the terms according to which media freedoms and societal claims can be exercised and reconciled. Much depends on the standardized characteristics of formats and genres and on the manner in which they are intended to portray social reality or are understood to do so by their audiences.

This question was illuminated through the case of television production in one country (Britain) by Elliott (1972), but his ideas could be applied to press media and to other national media systems. His typology (Figure 12.2) shows the variability of competence of the media organization over the giving or withholding of access to other would-be communicators. It portrays the inverse relationship between the degree of freedom of access available to society and the degree of extensiveness of control and action by media. The larger the scope of control by the media themselves (scope of production), the more limited the direct access by the society. There is a varying degree of intervention or mediation by the media as between the 'voice of society' or social reality on the one hand, and the society as audience on the other. This formulation underlines the basic conflict between media autonomy and social control. Access is bound to be a site of struggle.

Social reality content as a contested zone

Figure 12.2 shows the variable degree to which social 'reality' is filtered by the media, with news and documentary falling at a midpoint on the scale. The scope for producers to select and shape is more or less balanced against the scope for society to claim direct access to the audience. Editorial freedom is also in balance, with the scope for the audience to achieve a view of reality. Such 'actuality' material generally promises the audience a valid reflection of reality, but also retains the right of the media to set criteria of selection and presentation. Apart from its other merits, this typology reminds us that news, on which so much study of media selection has been concentrated, is only one of several kinds of message about reality that have to pass through the 'gates' of the media.

Scope of production/ media autonomy	Production function	Directness of access by society	Type of access for society	Television example
Limited	1 Technical facilitation	Total	1 Direct	Partly broadcast
↑	2 Facilitation and selection	↑	2 Modified direct	Education
	3 Selection and presentation		3 Filtered	News
	4 Selection and compilation		4 Remade	Documentary
↓	5 Realization and creation	↓	5 Advisory	Realistic social drama
Extensive	6 Imaginative creation	Zero	6 No control by society	Original television drama

Figure 12.2   A typology of production scope and directness of access by society: access by society is inversely related to communicator (editorial) autonomy (Elliott, 1972)

In practice, it is at the intermediate stages of the continuum (the sphere of actuality) where most potential for conflict arises and where media organizations have to defend their choices and priorities in relation to both society and public. This area extends beyond news and documentaries to encompass 'docudramas', historical dramas and many 'realistic' serials that portray police, medicine, the military, and so on. It also covers what is now often referred to as 'infotainment' (Brants, 1998). The more sensitive and powerful the external representatives of these domains of reality happen to be, the more careful the media have to be and the more obliged they are to avoid sensitive areas or to employ irony, allegory, fantasy and other long-known devices for evading direct accountability. It is not only self-interested authority that has a restraining influence, but also the possibility of unintended and unwanted effects on reality itself (such as causing panic, crime, suicide or terrorism).

Since the construction of this typology, there have been significant developments in broadcasting, especially the multiplication of channels, that do not invalidate the principles but introduce new possibilities and issues. A significant innovation has been that of audience participation in radio and television shows (Munson, 1993; Livingstone and Lunt, 1994; Shen, 1999). The phenomenon occurred first by way of radio call-in shows, usually in response to some expert, public figure or celebrity. There has since been an explosion of new formats and volume of output. The main variants of the new forms of 'reality television' are shown in Box 12.5.

New forms of 'reality' television **12.5** i

- Talk shows with a star presenter and famous guests before a live studio audience
- Public discussion and debate programmes with a live and participant studio audience
- Magazine shows with news and talk (as in *Good Morning America* and now many breakfast television shows)
- News interviews (without participation)
- Daytime talk shows on burning personal issues with audience participation, as pioneered by Oprah Winfrey
- 'Docudramas' and 'infotainment'
- Reality television shows such as *Big Brother*, with celebrity variants

---

The specific examples as well as the types are quite diverse and vary cross-culturally. In terms of the foregoing discussion of access, we can draw at least three conclusions. One is that there are novel forms of access for aspects of reality that were previously kept hidden, for instance the 'confessional' or sensational talk show. Secondly, we can conclude that there is a 'third voice' to be heard alongside the media professionals and the official or expert voices of society, and it is the voice of ordinary people. Thirdly, there is a large expansion of the intermediate types of access, as shown in Figure 12.2. In this territory the line between reality and fiction is very blurred and meanings are much more filtered and negotiated.

The Influence of Sources on News

Media of all kinds depend on having a readily available supply of source material, whether this is book manuscripts to publish, scripts to film, or reports of events to fill newspapers and television. Relations with news sources are essential to news media and they often constitute a very active two-way process. The news media are always looking for suitable content, and content (not always suitable) is always looking for an outlet in the news.

News people also have their own preferred sources and are also linked to prominent figures by institutional means – press conferences, publicity agents, and so on. Studies of news reporters (e.g. Tuchman, 1978; Fishman, 1980) make clear that one thing which they do not share with their colleagues is their sources and contacts. Elliott's (1972) study of the making of a television documentary about racial prejudice showed the importance of the 'contact chain'. Eventual content on screen was shaped by ideas and preconceptions held initially within the production team and by the personal contacts they happened to have. This suggests that the characteristics and personal values of media personnel may well be influential after all.

The practice of validating news reports by reference to dependable sources generally gives most weight to established authority and conventional wisdom. This is an almost inevitable form of unintended bias in mainstream news media, but it can end up as a consistent ideological bias, concealed behind the mask of objectivity. In the study of US television news content by Reese et al. (1994) referred to above, the three main types of 'source' interviewed or cited were institutional spokespersons, 'experts' and other journalists. The main finding of the study was the very high degree of interrelation between the same limited set of sources, making it difficult for a plurality of viewpoints to emerge. Reese et al. (1994: 85) write: 'By relying on a common and often narrow network of sources ... the news media contribute to [a] systematic convergence on the conventional wisdom, the largely unquestioned consensus views held by journalists, power-holders and many audience members.'

In times of national crisis or conflict, where foreign events are involved, the news media typically draw from official sources close to home, with an inevitable bias in terms of the framing of issues and events. There is evidence of this from the comparative analysis of news of recent wars in Kosovo, Afghanistan and Iraq. For example, Yang's (2003) comparison between Chinese and American press coverage of the Kosovo air strikes shows wide differences in sources and in the direction of coverage. Both press systems drew predominantly from their own national news sources and in both cases the news coverage reflected respective government views on the events.

The news media are often accused of bias, especially on issues where emotions are charged and opinion sharply divided. In the case of the first and second (Iraq) Gulf wars, the media of western participant countries were widely said to have failed to live up to their role of objective reporter and critical observer. Generally, such criticism is rejected by the media, but in May 2004 *The New York Times* took the unusual step of acknowledging serious failings in the run-up to the Iraq war. Not long after, *The Washington Post* made a similar admission. Excerpts from *The New York Times* editorial statement are reproduced in Box 12.6.

 12.6 *The New York Times* and Iraq: excerpts from editorial statement, 26 May 2004

Over the last year this newspaper shone the bright light of hindsight on decisions that led the United States into Iraq. We have examined the failings of American and allied intelligence ... We have studied the allegations of official gullibility and hype. It is time we turned the same light on ourselves ... [W]e found an enormous amount of journalism that we are proud of ... But we have found a number of instances of coverage that was not as rigorous as it should have been. In some cases, information that was controversial then, and seems questionable now, was insufficiently qualified or allowed to stand unchallenged ... Editors at several levels who should have been challenging reporters and pressing for more scepticism were perhaps too intent on rushing scoops into the paper. Accounts of Iraqi defectors were not always weighed against their strong desire to have Saddam Hussein ousted. Articles based on dire claims about Iraq tended to get prominent display, while follow-up articles that called the original ones into question were sometimes buried. In some cases, there was no follow-up at all.

The Westley–MacLean model described above (p. 69) shows communication organizations as brokers between would-be 'advocates' trying to convey their view of social reality and a public interested in reliable information about this reality. These advocates, for their part, initiate and maintain regular contact with news media in order to secure favourable access. One general result has been an inevitable degree of symbiosis between media and their sources. Even this does not exhaust the possibilities, especially by leaving out of the account the degree to which media serve as sources for each other in unchartable combinations and permutations. Any given medium tends to regard other media as the best initial guide to newsworthiness and celebrity status in making selections. Aside from the continuous feeding on each other by press and television, both as sources and as objects of information and comment, there are important relations of content provision from the film industry to television and from music to radio. This is one aspect of the 'intertextuality' of media (see p. 387).

The planning of supply

Ericson et al. (1987) even designate a special category of 'source media' whose main activity is to supply journalists with what they are looking for on behalf of source organizations of the kind mentioned. Source media consist of press conferences, press releases, public relations, and so on. In addition, the media are continually collecting their own material by direct observation, information gathering and reporting on a day-to-day and event-guided basis. They also routinely use the services of information suppliers, especially national or international news agencies, news film agencies, television exchange arrangements, and the like.

There are several aspects to note. First, there is the matter of the high degree of *planning* and predictability that goes with any large-scale continuous media production operation. The media have to have an assured supply for their own needs and thus have to 'order' content in advance, whether of news, fiction or other entertainment. This need is reflected in the growth of secondary organizations (such as news agencies) which provide content regularly. It also implies some inconsistency with the notion of media as neutral carriers or mirrors of the ongoing culture and news of the society. It conflicts with the ideals of novelty, spontaneity and creativity that are often part of the media self-image.

Secondly, there is the question of *imbalance* between information suppliers on the one hand and media takers of information on the other. Some sources are also more powerful than others or have more bargaining power because of their status, market dominance or intrinsic market value. Gandy (1982) has referred to the 'information subsidies' that are given selectively by powerful interest groups in order to advance their causes. Media organizations are far from equitable in the degree to which they allocate access to sources. According to Gans (1979), the sources who are most successful in gaining access to (elite) news media are likely to be powerful, well resourced and well organized for supplying journalists with the kind of 'news' they want at the right time. Such sources are both 'authoritative' and 'efficient' and they often enjoy 'habitual access' to the news media, in the sense meant by Molotch and Lester (1974). There is a potential limit to the independence and diversity of news media posed by the difficulty they have in turning away such source material.

Thirdly, there is the question of *assimilation* that arises when there exists a mutual interest on the part of the media and would-be external communicators (advocates or sources). There are obvious examples when political leaders want to reach large publics, but less obvious collusion arises in routine news coverage where reporters depend on sources likely to have both inside information and an interest in the way it is published. This applies to sources such as politicians, officials and the police. Assimilation can be said to occur if the degree of collaboration which exists for mutual benefit between reporter and source reaches a point where it conflicts with the 'distributive' role normally expected from those who claim to inform the public (Gieber and Johnson, 1961). Although this type of relationship may be justified by its success in meeting the needs of the public as well as those of the media organization, it also conflicts with expectations of critical independence and professional norms (Murphy, 1976; Chibnall, 1977; Fishman, 1980).

Public relations and news management

Molotch and Lester (1974) showed how news could be controlled by those in a position to manage publicity about events, if not the events themselves. They call these 'event promoters' and argue that, with reference to 'routine events', the event promoters have several opportunities for gaining access on their own terms. They can claim habitual access to the 'news assemblers' (that is, journalists), or they can use their power to disrupt the routine access of others and create 'pseudo-events' of their own which gain media attention. There is often a more or less institutionalized collusive relationship between politicians or officials and press which may serve a range of purposes without necessarily being manipulative in its effect (Tunstall, 1970; Sigal, 1973). This is especially evident in election campaigns, which lend themselves to the staging of 'pseudo-events', ranging from press conferences to major policy statements or demonstrations (Swanson and Mancini, 1996). In some spheres assimilation between news media and sources is virtually complete. Politics, government and law enforcement are three prime examples, but major sports provide another, and big business is not far behind in being able to claim uncritical media attention more or less at will and in having a good deal of control over the content and flow of information.

Assimilation in the sense used above is also promoted by the activities of professional public relations agencies. There is considerable evidence to suggest that well-organized suppliers of information can be effective and that a good deal of what is supplied by public relations agencies to the news media does get used (Turow, 1989; Shoemaker and Reese, 1991; Glenn et al., 1997; Cottle, 2003). A study by Baerns (1987), for instance, found that political reporting in one German *Land* was predominantly based on official press releases and news conferences. Schultz (1998: 56) reported research showing that about half the articles published in major Australian newspapers began as press releases. This reflects the fact that journalists rely differentially on official or bureaucratic sources for certain kinds of news (see Fishman, 1980). Journalists are normally suspicious of self-serving public relations handouts, but it does seem that rather little of the news we receive is the outcome of enterprise and investigation on the part of journalists (Sigal, 1973), though it may still be both reliable and relevant.

If anything, the process of attempting to influence news has accelerated in line with modern techniques of campaigning and opinion measurement (Swanson and Mancini, 1996). Political parties, government agencies and all the major institutions employ news managers and '**spin doctors**' whose task is to maximize the favourable presentation of policy and action and minimize any negative aspect (Esser et al., 2000). There is almost certainly an increasing importance attaching to 'symbolic politics', whether or not it is effective (Kepplinger, 2002). News media are less able to verify content themselves and the responsibility for truth is left to the source, more often than not. Not insignificantly, they try to influence foreign policy. Although it appears that the main beneficiaries of the increased use of professional public relations are likely to be the more powerful in society, Davis (2003: 40) argues that 'the resource-poor' and 'outsider' sources have also used public relations to gain more frequent and favourable coverage. The activities of environmental groups provide a number of examples (Anderson, 2003).

It is not only in political campaigns that news management plays an increasing role. Manheim (1998) has drawn attention to what he calls a 'third force in news-making' – the practice of '**strategic communication**', carried out by paid experts on behalf of well-resourced institutions, lobbies and interests. Strategic communicators use all forms of intelligence gathering and techniques of influence as well as mass media, and they are often operating outside the sphere of publicity. They may include governmental and political agencies, but also major corporations, well-funded parties to lawsuits, labour unions and foreign governments (Foerstal, 2001; and see pp. 290–91). News source theory predicts influence from several basic factors, as shown in Box 12.7.

Source access to news 12.7

Source access depends on:

- Efficient supply of suitable material
- Power and influence of source
- Good public relations and news management
- Dependency of media on limited source
- Mutual self-interest in news coverage

Media-Organizational Activity: Processing and Presentation

The organizational processes involved in the selection of news are typically very hierarchical rather than democratic or collegial, although *within* particular production units the latter may apply. Ericson et al. (1987) have shown how news organizations arrange the sequence of inputs and decisions. There are two main lines of activity, which start with 'ideas' for news (originating in other media, routine observations, agencies, and so on). Ideas lead to one line – that of story development – and ideas are also fed by a second 'sources' line. Sources can be reactive (routine) or proactive (enterprise). The two lines are closely connected since particular stories lead to the development of and search for sources. The two lines correspond more or less to the two stages of the 'double action' model of news flow described by Bass (1969) – essentially news gathering and news processing. The processing line follows from story assignments made by the assignment editor and goes through a sequence of news conference, play decisions (prominence and timing), layout or lineup, final news editing, content page makeup or television anchor script, and final lineup. This sequence can be fed up to the penultimate stage by source input. A schematic version of this is given in Figure 12.3.

In general, the sequence extends from a phase where a universe of substantive ideas is considered, through a narrowing down according to news judgements and to what is fed from the source channel, to a third phase, where format, design and presentation decisions are taken. In the final phase, technical decisions are likely to be paramount.

This model for news processing is compatible with what seems to occur in other situations, where reality content is also processed, although over a longer time scale and with more scope for production to influence content (see Figure 12.2). For instance, Elliott (1972), in his study of the making of a television documentary series, distinguishes three 'chains' (Box 12.8). The presentation chain included having plenty of illustrative film and having a well-known television personality to act as presenter. The subject and contact chains correspond to the 'ideas' and 'sources' routes in Figure 12.3, while presentation matters arise at the later stages of the 'production line'.

12.8 Three chains in documentary production (Elliott, 1972)

- A *subject* chain concerned with assembling programme ideas for the series
- A *contact* chain connecting producer, director and researcher with their contacts and sources
- A *presentation* chain in which realities of time slot and budget were related to customary ideas for effective presentation

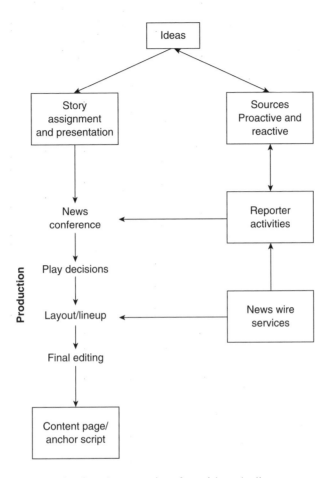

Figure 12.3   Intra-organizational processing, from ideas to the news: news as published has internal as well as external origins, and both types are processed jointly (based on Ericson et al., 1987)

An alternative model of organizational selection

These examples apply to cases where media processing takes place within the boundaries of the same organization. The music industry offers a different model, although there is still a sequence from ideas to transmission. Ryan and Peterson (1982) have drawn a model of the 'decision chain' in the popular music industry, which consists of six separate links. These are: (1) from songwriting to publishing; (2) from demo tape to recording (where producer and artist are selected); (3) and (4) from recording to manufacturing and marketing; (5) and (6) from there to consumption via radio, jukebox, live performance or direct sales (see Figure 12.4). In this case, the original ideas of songwriters are filtered through music publishers' ideas concerning presentation (especially artist and style), which then play a part in

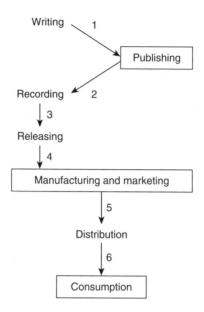

Figure 12.4 Decision sequence in the music industry: the elements in the sequence are often organizationally separate (Ryan and Peterson, 1982)

promoting the product in several different markets. Different from the previous examples is the linkage between several organizationally separate agencies and tasks. Processing takes place on the basis of a prediction about what the next gatekeeper in the chain will think, the key being the overall 'product image' (see below p. 332).

Bias as a result of internal processing

When content is subjected to organizational routines there is often an accentuation of the characteristics of any initial selection bias. This seems to happen not only to news but to other kinds of content as well since a high proportion of content acquired or started as projects never reaches distribution (this is especially true of the film industry, which is profligate with creative talent). This accentuation can mainly be accounted for by the wish to maximize output according to a tried and trusted product image. Some media products live on for years and are resold, remade or recycled indefinitely.

Media organizations tend to reproduce selectively according to criteria that suit their own goals and interests. These may sometimes be professional and craft criteria, but more weight is usually given to what sells most or gets highest ratings. The more that the same criteria are applied at successive stages of decision-making, the more pre-existing biases of form and content are likely to endure while variety, uniqueness and unpredictability will take second place. Bias in this sense may mean no more than favouring products which are both easy to reproduce and popular with audiences, but it also differentially reinforces certain elements of the media culture and increases conformity with organizational policy.

The tendency of media to look to other media for content and format ideas, for evidence of success and for validation of celebrity, also has a reinforcing effect on existing values. There is a spiralling and self-fulfilling effect that tends to work against experimentation and innovation, despite the necessity for innovation at some point.

Standardization and organizational logics

Although mass communication is a form of mass production, the standardization implied in this term relates in the first instance to multiple reproduction and distribution. The individual items of media content do not have to share all the characteristics of mass-produced products. They can easily be original, unique and highly differentiated (for instance, the one-off performance of a sports event, a television talk show or a news programme, which will never be repeated identically). In practice, however, the technology and organization of mass media production are not neutral and do exert a standardizing influence. Initial diverse and unique content items or ideas are fitted to forms that are both familiar to media producers and thought to be familiar to audiences. These forms are those most suitable for efficient production according to specifications laid down by the organization.

These specifications are of an *economic*, a *technological* and a *cultural* kind, and each entails a certain logic of its own which leaves a distinctive mark on the cultural product through its influence on production decisions. Pressures for *economic* efficiency stem from the need to minimize cost, reduce conflict and ensure continuity and sufficiency of supply. Cost reduction exerts pressure according to different time schemes: in the long run it may lead to the introduction of new technology, in the short run to maximizing output from existing staff resources and equipment and avoiding expensive or loss-making activities. The main pressures on media processors – to save time, use technology efficiently, save money and meet deadlines – are so interrelated that it is easier to see them in their combined consequences than in their separate operation. McManus (1994), in his study of local television news, showed that the lower the budget and smaller the staff, the greater the proportion of news that was 'discovered' in a 'passive' rather than 'active' way (meaning reliance on other media, agency and public relations material, lack of initiative or investigation). Picard (2004) points to the negative consequences for newspaper content of excessive reliance on advertising.

The *technological* logic is quite obvious in its effects, which keep changing as a succession of major new inventions has affected different media industries. There is an almost irresistible pressure sooner or later to adopt the latest innovations. Film was changed by the coming of sound and colour; the newspaper industry by continuous advances in printing and information transmission; and television by the portable video camera, satellites and now digitalization.

The pressure of technology is experienced mainly as a result of inventions which set higher technical standards for lower prices and which progressive media organizations have to keep up with (whether audiences know or care or not) in order to compete. The investment in technical facilities leads to pressure for their maximum use, and prestige as well as utility becomes a factor. New technology often means more speed, flexibility and capacity, but it establishes norms that put pressure on all media organizations to conform and eventually influences audience expectations about what is most professional or acceptable.

The Logic of Media Culture

The processing of media raw material requires a form of cultural standardization. It has already been suggested that media are constrained by their 'definitions' and associated expectations as to what they are 'good for' in general and what sort of content they can best offer and in what form. Within the media, the main types of content – news, sports, drama, entertainment, advertising – also follow standardized formats which are rooted in traditions (media-made or culturally inherited), ways of working, ideas about audience taste and interest, and pressures of time or space. Altheide and Snow (1979) were the first to use the term 'media logic' to capture the systematic nature of pre-existing definitions of what a given type of content should be like. The operation of a media logic implies the existence of a 'media grammar' which governs how time should be used, how items of content should be sequenced and what devices of verbal and non-verbal content should be used.

This refers to the influence of media (considered both as cultured technology and as formal organization) on 'real-world' events themselves as well as on their portrayal and constitution. Altheide and Snow (1991: 10) have described media logic as 'a way of seeing and interpreting social affairs ... Elements of this form [of communication] include the various media and the formats used by these media. Formats consist, in part, in how material is organized, the style in which it is presented, the focus or emphasis ... and the grammar of media communication.'

Because of the increased centrality of mass media for other institutions, there is an imperative to conduct affairs and stage events in ways that conform to the needs and routines of the mass media (in respect of timing and form). The idea of a staged 'media event' (or pseudo-event) belongs to the theory of media logic (Boorstin, 1961; Dayan and Katz, 1992). It has an obvious relevance to predominant modes of news coverage, in which familiar formats and routines predictably frame certain categories of event (Altheide, 1985). The general notion of media logic extends to include the influence of media requirements on a wide range of cultural happenings, including sport, entertainment and public ceremonies.

The concept has been especially useful for identifying the predilection of media producers for factors that they believe will increase audience attention and satisfaction. Many of the elements of media logic stem from the attention-gaining or publicity model outlined in Chapter 3 (pp. 72–3). However, there is an independent contribution that derives from media professionalism, especially when defined in terms of making 'good' TV, film, and so on. It has to be seen as a media-cultural phenomenon as much as a reflection of rational calculation. A very evident feature of media culture is its self-obsession and love of self-reference. The media are the main instrument for manufacturing fame and celebrity, whether in politics, sport or entertainment, and they are also captivated by it. It sometimes appears to be the primary resource and also criterion of value, when applied to people, products or performances. One of the driving forces of media logic is the search for new sources or objects of fame.

In relation to informational content, media logic places a premium on immediacy, such as dramatic illustrative film or photos, on fast tempo and short 'soundbites' (Hallin, 1992), and on personally attractive presenters and relaxed formats (such as the so-called 'happy news' format). Media logic also operates on the level of content: for instance, in political campaigns it leads to a preference for personalization, for controversiality and for attention to the 'horse-race' (for example, as measured by opinion polls) rather than the issues (Graber, 1976b; Hallin and Mancini, 1984; Mazzoleni, 1987b). Hallin (1992) demonstrated that there was a clear correlation in US news coverage of elections between 'horse-race coverage' and 'soundbite news': the more of the former, the shorter the latter (see also Chapter 19). The media qualities that contribute to media logic are summarized in Box 12.9

Main principles of media logic **12.9**

- Novelty
- Immediacy
- High tempo
- Personalization
- Brevity
- Conflict
- Dramatization
- Celebrity orientation

Alternative Models of Decision-making

In a review of the mechanisms according to which culture is produced in the commercial-industrial world of mass media, Ryan and Peterson (1982) describe five main frameworks for explaining how decisions are made in the media arts. Their first model is that of the *assembly line*, which compares the media production process to the factory, with all skills and decisions built into the machinery and with clear procedural rules. Because media-cultural products, unlike material goods, have to be marginally different from each other, the result is overproduction at each stage.

The second model is that of *craft and entrepreneurship*, in which powerful figures, with established reputations for judging talent, raising finance and putting things together, manage all the creative inputs of artists, musicians, engineers, and the like, in innovative ways. This model applies especially to the film business but could also hold for publications in which editors may play the role of personally charismatic and powerful figures with a supposed flair for picking winners.

The third model is that of *convention and formula*, in which members of a relevant 'art world' agree on a 'recipe', a set of widely held principles which tell workers how to combine elements to produce works in the particular genre. Fourthly, there is the model of *audience image and conflict*, which sees the creative production process as a matter of fitting production to an image of what the audience will like. Here decisions about the latter are central, and powerful competing entrepreneurs come into conflict over them.

The final model is that of the *product image*. Its essence is summarized in Box 12.10.

12.10 The product image: key quotation

Having a product image is to shape a piece of work so that it is most likely to be accepted by decision makers at the next link in the chain. The most common way of doing this is to produce works that are much like the products that have most recently passed through all the links in the decision chain to become successful. (Ryan and Peterson, 1982: 25)

This model does not assume there to be a consensus among all involved, or an entrepreneur, or an agreed audience image. It is a model which seems closest to the notion of 'professionalism', defined as the special knowledge of what is a good piece of media work, in contrast to the prediction of what will succeed commercially.

Most studies of media production seem to confirm the strong feeling held by established professionals that they know how best to combine all the available factors of production within the inevitable constraints. This may be achieved at the cost of not actually communicating with the audience, but it does secure the integrity of the product.

12.11 Five models of media decision-making

- The assembly line
- Craft and entrepreneurship
- Convention and formula
- Audience image and conflict
- Product image

Ryan and Peterson's typology is especially useful in stressing the *diversity* of frameworks within which a degree of regularity and predictability can be achieved in the production of cultural goods (including news). There are different ways of handling uncertainty, responding to outside pressures and reconciling the need for continuous production with artistic originality or journalistic freedom. The concepts of manufacturing or routine bureaucracy, often invoked to apply to media production, should be used with caution.

The Coming of Convergence Culture: Consumers as Producers

The concept of **convergence culture** may have been first coined by Jenkins (2004) ✱
but has gained wide currency. It refers to a range of related phenomena that follow on from and seem to be caused by purely technological convergence (Jenkins and Deuze, 2008). Primarily, they comprise the following: the participation of audiences in production; the blurring of the line between professional and amateur; and the breakdown of the line between producer and consumer. This last one has led to new terms such as 'prosumer' and 'produser'. Deuze (2007) gives some examples, as follows. Producers of fiction collect audience feedback to help develop new plotlines and characters. News services invite reader reactions and personal blogs. **Social net-** ✱
work sites such as *YouTube* largely depend on contributions from the Public. Amazon prints reader reviews. Wikipedia is written by volunteers. Google content is largely externally provided, with little own production. The significance and implications of all this are still unclear and there are many still unknown factors, such as those to do with finance and copyright. There seem to be potential consequences for media structures and professions and the former exclusive control by media of their own content is no more. On the other hand, much 'prosumerism' is also encouraged and managed by 'big media' for their own purposes and many such activities that began as innovative and grassroots in character have become normalized and commercialized.

Conclusion

The ground covered by this chapter has dealt mainly with processes of selection by and shaping within the formal media organization, as ideas and images are transformed into 'product' for distribution. The influences on this process are numerous and often conflicting. Despite certain recurring features and constants, media production still has a potential to be unpredictable and innovative, as it should be in a free society. The constraining economic, cultural and technological factors can also be facilitative, where there is enough money to buy freedom and cultural inventiveness and where technological innovation works to overcome obstacles.

We need to recall the dominant influence of the 'publicity' model compared with the 'transmission' or 'ritual' models of communication (as described in Chapter 3). The transmission model captures one image of the media organization – as a system for efficiently turning events into comprehensible information, or ideas into familiar cultural packages. The ritual model implies a private world in which routines are followed largely for the benefit of the participants and their clients. Both capture some element of the reality. The publicity model helps to remind us that mass communication is often primarily a business, and show business at that. Its roots are as much in the theatre and the showground as in politics, art or education. Appearance, artifice and surprise (the fundamentals of 'media logic') often count for more than substance, reality, truth or relevance when it comes to the essential matter of attracting attention. At the core of many media organizations, there are contrary tendencies that are often in tension, if not at open warfare, with each other, making illusory the search for any comprehensive theory of their work.

Further Reading

Deuze, M. (2007) *Media Work*. Cambridge: Polity Press.
A new and original interpretation of the general conditions in relation to society and of social-cultural trends that affect all forms of media work. Essentially this means the end of the industrial-bureaucratic model of production and of career development.

Tuchman, G. (1978) *The Manufacture of News: a Study in the Construction of Reality*. New York: Free Press.
A classic study of the consequences of work routines and technology on the picture of the world recorded and relayed to the public.

Whitney, D.C. and Ettema, J.S. (2003) 'Media production: individuals, organizations, institutions', in A.N. Valdivia (ed.), *The Companion to Media Studies*, pp. 157–87. Oxford: Blackwell.

Online Readings

Machill, M., Beiler, M. and Zenker, M. (2008) 'Search engine research: a European–American overview and systematization of an interdisciplinary and international research field', *Media, Culture and Society*, 30 (5): 591–608.
Schatz, T. and Perren, A. (2004) 'Hollywood', in J.D.H. Downing, D. McQuail, P. Schlesinger and E. Wartella (eds), *The Sage Handbook of Media Studies*, pp. 495–516. Thousand Oaks, CA: Sage.
Vasterman, P. (2005) 'Media hype: self-reinforcing news waves', *European Journal of Communication*, 19 (4): 449–645.
Wu, H.D. (2007) 'A brave new world for international news? Exploring the determinants of foreign news on US websites', *The International Communication Gazette*, 69 (6): 539–52.

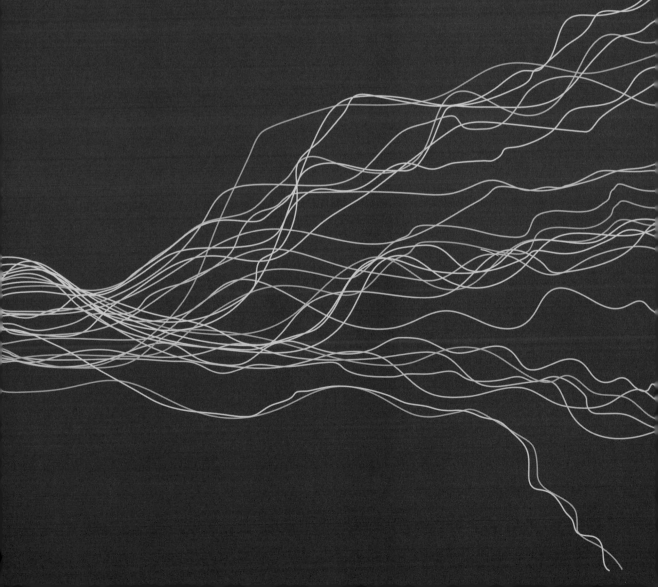

Part 5
Content

13

Media Content: Issues, Concepts and Methods of Analysis

The most accessible evidence of how mass communication works is provided by its content. In a very literal sense we can equate the media with the message, although it would be extremely misleading to do so. In this respect, the distinction between message and meaning is a significant one. The physical text of the message in print, sound or pictorial image is what we can directly observe and is in a sense 'fixed'. But we cannot simply 'read off' the meanings that are somehow 'embedded' in the texts or transmitted to audiences. These meanings are not self-evident and certainly not fixed. They are also multiple and often ambiguous.

Theory and research concerning mass media content are fissured by this distinction between message and meaning, which largely parallels the choice between a 'transport' and a 'ritual' (or cultural) model of communication (see p. 71). This remark exposes the difficulty in speaking about content at all with any certainty. Even so, we often encounter generalizations about the content of mass media as a whole, or a particular type of content, especially with reference to matters of media intention, 'bias', or probable effect. Our ability to generalize about these matters has been helped by the patterned and standardized forms which media content often takes.

The main purpose of this chapter is to review the alternative approaches to media content and the methods available. However, the choice of both approach and method depends on the purpose that we have in mind, of which there is some diversity. We mainly deal with three aspects of content analysis: content as information; content as hidden meaning (semiology); and 'traditional' quantitative content analysis. There is no coherent theory of media content and no consensus on the best method of analysis since alternative methods are needed for different purposes and kinds of content and for a variety of media genres. Consequently, we begin with the question of purpose.

Why Study Media Content?

The first reasons for studying media content in a systematic way stemmed either from an interest in the potential effects of mass communication, whether intended or unintended, or from a wish to understand the appeal of content for the audience. Both perspectives have a practical basis, from the point of view of mass communicators, but they have gradually been widened and supplemented to embrace a larger range of theoretical issues. Early studies of content reflected a concern about social problems with which the media were linked. Attention focused in particular on the portrayal of crime, violence and sex in popular entertainment, the use of media as propaganda and the performance of media in respect of racial or other kinds of prejudice. The range of purposes was gradually extended to cover news, information and much entertainment content.

Most early research was based on the assumption that content reflected the purposes and values of its originators, more or less directly; that 'meaning' could be discovered or inferred from messages; and that receivers would understand messages more or less as intended by producers. It was even thought that 'effects' could be discovered by inference from the seeming 'message' built into content. More plausibly, the content of mass media has often been regarded as more or less reliable evidence about the culture and society in which it is produced. All of these assumptions, except perhaps the last, have been called into question, and the study of content has become correspondingly more complex and challenging. It may not go too far to say that the most interesting aspects of media content are often not the overt messages, but the many more or less concealed and uncertain meanings that are present in media texts.

Despite these various complications, it is useful at this point to review the main motives that have guided the study of media content, as follows:

- *Describing and comparing media output.* For many purposes of analysis of mass communication (for instance, assessing change or making comparisons), we need to be able to characterize the content of particular media and channels.
- *Comparing media with 'social reality'.* A recurrent issue in media research has been the relation between media messages and 'reality'. The most basic question is whether media content does, or should, reflect the social reality, and if so, which or whose reality.
- *Media content as reflection of social and cultural values and beliefs.* Historians, anthropologists and sociologists are interested in media content as evidence of values and beliefs of a particular time and place or social group.
- *Hypothesizing functions and effects of media.* We can interpret content in terms of its potential consequences, whether good or bad, intended or unintended. Although content on its own cannot be taken as evidence of effect, it is difficult to study effects without intelligent reference to content (as cause).
- *Evaluating media performance.* Krippendorf (2004) uses the term 'performance analysis' to refer to research designed to find answers about the quality of the media as judged by certain criteria (see Chapter 8 and pp. 355–8).
- *The study of media bias.* Much media content has either a clear direction of evaluation in relation to matters of dispute or is open to the perception of favouring one side over another, even if unintentionally or unconsciously.
- *Audience analysis.* Since audiences are always defined at least in part by media content, we cannot study audiences without studying content.
- *Tackling questions of genre, textual and discourse analysis, narrative and other formats.* In this context, the text itself is the object of study, with a view to understanding how it 'works' to produce effects desired by authors and readers.
- *Rating and classification of content.* Regulation or media responsibility often requires that certain kinds of content are classified according to potential harm or offence, especially in matters of violence, sex, language, etc. The development of rating systems requires prior analysis of content.

Critical Perspectives on Content

The main grounds of criticism of mass media have already been introduced in earlier chapters. Here we look specifically at situations where the transmitted content is the main focus of attention. At issue are possible failings, omissions and bad intentions, especially in the way social life is represented, with particular reference to groupings based on social class, ethnicity, gender or similar differentiating factors. Another set of concerns relates to potential harm from content that is perceived as violent or otherwise offensive or dangerous. The cultural quality of media is also sometimes at issue, for example in debates about mass culture or the matter of cultural and national identity.

Marxist approaches

One main critical tradition has been based on a Marxist theory of ideology which relates mainly to class inequality but can also deal with some other issues. Grossberg (1991) has pointed to several variations of Marxist cultural interpretation that deal with the 'politics of textuality'. He identifies three 'classical' Marxist approaches, of which the most relevant derive from the Frankfurt School and ideas concerning 'false consciousness' (see Chapter 5). Two later approaches distinguished by Grossberg are 'hermeneutic' (interpretative) and 'discursive' in character, and again there are several variants. Compared with classical approaches, however, the main differences are, first, that 'decoding' is recognized as problematic and, secondly, that texts are seen as not just 'mediating' reality but actually constructing experience and shaping identity.

The Marxist tradition has paid most attention to news and actuality because of its capacity to define the social world and the world of events. Drawing on various sources, including Barthes and Althusser, Stuart Hall (1977) argued that the practice of signification through language establishes maps of cultural meaning which promote the dominance of a ruling-class ideology, especially by establishing a hegemonic view of the world, within which accounts of reality are framed. News contributes to this task in several ways. One is by 'masking' aspects of reality – especially by ignoring the exploitative nature of class society or by taking it for granted as 'natural'. Secondly, news produces a 'fragmentation' of interests, which undermines the solidarity of subordinate classes. Thirdly, news imposes an 'imaginary unity or coherence' – for instance, by invoking concepts of community, nation, public opinion and consensus as well as by various forms of symbolic exclusion.

Critique of advertising and commercialism

There is a long tradition of critical attention to advertising that sometimes adopts the Marxist approach as described, but also derives from other cultural or humanistic values. Williamson (1978), in her study of advertising, applies the familiar concept of 'ideology', which is defined by Althusser (1971) as representing 'the imaginary relationship of individuals to their real conditions of existence'. Althusser also says that 'All ideology has the function (which defines it) of "constituting" individuals as subjects.' For Williamson, the ideological work of advertising is accomplished (with the active co-operation of the 'reader' of the advertisement) by transferring significant meanings and ideas (sometimes myths) from experience (such as beauty, success, happiness, nature and science) to commercial products and by that route to ourselves.

The commercial product becomes a way to achieve the desired social or cultural state and to be the kind of person we would like to be. We are 'reconstituted' by advertising but end up with an imaginary (and thus false) sense of our real selves and of our relation to the real conditions of our life. This has the same ideological tendency as that attributed to news in critical theory – masking real exploitation and fragmenting solidarity. A very similar process is described by Williamson (1978) in terms of 'commodification', referring to the way advertising converts the 'use value' of products into an 'exchange value', allowing us (in our aspiration) to acquire (buy) happiness or other ideal states.

The ideological work of advertising is essentially achieved by constituting our environment for us and telling us who we are and what we really want (see Mills, 1951). In the critical perspective, all this is illusory and diversionary. What the effect of advertising might actually be is beyond the scope of any analysis of content, but it is possible to work back from content to intention, and the critical terminology of 'manipulation' and 'exploitation' is easier to justify than is the case with ideology in news.

On the question of cultural quality

Both the Marxist critique of mass culture and the elitist and moralistic critique that it replaced are out of fashion. Neither provided a clear definition of mass culture or offered subjective criteria for evaluating cultural quality. Even so, the issue is still a matter for public debate and even policy.

There have been a number of attempts to assess the quality of television in particular in recent years and in different countries, especially in response to the expansion and privatization of media. One example is the Quality Assessment of Broadcasting project of the Japanese public broadcaster NHK (Ishikawa, 1996). Notable in this project is the attempt to evaluate quality of output from different perspectives, namely that of 'society', of the professional broadcasters and of the audience. Of most interest is the assessment made by programme makers themselves. We find a number of criteria being applied. These relate especially to: degree and type of craft skill, resources and production values, originality, relevance and cultural authenticity, values expressed, integrity of purpose and audience appeal. There are other criteria and other ways of assessing quality because the range of content is so wide.

It has been suggested (Schrøder, 1992) that there are essentially three kinds of cultural standards to be applied: the aesthetic (there are many dimensions), the ethical (questions of values, integrity, intended meaning, etc.) and the 'ecstatic' (measured by popularity, pleasure and performative value, essentially aspects of consumption). Developments of cultural theory have significantly extended the scope for estimating the quality of cultural output according to stated criteria. Even so, such assessments are bound to remain subjective, based on approximate criteria and varied perception. Intrinsic quality cannot be measured.

Violence in the mass media

In terms of sheer volume of words written and salience in the public mind, the foremost critical perspective on mass media would probably belong under this heading. Despite the difficulty of establishing direct causal connections, critics have focused on the *content* of popular media. It has always been much easier to demonstrate that media portray violence and aggression in news and fiction to a degree quite disproportionate to real-life experience than to show any effects. Many studies have produced seemingly shocking statistics of average exposure to mediated violence. The argument of critics has been not just that it might cause violence and crime, especially by the young, but that it is often intrinsically undesirable, producing emotional disturbance, fear, anxiety and deviant tastes.

Accepting that thrills and action are a staple part of popular entertainment that cannot simply be banned (although some degree of censorship has been widely legitimated in this matter), content research has often been devoted to understanding the more or less harmful ways in which violence can be depicted (see Chapter 14, pp. 383–4). The scope of criticism was widened to include not only the questions of socialization of children, but also the issue of violent aggression directed at women. This occurs frequently, even in non-pornographic content.

Gender-based critique

There are several other varieties of critical *feminist* perspective on media content (see Chapter 5, pp. 120–3). Initially, these were mainly concerned with the stereotyping, neglect and marginalization of women that was common in the 1970s (see, for example, Tuchman et al., 1978). As Rakow (1986) points out, media content can never be a true account of reality, and it is less important to change media representations (such as having more female characters) than to challenge the underlying sexist ideology of much media content. Most central to critical feminist analysis is probably the broad question (going beyond stereotypes) of how texts 'position' the female subject in narratives and textual interactions and in so doing contribute to a definition of femininity in collaboration with the 'reader'. Essentially the same applies to masculinity, and both fall under the heading of 'gender construction' (Goffman, 1976).

For the feminist critique, two issues necessarily arise. The first is the extent to which media texts intended for the entertainment of women (such as soap operas or romances) can ever be liberating when they embody the realities of patriarchal society and family institutions (Radway, 1984; Ang, 1985). The second is the degree to which new kinds of mass media texts which challenge gender stereotyping and try to introduce positive role models can have any 'empowering' effect for women (while remaining within the dominant commercial media system).

Ultimately, the answers to these questions depend on how the texts are received by their audiences. Radway's (1984) study of romantic fiction argued that there is some element of liberation, if not empowerment, through what is essentially a woman's (own) genre, but she also acknowledged the patriarchal ideology of the form:

the romance also provides a symbolic portrait of the womanly sensibility that is created and required by patriarchal marriage and its sexual division of labour … [It] underscores and shores up the very psychological structure that guarantees women's commitment to marriage and motherhood. (1984: 149)

A variety of literary, discourse and psychoanalytic methods have been used in the critical feminist study of content, but there has been a strong emphasis on interpretation rather than quantification. The 'false consciousness' model, implying a more or less automatic 'transfer' of gender positioning, has also been discarded.

Structuralism and Semiology

One influential way of thinking about media content has origins in the general study of language. Basically, *structuralism* refers to the way meaning is constructed in texts, the term applying to certain 'structures of language', consisting of signs, narrative or myths. Generally, languages have been said to work because of inbuilt structures. The term 'structure' implies a constant and ordered relation of elements, although this may not be apparent on the surface and requires decoding. It has been assumed that such structures are located in and governed by particular cultures – much wider systems of meaning, reference and signification. *Semiology* is a more specific version of the general structuralist approach. There are several classic explications of the structuralist or semiological approach to media content (e.g. Barthes, 1967, 1977; Eco, 1977) plus numerous useful introductions and commentaries (such as Burgelin, 1972; Hawkes, 1977; Fiske, 1982).

Structuralism is a development of the linguistics of de Saussure (1915/1960) and combines with it some principles from structural anthropology. It differs from linguistics in two main ways. First, it is concerned not only with conventional verbal languages but also with any sign system that has language-like properties. Secondly, it directs attention less to the sign system itself than to chosen texts and the meaning of texts in the light of the 'host' culture. It is thus concerned with the elucidation of cultural as well as linguistic meaning, an activity for which a knowledge of the sign system is instrumental but insufficient on its own. Although semiology has declined in popularity as a method, the underlying principles are still very relevant to other varieties of discourse analysis.

Towards a science of signs

North American (Peirce, 1931–5) and British (Ogden and Richards, 1923) scholars subsequently worked towards the goal of establishing a 'general science of signs' (semiology or semiotics). This field was to encompass structuralism and other things besides, and thus all things to do with *signification* (the giving of meaning by means of language), however loosely structured, diverse and fragmentary. The concepts of 'sign system' and 'signification' common to linguistics, structuralism and semiology derive mainly from de Saussure. The same basic concepts were used in somewhat different ways by the three theorists mentioned, but the following are the essentials.

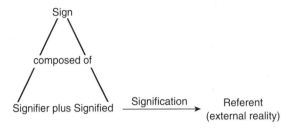

Figure 13.1   Elements of semiology. Signs in meaning systems have two elements: physical plus associated meanings in the culture and in use

A *sign* is the basic physical vehicle of meaning in a language; it is any 'sound image' that we can hear or see and which usually *refers* to some object or aspect of reality about which we wish to communicate, which is known as the *referent*. In human communication, we use signs to convey meanings about objects in the world of experience to others, who interpret the signs we use on the basis of sharing the same language or knowledge of the sign system we are using (for instance, **non-verbal communication**). According to de Saussure, the process of signification is accomplished by two elements of the sign. He called the physical element (word, image, sound) the *signifier* and used the term *signified* to refer to the mental concept invoked by a physical sign in a given language code (Figure 13.1).

Normally in (western) language systems, the connection between a physical signifier (such as a word) and a particular referent is arbitrary, but the relation between signifier and signified (meaning or concept conveyed) is governed by the rules of culture and has to be learned by the particular **'interpretative community'**. In principle, anything that can make a sense impression can act as a sign, and this sense impression has no necessary correspondence with the sense impression made by the thing signified (for instance, the word 'tree' does not look at all like a representation of an actual tree). What matters is the sign system or 'referent system' that governs and interrelates the whole process of signification.

Generally, the separate signs gain their meaning from the systematic differences, contrasts and choices which are regulated in the linguistic or sign-system code and from the values (positive or negative valence) which are given by the rules of the culture and the sign system. Semiology has sought to explore the nature of sign systems that go beyond the rules of grammar and syntax and regulate complex, latent and culturally dependent meanings of texts that can only be understood by reference to the culture in which they are embedded and the precise context in which they appear.

Connotation and denotation

This has led to a concern with *connotative* as well as *denotative* meaning – the associations and images invoked and expressed by certain usages and combinations of signs. **Denotation** has been described as the 'first order of signification' (Barthes, 1967) because it describes the relationship within a sign between the signifier (physical aspect) and signified (mental concept). The obvious straightforward meaning of a sign is its denotation. Williamson (1978) gives an example of an advertisement in which a photo of the film star Catherine Deneuve is used to advertise a French brand of perfume. The photo denotes Catherine Deneuve.

Connotation relates to a second order of signification, referring to the associated meaning that may be conjured up by the object signified. In the example of the advertisement, Catherine Deneuve is generally associated by members of the relevant language (and cultural) community with French 'chicness'. The relevance of this to advertisers is that the connotation of the chosen model (here a film star) is transferred by association to a perfume which she uses or recommends.

A seminal demonstration of this approach to text analysis was provided by Barthes (1977) in his analysis of a magazine advertisement for Panzani foods. This showed an image of a shopping bag containing groceries (the physical signifier), but these in turn were expected to invoke positive images of freshness and domesticity (the level of connotation). In addition, the red and green colours also signified 'Italianness' and could invoke a myth of culinary tradition and excellence. Thus, signification commonly works at two levels (or orders) of meaning: the surface level of literal meaning, and the second level of associated or connoted meaning. The activation of the second level requires some deeper knowledge or familiarity with the culture on the part of the reader.

Barthes extended this basic idea by introducing the concept of a *myth*. Often the thing signified by a sign will have a place in a larger discrete system of meaning, which is also available to the member of a particular culture. Myths are pre-existing and value-laden sets of ideas derived from the culture and transmitted by communication. For instance, there are likely to be myths about national character or national greatness, or concerning science or nature (its purity and goodness), that can be invoked for communicative purposes (as they often are in advertising).

Denotative meaning has the characteristics of universality (the same fixed meaning for all) and objectivity (references are true and do not imply evaluation), while connotation involves both variable meaning according to the culture of the recipient and elements of evaluation (positive or negative direction). The relevance of all this for the study of mass communication should be evident. Media content consists of a large number of 'texts' (in the physical sense), often of a standardized and repetitive kind, that are composed on the basis of certain stylized conventions and codes. These often draw on familiar or latent myths and images present in the culture of the makers and receivers of texts (Barthes, 1972).

Visual language

The visual image cannot be treated in the same way as the sign in Saussurian terminology (p. 345). There is no equivalent of the system of rules of a natural written language which enables us to intepret word signs more or less accurately. As Evans (1999: 12) explains it, a still image, such as a photograph of a woman, is 'less the equivalent of "woman" than it is a series of disconnected descriptions: "an older woman, seen in the distance wearing a green coat, watching the traffic, as she crosses the road'". She also tells us that pictures have no tense, and thus no clear location in time. For these and other reasons, Barthes famously described the photograph as a 'picture without a code'. It presents us, says Evans, with an object as a *fait accompli*.

Visual images are inevitably ambiguous and polysemic, but they also have certain advantages over words. One is their greater denotative power when used deliberately and effectively. Another is their capacity to become **icons** – directly representing some concept with clarity, impact and wide recognition. An example of the power of visual language is provided by the case of the photographs of torture and abuse at Abu Ghraib prison that were published worldwide in May 2004. Anden-Papadopolous (2008) describes these as iconic images that had the power to shape both news and public perceptions, beyond the power of the authorities to counter or control. They have also been transformed into sites of protest and opposition to the deeds they represent. Despite the lack of the equivalent of a true language, visual images, still or moving, can acquire a range of known meanings within the conventions and traditions of an art form (such as cinema or portrait painting) or a particular genre. This gives them considerable potential for skilful communication in certain contexts. Advertising is a primary example.

Given all that has happened by way of change in mass media, there is an even more pressing need to develop better concepts and methods for the analysis of many new formats and forms of expression, especially those that mix and innovate the codes employed. The initial outlook for progress is not very good.

Uses of semiology

The application of semiological analysis opens the possibility of revealing more of the underlying meaning of a text, taken as a whole, than would be possible by simply following the grammatical rules of the language or consulting the dictionary meaning of separate words. It has the special advantage of being applicable to 'texts' that involve more than one sign system and to signs (such as visual images and sounds) for which there is no established 'grammar' and no available dictionary. Without semiology, for instance, it would hardly have been possible for Williamson (1978) to have carried out her seminal study of advertisements.

However, semiological analysis presupposes a thorough knowledge of the originating culture and of the particular genre at issue. According to Burgelin (1972: 317), 'the mass media clearly do not form a complete culture on their own ... but simply a fraction of such a system which is, of necessity, the culture to which they belong'. Moreover, it follows from the theory summarized above that a text has its own immanent, intrinsic, more or less given and thus objective meaning, apart from the overt intention of the sender or the selective interpretation of the receiver. As Burgelin also comments (1972: 316), 'there is nobody, and nothing, outside the message which can supply us with the meaning of one of its elements'.

This body of theory supplies us with an approach, if not exactly a method, for helping to establish the 'cultural meaning' of media content. It certainly offers a way of describing content: it can shed light on those who produce and transmit a set of messages. It has a special application in opening up layers of meaning which lie beneath the surface of texts and deny simple description at the 'first level' of signification. It is also useful in certain kinds of evaluative research, especially as directed at uncovering the latent ideology and 'bias' of media content. The main tenets of these approaches are summarized in Box 13.1.

Structuralism/semiology: main tenets 13.1

- Texts have meanings built in by way of language
- Meanings depend on a wider cultural and linguistic frame of reference
- Texts represent processes of signification
- Sign systems can be 'decoded' on the basis of knowledge of culture and sign system
- Meanings of texts are connotative, denotative or mythical

Critical discourse analysis

The general term 'discourse analysis' has gradually become preferred to the expression 'qualitative content analysis', although there is not much specific meaning to the term that differentiates it. It may be simply that the latter expression was too closely identified with the content of mass media, while the term 'discourse' has a broader connotation and covers all 'texts', in whatever form or language they are encoded and also specifically implies that a text is constructed by those who read and decipher it as much as those who formulate it. Scheufele (2008) names four features shared by all discourses, as meant in the present context. First, discourses refer to political or social issues which are relevant for society, or at least for a major grouping of people. For instance, we can speak of a 'nuclear energy discourse' or a 'drug' discourse, Secondly, the elements of a discourse are called speech acts, emphasizing that they are a form of social interaction and wider patterns of social behaviour. Thirdly, discourse can be analysed by studying bodies of text of all kinds, including documents, transcripts of debates, media content. Fourthly, discourses are processes of collectively constructing social reality, often in the form of frames and schemata, which allow generalization. As to the purposes of discourse analysis, Scheufele reminds us that the primary aim is to uncover the substance or quality of a particular discourse, rather than to quantify the occurrence of different discourses.

According to Smith and Bell (2007), it is hard to give a precise definition of discourse analysis, but they say it is more common to find it referred to as 'critical discourse analysis' because of its attention to the role of power. This is in line with Scheufele's point about it usually being connected with some current significant social issue. Wodak and Meyer (2001: 2–3) define critical discourse analysis as being 'fundamentally concerned with analysing opaque as well as transparent structural relationships of dominance, discrimination, power and control as manifested in language'. This definition sounds as if it would cover, if not the theory, at least many of the applications of earlier and more formal structuralism and semiology, as described.

Media Content as Information

A completely different discourse around media content originates in the information theory approaches popularized by the work of Shannon and Weaver (1949). The roots are intermingled with the basic transmission model (see pp. 69–70), which conceives communication as essentially the intentional transfer of information from sender to receiver by way of (physical) channels which are subject to noise and interference. According to this model, communication is judged by the efficiency (volume and cost) and effectiveness in achieving the planned 'transfer'. The concept of information has proved difficult to define because it can be viewed in different ways, for instance as an object or a commodity, an agency, a resource, and so on. For present purposes, the central element is probably the capacity to 'reduce uncertainty'. Information is thus defined by its opposite (randomness or chaos).

Information theory

According to Frick (1959), the insight that led to the development of information theory was the realization that 'all the processes that might be said to convey information are basically selection processes'. The mathematical theory of communication provided an objective approach to the analysis of communication texts. The basis for objectivity (quantification) is the binary (yes/no) coding system, which forms the basis for digital computing. All problems of uncertainty can ultimately be reduced to a series of either/or questions; the number of questions required to solve a problem of meaning equals the number of items of information and is a measure of information quantity.

This line of thinking provides a tool for the analysis of the informative content of texts and opens up several lines of research. There is an inbuilt bias towards a view of communication content as embodying rational purposes of the producers and to an instrumental view of media messages (the transmission model again). The approach is also fundamentally *behaviourist* in its assumptions. For obvious reasons, most application of this kind of theory has been to 'informative' kinds of content (such as news). Nevertheless, all media texts that are systematically encoded in known 'languages' are open in principle to analysis in terms of information and uncertainty reduction. Photographs, for instance, at the level of denotation often present a series of 'iconic' items of information, signs that can be read as references to objects in the 'real world'.

Up to a point, iconic images are as informative as words, sometimes more so, and can also indicate certain kinds of relations between objects (such as relative distance) and give detailed information about colour, size, texture, and so on. Fictional narratives can also be treated as informational texts, by assuming what they represent to be informative. For purposes of quantifying the amount of information that is sent or received and for measuring some aspects of the quality of messages, it need not matter which type of media content is at issue.

Applications of information theory in the study of content

Examples of how the assumptions of information theory can be used in the analysis of media content can be found in certain measures of *informativeness*, *readability*, *diversity* and *information flow*. There are a number of different ways of measuring the *information value* (in the sense of capacity to reduce uncertainty) of media texts. The simplest approach is to count the number of 'facts' in a text, with alternative possibilities for defining what constitutes a fact (often it is conceived as a basic verifiable unit of objective information).

Research by Asp (1981) involved a measure of information value (or informativity) of news on certain controversial issues, based on three different indicators of news content, having first established a universe of relevant factual points in all news reports. One measure was of *density*: the proportion of all relevant points in a given report. A second was of *breadth*: the number of different points as a proportion of the total possible. The third was *depth*: the number of facts and reported motives helping to explain the basic points (some subjective judgement may be involved here). An *information value index* was calculated by multiplying the density score by the breadth score. While factualness can be formally measured in this and similar ways, it cannot be assumed that information density or richness will make communication any more effective, although it may represent (good) intentions on the part of the reporters and a potential for being informative.

An alternative is to measure *readability*, another valued quality of journalistic texts. Approaches to measurement have mainly followed the idea that news is more readable when there is more *redundancy* (the reverse of information density). The simple idea is that an 'information-rich' text packed full of factual information which has a high potential for reducing uncertainty is also likely to be very challenging to a (not very highly motivated) reader. This is also related to the variable of being closed or open: information-rich texts are generally closed, not leaving much room for interpretation.

There is experimental support for the view that the less information in a text, the easier it generally is to read and understand. The main (experimental) tool for measuring readability is called the *cloze procedure* (Taylor, 1953) and involves a process whereby a reader has to substitute words for systematically omitted words. The ease of substitution is the measure of ease of reading since texts with many redundant words give rise to fewer problems. This is not the only measure of readability, since measures of *sensationalism* achieve much the same result though without the same basis in information theory (Tannenbaum and Lynch, 1960).

If we can measure the information in media content, and if we can categorize items of information in a relevant way, it follows that we can also measure the (internal) *diversity* of texts. A typical diversity question (see below) might be the degree to which news gave equal or proportionate attention to the views of several different political parties or candidates. Chaffee (1981), for instance, suggested using Schramm's (1955) measure of *entropy*, which involved calculating the number of categories and the evenness of distribution of media space/time between categories (of information or opinion). There is more diversity where we find more categories (a wide range of opinion) and less diversity where there is very unequal attention to different categories (one opinion tends to dominate news coverage).

The evaluative dimension of information

From the examples given of the informational approach, it looks as if it is very one-dimensional and hard to apply to non-factual aspects of content. It seems insensitive to the different levels of meaning that have already been mentioned and offers no place for alternative interpretations of a message. From the informational perspective, ambiguous or open texts are simply more redundant or chaotic. It is also unclear how this kind of objective analysis can cope with the *evaluative* dimension of information (which is always present in news).

While this critique is valid, there are possibilities for the objective analysis of the value direction of texts. These depend on the assumption (which can be empirically supported) that signs often carry positive or negative loadings in their own natural languages or code systems, certainly for those who are members of the relevant 'interpretative community'. It follows that references to people, objects or events can objectively embody values.

The work of Osgood et al. (1957) on the evaluative structure of meaning in a language laid the basis for developing objective measures of value direction in texts. The essence of the approach (see van Cuilenburg et al., 1986) is to identify frequently ocurring words according to their 'common meaning' (their relative positive or negative weight in everyday use). Next, we record the extent to which words of different value direction are (semantically) connected with relevant attitude objects in the news (such as political leaders, policies, countries and events). In principle, by such procedures, it is possible to quantify the 'inscribed' evaluative direction of attitude in media content.

Moreover, it is possible to uncover *networks* of semantically associated 'attitude objects', and this sheds further light on value patterns (implied by association) in texts. This method does have the potential to allocate an evaluative meaning to whole texts, as well as to 'facts' or items of information, within a particular culture and society. Contextual knowledge is, however, a necessary condition, and the method departs from the purity of information theory. Box 13.2 summarizes the main points made above in relation to information.

Communication as information **13.2**

- Communication is to be defined as transfer of information from sender to individual receiver
- Media texts are bodies of information
- The essence of information is the reduction of uncertainty
- Information quality and the informativeness of texts are measurable
- The evaluative direction of information is measurable

Media Performance Discourse

There is an extensive body of research into mass media content according to a number of normative criteria, especially those discussed in Chapter 8. This tradition of research is usually based on some conception of the public interest (or good of society) that provides the point of reference and the relevant content criteria (McQuail, 1992). Although a given set of values provide the starting point for analysis of media, the *procedures* adopted are those of a neutral scientific observer, and the aim is to find independent evidence which will be relevant to public debate about the role of media in society (Stone, 1987; Lemert, 1989). The basic assumption of this tradition of work is that although quality cannot be directly measured, many relevant dimensions can be reliably assessed (Bogart, 2004). The NHK Quality Assessment project mentioned earlier (Ishikawa, 1996) is a good example of such work. The evidence sought should relate to particular media but needs also to have a general character.

It could be said that this particular discourse is about the politics of media content. It adjoins and occasionally overlaps with the critical tradition discussed earlier, but differs in that it stays within the boundaries of the system itself, accepting the goals of the media in society more or less on their own terms (or at least the more idealistic goals). The normative background and the general nature of the principles have already been sketched (Chapter 8). What follows are some examples of the testable expectations about the quality of media provision which are implied in the various performance principles.

Freedom and independence

Perhaps the foremost expectation about media content is that it should reflect or embody the spirit of free expression, despite the many institutional and organizational pressures that have already been described. It is not easy to see how the quality of freedom (and here the reference is primarily to news, information and opinion functions of media) can be recognized in content. Several general aspects of content can, even so, be identified as indicating more or less freedom (from commercial, political or social pressure). For example, there is the general question of editorial 'vigour' or activity, which should be a sign of using freedom and shows itself in a number of ways. These include: actually expressing opinions, especially on controversial issues; willingness to report conflict and controversy; following a 'proactive' policy in relation to sources (thus not relying on press handouts and public relations, or being too cosy with the powerful); and giving background and interpretation as well as facts.

The concept of 'editorial vigour' was coined by Thrift (1977) to refer to several related aspects of content, especially dealing with *relevant* and significant local matters, adopting an argumentative form and providing 'mobilizing information', which refers to information which helps people to *act* on their opinions (Lemert, 1989). Some critics and commentators also look for a measure of advocacy and of support for 'underdogs' as evidence of free media (Entman, 1989). Investigative reporting may also be regarded as a sign of news media using their freedom (see Ettema and Glasser, 1998).

In one way or another, most mass media content can be assessed in terms of the 'degree of freedom' exhibited. Outside the sphere of news, one would look for innovation and unexpectedness, non-conformity and experimentation in cultural matters. The most free media are also likely to deviate from conformity in matters of taste and be willing to be unpopular with audiences as well as with authorities. However, if so, they are not likely to remain mass media.

Content diversity

After freedom, probably the most frequently encountered term in the 'performance discourse' is diversity. It refers essentially to three main features of content:

- a wide range of choice for audiences, on all conceivable dimensions of interest and preference;
- many and different opportunities for access by voices and sources in society;
- a true or sufficient reflection in media of the varied reality of experience in society.

Each of these concepts is open to measurement (McQuail, 1992; Hellman, 2001; McDonald and Dimmick, 2003). In this context, we can really only speak of content diversity if we apply some external standard to media texts, whether of audience preference, social reality or (would-be) sources in society. Lack of diversity can be established only by identifying sources, references, events, types of content, and so on, which are missing or under-represented. In themselves, media texts cannot be said to be diverse in any absolute sense.

Essentially, diversity is another word for differentiation and is, in itself, rather empty of meaning, since everything we can distinguish is different, in some minimal sense of not being the very same thing, from everything else. The diversity value as applied to media content depends on some criteria of significant difference. These criteria are sometimes provided by the media themselves in the form of different formats, genres and types of culture. So, the same or different media channels can offer a changing supply of music, news, information, entertainment, comedy, drama, quiz shows, etc. External critics applying standards of social significance are usually more interested in differences of level and quality as well as format and genre. There are further criteria relating to the society in respect of representation of the whole range of social groupings, or providing for key minorities. The choice of criteria has to be made and justified by and according to the purpose at hand and the possibilities are virtually unlimited. However, the purpose is usually decided by reference to one or other of the three points made above – the matter of audience choice and preference; the access given to social groups and voices; the fair representation of social reality. Many questions about the effects of the media depend on having the concepts and means for measuring content diversity.

Objectivity and its Measurement

The standard of news objectivity has given rise to much discussion of journalistic media content, under various headings, especially in relation to some form of bias, which is the reverse of objectivity. As indicated already (Chapter 8), the ruling norms of most western media call for a certain practice of neutral, informative reporting of events, and it is against this positive expectation that much news has been found deficient. However, objectivity is a relatively complex notion when one goes beyond the simple idea that news should reliably (and therefore honestly) report what is really going on in the world.

The simplest version of the idea that news tells us about the real world can be referred to as *factuality*. This refers to texts made up of distinct units of information that are necessary for understanding or acting upon a news 'event'. In journalistic terms it means at least providing dependable (correct) answers to the questions 'Who?', 'What?', 'Where?', 'When?', and maybe 'Why?', and going on from there. A systematic approach to the assessment of factuality in the sense of 'information value' has already been discussed. News can be more or less 'information rich' in terms of the number of facts offered.

For analysing news quality, however, one needs more refined criteria. In particular, one asks if the facts given are *accurate* and whether they are sufficient to constitute an adequate account, on the criterion of *completeness*. Accuracy itself can mean several things, since it cannot be directly 'read' or 'measured' from inspection of texts alone. One meaning of accuracy is conformity to independent records of events, whether in documents, other media or eyewitness accounts. Another meaning is more subjective: accuracy is conformity of reports to the perception of the source of the news or the subject of the news (object of reporting). Accuracy may also be a matter of internal consistency within news texts.

Completeness is equally difficult to pin down or measure since complete accounts of even simple events are not possible or necessary. Although one can always make assessments and comparisons of news in terms of more or less information, the question really turns on how much information is needed or can reasonably be expected, which is a subjective matter. We are quickly into another dimension of factuality – that of the *relevance* of the facts offered. Again, it is a simple notion that news information is relevant only if it is interesting and useful (and vice versa), but there are competing notions and criteria of what counts as relevant. One source of criteria is what *theory* says news ought to be like; another is what professional *journalists* decide is most relevant; and a third is what an *audience* actually finds interesting and useful. These three perspectives are unlikely to coincide on the same criteria or on the same assessment of content.

Theory tends to equate relevance with what is *really* significant in the longer perspective of history and what contributes to the working of society (for instance, informed democracy). From this point of view, a good deal of news, such as that about personalities, 'human interest', sport or entertainment, is not regarded as relevant. Journalists tend to apply professional criteria and a feel for news values that balance the longer-term significance with what they think their public is interested in.

One study of US journalists (Burgoon, quoted in McQuail, 1992: 218) showed a decided split between perceptions of 'significance' and of 'interest' as factors in news judgement. Relevance was seen as having to do first with things 'which affect people's lives', secondly with things which are interesting or unusual, and thirdly with facts which are timely or relate to nearby or large-scale happenings. In the end, it is the audience that decides what is relevant, and there are too many different audiences for a generalization to be useful. Even so, it is clear that much of what theory says is relevant is not perceived as such by much of the audience much of the time.

The issue of what counts as *impartiality* in news seems relatively simple but can also be complex in practice, not least because there is little chance of achieving a value-free assessment of value freedom. Impartiality is appreciated mainly because many events involve conflict and are open to alternative interpretations and evaluations (this is most obviously true of political news, but much the same can be said of sports). Most generally, the normal standard of impartiality calls for balance in the choice and use of sources, so as to reflect different points of view, and also the presentation of two (or more) sides where judgements or facts are contested.

A summary example is given in Box 13.3 of the findings of research into whether a newspaper was biased or not in its reporting of a permanently contested situation – that of Israel and Palestine (Wu et al., 2002). It was concluded that the paper was reporting objectively, on the grounds that the assessed direction of reports was almost identical for the main parties (there was other evidence). The newspaper could claim to be balanced in respect of evaluative tendency. However, this might not satisfy someone convinced that one 'side' was clearly in the wrong for reasons outside the immediate events being reported. In many circumstances of conflict, one or other party is defined as at fault or with bad intentions and bad faith.

**An example of news judged as impartial: 13.3 eg
findings of a general reading of the
direction of news reports (*N* = 280) in the
Philadelphia Inquirer dealing with the Israel
and Palestine conflict, January to October
1998 (Wu et al., 2002)**

Entity	Positive	Neutral	Negative	Mixed	Total
Israel	17%	39%	39%	5%	100%
Palestine	14%	44%	39%	4%	100%
Other Middle East	21%	41%	35%	3%	100%
USA	34%	59%	7%		100%
UN	18%	82%			100%

Another aspect of impartiality is neutrality in the presentation of news: separating facts from opinion, avoiding value judgements or emotive language or pictures. The term 'sensationalism' has been used to refer to forms of presentation which depart from the objectivity ideal, and measures of news text sensationalism have been developed (e.g. Tannenbaum and Lynch, 1960). Methods have also been tested for application to visual content in news (Grabe et al., 2000, 2001).

There is also evidence to show that the choice of words can reflect and imply value judgements in reporting on sensitive matters, for instance relating to patriotism (Glasgow Media Group, 1985) or race (Hartman and Husband, 1974; van Dijk, 1991). There are also indications that particular uses of visuals and camera shots can lead the viewer in certain evaluative directions (Tuchman, 1978; Kepplinger, 1983). Impartiality often comes down in the end simply to the absence of intentional or avoidable 'bias' and 'sensationalism'. Unfortunately, it is never that simple since bias is as much, if not more, a matter of perception as of measurable dimensions of content (D'Alessio and Allen, 2000; D'Alessio, 2003).

Reality reflection or distortion: the question of bias

Bias in news content can refer, especially, to distorting reality, giving a negative picture of minority groups of many kinds, neglecting or misconstruing the role of women in society, or differentially favouring a particular political party or philosophy (see Shoemaker and Reese, 1991). There are many such kinds of news bias which stop short of lies, propaganda or ideology, but often overlap with and reinforce similar tendencies in fictional content. In general, this category can be classified as 'unwitting bias', arising from the context of production, as explored in Chapter 12. While the territory of media bias is now almost boundless and still extending (American Behavioral

Scientist, 2003), we can summarize the most significant and best-documented generalizations in the following statements about news content, derived from numerous sources and examples:

- Media news over-represents the social 'top' and official voices in its sources.
- News attention is differentially bestowed on members of political and social elites.
- The social values which are most emphasized are consensual and supportive of the status quo.
- Foreign news concentrates on nearer, richer and more powerful nations.
- News has a nationalistic (patriotic) and ethnocentric bias in the choice of topics and opinions expressed and in the view of the world assumed or portrayed.
- More attention and more prominence are given to men than to women in the news.
- Ethnic minorities and immigrant groups are differentially marginalized, stereotyped or stigmatized.
- News about crime over-represents violent and personal crime and neglects many of the realities of risk in society.
- Health news gives most attention to the most feared medical conditions and to new cures rather than prevention.
- Business leaders and employers receive more favoured treatment than unions and workers.
- The poor and those on welfare are neglected and/or stigmatized.
- War news typically avoids images of death or personal injury – sanitizing the reality.
- Well-resourced and well-organized news sources have more chance of defining news on their own terms.

Content analysis of fiction and drama has showed up similar systematic tendencies to allocate attention and esteem to the same groups who benefit from prominence in the news. Correlatively, the same minorities and outgroups tend to be stereotyped and stigmatized. Similar tendencies to give an unrealistic representation of crime, health and other risks and rewards are to be found. The evidence has normally been derived by applying methods of quantitative analysis to the overt content of texts, on the assumption that relative frequency of references will be taken as reflecting the 'real world'.

A critique of the reality reflection norm

It is striking how much the evaluation of media content comes down to the question of relation to reality, as if media ought to reflect more or less proportionately some empirical reality and ought always be 'fair' as between the advantaged and the disadvantaged. This is referred to by Kepplinger and Habermeier (1995) as the 'correspondence assumption' often attributed to the audience. The assumption that media ought to reflect reality in some direct and proportional way has been the basis for much criticism of media performance and has often been a key ingredient in research on media effects (for instance, in **cultivation analysis**) but is itself open to question. According to Schulz (1988), it derives from an antiquated 'mechanistic' view of the relationship between media and society, more or less akin to the 'transportation model' of communication effects. It fails to recognize the essential specificity, arbitrariness and, sometimes, autonomy of media texts and neglects the active participation of the audience in the making of meaning. Perhaps most telling is the absence of evidence that the audience does actually assume any statistical correspondence between media content and reality.

Apart from this fundamental doubt about the expectation of proportional reality reflection, there are several reasons why media content should *not* normally be expected to 'reflect' reality in any literal (statistically representative) way. Functionalist theory of media as agents of social control, for instance, would lead us to expect that media content would over-represent the dominant social and economic values of the society. We would also expect social elites and authorities to have more visibility and access. Indeed, the media do reflect the social reality of inequality when they tip the scales of attention towards the powerful in society and towards powerful nations in the world. The complaint is really that in so doing they may reinforce it.

The analysis of media organizations has shown how unlikely it is that news will match some 'average' of reality. The need for authoritative news sources and the requirements of 'news values' are obvious sources of statistical 'distortion'. Drama, celebrity, novelty and conflict are, by definition, abnormal. In addition, fictional media often deliberately seek to attract an audience by over-populating their stories with characters who lead more exciting lives and are richer, younger, more fashionable and more beautiful than the typical audience member (Martel and McCall, 1964). The study of 'key events' and 'framing' of news makes it both clear and understandable that 'reality' cannot be treated as if all happenings were of equal significance, even within the same category.

The simple fact that mass media are generally oriented to the interests of their audiences as 'consumers' of information and entertainment can easily account for most of the evidence of reality distortion summarized above. It is clear that audiences like many things which are inconsistent with reality reflection, especially fiction, fantasy, the unusual and bizarre, myths, nostalgia and amusement. The media are often sought out precisely as an alternative to and an escape from reality. When people look for models to follow or for objects of identification, they are as likely to seek an idealized as a realistic object or model. From this point of view, the reality 'distortions' observed in content are not in themselves surprising or necessarily regrettable. However, a significant determinant is also the efforts of interested agents to shape their own image and dominate the flow of communication.

Questions of Research Method

The various frameworks and perspectives for theorizing about media content that have been discussed often imply sharp divergences of methods of research. The full range of alternatives cannot be discussed here since there are many different methods for different purposes (several have already been introduced). Methods range from simple and extensive classifications of types of content for organizational or descriptive purposes to deeply interpretative enquiries into specific examples of content, designed to uncover subtle and hidden potential meanings. Following the line of theoretical demarcation introduced in Chapter 3, we can broadly distinguish between quantitative and descriptive enquiry into overt meaning on the one hand, and more qualitative, deeper and more interpretative enquiry on the other. There are also enquiries directed to understanding the very nature of the various 'media languages' and how they work, especially in relation to visual imagery and sounds.

Where is meaning?

Theory has been perennially preoccupied with the question of the 'location' of meaning. Does meaning coincide with the intention of the sender, or is it embedded in the language, or is it primarily a matter of the receiver's interpretation (Jensen, 1991)? As we have seen from the previous chapters, mass communicated information and culture are produced by complex organizations whose purposes are usually not very specific and yet often predominate over the aims of individual communicators. This makes it hard to know what the 'sender's' intention really is: who can say, for instance, what the purpose of news is, or whose purpose it is? The option of concentrating on the message itself as the source of meaning has been the most attractive one, partly for reasons of practicality. The physical texts themselves are always available for direct analysis, and they have the advantage (compared with human respondents) of being 'non-reactive' to the investigator. They do not decay with time, although their context does decay and with it the possibility of really knowing what they originally meant to senders or to receivers.

It is impossible to 'extract' meaning from media content texts without also making assumptions which themselves shape the meaning extracted – for instance, the assumption that the amount or frequency of attention to something is a reliable guide to message meaning, intention and effect. The findings of content analysis can never 'speak for themselves'. In addition, the 'languages' of media are far from simple and are still only partially understood, especially where they involve music and visual images (both still and moving) in many combinations, drawing on numerous and varied codes and conventions.

Dominant versus alternative paradigms again

The choices of research method generally follow the division between a dominant empirically oriented paradigm and a more qualitative (and often critical) variant (see Chapter 3). The former is mainly represented by traditional content analysis, which was defined by Berelson (1952: 18) as 'a research technique for the objective, systematic and quantitative description of the manifest content of communication' (see pp. 362–3). This assumes that the surface meaning of a text is fairly unambiguous and can be read by the investigator and expressed in quantitative terms. In fact, it is assumed that the numerical balance of elements in the text (such as the number of words or the space/time allocated to a set of topics) is a reliable guide to the overall meaning. Several relatively sophisticated forms of quantitative content analysis have been developed which go well beyond the simple counting and classifying of units of content that were characteristic of early research. There remains, even so, a fundamental assumption that media content is encoded according to the same language as the reality to which it refers.

The alternative approach is based on precisely the reverse assumption – that the concealed or latent meanings are the most significant, and these cannot be directly read from the numerical data. In particular, we have to take account not just of relative frequency but of links and relationships between elements in the text, and also to take note of what is missing or taken for granted. We need to identify and understand the particular discourse in which a text is encoded. In general, we need to be aware of the conventions and codes of any genre that we study since these indicate at a higher level what is going on in the text (Jensen and Jankowski, 1991). In contrast, content analysis may permit the conflation of several different kinds of media text, ignoring discursive variety.

Both varieties of analysis can claim some measure of scientific reliability. They deploy methods which can, in principle, be replicated by different people, and the 'findings' should be open to challenge according to some (not always the same) canons of scientific procedure. Secondly, they are both designed to deal with regularity and recurrence in cultural artefacts rather than with the unique and non-reproducible. They are thus more appropriate for application to the symbolic products of the culture industries than to those of the 'cultural elite' (such as 'works of art'). Thirdly, they avoid judgements of moral or aesthetic value (another sense of being objective). Fourthly, all such methods are, in principle, instrumental means to other ends. They can be used to answer questions about the links between content, creators, social context and receivers (Barker, 2003).

Non-verbal communication

Some attention has already been given in this chapter to the problems and possibilities for analysing non-verbal text. In fact, the analysis of media content has concentrated overwhelmingly on verbal texts or on verbal descriptions of visual elements (e.g. in relation to representations of violence). The objective representation of non-verbal communication in formal analysis has proved extraordinarily difficult. As noted above, semiological methods have been applied to photographs and moving images, but as Barthes observed, a photo is a message without a code and by definition cannot be coded. Film and television can only be coded in so far as film-makers consciously employ some conventions of visual symbolism that are little different from clichés (see Monaco, 1981; Newbold, 2002). Music has proved even harder to code and few have attempted it (Middleton, 2000).

Some features of television news have been interpreted in terms of meaning and direction, especially the use of certain kinds of shots and framing (Tuchman, 1978; Kepplinger, 1983, 1999). There is some experimental evidence to validate ideas of how visual framing works, but no established method of analysis. Many visual and aural aspects of communication can be recorded (for instance, the dimensions of sensationalism: Grabe et al., 2001), but the problem of imputing meaning on the part of the sender or receiver remains.

Traditional Content Analysis

Basics

'Traditional' content analysis, following Berelson's (1952) definition (see above), is the earliest, most central and still most widely practised method of research. Its use goes back to the early decades of the century (see Kingsbury and Hart, 1937). The basic sequence in applying the technique is set out as follows:

- Choose a universe or sample of content.
- Establish a category frame of external referents relevant to the purpose of the enquiry (such as a set of political parties or countries which may be referred to in content).
- Choose a 'unit of analysis' from the content (this could be a word, a sentence, an item, a whole news story, a picture, a sequence, etc.).
- Seek to match the content to the category frame by counting the frequency of the references to relevant items in the category frame, per chosen unit of content.
- Express the results as an overall distribution of the complete universe or chosen content sample in terms of the frequency of occurrence of the sought-for referents.

The procedure is based on two main assumptions. The first is that the link between the external object of reference and the reference to it in the text will be reasonably clear and unambiguous. The second is that the frequency of occurrence of chosen references will validly express the predominant 'meaning' of the text in an objective way. The approach is, in principle, no different from that adopted in surveys of people. One chooses a population (here a media type or subset), draws a sample from it of respondents representative of the whole (the units of analysis), collects data about individuals according to variables and assigns values to these variables. As with the survey, content analysis is held to be reliable (reproducible) and not unique to the investigator. The method produces a statistical summary of a much larger media reality. It has been used for many purposes but especially for comparing media content with a known frequency distribution in 'social reality'.

Limits to content analysis

The traditional approach has many limitations and pitfalls, which are of some theoretical interest as well as practical relevance. The usual practice of constructing a category system before applying it involves the risk of an investigator imposing a meaning system rather than discovering it in the content. Even when care is taken to avoid this, any such category system must be selective and potentially distorting. The outcome of content analysis is itself a new text, the meaning of which may, or even must, diverge from the original source material. This result is also based on a form of 'reading' of content that no actual 'reader' would ever, under natural circumstances, undertake. The new 'meaning' is neither that of the original sender, nor that of the text itself, nor that of the audience, but a fourth construct, one particular interpretation. Account cannot easily be taken of the context of a reference within a text or of the text as a whole. Internal relationships between references in texts may also be neglected in the process of abstraction. There is an assumption that 'coders' can be trained to make reliable judgements about categories and meanings.

The boundaries of the kind of content analysis described are, in fact, rather elastic, and many variants can be accommodated within the same basic framework. The more one relaxes requirements of reliability, the easier it is to introduce categories and variables that will be useful for interpretation but 'low' in 'objectivity' and somewhat ambiguous. This is especially true of attempts to capture references to values, themes, settings, style and interpretative frameworks. Content analyses often display a wide range of reliability because of attempts to include some more subjective indicators of meaning.

The extensive digitization of current and past media content (especially print media such as newspapers) has opened up many new possibilities for computer-assisted quantitative analysis of very large quantities of material. It has even become the normal method of analysing newspapers. However, there are serious pitfalls, as Deacon (2007) has pointed out, on the basis of an exploratory testing. Aside from defects in particular databases (for example, gaps or duplications in the archives) that are unintended but also often unknown, there are several intrinsic obstacles that are not easy to overcome. For instance, it is not easy to capture complex thematic issues by way of key words. Large bodies of text have to be divided up for counting purposes, but the choice of unit is not fixed. Visuals are generally not included in analyses. The specific context of verbal references cannot easily be recovered. All in all, Deacon concludes that content should wherever possible be studied in its original form.

Quantitative and Qualitative Analysis Compared

The contrast between traditional content analysis and interpretative approaches can now be summarized. Some differences are self-evident. First, structuralism and semiology (the main interpretative approaches: see pp. 345–8) do not involve quantification, and there is even an antipathy to counting as a way of arriving at significance, since meaning derives from textual relationships, oppositions and context rather than from number and balance of references. Secondly, attention is directed to latent rather than to manifest content, and latent (thus deeper) meaning is regarded as actually more essential. Thirdly, structuralism is systematic in a different way from content analysis, giving no weight to procedures of sampling and rejecting the notion that all 'units' of content should be treated equally.

Fourthly, structuralism does not allow the assumption that the world of social and cultural 'reality', the message and the receiver, all involve the same basic system of meanings. Social reality consists of numerous more or less discrete universes of meaning, each requiring separate elucidation. The 'audience' also divides up into 'interpretative communities', each possessing some unique possibilities for attributing meaning. Media content, as we have seen, is also composed on the basis of more than one code, language or sign system. All this makes it impossible, even absurd, to assume that any category system of references can be constructed in which a given element is likely to mean precisely the same in the 'reality', in the content, to the audience member and to the media analyst. It follows from structuralist theory that it is very difficult to carry out research that relates findings in one of these 'spheres' to findings in another.

Mixed methods are possible

This comparison does not indicate the superiority of one approach over the other, since, despite the claim at the outset that these methods have something in common, they are essentially good for different purposes. Structuralism does not offer a systematic method and is not accountable in its results according to normal standards of reliability. Neither is it easy to generalize from the results to other texts, except perhaps in relation to form (for instance, comparing one genre with another). It is certainly not a way of summarizing content, as content analysis often can be.

For some purposes, it may be permissible and necessary to depart from the pure form of either 'Berelsonian' or 'Barthian' analysis, and a number of studies have used combinations of both approaches, despite their divergent assumptions. An example of such a hybrid approach is the work on British television news by the Glasgow Media Group (1976, 1980, 1985), which combined rigorous and detailed quantitative analysis of industrial news with an attempt to 'unpack' the deeper cultural meaning of specific news stories. The school of 'cultural indicators', as represented by Gerbner and colleagues, has also sought to arrive at the 'meaning structure' of dominant forms of television output by way of systematic quantitative analysis of overt elements of television representation.

There are methods that do not easily belong to either of the main approaches described. One is the psychoanalytic approach favoured at an early stage of content study. This focuses on the motivation of 'characters' and the underlying meaning of dominant themes in the popular (or less so) culture of a given society or period (e.g. Wolfenstein and Leites, 1947; McGranahan and Wayne, 1948; Kracauer, 1949). It was also taken up for studying gender issues and the meaning and influence of advertising (e.g. Williamson, 1978).

Other variants of analysis method have already been noted – for instance, the analysis of narrative structure (Radway, 1984) or the study of content functions. Thus, Graber (1976a) named the following set of functions in political communication: to gain attention; to establish linkages and define situations; to make commitments; to create policy-relevant moods; to stimulate action (mobilize); to act directly (words as actions); and to use words as symbolic rewards for actual or potential supporters.

Such possibilities are a reminder of the *relative* character of most analysis of content, in that there has always to be some outside point of reference or purpose according to which one chooses one form of classification rather than another. Even semiology can supply meaning only in terms of a much larger system of cultural meanings and sense-making practices. The main differences between essentially quantitative and qualitative approaches are given in Box 13.4. Whether these differences are advantages or not depends on the purpose.

Types of media content analysis compared 13.4

Message content analysis	Structural analysis of texts
Quantitative	Qualitative
Fragmentary	Holistic
Systematic	Selective
Generalizing, extensive	Illustrative, specific
Manifest meaning	Latent meaning
Objective	Relative to reader

One recurrent problem with all methods and approaches is the gap that often exists between the outcome of content analysis and the perceptions of the creators or the audience. The creators tend to think of what is unique and distinctive in what they do, while the audience is inclined to think of content in terms of a mixture of conventional genre or type labels and a set of satisfactions which have been experienced or are expected. The version extracted by the content analyst is thus not very recognizable to the two main sets of participants in the mass communication enterprise (producers and receivers) and often remains a scientific or literary abstraction.

Conclusion

The future of content analysis, one way or another, has to lie in relating 'content' as sent to the wider structures of meaning in a society. This path can probably best be followed by way of discourse analysis, which takes account of other meaning systems in the originating culture, or by way of audience reception analysis, which takes seriously the notion that readers also make meanings. Both are necessary in some degree for an adequate study of media. The various frameworks and perspectives for theorizing about media content that have been introduced often imply sharp divergences of methods of research as well as differences of purpose. The full range of alternative methods cannot be discussed here, but the main options will be set out in Chapter 14.

Further Reading

Barthes, R. (1967) *Image, Music, Text: Essays*. Selected and translated by Stephen Heath. London: Fontana.
Some of the key writings by one of leading theorists of semiology in accessible form. Especially interesting is the treatment of the photographic image.

Krippendorf, K. (2004) *Content Analysis*, 2nd edn. Thousand Oaks, CA: Sage.
A standard work of reference and explication dealing with all main methods of empirical analysis of content, by one of the early authorities and practitioners.

Matheson, D. (2005) *Media Texts: Analysing Media Texts*. Maidenhead: Open University Press.
Provides clarification of the central term of discourse 'analysis' and illustrations of applications.

van Dijk, T.A. (1993) 'Principles of critical discourse analysis', *Discourse and Society*, 4 (2): 249–83.
A good concise summary of key ideas, by one of main founders of critical discourse analysis, especially in relation to racism and the news.

Williamson, J. (1978) *Decoding Advertisements*. London: Boyars.
Judith Williamson applies critical theory and various methods of content analysis to unpack the open and hidden meanings of a range of different kinds of visual display advertisements, in a series of case studies.

Online Readings

Deacon, D. (2007) 'Yesterday's news and today's technology', *European Journal of Communication*, 22 (1): 5–25.
Hellman, H. (2001) 'Diversity: an end in itself?', *European Journal of Communication*, 16 (2): 281–308.
Philo, G. (2007) 'News content studies, Media Group methods and discourse analysis: a comparison of approaches', in E. Devereux (ed.), *Media Studies*, pp. 103–33. London: Sage.
Smith, P. and Bell, A. (2007) 'Unravelling the web of discourse analysis', in E. Devereux (ed.), *Media Studies*, pp. 78–100. London: Sage.
Wodak, R. and Busch, B. (2004) 'Approaches to media texts', in J.D.H. Downing, D. McQuail, P. Schlesinger and E. Wartella (eds), *The Sage Handbook of Media Studies*, pp. 105–22. Thousand Oaks, CA: Sage.

Media Genres and Texts

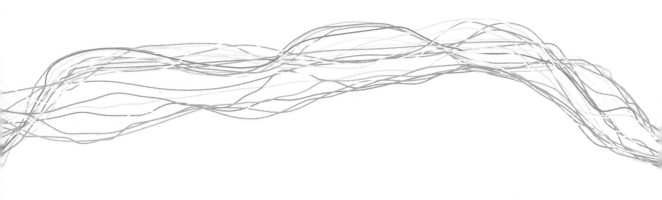

The aim of this chapter is to look more closely at some examples of typical media content as revealed by applying some of the approaches and the methods outlined in Chapter 13. It also introduces some of the concepts which are used to classify the output of mass media. In particular we explore the concepts of media format, genre and text.

Questions of Genre

In general use, the term 'genre' simply means a kind or type and it is often loosely applied to any distinctive category of cultural product. In film theory, where it originates, the term has been controversial because of the tension between individual creative authorship and location in a genre (Andrew, 1984). An emphasis on the genre tends to credit the value of a work to a cultural tradition rather than to an individual artist, who simply follows the rules laid down by the particular school of production. In relation to most mass media content, however, the concept of genre is useful and not especially controversial since the question of artistic authorship does not usually arise.

For our purpose, genre can refer to any *category* of content that has the following characteristics:

- Its collective identity is recognized more or less equally by its producers (the media) and its consumers (media audiences).
- This identity (or definition) relates to purposes (such as information, entertainment or subvariants), form (length, pace, structure, language, etc.) and meaning (reality reference).
- The identity has been established over time and observes familiar conventions; cultural forms are preserved, although these can also change and develop within the framework of the original genre.
- A particular genre will follow an expected structure of narrative or sequence of action, draw on a predictable stock of images and have a repertoire of variants of basic themes.

The genre may be considered as a practical device for helping any mass medium to produce consistently and efficiently and to relate its production to the expectations of its audience. Since it helps individual media users to plan their choices, it can also be considered as a mechanism for ordering the relations between producers and consumers. According to Andrew (1984: 110), genres (of film)

> are specific networks of formulas that deliver a certified product to a waiting customer. They ensure the production of meaning by regulating the viewers' relation to the image and narrative construction for him or her. In fact, genres construct the proper spectators for their own consumption. They build the desires and then represent the satisfaction of what they have triggered.

This view overrates the extent to which the media can determine the response of an audience, but it is at least consistent with the aspirations of media themselves to control the environments in which they operate. In fact, there is a good deal of evidence of audience recognition and use of genre categories in discourse about media. Hoijer (2000), for instance, applied a reception analysis to the interpretation of different television genres and found that each genre generated certain expectations. Popular fiction in the realistic mode is expected to provide a valid reflection of everyday reality. Ideas of this kind were used by the audience as standards of criticism. Distinctions are made according to text characteristics of specific genre examples. For instance, expectations about realism were lower for American than for European serials.

Genre examples

The origin of genre analysis is credited by Berger (1992) to Stuart Kaminsky (1974: 3), who wrote that

> genre study of the film is based in the realization that certain popular narrative forms have both cultural and universal roots, that the Western of today is related to archetypes of the past 200 years in the United States and to the folk tale and the myth.

Stuart Hall (1974/1980) also applied the genre idea to the 'B-movie western'. In his analysis, genre depends on the use of a particular 'code' or meaning system, which can draw on some consensus about meaning among users of the code (whether encoders or decoders) in a given culture. According to Hall, we can speak of a genre where coding and decoding are very close and where meaning is consequently relatively unambiguous, in the sense of being received much as it is sent.

The classic western movie is then said to derive from a particular myth concerning the conquest of the American West and involving such elements as displays of masculine prowess and womanly courage, the working out of destiny in the wide open spaces and the struggle of good versus evil. The particular strength of the western genre is that it can generate many variant forms that can also be readily understood in relation to the original basic form. For instance, we have seen the psychological western, the parody western, the spaghetti western, the comedy western and the soap opera western. The meaning of the variant forms often depends on the reversal of elements in the original code.

Many familiar examples of media content can be subjected to a genre analysis designed to uncover their essential recurring features or formulas, as Radway (1984) has done for the romance story, by exposing the typical 'narrative logic' (see Figure 14.2 on p. 389). It is also possible to classify the different variants of the same genre, as Berger (1992) does for the detective mystery. According to Berger, the 'formula' is a subcategory or genre and involves the conventions of that genre, with particular reference to time, place, plots, costumes, types of hero, heroine and villain, and so on. A western, for instance, has a certain range of possibilities for the formulaic elements that will be known to experienced audience members. This knowledge enables the content to be read correctly when certain signs appear: for instance, white hats identifying good guys, and the music that heralds the approaching cavalry.

More recent developments in media-cultural studies have given prominence to several familiar television genres and provided the boundaries for new fields of inquiry. A noteworthy example is the attention paid to soap operas, partly on account of their identification as a *gendered* form of television (Modleski, 1982; Allen, 1987, 1989; Hobson, 1989; Geraghty, 1991; Liebes and Livingstone, 1998; Brunsdon, 2000). The more feminine characteristics of the soap opera genre were said to reside in its form of narrative, preference for dialogue over action, and attention to the values of extended families and the role of mothers and housewives.

The soap opera is also a very typical example of a serial form of narrative. The great interest in the serial *Dallas* during the 1980s (Ang, 1985; Liebes and Katz, 1990), for somewhat different reasons, also drew attention to the soap opera as a genre. The particular example also stretched the meaning of the term to include a media product which was very different from the early North American radio or television daytime serial. Even so, the wide and long currency of the term 'soap opera' applied to different kinds of drama confirms, in some measure, the validity and utility of the concepts of genre and soap opera.

One of the strengths of the genre idea is its capacity to adapt and extend to cope with dynamic developments. This is well represented in the even more recent rise of the 'talk show' genre, which began as entertainment interviews with celebrities and as a 'breakfast television' format and has expanded luxuriantly throughout the world in manifestations that range from the sensationalist knockabout to very serious occasions for political participation. The common elements holding the genre together are not easy to identify, apart from the centrality of talk and the presence of a key anchor personality. But they often include some audience presence or participation, some conflict or drama, some degree or illusion of actuality, a strong dose of personalization and an illusion of intimacy (see Munson, 1993). The genre of reality television similarly moved from modest beginnings in which real-life scenes from a variety of sources were repackaged thematically (e.g. police, accidents, weather, crime, pets, etc.) as entertainment and then into new forms in which volunteers were subjected to a variety of controlled contest or stress situations to produce a voyeuristic and engaging 'live' experience for the audience, which could also intervene in some way.

A typology of genres

So far it has seemed that genre analysis can only be applied to discrete categories of content, each with certain key dimensions. At least one attempt has been made at more of a meta-analysis. Berger (1992) suggests that all television output can be classified according to four basic types, produced by two dimensions: degree of emotionality and degree of objectivity. The typology is shown in Figure 14.1. The explanation of the terms is as follows:

- *Contests* are programmes with competition involving real players, including game shows, quizzes and sports. They are both real and emotionally involving (in intention).
- *Actualities* include all news, documentary and reality programming. They are objective and unemotional in principle.

		Objectivity	
		High	*Low*
Emotionality	*Strong*	**Contests**	**Dramas**
	Weak	**Actualities**	**Persuasions**

Figure 14.1   The structure of television genres: a typology (Berger, 1992: 7)

- *Persuasions* are low on both dimensions and reflect an intention by the sender to persuade, especially by advertising or some form of advocacy or propaganda.
- *Dramas* cover almost all fictional storytelling and a wide range of genres.

As Berger notes, the application of this scheme is complicated by the fact that new and mixed genres are continually being created that do not belong to a unique category. Familiar examples are those of 'docudrama' and other kinds of 'infotainment'. But this is also a feature of individual genres and can be helpful in tracking and analysing what is happening. The category of 'reality television' in any given instance (e.g. *Big Brother*) does not easily fit into one unique category, although there is an important element of contest in the format. This indicates a limitation in the typology.

While genre is a useful concept for finding one's way in the luxuriant abundance of media output and for helping to describe and categorize content, it is not a very powerful tool of analysis since there are simply too many possibilities for applying it. The distinction between one genre and another is not easy to ascertain objectively, and the correspondence of recognition and understanding by producers and audience, named above as a characteristic of a genre, is not easy to demonstrate. It may be a more useful term in relation to films and books, where individual acts of choice are made and paid for, guided by experience, taste and publicity, and lead to established preference. It has also been shown that inter-genre differences can be used to differentiate types of television producer (Tunstall, 1993).

Media format

The genre concept has also been useful in a somewhat adapted form for analysing media formats. Altheide and Snow (1979), for instance, developed a mode of analysis of media content, employing the terms *media logic* and *media format*. The first refers essentially to a set of implicit rules and norms that govern how content should be processed and presented in order to take most advantage of the characteristics of a given medium. This includes fitting the needs of the media organization (including the media's perception of the needs of the audience). Altheide sees content as tailored to fit media formats, and formats as tailored to fit listener/viewer preferences and assumed capacities. Formats are essentially sub-routines for dealing with specific themes within a genre. For instance, Altheide (1985) describes a 'format for crisis' in television news, which transcends the particularities of events and gives a common shape to the handling of different news stories. The main conditions necessary for the news handling of a crisis on a continuing basis are accessibility (to information or to the site of the crisis), visual quality (of film or tape), drama and action, relevance to the audience and thematic unity. There is some affinity with the concept of framing.

Graber (1981) has made notable contributions to the study of political languages in general and its television versions in particular. She confirms the points made by Altheide in her comment that 'television journalists have developed repertoires – another possible term for frames, logics or sub-genre formats of highly stereotyped cues for many specific situations in politics'. She argues convincingly that the encoding and decoding of audiovisual languages is essentially *different* from that of verbal languages in being more associational, connotative and unstructured and less logical, clearly defined and delimited. The systematic analysis of audiovisual languages is, nevertheless, still at an early stage.

Before leaving the subject of genres, formats and related concepts, it is worth emphasizing that they can, in principle, cut across the conventional content categories of media output, including the divide between fiction and non-fiction. Fiske (1987) underlines the essential *intertextuality* of genres. This is not too surprising, given the long tradition that allows fiction to draw on real-life situations or historical events for its subject matter, although it may undermine the reality claims of media news and information.

Genre and the Internet

For the most part, the recognition of specific genres has taken place within the boundaries of a single medium (film, television, radio, etc.). There does not seem yet to have been an attempt to apply the general concept of genre to the Internet, although observations can be made. First, the Internet is a multimedia platform providing a vehicle for all existing genres. Secondly, certain forms and formats at least have already developed on the basis of the special features of the Internet. These include various forms of bulletin board, forum, social networking sites, different kinds of blog and many types of selling and buying sites (with e-bay as the most innovative and successful) and the 'search engine'. Many of the examples that could be named, although with some uncertainty about whether or not they are really genres, do conform to several features of the concept, as given above. For instance, there is usually an agreed definition or perception as between producers and users, with established expectations about purposes and the rules or guidelines to be followed. However, it is still too early for many formats to achieve any stability and the boundaries between them are unclear.

The search engine as a new media form

There are some fundamental innovations of the Internet that set it aside from earlier media and require new ways of thinking. Two such important features are the vastly expanded scope for consultation and search at the will of the user and the greatly enhanced provision of connectivity (of all kinds) that existed only in limited ways up until recently. Attention is also due to the relatively new idea and reality of the Internet portal, a term with a rich array of meanings (Kalyanaraman and Sundar, 2008) that is essentially different from a medium as previously known (the quite vague term 'cyberspace' still seems useful for identification) (see p. 153). In this connection, we also need to take stock of the 'search engine' as a new and very influential presence in the sphere of public communication. There has been nothing like it before and it has a potential, as yet unknown, for affecting existing genres.

The search engine is essentially an index to, or catalogue of, content on the Web, and as such clearly not entirely new in concept, even if with enhanced features of search-ability. Consulting a search-engine may now be the single most widespread and most frequent form of use. Apart from this, the search engine has achieved great significance and become indispensable for many personal, social and commercial purposes (Halvais, 2009), especially as in many cases it provides the main entry point to the world of cyber-space, the clearest example of a portal. Its importance is comparable in many ways to that of the news. We can locate it on our notional map of mass media types, with refer-ence to Figure 6.1 (see p. 137), as essentially a consultation medium. Its characteristics also reflect the undetermined, mixed nature of online media, as described in Chapter 6, having many different potential uses for both senders and receivers. It is still unclear whether we should call it an applied technology, a media form or a genre, being all three in some respects, but we opt provisionally here for the second term. Certainly, it is also similar to a genre in showing a tendency to differentiate into a number of sub-genres, especially by topic or type of user (e.g. professional) or the nature of content searched (e.g. images). With a good deal of speculation, the emerging perceptions of the Internet search engine as a media form are given in Box 14.1.

Emerging perceptions of the Internet search engine as a media genre **14.1**

- An accessible gateway to the universe of content in cyberspace
- Primary purpose is informative
- It is a neutral, unedited, uncensored and comprehensive source
- It is freely and equally open to all senders and receivers
- Its form allows the user to follow any of innumerable search paths and linkages
- There are no indications of status or value, except as perceived by the searcher

---

These perceptions are not necessarily well founded, as is also the case with com-mon perceptions of the news genre, but they do tend to govern behaviour. There is still too little settled experience with the form and little 'performance' research to make an independent assessment. Even so, there is already evidence of some disturbing features, especially the following:

- The impression that all public knowledge can be accessed is misleading since the capacity to search the whole Web does not exist.
- The form has a natural tendency to monopoly and there is already a very high level of concentration on two or three services, much beyond the level that is tolerated for other media (Machill et al., 2008).
- Search engines are financed almost entirely by advertising or by payments for inclusion, inevitably affecting the order of the display of items. There is very limited transparency about the criteria for the ordering of presentation.
- Advertising and other information are not clearly distinguished, as is conventionally the case with other mass media.
- Exclusion and censorship are practised, either by the choice of the provider or in response to local (i.e. national) laws or other pressures.
- The search engine has been partly assimilated with journalism (Machill et al., 2008), with potentially negative consequences for news quality. An example is the evidence that news search engines reduce the scope for journalists to structure news items in order of significance or provide context, leaving both matters to the individual user (Carlson, 2007).
- The ease of use is misleading, with many possibilities for search errors. There are large amounts of useless and decontextualized 'information' in circulation.
- The editing and updating process eliminates much information that was valid at an earlier point, thus tending to rewrite history (Hellstein et al., 2006).

These and other matters that go beyond the question of genre characteristics open up a large number of questions about the wider and longer impact of the search engine.

The News Genre

In the following sections, attention focuses on the news genre, partly because it has such a long history and is so central in accounting for the position of the media as a privileged social institution. The newspaper is, arguably, the archetype as well as the prototype of all modern mass media (Tunstall, 1977: 23), and 'news' is the central ingredient of the newspaper (though far from the only one). To some extent, radio and television were modelled on the newspaper, with regular news as their chief anchor point. News merits special attention in a discussion of media content just because it is one of the few original contributions by the mass media to the range of cultural forms of expression. It is also the core activity according to which a large part of the journalistic (and thus media) occupation defines itself.

News provides the component that distinguishes something called a newspaper from other kinds of print media and often earns it a special status or protection in society, allowing it to express opinion in the name of the public. Media institutions can barely exist without news, and news cannot exist without media institutions. Unlike almost all other forms of authorship or cultural creation, news-making cannot be done privately or even individually. The institution provides both the machinery for distribution and the organization for reception, plus a guarantee of credibility and authority.

Arguably, this feature of the news genre has been undermined by the rise of blogging, which is outside the control of the media. Certainly, there is no longer a monopoly on news publication and there is already evidence of changes in news as a result of the Internet. For instance, a comparison of Google news service with traditional journalism concluded that the difference is essentially between an 'interpretative' mode of structuring news in an orderly way and the Google mode of more fragmentary information from multiple sources that promotes diversity of viewpoint, but gives no indication of preference or relative legitimacy. Blogging is now recognized as a genre that is different from traditional news, with several different varieties (Domingo and Heinonen, 2008). A study of war blogs by Wall (2005) found that they encourage audience participation, personalization, have fragmented story forms and are interdependent with other websites. As yet, we cannot say if changes and differences like this are fundamental or merely rearranging familiar elements of the overall existing news genre. After all, one origin of the newspaper was the personal letter.

What is news?

Despite the central position of news in the media, the question 'What is news?' is one which journalists themselves find distinctly metaphysical and difficult to answer except in terms of their intuition, 'feel' and innate judgement. Attempts to answer it by analysis of media content have not been very revealing. It happens that the two 'founding fathers' of the sociology of news were both former or practising journalists and drew on their own experience in tackling the question of the nature of the news. Walter Lippmann (1922: 216) focused on the process of news gathering, which he saw as a search for the 'objective clear signal which signifies an event'. Hence, 'news is not a mirror of social conditions, but the report of an aspect that has obtruded itself'.

The second early commentator on news, Robert Park (1940/1967), paid more attention to the essential properties of the news report. His starting point was to compare it with another 'form of knowledge', history, which is also a record of past events, and to place news on a continuum that ranges from 'acquaintance with' to 'knowledge about'. News is located somewhere in the middle of this continuum. The result of Park's comparison of news with history can be distilled into a few main points, as follows:

- News is timely: it is about very recent or recurrent events.
- News is unsystematic: it deals with discrete events and happenings, and the world seen through news alone consists of unrelated happenings.
- News is perishable: it lives only when the events themselves are current, and for purposes of record and later reference other forms of knowledge will replace news.
- Events reported as news should be unusual or at least unexpected, qualities that are more important than their 'real significance'.
- Apart from unexpectedness, news events are characterized by other 'news values' that are always relative and involve subjective judgements about likely audience interest.
- News is mainly for orientation and attention direction and not a substitute for knowledge.
- News is predictable.

The paradoxical and provocative final statement that news is predictable was explained by Park as follows:

> if it is the unexpected that happens it is not the wholly unexpected which gets into the news. The events that have made news in the past, as in the present, are actually the expected things ... it is on the whole the accidents and incidents that the public is prepared for ... the things that one fears and that one hopes for that make news. (1940/1967: 45)

Apart from this, as we have seen, much news consists of diary events, known well in advance. A similar point was put more succinctly by Galtung and Ruge (1965) in the remark that 'news' are actually 'olds'. Warren Breed (1956) listed the following terms as descriptive of news: 'saleable', 'superficial', 'simple', 'objective', 'action centred', 'interesting' (as distinct from significant), 'stylized' and 'prudent'. He also suggested dimensions along which an item of news might be placed: news versus truth; difficult versus routine (in terms of news gathering); and information versus human interest.

The facticity of news

Many aspects of news form are clearly related to the pursuit of objectivity in the sense of facticity or factualness. The language of news is 'linear', elaborating an event report along a single dimension with added information, illustration, quotation and discussion. Tuchman (1978) describes some of the familiar features of news narrative – for instance that it is told in the past tense, with headlines in the present tense, and that it avoids conventions associated with fiction. She also observes an equivalent narrative style for television news film, as follows:

> News film casts an aura of representation by [the fact that] ... its uses of time and space announce that the tempo of events and spatial arrangements have *not* been tampered with to tell this story. By seeming *not* to arrange time and space, news films claim to present facts, not interpretations. That is, the web of facticity is embedded in a supposedly neutral, not distorted, synchronization of film with the rhythm of everyday life. (1978: 109–10)

There is little doubt that facticity is vital to the news genre. Tuchman (1978) tells us that a key element of facticity is attribution to very credible or positively verified sources. As Smith puts it, 'The whole idea of news is that it is beyond a plurality of viewpoints' (1973: 174). In his view, without an attribution of credibility by the audience, news could not be distinguished from entertainment or propaganda. This may point to one reason why the secular trend in news development has been away from ideology and towards neutrality. Despite this, there is little reason to modify Gerbner's (1964) conclusion from a study of the French press that 'there is no fundamentally non-ideological, apolitical, non-partisan news-gathering and reporting system'. Box 14.2 outlines the main features of news as an established genre.

The news genre: main attributes 14.2

- Timeliness and recency
- Unexpectedness
- Predictability of type
- Fragmentary nature
- Perishability
- Signalling function or effect
- Shaped by values
- Interesting
- Facticity

News and human interest

In Breed's characterization of news, it is at one point contrasted with human interest, implying that the former has to do with serious information, the latter with something else perhaps entertaining, personalized or sensational. In practice it is hard to separate the two, and both have been elements in the newspaper since its earliest appearance. A classic study by a pupil of Park, Helen McGill Hughes (1940), examined the relationship between the two forms of content and concluded that the (US) newspaper had been 'transformed from a more or less sober record into a form of popular literature'. In her view, a human interest story is not intrinsically different from other news stories but takes its character from the particular attitude which the writer adopts towards the reader. It is a story that is intended to divert, but also one which is told, as it were, from the reader's point of view. As a result, it can only be told by a reporter who is 'able to see the world as his or her readers do'. Hence it is more akin to gossip or the folk tale. The characteristics of news are derived in part from much older traditions of storytelling (Darnton, 1975). Certainly, readers are often more attracted to 'human interest' than to 'news' about politics, economics and society (Curran et al., 1981; Dahlgren and Sparks, 1992). From this point of view, it has a positive contribution to make to democratic communication.

As with other genres, there are several variants that depend on the central code of the news. One example is that of gossip, especially concerning media stars or other celebrities, which purports to offer objective information but usually has no deep significance or any material relevance. The conventions and codes of the news genre can also be used in advertising or in satirical media performances, which outwardly observe the news form but are totally inverted. So-called 'tabloid television' – sensational, gossipy, weird information – is another example of the stretching of a genre. The news genre is also capable of adaptation and extension to new circumstances. News had to be in some degree reinvented for radio, television and pictorial possibilities. The 'happy news format' of television news (with presenters interacting informally), which was introduced in the 1970s for greater audience appeal, has since been widely adopted (Dominick et al., 1975).

The Structure of News: Bias and Framing

One general conclusion from the many content studies is that news exhibits a rather stable and predictable overall pattern when measured according to conventional categories of subject matter. Many of the reasons for this have already been discussed in relation to the production of news (Chapters 11 and 12) and in discussing the news genre.

In this context, much attention has been paid to the question of how news information is presented or 'framed'. Tuchman (1978) cites Goffman (1974) as the originator of the idea that a frame is needed to organize otherwise fragmentary items of experience or information. The idea of a 'frame' in relation to news has been widely and loosely used in place of terms such as 'frame of reference', 'context', 'theme', or even 'news angle'. In a journalistic context, stories are given meaning by reference to some particular 'news value' that connects one event with other similar ones. While it is a common-sense notion, it is also necessary to use the term with some precision, especially when the aim is to study the possible effects of the framing of news. In that case the content frame has to be compared with the frame of reference in the mind of an audience member. According to Entman (1993), 'Framing involves *selection* and *salience*.' He summarizes the main aspects of framing by saying that frames define problems, diagnose causes, make moral judgements and suggest remedies. It is clear that a very large number of textual devices can be used to perform these activities. They include using certain words or phrases, making certain contextual references, choosing certain pictures or film, giving examples as typical, referring to certain sources and so on. The possible effects of all this are discussed in Chapter 19 (pp. 511–12).

Framing is a way of giving some overall interpretation to isolated items of fact. It is almost unavoidable for journalists to do this and in so doing to depart from pure 'objectivity' and to introduce some (unintended) bias. When information is supplied to news media by sources (as much often is), then it arrives with a built-in frame that suits the purpose of the source and is unlikely to be purely objective. Entman (2007) distinguishes between deliberate falsification or omission, 'content bias', where the reality of the news seems to favour one side over another in a conflict situation and 'decision-making' bias, where the motivation and mindset of journalists are unintentionally influential. It is in the second two instances that framing comes into play. There are numerous examples of framing in the literature of content analysis. Race relations issues, for instance, have often been presented in the media as problematic for society rather than for immigrant minorities (Horsti, 2003; Downing and Husband, 2005). Van Gorp's (2005) account of Belgian press coverage of asylum seekers showed a division between a frame of 'victim' that invited sympathy and a frame of 'intruder' that raised public fears and opposition. Almost all news about the Soviet Union and Eastern Europe was for decades reported in terms of the Cold War and the Soviet 'enemy' (McNair, 1988). Much the same was true for China, until it became too important to offend.

Inevitably, framing reflects both the sources that are chosen and the national context in which news is produced, thus also the foreign policies of countries concerned. The Iraq war produced much evidence of the alignment of national media systems with their government and public opinion (e.g. Tumber and Palmer, 2004; Aday et al., 2005; Ravi, 2005). Similar patterns were found in online news by Dimitrova et al. (2005). Bird and Dardenne (2009) contrast US and British reporting of the 'shock and awe' bombing of Baghdad, which was described by the former in admiring terms as a demonstration of power and by the latter as catastrophic, destructive and outrageous.

Entman (1991) describes US reporting of two similar air tragedies in which military action caused the deaths of large numbers of civilians. One was the Korean aircraft (KAL 007) shot down in 1983 by a Soviet plane; the other was an Iranian civil flight (Iran Air 655) shot down in 1988 by a US naval vessel in the Persian Gulf. The events were reported quite differently, in ways that reflected both ethnocentrism and the international tensions of the times. The manner of reporting, in words, tone and problematizing, constituted different frames in the sense under discussion. The key differences are summarized in Box 14.3.

Differential framing in US media of two comparable air disasters caused by Soviet and US military action respectively 14.3

Predominant definition of events

	KAL 007	Iran Air 655
Motive	Deliberate	A mistake
Report tone	Emotional/human	Neutral/technical
Characterization	An attack	A tragedy

The analysis of texts according to framing theory often produces clear and interesting results, in a transparent and communicative way, even if we are left at the end without a clear measure of strength and extent of the 'frames' uncovered. There are many cues to draw on, presumably the same ones that are available to the audience that give rise to supposed effects. These include visuals, language usage, labels, similes and metaphors, familiar narrative structures, and so on.

Manheim (1998) describes the misleading public relations campaign designed to gain American public support for action to liberate Kuwait in 1990 and 1991. Research indicated that an appeal to justice did not help as much as the demonization of Saddam Hussein as a latter-day Hitler. In the 1999 Kosovo conflict, NATO propaganda aimed from the start of the air attack on Yugoslavia to frame the event as both a necessary and a 'humanitarian' war against 'genocide', also calling up images of the Holocaust, comparing Milošević to Hitler and generally demonizing the Serbs (Norstedt et al., 2000; Thussu, 2000; Vincent, 2000; Wolfgram, 2008). Foerstal (2001) describes a PR campaign on behalf of Kosovo Albanians as very similar to the discredited Kuwaiti PR campaign. The purpose was to raise support in western public opinion and to combat criticism of the action. The materials for framing were readily available to the media from the previous years of savage Balkan conflict, and the propaganda offensive was largely successful. To some degree, the same media control tactics were followed by the American-led coalition in the war against Iraq in 2003, although the situation was complicated by the need to keep in play a frame of 'liberation' rather than a pre-emptive strike against a dangerous tyrant.

Framing also undergoes changes that reflect the goals of sources as well as changing realities. Schwalber et al. (2008) analysed visuals in US media over the early weeks of the invasion of Iraq and observed a shift from a master narrative of patriotic endeavour to a more fragmented and ambivalent view as the war dragged on. Framing analysis offers an apparently convincing impression of underlying meanings and assumptions, but Kitzinger (2007) reminds us that the most powerful frame may well be invisible or so transparently obvious that it is taken for granted. For instance, an issue that is treated as problematic in the news may lead to the alternative framing of narratives and solutions, while the framing of an issue in itself as a problem is unquestioned. She gives the example of homosexuality in the past, but there are plenty of contemporary examples, including immigration, security, law enforcement, and so on.

The form of the news report

The strength of the news genre is attested to by the extent to which certain basic features are found across the different media of print, radio and television, despite the very different possibilities and limitations of each. Some of these features of regularity are found to be much the same in different countries (Rositi, 1976; Heinderyckx, 1993). What is striking is the extent to which a presumably unpredictable universe of events seems open to incorporation, day after day, into much the same temporal, spatial and topic frame. It is true that deviations occur, at times of crisis or exceptional events, but the news form is posited on the normality and predictability of the world of events.

The news form provides indications of the relative significance of events and of types of content. Significance is mainly indicated by the sequencing of content and by the relative amount of space or time allocated. According to what the Glasgow Media Group (1980) called 'viewers' maxims', it will be understood that first-appearing items in television news are most 'important' and that, generally, items receiving more time are also more important. Television news bulletins are also generally constructed with a view to arousing initial interest by highlighting some event, maintaining interest through diversity and human interest, holding back some vital information to the end (sports results and weather forecast), then sending the viewer away at the close with a light touch. The Glasgow Media Group argued that the hidden purpose or effect of this is to reinforce a 'primary framework' of normality and control and a view of the world that is essentially ideological. The world is 'naturalized' (see also Tuchman, 1978).

The regularities described characterize the dominant western news form, and it is possible that media operating under different 'press theories' will exert different kinds of regularity. There are almost certainly significant and systematic differences between television news-giving in different societies, although these are more likely to follow cultural and institutional lines of demarcation which are different from national and language frontiers. A comparison of US and Italian television news, for instance, led to the conclusion that each system's news gives a significantly different conception of what politics is about (Hallin and Mancini, 1984). The main differences were attributed to the much larger space occupied by a public sphere, other than the state, in the case of Italy. As a result, journalists in the USA have a much larger role as representatives of the public than they adopt, or are credited with, in Italy.

News as Narrative

Text as narrative has long been an object of study, and the narrative concept has proved useful in understanding a variety of media contents. Basic narrative forms span a wide range of types, including advertisements and news 'stories' as well as the more obvious candidates of drama and fiction. In one way or another, most media content tells stories, which take rather patterned and predictable forms. The main function of narrative is to help make sense of reports of experience. It does this in two main ways: by linking actions and events in a logical, sequential or causal way; and by providing the elements of people and places that have a fixed and recognizable (realistic) character. Narrative helps to provide the logic of human motive that makes sense of fragmentary observations, whether fictional or realistic. When news is considered as narrative, we can appreciate the way in which it draws on and retells the recurrent and dominant myths of a society, inevitably with some 'ideological' loading (Bird and Dardenne, 2009).

Darnton (1975) argues that our conception of news results from 'ancient ways of telling stories'. News accounts are typically cast in narrative form, with principal and minor actors, connected sequences, heroes and villains, a beginning, middle and end, signalling of dramatic turns and a reliance on familiar plots. The analysis of news narrative structure has been formalized in the 'discourse analysis' tradition, especially by van Dijk (1983, 1985), who developed an empirically based framework for the analysis of news based on the concept of 'news schemata', which provide a syntax of news stories. Bell (1991) reminds us that news cannot follow normal narrative, because news structure requires an abstract of the story at the start and also a sequence that reflects the varying news values of actors and events. Fragments of information are reassembled by journalists in newsworthy rather than chronological order.

Television Violence

One category of media content that has been studied as intensively and as long as news is that of television programming containing violence. Of course, this is not a genre as such since violence can appear in virtually all television genres. However, there is a smaller category of television programming which is identifiable by its heavy reliance on violence for its audience appeal. Such content does share certain features of purpose, style and meaning in a similar way to more overtly recognized genres, to the extent of their being various sub-genres (e.g. war, gangland, humorous, cartoon, sadistic crime, etc.). The main purpose here is to indicate briefly how the key features of 'violent television' have been identified and described, primarily with a view to protecting children from harmful influence and waging an anti-violence campaign.

The history of research in this area goes back to the earliest days of communication research, although a major landmark was the Report of the (US) National Commission on the Causes and Prevention of Violence (Baker and Ball, 1969). This study provided the first accounts of the methods and findings of Gerbner's cultivation research programme (see Gerbner et al., 2002). More recent US research, under the aegis of the National Television Violence Study, has continued in much the same tradition and their work provides the source for a description of the aims and methods in the mainstream tradition (see Wilson and Smith, 2002). The study defines violence as 'any overt depiction of a credible threat of physical force, or the actual use of such force intended to physically harm an animate being or a group of beings. Violence also includes certain depictions of physically harmful consequences against an animate being or group that occur as a result of unseen violent means.' Wilson et al. name four foundations for their choice of method in recording the type and incidence of violence on television, as follows:

- TV violence contributes to antisocial effects on viewers.
- There are three primary types of effects from viewing TV violence: learning aggressive attitudes and behaviour; desensitization to violence; increased fear of being victimized by violence.
- Not all violence poses the same degree of these harmful effects.
- Not all viewers are affected by violence in the same way.

In line with these principles and the research and theory that supports them, the analysis sought to establish the characteristics of programmes on television according to the main contextual indicators of any violence depicted, which has relevance for effects. These are shown in Box 14.4.

14.4 Contextual factors in the portrayal of violence

- The relative appeal of the perpetrator
- The relative appeal of the victim
- The reasons for violence
- The weapons used
- The extensiveness and graphicness of the depiction

> - The realism with which violence is portrayed
> - Rewards and punishments for acts
> - The consequences as shown in terms of pain and harm
> - Humour, its presence or absence

The variables in Box 14.4 were applied at three levels: to each violent incident; to each scene; and to a programme as a whole. The main conclusions from the study of nearly 3,000 programmes in 1995–6 were that:

- most programmes of all kinds contain some violence (61%);
- there are few programmes with an anti-violence theme;
- most violence on television is sanitized;
- portrayals with a high risk of teaching aggression to children under age 7 are concentrated in the very programmes and channels targeted to young viewers;
- for older children and teens, high-risk portrayals that encourage aggression are found most in movies and dramas.

The Cultural Text and Its Meanings

A new form of discourse concerning media texts has emerged, especially with the rise of cultural studies and its convergence on an existing tradition of mass communication research. The origins of cultural studies are somewhat mixed, including traditional literary and linguistic analysis of texts, semiology and Marxist theory. A convincing effort has been made by Fiske (1987) to bring much disparate theory together, especially for the purposes of analysing and understanding popular (television) culture. New definitions of the media text have been introduced along with ways of identifying some key features.

The concept of text

The term 'text' has been mainly used in two basic senses. One refers very generally to the physical message itself – the printed document, film, television programme or musical score, as noted above. An alternative usage, recommended by Fiske, is to reserve the term 'text' for the meaningful outcome of the encounter between content and reader. For instance, a television programme 'becomes a text at the moment of reading, that is, when its interaction with one of its many audiences activates some of the meanings/pleasures that it is capable of provoking' (1987: 14). It follows from this definition that the same television programme can produce many different texts in the sense of accomplished meanings. Summing up this point, Fiske tells us that 'a programme is produced by the industry, a text by its readers' (1987: 14). It is important, from this perspective, to see that the word 'production' applies to the activities of both the 'mass communicators' and the audiences.

This is a central point in what is essentially a theory of media content looked at from the point of view of its reception rather than its production or intrinsic meaning. Other essential elements in this approach are to emphasize that the media text (in the first or 'programme' sense) has many potential alternative meanings that can result in different readings. Mass media content is thus in principle *polysemic*, having multiple potential meanings for its 'readers' (in the generic sense of audience members). Fiske argues that polysemy is a necessary feature of truly popular media culture since the more potential meanings there are, the greater the chance of appeal to different audiences and to different social categories within the total audience.

Multiplicity of textual meaning has an additional dimension, as Newcomb (1991) reminds us. Texts are constituted out of many different languages and systems of meaning. These include codes of dress, physical appearance, class and occupation, religion, ethnicity, region, social circles and many more. Any words in a spoken language or interactions in a drama can have different meanings in relation to any or several of these other languages.

Differential encoding and decoding again

Despite this polysemic character, the discourses of particular examples of media content are often designed or inclined to control, confine or direct the taking of meaning, which may in turn be resisted by the reader. This discussion relates to Hall's (1974/1980) model of *encoding/decoding* (discussed in Chapter 3), according to which there is usually a *preferred reading* encoded in a text – the meaning which the message producer would like the receiver to take. On the whole, it is the 'preferred readings' that are identified by analysis of overt content – the literal or surface meaning plus the ideology. One aspect of this relates to the notion of the **'inscribed reader'** (Sparks and Campbell, 1987). Particular media contents can be said, in line with the theory of Bourdieu (1986), to 'construct' a reader, a construction which can to some extent be 'read back' by an analyst on the basis of the set of concerns in the text as written. The 'inscribed reader' is also the kind of reader who is primarily *addressed* by a message. A similar concept is that of the 'implied audience' (Deming, 1991).

The process by which this works has also been called *interpellation* or appellation, and usually refers back to the ideology theories of Althusser (1971). According to Fiske (1987: 53), 'interpellation refers to the way any use of discourse "hails" the addressee. In responding … we implicitly accept the discourse's definition of "us", or … we adopt the subject position proposed for us by the discourse.' This feature of discourse is widely exploited in advertising (Williamson, 1978), where advertisements commonly construct and project their image of a model consumer of the product in question. They then invite 'readers' to recognize themselves in these images. Such images normally associate certain desirable qualities (such as chicness, cleverness, youth or beauty) with using the product, and generally this is flattering to the consumer as well as to the product.

Intertextuality

As Fiske (1987) also reminds us, the text as produced by the reader is not con-fined in its meaning by the boundaries that are set on the production side between programmes or between content categories. A 'reader' of media texts can easily combine, for instance, the experience of a programme with that of advertisements inserted in it, or with adjoining programmes.

This is one aspect of the intertextuality of media, and it applies also to cross-ing boundaries between media (such as film, books and radio). Intertextuality is not only an accomplishment of the reader, but also a feature of media themselves, which are continually cross-referencing from one medium to another, and the same 'mes-sage', story or type of narrative can be found in very different media forms and genres. The expansion of marketing based on media images has extended the range of inter-textuality from media content 'texts' to all kinds of consumption articles. Television, according to Fiske (1987), gives rise to a 'third level of intertextuality' – referring to the texts that viewers make themselves and reproduce in conversation or in writing about the media experience. Ethnographic researchers into media audiences draw on such 'third-level' texts when they listen in on conversations or organize group discus-sions to hear about how the media are experienced (e.g. Radway, 1984; Ang, 1985; Liebes and Katz, 1986).

Codes are systems of meaning whose rules and conventions are shared by mem-bers of a culture or by what has been called an 'interpretative community' (for instance, a set of fans of the same media genre, author or performer). Codes help to provide the links between media producers and media audiences by laying the foundations for interpretation. We make sense of the world by drawing on our understanding of com-municative codes and conventions. Particular gestures, expressions, forms of dress and images, for example, carry more or less unambiguous meanings within particular cultures that have been established by usage and familiarity. An example of a film code (Monaco, 1981) is an image combining a weeping woman, a pillow and money, to symbolize shame.

Open versus closed texts

In the particular discourse about media content under discussion, the content may be considered to be more or less 'open' or 'closed' in its meanings. According to Eco (1979), an open text is one whose discourse does not try to constrain the reader to one particular meaning or interpretation. Different kinds and actual examples of media text can be differentiated according to their degree of openness. For instance, in gen-eral, news reports are intended not to be open but to lead to a uniform informational end, while serials and soap operas are often loosely articulated and lend themselves to varied 'readings'. This differentiation is not always consistent between genres, and there can be large variations within genres in the degree of textual openness. In the case of commercial advertisements, while they are intended to achieve a long-term goal benefiting the product advertised, the form of advertisement can range from the playful and ambiguous to the one-dimensional 'hard sell' or simple announcement. It has also been argued that television in general has a more open and ambiguous text than cinema film (Ellis, 1982).

The distinction between open and closed texts has a potential ideological significance. In their discussion of the television portrayal of terrorism, for instance, Schlesinger et al. (1983) argued that a more open portrayal also leads to alternative viewpoints, while a closed portrayal tends to reinforce the dominant or consensual view. They make another distinction between a 'tight' or a 'loose' storyline, reinforcing the tendency of the closed versus open choice. They conclude that television news is in general both closed and tight, while documentary and fiction are more variable. They observe that, in the case of fiction, the larger the (expected) audience, the more closed and tight the representation of terrorism, thus converging on the 'official' picture of reality as portrayed on the news. This suggests some form of ideological control (probably self-censorship), with risks not being taken with a mass audience.

Seriality

There has been a revival of interest in narrative theory (Oltean, 1993), especially as a result of the great attention given to television drama, serials and series in media studies (e.g. Seiter et al., 1989). The topic of seriality now has a place in narrative theory. Narrative theory itself owes much to the work of Propp (1968), who uncovered the basic similarity of narrative structure in Russian folk tales. Modern popular media fiction also testifies to the high degree of constancy and similarity of a basic plot. For instance, Radway (1984) described the basic narrative logic of mass-produced romance stories for women in terms of a series of stages (see Figure 14.2). It starts with a disturbance for the heroine, through an antagonistic encounter with an aristocratic male, by way of a separation, to a reconciliation and a sexual union, concluding with a restoration of identity for the heroine.

While basic plots can be found in many different genres, with a range of established but familiar variations, there are other narrative differences to note. Television *series* can, for instance, be clearly differentiated from *serials*, using narrative theory. The series consists of a set of discrete stories which are terminated in each episode. In the cases of serials, the story continues without end from one episode to the next. In both cases there is continuity, primarily achieved by retaining the same principal characters. However, there is a difference. In series, the heroes and heroines (subjects) remain constant, while the villains (objects) differ from one episode to another. The same characters go through different narrative sequences in the same settings. In between episodes, as Oltean (1993) remarks, 'the marionettes stay put in a cabin placed outside the fictional reality'. By contrast, with serials (such as normal soap operas, which in their original form were broadcast daily) the same cast of characters appears each time, and an illusion is fostered that they continue their life actively between episodes. They 'remain fictively active'.

Another aspect of narrative underlined by Oltean is the difference between 'linear' and 'parallel' processing. In serials there is a transition from one storyline to the

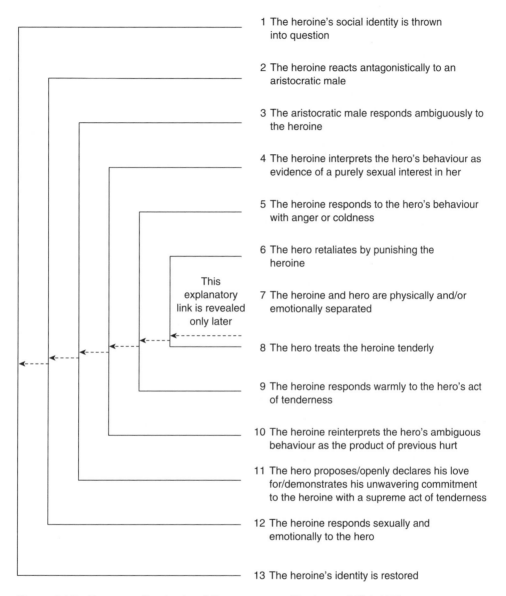

1 The heroine's social identity is thrown into question

2 The heroine reacts antagonistically to an aristocratic male

3 The aristocratic male responds ambiguously to the heroine

4 The heroine interprets the hero's behaviour as evidence of a purely sexual interest in her

5 The heroine responds to the hero's behaviour with anger or coldness

6 The hero retaliates by punishing the heroine

This explanatory link is revealed only later

7 The heroine and hero are physically and/or emotionally separated

8 The hero treats the heroine tenderly

9 The heroine responds warmly to the hero's act of tenderness

10 The heroine reinterprets the hero's ambiguous behaviour as the product of previous hurt

11 The hero proposes/openly declares his love for/demonstrates his unwavering commitment to the heroine with a supreme act of tenderness

12 The heroine responds sexually and emotionally to the hero

13 The heroine's identity is restored

Figure 14.2   The narrative logic of the romance (Radway, 1984: 150)

next, while in series there is a 'meta-story' (concerning the permanent characters), with several different storylines as they encounter their new adventures week by week. The series organizes stories according to a principle of linearity, while serials (such as soap operas) prefer parallel processing with a network of concurrent storylines involving different subgroups of the permanent cast of characters interacting and interweaving on varying time scales.

Realism

Narrative often depends on assumptions about realism and helps to reinforce a sense of reality, by invoking the logic, normality and predictability of human behaviour. The conventions of realistic fiction were established by the early forms of the novel, although they were preceded by realism in other arts. On the one hand, realism of media depends on a certain attitude that what is portrayed is 'true to life', if not literally true in the sense of having actually occurred. Realistic fiction depends on the belief that it *could* occur or might have done so. Even fantastic stories can be made realistic if they use actual settings and social backgrounds and gain verisimilitude from applying plausible logics of action. In fact, realism is not a simple concept. Research by Hall (2003), based on an exploration of audience evaluations, indicates that there are a number of dimensions. She identifies six of these under the following headings: plausibility, perceptual persuasiveness, typicality, factuality, emotional involvement and narrative consistency. She concludes that different genres require different concepts of realism.

There are techniques of writing and filming that emphasize realism. In the former case, accurate documentary-like descriptions and concrete, logical and sequential storytelling achieve this result. In filming, aside from representing real places, a continuous flow of action serves to create a realistic illusion. Sometimes black and white film stock is inserted (for instance, in flashbacks) to indicate that scenes have a real or documentary character. There are also classic realistic stylistic devices (Monaco, 1981). One of these is the 'shot, reverse shot', which moves the camera from one speaker to a partner in a dialogue to create the illusion for the spectator of involvement in the ongoing conversation (Fiske, 1987).

Film and television can also employ in fiction the 'documentary' mode or style, which is established on the basis of learned conventions. In general, documentary style relies on real places and social settings to create the illusion of actuality. According to Fiske (1987), media realism leads in a 'reactionary' (rather than a radical) direction because it 'naturalizes' the status quo – making it seem normal and therefore inevitable. In the terms used above, realism goes in the direction of 'closure', since the more real the portrayal seems, the more difficult it is for the reader, who is likely to take the reality of the world for granted, to establish any alternative meanings. This relates back to Schlesinger et al.'s (1983) evidence about differing degrees of openness and closure in news and fiction.

Gendered media texts

The concept of an inscribed (written into) or interpellated reader can be used to analyse the audience image sought by particular media, in terms of class, cultural taste, age or lifestyle. Many kinds of media content, following the same line of argument, are differentially gendered. They have a built-in bias towards the supposed characteristics of one or other gender, presumably for reasons of appealing to a chosen audience, or simply because many language codes are innately gendered.

Fiske (1987) gives an example based on the television police series *Cagney and Lacey*, which features two women as the chief protagonists. In the series, 'the discourse of gender … underwrites a number of codes to discourage us from adopting the masculine point of view that is normal in patriarchal television'. The female active role is 'represented as a controlling, active person upon whom the camera dwells not in order to display her sexual attractiveness, but to explore and convey the manner in which she is controlling the scene' (1987: 53).

A number of writers (e.g. Geraghty, 1991) have argued that the soap opera as a genre is intrinsically 'gendered' as female narrative, by way of its characterizations, settings and dialogue, and the positioning of male and female roles. Modleski (1982) suggested that the loose structure of the typical soap opera matches the fragmented pattern of the housewife's daily work. By contrast, television action serials can often be said to be gendered in a masculine way. Some of the differences (as with advertising) are certainly caused by simply planning to appeal to different audience groups, following conventional and often stereotyped ideas about male–female differences. Mass-produced romances of the kind described by Radway (1984) are clearly 'gendered' from the start and mostly written by women as well as openly for women. However, this is not likely to be the whole explanation, and 'gendering' can take subtle and not always intended forms, which makes the pursuit of the topic worthwhile.

For example, a study of female and male film directors by Patsy Winsor, reported by Real (1989), showed a number of significant differences in the content of popular films made by men and women. Female film directors were noticeably less inclined to include acts of physical aggression or to associate them so strongly with men. They showed women in more active roles, and in several different and less predictable ways produced distinctive texts. The study concluded that, notwithstanding the constraints of popular film-making, there was some evidence of the emergence of a 'women's aesthetic'. There is other evidence that the gender of producers can affect the outcome, although there are more powerful organizational factors at work. For instance, Lanzen et al. (2008) analysed a sample of US prime-time network shows and found the usual tendency to gender stereotyping, but those with one or more female writer/creator were more likely to include male characters in interpersonal roles compared to all-male production teams.

Studying the popular

The approach to content which has been reviewed under the heading of 'cultural text' has seemed suited to the study of popular mass entertainment, especially fictional and dramatic forms, which seek to involve the reader in fantasy but usually in realistic settings. The aim of such media content is not to convey any specific meaning but simply to provide 'entertainment' – taking people out of themselves and into other worlds of the imagination, caught up in dramatic actions and emotions. The texts employed for this purpose tend to be relatively 'open' and do not have to work hard at the cognitive level.

Outside the sphere of popular fiction, there is likely to be a greater tension between the postulate of *polysemy* and the view that texts are structured in certain ways to achieve their audience and their effect. The inscribed texts of media news, for instance, are much more closed and determinate in their informational purpose, even if they also can be differentially or even aberrantly 'decoded' (Eco, 1979).

14.5 The cultural text approach

- Texts are jointly produced with their readers
- Texts are differentially encoded
- Texts are 'polysemic', i.e. have many potential meanings
- Texts are related to other texts (intertextuality)
- Texts employ different narrative forms
- Texts are gendered

Conclusion

Generalization about the content of mass media has become progressively more difficult as the media have expanded and diversified and multimedia forms have come to predominate. Established genres have multiplied and mutated, casting doubt on genre analysis as a stable framework for describing media output. Our capacity to analyse and understand how texts work has not kept pace with the variety of output even of conventional media, let alone of the Internet and the other new forms of delivery. We still have to live with the puzzle that has always faced us of where 'meaning' can be found: in the intention of the producer, the perception of the receiver, or the text itself. This catalogue of problems is discouraging, but it is still possible to analyse content if we have a clearly defined purpose in mind, a viable method and an awareness of pitfalls and opportunities.

Further Reading

Berger, A. (1979) *Popular Culture Genres*. Newbury Park, CA: Sage.
A still largely valid typology and characterization of the underlying principles of popular culture genres, although with a strong bias towards forms found on television. Provides a framework for identifying innovation.

Bird, S.E. and Dardenne, R.W. (2009) 'Rethinking news and myth as storytelling', in K. Wall-Jorgenson and T. Hanitsch (eds), *The Handbook of Journalism Studies*, pp. 205–17. London: Routledge.
A fresh look at the narratology tradition of news theorizing.

Creeber, G. (ed.) (2006) *The Television Genre Book*. London: BFI Publishing.
An introduction to the study of television genre, with identification and illustration of the main forms.

Radway, J. (1984) *Reading the Romance*. Chapel Hill, NC: University of North Carolina Press.
A classic genre study combining literary analysis with audience research more or less according to the principles of the media 'uses and gratifications' approach.

Online Readings

Akass, K. and McCabe, J. (2007) 'Analyzing fictional television genres', in E. Devereux (ed.), *Media Studies*, pp. 283–301. London: Sage.

Anden-Papadopolous, K. (2008) 'The Abu-Ghraib torture photographs: news frames, visual culture and the power of images', *Journalism*, 9 (1): 5–30.

Brants, K. (1998) 'Who's afraid of infotainment?', *European Journal of Communication*, 13 (3): 315–56.

Newcomb, H. (2004) 'Narrative and genre', in J.D.H. Downing, D. McQuail, P. Schlesinger and E. Wartella (eds), *The Sage Handbook of Media Studies*, pp. 413–28. Thousand Oaks, CA: Sage.

Reese, S.D., Rutigliano, L., Hyun, K. and Jeong, J. (2007) 'Mapping the blogosphere', *Journalism*, 8 (3): 235–61.

Part 6
Audiences

15

Audience Theory and Research Traditions

This chapter begins with a discussion of the origins of the audience concept, which has a number of different meanings and manifestations. Different types of audience are identified. The main issues that have guided audience theory are explained and the purposes of audience research outlined. A typology of audiences is proposed as a framework of analysis. The question of relations between media communicators and their audiences, actual or imagined, is addressed. The chapter continues with a discussion of various measures of media reach and concludes with an assessment of ideas about audience selectivity and different types and degrees of activity.

The Audience Concept

The word 'audience' is very familiar as the collective term for the 'receivers' in the simple sequential model of the mass communication process (source, channel, message, receiver, effect) that was deployed by pioneers in the field of media research (e.g. see Schramm, 1955). It is a term that is understood by media practitioners as well as theorists and is recognized by media users as an unambiguous description of themselves. Nevertheless, beyond common-sense usage, there is much room for differences of meaning and theoretical disputes. These stem mainly from the fact that a single word is being applied to an increasingly diverse and complex reality, open to alternative and competing formulations. It has been suggested that 'what is occurring is the breakdown of the *referent* for the word audience in communication research from both the humanities and the social sciences' (Biocca, 1988a: 103). In other words, we keep the familiar word, but the thing itself is disappearing.

To start with, the audience concept implies an attentive, receptive but relatively passive set of listeners or spectators assembled in a more or less public setting. The actual reception of mass media is a varied and messy experience with little regularity and does not match this version. This is especially so in a time of mobility, individualization and multiplicity of media usage. Secondly, the rise of new media has introduced entirely new forms of behaviour, involving interactivity and searching, rather than watching or listening. Thirdly, the line between the producers and audiences has become blurred for reasons given earlier (see p. 333).

Audiences are both a product of social context (which leads to shared cultural interests, understandings and information needs) and a response to a particular pattern of media provision. Often they are both at the same time, as when a medium sets out to appeal to the members of a social category or the residents of a certain place. Media use also reflects broader patterns of time use, availability, lifestyle and everyday routines.

An audience can thus be defined in different and overlapping ways: by *place* (as in the case of local media); by *people* (as when a medium is characterized by an appeal to a certain age group, gender, political belief or income category); by the particular type of *medium* or *channel* involved (technology and organization combined); by the *content* of its messages (genres, subject matter, styles); by *time* (as when one speaks of the 'daytime' or 'primetime' audience, or an audience that is fleeting and short term compared with one that endures).

There are other ways of characterizing the different kinds of audience that have emerged with changing media and changing times. Nightingale (2003) offers a new typology that captures key features of the new diversity, proposing four types as follows:

- *Audience as 'the people assembled'*. Essentially the aggregate measured as paying attention to a given media presentation or product at a given time. These are the known 'spectators'.
- *Audience as 'the people addressed'*. Referring to the group of people imagined by the communicator and for whom content is shaped. This is otherwise known as the 'inscribed' or 'interpellated' audience (see p. 386).
- *Audience as 'happening'*. The experience of reception alone or with others as an interactive event in daily life, contextualized by place and other features.
- *Audience as 'hearing' or 'audition'*. Essentially refers to participatory audience experience, when the audience is embedded in a show or is enabled to participate by remote means or to provide a response at the same time.

There are some other possibilities for defining a distinctive kind of audience, depending on the medium concerned and the perspective adopted. The Internet provides for new kinds of communicative relations that do not fit the typologies created for mass communication.

The Original Audience

The early origins of today's media audience lie in public theatrical and musical performances as well as in the games and spectacles of ancient times. Our earliest notions of audience are of a physical gathering in a certain place. A Greek or Roman city, for example, would have a theatre or arena, and it was no doubt preceded by less formal gatherings for similar events and for religious or state occasions. The original audience had many features that are familiar today in other areas of public performance, including those listed in Box 15.1.

Characteristics of the original audience 15.1

- Planning and *organization* of viewing and listening as well as of the performances themselves
- Events with a *public* and 'popular' character
- *Secular* (thus not religious) content of performance – for entertainment, education and vicarious emotional experience
- *Voluntary*, individual acts of choice and attention
- *Specialization of roles* of authors, performers and spectators
- Physical *locatedness* of performance and spectator experience

The audience as a set of spectators for public events of a secular kind was thus already institutionalized more than 2000 years ago. It had its own customs, rules and expectations about the time, place and content of performances, conditions for admission, and so forth. It was typically an urban phenomenon, often with a commercial basis, and content varied according to social class and status. Because of its public character, audience behaviour was subject to surveillance and social control.

The modern mass-media audience shares some of these features but is also very different in some obvious ways. The audiences for mass media are much more diverse, in terms of content available and the social behaviour involved. There is no element of public assembly. The audience remains in a state of continuous existence, rather than reforming occasionally for specific performances. The mass-media audience attracts a supply of content to keep it satisfied instead of reforming in response to some periodic performance of interest. The more one thinks about it, the less relevant the original concept appears to be. In several linguistic cultures other than English, the term 'public' is conventionally used rather than 'audience', but this too has a number of similar limitations, including the fact that much media use is not at all public in the primary meaning of this term.

From Mass to Market

Although many observers commented on the amazing new possibilities for reaching so many disparate people so quickly by the press, film or radio, the first theoretical formulation of the media audience concept stemmed from a wider consideration of the changing nature of social life in modern society. As recounted in Chapter 3, Herbert Blumer (1939) first provided an explicit framework in which the audience could be exemplified as a new form of collectivity made possible by the conditions of modern societies. He called this phenomenon a 'mass' and differentiated it from older social forms – especially the group, the crowd and the public (see pp. 56–8).

The mass audience was large, heterogeneous and widely dispersed, and its members did not and could not know each other. This view of the mass audience is less a description of reality than an accentuation of features typical of conditions of mass production and distribution of news and entertainment. When used by early commentators, the term generally had a pejorative connotation, reflecting a negative view of popular taste and mass culture.

Rediscovery of the audience as a group

The inadequacy of this concept of audience has long been apparent. The reality of people's experience of mass print and film was always very diverse. While impersonality, anonymity and vastness of scale might describe the phenomenon in general, much actual audience experience is personal, small-scale and integrated into social life and familiar ways. Many media operate in local environments and are embedded in local cultures. Since most people make their own media choices freely, they do not typically feel manipulated by remote powers. The social interaction that develops around media use helps people to incorporate it into everyday life as a friendly rather than an alienating presence. At an early point in the history of media research, actual audiences were shown to consist of many overlapping networks of social relations based on locality and common interests, and the 'mass' media were incorporated into these networks in different ways (Delia, 1987). The communal and social group character of audiences was restored to conceptual prominence (e.g. Merton, 1949; Janowitz, 1952; Katz and Lazarsfeld, 1955). Critical thinkers (e.g. Gitlin, 1978) objected that this supposed protection of the individual from manipulation was in itself an ideological move to obscure the much more typical vulnerability of the individual in the mass and allay fears of mass society.

Audience as market

The press and film were already established as very profitable businesses when broadcasting made its uncertain appearance on the scene in the 1920s. The radio and television audience rapidly developed into an important consumer market for hardware and software. At first sight, the widely used expression 'media market' seems to offer a more objective alternative to other, more value-laden terms to describe the audience phenomenon. As the media have become bigger business, the term 'market' has gained in currency. It can designate regions served by media, social-demographic categories, or the actual or potential consumers of particular media services or products. It may be defined as an aggregate of actual or potential consumers of media services and products, with a known social-economic profile.

While the market concept is a pragmatic and necessary one for media industries and for analysing media economics, it is also problematic and not really value-free. It treats an audience as a set of consumers rather than as a group or public. It links sender and receiver in a 'calculative' rather than a normative or social relationship, as a cash transaction between producer and consumer rather than a communication relationship. It ignores the internal social relations between individuals since these are of little interest to service providers. It privileges social-economic criteria and focuses on media *consumption* rather than reception.

Effective communication and the quality of audience experience are of secondary importance in market thinking. The significance of audience experience for the wider public sphere is also de-emphasized. The view of audience as market is inevitably the view 'from the media' (especially of their owners and managers), and within the terms of the media industries' discourse. People in audiences do not normally have any awareness of themselves as belonging to markets, and the market discourse in relation to the audience is implicitly manipulative.

In an innovative and sophisticated move, the Canadian Dallas Smythe (1977) gave birth to the theory that audiences actually *work* for advertisers (thus, for their ultimate oppressors). They do so by giving their free time to watch media, with this labour then packaged and sold by the media to advertisers as a new kind of 'commodity'. The whole system of commercial television and the press rests on this extraction of surplus value from an economically exploited audience. The same audience has to pay yet again for its media, by way of the extra cost added to the advertised goods. It was an ingenious and convincing piece of theorizing which revealed the mass audience phenomenon in quite a new light (see Jhally and Livant, 1986). It is plausible to suppose that the media need their audience more than audiences need their media, and there is also reason to view audience research as primarily a tool for the close control and management (call it manipulation) of media audiences.

This line of argument is, in some respects, even more applicable to the Internet-based media that are almost entirely financed by advertising and also (perhaps for that reason) require a good deal more 'work' from their users than simply attending to advertisements, in the form of self-produced content (see p. 393). A new political economic interpretation along these lines has been provided by Fuchs (2009). However, Dallas Smythe's argument has also been questioned by Bermejo (2009), mainly on the grounds that it is not very clear just what is being produced and sold. It is not the attention and time of an audience in a conventional sense. Essentially, this had first to be converted into 'ratings', based on time spent. However, the same time-based ratings system does not apply to the Internet. In some respects, the Internet user does work much harder than the passive watcher of television, but it is not clear who benefits from this work. Bermejo suggests that in the case of search engines, it is not the watching time of audiences that is sold to advertisers, but words.

With respect to television, the media industry is routinely transforming the actual television audience into a piece of commercial information called 'ratings' (Ang, 1991). Ratings are described as forming 'the basis for the agreed-upon standard by which advertisers and networks buy and sell the audience commodity' (1991: 54). Ang reminds us that 'watching television is an ongoing, day-to-day cultural practice engaged in by millions of people' and the 'ratings discourse' serves to 'capture and encompass the viewing practice of all these people in a singular, objectified, streamlined construct of "television audience"'. These comments essentially label the industry view of the audience as intrinsically dehumanizing and exploitative. Again, it reflects the view that commercial mass media are served by their audiences rather than vice versa. Ang (1991) argued that media institutions have no real interest in *knowing* their audiences, only in being able to prove they exist by way of systems and techniques of measurement (e.g. 'people meters') which convince their clients but which can never begin to capture the true essence of 'audiencehood'. Much the same critique applies to the Internet, where ratings are also pursued assiduously, albeit in new and even more detailed terms. The main theoretical features of the audience as market are reviewed in Box 15.2.

The audience as a market: main theoretical features 15.2

- Audiences are aggregates of many potential or actual consumers
- Members are unrelated to each other and have no shared identity of their own
- Boundaries assigned to audiences are based mainly on socio-economic criteria
- Audiences are objects of management and control by media providers
- The formation is temporary
- Public significance is subordinate
- Relations of audience with media are mutually calculative, not moral

Goals of Audience Research

Since the audience has always been a contested category, it is not surprising that the purposes of doing research into audiences are varied and often inconsistent. All research shares the general characteristic that it helps to 'construct', 'locate' or 'identify' an otherwise amorphous, shifting or unknowable social entity (Allor, 1988). But the methods used, the constructions of the audience arrived at, and the uses to which they are put all diverge considerably. Leaving aside the purpose of theory building, we can classify research goals in terms of the main uses to which information about the audience can be put. These are shown in Box 15.3.

Varied goals of audience research 15.3

Media-centred goals

- Measuring actual and potential reach for purposes of book-keeping and advertising (sales and ratings)
- Managing audience choice behaviour
- Looking for new audience market opportunities
- Product testing and improving effectiveness from the perspective of the sender

Audience-centred goals

- Meeting responsibilities to serve an audience
- Evaluating media performance from an audience perspective
- Charting audience motives for choice and use
- Uncovering audience interpretations of meaning
- Exploring the context of media use
- Assessing actual effects on audiences

Perhaps the most fundamental division of purpose is that between media industry goals and those that take the perspective and 'side' of the audience. Research can, as it were, represent the voice of the audience, or speak on its behalf. Although it is not at all sure that audience research can ever truly serve the audience alone, we can provisionally view the different purposes of research as extending along a dimension ranging from audience control to audience autonomy. This division approximates to that shown in Box 15.3. Eastman (1998) has sketched the history of audience research as a permanent tug-of-war between the media industry seeking to manage audience behaviour, and people seeking to satisfy their media needs.

By far the greatest quantity of audience research belongs at the control end of the spectrum, since this is what the industry wants and pays for (Beniger, 1986; Eastman, 1998). Few of the results of industry research appear in the public domain, and they are consequently neglected in academic accounts of the audience. Curiously enough, according to Eastman, scholarly research on the audience has made no impact on the media industry. Despite this overall imbalance and general disconnection of research effort, the clearest line of development in audience theory has been a move away from the perspective of the media communicator and towards that of the receiver. It seems as if the media industry has also accepted this as a pragmatic trend as a result of the steadily increasing competition for audience attention. Accounts of audience research have increasingly tended to emphasize the 'rediscovery' of people, in the sense of recognizing that the initiative for choice, interpretation and response lies primarily much more with receivers than with senders, and the notion of an active and obstinate audience in the face of attempted manipulation. The preferences of audiences are still the driving forces of media use.

Alternative Traditions of Research

For present purposes, it is convenient to identify three main traditions of research, under the headings 'structural', 'behavioural' and 'social-cultural'.

The structural tradition of audience measurement

The needs of media industries gave rise to the earliest and simplest kinds of research, which were designed to obtain reliable estimates of what were otherwise unknown quantities. These were especially the size and reach of radio audiences and the 'reach' of print publications (the number of potential readers as opposed to the circulation or print run). These data were essential to management, especially for gaining paid advertising. In addition to size, it was important to know about the social composition of audiences in basic terms – the who and where of the audience. These elementary needs gave rise to an immense industry interconnected with that of advertising and market research.

The behavioural tradition: media effects and media uses

Early mass communication research was mainly preoccupied with media effects, especially on children and young people and with an emphasis on potential harm. Nearly every serious effects study has also been an audience study, in which the audience is conceptualized as 'exposed' to influence or impact, whether of a persuasive, learning or behavioural kind. The typical effects model was a one-way process in which the audience was conceived as an unwitting target or a passive recipient of media stimuli. The second main type of 'behavioural' audience research was in many ways a reaction from the model of direct effects. Media *use* was now central, and the audience was viewed as a more or less active and motivated set of media users/consumers, who were 'in charge' of their media experience, rather than passive 'victims'. Research focused on the origin, nature and degree of motives for choice of media and media content. Audiences were also permitted to provide the definitions of their own behaviour (see Blumler and Katz, 1974). The 'uses and gratifications' approach is not strictly 'behavioural' since its main emphasis is on the social origins of media gratification and on the wider social functions of media, for instance in facilitating social contact and interaction or in reducing tension and anxiety.

The cultural tradition and reception analysis

The cultural studies tradition occupies a borderland between social science and the humanities. It has been almost exclusively concerned with works of popular culture, in contrast to an early literary tradition. It emphasizes media use as a reflection of a particular social-cultural context and as a process of giving meaning to cultural products and experiences in everyday life. This school of research rejects both the stimulus–response model of effects and the notion of an all-powerful text or message. It involves a view of media use as in itself a significant aspect of 'everyday life'. Media reception research emphasized the deep study of audiences as 'interpretative communities' (Lindlof, 1988). Drotner (2000) characterizes audience ethnography by three main features: it looks at a group of people rather than the media or content; it follows the group in different locations; and it stays long enough to avoid preconceptions. Reception analysis is effectively the audience research arm of modern cultural studies, rather than an independent tradition.

The main features of the culturalist (reception) tradition of audience research can be summarized as follows (though not all are exclusive to this approach):

- The media text has to be 'read' through the perceptions of its audience, which constructs meanings and pleasures from the media texts offered (and these are never fixed or predictable).
- The very process of media use and the way in which it unfolds in a particular context are central objects of interest.
- Media use is typically situation-specific and oriented to social tasks which evolve out of participation in 'interpretative communities' (Lindlof, 1988).

	Structural	Behavioural	Cultural
Main aims	Describe composition; enumerate; relate to society	Explain and predict choices, reactions, effects	Understand meaning of content received and of use in context
Main data	Social-demographic, media and time use	Motives; acts of choice; reactions	Perceptions of meaning regarding social and cultural context
Main methods	Survey and statistical analysis	Survey; experiment; mental measurement	Ethnographic; qualitative

Figure 15.1   Three audience research traditions compared

- Audiences for particular media genres often comprise separate 'interpretative communities' which share much the same forms of discourse and frameworks for making sense of media.
- Audiences are never passive, nor are all their members equal, since some will be more experienced or more active fans than others.
- Methods have to be 'qualitative' and deep, often ethnographic, taking account of content, act of reception and context together.

The three traditions are summarily compared in Figure 15.1.

There are some indications of increasing convergence in research approaches (Schrøder, 1987; Curran, 1990), especially in the combination of quantitative and qualitative methods. Large differences in underlying philosophy and conceptualization remain between the alternative schools, although increasing attention is being given to methodological issues raised by qualitative audience research (Barker, 2003; Hoijer, 2008).

Audience Issues of Public Concern

This brief review of alternative research approaches helps us to identify the main issues and problems that have shaped thinking and research about mass media audiences, aside from the obvious practical need to have basic information about the audience. As we will see, the transformation of a straight question about the audience into an 'issue' or a social problem normally requires the injection of some value judgements, as described in the following paragraphs.

Media use as addiction

'Excessive' media use has often been viewed as harmful and unhealthy (especially for children), leading to addiction, dissociation from reality, reduced social contacts, diversion from education and displacement of more worthwhile activities.

Television has been the most usual suspect, but previously films and comics were regarded similarly, while video games, computers and the Internet have become the latest perpetrators.

The mass audience and social atomization

The more an audience is viewed as an aggregate of isolated individuals rather than a social group, the more it can be considered as a mass with the associated negative features of irrationality, lack of normative self-control and vulnerability to manipulation. In a curious reversal of this fear of the mass, it has been argued that the contemporary fragmentation of the audience poses a new threat of loss of national cohesion, following the decline of central broadcasting institutions.

Audience behaviour as active or passive

In general, active is regarded as good and passive as bad, whether for children or adults. The media are criticized for offering mindless and soporific entertainment instead of original and stimulating content. The results are found, for instance, in escapism and diversion from social participation. Alternatively, the audience is criticized for choosing the easy path. While media use is by definition somewhat inactive, it can show signs of activity by way of selectivity, motivated attention and critical response.

Manipulation or resistance

Early formulations of the audience viewed it as readily available as an object of manipulation and control, open to suggestion and foolish in its adulation of media celebrity. The idea of an 'obstinate' audience was an early development in audience theory. Later, reception research emphasized the fact that audiences often have social and cultural roots and supports that protect them against unwanted influence and make for autonomy in choice and response to what they receive.

Minority audience rights

Inevitably, mass communication tends to work against the interests of small and minority audiences. An audience research project that is independent and people-centred should pay attention to the needs and interests of minorities by way of recognition and finding ways to promote their viability. In this context, minority covers a potentially wide range of factors, including gender, political dissent, locality, taste, age, ethnicity and much besides.

The implications of new media technology

Finally, there is the question of the future of the audience, especially in the light of changes in communication technology, making for abundance and interactivity (Livingstone, 2003). One proposition is that audiences (sets of users) will become more and more fragmented and atomized and lose their national, local or cultural identity. On the other hand, new kinds of integration based on interactivity may compensate for the loss of older forms of shared experience. More options for audience formation based on shared interests are available to more people and there could be greater freedom and choice.

Types of Audience

Audiences originate both in society and in media and their contents: either people stimulate an appropriate supply of content, or the media attract people to the content they offer. If we take the first view, we can consider media as responding to the needs of a national society, local community, pre-existing social group or some category of individuals that the media choose as a 'target group'. Alternatively, if we consider audiences as primarily created by the media, we can see that they are often brought into being by some new technology (as with the invention of film, radio or television) or they are attracted by some additional 'channel', such as a new magazine or radio station. In this case, the audience is defined by the media source (e.g. the 'television audience' or the 'readers of newspaper X') rather than by their shared characteristics.

The media are continuously seeking to develop and hold new audiences, and in doing so they anticipate what might otherwise be a spontaneous demand, or identify potential needs and interests which have not yet surfaced. In the continual flux of media audience formation and change, the sharp distinction made at the outset is not easy to demonstrate. Over time, media provision to pre-existing social groups has become hard to distinguish from media recruitment of social categories to the content offered. Media-created needs have also become indistinguishable from 'spontaneous' needs, or both have fused inextricably. Nevertheless, the theoretical distinction between receiver- and sender-created demand is a useful one for mapping out different versions of audience that have been introduced. The distinction is set out in Figure 15.2, first of all between society- and media-created needs and, secondly, between the different levels at which the process operates, namely macro or micro.

		Source	
		Society	Media
Level Macro		Social group or public	Medium audience
Micro		Gratification set	Channel or content audience

Figure 15.2 A typology of mass media audience formation

The four main types that are identified in Figure 15.2 are further described in the following sections.

The Audience as a Group or Public

Today, the most common example of a media audience which is also in some sense a social group is probably the readership of a local newspaper or the listener group of a community radio station. Here the audience shares at least one significant social/cultural identifying characteristic – that of shared space and membership of a residential community. Local media can contribute significantly to local awareness and sense of belonging (Janowitz, 1952; Stamm, 1985; McLeod et al., 1996; Rothenbuhler et al., 1996; Stamm et al., 1997). Local residence defines and maintains a wide range of media-relevant interests (e.g. leisure, environmental, work-related, social networks, etc.) and local media advertising serves local retail trade and labour markets as well as residents of the area. Social and economic forces together reinforce the integrative role of local media. Even if a local medium goes out of business, the local community that forms its audience will persist.

Beyond the case of local media, there are other circumstances where shared characteristics, relative homogeneity and stability of composition indicate the existence of some independent and group-like qualities in the audience. Newspapers are often characterized by readerships of varying political leaning, and readers express their political identity by their choice of paper as well as finding reinforcement for their beliefs. Newspapers and magazines may respond by shaping their contents and expressing opinions accordingly.

The conditions of society that militate against the formation of audiences as groups and publics include especially totalitarian government and very high levels of commercially monopolized media. In the first case, there is no autonomy for social groups; and in the second, audience members are treated as customers and consumers, but with little power in the media market to realize their diverse wants. There are some other relevant examples of audience groups and special publics. For example, the broad term 'radical' media (Downing, 2000) embraces a wide range of more or less oppositional media channels which can be considered to carry on the tradition of the early radical and party press, especially in developing countries. Many such media are 'micro-media', operating at grass-roots level, discontinuous, non-professional, sometimes persecuted or just illegal. The *samizdat* publications forbidden under communism, the opposition press in Pinochet's Chile, or the underground press of occupied Europe during the Second World War are well-known examples. The publics for such media are often small, but they are likely to be intensely committed. They usually have clear social and political goals. Less unusual and more enduring examples are provided by the many minority ethnic and linguistic publications and channels that have grown up in numerous countries to serve immigrant groups. New media have opened up new opportunities for the formation of very small audiences based on many different aims and identities and with the advantage of being able to serve very dispersed groups.

The Gratification Set as Audience

The term 'gratification set' is chosen to refer to multiple possibilities for audiences to form and re-form on the basis of some media-related interest, need or preference. The use of the word 'set' implies that such audiences are typically aggregates of dispersed individuals, without mutual ties. While the audience as 'public' often has a wide range of media needs and interests, and derives its unity from shared social characteristics, the 'gratification set' is identified by a particular need or type of need (which may, nevertheless, derive from social experience). To a certain degree, this type of audience has gradually supplanted the older kind of public, the result of differentiation of media production and supply to meet distinctive consumer demands. Instead of each public (whether based on place, social class, religion or party) having its own dedicated medium, many self-perceived needs have stimulated their own corresponding supply.

The phenomenon is not new since popular newspapers, as well as gossip, fashion and 'family' magazines, have long catered for a diverse range of specific but overlapping audience interests. More recently, the range of interests covered has widened, with each type of medium (film, book, magazine, radio, phonogram, etc.) packaging its potential audience appeal in a variety of ways. The sets of readers/viewers/listeners that result from a highly differentiated and 'customized' supply are unlikely to have any sense of collective identity, despite some shared social-demographic characteristics.

*   Relevant here is the concept of **'taste culture'** which was coined by Herbert Gans (1957) to describe something like the audience brought into being by the media based on a convergence of interests, rather than on shared locality or social background. He defined it as 'an aggregate of similar content chosen by the same people' (in Lewis, 1981: 204). Taste cultures are less sets of people than sets of similar media products – an outcome of form, style of presentation and genre which are intended to match the lifestyle of a segment of the audience. The more this happens, the more there is likely to be a distinctive social-demographic profile of a taste culture.

Research in the tradition of 'media uses and gratifications' has shed light on the nature of the underlying audience demands and on the way in which they are structured. The motivations expressed for choice of media content and the ways in which this content is interpreted and evaluated by the audience point to the existence of a fairly stable and consistent structure of demand. These points are taken up in Chapter 16.

The Medium Audience

The third version of the audience concept (Figure 15.2) is the one that identifies it by the choice of a particular type of medium – as in the 'television audience' or the 'cinema-going public'. The earliest such usage was in the expression the 'reading public' – the small minority who could and did read books when literacy was not very common. The reference is usually to those whose behaviour or self-perception identifies them as regular and attracted 'users' of the medium concerned.

Each medium – newspaper, magazine, cinema, radio, television, phonogram – has had to establish a new set of consumers or devotees, and the process continues with the diffusion of 'new media' such as the Internet or multimedia. It is not especially problematic to locate relevant sets of people in this way, but the further characterization of these audiences is often crude and imprecise, based on broad social-demographic categories.

This type of audience is close to the idea of a 'mass audience' as described above (p. 400), since it is often very large, dispersed and heterogeneous, with no internal organization or structure. It also corresponds to the general notion of a 'market' for a particular kind of consumer service. By now, most such audiences are so overlapping that there is little differentiation involved, except in terms of subjective affinity and relative frequency or intensity of use. The audience for any one mass medium is often identical with the audience for another.

The audience continues to distinguish between media according to their particular social uses and functions or according to their perceived advantages and disadvantages. Media have fairly distinctive images (Perse and Courtright, 1992). Research has shown that some media are substitutable for each other for certain purposes, while others have distinctive uses (Katz et al., 1973). Competition between different media for audience and advertising income is intense and these differences play a part. The 'medium audience' is an important concept for those who want to use the media for purposes of advertising and other campaigns, despite the lack of exclusivity. A key decision in advertising is often that concerning the 'media mix' – the division of an advertising budget between the alternatives, taking into account the characteristics of each medium, the audience it reaches and the conditions of reception.

In media economics, the issue of media *substitutability* continues to be important and often turns on the extent to which distinctive medium audiences persist (Picard, 1989). Several considerations come into play, aside from the questions of audience size and demographics. Some messages are best delivered in a domestic or family context, indicating a choice of television, while others may be individual and more *risqué*, indicating posters or magazines. Some may be appropriate in an informational context, others against a background of relaxation and entertainment. From this perspective, the medium audience as target is chosen not only on the basis of socio-economic characteristics, but with reference to typical content carried and the social-cultural associations and context of the media behaviours concerned.

The familiar division of the media landscape according to media type is yet another casualty of the rise of the Internet and other multimedia platforms. There is really no 'Internet audience' as such, in any meaningful sense, although it is possible to identify more or less intensive (even addicted) users and to classify use according to certain kinds of satisfaction obtained and in other ways.

Audience as Defined by Channel or Content

The identification of an audience as the readers, viewers or listeners of a *particular* book, author, film, newspaper title or television channel and programme is relatively straightforward. It is the usage with which audience research in the 'book-keeping' tradition is most comfortable, and it seems to pose few problems of empirical measurement. There are no hidden dimensions of group relations or consciousness to take account of, no psychological variables of motivation that need to be measured. It is the audience in this very concrete sense on which the business of the media turns most of all. For this reason, specific content or channel has usually been privileged as a basis for defining audiences, especially in industry-related research.

This version of audience is also consistent with market thinking, according to which audiences are sets of consumers for particular media products. The audience consists either of paying customers, or of the heads and pockets delivered to advertisers per unit of media product and charged for accordingly. It is expressed as the 'ratings', the 'numbers' which are central to the media business. It provides the main criteria of success in any game of media politics, even where profit is not involved. Increasingly, it is the dominant meaning of the term 'audience', the only one with immediate practical significance and clear market value. It also involves a view of the audience as a *product* of the media – the first and indubitable *effect* of any medium.

This sense of audience is a valid one, but we cannot be limited to it. There are, for instance, audiences in the sense of 'followers' or fans of television or radio serials and series, which cannot be unambiguously measured. There are also audiences for particular films, books, songs and also for stars, writers and performers, which only accumulate over time to a significant number or proportionate reach. In addition, content is often identified by audience according to genres, usually within the boundaries of a given medium. All of these are relevant aspects of the audience experience, though they usually evade any but the most approximate measurement.

This brings us to the yet more complex question of fans and *fandom*. The term can refer to any set of extremely devoted followers of a media star or performer, performance or text (Lewis, 1992). They are usually identified by great, even obsessive attachment to their object of attraction. Often they show a strong sense of awareness and fellow-feeling with other fans. Being a fan also involves a pattern of supplementary behaviour, in dress, speech, other media use, consumption, and so on. The topic of fandom is discussed in Chapter 16, pp. 442–3.

Questions of Audience Reach

The least problematic version of the audience concept is probably that which underlies the 'ratings' in their various forms. Media providers need to know a great deal about the extent of media reach (which is at the same time a measure of audience attention), for reasons of finance or policy or for organization and planning. These concerns create a strong vested interest in the 'canonical audience' referred to by Biocca (1988b: 127). This concept derives from the theatre and cinema and refers to a physical body of identifiable and attentive 'spectators'. A belief in the existence of such an audience is essential to the routine operation of media and provides a shared goal for the media organization (Tunstall, 1971). The fact of having an audience, and the right one as well, is a necessary condition of media organizational survival and it has to be continually demonstrated.

However, this requirement is less easy to meet than it seems because of the differences between media and different ways of defining the 'reach' of a given medium or message. Leaving intermedia differences aside, there are at least six relevant concepts of audience reach, as follows:

- the *available* (or potential) audience: all with the basic skills (e.g. literacy) and/or reception capability;
- the *paying* audience: those who actually pay for a media product, whether newspaper, film entrance, video rental, CD or book;
- the *attentive* audience: those who actually read, watch, listen, etc., to particular content;
- the *internal* audience: those who pay attention to particular sections, types or single items of content;
- the *cumulative* audience: the overall proportion of the potential audience that is reached over a particular period of time;
- the *target* audience: that section of a potential audience singled out for reach by a particular source (e.g. an advertiser).

There is also the question of listening or viewing as primary or secondary activity, since both can and do accompany other activities, radio more so than television. Conceptually, this is not very crucial, but it matters greatly for measurement (see Twyman, 1994). Other less conventional audiences can also be distinguished, for instance for outdoor billboards and video screens, direct mail, audiotext, telephone selling campaigns, and so on. The content and uses of old media also change. The terms and definitions presented here are not fixed. However, the principles of classification remain much the same and we can adapt these to new circumstances.

The basic features of audience reach, as viewed by the would-be communicator, are shown in Figure 15.3, derived from the work of the Belgian researcher Roger Clausse (1968). Although this model was developed for the case of broadcasting, it can apply, in principle, to all mass media to cover most of the distinctions made above. The outer band represents the almost unlimited potential for the reception of broadcast messages. In effect, it equates audience with a near-universal distribution system. The second band indicates the realistic maximum limits which apply to reception; these delineate the *potential* media public, which is defined by residence in a geographical area of reception, and by possession of the necessary apparatus to receive, or the means to purchase or borrow publications, phonograms, video recordings, and the like. It is also determined by the degree of literacy and possession of other necessary skills.

The third band identifies another level of media public – the *actual* audience reached by a radio or television channel or programme or any other medium. This is what is usually measured by sales, admission and subscription figures, reading surveys and audience ratings (often expressed as a percentage of the potential audience), and so on. The fourth and the central band relates to the *quality* of attention, degree of impact and potential effect, some of which are empirically measurable. In practice, only a small fragment of the total of *actual* audience behaviour can ever be measured and the rest is extrapolation, estimate or guesswork.

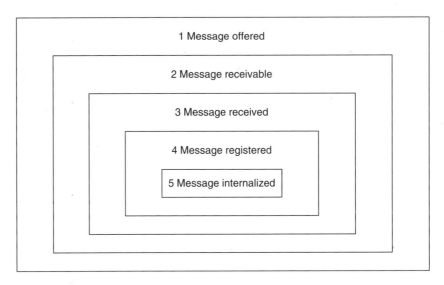

Figure 15.3   A schema of differential audience reach (Clausse, 1968)

From the point of view of the communicator, Figure 15.3 shows that there is a high degree of 'wastage' in mass communication, although this may not carry much extra cost. The question of differential reach and impact of mass media is of more than theoretical interest since it has to be taken into account in planning communication – especially in campaigns for commercial, political or informational ends (see Windahl et al., 1992). Most campaigns operate with a notion of a 'target group' (of voters, consumers, and the like) that becomes the audience which a campaign tries to reach.

Activity and Selectivity

Research into audience selectivity was originally stimulated by fears about the effects of mass communication. Critics of mass culture feared that a large and *passive* audience would be exploited and culturally harmed and that passive and unselective attention, especially by children, should be discouraged. In addition, the media, especially television, were thought to encourage passivity in children and adults alike (e.g. Himmelweit et al., 1958; Schramm et al., 1961). A distinction has been made between 'ritualized' and 'instrumental' patterns of use (Rubin, 1984). The former refers to habitual and frequent viewing by people with a strong affinity with the medium. Instrumental use is purposeful and selective, and thus more likely to qualify as active. Use of other media, especially radio, music and newspapers, can be similarly patterned. This version of the activity concept seems to imply that more active users are more sparing with their time.

The whole issue has also been defined in a normative way, with passivity as harmful, and active use of media as good. However, there are significant industry interests at stake, since too much audience activity can be interpreted as trouble for those who seek to control the audience by manipulation of programming and by exploiting the routine character and inertia of much media use (Eastman, 1998).

There has continued to be controversy about how active the typical media audience really is and about what activity means. The extensive and detailed studies of time use by Kubey and Csikszentmihalyi (1991), based on self-reports, leave little doubt about the generally uninvolving and secondary character of television viewing, although this should not be confused with lack of significance. On the other hand, reading and film going are likely to be more personally involving.

Biocca (1988a) has reviewed the different meanings and concepts of *audience activity*, proposing five different versions that are to be found in the literature, as follows:

- *Selectivity*. We can describe an audience as active, the more that choice and discrimination are exercised in relation to media and content within media. This is mainly likely to show up in evidence of planning of media use and in consistent patterns of choice (including buying, renting or borrowing films or books). Very heavy media use (especially of television) is likely to be accounted as by definition 'unselective' and therefore inactive.
- *Utilitarianism*. Here the audience is the 'embodiment of the self-interested consumer'. Media consumption represents the satisfaction of some more or less conscious need, such as those postulated in the 'uses and gratifications' approach.
- *Intentionality*. An **active audience**, according to this definition, is one which engages in active cognitive processing of incoming information and experience. It is often implied by the various forms of subscription to media. ✳
- *Resistance to influence*. Following the lines of the 'obstinate audience' concept (Bauer, 1964), the activity concept here emphasizes the limits set by members of the audience to unwanted influence or learning. The reader, viewer or listener remains 'in control' and unaffected, except as determined by personal choice.
- *Involvement*. In general, the more an audience member is 'caught up' or 'engrossed' in the ongoing media experience, the more we can speak of involvement. This can also be called 'affective arousal'. Involvement may also be indicated by such signs as 'talking back' to the television.

These different versions of the audience activity concept do not all relate to the same moment in the sequence of media exposure. As Levy and Windahl (1985) point out, they may relate to *advance* expectations and choice, or to activity *during* the experience, or to the *post-exposure* situation, for instance the transfer of satisfactions gained from the media to personal and social life (e.g. in conversation about media, or based upon media-derived topics).

There are some other aspects of active media use that may be missed by the five variants outlined. For instance, audience activity can take the form of direct response by letter or telephone, whether or not encouraged by the media. Local or community media, whether print or broadcast, may generally have more active audiences, or have more opportunity to do so. Critical reflection on media experience, whether openly expressed in 'feedback' or not, is another example of audience activity, as is conscious membership of a fan group or club.

In the case of television, audience appreciation ratings, which are either unusually high or low, often indicate the presence within a programme audience of a set of active viewers who respond very positively or very negatively. The act of recording and replaying from radio or television is another indication of above-average engagement. Finally, we can note the view, examined later in more detail, that audiences often participate in the media experience by giving meaning to it, thus actively *producing* the eventual media 'text' (Fiske, 1987, 1992).

The general notion of 'audience activity' is evidently an unsatisfactory concept. It is open to diverse definitions, its indicators are very mixed and ambiguous, and it means different things with different media. It is sometimes manifested in behaviour, but sometimes it is only a mentalistic construct (an attitude or feeling). According to Biocca, it is almost empty of meaning in general because it is *unfalsifiable*: 'It is, by definition, nearly impossible for the audience *not* to be active' (1988a: 59). This is even more true of interactive online media.

Conclusion

As we have seen, the apparently simple idea of an audience turns out to be quite complicated. The very concept is understood differently from quite different perspectives. For most of the media industry it is more or less the equivalent of a market for media services, and is categorized accordingly. From the point of view of the audience, or those who take the audience perspective, this view of an audience is peripheral or unrecognized. The audience experience as a social event or cultural event takes precedence. Being in an audience is often the outcome of quite varied motives. Yet other possibilities arise when the view of the sender or communicator is taken, in terms not of selling services but of trying to communicate meaning. Audiences may be thought of by communicators in terms of their tastes, interests, capacities or their social composition and their location. The situation is even more complicated by the arrival of new means of communication, with implications for many of the factors mentioned.

Further Reading

Alasuutari, P. (ed.) (1999) *Rethinking the Media Audience*. London: Sage.
Assembles a strong and varied collection of articles on the application of qualitative reception research.

LaRose, R. and Estin, M.S. (2004) 'A social cognitive theory of internet use and gratifications: towards a new model of media attendance', *Journal of Broadcasting and Electronic Media*, 48 (3): 358–77.
This exploratory article sets out a number of relatively new kinds of gratification as offered by the Internet.

Liebes, T. and Katz, E. (1990) *The Export of Meaning: Cross-cultural Readings of 'Dallas'*. Oxford: Oxford University Press.

Although not the first to demonstrate the alternative readings of popular television fiction, it was very influential on research, especially because it demonstrated such a clear cross-cultural dimension.

Rosengren, K.-E., Palmgreen, P. and Wenner, L. (eds) (1985) *Media Gratification Research: Current Perspectives*. Beverly Hills, CA: Sage.
Although it can no longer count as current, this collection of chapters on theory and research in the uses and gratifications tradition marks a high point and a useful source for reconsideration and rescue, where appropriate.

Ross, S.M. (2008) *Beyond the Box*. Malden, MA: Blackwell.
An exploration of the ways in which the coming of the Internet is changing the way television is viewed and especially the way in which fans participate in the experience and connect with each other. Main illustrations are with reference to *American Idol* and *Buffy the Vampire Slayer*.

Online Readings

Bakker, P. and Sadaba, C. (2008) 'The impact of the Internet on users', in S. Küng et al. (eds), *The Internet and the Mass Media*, pp. 86–101. London: Sage.

Bermejo, F. (2009) 'Audience manufacture in historical perspective: from broadcasting to Google', *New Media and Society*, 11 (1/2): 133–154.

Finn, S. (1997) 'Origins of media exposure: linking personality traits, TV radio, print and film use', *Communication research*, 24 (5): 507–29.

Kitzinger, J. (2004) 'Audience and Readership research', in J.D.H. Downing, D. McQuail, P. Schlesinger and E. Wartella (eds), *The Sage Handbook of Media Studies*, pp. 167–82. Thousand Oaks, CA: Sage.

Vandebosch, H. (2000) 'A captive audience? The media use of prisoners', *European Journal of Communication*, 15 (4): 529–44.

16

Audience Formation and Experience

This chapter looks at the reasons why audiences form in the first place – essentially the motives for attending to mass media and the satisfactions expected or derived. There are different theories about this, since being in the audience not only is the result of personal choice, but also depends on what is available to choose from, our social milieu or lifestyle, and the circumstances of the moment. The chapter is also concerned with other aspects of the audience experience, including its relationship to the social and cultural context. Media use is a social and often sociable activity and is governed to some extent by expectations and norms that vary from place to place and the type of media involved. Finally, the chapter looks at the implications of changing media for the audience, especially the question of the decline of the mass audience.

The 'Why' of Media Use

In line with earlier remarks, we can approach the question of accounting for media use either from the 'side' of the audience, asking what influences individual choices and behaviours, or from the side of the media, asking what factors of content, presentation and circumstance help to draw and keep audience attention. There is no sharp division between the two since questions of personal motivation cannot be answered without some reference to media products and contents.

We can also choose to follow one or more of the audience research schools described in Chapter 15, each of which suggests a somewhat different kind of explanation for media use behaviour. The 'structural' tradition emphasizes the media system and the social system as primary determinants; the behavioural (functionalist) approach takes individual needs, motives and circumstances as the starting point; while the social-cultural approach emphasizes the particular context in which an audience member is located and the way in which media alternatives are valued and given meaning. As we have seen, each approach has different theoretical foundations and entails different kinds of research strategy and methods.

A good deal is known about the general factors shaping audience behaviour, which has been quite stable and predictable (see, for example, Bryant and Zillman, 1986), although changing. Broad patterns of attention to media alter only slowly and usually for obvious reasons, such as a change in media structure (e.g. the rise of a new medium) or because of some wider social change (e.g. the development of a youth culture or the transition from communism to capitalism). For instance, the long dominance of American television by three big networks lasted forty or so years and in Europe, similarly, viewing was monopolized by two or three channels before the audience broke up at the turn of the century. There are always random influences and chance combinations of factors, but audience research is mostly a matter of routine recording of very predictable outcomes. Such mystery as there is relates to questions of detailed choice within a media sector, between channels or products, or concerns the success or failure of some specific innovation or item of content. If there were no mystery, the media business would not be as risky as it is and every film, song, book or show could be a hit.

These remarks are a reminder that there has always been a disjunction between the *general* pattern of mass media use and what happens on a day-to-day basis. In one respect this can be understood as the difference between a long-term average, based on much data, and the observation of a single case, where the latter might be one day's pattern or one person's habitual media use. As individuals, we usually have a fairly stable pattern of media preferences, choices and time use (although one 'pattern' may be of instability), but each day's media experience is unique and affected by varying and unpredictable circumstances.

In the following sections we look at some alternative theoretical models for accounting for the recruitment and composition of media audiences.

A Structural Approach to Audience Formation

The basic premise, as indicated already, is that media use is largely shaped by certain relatively constant elements of social structure and media structure. Social structure refers to 'social facts' such as those of education, income, gender, place of residence, position in the life-cycle, and so on, which have a strong determining influence on general outlook and social behaviour. Media structure refers to the relatively constant array of channels, choices and content that is available in a given place and time. The media system responds to pressures and to feedback from audiences, so as to maintain a stable self-regulating balance between supply and demand.

The processes at work are sketched in the model shown in Figure 16.1, slightly adapted from Weibull (1985), which depicts the relationship between that habitual pattern of media use behaviour and the particular choices, for instance on a given day. In the figure, the upper section shows an individual's habitual pattern of media use as an outcome of two main factors which themselves reflect the overall social structure. One is the more or less fixed *social situation* in which a person is located along with the associated media-related *needs* (e.g. for certain information, relaxation, social contact, and the like). The second factor (shown as 'mass media structure') consists of the available media possibilities in the particular place, given a person's economic and educational circumstances. Between them, these two factors lead not only to a regular pattern of *behaviour*, but also to a fairly constant disposition, tendency or 'set', which is called a person's *media orientation*. This is a joint outcome of social background and past media experience and takes the form of an affinity for certain media, specific preferences and interests, habits of use, expectations of what the media are good for, and so on (see McLeod and McDonald, 1985; McDonald, 1990; Ferguson and Perse, 2000). This provides the connection to what is contained in the lower part of the figure. Here we find the particular daily situation in which specific choices of media and content are made. These are likely to be influenced by three main variables:

- the specific daily menu of content on offer and the form of presentation (shown as 'media content');
- the circumstances of the moment, for instance amount of free time, availability to attend, range of alternative activities available (labelled as 'individual's circumstances');
- the social context of choice and use, for example the influence of family and friends.

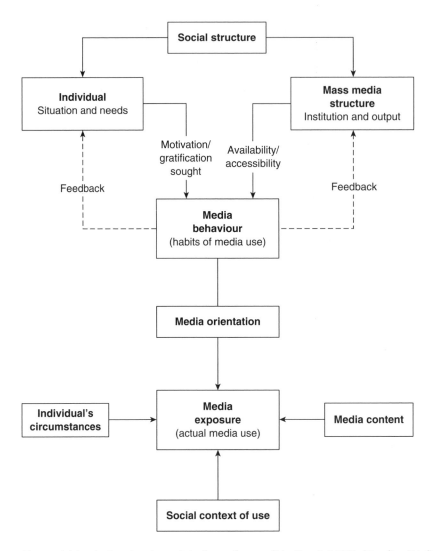

Figure 16.1   A structural model of media use (McQuail, 1997: 69, after Weibull, 1985)

Up to a point, what happens on a day-to-day basis is predictable from a person's 'media orientation', but the specifics are contingent on many unpredictable circumstances.

Weibull has tested this model with newspaper reading and concluded that 'when an individual is highly motivated to obtain specific gratifications (for instance, a particular item of sports news) he or she is less affected by media structure ... Individuals with less interest in the media seem to be more influenced by specific contents or by content composition' (1985: 145). This is a reminder of the high degree of freedom we all have in principle to deviate from the general patterns arising from social and media structure. It also helps to explain why evidence about general tastes and preferences does not have a great short-term or individual predictive value.

While many features of daily media use can be traced back to their origins in social and media structure, this kind of model is no more than a preliminary orientation to the question of actual audience formation, which is based on many personal choices. It does have the advantage, however, of showing the connection between a media system (or structure) and an individual audience member's social position. The media system reflects the given facts of a society (e.g. economic, cultural and geographical conditions) and also responds to audience demands, which are partly determined by social background factors, partly those that are idiosyncratic and contingent.

The Uses and Gratifications Approach

The idea that media use depends on the perceived satisfactions, needs, wishes or motives of the prospective audience member is almost as old as media research itself. As noted in Chapter 15, audiences are often formed on the basis of similarities of individual need, interest and taste. Many of these appear to have a social or psychological origin. Typical of such 'needs' are those for information, relaxation, companionship, diversion or 'escape'. Audiences for particular media and kinds of media content can often be typified according to such broad motivational types. The approach has also been applied to studying the appeal of new electronic media (Perse, 1990) and even to uses of the telephone (Dimmick and Rothenbuhler, 1984). Relative affinity with different media is associated with differences of expectation and gratifications sought.

This way of thinking belongs to a research school which became known as the 'uses and gratifications approach', the origins of which lie in the search for explanations of the great appeal of certain staple media contents. The central question posed is: *why* do people use media, and what do they use them for? Functionalist sociology (see Wright, 1974) viewed the media as serving the various needs of the society – for example, for cohesion, cultural continuity, social control and a large circulation of public information of all kinds. This, in turn, presupposes that individuals also use media for related purposes, such as personal guidance, relaxation, adjustment, information and identity formation.

The first such research dates from the early 1940s, and focused on the reasons for the popular appeal of different radio programmes, especially 'soap operas' and quizzes, and also looked at daily newspaper reading (Lazarsfeld and Stanton, 1944, 1949). These studies led to some unexpected findings, for instance that daytime radio soap operas, although often dismissed as superficial and mindless stories to fill time, were also found significant by their (women) listeners. They provided a source of advice and support, a role model of housewife and mother, or an occasion for emotional release through laughter or tears (Herzog, 1944; Warner and Henry, 1948). From talking to newspaper readers, it was also discovered that these were more than just sources of useful information, but also important for giving readers a sense of security, shared topics of conversation and a structure to the daily routine (Berelson, 1949).

Uses and gratifications rediscovered

The basic assumptions of the approach when it was rediscovered and elaborated twenty years later (in the 1960s and 1970s) were as follows.

- Media and content choice is generally rational and directed towards certain specific goals and satisfactions (thus the audience is active and audience formation can be logically explained).
- Audience members are conscious of the media-related needs which arise in personal (individual) and social (shared) circumstances and can voice these in terms of motivations.
- Broadly speaking, cultural and aesthetic features of content play much less part in attracting audiences than the satisfaction of various personal and social needs (e.g. for relaxation, shared experience, passing time, etc.).
- All or most of the relevant factors for audience formation (motives, perceived or obtained satisfactions, media choices, background variables) can, in principle, be measured.

In line with these assumptions, the process of media selection was described by Katz et al. (1974: 20) as being concerned with:

(1) the social and psychological origins of (2) needs which generate (3) expectations of (4) the mass media or other sources which lead to (5) differential exposure (or engaging in other activities), resulting in (6) need gratification and (7) other consequences.

A longer-term aim of the research school was to reach some general theoretical framework within which to place the many particular findings about audience motivations. McQuail et al. (1972), after studying a number of different radio and TV programmes in Britain, proposed a scheme of 'media–person interactions' (a term which reflects the dual origin of the media gratification concept) that capture the most important media satisfactions. This is shown in Box 16.1.

16.1 A typology of media–person interactions (McQuail et al., 1972)

- *Diversion*: escape from routine or problems, emotional release
- *Personal relationships*: companionship, social utility
- *Personal identity*: self-reference, reality exploration, value reinforcement
- *Surveillance* (forms of information seeking)

A more psychological version of the theory of audience motivation was suggested by McGuire (1974), based on the general theory of human needs. He distinguished first between cognitive and affective needs, then added three further dimensions: 'active' versus 'passive' initiation; 'external' versus 'internal' goal orientation; and orientation to 'growth' or to 'stability'. When interrelated, these factors yield 16 different types of motivation which apply to media use. For instance, the motivation to read newspapers in order to attain cognitive consistency (meaning essentially to bring one's opinions into line with those of like-minded others and other relevant information) belongs to the category of active, externally-directed behaviour that is oriented to maintaining stability. An example of an effective type of motive would be watching television drama 'in order to find models of personal behaviour'. This type of motive is also active, but internal to the person and oriented to growth and change rather than stability. In the nature of psychological theory of this kind, the media user is unlikely to be conscious of the underlying causes of motivations, expressed in these terms. Even so, there has been some research that shows a relationship between the McGuire factors and different motivational patterns of television use (Conway and Rubin, 1991).

There have been a number of other attempts to write a model of the uses and gratifications process. Renckstorf (1996) has outlined a 'social action' model of audience choice, based on symbolic interactionism and phenomenology. Essentially, he sees media use as a form of social action, shaped by a personal definition of the situation and oriented towards solving some newly perceived 'problem' in the social environment, or as an everyday routine designed to deal with unproblematic situations.

Comment on uses and gratifications theory

This general approach was criticized in its own time as being too behaviourist and functionalist. It also failed to provide much successful prediction or causal explanation of media choice and use (McQuail, 1984). The reasons for poor prediction may lie partly in difficulties of measurement of motives and partly in the fact that much media use is actually very circumstantial and weakly motivated. The approach seems to work best in relation to specific types of content where motivation might be present, for example in relation to political content (Blumler and McQuail, 1968), news (Levy, 1977, 1978) or erotica (Perse, 1994). In fact, the connection between attitude to the media and media use behaviour is actually quite weak and the direction of the relationship is often uncertain. Typologies of 'motives' often fail to match patterns of actual selection or use, and it is hard to find a logical, consistent and sequential relation between the three factors of *liking/preference*, actual *choosing* and subsequent *evaluation*.

The extent to which audience behaviour is guided by specific and conscious motives has always been in dispute. Babrow (1988) proposed that we think more in terms of 'interpretative frameworks', based on experience. Thus, some audience choice is meaningful in terms of such frameworks, while other exposure is based only on habit and reflex and may be considered unmotivated (Rubin, 1984). These ideas are in line with the concept of 'media orientation' introduced earlier in this chapter and the idea of a general preference set included in Figure 16.3.

In discussing the status of 'uses and gratifications' theory, Blumler (1985) made a distinction, based on extensive evidence, between 'social origins' and ongoing social experiences. The former seem to go with predictable constraints on the range of choice as well as with compensatory, adjustment-oriented, media expectations and uses. The latter – ongoing experience and current social situation – are much less predictable in their effects. They often go with 'facilitatory' media uses – with positive choice, and application, of media for personally chosen ends. This means that media use is an outcome of forces in society, of the personal biography of the individual and also of immediate circumstances. The *causes* of audience formation are located in the past as well as in the very immediate present and at points in between. It is not surprising that attempts at general *explanation* of actual audience realities have had so little success.

The steady diversification of the media environment has made it even more difficult to find any single explanatory framework of audience patterns. It is likely that an increasing amount of media use can only be explained by reference to 'media side factors' (see Figure 16.3), especially specific content and publicity. The approach is appropriate for application to the Internet and other new media, especially for comparison and description, and is increasingly being applied (Perse and Dunn, 1998; Kaye and Johnson, 2002; Livingstone, 2002; Webster and Lin, 2002).

Expectancy-value theory

Essential to most theory concerning personal motivations for media use is the idea that the media offer rewards which are expected (thus predicted) by potential members of an audience, on the basis of relevant past experience. These rewards can be thought of as psychological effects which are valued by individuals (they are sometimes called media 'gratifications'). Such rewards can be derived from media use as such (e.g. 'having a good read') or from certain favourite genres (e.g. detective stories) or actual items of content (a particular film), and they provide guidance (or feedback) for subsequent choices, adding to the stock of media-relevant information. A model of the process involved has been proposed by Palmgreen and Rayburn (1985), based on the principle that attitudes (towards media) are an outcome of empirically located beliefs and also of values (and personal preferences). The resulting 'expectancy-value' model is depicted in Figure 16.2.

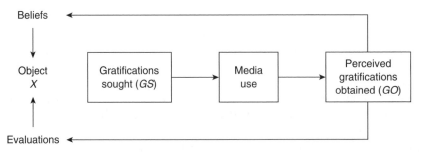

Figure 16.2   An expectancy-value model of media gratifications sought and obtained (Palmgreen and Rayburn, 1985)

The elements in the model are formally related as follows:

$$GS_i = b_i e_i$$

where GS_i is the ith gratification sought from some media object X (medium, programme or content type); b_i is the belief (subjective probability) that X possesses some attribute or that a behaviour related to X will have a particular outcome; and e_i is the affective evaluation of the particular attribute or outcome.

In general, the model expresses the proposition that media use is accounted for by a combination of *perception* of benefits offered by the medium and the differential *value* of these benefits for the individual audience member. This helps to cover the fact that media use is shaped by *avoidance* as well as by varying degrees of positive choice among the potential gratifications expected from the media. The model distinguishes between expectation (gratifications sought) and satisfaction (gratifications obtained) and identifies an *increment* over time from media use behaviour. Thus, where *GO* (gratifications obtained) is noticeably higher than *GS* (gratifications sought) we are likely to be dealing with situations of high audience satisfaction and high ratings of appreciation and attention. The reverse pattern can also occur, providing clues to falling circulation, sales or ratings, and channel switching in the case of television. This theoretical refinement has not altered the fact that audience motivational theory is not easy to translate into a sharp empirical tool.

An overview of the main gratifications from media use that have been identified is given in Box 16.2.

Media gratifications sought or obtained 16.2

- Information and education
- Guidance and advice
- Diversion and relaxation
- Social contact (see Box 16.3)
- Value reinforcement
- Cultural satisfaction
- Emotional release
- Identity formation and confirmation
- Lifestyle expression
- Security
- Sexual arousal
- Filling time

An Integrated Model of Audience Choice

We can combine a number of the influences on media choice into a single heuristic model, which provides a guide to understanding the sequential process of audience formation. The

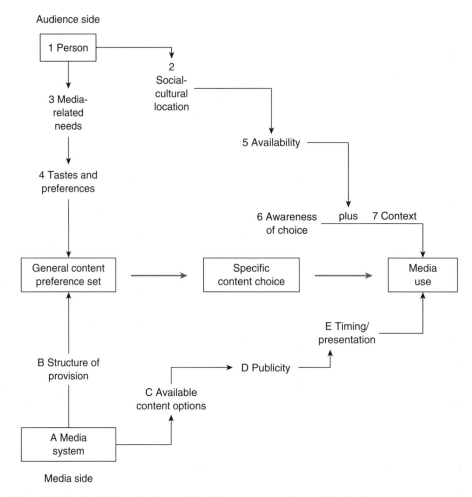

Figure 16.3   An integrated model of the process of media choice

main entries in the model (Figure 16.3) operate either on the 'audience side' of the media–person interaction or on the 'media side'. While described separately, the two sets of factors are not independent of each other but the result of a continuing process of mutual orientation and adjustment. The form of the model as presented here was influenced initially by the work of Webster and Wakshlag (1983), who sought to explain television viewer choice in a similar way. The version shown here is intended, in principle, to apply to all mass media and not just television. First, the main explanatory factors can be introduced.

'Audience side' factors

1 *Personal attributes* of age, gender, family position, study and work situation, level of income; also 'lifestyle', if relevant. There is some indication that personality differences may play a part (see Finn, 1997).

2 *Social background and milieu*, especially as reflected in social class, education, religious, cultural, political and family environment and region or locality of residence. We can also refer here to what Bourdieu (1986) calls 'cultural capital' – learnt cultural skills and tastes, often transmitted intergenerationally by way of family, education and the class system.

3 *Media-related needs*, of the kind discussed above, for such personal benefits as company, distraction, information, and so on. These needs are widely experienced, but the particular balance between them depends on personal background and circumstances.

4 *Personal tastes and preferences* for certain genres, formats or specific items of content.

5 *General habits of leisure time media use* and availability to be in the audience at a particular time. Since media are used in space as well as time, availability also refers to being in the appropriate places to receive (e.g. at home, in trains, driving, etc.). Availability also refers to the economic potential to be in an audience, for instance being able and willing to pay the price of a cinema ticket or a music recording.

6 *Awareness* of the choices available and the amount and kind of information possessed also play a part in audience formation. More active audience members can be expected to plan their media use accordingly.

7 *Specific context of use*. This varies according to medium but generally refers to sociability and location of use. Most relevant is whether one is alone or in company (friends, family, others). Where media are used (e.g. at home, work, travelling, in a cinema, etc.) can also influence the character of the experience as well as the process of choice-making.

8 *Chance* often plays a part in media exposure, and its intervention reduces the ability to really *explain* choice or audience composition.

'Media side' factors

A *The media system*. Preferences and choices are influenced by the makeup of the (national) media system (number, reach and type of media available) and by the specific characteristics of different media outlets.

B *Structure of media provision*. This refers to the general pattern of what the media provide in a given society, which exerts a long-term influence on audience expectations.

C *Available content options*. The specific formats and genres that are on offer to the potential audience at particular times and places.

D *Media publicity*. This includes advertising and image-making by the media on their own behalf as well as intensive marketing of some media products.

E *Timing and presentation*. Media selection and use are likely to be influenced by specific strategies of timing, scheduling, placement, content and design of the media message according to competitive audience-gaining strategies. This factor is less influential due to time-shifting possibilities, but remains valid.

Figure 16.3 represents the general process of choice-making, in which influences of both kinds (from society and from media) are shown sequentially according to their relative 'distance' from the moment of choice or attention (*media use*). Most distant (and more or less fixed) are social and cultural background and (for most adults at least) general sets of tastes and preferences, likes and interests. Thus, our social background has a strongly orienting and dispositional influence on our choice behaviour.

The other, almost equally distant (but less constant) factor is the general makeup of different media and the mix of genres, of which we have accumulated knowledge and experience. There is both a cognitive and an evaluative aspect to our dispositions (see the expectancy-value model above).

Personal knowledge of this kind and the related attitudes shape our tastes and preferences. The combination of the two (perception and evaluation) leads to a *general content preference set*. This is a hypothetical construct, but it shows up in consistent and thus predictable patterns of choice-making and also in more or less coherent patterns and types of media usage (these are close to what are sometimes called 'taste cultures'). We can think of it in terms of the 'repertoire' of available sources and content types with which we are familiar and from which we make actual choices (see Heeter, 1988). It is also very close to Weibull's 'media orientation' in the structural model (see Figure 16.1) and includes affinity for media as well as for types of content. Patterns of choice-making are, of course, always adapted according to changes in circumstances and experience with the media. There is a continuous process of response, feedback, learning and evaluation.

At a point much closer in time or place to media use, the circumstances of the potential audience member and the availability of the media coincide, resulting in actual audiences. These are never fully predictable, although the broad shape in aggregate terms is, as noted above, rather constant. It is the internal composition that is always shifting, since individual choice behaviour is affected by circumstances.

The complexity and multiplicity of audience formation preclude any simple descriptions or single theoretical explanation. We can certainly conclude that audiences are rarely what they seem from ratings alone. They are often shifting aggregates without clear boundaries. Motives and orientations are always mixed. Sometimes there are no motives. Even if motives were clearer and less mixed, they would not be 'readable' from the content alone, although in an efficient media market we may suppose that content and audience composition are well matched. There are enormous inbuilt uncertainties that cannot be eliminated. Nevertheless, within the complexity and seeming confusion there are some islands of stability and order – occasions where people and media meet to mutual satisfaction and stay with each other. However, this state is one that, by definition, is not easy to achieve by manipulation and publicity, but comes either from genuine social needs or from chance conjunctures of media creativity and public taste.

Public and Private Spheres of Media Use

As noted, certain forms of media use have a distinctly public character, both in the sense of taking place outside the home (as with cinema or concerts) and also in having a wider significance as a shared response to public performances and to public events. Saenz (1994: 576) refers to the continued significance of a 'widely shared, collectively appreciated performance, an immediate delivery ... to a large and general audience'. He adds: 'The sense of performance and cultural currency in television programming constitutes an important dimension in viewers' appreciation of television drama as a prominent cultural event.' The term 'public' can have a reference to the type of content, the location of an event and also to the degree of shared, collective experience.

Mass media which are located in their use primarily in the home (especially television, video, music and books) can be considered to bridge the gap between the private, domestic world and the concerns and activities of the wider society. Under some conditions, being a member of an audience has the meaning of sharing in the wider life of society, while in other circumstances it is a self-initiated experience which may be entirely personal or shared only by a small circle of friends or family members. It is not so much the physical location of the audience experience (for instance, cinema and theatre versus home) which matters as the definition of its meaning as more public or more private.

The public type of audiencehood is typified by occasions of consciously motivated attention to reports of events which are of wide social significance (e.g. election results, major disasters, world crises), or which involve the watching of major live sporting events on television (Rothenbuhler, 1987) or big entertainment events (e.g. live concerts). Public audience experience normally involves some degree of identification with a wider social grouping – whether defined as fans, or citizens, or a local population, or a taste culture. It may also be an experience associated with some more or less public role, for instance citizen, voter or worker. Increasingly, this version of audiencehood involves a cross-over with the Internet, which serves to construct a network of contacts in response to mass media content.

In their study of 'media events', Dayan and Katz (1992) draw attention to a special category of occasions when the media (especially television) unite a population in a near-ritual manner to celebrate and join in some wider national or global experience. Such media events are always special and constitute interruptions of routine. Aside from their significance, they are typically pre-planned, remote and live. Rothenbuhler (1998) developed the concept of ritual communication to apply to participation by way of the media in the rites and ceremonies of public life. To be in the (media) audience for such events is to participate more fully in the public life of the nation or another significant membership group. This research reminds us again of the collective character of 'audiencehood'.

The private type of audience experience is constructed according to personal mood and circumstance and does not involve any reference to society or even to other people. When not purely introspective, it is likely to be concerned with self-comparison and matching with a media model, role or personality in the search for an acceptable identity for public self-presentation. The difference between the public and the private type of audience experience depends on a combination of factors: the type of medium and content and the frame of mind of (or definition supplied by) the audience member. Expansion and development of media seem to be opening up relatively more possibilities for private audiencehood, by bringing more of media experience within the control of the individual to choose at will (see Neuman, 1991). Put differently, the fragmentation of audiences is reducing the public significance of audience experience.

Subculture and Audience

Early critics of 'mass society' theory pointed to the high degree of social differentiation of the seemingly homogeneous 'mass' audience. As media industries have developed and sought more new and 'niche' audience markets they have needed no persuasion on this point, and have even entered the business of trying to define and create new social and cultural subgroups, based on taste or lifestyle, with which potential media consumers might identify. There is a continuous process of creating media-based styles or pseudo-identities which are intended to strike a responsive chord in an audience.

Nevertheless, media use is always likely to be shaped predominantly according to early experience and identifications forged in personal social life or in line with the social context of the moment. After the particular social milieu of one's family comes the peer group of school classmates or neighbourhood friends which influences taste and media consumption, especially in respect of music and television – the two most popular media for the young. There are many layers of differentiation, aside from the sometimes fine age grading of youthful preferences (von Feilitzen, 1976; Livingstone, 2002) and the general separation out of a 'youth culture' as distinct from that of adults. Young adult experience is reshaped by social contacts at work and in leisure. Such general environmental influences are cross-cut by many other specific factors, not least that of gender.

There is much evidence that media use can play an important role in the expression and reinforcement of identity for subgroups of different kinds (Hebdige, 1978). This is not surprising, since media are part of 'culture', but there is a particular point in noting the strong connection between more deviant and alternative subcultures in modern society and, especially, youth musical taste (Murdock and Phelps, 1973; Avery, 1979; Roe, 1992). The focus of resistance to dominant forces of society has often been music and dance forms which are appropriated by subcultures and become a symbol of resistance (Hall and Jefferson, 1975; Lull, 1992). Much of what counts as modern music is perennially anathema to parents, teachers and established society generally. Rap music has been accused of demeaning women, and cults of violence disseminated in rap lyrics have been linked to extreme cases of unmotivated killing (as at Columbine High School).

Lifestyle

The concept of lifestyle has often been used in describing and categorizing different patterns of media use, often as part of a constellation of other attitudes and behaviour (e.g. Eastman, 1979; Frank and Greenberg, 1980; Donohew et al., 1987; Vyncke, 2002). The pioneering work of the French sociologist Pierre Bourdieu (1986) represents a long tradition of inquiry relating various expressions of cultural taste with social and family background. In one respect, the lifestyle concept offers an escape from the presumption that media taste (unlike traditional aesthetic and artistic taste) is determined by social class and education, since lifestyles are, to some extent, self-chosen patterns of behaviour and media use choice.

In commercial marketing research, the lifestyle concept is helpful for classifying consumers into various types in ways which assist the targeting and design of advertising. For such purposes it is desirable to go beyond basic social-demographic categories and to make finer distinctions, especially with psychological dimensions. The combination of demographic and psychological characteristics has been referred to as 'psychographics'. Lifestyle research involves studying a wide range of social positional variables, behaviours (including media use and other leisure and consumption practices) and attitudes, tastes and values. There is in fact no limit to the potential scope of such research or, perhaps, to the number of media-relevant lifestyles which can be identified (see Finn, 1997). Vyncke (2002) has described the construction of a typology intended to indicate segmented lifestyles. He found that the inclusion of media use variables significantly increased the power of the typology to discriminate. This suggests that media use plays an important role in expressing and forming lifestyle identity.

Johansson and Miegel (1992) distinguish three levels of analysis: that of the whole society (for international comparisons), that of differences within societies and cultures, and that of the individual. One of the main problems with the concept is finding an appropriate level. The second level is the most commonly applied, often with rather confusing results. Of the third level, they say that 'lifestyles are expressions of individuals' ambitions to create their own specific, personal, social and cultural identities' (1992: 23). There are potentially as many lifestyles as there are individuals. Nevertheless, the concept is helpful in understanding the many different ways in which media are meaningfully interrelated with social and cultural experience.

Gendered Audiences

The idea that media use is notably and persistently 'gendered' has also been developed in reception research, under the influence of feminist theory (Seiter et al., 1989). The differentiation of media use according to sex has long been recognized, and certain types of media are specifically produced for female audiences, often by women, especially perhaps certain magazines (Ferguson, 1983) and types of fiction (e.g. romance). Male audiences are also served by distinctive media types and genres. What is new is a greater curiosity about the meaning of these differences and a search for an understanding of how the social construction of gender also influences media choice and vice versa.

Gendered audience experience is a complex outcome of a certain kind of media content, typical everyday routines and the wider structure of what may still be described as 'patriarchal society' – or a 'man's world' as far as power is concerned. A much-cited example is Radway's (1984) research into one set of devoted (that is, really addicted) women readers of mass-produced romance fiction. Radway set out to account for the compulsive appeal of romance fiction by accepting in the first instance the main explanations offered by women readers themselves. From this perspective, romances offer an escape specifically designed for women, first by way of the act of reading, which establishes a private 'space' and time protected from incursion by husbands and family duties, and secondly by providing versions, albeit in fantasy form, of the ideal romance, which can be emotionally nurturing.

The notion of gendered audience has also been invoked in relation to another genre which attracts a largely female audience – that of radio and television 'soap operas' (e.g. Hobson, 1982, 1989; Allen, 1989; Geraghty, 1991) (see Chapter 14, p. 390). Studies have linked their narrative form (continuity, indeterminacy) to typical features of the housewife's daily routine, which is fragmented and distracted (preventing continuous attention) but also flexible. Soap operas in general are significantly preferred and more watched by women, even when they recognize the low status of the genre (e.g. Alasuutari, 1992). Ethnographic research into female soap opera viewers indicates that the genre is widely appropriated as especially meant for women and often serves for conversation and reflection about viewers' own everyday experiences (Livingstone, 1988).

In respect of the audience for women's magazines, Hermes (1995) identified a set of interpretative 'repertoires' or structures of meaning in terms of which women readers account for their reading behaviour and their relative attraction to the different varieties of the genre (ranging from feminist to traditional publications). Repertoires refer, for instance, to the sense of duty to support the cause of women or the mild guilt at reading traditional women's magazines. These sets of ideas are often mutually inconsistent or in dialogue with each other, but contradictions are made easier to handle by the relative lack of significance attached to the magazine medium by even their most faithful readers.

The essence of a gendered audience is not the sex ratio of its composition, but the degree to which conscious membership of an audience (audiencehood) is given some distinct meaning in terms of specific female or male experience. There are numerous indications in research into media use that gendered differences are associated with different preferences and satisfactions. For instance, Anderson et al. (1996) found that stressed women watched more game and variety shows, while stressed men watched more action and violent programming, thus accentuating differences which show up in the general audience. Despite gender difference, there is much evidence of shared purpose, behaviour and understanding across gender lines.

Another aspect of audience gendering is the degree to which the complex social act of using a domestic medium such as television is influenced by relations between the sexes and by particular sex roles. The classic exploration is probably that of Morley (1986), whose ethnographic study of family viewing emphasized the many unwritten rules, understandings and patterns of behaviour that develop in the micro-audience environment of even one family. Typically, the power to control (evening) viewing was exercised by the man (see also Lull, 1982).

Women, in general, were found less likely to plan viewing or to watch continuously. They were more likely to do other things while viewing, to give way to the preferences of other family members for social reasons, to talk while viewing, to feel guilty for viewing alone. Women would be inclined to treat television as a resource for easing family tensions, reconciling quarrels, and encouraging varying degrees of privacy or sociability in a viewing situation. Morley (1986) cites the example of men using their power of control to 'get even' with their wives in some dispute, for instance by watching sport exclusively. Presumably women do something similar in return, when they get the chance. Finally, there is now an expanding field of research addressed to the influence of gender on the acquisition and use of new communication technologies in the home (Rakow, 1986; Frissen, 1992; Moores, 1993; Slack and Wise, 2002).

Sociability and Uses of the Media

It had not escaped early audience researchers that media use was shaped by circumstances of time and place, and by social and cultural habits. People joined audiences for various social reasons (e.g. for conversation, or organizing daily routine) as much as for some communicative value or purpose (such as learning from the news). For instance, 'going to the movies' has nearly always been viewed more as a social activity than as an occasion for seeing particular films (Handel, 1950). Eliot Friedson (1953) emphasized the group character of much actual media experience (in contrast to what the theory of mass behaviour proposed), drawing on the then contemporary evidence of film and broadcast audiences. He wrote:

> Much audience behavior, then, takes place in a complex network of local social activity. Certain times of day, certain days, certain seasons are the appropriate times for engaging in particular activities connected with various mass media. The individual is frequently accompanied by others of his social group ... [and] participates in an interpersonal grid of spectators who discuss the meaning of past experience with mass communication and the anticipated significance of future experience.

The media occasion had a significance beyond that of any 'message' communicated or any individual gratification obtained. Seeing a 'bad' movie could be just as satisfying as seeing a 'good' one. Much the same could be said of radio, phonograph listening and television viewing, although, unlike the cinema, these have nearly always taken a secondary place in complex patterns of family life. 'Watching television' is generally a more accurate description of what is going on than 'watching television programmes', but it too overstates the significance of the ubiquitous flickering screen.

Despite the above, mass media use was often associated with forms of social isolation (Maccoby, 1954; Bailyn, 1959), and there have been similar anxieties about computer games and the Internet. There are obviously many individuals who are both socially isolated and also strongly addicted to media use behaviours that might reinforce their isolation. The term 'addiction' has been viewed as both too loaded a word and also too vague to be useful. Efforts have been made to make it more precise and relevant. For instance, Horvath (2004) proposed a new scale for measuring TV addiction, with the following main factors: (1) actual time spent; (2) evidence of withdrawal problems; (3) degree to which unintended; (4) displacement effects on other activities; (5) continuation despite problems caused; and (6) repeated attempts to cut down. An understandable concern about addiction to media has diverted attention from the more typical meanings of media attractiveness. Most uses of the media have been effectively rendered sociable. Media use is itself a ubiquitous form of normal social behaviour and an acceptable substitute for actual social interaction. It is also widely perceived as a significant 'agent of socialization' – an occasion for social learning and a means towards participation in the wider society.

The sociability of the audience experience is indicated by certain familiar (and well-attested) features of media use, apart from just sharing the activity. The media (e.g. television or music) are often used to entertain other people or to ease social interaction. Media use is often accompanied by talk about the ongoing experience. The content of media (news items, stories, performances) provides an object of shared attention for many as well as topics of conversation. Media-related talk is especially useful in providing a non-intrusive basis of contact with strangers. Media in the home are frequently a background to virtually every other kind of activity, without necessarily impeding or displacing these activities. Kubey and Csikszentmihalyi (1991: 75), for instance, reported that '63.5% of the time television was being viewed, people reported doing something else as well'.

There is no clear evidence that the classic forms of interpersonal 'sociability', such as conversation and 'hanging out', have disappeared, although it is very likely that some domestic entertainments which were sociable, like card-playing, musical parties and family games, have declined (although for other reasons as well). Rosengren and Windahl (1989), in their overview of findings of the long-term Swedish Media Panel research into child development, have found much evidence of varied and complex patterns linking media use with other social activities. They find (1989: 200) 'on the whole positive relations between children's television viewing and their social interaction'. Age (grade in school), gender and social class all played a part in mediating the link (see Buckingham, 2002).

Most media use can be as sociable or not as one chooses, depending on our real-life resources (in terms of money, mobility, available friends and social contacts). This is what Rosengren and Windahl (1972) termed 'interaction potential'. In providing a substitute to 'real-life' social contact, which might simply not be available, especially in modern urban living, the media often help to alleviate loneliness and stress caused by isolation.

Mass-mediated social contact can supplement and complement, as well as displace, real personal contacts with others. As a result, the potential for social interaction can just as easily be enlarged by mass media as reduced. In so far as there is a general empirical answer to the question of relationship between social interaction and media use, it seems that higher levels of 'real' social contact are often accompanied by above-average levels of contact with the media. This finding does not settle the issue, but the correlation can be understood as supporting the claim that being in an audience is most correctly to be defined as 'social' rather than 'non-social'. There is a variety of ways in which media use becomes intertwined with everyday life, especially in the case of television, which is such a ubiquitous accompaniment to domesticity. James Lull (1982) suggested a typology of social uses of television, based on participant observation of families. Some of the points also apply to other media. The first type is referred to as *structural* and identifies the numerous ways in which the media provide a time-frame for daily activities. This begins with an early news bulletin, an accompaniment to breakfast, and continues, according to the daily schedule, to mark breaks from work, mealtimes, the return from work and evening relaxation with familiar and suitable programming on radio and television. This is what Mendelsohn (1964) referred to as the function of radio in 'bracketing the day'. A media-derived structure of this kind provides a sense of companionship and marks off phases of the day, helping to establish appropriate moods. A second type is called *relational* and covers the points made earlier about content as a conversational 'coin of exchange' and a way of easing social contacts of an informal but non-intimate kind.

The third category is summarized in terms of *affiliation* and *avoidance*, referring to the fluctuating dynamics of social relations in which people want to be, by turns, socially close to, or separate from, others with whom they share the same physical space. Different media offer different opportunities for one or the other option. Affiliation is expressed by joining in the same spectatorship (e.g. a football match on TV) in varying degrees of participation. Avoidance takes more diverse forms. Some involve the use of particular media that are, by definition, solitary in use, like books, headphone music or mobile phones (sometimes). In public as well as private places, reading newspapers often expresses a wish to be left alone. Having separate television and radio receivers in different parts of a house helps in the dispersal of members of a household. These social devices are usually understood and accepted as legitimate, thus avoiding offence to others. It is impossible to separate out the more 'legitimate' media use motives from the less acceptable aspect of self-isolation. In families, as children grow up, there is a fairly clear pattern of increasing dispersal of individual activities, which is closely related to the use of different media (von Feilitzen, 1976; Livingstone, 2002).

Of the remaining social uses named by Lull, one – *social learning* – covers a wide range of socializing aspects of media use (e.g. adopting certain role models) and a fifth carries the label *competence/dominance*. This refers to the socially structured power to control media use in a household, ranging from a decision to choose a daily newspaper to the use of the TV remote control, and including decision-making over the acquisition of media hardware and software. It also refers to the uses made of media-derived information and expertise to play the role of **opinion leader** in social contacts with family and friends (Katz and Lazarsfeld, 1955). Ethnographic research in domestic settings makes it clear that media use is often governed by quite complex, usually unspoken, rules and understandings which vary from one family to another (see Morley, 1986). The main social uses of the media that have been uncovered are listed in Box 16.3.

Social uses of the media 16.3

- Managing relations with others
- Conversation and social exchange
- Social attachment and avoidance
- Social learning and identification with role models
- Having control of media choice
- Sharing activity
- Vicarious companionship
- Filling time
- Framing daily activity

Normative Framing of Media Use

The preceding discussion is a reminder of the extent to which research into the media audience has taken place within a normative, even judgemental, framework (see Barwise and Ehrenberg, 1988: 138ff), itself a sign that media use has been thoroughly incorporated in the socialization process. Although, as we have seen, high media use does not in itself have to be viewed as harmful, the most basic norm applied to the media has been that you can have too much, even of a good thing. The normative framing of media use seems at first to run counter to the view that media use is a voluntary, free-time, 'out-of-role' and generally pleasurable activity, more or less unrelated to any social obligation. Yet audience research continually uncovers the existence of value systems which informally serve to regulate media behaviour. As Kramer (1996: 251) observes, 'families have as many rules and disagreements about TV viewing as they do about such diverse topics as homework, eating habits and religious obligations'. It is from the imposition of norms for media use in family contexts (with reference to parental responsibility) that we are most aware of normative control of media (Geiger and Sokol, 1959; Brown and Linné, 1976; Hedinsson, 1981; Rosengren and Windahl, 1989).

There is plenty of evidence that the media are widely regarded by their own audiences as potentially influential for good or ill and thus in need of direction and control by society. At the very least they should be supervised by parents. For instance, Gunter and Winstone (1993) reported that 90% of a British sample thought parents should discourage their children from watching too much TV, and large majorities support control over viewing in general. In the same survey, about 50% thought British television was strongly regulated, and 75% were satisfied with this or wanted even more control than was exercised at present.

While no doubt much of the normative concern about media stems from fears of unwanted influences, media use in itself can be regarded as morally dubious (as noted above). Steiner (1963) long ago found a tendency for viewers to show guilt over their own high levels of television use, which he attributed to a legacy from the Protestant ethic, which frowns on 'unproductive' uses of time. Among middle-class audiences, especially, a sensitivity to this value persists. Radway found similar kinds of guilt feelings among keen female readers of romantic fiction and for similar reasons: 'guilt is the understandable result of their socialization within a culture that continues to value work above leisure and play' (1984: 105). In both examples, guilt was more evidenced in words than in behaviour, reflecting the influence of social desirability. This is confirmed by Hagen's (2000) qualitative evidence relating to television viewing in Norway. Television was identified as a 'time stealer' and rated morally and aesthetically lower than other activities.

In her study of readers of women's magazines, Hermes (1995) found that within the 'interpretative repertoires' (ideas which frame reading experiences) of women readers, there was a place both for feelings of duty to read a feminist publication and guilt at enjoying traditional women's magazines. Barwise and Ehrenberg (1988) and Kubey and Csikszentmihalyi (1991) suggest that such guilt feelings (in relation to television) are typically quite weak (Hermes would probably agree in respect of magazines), but their persistence and ubiquity is nevertheless striking in a supposedly hedonistic age as regards such a harmless pleasure.

Audience Norms for Content

Normative expectations relate not only to media use behaviour, but also to aspects of media content. People voice complaints about, as well as appreciation of, the media.

Positive response usually outweighs criticism, but what is striking is the fact that the performance of the media is so widely regarded as a proper topic for the expression of public attitudes, judgements and opinion. Audiences expect media to conform to certain norms of good taste and morality, and sometimes also to other values, such as those of the local community, patriotism and democracy. Norms for what is appropriate in fiction and entertainment usually refer to bad language, violence, sex and the models of behaviour offered by media. Here family life, the protection of children and the personal susceptibilities and moral standards of adults are the main point of reference.

Morals aside, it is notable also that audiences are sensitive to the quality of media on the grounds of political bias and fairness, often placing more emphasis on impartiality and reliability than on the media's own rights to freedom of expression (e.g. Comstock, 1988; Gunter and Winstone, 1993; Fitzsimon and McGill, 1995; Golding and van Snippenburg, 1995; McMasters, 2000). Audiences can often seem intolerant of the public expression in the mainstream media of extreme or deviant political views. Questions about censorship tend to reveal unexpected variations in public attitudes. For instance, Paek et al. (2008) found that among a sample of students there was more support for advance censorship and for punishment of 'anti-government pamphlets' than for propaganda. Adults were somewhat more inclined the other way. The norms applied by the audience to media information commonly refer to completeness and accuracy, balance and diversity of opinion. News sources are often judged according to their relative credibility (Gaziano and McGrath, 1987). By various accounts, the media have been losing trust and, once lost, it is hard to regain, just as it is hard for new media (e.g. online news) to acquire trust in the first place (Althaus and Tewkesbury, 2000; Schweiger, 2000; Johnson and Kaye, 2002).

Despite the evidence of critical public attitudes, relatively few people seem personally offended by the media, and actual use behaviour shows a state of relative normlessness (see, for example, Gunter and Winstone, 1993). This paradox may reflect the existence of private norms based on personal taste and preferences which, as with many aspects of behaviour, do not correspond with the public norm. It also suggests that evaluative attitudes expressed towards media are somewhat superficial and learnt as socially desirable rather than deeply internalized. This is not to say that personal preferences in choosing and responding to media content will not be influenced by an individual's own personal values (see Johansson and Miegel, 1992). Rather, these value influences are often implicit and beneath the surface.

Values applied to content often involve fine distinctions between one medium and another and one genre and another. For example, Alasuutari (1992) showed that Finnish television viewers deployed a sort of 'moral hierarchy', according to which news and information were highly regarded and soap operas were seen as a 'low' form of content. This applied even to fans of soap operas (this perception is quite widespread; see, for example, Ang, 1985; Morley, 1986; Seiter et al., 1989). They were expressing a consensus of judgement that they were aware of, without feeling personally bound to follow it. The nature of the hierarchy is not very surprising since it reflects traditional cultural values and tastes, especially a respect for reality and information.

Other forms of critical distance include an objection to some aspects of content on moral or ideological grounds. In other words, it seems that 'experienced' audience members (these kinds of data came from regular and articulate viewers) have a fairly extensive repertoire of positions they can take up in respect of particular media contents. Box 16.4 summarizes the main norms applied to use of television and other media.

16.4 Audience norms for media conduct and content

- Too much media use, especially TV, is bad, especially for children
- Children's TV use should be protected and supervised
- Different genres and media received different valuations
- Audiences expect accuracy and impartiality in news
- General audience content should not offend against dominant moral and social norms
- Media should not be free to damage national interest or security

The View from the Audience

As noted in Chapter 12, mass communicators solve the 'problem' of orientation to an essentially unknown audience in a variety of ways, depending on their particular role conception and type of medium or concept. Here we look briefly at the communicator–audience relationship from the other 'end', having already described normative concerns about content. In general, the audience does not experience its relations with the media and media communicators as problematic on a day-to-day basis. Under conditions of freedom and diversity, audiences choose their own media sources according to personal likes and perceptions of what is relevant and interesting. Nevertheless some effort is required on the part of the audience and some discomfort may be entailed. The first dimension to consider in audience–source relations is that of *affective direction*.

Although media are freely chosen by their audiences, actual people in audiences may not have personally chosen their media or the specific content to which they find themselves exposed. This applies where members of families, households or other groups are subject to the choices of others about what is available to read, view or listen to. Such media 'micro-gatekeepers' may be parents, partners, friends, and the like. It also applies where there are few or no real alternatives, for instance where there is only one local or city newspaper which is hard, in practice, to ignore.

There is usually a large flow of unrequested and often unwanted media messages by way of media advertising of all kinds, for example mail, telephone, and so on, which gives rise to a similar situation. Even where we do choose our own media channel, source and content, we can easily be dissatisfied with some aspects of media performance and there is much scope for negative responses to the media. We are continually faced with the need to select and evaluate, and this includes making choices *against* what we dislike.

Apart from the existence of positive or negative feelings towards source, medium or message, we need to consider the degree of audience *involvement* or *attachment*, which can vary from that of casual spectatorship to a high sense of personal commitment to a media person or performance. From the earliest days of radio, communicators sought to establish an illusion of personal contact and intimacy with the invisible audience by using familiar forms of address, by incorporating sound effects to simulate the presence of audiences or by encouraging audience participation. There has always been much pseudo-participation associated with radio and television, more now than ever, and it is not surprising that it evokes some response in the audience, as shown by the phenomenon of fandom (p. 442). In practice it is difficult to empirically distinguish 'real' attachment from 'artificial' attachment. But, as Hermes (1999: 74) points out: 'Seeing media figures as real and as part of our everyday cultural and emotional experience is part and parcel of how media texts come to have meaning.'

The concept of **parasocial interaction** was introduced by Horton and Wohl (1956) to describe the displacement of a human interlocutor by a media character or personality, treating it, by implication, as less satisfactory than real social interaction. However, it may be considered as better than nothing, or as a reaction to a lack of real social contact. Scales have been developed to measure the degree of parasocial interaction (PSI) (Austin, 1992), following a definition of PSI by Rubin et al. (1990: 250) as 'the degree to which audience members feel they interact with their favourite TV news persona'.

Rosengren and Windahl (1989) proposed a fourfold typology of 'television relations', which they derived from two main dimensions of audience relations with the media. One of these they call *interaction* – having the feeling of interacting with actors on the screen. The second is the variable of degree of *identification* (involvement with some media figure). The extreme case of attachment to media occurs when a high degree of interaction coincides with a high degree of identification. Rosengren and Windahl, refer to this situation as one of *capture*. The reverse condition, with low identification and low involvement, is referred to as 'detachment'. Noble (1975) reported on the strong attachment shown by children in care to television personalities. Television characters provided something akin to a 'screen community'. The attraction ranged from simple recognition to very positive 'identification', which leads to sharing the emotions of the character and a loss of contact with reality. The meaning of identification has been problematic. Cohen (2001) distinguishes it from parasocial interaction, from affinity with media characters and from merely liking them. He defines it as 'an imaginative response through which an audience member assesses the identity, goals and perspectives of characters' (2001: 261). Different forms and degrees of personal orientation to media personalities and characters are given in Box 16.5.

16.5 Types of audience orientation to media

- Liking or affinity
- Involvement
- Parasocial interaction
- Interactivity
- Attachment
- Identification
- Capture
- Fandom

Media Fandom

Audiences are connected to 'distant' media sources in several different ways, perhaps especially through the mediation of their family, friends and others in their social milieux. It is also relevant to include institutionalized 'fandom' in this same category, even if often it is not very spontaneous and is engineered or manipulated by the media. Audience experience has always been characterized by occasions of greatly accentuated and specified attachment to particular performers (most especially), but also to certain kinds of performance (types of music, genres of film or fiction). The weakest kind of fandom is simply an attraction to a medium (as in the old expression 'film fan'). The strongest version involves a high degree of emotional investment and activity centring on a media personality. Something rather similar, but less intense, can occur with followers of a particular television series, when attachment to a fictional character gets mixed up with attachment to the actor, or when the distinction between fiction and reality is lost sight of.

Fandom is often associated in the view of critics with immaturity and irrationality, an outcome of mass culture and an example of mass behaviour. As Jensen (1992) has pointed out, we do not take the same view of *aficionados* in many other areas of cultural activity, although it is hard to say how a fan of a pop group differs in principle from, say, an opera buff. Fandom has also been interpreted as evidence of manipulation and exploitation – something encouraged by the media to strengthen ties with products and performers, to help with publicity and to make extra money from merchandising and other media 'spinoffs'. It helps in extending the life of products and maximizing profit (Sabal, 1992). While this is true, there is an alternative perspective, according to which fandom shows not manipulation by the media but the 'productive power' of audiences (Fiske, 1992). According to this view, the fans actively create new meaning out of the materials offered, building up systems of cultural discrimination, stylistic display, social identification and association which serve to detach the fan group from the manipulative grip of the media.

Fandom is best considered as something collective – a consciously shared feeling of more or less intense attraction. There are individual fans, of course, but it would be hard to be a lone fan, and the concept would be redundant. Fandom is also generated by fans themselves, when they associate with each other and express their attachment in public ways (T-shirts, fanzines, style, etc.). By definition fandom defines relations with the media in a satisfying way and bridges the inevitable real 'distance' between star and stargazer. Nevertheless, it can also be a painful experience, involving high expectations and vicarious emotional attachments that make the fan potentially vulnerable. Fandom can also have a downside for the object of affection since fans can be fickle and unforgiving and will ultimately desert. They also treat stars as objects of gossip, envy and dislike (Alberoni, 1972), often encouraged in this by other media (Turner, 2004).

Of the many ways in which the arrival of the Internet is affecting how television is both made and viewed, the impact on the relationship with fans is one of the most striking. A case study of the views and behaviour of fans of several cult TV shows, including *Buffy the Vampire Slayer* by Sharon Ross (2008), as summarized in Box 16.6, helps to show how the Internet has become integral to the whole phenomenon of fandom and to the development of cult status.

Tele-participation as new form of fandom 16.6 eg

Fandom is about participating somehow in the story and becoming part of the social audience surrounding the show. The Internet makes this possible by extending the TV text beyond the story on the set. Even when viewers are not actively using the possibilities, they know it is going on and has become part of a generalized idea of what it means to 'watch TV'. The effects are not confined to audiences since producers and creative professionals are working on the same assumptions. Ross writes: 'Key amongst these changes is the development of an aesthetics of multiplicity. Shows that have marked tele-participation feature narratives with multiple points of view, typically through the use of ensemble casts and often ... complex narrative structures. These programs also focus on incomplete stories, typically relying on seriality and interruption' (Ross, 2008: 255).

The End of the Audience?

As we noted at the beginning of Chapter 15, the audience concept has always been more problematic than it seems, because it can be defined and constructed in so many ways and has no fixed existence. The problems are compounded the more we take the view of the audience itself rather than the media industry. New and different audiences can be constituted by people themselves based on some shared interest or identity. New technologies are bringing into question the clear distinction between sender and receiver which is crucial to the original idea of the media audience, as well as introducing new forms of use of media (see Chapter 6). Interactive and consultative uses of media take away the spectatorship that was so characteristic of the original mass audience. Aside from radically new communication technologies, there are many changes to the 'old technologies' and to media industries that have implications for the audience (Livingstone, 2003).

The effects of change are quite mixed, however. On the one hand, they increase the size of audiences for particular products and performers, as a result of concentration and monopoly forming and the exploitation of the same content in many different markets. Internationalization is also a route towards much larger (cumulative) audiences for certain high-profile types of content. On the other hand, 'actual' audiences are being diversified as a result of channel multiplication and specialization. There are many more, but often smaller and more homogeneous, audiences. Instead of audiences being recruited from a given geographical area or social class, they are based more on tastes and lifestyles. The term *segmentation* is used to refer to the process by which media supply is matched more precisely to a relevant set of media consumers, and the process is aided by the greater possibility of selection on the part of consumers themselves. Evidence from the USA already indicates that the homogeneity of composition of cable channel audiences is much greater than for national broadcast channels (Barnes and Thomson, 1994: 89).

Another process, that of *fragmentation*, involves the dispersal of the same amount of audience attention over more and more media sources. Ultimately, nearly all choices could be individualized, spelling the end of the audience as a significant social collectivity. Media users will come to have no more in common with each other than owners of any other consumer article. Along with fragmentation of audiences and individualization of use comes a decline in the strength of ties that bind people to their chosen media source and a loss of any sense of identity as an audience.

The analysis of electronically collected data by people meters has shed more light on patterns of television use in the age of 'media abundance', providing evidence for some of these generalizations. Studies of German and Swiss audiences reported by Krotz and von Hasebrink (1998) and von Hasebrink (1997) captured some of the changes taking place in television use behaviour in Europe, indicating four important trends. First, decline of the 'typical' collective family viewing situation, since the overwhelming amount of viewing is by one or only two persons. Secondly, the prevalence of a type of viewing that involves 'many and short' viewing periods, especially among children and younger people. Thirdly, despite much greater choice, there is still quite a strong channel loyalty, with many viewers using a limited number of channels. Fourthly, there is clear evidence that content preferences play a larger part in selection than they did in the days of limited television provision (Goodhart et al., 1975; Eastman, 1998).

We can summarize the audience trends discussed in terms of four succeeding stages, as shown in Figure 16.4. This applies especially to television, but it has a wider reference. In the early years of television (1950s and 1960s) the majority of viewers in most countries had a very limited choice of up to three national channels (the USA had somewhat more choice). The same media experience was widely shared by nearly everyone. This *unitary model* implies a single audience more or less coextensive with the general public. As supply of content and channels increase, there is more diversity, and more distinctive options begin to emerge within the framework of a unitary model (e.g. daytime and night-time television, regional variations, more private television in Europe). This pattern of limited internal diversification can be called a *pluralism model*. The third stage, the *core–periphery model*, is one in which the multiplication of

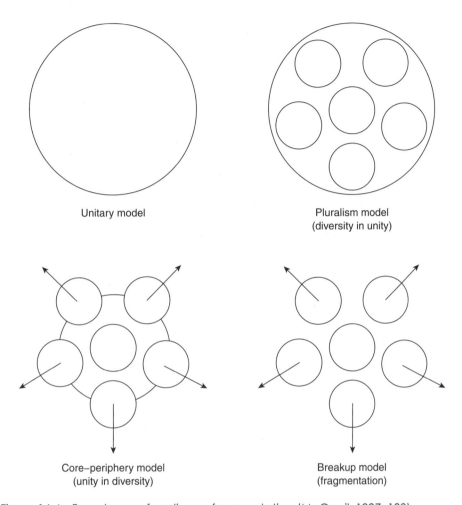

Figure 16.4   Four stages of audience fragmentation (McQuail, 1997: 138)

channels undermines the unity of the framework. It becomes possible, as a result of cable and satellite transmission, recording technology and other new media, to enjoy a television diet that differs significantly from the majority or mainstream. We are already in that situation in most developed countries. The final stage envisaged in Figure 16.4 is that of the *breakup model*, where fragmentation accelerates and there is no longer any 'centre', just very many and very diverse sets of media users.

The 'Escape' of the Audience

The apparent changes in the general character of audiences can be assessed in different ways. The problems for the media industry are well summed up by the title of Ien Ang's book *Desperately Seeking the Audience* (1991). It has become more difficult to keep track of the audience, to manage or predict its composition and the direction of its interests, even if new technology such as that of the people meter and other forms of computer analysis of system users also improves the flow of information back to the media. However, the potential 'escape' of the audience from management and control, as well as the greatly increased choice, seem to be entries on the credit side in the balance of audience power.

On the face of it, there has been a shift in favour of media consumers in the market-place and even perhaps as individual citizens. There are more channels of relevant political and civic information and less likelihood of a mass audience being the object of semi-monopolistic propaganda or biased information. It is generally harder for would-be persuaders, whether political or commercial, to reach any large general public. The audience is also less attentive to messages received than was the case in the early days of radio and television. The over-abundance of supply outstrips the capacity of people to notice or make use of it. Even when attention is given, the likelihood of influence is lower than it used to be. Neuman and Pool (1986) invoked the idea of an equilibrium model, according to which audience discomfort at overload is avoided by reducing the 'quality' of attention. The typical media user has less time and motivation and, according to comments made above, lacks the social or normative connection with a media source that would support influence. The quality as well as the quantity of potential influence has been diluted.

The increased 'power' of the audience should not be overstated since there are gains as well as losses. The more audiences become just another set of consumer markets, the more they lose collective social power. According to Cantor (1994: 168): 'Audiences as market segments rather than audiences as cultural politicians remain the most powerful influence on television content.' Aggregate market influence is far removed from that of public opinion or organized collective action. One of the continued advantages of public service television is that the audience has some collective rights as a body of citizens that still has formal control over media channels. Changes affecting the audience as a concept and reality are summarized in Box 16.7.

16.7 Media changes affecting the audience

- Multiplication of channels
- Conglomeration increasing some audience sizes
- Fragmentation of the mass audience
- Segmentation according to market characteristics
- Escape of the audience from management and measurement
- New types of audience emerge: interactive and consultative

The Future of the Audience

At the present time, despite the trends discussed, it is too early to conclude that the mass audience will fade away. It still exists, albeit in changing forms, and the mass media industries have shown a remarkable capacity to survive. Despite the multiplication of channels for television, the greater ease of entering the media market with new technology and the increased capacity of individuals to exercise choice, the overall structure of media audiences has not yet changed fundamentally. Webster and Phalen (1997: 114) noted that 'traditional mass appeal network television still dominates media consumption in the United States'. Ten years later the three largest US networks plus Fox had barely 64% audience share and falling (Hindman and Wiegand, 2008; Turow, 2009: 191), but the industry is still driven by the search for successful formats that will reach the largest possible audiences at home and internationally. In most European countries, the multiplication of channels has not yet led to a general fragmentation of audiences, although there are warning signs. Audience share is still the touchstone of success. Change has been very gradual, and much the same can be said of the newspaper press in most countries.

It is still plausible to conclude, along with Neuman (1991), that there is a considerable inertial force that limits fundamental change in audience formation. One aspect of the resistance is attributable to 'the social psychology of media use', expressed in 'deeply ingrained habits of passive, half-attentive use' (1991: 42). The other pressure is the communications industry itself. According to Neuman (1991: 42): 'Economies of scale push in the direction of common-denominator, one-way mass communications, rather than promoting narrowcasting and two-way communications.' There are also powerful and varied social forces influencing media production and use that have deep roots and are resistant to the influence of technological change on its own. The shape of audiences reflects the structure, dynamics and needs of social formations, ranging from national societies to families. These forces do not all work in the same direction to support the mass audience, and some are likely to favour new uses of new media and thus new audience realities. As a result, we cannot make any certain predictions, even about the strength and direction of broad trends.

The Audience Concept Again

Sufficient reasons have already been given to wonder whether the term 'audience' is still a useful one, especially as there are so many kinds of use of many different communications media. The term 'audience' cannot easily be divested of its strong connotation of 'spectatorship' – of rather passive watching and listening. It is also closely tied in meaning to the reception of some 'message', despite the fact that we know audience behaviour to involve several equally important motives or satisfactions – for instance, social togetherness and the pleasures of actual use of a medium, regardless of content. Despite this, there seems to be no viable alternative term, and we will probably have to go on using it to cover very diverse occasions. In its early manifestation as a mass audience for the 'industrial' media, it was always something of a caricature, ignoring the degree of sociability and negotiation involved in attending to media. We can agree with Livingstone (2003: 353) that 'the term "audience" can only be satisfactorily applied to the activities of listening and watching… [while] the term "user" seems to allow for a greater variety of modes of engagement, although it tends to be overly individualistic and unstructured, losing the sense of collectivity that is central to the "audience" and with no necessary relation to "communication" at all'. She concludes that no single term will serve to cover the many ways that technologies mediate in relations between people and suggests that we reconceptualize audience as 'relational and interactional construct' that can also relate people to their social and cultural contexts. She emphasizes that what is central is the nature of the relationship, rather than an artificially created concept.

Even so, we can always differentiate for specific purposes. By way of indicating and summarizing the diverse possibilities, Box 16.8 offers a list of the main dimensions of audience. Each variable shown can be used to describe and classify one or other of the many types of audience that now exist, and each has a history in theory and research.

16.8 The main dimensions of the audience

- Degree of activity or passivity
- Degree of interactivity and interchangeability
- Size and duration
- Locatedness in space
- Group character (social/cultural identity)
- Simultaneity of contact with source
- Heterogeneity of composition
- Social relations between sender and receiver
- Message versus social/behavioural definition of situation
- Degree of perceived 'social presence'
- Sociability of context of use

Conclusion

This book is about mass communication, and we stop at the frontier where new and related phenomena begin, especially those based on the use of the computer and other new media. As we have seen, the concept of audience shades into other terms to describe the use of other communication technologies. However, there is shared ground that straddles the boundary between communication forms, especially when we consider: alternative ways of using spare time; various functions that can be met by different means; the fact of multiple dependencies on technology; the ownership and organization of mass and new media; and some of the forms of content. It is clear that quite a lot of audience theory also applies to non-mass communication situations, albeit in adapted or extended forms.

Further Reading

Ettema, J.S. and Whitney, D.C. (eds) (1994) *How the Media Create the Audience*. Thousand Oaks, CA: Sage.
Provides a set of authoritative views on the possible manipulation of audiences, with general principles explained that are still relevant.

Liebes, T. (2005) 'Viewing and reviewing the audience: fashions in communication research', in J. Curran and M. Gurevitch (eds), *Mass Media and Society*, 4th edn, pp. 356–74. London: Hodder Arnold.
Argues the case for distinguishing Internet users from the media audience and reviews the history of views about the audience as media scarcity turned to plenty.

Neuman, W.R. (1991) *The Future of the Mass Audience*. Cambridge: Cambridge University Press.
An early and perspicacious account of the changes in prospect for mass media audiences, providing a framework for charting changes that have actually occurred and identifying the constant factors in audience behaviour.

Webster, J.G. (2005) 'Beneath the veneer of fragmentation – TV audience polarization in a multi-channel world', *Journal of Communication*, 55 (2): 366–82.
Presents data and reflection on the consequences of fragmentation, showing an unclear relation between audience size and degree of attachment and loyalty.

Online Readings

Elvestad, E. and Blekesaune, A. (2008) 'Newspaper readers in Europe: a multilevel study of individual and national differences', *European Journal of Communication*, 23 (4): 425–48.
Livingstone, S. (2007) 'From family television to bedroom culture: young people's media at home', in E. Devereux (ed.), *Media Studies*, pp. 302–21. London: Sage.
McBeth, T.M. (2004) 'Psychology of media use', in J.D.H. Downing, D. McQuail, P. Schlesinger and E. Wartella (eds), *The Sage Handbook of Media Studies*, pp. 201–26. Thousand Oaks, CA: Sage.
Peter, J. and Valkenberg, P. (2006) 'Individual differences in perception of internet communication', *European Journal of Communication*, 21 (2): 213–26.

Part 7
Effects

17

Processes and Models of Media Effects

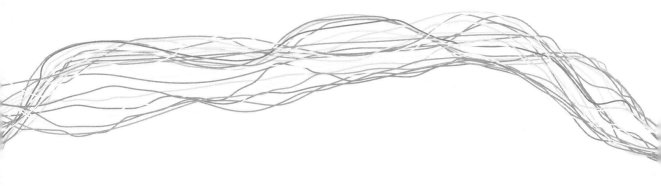

This chapter provides a general overview of theories and models of mass media effect. It begins with a paradox. There is a widespread belief, nearing on certainty, that the mass media are a powerful instrument of influence on opinion and of effects on behaviour. At the same time, there is great difficulty in predicting effects, engineering them by design or in proving that they have happened, after the event. Despite this difficulty, knowledge about the processes involved has gradually increased and as a result we are in a better position to say when and which effects are more or less likely. The chapter charts the development of theory and explains the different kinds of effect that are involved and the main alternative models according to which they occur.

The Premise of Media Effect

As noted above, the entire study of mass communication is based on the assumption that the media have significant effects, yet there is little agreement on the nature and extent of these assumed effects. This uncertainty is the more surprising since everyday experience provides countless, if minor, examples of influence. We dress for the weather as forecast, buy something because of an advertisement, go to a film mentioned in a newspaper, react in countless ways to media news, to films, to music on the radio, and so on. Good or bad economic news clearly affects business and consumer confidence. There are many cases of negative media publicity concerning, for instance, food contamination or adulteration, leading to significant changes in behaviour, sometimes with large economic impact. Public figures in all walks of life as well as firms and institutions are extremely sensitive about their image in the media. Acts of violence or suicide appear to be copied from, or stimulated by, media portrayals of such acts. Much policy and regulation are directed at preventing the media from causing harm, and encouraging the media to do some good.

Our minds are full of media-derived information and impressions. We live in a world saturated by media sounds and images, where politics, government and business operate on the assumption that we know what is going on in the wider world. Few of us cannot think of some personal instance of gaining significant information or of forming an opinion because of the media. Much money and effort are also spent on directing the media to achieve such effects, especially by way of advertising and public relations, and it is hard to believe that this would happen without a conviction that it works, more or less according to plan. Certainly, the media themselves seem confident of their capacity to achieve intended effects.

And yet considerable areas of uncertainty remain. We know that under some conditions – for instance, of consistency and consensus of message, prominence of news reports from trusted sources, coupled with large audiences – we can expect there to be certain effects on public knowledge and on opinions, but we cannot be sure of the degree of change that will occur, nor of which sectors of the audience will respond most, never mind the case of one individual. The media are rarely likely to be the only necessary or sufficient cause of an effect, and their relative contribution is extremely hard to assess. There are many reasons for this uncertainty, and even common sense wavers when faced with questions of media effect in the contested areas of morals, opinion and deviant behaviour, which have attracted most public notice. On such matters the media are unlikely to be a primary or sufficient cause, and it would be impossible to take full account of all the possible psychological, social and cultural factors involved. Furthermore, it makes little sense to speak of 'the media' as if they were one thing rather than the carriers of an enormously diverse set of messages, images and ideas. Most of this material does not originate with the media themselves but 'comes from society' and is 'sent back' to society by way of the media.

Most effect research has been initiated from *outside* rather than within the media, especially by social critics, politicians, interest groups, and so on. The underlying premise has usually been that mass media are some kind of 'problem' for the rest of society and problematic aspects of media effects still tend to shape public debate on the media, including newer forms such as the Internet. There remains a large gap between those who either claim great power for the media (usually for self-interested reasons) or who are fearful of media power to cause harm and those who dismiss the claims and fears as largely unproven. It is not going too far to say that there is a 'media power belief system' whose adherents do not need detailed proof of the kind demanded by sceptics. On the other hand, the rejection of all claims to media power on grounds of lack of empirical proof can lead to another kind of error. Many of the potential effects of mass media are either too complex, subtle or long-term to be captured by the still rudimentary forms of measurement available. However, this conflict of view can be fruitful. It is a reminder that we have to be careful not to accept the claims of the 'persuaders' or of the critics too readily, that we should not confuse particular messages with the medium as a whole, and that we should discriminate carefully between different types of effect and different situations. Most important, we should give due weight to the fact that the effects are determined at least as much by the receiver as by the sender.

The Natural History of Media Effect Research and Theory: Four Phases

The development of thinking about media effects may be said to have a 'natural history', in the sense of its being strongly shaped by the circumstances of time and place. It has also been influenced by several 'environmental' factors, including the interests of governments and law-makers, changing technology, the events of history, the activities of pressure groups and propagandists, the ongoing concerns of public opinion, and even the findings and the fashions of social science. It is not surprising that no straight path of cumulative development of knowledge can be discerned. Even so, we can distinguish a number of stages in the history of the field which indicate some degree of ordered progression.

Phase 1: all-powerful media

In the first phase, which extends from the turn of the century until the 1930s, the then new media of press, film and radio were credited with considerable power to shape opinion and belief, to change habits of life and to mould behaviour more or less according to the will of their controllers (Bauer and Bauer, 1960). This view was based not on scientific investigation but on awe at the possibilities for mass persuasion that seemed to open up and on observation of the enormous popularity of these media that intruded into many aspects of everyday life as well as public affairs.

In Europe, the use of media by advertisers, by First World War propagandists, by dictatorial states in the inter-war years and by the new revolutionary regime in Russia, all appeared to confirm what people were already inclined to believe – that the media could be immensely powerful. Against the background of such beliefs, systematic research using survey and experimental methods, and drawing heavily on social psychology, was begun during the 1920s and 1930s, although mainly limited to the United States. Many books were written about the power of propaganda in this period (e.g. Lasswell, 1927; see also Jowett and O'Donnell, 1999).

Phase 2: theory of powerful media put to the test

The transition to empirical enquiry led to a second phase of thinking about media effects. Its beginning is well exemplified in the research literature by the series of Payne Fund studies in the United States in the early 1930s (Blumer, 1933; Blumer and Hauser, 1933; Peterson and Thurstone, 1933). These studies were primarily concerned with the influence of films on children and young people. The results confirmed many ideas about the effects on the emotions, attitudes and behaviour of young people. This era of research into media effects continued until the early 1960s, with particular reference to the effects of television when it arrived in the post-war years (e.g. Himmelweit et al., 1958). Many separate studies were carried out into the effects of different types of content and media, of particular films or programmes and of entire campaigns. Attention was mainly concentrated on the possibilities of using film and other media for planned persuasion or information.

Hovland et al. (1949), for instance, reported a series of large-scale experimental studies that assessed the value of using film material to 'indocrinate' American military recruits into awareness of and support for the aims of the Second World War. Star and Hughes (1950) reported a campaign designed to improve public support for the United Nations. Lazarsfeld et al. (1944) initiated a long tradition of investigating the effectiveness of democratic election campaigns.

In the immediate post-war era, research into media effects become much more sophisticated. More account was taken of the intervening effects of social and demographic variables, such as age, education and sex, and also of social psychological factors, such as predispositions and prior attitudes, personality type, persuadability, degree of interest and motivation, trust in the source, etc. The influence of personal social contacts was also included in the range of potential variables as well as of the different motives for attending to media in the first place. The more variables that were added, the more difficult it became to pin down and quantify the precise contribution of the media to any change and the suspicion grew that this might be typically quite small.

What now seems like the end of an era was marked by expressions of disillusion with the outcome of this kind of media effect research. One leading researcher, Berelson (1959), suggested that the field of mass communication research might be withering away. It was Berelson who summed up the achieved wisdom of research into media effects in a much-quoted conclusion (Box 17.1). This sounds like a confession of despair, but it also points to the key factors that need to be examined in any research into effects.

Berelson on media effects: key quote 17.1

Some kinds of communication on some kinds of issues have brought to the attention of some kinds of people under some kinds of conditions have some kinds of effects. (Berelson, 1948: 172)

There were new statements of conventional wisdom which assigned a much more modest role to media in causing any planned or unintended effects. The still influential and useful summary of early research by Joseph Klapper, published in 1960 (though dating largely from 1949), appeared to set the seal on this research phase. It concluded that 'mass communication does not ordinarily serve as a necessary or sufficient cause of audience effects, but rather functions through a nexus of mediating factors' (1960: 8).

It was not that the media had been found to be without effects or influence; rather there was no direct or one-to-one link to be expected between media stimulus and audience response. Media were shown to operate within a pre-existing structure of social relationships and a particular social and cultural context. These factors took primacy in shaping the opinions, attitudes and behaviour under study and also in shaping media choice, attention and response on the part of audiences. It was also clear that information acquisition could occur without related attitude change, and attitude change without changes in behaviour (e.g. Hovland et al., 1949; Trenaman and McQuail, 1961).

The new sobriety of assessment was slow to modify opinion outside the social scientific community. It was particularly hard to accept for those who made a living from advertising and propaganda and for those in the media who valued the myth of their great potency. Those with political or commercial motives for using or controlling the media did not feel they could risk accepting the message of relative media impotence which research had produced. There was still room for varying assessments since the message of limited effect was heavily qualified and was itself a reaction against unrealistic claims. The failure of research to find powerful effects could well be attributed to the complexity of the processes and the inadequacy of research designs and methods.

Phase 3: powerful media rediscovered

Hardly had the 'no (or minimal) effect' conclusion been written into the textbooks when it was being challenged by those who doubted that the whole story had been written. There was plenty of contemporary evidence of a circumstantial nature that the media could indeed have important social effects and be an instrument for exercising social and political power. Authoritative retrospective accounts of the period (e.g. McGuire, 1973; Lang and Lang, 1981; McLeod et al., 1991) shed considerable doubt on whether there ever was a watershed at this time between a belief in media power and one in media impotence.

In relation to public opinion effects, Lang and Lang (1981) argue that the 'minimal effect' conclusion is only one particular interpretation which has gained undue currency (see also Chaffee and Hochheimer, 1982). Lang and Lang (1981: 659) write: 'The evidence available by the end of the 1950s, even when balanced against some of the negative findings, gives no justification for an overall verdict of "media impotence".' In their view, the 'no effect' myth was due to a combination of factors. Most notable was the undue concentration on a limited range of effects, especially short-term effects on individuals (for instance, during elections) instead of on broader social and institutional effects, and the undue weight given to two publications: Katz and Lazarsfeld's *Personal Influence* (1955) and Klapper's *The Effects of Mass Communication* (1960). Nevertheless, they conceded that the myth was influential enough to close off certain avenues of research temporarily.

One reason for the reluctance to accept a 'minimal effect' conclusion was the arrival of television in the 1950s and 1960s as a new medium with even more power of attraction (if not necessarily of effect) than its predecessors and with seemingly major implications for social life. The third phase of theory and research was one in which potential effects were still being sought, but according to revised conceptions of the social and media processes likely to be involved. Early investigation had relied very heavily on a model (borrowed from psychology) in which correlations were sought between degree of 'exposure' to media stimuli and measured changes of, or variations in, attitude, opinion, information or behaviour, taking account of numerous intervening variables.

The renewal of effect research was marked by a shift of attention towards long-term change, towards what people learn from the media directly or indirectly than direct effects on attitudes and opinions. More attention was also paid to collective effects on climates of opinion, definitions of social reality, ideology and to the structure of opinion and belief in a given population. Other kinds of effect were also considered, especially in cultural patterns and on institutional behaviour. For instance, there were changes in political communication following the arrival of television and further changes as a result of newer communication media. Also important was the realization that the way media select, process and shape content for their own purposes can have a strong influence on how it is received and interpreted and thus on longer-term consequences.

Much of what follows is taken up with a review of these newer theories of effect and of modifications of early direct-effect models. While there are many contributors to, and causes of, the revival of interest, it was Noelle-Neumann (1973) who coined the slogan 'return to the concept of powerful mass media', which serves to identify this research phase. The upsurge of critical theory in the 1960s (the new left) also made an important contribution by crediting the media with powerful legitimating and controlling effects in the interests of capitalist or bureaucratic states.

Phase 4: negotiated media influence

Beginning in the late 1970s, an approach to media effects emerged that can best be termed 'social constructivist' (Gamson and Modigliani, 1989). In essence, this involves a view of the media as having their most significant effects by constructing meanings. The media tend to offer a 'preferred' view of social reality (one that purports to be widely accepted and reliable). This includes both the information provided and the appropriate way of interpreting it, forming value judgements and opinions and reacting to it. These are the ready-made meanings that the media systematically offer to their audiences. It is up to the audience member to decide whether or not to adopt the views offered, although they are often the only material available for forming an opinion on distant matters. The alternative sources could include influences from personal experience or from the social or cultural environment that might even be a basis for active resistance to influence. Thus there is no automatic or direct transfer of meaning but a negotiation between what is offered and what a receiver is inclined to accept. This view of the process is a break from the 'all-powerful media' paradigm and is also marked by a shift from quantitative and behaviourist methods towards qualitative, deeper and ethnographic methods.

The origins of the last research phase are diverse and lie quite deep in the past. The thinking has some points of similarity with early 'powerful media' theory, including, for example, the theory of ideology and false consciousness, Gerbner's cultivation theory (Signorielli and Morgan, 1990) and the ideas elaborated by Noelle-Neumann (1974) in her **'spiral of silence'** theory. These are discussed later in this book. This emerging paradigm of effects has two main thrusts. First, media 'construct' social formations and even history itself by framing images of reality (in fiction as well as news) in predictable and patterned ways. Secondly, people in audiences construct for themselves their own view of social reality and their place in it, in interaction with the symbolic constructions offered by the media. The approach allows both for the power of media and for the power of people to choose, with a terrain of continuous negotiation in between, as it were. In general, it is a formulation of the effect process which accords well with the mediation perspective outlined in Chapter 4.

There are by now a good many studies which operate within this framework, with attention often directed at how media interact with significant social movements in society (for instance, in relation to the environment, peace and the advance of women and minorities). One example is offered by Gitlin's (1980) account of the US student movement in the late 1960s. This showed how the US media (for their own purposes) promulgated an image of the movement as activist and celebrity-led and inclined to violence, an image which shaped public opinion and caused the movement in some ways to live up to public expectations as portrayed in the media. A more recent study by van Zoonen (1992) of the rise of the women's movement in The Netherlands has adopted a 'social constructivist' approach to assessing the contribution of the media to events. She explains the perspective essentially as follows. The media are more than plain transmitters of movement messages and activities, but they do this selectively; it is not the transmission which counts so much as 'a particular *construction* of the movement's ideas and activities', influenced by many negotiations and conflicts within the news organization. She comments: 'The media image of the movement is the result of an intricate *interaction* between movement and media', leading to a certain *public identity* and *definition*.

The constructivist approach does not replace all earlier formulations of the effect process – for instance, in matters of attention-gaining, direct stimulus to individual behaviour or emotional response. It is also consistent with a good deal of earlier theory, although it departs radically in terms of method and research design by calling for much deeper, broader and more qualitative kinds of evidence, especially about the context of 'critical events' (a term for key moments in society when change is in play for good or ill, awareness of events is heightened, decisions are made and new paths are opened up) during which constructions are forged. It clearly owes more to the cultural than to the structural and behavioural traditions outlined earlier (Chapter 3). But it does not stand entirely apart from the latter, since investigation has to be located in a societal context and it assumes that eventual constructions are the outcome of numerous behaviours and cognitions by many participants in complex social events. The approach can be applied to a good many situations of presumed media influence, especially in relation to public opinion, social attitudes, political choice, ideology and many cognitions. The various formulations of frame and schema theory (Graber, 1984) can usefully be located under the same general heading (see pp. 506–7).

The four-phase account of the development of thinking about media effects is only one interpretation. In her overview of the field, Perse (2001) suggests that this and similar accounts of the development of effect theory are an oversimplification and may be misleading, especially by not recognizing the differences between various research areas. For instance, researches on children and on political communication have different histories. Instead of the historical account, she proposes to deal with key differences in terms of alternative models of effect. The four models she names are:

- direct effects;
- conditional effects (varying according to social and psychological factors);
- cumulative effects (gradual and long term);
- cognitive-transactional effects (with particular reference to schemata and framing).

In fact, these models correspond quite closely to the four phases described above. Figure 17.1 (from Perse, 2001) summarizes the main features of these models.

Models of media effects

	Nature of effects	Media content variables	Audience variables
Direct	Immediate, uniform, observable Short term Emphasis on change	Salience, arousal, realism	Not relevant
Conditional	Individualized Reinforcement as well as change Cognitive, affective and behavioural Long or short term	Not relevant	Social categories Social relationships Individual differences
Cumulative	Based on cumulative exposure Cognitive or affect Rarely behavioural Enduring effects	Consonant across channels Repetition	Not relevant
Cognitive-transactional	Immediate and short term Based on one-shot exposure Cognitive and affective; behavioural effects possible	Salience of visual cues	Schema make-up Mood Goals

Figure 17.1   Four models of media effects (Perse, 2001: 51)

Media power can vary with the times

Before leaving the historical aspect of research into media effects, it is worth reflecting on a suggestion by Carey (1988) that variations in *belief* in the power of mass communications may have a historical explanation. He writes: 'It can be argued that the basic reason behind the shift in the argument about the effects from a powerful to a limited to a more powerful model is that the social world was being transformed over this period.' Powerful effects were indeed signalled in a time of world upheaval around the two world wars, while the quieter 1950s and 1960s seemed more stable, until peace was again upset by social upheaval. It does seem that whenever the stability of society is disturbed, by crime, war, economic malaise or some 'moral panic', the mass media are given some of the responsibility. This suggestion is confirmed by claims made that the media contributed to the banking and credit crisis of 2008–9 by fuelling the earlier boom and failing to warn of impending bust. Some parts of the charge are convincing, but as usual the media are unlikely to have been more than a contributory factor.

We can only speculate about the reasons for such associations in time, but we cannot rule out the possibility that media *are* actually more influential in certain ways at times of crisis or heightened awareness. This might apply to the impact of the fall of communism in Europe or to international conflicts such as the Gulf and Balkan wars of the 1990s and the Afghanistan and Iraq wars that followed 9/11. There are several reasons for this possibility. People often know about the more significant historical events only through the media and may associate the message with the medium. In times of change and uncertainty, it is also highly probable that people are more dependent on media as a source of information and guidance (Ball-Rokeach and DeFleur, 1976; Ball-Rokeach, 1985, 1998). Media have also been shown to be more influential on matters outside immediate personal experience. Under conditions of tension and uncertainty, government, business and other elites and interests often try to use media to influence and control opinion. Perse (2001: 53–82) gives close attention to the role of the media at times of crisis and concludes that this role can be best accounted for in terms of functional theory (see pp. 98–9). She points out that media help to reduce uncertainty and fear by providing information and explanation. They also contribute to solidarity and mobilization in response to dangers and threats.

In a somewhat different context (that of the socializing effects of television on children), Rosengren and Windahl (1989) suggest that variations in evidence about the influence of television itself may reflect the fact that television was actually different in content and as a social experience in the 1980s compared with the 1950s when the first research was undertaken. It is also different in different societies. If that was true, then it has implications for today when television experience has again changed in many ways. The important if obvious point is that the media are not constant as a potential or actual influence, over time and between places.

Types of Communicative Power

The concept of power in human affairs has proved difficult to pin down, and not only in relation to the media. Where it has been defined, two alternative paths have been followed. One takes a behavioural and causal line of reasoning that is consistent with stimulus–response thinking and in which power is equated with the probability of achieving some given outcome, intended or not. The other model is sociological and derives from Max Weber's definition of power as the 'chance of a man or number of men to realize their will in a communal action even against the resistance of others who are participating in the action' (1964: 152). In this view of power, a relationship is presumed to exist between the partners to action and coercion is possible to achieve some aim. There are also winners and losers (a zero-sum situation).

While both models are relevant to the question of media effects, the second has proved to have more explanatory potential, even where effects are not intended, since the achievement of most effects requires the co-operation or compliance of the person to be influenced. However, when applied to mass communication, there may not be obvious partners to action and there is no chance of true coercion. Communicative or symbolic power is generally different from other kinds of power since it depends on non-material factors (trust, rationality, respect, affection, etc.). The point to underline here is also that there are different ways in which symbolic power can be used. The main types are as follows:

- by way of information;
- by stimulation to action;
- by directing attention differentially;
- by persuasion;
- by defining situations and framing 'reality'.

While there is some evidence of media effect according to each of these routes, they do not have an equal potential, at least not for an independent communication effect. For a number of reasons (especially the lack of resistance and low threshold for an effect), more effects from media occur as a result of defining situations and framing reality, provision of information or the differential direction of attention (including the amplification of certain images and ideas) than from persuasion or stimulation to action. These points are largely indicated by and consistent with the 'negotiated influence' phase described above.

Levels and Kinds of Effects

Media 'effects' are simply the consequences of what the mass media do, whether intended or not. The expression 'media power', on the other hand, refers to a general potential on the part of the media to have effects, especially of a planned kind. 'Media effectiveness' is a statement about the *efficiency* of media in achieving a given aim and always implies intention or some planned communication goal. Such distinctions are important for precision, although it is hard to keep to a consistent usage. Even more essential for research and theory is to observe the distinction between 'levels' of occurrence, especially the levels of individual, group or organization, social institution, national society, and culture. Each or all can be affected by mass communication, and effects at any one level (especially a 'higher' level) often imply some effects at other levels. Most media effect research has been carried out, methodologically, at the individual level, though often with the aim of drawing conclusions relating to collective or higher levels.

Perhaps the most confusing aspect of research on effects is the multiplicity and complexity of the phenomena involved. Broad distinctions are normally made between effects which are cognitive (to do with knowledge and opinion), effects which are affectual (relating to attitude and feelings) and effects on behaviour. This threefold distinction was treated in early research as following a logical order from the first to the third, and with an implied increase in significance (behaviour counting more than knowledge). In fact, it is no longer easy to sustain the distinction between the three concepts or to accept the unique logic of that particular order of occurrence (see p. 469). Nor is behaviour (such as acts of voting or purchasing) necessarily more significant than other kinds of effect.

There are several ways of differentiating between the types of media effect. Klapper (1960) distinguished between *conversion, minor change* and *reinforcement*, which are respectively: change of opinion or belief according to the intention of the communicator; change in form or intensity of cognition, belief or behaviour; and confirmation by the receiver of an existing belief, opinion or behaviour pattern. This threefold distinction needs to be widened to include other possibilities, especially at levels above that of the individual (see Chapter 1). The main options are listed in Box 17.2. The two effect types that imply absence of any effect involve different conceptions of media processes. In the case of an individual, reinforcement is a probable consequence of selective and persistent attention on the part of the receiver to content that is congruent with his or her existing views.

17.2 Main kinds of media-induced change

The media can:

- Cause intended change
- Cause unintended change
- Cause minor change (form or intensity)
- Facilitate change (intended or not)
- Reinforce what exists (no change)
- Prevent change

Any of these changes may occur at the level of the individual, society, institution or culture.

'Preventing change', on the other hand, implies the deliberate supply of one-sided or ideologically shaped content in order to inhibit change in a conforming public. Often this just refers to the repetition of consensual views and absence of any challenge. The 'no change' effect from the media, of which we have so much evidence, requires very close attention because of its long-term implications. It is a somewhat misleading expression, since anything that alters the probability of opinion or belief distribution in the future is an intervention into social process and thus an effect.

Lang and Lang (1981) pointed to yet other types of effect that have been observed, including 'reciprocal', 'boomerang' and **'third-party' effects**. The first refers to the consequences for a person or even an institution of becoming the object of media coverage. A planned event, for instance, is often changed by the very fact of being televised. There is often an interaction between media and the objects of reporting. Gitlin (1980) showed, for example, how the US student movement in the 1960s was influenced by its own publicity. A 'boomerang' effect, causing change in the opposite direction to that intended, is a very familiar phenomenon (or risk) in campaigning. A 'third-party' effect refers to the belief, often encountered, that other people are likely to be influenced but not oneself. The term 'sleeper effect' has also been used to refer to effects that do not show up until much later.

In their discussion of dimensions of effects, McLeod et al. (1991) also point to the difference between effects which are diffuse or general (such as the supposed effects of television as a medium) and those that are content specific. In the latter case, a certain inbuilt structure or tendency (for instance, a political bias) is singled out as the potential cause of change.

Processes of Media Effect: a Typology

In order to provide an outline of developments in theory and research, we begin by interrelating two of the distinctions already mentioned: between the intended and the unintended, and between the short term and the long term. This device was suggested by Golding (1981) to help distinguish different concepts of news and its effects. He argued that, in the case of news, intended short-term effects may be considered as 'bias'; unintended short-term effects fall under the heading of 'unwitting bias'; intended long-term effects indicate 'policy' (of the medium concerned); while unintended long-term effects of news are 'ideology'. Something of the same way of thinking helps us to map out, in terms of these two co-ordinates, the main kinds of media effect process which have been dealt with in the research literature. The result is given in Figure 17.2.

The main entries in the figure can be briefly described, although their meaning will be made more explicit in the discussion of theory that follows.

Planned and short term

- *Propaganda*. Defined as 'the deliberate and systematic attempt to shape perceptions, manipulate cognitions, and direct behaviour to achieve a response that furthers the desired intent of the propagandist' (Jowett and O'Donnell, 1999). Propaganda can also be long term.
- *Individual response*. The process by which individuals change, or resist change, following exposure to messages designed to influence attitude, knowledge or behaviour.
- *Media campaign*. The situation in which a number of media are used in an organized way to achieve a persuasive or informational purpose with a chosen population.
- *News learning*. The short-term cognitive effect of exposure to mass media news, as measured by tests of audience recall, recognition or comprehension.
- *Framing*. As a media effect, refers to the adoption by the audience of the same interpretative frameworks and 'spin' used to contextualize news reports and event accounts. An associated process is that of **priming** (where media foreground the criteria for assessing public events or figures).   ✱
- *Agenda-setting*. The process by which the relative attention given to items or issues in news coverage influences the rank order of public awareness of issues and attribution of significance.

Unplanned and short term

- *Individual reaction*. Unplanned or unpredicted consequences of individual exposure to a media stimulus. This has mainly been noticed in the form of imitation and learning, especially of aggressive or deviant acts (including suicide). The term 'triggering' has also been used. Related types of effect include strong emotional responses, sexual arousal, and reactions of fear or anxiety.
- *Collective reaction*. Here some of the same effects are experienced simultaneously by many people in a shared situation or context, leading to joint action, usually of an unregulated

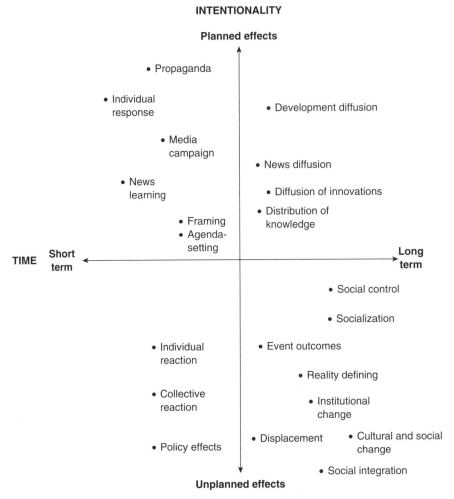

Figure 17.2 A typology of media effects. Effects can be located on two dimensions: that of time span and that of intentionality

and non-institutional kind. Fear, anxiety and anger are the most potent reactions, which can lead to panic or civil disturbance.

- *Policy effects*. The unintended impact of news on government policy and action by the highlighting of some crisis, abuse, danger, and so on. The chief example is the so-called CNN effect on foreign policy.

Planned and long term

- *Development diffusion*. The planned use of communication for purposes of long-term development, campaigns and other means of influence, especially the interpersonal network and authority structure of the community or society.

- *News diffusion*. The spread of awareness of particular (news) events through a given population over time, with particular reference to the extent of penetration (proportion ultimately knowing) and the means by which information is received (personal versus media sources).
- **Diffusion of innovations**. The process of takeup of technological innovations within a given population, often on the basis of advertising or general publicity. It can be an unintended as well as an intended effect.　　　　　　　　　　　　　　　　＊
- *Distribution of knowledge*. The consequences of media news and information for the distribution of knowledge as between social groups. The main reference is to the closing or widening of '**knowledge gaps**'. A related phenomenon is the 'digital divide'.　＊

Unplanned and long term

- *Social control*. Refers here to systematic tendencies to promote conformity to an established order or a pattern of behaviour. Depending on one's social theory, this can be considered either as a deliberate or as an unintended extension of socialization.
- *Socialization*. The informal contribution of media to the learning and adoption of norms, values and expectations of behaviour in particular social roles and situations.
- *Event outcomes*. Referring to the part played by media in conjunction with institutional forces in the course and resolution of major 'critical' events (see Lang and Lang, 1981). Examples could include revolution, major domestic political upheavals and matters of war and peace. Less significant events, such as elections, could also figure here (Chaffee, 1975).
- *Reality defining and construction of meaning*. Effects on public cognitions and frames of interpretation. This kind of effect requires the more or less active participation of receivers in the process of constructing their own meaning.
- *Institutional change*. The adaptation by existing institutions to developments in the media, especially those affecting their own communication functions (see the notion of 'reciprocal effects').
- *Displacement*. The many possible consequences of allocation of time to media use away from other (mainly free-time) pursuits, including social participation.
- *Cultural and social change*. Shifts in the overall pattern of values, behaviours and symbolic forms characterizing a sector of society (such as youth), a whole society or a set of societies. The possible strengthening or weakening of cultural identity may also be an example of effect.
- *Social integration*. Integration (or its absence) may be observed at different levels, especially group, local community or nation, which also correspond with the distribution areas of media. Effects can also be short term, as in response to a shared public disaster or emergency.

Individual Response and Reaction: the Stimulus–Response Model

The dimensions according to which types of effect have been classified in Figure 17.2 are not the only possibilities, and the resulting typology may not always seem completely logical. At the heart of the problem is the fact that any process of media effect on individuals must begin with attention, or 'exposure' to some media message. The results of this event extend through time and take different, often collective forms. The effects themselves, for instance acquiring knowledge of events by way of news, are not uniquely short or long term, but can be treated as both. Because the 'inputs' from media are so numerous, varied and interrelated, we cannot in practice separate them according to these or other dimensions, although we have to do so for purposes of analysis. However, the stimulus–response model is unambiguously short term and individualistic. Two of the entries in Figure 17.2 – *individual response* and *individual reaction* – share this same underlying behavioural model. The model's main features can be simply represented as follows:

single message   →   individual receiver   →   reaction

This applies more or less equally to intended and to unintended effects, although there is a significant difference between a *response* (implying some interaction with the receiver and also a learning process) and a *reaction* (which implies no choice or interaction on the part of the receiver and is essentially a behavioural reflex). A more extended version of the basic response and learning process as it occurs in persuasion and opinion formation is indicated by McGuire (1973) in the form of six stages in sequence: presentation, attention, comprehension, yielding, retention and overt behaviour.

This elaboration is sufficient to show why stimulus–response theory has had to be modified to take account of selective attention, interpretation, response and recall. The model, in whatever form, is highly pragmatic: it predicts, other things being equal, the occurrence of a response (verbal or behavioural act) according to the presence or absence of an appropriate stimulus (message). It presumes a more or less direct behavioural effect in line with the intention of the initiator and consistent with some overt stimulus to act in a certain way which is built into the message. In discussions of media effect, this has sometimes been referred to as the 'bullet' or 'hypodermic' theory, terms that far exaggerate the probability of effect and the vulnerability of the receiver to influence. No adequate account can be taken of the many mediating effects that apply in natural settings of media influence. Nor can it take account of effects that occur over time, long after the moment of the 'stimulus'.

Mediating Conditions of Effect

The revision of the stimulus–response model involved the identification of the conditions that mediate effects. McGuire (1973) indicated the main kinds of variable as having to do with source, content, channel, receivers and destination. There is reason to believe that messages stemming from an authoritative and credible source will be relatively more effective, as will those from sources that are attractive or close (similar) to the receiver. As to content, effectiveness is associated with repetition, consistency and lack of alternatives (a monopoly situation). It is also more likely where the subject matter is unambiguous and concrete (Trenaman, 1967).

In general, effect as intended is also likely to be greater on topics that are distant from, or less important for, the receiver (lower degree of ego involvement or prior commitment). Variables of style (such as personalization), types of appeal (such as emotional versus rational) and order and balance of argument have been found to play a part, but too variably to sustain any general prediction. Channel (medium) factors have often been investigated, with mixed results, mainly because content and receiver factors dominate learning outcomes. It is also hard to discriminate between intrinsic channel differences and the differences between media in which channels are embedded (such as press versus television).

Generally, research has failed to establish clearly the relative value of different modes (audio, visual, and so on) in any consistent way, although the written or spoken verbal message seems to take primacy over pictorial images, according to measures of recall or comprehension (e.g. Katz et al., 1977). However, this finding relates to cognitive learning from news information when averaged out. It leaves out of the account the emotionally compelling power of certain vivid images that seem to speak clearly for themselves. The example of the Abu Graib photographs of prisoner abuse in Iraq again comes to mind, whatever their real status as evidence might have been (Bennett et al., 2007). As we have seen, a number of obvious receiver variables can also be relevant to effect, but special notice should perhaps be given to the degree of motivation, interest and level of prior knowledge. The degree of motivation or involvement has often been singled out as of particular importance in the influence process and in determining the sequence in which different kinds of effect occur (Krugman, 1965).

According to Ray (1973), the normal 'effect hierarchy' as found, for instance, in the work of Hovland et al. (1949) on wartime propaganda films, is a process leading from cognitive learning (the most common effect) to affective response (like or dislike, opinion, attitude) to 'conative' effect (behaviour or action). Ray argues, with some supporting evidence, that this model is normal only under conditions of high involvement (high interest and attention). With low involvement (common in many television viewing situations and especially with advertising) the sequence may go from cognition directly to behaviour, with affective adjustment occurring later to bring attitude into line with behaviour (reduction of dissonance: Festinger, 1957).

In itself, this formulation casts doubt on the logic and design of many persuasive communication campaigns which assume attitude to be an unambiguous correlate and predictor of behaviour. There is also a question mark against campaign evaluations based on measures of attitude change alone. The question of consistency between the three elements is also at issue. According to Chaffee and Roser (1986), high involvement is also likely to be a necessary condition for consistency of effects, and thus for a stable and enduring influence. Their preferred model of media effect involves a repetitive sequence from low involvement, through perception of dissonance and then to learning, with cumulative results. In this view, shallow and easily forgotten information can develop into a reasoned set of ideas and into action, especially under conditions of repeated exposure (as in a systematic campaign).

In any natural (non-laboratory) media situation, individual receivers will choose which stimulus to attend to or to avoid, will interpret its meaning variably and will react or not behaviourally, according to choice (Bauer, 1964). This seriously undermines the validity of the conditioning model, since the factors influencing selectivity are bound to be strongly related to the nature of the stimulus, working for or against the occurrence of an effect. Our attention should consequently be drawn away from the simple fact of experiencing a stimulus and towards the mediating conditions described above, especially in their totality and mutual interaction.

Source–Receiver Relations and Effect

As has been noted, trust in and respect for the source can be conducive to influence. There have been several attempts to develop theories of influence taking account of relationships between sender (or message sent) and receiver. Most of these theories refer to interpersonal relations. One framework has been suggested by French and Raven (1953), indicating five alternative forms of communication relationship in which social power may be exercised by a sender and influence accepted by a receiver. The underlying proposition is that influence through communication is a form of exercise of power that depends on certain assets or properties of the agent of influence (the communicator).

The first two types of power asset are classified as *reward* and *coercion*, respectively. The former depends on there being gratification for the recipient from a message (enjoyment, for instance, or useful advice); the latter depends on some negative consequence of non-compliance (uncommon in mass communication). A third type is described as *referent* power and refers to the attraction or prestige of the sender, such that the receiver identifies with the person and is willingly influenced, for affective reasons.

Fourthly, there is *legitimate* power, according to which influence is accepted on the assumption that a sender has a strong claim to expect to be followed or respected. This is not very common in mass communication but may occur where authoritative messages are transmitted from political sources or other relevant institutional leaders. This type of power presumes an established relationship between source and receiver that predates and survives any particular instance of mass communication. Finally, there is *expert* power, which operates where superior knowledge is attributed to the source or sender by the receiver. This situation is not uncommon in the spheres of media news and advertising, where experts are often brought in for explanation, comment or endorsement. Examples of exploitation of all five types of media power can be found in advertising and informational campaigns, and more than one of these power sources is likely to be operative on any given occasion.

A rather similar attempt to account for effects (especially on individual opinion) was made by Kelman (1961). He named three processes of influence. One of these, *compliance*, refers to the acceptance of influence in expectation of some reward or to avoid punishment. Another, *identification*, occurs when an individual wishes to be more like the source and imitates or adopts behaviour accordingly (similar to 'referent' power). A third, *internalization*, describes influence that is guided by the receiver's own pre-existing needs and values. This last-named process may also be described as a 'functional' explanation of influence (or effect), since change is mainly explicable in terms of the receiver's own motives, needs and wishes. According to

Katz (1960), a 'functional' approach is generally preferable to one that assumes the audience is either irrational and prey to powerful suggestions or highly rational and able to critically process and evaluate competing sources of information.

The Campaign

Basic features

There are many different kinds of campaign. These include: public information campaigns designed to benefit the recipient on matters such as health and safety or to provide a public service; election campaigns for parties or candidates; advocacy campaigns for a particular cause; campaigns in developing countries for some aspect of 'modernization'; commercial advertising; government corporate image-making; propaganda or **'public diplomacy'** on behalf of national foreign policy. These types are likely to differ not only in terms of goals, but according to the norms and rules, the degree of social support they enjoy, the methods and strategies applied and also the relative significance of the media contribution relative to other resources (e.g. economic incentives or personal contact). Campaigns have specific and overt aims and a limited timespan. The population targeted for influence is usually large and dispersed.

  The summary presentation in Box 17.3 draws attention to key features of the general process. First, the originator of the campaign is almost always a collectivity – a political party, government, church, charity, pressure group, business firm, and so on – rather than an individual. The known position in society of the source will strongly affect its chances of success in a campaign. Secondly, campaigns are also often concerned with directing, reinforcing and activating existing tendencies towards socially approved objectives such as voting, buying goods, raising money for good causes or achieving better health and safety. The scope for novelty of effect or major change is thus often intrinsically limited, and the media are employed to assist other institutional forces.

Typical elements and sequence of a public media campaign **17.3**

A collective *source* with
socially approved *goals*, uses
several *channels* and
with different *messages*
for different *target groups*,
subject to *filter conditions*
and variable *information processing*
in order to achieve *planned effects*
that have to be *evaluated*.

Thirdly, a campaign usually consists of many messages distributed through several media, with the chances of reach and effect varying according to the established nature of the channels and the message content. A key consideration is the degree to which the identified target group within the public as a whole is actually reached. A distinctive feature of many campaigns is that they aim to *redistribute* a limited amount of public attention, action or money (thus a zero-sum condition). This applies especially to advertising, but it is also true of politics and, in practice, to most fund-raising for charitable purposes.

This simple presentation does not really do justice to the complexity of campaigning in the contemporary world, especially with the availability of entirely new kinds of media or 'platforms'. The number of possibilities is too large to describe, but special mention should be given to social networking sites and search engines. In addition, there are many ways of obtaining visibility in media content without being identified as a persuasive campaigner. The complexity defies any close evaluation except in terms of goals reached or not.

Filter conditions

There is a set of 'filter conditions' or potential barriers that can facilitate or hinder the flow of messages to the whole or chosen public. Several of these have already been discussed and they are to some extent predictable in their operation, although only in very broad terms. *Attention* is important because without it there can be no effect, and it will depend on the interest and relevance of content for the receivers, on their motives and predispositions, and on channel-related factors. *Perception* matters because messages are open to alternative interpretations, and the success of a campaign depends to some extent on its message being interpreted in the same way as intended by the campaign source. Research has indicated the occurrence of 'boomerang' effects – for instance, in attempts to modify prejudice (e.g. Cooper and Jahoda, 1947; Vidmar and Rokeach, 1974) – and it is a constant preoccupation of commercial and political campaigners to try to avoid counter-effects which will aid the 'opposition'. Unwanted side-effects also occur in campaigns to raise money for good causes. For instance, appeals on behalf of the Third World may also create an image of incompetence and inferiority of the region or peoples involved (Benthall, 1993).

Motivation also plays a part, especially the variable of type and degree of expected satisfaction on the part of the audience member that can influence either learning or attitude change. These 'filter conditions' together determine the composition of the public reached, and the success of a campaign is ultimately dependent on a reasonable 'fit' between the composition of the planned 'target' public and the actual public reached.

Personal influence

The *group situation* of the receiver can mediate the effects of campaigns that originate 'outside' the many groups to which people belong, according to age, life circumstances, work, neighbourhood, interest, religion, and so on. Group allegiance, or its absence, has consequences for whether messages are noticed and then accepted or rejected. While the concept is relevant to any effect, it originated in the study of campaigns, and the circumstances of medium-term and deliberate attempts to persuade and inform are most conducive to the intervention of personal contacts as sources of influence. The underlying idea of personal influence is a simple one; its originators expressed it, in the course of their research into the 1940 US presidential election campaign (Lazarsfeld et al., 1944: 151), as follows: 'ideas often flow from radio and print to the opinion leaders and from them to the less active sections of the population'.

Thus, two elements are involved. The first is the notion of a population stratified according to interest and activity in relation to media and to the topics dealt with by mass media (in brief, 'opinion leaders' and 'others'). The second is the notion of a 'two-step flow' of influence rather than direct contact between 'stimulus' and 'respondent'. These ideas were further developed and elaborated by Katz and Lazarsfeld (1955). While confirming the importance of conversation and personal contact as an accompaniment to and perhaps modifier of media influence, subsequent research has not yet clearly shown that personal influence always acts as a strong independent or *counteractive* source of influence on the matters normally affected by mass media.

It has become clear that the division between opinion 'leaders' and 'followers' is variable from topic to topic; the roles are interchangeable, and there are many who cannot be classified as either one or the other (and may thus be outside the scope of group influence) (Robinson, 1976). It also seems probable that what occurs is as likely to be a multi-step as a two-step flow. It is also clear that direct effects from the media can and do occur without 'intervention' from opinion leaders, and it is highly probable that personal influence is as likely to reinforce the effects of media as to counteract them (see Chaffee and Hochheimer, 1982; Bandura, 2002), although such sources of influence operate spontaneously and are not easy to manipulate for planned communication. The newer media, as mentioned above, seem particularly suited to developing the power of personal influence and advertisers often mention the desirability of 'word of mouth' endorsement and the possibilities of '**viral advertising**', where consumers themselves do the work of onward transmission.

In whose interest?

Another dimension that should also be kept in mind is that campaigns can differ according to what Rogers and Storey (1987) call the 'locus of benefit'. Some campaigns purport to be in the interests of the recipient (such as health and public information campaigns), while others are clearly on behalf of the sender – most commercial advertising and most 'propaganda'. This does not necessarily give the former a decisive advantage, if they fail to meet other basic conditions of success (such as reaching the intended target audience or choosing the right message), though it may endow them with the advantages of receiver trust and goodwill.

Conclusion

This chapter has provided a general introduction to the question of media effects and their measurement. That media have effects is not in doubt, although it is difficult to establish when and to what degree an effect has occurred or is likely to occur. This difficulty is not primarily due to methodological obstacles, although these do exist. It mainly arises from the very number and variety of possible effects and of the facts and conditions that relate to the occurrence of effects. Not least problematic is the fact that effects, when they do occur, involve not only the actions of communicators, but the orientations and actions of the audience. Most effects are in some degree interactions between senders and receivers. Many longer-term effects of mass media do not involve the initial or immediate audience at all, but are the secondary responses of others.

Further Reading

Bennett, W.L. and Iyengar, S. (2008) 'A new era of minimal effects? Changing foundations of political communication', *Journal of Communication*, 58 (4): 707–31.
The authors interpret current trends of diversification of channels and fragmentation of audience attention as reducing the possibilities once inherent in mass media for major society-wide effects.

Bryant, J. and Zillman, D. (2002) *Perspectives on Media Effects*, 3rd edn. Hillsdale, NJ: Erlbaum.
A wide-ranging assemblage of key chapters of theory-based research articles by different authors covering the whole field.

Grabe, M.E., Karnhaus, R. and Yelyan, N. (2009) 'Informing citizens: how people with different levels of education process TV, newspaper and Web news', *Journal of Broadcasting and Electronic Media*, 53 (1): 90–111.
Reports experimental findings which indicate that the higher the educational level, the more people learn from Web news, the reverse being true for television news. This suggests that the Internet could lead to a widening information gap in society.

Graber, D. (1990) 'Seeing is remembering: how visuals contribute to TV news', *Journal of Communication*, 40 (3): 134–55.
Convincing evidence of the contribution of visuals to news learning, although some biases are involved and the effects vary according to personal factors.

Lowery, S.A. and DeFleur, M.L. (eds) (1995) *Milestones in Mass Communication Research*, 3rd edn. New York: Longman.
Contains summaries of many early influential studies, mainly concerned with effects, all based in the USA.

Perse, E.M. (2001) *Media Effects and Society*. Mahwah, NJ: Erlbaum.
A comprehensive, integrated overview of nearly all aspects of empirical research on mass media influence, with good explanations of concepts and theories. Probably still the best such volume available.

Online Readings

De Vreese, C. (2006) 'Media message flows and interpersonal communication', *Communication Research*, 33 (1): 19–37.

Graber, M.E., Lang, A. and Zhao, X. (2002) 'News content and form: implications for memory and audience evaluation', *Communication Research*, 30 (4): 387–413.

McDonald, D.G. (2004) 'Twentieth century media effect research', in J.D.H. Downing, D. McQuail, P. Schlesinger and E. Wartella (eds), *The Sage Handbook of Media Studies*, pp. 183–200. Thousand Oaks, CA: Sage.

Schulz, W. (2004) 'Reconstructing mediatization as an analytic concept', *European Journal of Communication*, 19 (1): 87–102.

18

Social-Cultural Effects

This chapter deals with a wide range of media effects, including both short- and long-term processes, those that are collective as well as individual, considered either negative or positive. For the most part, they are effects not directly intended by the media, although they may be predictable. They are united by having a predominant reference to social or cultural aspects of media effects, in line with theories of mass communication discussed at the start of the book (especially in Chapters 4 and 5). Intended informational and political effects are reserved for discussion in the following chapter, although there is no sharp division since unintended social effects also involve learning and other cognitive processes. The effects dealt with often have a social problematic character, especially where they relate to children and young people and to antisocial tendencies generally. This is a bias that has shaped research into mass communication since its earliest days and should not be taken to mean that the actual effects of mass media are more negative than positive. For the most part, the basic theories and processes of effects have been outlined in Chapter 17, although some additions are made, especially the model of behavioural effect, with which the chapter begins. The main aim here is to assess briefly, with reference to the evidence, a number of hypotheses about the social and cultural influence of the media, especially television.

A Model of Behavioural Effect

The developments of theory described in Chapter 17 take one a good way from the simple conditioning model and help to account for some of the complexities encountered in research. It is obvious that in situations of unintended effect, some individuals will be more prone than others to react or respond to stimuli, 'more at risk' when harmful effects are involved. An elaboration of the basic stimulus–response model for the case of television viewing has been developed by Comstock et al. (1978) to help organize the results of research in this field, especially relating to violence. It rests on the presupposition that media experience is no different in essence from any other experience, act or observation which might have consequences for learning or behaviour.

The process depicted by the model, and shown in Figure 18.1, takes the form of a sequence following the initial act of 'exposure' to a form of behaviour on television ('TV act'). This is the first and main 'input' to learning or imitating the behaviour concerned. Other relevant inputs (enclosed within the box in Figure 18.1) are the degree of excitement and arousal ('TV arousal') and the degree to which alternative behaviours ('TV alternatives') are depicted: the more arousal and the fewer behaviours (or more repetition), the more likely learning is to take place. Two other conditions (inputs) have to do with the portrayal of consequences ('TV perceived consequences') and the degree of reality ('TV perceived reality'): the more that positive consequences seem to exceed negative ones and the more true to life the television behaviour, the more likely is learning ('P TV act') to take place. Where the conditions for effect are not met ($P = 0$), the individual returns to the start of the process; where some probability of effect exists ($P > 0$), the question of opportunity to act arises.

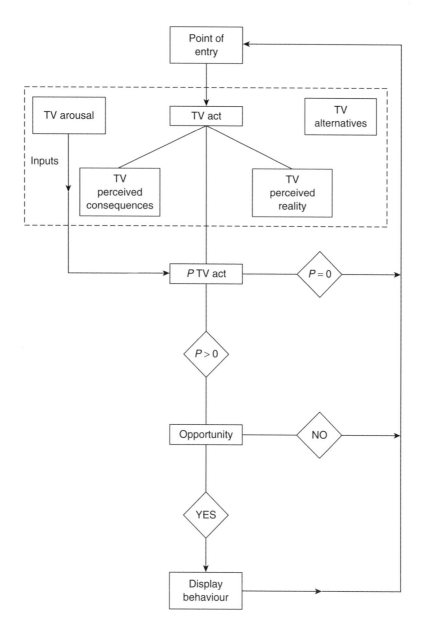

Figure 18.1   A simplified version of Comstock et al.'s (1978) model of television effects on individual behaviour. The effect process is a continuous sequence of repeated exposure to representations of behaviour ('TV acts'); effects depend on the way the behaviour is perceived, on inputs from the situation and on opportunities to act out and display the behaviour concerned (McQuail and Windahl, 1993)

All the inputs mentioned affect the probability of learning the action (the effect), but ultimately any resulting behaviour is conditional on there being an opportunity to put the act into practice. Apart from opportunity, the most important condition is 'arousal', since without arousal (connoting also interest and attention) there will be no learning. While full confirmation of this model from research is not yet available, it is an advance on the simple conditioning model and useful for directing attention to key aspects of any given case.

The Media, Violence and Crime

Much attention has focused on the potential of media to encourage, if not cause, crime, violence, and aggressive, antisocial and even criminal behaviour. The reason for concern lies primarily in the repeated demonstration of the high level of portrayal of crime and violence in popular media of all kinds (see Smith et al., 2002; and Chapter 14). A secondary reason is the widespread perception, whether correct or not, that the social evils mentioned grew step by step with the rise of the mass media during the twentieth century. Each new popular medium has given rise to a new wave of alarm about its possible effects. More recently, both the Internet and popular music have been linked to random acts of violence perpetrated by young people in particular. Aside from the 'problem' posed by new media outside the control of society and parents, there has been a general change in media that has encouraged a fresh look at an old issue. There has been a proliferation of television channels, a decline in regulation and a lowering of thresholds about what is acceptable, making it likely that children will have a much larger diet of televised violence (and also 'adult content') than ever before.

The persistent belief that screen violence (especially) is a cause of actual violence and aggression has led to many thousands of research studies, but no great agreement on the degree of causal influence from the media. Nevertheless, the programme of research carried out for the US Surgeon General at the end of the 1960s resulted, according to Lowery and DeFleur (1995), in three main conclusions:

- Television content is heavily saturated with violence.
- Children are spending more and more time exposed to violent content.
- Overall, the evidence supports the hypothesis that the viewing of violent entertainment increases the likelihood of aggressive behaviour.

These conclusions still appear to stand more than thirty years later.

Theory

The main components of hypotheses about violent effects have remained fairly constant. Wartella et al. (1998: 58–9) outline three basic theoretical models for describing the process of learning and imitation of television violence. One is the 'social learning theory' of Albert Bandura, according to which children learn from media models what behaviour will be rewarded and what punished. Secondly, there are 'priming' effects (Berkowitz, 1984): when people view violence it activates or 'primes' other related thoughts and evaluations, leading to a greater predisposition to use violence in interpersonal situations. Thirdly, Huesmann's (1986) script theory holds that social behaviour is controlled by 'scripts' that indicate how to respond to events. Violence on television is encoded in such a way as to lead to violence, as a result of aggressive scripts.

In addition to learning and modelling effects, there is a widespread belief that exposure to portrayals of violence leads to a general 'desensitization' that lowers inhibitions against, and increases tolerance of violent behaviour. As with all such theories, there are many variables influencing the disposition of a person and several relating to the depiction of violence. The main contextual factors (in content) influencing audience reactions have already been indicated in Chapter 14 (Box 14.4) and in Figure 18.1. In addition to variables of personal disposition and content, there are also variables of the viewing situation that are important, especially being alone or being with parents or peers. The model of behavioural effect outlined in Figure 18.1 applies especially to several of the effects mentioned.

Content

The main findings of the Surgeon General's report, as summarized above, have often been confirmed (see, for example, Comstock, 1988; Bryant and Zillman, 2002; Oliver, 2003). There has continued to be a great deal of violence portrayed on television, and it exerts a great attraction for the young. Wilson and Smith (2002) found from the 1998 US National Television and Violence Study that programmes targeted at children actually contained more violence than other types of programme (see also Smith et al., 2002). It is less easy to say if the average degree of exposure has increased or not over time, but the potential to see screen violence has gradually extended to most parts of the world, along with the means of viewing. Groebel (1998), reporting on a global survey of violence on television on behalf of Unesco, involving 5,000 children in 23 countries, commented on the universality of media violence and on the widespread fascination with aggressive media hero figures, especially among boys. For instance, he found that 88% of the world's children knew Arnold Schwarzenegger's *Terminator* (1998: 182).

Evidence of effect

The third finding noted above, concerning effects on behaviour, is much less unanimous and has always been controversial because of the industry and policy implications. It is not easy to be certain on this matter, and any general authoritative statement takes on a political character (Ball-Rokeach, 2001). The American Psychological Association (2003) concluded that 'there is absolutely no doubt that those who are heavy viewers of this [television] violence demonstrate increased acceptance of aggressive attitudes and increased aggressive behavior' (cited in Wartella et al., 1998). However, even this falls short of a clear statement of causation and leaves aside the question of other influences, such as environment. Groebel (1998) noticed in his finding that children from high-aggression environments (crime and war) and who were in a 'problematic emotional state' were much more likely to view and be attracted by aggressive violence than were others.

In her survey of the views of European academic researchers into media and violence, Linné (1998) asked their opinion of the causal link between violence in the media and violence in society. Twenty-two per cent thought there was an 'evident causal link', 33% a 'vague causal link and only for some children' and 4% 'no causal link'. The remainder found the issue too problematic to be given such a simple answer. In general, Linné found that research had shifted from the question of causation towards that of understanding the appeal of violence that undoubtedly exists.

From Groebel's research (see above) comes the observation (1998: 195) that 'children's aggressive behaviour patterns and perceptions are a mirror of what they experience in their real environment: frustration; aggression; problematic circumstances'. He goes on to say (1998: 198): 'Media violence … is primarily presented in a rewarding context … [and] satisfies different needs. It "compensates" own frustrations and deficits in problem areas.' It offers 'thrills for children in a less problematic environment. For boys it creates a frame of reference for "attractive role models" … The "reward characteristics" of aggression are more systematically promoted than non-aggressive ways of coping with one's life.' These findings are not novel and echo the lessons of much earlier research. We know for sure that undesirable effects occur following attention to television violence, although they are generally mediated by way of other factors that may well be the 'real' or fundamental cause.

The possibility that media portrayals of violence and aggression might have some positive effects by allowing a vicarious and harmless release of emotion and aggression has sometimes been advanced (see Perse, 2001: 220–1). The term **'catharsis'**, derived from Aristotle's theory of drama, has been applied to this process. Although it is clear that most aggression aroused by media portrayals is vicariously released without harm to others, there is little empirical support for a theory that sees a benefit in exposure to violence.

Inducement of fright

Another frequently observed effect of violent and 'horror' content is the arousal of fear and emotional disturbance (Cantor, 2002). Adults as well as children often seek out fright-inducing content for thrills and entertainment, but there are also unintended and negative consequences for some individuals. Fear induced by media can often be intense and endure for long periods. It is not always easy to predict which content will be disturbing. In assessing the likely degree of and harm of frightening content, we need to distinguish according to types of content (e.g. physical or psychological threat), degree of realism, motivation for 'exposure', plus receiver variables of age personality and emotional stability. Girls do seem more susceptible than boys to media-induced fear (Cantor, 2002). The context of exposure can also play a part. Valkenburg et al. (2000) found that 31% of children surveyed in Holland reported being frightened by television, but nearly always by films or adult series.

Media and crime

Although the media have often been invoked as a potential cause of real crime (leaving aside aggression and violence), research has uncovered no such causal connection. The reasons for treating media as a suspect are largely circumstantial. The theoretical arguments include the possibility that media glamorize the criminal lifestyle, show the rewards of crime and teach techniques. Nevertheless, the overwhelming message of the media has always been that crime does not pay and that criminals are not attractive people. While there are doubts about the effects on behaviour of media portrayals of crime, in fact and fiction, there is little doubt that they influence opinions about the incidence of crime (see, for example, Lowry et al., 2003) and about the risks of being a victim (see below on 'cultivation analysis'). In doing so, media portrayals can shape attitudes and normative standards generally. For instance, Krcmar and Vierig (2005) showed that exposure to TV violence (even of a fantasy sort) has a negative effect on a child's moral reasoning about justified violence.

The possible link between media portrayal and actual violence has been highlighted by some cases of apparently motiveless killing, where an association of the perpetrators with certain media can be established, as with the 1999 Columbine School massacre and the similar event in Erfurt, Germany, in 2002. There have been a number of court cases in the United States alleging media stimuli as a cause of violence, although none has succeeded. Dee (1987) found that liability was thought to depend mainly on the question of negligence, which depends on whether the media took unreasonable risks. The extreme rarity of such cases of alleged effect makes it difficult to support a case against media, without leading to widespread suppression and censorship.

A similar problematic issue arises in the case of the effects of sexually explicit content. Perse concluded from her review of research that such material does encourage the acceptance of violence against women and desensitizes those exposed to it: 'exposure to pornography seems to be associated with harmful consequences' (2001: 229). Even so, the issue remains unsettled. Einseidel (1988) reviewed the findings of three public commissions (in Britain, Canada and the USA) and concluded that social scientific evidence has been unable to settle the issue. Political and ideological considerations cannot be excluded from the interpretation of evidence. There is also a potential inconsistency between legal thinking that typically adopts a direct model of effects, and content and media theory that has cast doubt on this model (see Calvert, 1997; Wackwitz, 2002).

A category of media effect not covered by the preceding discussion concerns violence that may be perpetrated at the instigation of the media against certain minorities, outgroups or hate figures. Although media are forbidden by law to incite violence openly, they can knowingly demonize identifiable persons or groups in such a way that there is a real risk of violence by individual or collective action. There is circumstantial evidence that violence has been directed at such groups as child sex offenders, other sexual deviants, ethnic minorities of different kinds, conscientious objectors, alleged terrorists, gypsies, migrants and so on, with a plausible connection to (effectively) hate campaigns in certain media. Other conditions have to be present, but there is little doubt of some causal contribution by media to some of the many cases recorded. There is a larger question concerning media incitement to civil or national war. There is some reason to believe that the media played a part in triggering the ethnic violence at the start of the wars in Yugoslavia in the early 1990s.

Media, Children and Young People

Expectations and fears (mostly the latter) abound in the general and research literature about the influence of media on children, aside from the issue of violence and delinquency. Much research has been carried out into children's use of and response to media (especially television) from early to recent times (e.g. Himmelweit et al., 1958; Schramm et al., 1961; Noble, 1975; Brown, 1976; Carlsson and von Feilitzen, 1998; Buckingham, 2002; Livingstone, 2002). Among the ideas expressed and tested about undesirable effects are the following expectations from media:

- an increase in social isolation;
- reduction of time and attention to homework;
- increased passivity;
- reduced time for play and exercise (displacement);
- reduced time for reading (due to television);
- undermining of parental authority;
- premature sexual knowledge and experience;
- unhealthy eating and obesity;
- promotion of anxiety about self-image leading to anorexia;
- depressive tendencies.

Beneficial effects attributed to media include:

- provision of a basis for social interaction;
- learning about the wider world;
- learning of prosocial attitudes and behaviours;
- educational effects;
- help in forming an identity;
- developing the imagination.

Many of the above hypotheses can be supported as plausible according to social learning theory (see pp. 491–2) and a number have been investigated (see Perse, 2001). No general conclusion is possible and none of these can be regarded as either fully proven or entirely ruled out. Experience of research reminds us to be cautious about the many other influences that contribute to any one of these 'effects'. Despite this, there still does seem to be a consensus among researchers that children are better off, on the whole, without high exposure to television. But as Seiter (2000) shows, adult attitudes to the dangers of television vary according to social class, gender and other factors.

Hargrave and Livingstone (2006) provide a detailed review of evidence of harm and offence caused by media, with particular reference to young people and to the UK. In line with earlier assessments, they find only modest effects, usually in combination with other factors. The most vulnerable are likely to be young males. The rise of a 'bedroom culture' has also been chronicled by Livingstone (2007) and will now be familiar to most parents. It means that children from an early age now determine their own media environment. This means at the very least a reduction in parental control and supervision, although it can also connect a child with a wider peer culture (and also be separating). One probable consequence is a higher level of consumption of media, but beyond that it is hard to generalize. In one study of 12–14-year-olds in the USA, quite large differences in media use were found between black and white adolescents (Jackson et al., 2008). In particular, white adolescents with bedroom television were more likely than other children to watch 'mature' content on television and were also more likely to have tried smoking and had had sexual experience. These relationships did not apply to black children in a similar position.

Collective Reaction Effects

Collective response to mass media can be dealt with according to the logic of the stimulus–response model, although other elements are present. The new elements mainly relate to the manner in which reactions are transmitted to others, often at great speed and with considerable amplification of overall effects. Often there is a self-generating and self-fulfilling process at work. The concept of 'contagion' has been applied in such circumstances, especially where crowds gather physically, but also where individuals are dispersed and reached by mass media as well as by personal contacts. One important kind of effect is manifested in widespread panic in response to alarming, incomplete or misleading information. This was instanced by the much-cited (but now doubted) panic reaction to the Orson Welles radio broadcast of *The War of the Worlds* in 1938, when simulated news bulletins reported a Martian invasion (Cantril et al., 1940). It was also exemplified by the hypothesized effect of the media in stimulating civil disorder in some US cities in the late 1960s. The collective reaction to the terrorist bomb outrage in Madrid in 2004 that immediately preceded a general election was thought to have been facilitated by personal contacts and influenced by distrust of official accounts of the event as given on mass media. In all these cases, the part played by mass media is somewhat ambiguous. The fairly obscure original publication of cartoons depicting the Prophet Muhammad in a Danish magazine in 2006 sparked off a global wave of protest and rioting that probably owed much to media amplification. However, the causes lie much deeper and the media were essentially only the messenger.

The relevance of such effects has been increased by the greater risk of unexpected terrorist outrages, although natural disasters such as earthquakes and industrial emergencies such as power breakdowns and nuclear accidents offer quite enough potential stimuli. There is little doubt that in some circumstances the conditions for a panic reaction to news do arise. We are dealing here with a special case of **rumour** (see Shibutani, 1966), which typically involves an urgent need for information coupled with a restricted supply. The media contribute the element of reaching large numbers of separate people at the same moment with the same item of news (which may not be open to independent verification) which can either provoke panic or help to alleviate it. The other related conditions for a panic response are anxiety, fear and uncertainty. Beyond this, precipitating features of panic seem to be incompleteness or inaccuracy of information, leading to the urgent search for information, usually through personal channels, thus giving further currency to the original message (Rosengren, 1976).

Much terrorist violence is either planned, threatened or carried out for political objectives by people seeking, however indirectly, to use the media for their own purposes. This gives rise to a complex interaction between the two. The hoped benefits for terrorists include drawing attention to their cause and arousing public fear and alarm. Blackmail may also be involved. Schmid and de Graaf (1982) have also argued that violence is a means of access to media channels and a message in itself. The media are caught between two strong pressures, the first to apply normal news values to dramatic events, and the second to avoid being an instrument of harm and a hindrance to counter-terrorism. Despite a good deal of research (e.g. Alali and Eke, 1991), there is no clear assessment in respect of the popular belief that the media actually encourage the spread of terrorism.

Studies of the reaction to the 9/11 terror attacks on New York suggest that despite the intensity of shock and horror and the complete unpreparedness for such events, there was no widespread public panic (Greenberg et al., 2002). We can suppose that full media coverage, beyond the immediate scene, contributed to calming the situation. The experience of the great Hanshin (Kobe) earthquake of 1995 taught many lessons about the value of media in disasters and the effects of media breakdown (Takahiro, 2004).

A different example of possible contagion effects is the sequence of aircraft hijacking crimes in 1971–2, which showed clear signs of being modelled on news reports. Holden (1986) reported correlational evidence of a similar kind that seems to point to an influence from media publicity. There has been other empirical support for the theory that press reports can 'trigger' individual but widespread actions of a pathological kind. Phillips (1980) showed that suicides, motor vehicle fatalities and commercial and non-commercial plane fatalities had a tendency to increase following press publicity for suicides or murder-suicides. He was also (Phillips, 1982) able to statistically link the portrayal of suicide in television fiction with the real-life occurrence of suicide, although the findings have been challenged on methodological grounds (Hessler and Stipp, 1985). There seems, at least, some evidence to make a plausible case for an imitation or 'contagion' effect. Ever since Goethe's book *The Sorrows of Young Werther* was published in 1774, there have been recurrent reports of suicide being stimulated by fiction and news. The evidence is discussed by Jamieson et al. (2003) and suggestions are made for ways in which reporting should be handled to minimize risks to vulnerable individuals. More recent evidence has given new support to the contagion effect of local news (Romer et al., 2006). The findings also suggested that suicide could be inhibited by the right kind of news presentation.

Civil disorder

Because of the potential threat to the established order, non-institutionalized and violent collective behaviour has been extensively studied, and the media have been implicated in the search for causes of such behaviour. It has been suggested that the media can, variously, provoke a riot, create a culture of rioting, provide lessons on how to riot, and spread a disturbance from place to place. The evidence for or against these propositions is thin and fragmentary, although it seems to be acknowledged that personal contact plays a larger part than media in any riot situation. There is some evidence, even so, that the media can contribute by simply signalling the occurrence and location of a riot event (Singer, 1970), by publicizing incidents which are themselves causes of riot behaviour, or by giving advance publicity to the likely occurrence of rioting. In general, it seems likely that the media do have a capacity to define the nature of events, and even if they are ultimately 'on the side' of established order, they can unintentionally increase the degree of polarization in particular cases.

While the media have not been shown to be a primary or main cause of rioting (see, for example, Kerner et al., 1968; Tumber, 1982), they may influence the timing or form of riot behaviour. Spilerman (1976) lends some support to this and other hypotheses, on the basis of rather negative evidence. Despite extensive research, he failed to find a satisfactory structural explanation of many urban riots in the United States (that is, explanations in terms of community conditions). He concluded that television and its network news structure were primarily responsible, especially by creating a 'black solidarity that would transcend the boundaries of community'. In our own time, mobilization to collective action seems likely to be conducted by mobile phone or the Internet rather than as an unintended effect from mass media. Examples include the Madrid case cited above, and the organized protest actions directed at world economic summits, starting with Seattle in 1998 (Kahn and Kellner, 2004).

In treating together the topic of panic and rioting, it is worth noting that the most canvassed solution to the dangers just signalled, the control or silencing of news (Paletz and Dunn, 1969), might itself entail a local panic through lack of any explanation for observable neighbourhood disturbances.

Diffusion of Innovation and Development

Most evidence relates to the many attempts since the Second World War to harness mass media to campaigns for technical advance or for health and educational purposes in developing countries, often following models developed in the rural United States (Katz et al., 1963). Early theory of media and development (e.g. Lerner, 1958) portrayed the influence of media as 'modernizing' simply by virtue of promoting western ideas and consumer aspirations. The mainstream view of media effect has been as a mass educator in alliance with officials, experts and local leaders, applied to specific objectives of change.

A principal chronicler of this tradition has been Everett Rogers (1962; Rogers and Shoemaker, 1973), whose model of information diffusion envisaged four stages: information, persuasion, decision or adoption, and confirmation. This sequence is close to McGuire's (1973) stages of persuasion (see p. 468). However, the role of the media is concentrated on the first (information and awareness) stage, after which personal contacts, organized expertise and advice, and actual experience take over in the adoption process. The early diffusionist school tended to emphasize organization and planning, linearity of effect, hierarchy (of status and expertise), social structure (thus also personal experience), reinforcement and feedback. Rogers (1976) has himself signalled the 'passing' of this 'dominant paradigm', its weakness lying in these same characteristics and its over-reliance on 'manipulation' from above.

Rogers and Kincaid (1981) have put forward an alternative 'convergence model' of communication which emphasizes the need for a continual process of interpretation and response, leading to an increased degree of mutual understanding between sender and receiver (see also Rogers, 1986). Critical theory in the 1970s linked attempts at development from outside with the maintenance of dependency. Newer theories of development allot to mass media a more limited role, with success depending on their remaining close to the base of the society and to its native culture. The idea of participatory communication has been advocated and increasingly practised (Servaes, 1999; Huesca, 2003). It is worth noting that mass communication is itself an innovation which has to be diffused before it can play a part in diffusion processes of the kind familiar in modern or developed societies (DeFleur, 1970; Rogers, 1986). For media to be effective, other conditions of modernity may also have to be present – such as individuation, trust in bureaucracies and in technology, and understanding of the basis of media authority, legitimacy and objectivity.

While development aid continues to be given by donor countries for communication projects and the improvement of mass media infrastructure, there is now much less expectation of direct large-scale effects on levels of development. There is more awareness of the limitations of information-technological solutions and of the unequal distribution of any benefits. There is also more emphasis on the need to improve public communication for the mass of the people and communication freedom as a human right as preconditions of progress. The main propositions of media development theory are set out in Box 18.1.

18.1 Mass media and development: propositions

Mass media serve as agents of development by:

- Disseminating technical know-how
- Encouraging individual change and mobility
- Spreading democracy (elections)
- Promoting consumer demand
- Aiding literacy, education, health, population control, etc.

The Social Distribution of Knowledge

Here we deal briefly with one widely expected and major media effect – their capacity to inform and keep informed a large-scale society in a manner consistent with the needs of a modern economy and a participant democratic process. While mass-mediated information considerably raises the average and minimum level of 'knowledge' in a society and the speed of circulation of information, there is a good deal of dispute about continued inequalities and about the varying capacity of different media to achieve these results. The debate has been given fresh life and urgency by the arrival of the Internet, with its great informative potential but variable diffusion and actual use. It has led to the coining of a new expression – that of the 'digital divide' – in place of the older term 'knowledge gap' (Norris, 2002).

It has long been assumed that the press and broadcasting have added so greatly to the flow of public information that they will have helped to modify differences of knowledge resulting from inequalities of education and social position (Gaziano, 1983). There is some evidence from political campaign studies to show that such 'information gap-closing' between social groups can occur in the short term (e.g. Blumler and McQuail, 1968). However, there has also been evidence of the reverse effect, showing that an attentive minority gains much more information than the rest, thus widening the gap between certain sectors of the public.

Tichenor et al. (1970) wrote of the 'knowledge gap hypothesis' that it 'does not hold that lower status population segments remain completely uninformed (or that the poorer in knowledge get poorer in an absolute sense). Instead the proposition is that growth of knowledge is relatively greater among the higher status segments.' There is certainly a class bias in attention to 'information-rich' sources, and strong correlations are persistently found between social class, attention to these sources and being able to answer information questions on political, social or economic matters.

There are two main aspects to the knowledge gap hypothesis: one concerning the general distribution of aggregate information in society between social classes, the other relating to specific subjects or topics on which some are better informed than others. As to the first 'gap', it is likely to have roots in fundamental social inequalities which the media alone cannot modify. As to the second, there are many possibilities for opening and closing gaps, and it is likely that the media do close some and open others. A number of factors can be named as relevant to the direction of the media effect. Donohue et al. (1975) put special emphasis on the fact that media operate to close gaps on issues that are of wide concern to small communities, especially under conditions of conflict, which promote attention and learning.

In general, motivation and perceived utility influence information seeking and learning, and these factors come more from the social context than from the media. It has, however, been argued that different media may work in different ways and that print media are more likely to lead to a widening of gaps than is television (Robinson, 1972) because these are the favoured sources for the favoured classes. The suggestion that television can have a reverse effect (benefiting the less privileged) is based on the fact that it tends to reach a higher proportion of a given population with much the same news and information and is widely regarded as trustworthy. However, much depends on the institutional forms adopted in a given society.

Public broadcasting arrangements in Western Europe and, to a lesser extent, the national network system in the USA used to ensure (in part due to their *de facto* oligopoly) that television would provide a popular and homogeneous source of shared information about national and international concerns. Curran et al. (2009) compared countries with public broadcasting systems with the USA (a purely market model) and found the former to have lower levels of knowledge gaps between the advantaged and disadvantaged, seemingly a result of the deliberate informational policy of still popular public broadcasting services (see Box 18.2). The authors attributed these results to the difference of media system, especially the role of public broadcasting, although recognizing that greater economic inequality in the USA is probably a more underlying cause. Even so, they warn against the potential effects of further deregulation and privatization. These results might also follow on from the process of fragmentation of the national audience.

18.2 Media systems and knowledge gaps

Curran et al. (2009) analysed the content of television news services and the press in the USA, the UK, Finland and Denmark and surveyed the audience in each country to establish levels of knowledge of news events. The results showed that, as expected, the US media payed significantly less attention to international news (aside from Iraq) than the other countries. The survey 'revealed Americans to be especially uninformed about international public affairs'. They were also less well informed about soft news, except domestically. The main reasons cited for these findings were the relatively low attention paid to conventional media. In European countries there were much higher levels of knowledge and much less difference between social groups, as shown in the following figures:

Education: *Hard news % knowledge score*

	US	UK	FIN	DEN
Low	31.4	57.4	65.0	71.1
Medium	52.0	59.7	67.6	73.0
High	71.0	70.9	78.4	70.3

Source: James Curran, 2009 Shanto Iyengar, Anker Brink Lund and Inka Salovaari-Moring, *European Journal of Communication*, 24, 1: 5–26.

Under more recent trends towards channel multiplication, greater competition and audience fragmentation, this large audience for information is vanishing. Television is becoming a more differentiated source of information, more akin to print media, and without any captive mass audience. Robinson and Levy's (1986) evidence concerning news learning from television does not give much confidence in the capacity of television to close knowledge gaps, even in the days of mass viewing. A review by Gaziano (1997) of 39 studies of the knowledge-gap hypothesis concluded that the effect of the media on closing or narrowing gaps remains uncertain, but the gaps continue (see also Visvanath and Finnegan, 1996). Bennett and Iyengar (2008) make a strong case for the view that the decline of network television and other mass media will result in lower chance exposure to public information and thus wider knowledge gaps.

The differential diffusion of new computer-based information technology also works towards increasing the division between the information rich and the information poor (Katz and Rice, 2002). Knowledge-gap theory would indicate a widening of the gaps as a result, since people who are already information rich, with higher information skills and more resources, would move even further ahead of informationally poorer strata. It can be questioned if 'knowledge-gap' theory is still relevant. It supposes a basic corpus of knowledge that we all need in order to operate in society. Under conditions of abundance and specialization of knowledge, this premise looks increasingly doubtful, although it may still be valid for the democratic political process of electing governments.

As noted above, high expectations have been generated by the coming of web-based news information. Comparisons with traditional media have been made, with initial results not very promising for a more equally informed society. Graber et al. (2009) found that television was easier for the less educated to process and learn from that newspapers or the Web, with a reverse pattern for the better educated. Schoenbach et al. (2005) found newspapers to do better than online news at widening the public agenda. Some research points to a new form of digital divide based on different levels of skill at using information sources (Selwyn, 2004; Hargittai and Hinnant, 2008).

Social Learning Theory

A widely referenced model of media effects, especially in relation to children and young people, is Bandura's (1986) social learning (or observational learning) theory. The basic idea is that we cannot learn all or even much of what we need to guide our own development and behaviour from direct personal observation and experience alone. We have to learn much from indirect sources, including mass media. Bandura's model posits four basic processes of social learning that occur in sequence: attention, retention, production and motivation. Our attention is directed at media content of potential relevance to our lives and personal needs and interests. We may then retain what we have learnt and add it to our stock of prior knowledge. The third stage – that of production – refers to the actual application in behaviour of lessons learnt, where it may be rewarded (reinforced) or punished, leading to greater or less motivation to follow any particular path.

The theory has a general application to socializing effects of media and the adoption of various models of action. It applies to many everyday matters, such as clothing, appearance, style, eating and drinking, modes of interaction and personal consumption. It can also support long-term trends. According to Bandura (1986), the theory only applies to behaviour that is directly represented in symbolic form. The theory also implies an active engagement on the part of the learner, and on the individual's self-reflective capability. It is not the same as imitation or mimicry. Mass media are rarely the only source of social learning and their influence depends on other sources, such as parents, friends, teachers, and so on. There are strong collective influences on social learning. Even so, social learning theory holds that media can have direct effects on people and their influence does not have to be mediated by personal influence or social networks (see Bandura, 2002: 140).

Socialization

That the media play a part in the early socialization of children and the long-term socialization of adults is widely believed, although in the nature of the case it is difficult to prove. This is partly just because it is such a long-term process and partly because any effect from media interacts with other social background influences and variable modes of socialization within families (Hedinsson, 1981). Rare longitudinal studies of development have sometimes produced prima facie evidence of socialization from media (e.g. Rosengren and Windahl, 1989). Nevertheless, certain basic assumptions about the potential socialization effects from media are often built into policies for control of the media, decisions by media themselves and the norms and expectations which parents apply or hold in relation to the media use of their own children. The thesis of media socialization has, in fact, two sides to it: on the one hand, the media can reinforce and support other agencies of socialization; on the other, they are also viewed as a potential threat to the values set by parents, educators and other agents of social control.

The main logic underlying the thesis is that the media can teach norms and values by way of symbolic reward and punishment for different kinds of behaviour as represented in the media. An alternative view is that it is a learning process whereby we all learn how to behave in certain situations and the expectations which go with a given role or status in society. Thus the media are continually offering pictures of life and models of behaviour in advance of actual experience. In doing so, media portrayals can shape attitudes and normative standards. For instance, Krcmar and Vierig (2005) show that exposure to television can have a negative effect on a child's moral reasoning about justified violence.

Early studies of children's use of media revealed a tendency for children to find lessons about life and to connect these with their own experience. Studies of content also drew attention to the systematic presentation of images of social life which could strongly shape children's expectations and aspirations. Socialization theory does tend to emphasize the conformist role of media. In this view, the media are neither 'prosocial' nor 'antisocial' but tend to favour the most dominant and established values. Of course, such established values are by definition 'pro-social'. An extensive study of American television content by Smith et al. (2006) showed quite high levels of altruism in action in the form of helping and sharing. They found that 73% of programmes sampled contained at least one such action and in general they were supported by the context. The effects of such portrayals have rarely been studied, reflecting a bias in research towards problematic issues. In whichever formulation, the general proposition that media have a socializing effect is clearly supported, but it is only indirectly founded on empirical evidence.

Social Control and Consciousness Formation

There is a continuum of theoretical positions about the degree and purposefulness of the mass media as an agent of social control. A common view is that the media act non-purposively to support the values dominant in a community or nation, through a mixture of personal and institutional choice, operational requirements, external pressure and anticipation of what a large and heterogeneous audience expects and wants. A stronger and more critical version of this position sees the media as essentially conservative because of a combination of market forces (especially ownership by large firms) and subordination to the interests of nation and state. These alternative theories tend to draw on much the same kind of evidence, most of it relating to systematic tendencies in content, with very little directly about effects.

A hybrid critical theory of systematic long-term effect has been developed by Herman and Chomsky (1988) in the form of a 'propaganda model'. This says that news in capitalist countries has to be 'strained' through several 'filters', especially the financial integration of the media with the rest of the economy, advertising, news management campaigns, the dominant ideology of the society and reliance on official sources of information. Herman and Chomsky found a good deal of circumstantial evidence of the last-named filter at work, as have other researchers, for instance Reese et al. (1994) and Manheim (1998).

Herman and Chomsky took the title of their book, *Manufacturing Consent*, from Walter Lippmann, who wrote (1922: 158) that the 'manufacture of consent is capable of great refinements ... and the opportunities for manipulation open to anyone who understands the process are plain enough'. Lippmann's views exemplify what was referred to above as the first phase (that of 'all-powerful media') in the evolution of thinking about the power of the media, and the weakness of the Herman and Chomsky position is that they take so little account of later research and evidence (Klaehn, 2002).

The content of media with the largest audiences does appear broadly supportive of reigning social norms and conventions (an aspect of socialization and of 'cultivation'). Fundamental challenges to the national state or its established institutions are hard to find in the mass media. The argument that mass media tend towards the confirmation of the status quo is thus based on evidence both about what is present and about what is missing in media content. The former includes the rewarding (in fiction) of 'conformist' or patriotic behaviour, the high degree of attention and privileged (often direct) access given to established elites and points of view, and the often negative or unequal treatment of non-institutional or deviant behaviour. The mass media are repeatedly shown as supportive of national or community consensus, and as tending to show problems as soluble within the established 'rules' of society and culture.

Correlatively, the media commonly define certain kinds of behaviours and groups as both deviant from, and dangerous to, society. Apart from the obviously criminal, these include groups such as teenage gangs, drug-takers, 'football hooligans' and some sexual deviants. It has been argued that the media often demonstrably exaggerate the real danger and significance of such groups and their activities (Cohen and Young, 1973) and tend to create 'moral panics' (Cohen, 1972). Within the category of anti-social elements, those who rely on state benefit payments may also come to be included under the label of 'welfare scroungers' (Golding and Middleton, 1982; Sotirovic, 2001), and the same can happen to immigrants, refugees or travelling people (Horsti, 2003) and even just the poor (Clauson and Trice, 2001). The process has been called 'blaming the victim' and is a familiar feature of collective opinion forming, to which the media can make an important contribution. The effect is to provide society with scapegoats and objects of indignation, to divert attention from real evils with causes lying in the institutions of society, and to rally support for the agencies of law and order.

The evidence of media omission is, in the nature of things, harder to assemble, but comparative content analyses of news in several countries have added evidence of systematic omission in the attention given to certain issues and parts of the world (Golding and Elliott, 1979). Detailed studies of news content such as those by the Glasgow Media Group (1976, 1980, 1985) have also documented some significant patterns of omission. In considering the often eloquent and plausible theoretical arguments for the ideological effects of the media, we should also keep in mind the equally plausible theories concerning the limited potential for media effect. Especially relevant is the evidence of audience selectivity and 'differential decoding' (Jensen, 1986, 1998; Liebes and Riback, 1994). Most of the theories about ideological or hegemonic effects are based on observation of media and content, not of audience or 'effects'. The lessons of 'reception' research offer a counterweight, even though they derive originally from the same critical school.

It is almost impossible to give any useful assessment of the degree to which the effects posited by this body of theory and research actually occur. Nevertheless, the media are mainly owned and controlled either by (often large) business interests or (however indirectly) by the state – and thus by the interests which also have most political and economic power (Dreier, 1982). There is a good deal of prima facie evidence that such controlling power over the media is valued (by its possessors) beyond its immediate economic yield, especially for political and social influence and status. The effects are not uniformly consensual or supportive of the status quo. Gans' (1979: 68) judgement that 'news is not so much conservative or liberal as it is reformist' probably still applies very widely. The media are committed by their own self-defined task and their ideology to serve as a carrier for messages (for instance, about scandals, crises, social ills and also innovations) which can also be an impulse to change. They probably do stimulate much activity, agitation and anxiety that disturb the existing order, within the limits of systems which have some capacity for generating change.

Cultivation

Among theories of long-term media effect, the cultivation hypothesis of Gerbner (1973) remains probably the best documented and most investigated (see Signorielli and Morgan, 1990). It holds that television, among modern media, has acquired such a central place in daily life that it dominates our 'symbolic environment', substituting its (distorted) message about reality for personal experience and other means of knowing about the world. Television is also described as the 'cultural arm of the established industrial order [which] serves primarily to maintain, stabilize and reinforce rather than to alter, threaten or weaken conventional beliefs and behaviours' (Gross, 1977: 180). This statement brings the cultivation effect very close to that posited by the critical theorists of the Frankfurt School and not far from later Marxist analysis. According to Signorielli and Morgan (1990: 15):

> Cultivation analysis is the third component of a research paradigm called 'Cultural Indicators' that investigates (1) the institutional processes underlying the production of media content, (2) images in media content, and (3) relationships between exposure to television's message and audience beliefs and behaviors.

The theory

The central hypothesis of the research was that viewing television gradually leads to the adoption of beliefs about the nature of the social world which conform to the stereotyped, distorted and very selective view of reality as portrayed in a systematic way in television fiction and news. Cultivation is said to differ from a direct stimulus–response effect process mainly because of its gradual and cumulative character. It involves, first, learning and, secondly, the construction of a view of social reality dependent on personal circumstances and experience (such as of poverty, race or gender) and also on reference-group membership. It is also seen as an interactive process between messages and audiences.

In this theory of media effect, television provides many people with a consistent and near-total symbolic environment that supplies norms for conduct and beliefs about a wide range of real-life situations. It is not a window on or a reflection of the world, but a world in itself. The resulting research has two main thrusts: one directed to testing the assumption about the consistency (and distortion) of the television 'message system'; the other designed to test, by way of survey analysis, a variety of public beliefs about social reality, especially those which can be tested against empirical indicators. The core of the ensuing analysis is the comparison between beliefs about reality and actual reality, taking account of varying degrees of habitual exposure to television. There is some basic similarity to the ideas underlying the 'agenda-setting' hypothesis (see pp. 512–14).

Testing the theory

Those who watch increasing amounts of television are predicted to show increasing divergence of perceptions of reality away from the known picture of the social world and towards the 'television' picture of the world. A major focus of the research has always been on questions concerning violence and crime, with cultivation research paying attention to its television portrayal, its actual incidence and its differential risks on the one hand, and to public awareness of and attitudes towards crime on the other. Early cultivation research findings (Gerbner and Gross, 1976) showed that the more television people viewed, the more likely they were to exaggerate the incidence of crime in the real world and the personal risks they run. This relationship still seems to hold (Romer et al. 2003), at least in the USA. Other topics of political and social concern have also been studied, including the media production of political consensus. Gerbner et al. (1984) applied their concept of 'mainstreaming' to the political sphere and found evidence that exposure to television shifted opinion in the direction of 'moderate' opinion. Some details are given in Box 18.3.

18.3 Mainstreaming: political correlates of television viewing

Cultivation theory holds that the more time a person spends watching television (of all kinds) the more he or she will adopt the predominant outlook of the world that is expressed on the medium. This should also apply to politics since it is (or was) the main source of political information for most people. The study summarized here is based on the assumption that television (under pressure from networks and advertisers) seeks to avoid extremes, staying safely in the 'non-ideological middle ground that holds the largest possible audience'. This leads to favouring 'moderate' or centrist political positions (or mainstreaming). The timing of the study (1981) was one of a shift to the right after a decade of upheaval in the USA. It was conducted using very large random sample surveys, with basic questions asked about amount of viewing and personal political outlook as either liberal, moderate or conservative. Controls for other variables were applied. The results confirmed the expectation. In the nine surveys (different years), heavy viewers were more likely than light viewers to choose the 'moderate' self-designation in all but one case. This relationship did not hold for other media. Newspaper readers were likely to be more conservative, radio users more liberal. The authors warn that the meanings of the labels are not straightforward or stable. Specifically, they say that television is not genuinely a force for moderation. (Gerbner et al., 1984)

In an extensive review of numerous studies of the television construction of reality, Hawkins and Pingree (1983) found many scattered indications of the expected relationships, but no conclusive proof of the *direction* of the relationship between television viewing and ideas about social reality. They say that television *can* teach about social reality and that the relationship between viewing and social reality may be reciprocal: television viewing causes a social reality to be constructed in a certain way, but this construction of social reality may also direct viewing behaviour. In a recent extensive overview of cultivation research, Morgan and Shanahan (1997) draw the conclusion that cultivation effects do occur but are on average quite small.

The television experience is now almost certainly more differentiated and non-cumulative than allowed for in the theory as production and supply increase (both in the USA and elsewhere). Hypotheses have to be much more specific about content and effects. For instance, a study of the cultivation effects of television on expectations about marriage (Segrin and Nabi, 2002) found that TV viewing of genre-specific 'romantic' content was associated with unrealistic expectations, but not general TV viewing. Sotirovic (2001) found negative images of welfare recipients among viewers of cable TV news and entertainment shows, as opposed to other sources. Rössler and Brosius (2001) also found limited cultivation effects in Germany from specific talk show contents, but not from all TV or the genre as a whole. Active audience theory (see Chapter 15) also challenges the assumption of the long-term cumulative effect of powerful 'message systems'. Several authors have raised doubts about the causal relationship posited between television use data and survey data concerning values and opinions (Hirsch, 1980, 1981; Hughes, 1980). The 'cultivation' effect was first identified in the United States, where (mainstream) television content was more commercial and probably less diverse.

The evidence from other countries is still mixed, despite the amount of work that has been done. In relation to images of a violent society, Wober (1978) found no support from British data, and Doob and McDonald (1979) reported similarly from Canada. A longitudinal study of Swedish children (Hedinsson, 1981: 188) concluded, however, that evidence amounted to 'if not a direct support, at least a non-refutation of Gerbner's theory'. Rosengren and Windahl (1989) report a number of findings of longer-term changes in relation to the television experience of the young that could be taken as support for the cultivation hypothesis. One example appears in the 'mental maps' of the world that differ significantly according to the amount of television viewing. For high-viewing adolescent boys, the world outside Sweden consists of little apart from North America.

Evidence of cultivation does still arrive from new sources. Yay et al. (2008) found that consumption of American television content in South Korea and in India was associated with dissatisfaction with personal life (India) and dissatisfaction with society (in both countries). Cultivation effects from television on gender-role attitudes have also been found in Japan. According to Saito (2007), these effects were specific to certain subgroups. Thus television decelerated social change by cultivating traditional attitudes among many viewers, although it also seemed to liberate the most conservative people. These findings are approximately in line with the 'mainstreaming' effects described above (Box 18.3).

However plausible the theory, it is almost impossible to deal convincingly with the complexity of posited relationships between symbolic structures, audience behaviour and audience views, given the many intervening variables. It is also hard to separate out any process of 'cultivation' from general socialization. Despite all this, it appears that the line of enquiry represented by cultural indicators and cultivation research is not a spent force and can lend itself to more specified and nuanced enquiries on particular topics.

Media and Long-term Social and Cultural Change

The theories of mass communication outlined in Chapters 4 and 5 all in some way posit a variety of significant social and cultural effects. The same is true of the effects of globalization, as discussed in Chapter 10. However, any such effects are likely to be gradual, long-term and difficult to measure. There are also often divergent and even inconsistent possibilities. For instance, mass media have been said to lead to personal isolation, individuation and social diversity or even fragmentation. Putnam (2000) has blamed television use in particular for the decline in 'social capital' in America and a consequent reduction in participation in civic and social life. Some support for the thesis of fragmentation was found by Moy et al. (1999).

Other theorists have credited the media with (or accused them of) promoting homogeneity and social cohesion, sometimes to an excessive degree of conformity (see pp. 493–4). The media have been blamed for declining cultural standards (and reducing content to the lowest common denominator) and also praised for disseminating traditional and contemporary culture more widely. Despite the plausibility of these and other ideas about the influence of mass media on culture and society, there is little firm evidence of the general effects posited.

Central to the process by which the media contribute to social and cultural change is their capacity to define situations, provide frames of reference and disseminate images of social groups. They also tend to constitute the 'collective memory' of a given national society, in the absence of extensive historical knowledge. The media are not primary inventors or sources of any of these, but they put them together in more or less consistent and repetitive narratives that become the secondary sources for ideas that people have about their own society and their place in it. The media have an insatiable appetite for novelty as well as continuity, and contribute to change by picking up on every new fashion, fear or significant fact that might become part of a larger story, whether in news or fiction. For the majority of people, the media become effectively the gatekeepers of change, especially when they seem to agree on the same selection and perception of what is going on.

In determining these and other questions, much depends on the perspective of the assessor and the initial assumptions made about the problem at issue. We should also keep in mind the fact that there is a continuous interaction between media and society. The media, whether as technology or as cultural content, do not have a simple one-way causal relation with cultural and social change. The outcomes of these interactions are very variable, unpredictable and different from one set of circumstances to another. As the media have developed they have, without doubt, diverted time and attention from other activities (displacement effects); become a channel for reaching more people with more information than was available under 'pre-mass-media' conditions; and changed the way in which information and ideas circulate. These facts have implications for any social institution that needs to gain public attention and to communicate to the society at large. Other institutions are under pressure to adapt or respond in some way to the mass media, or to make their own use of mass media channels. In doing so, they are likely to change their own practices.

The influence of media is generally likely to be indirect. They work to change public expectations, the possibilities for meeting needs and, especially, the way things are done in other social institutions. These have become more and more dependent on the media for their communicative links to their publics, and communication has adapted to what has been called a 'media logic' (see p. 333), which has profound effects on their conduct. As Altheide and Snow (1991: ix) have remarked, 'today all social institutions are media institutions'. The case of the political institution is assessed in Chapter 19, but similar conclusions apply to cultural and social institutions. In her presidential address to the International Communication Association in 2008, Sonia Livingstone (2009) commented on the fact that almost every dimension of society life was now said to be 'mediated' in one way or another and called for more precision about what this might mean. There are certainly different possible meanings, but in the present context the most central claim is that requirements of message and medium take precedence over the meaning of content.

Entertainment Effects

The largest category of media content can probably be labelled as 'entertainment' and it is the main reason why media are so popular. We are reminded by Zillmann and Bryant (1994) that entertainment also has many effects beyond the unintended negative consequences so often studied and that entertainment is also an effect in itself, intended as such by producers and audiences. Entertainment has proved difficult to define, although the essential idea seems to be of diversion and getting caught up in some story or spectacle. It can also be considered in terms of more specific kinds of effect, including being amused; emotionally aroused so as to experience sadness, happiness, anger, relief, excitement, fear, etc.; diverted from anxiety, and so on. Music, in particular, has also been credited with a number of effects, especially on moods and dispositions and on arousal (Knobloch and Zillmann, 2002).

Zillmann (1980) identified the appeal of drama in terms of enjoyment and annoyance induced by the changing fortunes of positively or negatively portrayed characters. Zillmann and Bryant (1994) raise more questions than they can answer about the appeal of suspense, and especially also about the apparent appeal of news presentations of tragic events, which seem to fascinate even where, unlike in much fiction, there is no reason to dislike the main victims. The 'uses and gratifications' tradition of research offers some ways of uncovering the satisfactions (intended effects) sought out by audiences and some relevant findings, but there is still little clear conceptualization in this neglected area of media effects. The concept of 'escapism' is inadequate to account for entertainment effects, and the various theories of pleasure that have been put forward (see Bryant and Miron, 2002) do not lend themselves to precise formulation and testing.

Conclusion

The social and cultural effects of mass communication are difficult to assess for the reasons given. There are some possibilities for observing short-term changes affecting individuals, which can then sometimes be generalized to larger aggregates and even the society as a whole. However, we hardly have the methodological capacity to measure larger trends at the higher level of analysis with any reliability and have to depend on theory and argument. There is little doubt that media do have many effects and they probably do account for some general trends. However, their effects are often inconsistent and cancel each other out, and complex societies are often characterized by different lines of development at the same time. The media are unlikely to be the main driving forces of fundamental long-term change, although consequences of increasingly rapid and penetrating diffusion of information, ideas and images on a global scale should not be underestimated.

Further Reading

Gitlin, T. (1980) *The Whole World is Watching: Mass Media in the Making and Unmaking of the New Left*. Berkeley, CA: University of California Press.
A participant observation study of the public campaigning for change on the part of the Students for a Democratic Society movement in the USA during the later 1960s and early 1970s. A central conclusion is that the movement gradually adapted itself to the expectations of the news media in ways that changed it in some fundamental ways.

Hargrave, A.M. and Livingstone, S. (2006) *Harm and Offence in Media Content*. Bristol, UK: Intellect.
A systematic review of the literature on hypotheses and evidence relating to potential harms from different kinds of media, with particular reference to children.

Jackson, C., Brown, J.D. and Pardon, C.J. (2008) 'A TV in the bedroom: implications for viewing habits and risk behaviors', *Journal of Broadcasting and Electronic Media*, 52 (3): 349–67.
Interesting evidence of differences between white and black teenagers in the correlates of having bedroom television and behaviours relating to drugs, early sex experience, etc.

Rosengren, K.E. and Windahl, S. (1989) *Media Matter*. Norwood, NJ: Ablex.
Presents the results of a rare longtitudinal study of the relationship between television viewing and other aspects of child development, following the tradition of cultural indicators, but with other methods and theory as well. Location was Sweden.

Yay, H., Ranasubranuanian, S. and Oliver, M.B. (2008) 'Cultivation effect on quality of life indicators', *Journal of Broadcasting and Electronic Media*, 52 (2): 247–67.
Relatively unusual study reporting prima facie evidence of a cultivation effect in countries undergoing development.

Online Readings

Krcmar, M. and Vierig, E.V. (2005) 'Imitating life, imitating television', *Communication Research*, 32 (3): 267–94.

Van den Bulck, J. and Beullens, K. (2007) 'The relationship between Docu-Soap exposure and adolescents' career aspirations', *European Journal of Communication*, 22(3): 355–366.

Smith, S.L., Moyer-Gusé, E. and Donnerstein, E. (2004) 'Media violence and sex: what are the concerns, issues and effects?', in J.D.H. Downing, D. McQuail, P. Schlesinger and E. Wartella (eds), *The Sage Handbook of Media Studies*, pp. 541–68. Thousand Oaks, CA: Sage.

Valkenberg, P., Cantor, J. and Peeters, A.L. (2000) 'Fright reactions to TV', *Communication Research*, 27 (1): 82–94.

19

News, Public Opinion and Political Communication

This chapter deals with another diverse set of possible media effects, distinguished primarily by their relation to informational media content of several kinds, but especially news and various forms of political communication. The effects concerned relate to public 'knowledge', opinions and attitudes, especially of a short- or medium-term kind. Some of the effects are intended (as with election campaigning and propaganda), others are not (as with general news), but the line between the two is uncertain. Intentional communication can have unintended consequences, and unintended communication can have some systematic and predictable effects (for instance, an unwitting bias is present in supposedly objective news). Moreover, it has become a commonplace to observe that intentional communicators (propagandists of various kinds) often try to include their advocacy in concealed form within the 'news', or simply try to gain attention and free publicity.

News and political communication generally comprise an area of mass communication where traditional media are most open to competition and challenge from new online media, especially the Internet. The Internet can, in principle, offer many more sources and more diverse news than any given newspaper or television channel, and allows the receiver to select according to personal interests (although the reality falls a good deal short of the potential). It also adds the potential for interaction with and response to sources of news. There are also limitations and obstacles to audience use of the new potential and therefore limits to effects. Some of the general models and processes effect introduced in Chapter 17 are relevant, but some new models of particular processes are introduced.

Learning from News

News does not typically set out with learning goals, but simply offers a service in which diverse items of information are made available to members of an audience to select according to their interests. The circumstances of mass media news consumption are typically quite different from other informational situations, especially in the voluntariness of attention, the frequent lack of specific motivation and the high level of inattention that accompany broadcast news use in particular. The content of news is often very perishable and peripheral. Nevertheless, the overall purpose is informative and news content is usually judged both sender and receiver according to some criteria of information value. Moreover, people do learn from the news and become more informed as a result. The extent to which news has effects depends on its reaching an audience that pays some attention to the content, understands it and is able to recall or recognize some of it after the event.

As with other kinds of effect, comprehension and recall depend on both message and sender factors and also on audience factors. News messages can be more or less relevant, attention-gaining, interesting and comprehensible. News sources are likely to vary according to the trust and credibility they have established among the audience. On the audience side, the main factors are likely to be general motivation for following news, previous familiarity with the topics and general educational level. It is fairly clear that much news is 'received' without much attention and with little active 'processing'.

Published research into learning from news is fairly thin on the ground (although important contributions have been made, especially by Findahl and Hoijer, 1981, 1985; Robinson and Levy, 1986; Woodall, 1986; Gunter, 1987, 1999; Davis and Robinson, 1989; Robinson and Davis, 1990; Newhagen and Reeves, 1992). The results so far have tended to confirm the outcome of much basic communication research of decades past (Trenaman, 1967). Thus the interest, relevance and concreteness of news stories aid comprehension, and both prior knowledge and the habit of discussion of news topics with others are still important, in addition to favourable educational background. Not too surprisingly, there is evidence that the presence of a narrative structure in television news contributes to recall and comprehension (Machill et al., 2007).

Although television is routinely cited by the public as the main source of news, Robinson and Levy (1986) judged it to be overrated as a source of knowledge of public affairs. They also found that several common news production and presentation practices often worked against adequate comprehension of news by audiences (see also Cohen, 2001). Graber (1990) confirmed this, but also showed that visuals do have some potential under the right circumstances. The main findings of her research on this question are summarized in Box 19.1.

The contribution of visuals to learning from television news (Graber, 1990) 19.1

This study examined audience response to 189 news stories on US television in 1985. All stories were coded in detail for verbal and visual components. This analysis suggested that television news does 'militate against learning', as widely claimed. The reasons for this were: (1) news items are very short and crowded with visual scenes – 79% of items were less than three minutes long and only 13% had any scene lasting more than 30 seconds; (2) the pictures did not supply much factual learning; (3) scenes were routine and stereotypical; (4) in more than half the items, the pictorial information failed to enhance the story line.

In order to test audience learning, a sample of 48 adults was recruited, all educated and interested (thus a best-case scenario for learning). Open-ended methods were used. The main findings were: (1) the level of (aided) recall of both verbal and visual themes was low, varying with the topic – in about half of both sets, recall was rated as 'low' (less than 25%); (2) visual themes were more spontaneously remembered than verbal ones; (3) people process stories according to their own schemas, leading to error; (4) the main perceived contribution of visuals was to add reality, followed by clarity and emotional impact; (5) there was little agreement among the audience on which visuals for a given story were helpful or not.

The overall conclusion: visuals have many limitations but they do add to general understanding and also some unique 'visual' information as well as some extra reality and feeling. There is a need to reconsider 'print-age' values.

The general conclusion from (television) news research is that the average level of learning, as measured by either comprehension or recall, is very low and what is learnt is fragmentary. Findahl (2001) estimated that people in natural situations remember less than 5% of news. Even so, what is learnt is shaped by selection and framing of content as presented. It is impossible to say what a satisfactory figure, given in such terms, would be. It depends on the potential value of the information provided and on which parts are remembered. Quite probably much of the effect of news is in the form of reinforcement of familiar themes and reaffirming the known content of the news agenda. Certainly, at moments of 'breaking' news of dramatic and relevant events, the degree of learning is likely to be much higher than the routine average. As Graber (1990) also reminded us, there are certain kinds of impressions and information that may be conveyed by news but are difficult to measure by social scientific methods.

News schemata and news processing

News content research has shown that much news is presented within frameworks of meaning which derive from the way news is gathered and processed (see Chapter 14). News is topically and thematically 'framed' for easier understanding, and it is reasonable to suppose that audiences employ some of the same frames in *their* processing of incoming news. Graber (1984) applied this line of thinking to news processing. The interpretative frames or schemata mentioned earlier (see Chapter 14, p. 380) provide guides to selection, relevance and cognition and are collectively constructed and often widely shared. Graber defined a schema as a 'cognitive structure consisting of organized knowledge about situations and individuals that has been abstracted from prior experiences. It is used for processing new information and retrieving stored information' (1984: 23). Schemata help in evaluating new information and filling gaps when information is missing or ambiguous. They are also aids to remembering news.

The broadest and most enduring frames may have an international currency (for instance, the 'global recession', 'international terrorism' or 'threat to global environment'), but others may be local and specific. Graber found the actual 'schemata in people's minds' were very diverse, fragmentary and poorly organized. The ways in which schemata were used in responding to news information were also varied, with several different strategies being observed. A simplified version of Graber's model of the way news is processed is given in Figure 19.1.

According to this model, news learning can be conceived as the integration of new information into pre-existing schemata. This partly accounts for the fact that prior knowledge is associated with greater learning capacity. An active process by the receiver is presumed, although it is also the case that information is frequently presented in the form of pre-existing schemata that are simply taken over by a receiver rather than being critically examined.

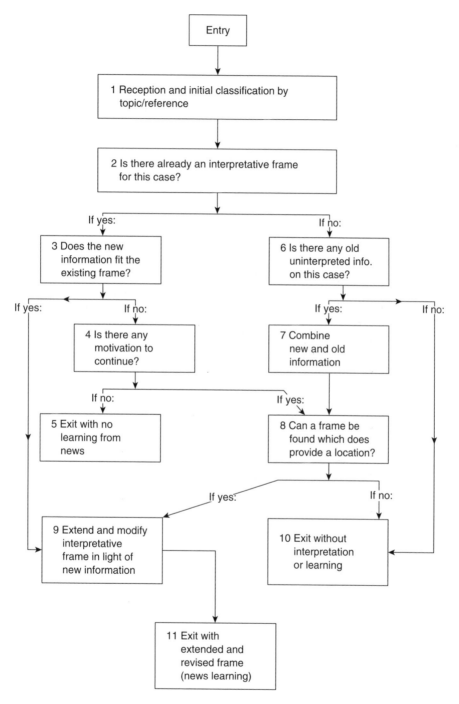

Figure 19.1   Schema theory news processing model (McQuail and Windahl, 1993, adapted from Graber, 1984)

Exemplification

One of the typical features of news that has been investigated in respect of effects is the use of 'exemplification' – the citing of specific concrete cases to illustrate more general themes and justify general conclusions. This is one form of framing. However, the practice can lead to misinformation or bias, where the case is not in fact representative. Zillmann (2002) points to four possible effects. There will be greater influence on the perception of issues where concrete examples are used rather than abstract points; where examples are emotionally arousing; where multiple examples of the same kind are given; and where presentation is vivid. Generally, research has confirmed these propositions (Zillmann and Brosius, 2000).

Differential reception

Other research, in the tradition of 'reception analysis', has supported the view that actual interpretations of news are strongly influenced at the point of reception by the circumstances, outlook and prejudices of the individual audience member in a domestic and 'everyday life' situation (see Jensen, 1986, 1998). Gurevitch and Levy (1986: 132) described the frames of interpretation brought by viewers to television news as 'meta-messages', 'latent meanings that are embedded in audience decodings', which help to link individual sense-making to larger stories. They assume that audiences, much as journalists, have 'tacit theories' to frame their understanding of events in the world and to help in their processing of information.

This view was confirmed by Jensen (2001) on the basis of a comparison of news reception in different countries. He found that the themes deployed by less educated and interested news audience members do not correspond with the 'super-themes' used by journalists to frame news accounts. The perspectives arising often cut across the actual topics of the news, especially international news. Jensen distinguished four dimensions by which audiences made sense of news, as follows:

- *Space*. Audiences decide if and how distant events might affect themselves.
- *Power*. Audiences are likely to see news as concerning themselves as well as the more powerful.
- *Time*. Audiences see events in terms of their own past and future history.
- *Identity*. Audiences link or disassociate themselves with events, places and people in the news.

The earliest types of news reception research (see Alasuutari, 1999) were based on the encoding/decoding model of Stuart Hall (1974/1980) and involved the hypothesis that news could be decoded in 'hegemonic', 'negotiated' or 'oppositional' ways according to the outlook of the individual receiver. The evidence for this is not easy to come by, but a study of Palestinian and Jewish responses to news of the *Intifada* seems to offer clear support (Liebes and Riback, 1994). 'Extremists' on both sides tended to read the news in either a 'hegemonic' or an 'oppositional' way, while moderates on both sides applied a 'negotiated' mode of interpretation. A summary of factors relevant to news learning is given in Box 19.2.

Factors associated with news learning **19.2**

- Prior knowledge and interest on part of audience
- Perceived relevance of topic
- Credible and trusted news channel or source
- Visual illustration
- Concrete subject matter and 'hard news' character
- News fits an available frame of interpretation
- Repetition of news
- Narrativity of text

News credibility

A condition of news to achieve learning effects, as shown in Box 19.2, is the attribution of believability by an audience. Essentially, some trust is required for a news source to be effective, although there is plenty of evidence that people do habitually pay attention to media sources that they do not trust (see Isfati and Capella, 2003). Gaziano and McGrath (1987) found that credibility had more to do with perceived fairness, lack of bias and good faith rather than perceived accuracy or reliability of information as such. It is the quality of the source rather than the information that matters. A relevant component was a perception of a medium as having the interest of the public at heart. In the United States and the UK television rapidly outstripped newspapers after the 1960s as the most trusted source of news. Although the assumption that pictures are more dependable than words plays a part, the regulated impartiality of television is also a reason for public trust. In some countries a clear distinction appears between a more trusted public and a less trusted private television (in Germany, Japan and the UK). Survey evidence also shows public awareness of different degrees of credibility between newspapers, especially between quality and 'tabloid' variants.

There are also cross-country variations. Within Europe, the newspaper press in the UK is much less trusted than the press in nearly all other countries of Western Europe (Eurobarometer, 1999). It seems that perceptions of credibility do reflect real differences between sources and can change. There remains a problem of what precisely is being measured.

The issue of credibility has been revived with the appearance of the Internet as a news medium. There are intrinsic difficulties for users in assessing the credibility of information on the Internet unless it comes from established media names, but there is also a high general public expectation that the Internet can provide solutions to uncertainty. It is still too early for a clear pattern of public attitudes to emerge, and the findings of research have been mixed. Research comparing the Internet with television and newspapers as news sources in Germany (Schweiger, 2000) and the USA (Flanagan and Metzger, 2000; Kiousis, 2001; Johnson and Kaye, 2002; Metzger et al., 2003) showed the Internet lagging somewhat in perceived trust. In a later study Flanagan and Metzger (2007) reported that perception of credibility of web information was based on website features rather than familiarity with sources. Younger (student) users also seem to trust online sources more than others (Bucy, 2003). Those who are generally more sceptical about politics prefer to go to non-mainstream sources, including the Internet, consistent with the idea that there is greater diversity.

News Diffusion

The **diffusion of news** in the sense of its takeup and incorporation into what people 'know' is mainly a short- or medium-term matter. Most early news effect research focused on 'diffusion' – the spread of news as measured by the capacity to recall certain named events. Four main variables have been at the centre of attention in this matter. They are the extent to which people (in a given population) know about a given event; the relative importance or perceived salience of the event; the volume of information about it that is transmitted; and the extent to which knowledge of an event comes first from news media or from personal contact. The possible interactions between these four are complex, but one model of the interaction is expressed by the J-curved relationship between the proportion who are aware of an event and the proportion who heard of the same event from an interpersonal source (Greenberg, 1964).

The J-shape expresses the following findings: when an event is known about by virtually everyone (such as the assassination of John F. Kennedy in 1963, the death of Princess Diana in 1997 or the attacks of 9/11), a very high proportion (over half) are likely to have been told by a personal contact (associated conditions here being high event salience and rapid diffusion). When events are known by decreasing proportions of the population, the *percentage* of personal contact origination falls and that of media source rises (associated conditions are lower salience and slower diffusion rates). However, there is a category of events which is known about ultimately only by rather small proportions of a whole population. These comprise minorities for whom the event or topic is highly salient, and the proportion of knowledge from personal contact rises again in relation to media sources because personal contact networks are activated in these circumstances.

The pattern of news information diffusion can take a variety of forms which deviate from the 'normal' S-curve of diffusion (a slow start, then an acceleration, then a flattening as the upper limit is reached). The J-curve, just described, is one important variant type. Chaffee (1975) has suggested three alternative patterns that are sometimes found: incomplete diffusion, very rapid early acceleration, and unduly slow acceleration. We should look for different explanations in terms of either 'content-specific' factors or source variables or receiver variables, often working in combination.

Theory about news diffusion is still held back by the bias of research towards a certain class of events, especially towards 'hard news', which has a high measure of unexpectedness (Rosengren, 1973, 1987). In order to have a fuller picture of processes of news diffusion we would need more evidence about 'soft news' and more about routine or anticipated events. We are also limited by the difficulty of estimating event importance independently of the amount of attention given by the media, bearing in mind the varying interests of different sectors of the society.

The diffusion of news has been made more complex by the increase in the number of channels available and the relative decline of centralized mass news channels. The fact noted above that word of mouth plays a key part in the dissemination of certain kinds of dramatic news is continually reconfirmed, despite the alleged decline of social contacts in modern society. In the case of the 9/11 terrorist attack on New York, interviews conducted a day later on people's immediate news source showed 50% hearing first from someone else, 33% from television, and 15% from radio. It took two hours for full diffusion to be achieved (Greenberg, 2002).

Framing Effects

The idea of framing (explained in Chapter 14, p. 380) is an attractive one and provides a strong hypothesis that an audience will be guided by journalistic frames in what it learns. It will also learn the frames themselves. However, it is not obvious how framing will work as an effect process. As Cappella and Jamieson put it (1997: 98), 'The way the news is framed by journalists and how the audience frames news may be similar or different.' The same authors proposed a model of framing effects, with the central idea that news frames activate certain inferences, ideas, judgements and contrasts concerning issues, policies and politicians. Their particular concern was to assess whether consistent framing of political news as either 'strategic' (dealing with attempts to gain campaign advantage) or 'conflict oriented' (as opposed to objectively reporting substance) would contribute to greater public cynicism about politics. Their evidence supports the idea of a cumulative (spiralling) process of increased cynicism as a media effect.

Scheufele (1999) has suggested a process model of framing effects that recognizes them as outcomes of interaction between three different kinds of actor: interested sources and media organizations, journalists (media) and audiences. As he notes, we are dealing with two kinds of frame: media frames and individual (receiver) frames. Both kinds of frame can be either independent (a cause) or dependent (an effect). According to the model, there are four interrelated framing processes involving these actors. First, there is the construction and use of media frames by journalists and others working in news organizations under routine pressures, constantly dealing with sources and applying 'news values' and 'news angles' to event reports. Secondly, there is the transmission of 'framed' news reports (e.g. a cynical view of politicians) to the audience. Thirdly, there is an acceptance of certain frames by members of the audience, with consequences for their attitudes, outlook (e.g. cynicism) and behaviour (e.g. non-participation).

The groundwork for much framing research was laid by Entman (1993), but there has been some criticism of his ambition to construct a single general paradigm of the framing process. D'Angelo (2002) argues that the literature indicates the existence of at least three different framing paradigms. The first of these is a *cognitivist* model, according to which the texts of journalistic accounts become embodied in the thoughts and words of those affected. Secondly, there is a *constructionist* variant of the process, which sees journalists as providing 'interpretative packages' of the positions of sponsors (i.e. sources) of news. Thirdly, there is a *critical* paradigm that sees frames as the outcome of news gathering routines and the values of elites. This attributes a hegemonic influence to framing. There has been some criticism of the general failure of framing research to pay much attention to power, although Entman (1993), in his founding presentation, did say that frames in news stories reveal the 'imprint of power'. Canagee and Roefs (2004) emphasized that frames are much more than story topics and do usually embody some direction of valuation.

Despite the complexities, there is sufficient evidence, especially from political communication research, to demonstrate the occurrence of effects on audiences that are in line with news frames. Iyengar (1991) showed that the way in which news about social problems was framed affected whether audiences were more or less likely to 'blame the victim' for their troubles. Research into the 1991 Gulf War showed that framing of news encouraged audiences to endorse military rather than diplomatic solutions (Iyengar and Simon, 1997). In the case of the news reporting of the two air disasters mentioned in Chapter 14 (Box 14.3), Entman (1991) found strong evidence of public opinion forming in line with the inbuilt news frames: the Soviets were strongly condemned for the loss of the Korean plane, and the Americans were largely absolved of responsibility for the Iranian loss. McLeod and Detenber (1999) found that differently framed news reports of the same protests had different effects on viewers. As noted on p. 530, Jamieson and Waldman (2003) attribute the failure of Al Gore in his challenge to George W. Bush over the contested US presidential election outcome to the way the issue was framed. Several accounts of the early stages of the Iraq war confirm that the US administration sources successfully injected frames favourable to the war into mainstream news reports (Schwalber et al., 2008), which in turn seemed to mobilize popular support, although gradually discordant and critical elements crept into news and support declined.

Agenda-setting

The term '**agenda-setting**' was coined by McCombs and Shaw (1972, 1993) to describe a phenomenon which had long been noticed and studied in the context of election campaigns. The core idea is that the news media indicate to the public what the main issues of the day are and this is reflected in what the public perceives as the main issues. As Trenaman and McQuail (1961: 178) pointed out, 'The evidence strongly suggests that people think *about* what they are told but at no level do they think *what* they are told.' The evidence collected at that time, and much since, consists of data showing a correspondence between the order of importance given in the media to 'issues' and the order of significance attached to the same issues by politicians and the public. Dearing and Rogers (1996) define the process as 'an ongoing competition among issue protagonists to gain the attention of media professionals, the public and policy elites'. Lazarsfeld et al. (1944) referred to it as the power to 'structure issues'. Politicians seek to convince voters that the most important issues are those with which they are most closely identified. This is an essential part of advocacy and attempts at influencing public opinion. As a hypothesis, agenda-setting (set out in summary form below in Box 19.3) seems to have escaped the general conclusion that persuasive campaigns have small or no effects.

This is the essence of the agenda-setting hypothesis, but such evidence is insufficient to show a *causal* connection between the various issue 'agendas'. For that we need to know the content of party programmes, evidence of opinion change over time in a given section of the public (preferably with panel data), plus content analysis showing media attention to different issues in the relevant period. We also need some indication of relevant media use by the public concerned. Such data have rarely, if ever, been produced at the same time in support of the hypothesis of agenda-setting. The further one moves from the general notion that media direct attention and shape cognitions and towards examining actual cases, the more uncertain it becomes whether such an effect actually occurs.

Davis and Robinson (1986) criticized previous agenda-setting research for neglecting possible effects on what people think concerning *who* is important, *where* important things happen, and *why* things are important. According to Rogers and Dearing (1987), we need to distinguish clearly between three different agendas: the priorities of the media, those of the public and those of policy. These interact in complex ways and may have effects in different directions. The same authors also note that media vary in their credibility, that personal experience and the media picture may diverge, and that the public may not share the same values about news events as the media. In addition, 'real-world events' may intervene in unexpected ways to upset previous agendas (Iyengar and Kinder, 1987). Reese (1991) has pointed out that much depends on the relative balance of power between media and sources, a factor that varies considerably from case to case. Agenda-setting effects are not unlike most other known effects in that they are also contingent on the right combination of factors in respect of the topic, the type of media and the larger context (Walgrave and Van Aelst, 2006).

Each of these comments introduces new sources of variation. Despite the difficulties, agenda-setting has attracted mass communication researchers because it seems to offer an alternative to the search for directional media effects on individual attitudes and behaviour change. Dearing and Rogers (1996: 15) write that agenda-setting is related to several other kinds of effects, including: the bandwagon effect, the spiral of silence, the diffusion of news, and media gatekeeping. Most evidence (e.g. Behr and Iyengar, 1985) is inconclusive, and assessments (among them by Kraus and Davis, 1976; Becker, 1982; Reese, 1991; Rogers et al., 1993) tend to leave agenda-setting with the status of a plausible but unproven idea.

The doubts stem not only from the strict methodological demands for proof of a causal connection, but also from theoretical ambiguities. The hypothesis presupposes a process of influence, from the priorities of political or other interest groups to the news priorities of media, in which news values and audience interests play a strong part, and from there to the opinions of the public. There are certainly alternative models of this relationship, of which the main one would reverse the flow and state that underlying concerns of the public will shape issue definition by both political elites and the media. Such a process is fundamental to political theory and to the logic of free media. It is likely that the media do contribute to a *convergence* of the three 'agendas' mentioned above, but that is a different matter from setting any particular one of them.

Dearing and Rogers (1996) offer several generalizations about agenda-setting. One is that different media do tend to agree about the relative salience of a set of issues. Secondly, media agendas do not closely match 'real-world' indicators. It is not the absolute significance of an issue that counts, but the relative strength of forces and people trying to define and promote an issue. Finally, the 'position of an issue on the media agenda importantly determines that issue's salience in the public agenda' (1996: 192). It is interesting to note that despite the centrality of agenda-setting to political communication effects research, the effect itself is likely to be accounted a 'peripheral' effect in terms of the ELM model (see p. 517), since it arises from incidental cues of significance given by presentation (Perse, 2001: 100). This does not make such effects less significant, since they contribute to shaping public perceptions of political and social reality. One common condition for agenda-setting is that different mass media tend to share the same set of news priorities. This condition is challenged by the availability of many new online news services, plus the greater chance for a 'news user' to seek news according to a personal agenda (see p. 533).

Priming

Reference is sometimes made (especially in political communication research) to 'media priming' effects, as a more specific aspect of agenda-setting. The idea of priming originated in social learning theory and the study of effects in aggression. It also has a long history in election campaign research in the attempts by politicians to be associated with the issues on which they have the strongest reputation. The authors of this idea (Iyengar and Kinder, 1987) show that the political issues that receive most attention (highest on the agenda) also figure more prominently in public assessments of the performance of political actors. The general assessment of a party or a politician thus depends on the perception of how they do on the most salient issues.

The priming 'effect' is essentially one of promoting certain evaluative criteria and it plays a part in attempts to manage news. For instance, the often suspected attempts of national leaders to divert attention from domestic failure by some foreign policy success, or even military adventure, is an extreme example of priming. Like agenda-setting, although it seems true to what is going on, it is difficult to prove in practice. Pan and Kosicki (1997) investigated the process in relation to public assessments of the US President's media performance and concluded that any priming effect of media is too weak in relation to other influences to be demonstrated.

The agenda-setting hypothesis 19.3

- Public debate is represented by a set of salient issues (an agenda for action)
- The agenda originates from public opinion and the proposals of political elites
- Competing interests seek to promote the salience of 'their' issues
- Mass media news selects issues for more or less attention according to several pressures, especially those from interested elites, public opinion and real-world events
- The outcome in media (relative degree of prominence of issues) both gives public recognition to the current agenda and has further effects on opinion and the evaluation of the political scene
- Agenda effects are peripheral and short term

Effects on Public Opinion and Attitudes

Mass communication research began with the expectation of finding significant influences from mass media on public opinion and attitudes. The distinction between the various types of effect, especially information, behaviour, opinions and attitudes, mentioned in Chapter 17, is important and calls for some comment. The first two are least problematic in respect of conceptualization and observation. Opinion and attitude cannot be observed directly or defined precisely enough to allow unambiguous measurement. Attitudes are underlying dispositions or mental sets towards some object that are generally measured in terms of verbal responses to evaluative statements. These responses are typically converted into a scale showing an individual's direction and strength of leaning in respect of an object (for instance, a political party or leader or issue). Attitudes towards different objects are thought to be related such that a person has a structure of more or less consistent attitudes. Attitudes are primarily valuations and attributions made by individuals, although it is possible to speak of 'public attitudes' as an assessment of the predominant tendency in a group or aggregate.

An opinion is a statement of preference for one side of an argument or choice presented. It is also as much cognitive as evaluative. It has a specific and provisional character and a person can have many opinions on different topics, without any necessary cohesion. Opinions vary in the strength to which they are held and in the degree to which they are based on correct information. Opinions are also individual, although they can be aggregated to form something called public opinion, which is usually taken to mean the predominant leaning, or sum of views, of the population as a whole. Public opinion does, however, have a certain independence from the individuals contributing to it. This is evident by the fact that individuals have a perception, whether accurate or not, of public opinion as the prevailing view and the view of others. This perception can have effects, as shown below. Secondly, 'public opinion' acquires a certain independence when it is embodied in media accounts. It becomes an objective 'social fact' that has to be taken account of by political and other actors.

The relevance for ideas about media effects is as follows. The media are expected to have considerable potential for influence on the opinions of individuals, although mostly without intention, by providing the information that issues exist and indicating the options. By publishing opinion poll results or by stating editorially what the public view is on a given topic, they add another element of potential influence. Media are much less likely to influence attitudes than opinions, even when they bring new and relevant evaluative information. Attitudes only change slowly and are resistant. They are anchored by each other in a larger outlook on the world.

One basic principle of organization of both attitude and opinion is their grounding in membership of social groups and the influence of the social milieu in which we move. A second principle is that of consistency or balance. We are more comfortable when our various likes and dislikes and our opinions are compatible with each other. This is expressed in the idea of 'cognitive consistency'. The theory of **cognitive dissonance** (the reverse condition) predicts that we will tend to look for information or ideas that maintain consistency and avoid the discomfort of incompatible opinions (Festinger, 1957). This also means that new information can unsettle existing attitudes and lead to realignments. This is one reason why the established learning or informational effects of mass media are more important in the longer term.

Expectations of finding proof of causal connections between media and opinions and attitudes are much lower than in earlier days. The main factors whose presence or absence affects the chances of media effects occurring are summarized in Box 19.4.

19.4 Factors affecting the chances of media effects on opinion and attitude

- The perceived authority, legitimacy and credibility of the source
- Consistency of content of media messages
- Attachment and loyalty to sources
- Motives for attention to media
- Congruence of content with existing opinion or belief
- Amount and quality of attention paid
- Skill and appeal of message and presentation
- Support from personal contacts and environment

These factors have to be considered in combination with each other. For instance, a legitimate source may not be liked or trusted personally. The factors apply in various forms and ways. For example, 'consistency of messages' can derive from a media monopoly situation or from essential agreement between independent media and sources. The factor 'attention' is especially tricky since, apart from a minimum requirement, more attention paid does not necessarily mean more effect. Under some circumstances it is the less attentive and less motivated who are more influenced. Motives are quite diverse and differ in their implications for effects (Blumler and McQuail, 1968). Finally, there is no guarantee that professional skill leads to more persuasion and more communication than its reverse.

Research attention has shifted to more indirect ways in which the media have an influence (for instance, by framing, agenda-setting and informational increments) and to special circumstances where media may play an enhanced role. In the following section, a model of the influence process is presented which takes account of incidental influence (whether given or taken).

The Elaboration-Likelihood Model of Influence

There are a number of models that represent the way that information and impressions are processed in any attempt at influence or persuasion, leaving aside the different variants of conditioning. One cognitive processing model in particular that has often been applied is Petty and Cacioppo's (1986) elaboration-likelihood model (ELM). Elaboration refers to the extent to which a person thinks about the issue and about relevant arguments contained in a message. The model is based on the assumption that people are motivated to hold 'correct attitudes' in the sense of their being rational, coherent and consistent with other views. At the same time, not everyone has the time or capacity to devote to developing such attitudes and we are selective in our attention to issues and arguments. We devote more effort to understanding and evaluating matters of greater personal interest and relevance. This is reflected in the way we process incoming information, either *centrally* (high elaboration) or *peripherally*. In the former case, we draw on our knowledge and experience to scrutinize information. In the second case, we rely more on incidental cues, such as the perceived credibility or attractiveness of the source or the appeal of the presentational form rather than the cognitive content of the message itself. Whether or not we adopt a central or peripheral mode is affected by 'receiver' variables as well as 'message' variables. The difference between modes opens the way for matching the persuasive strategies of would-be communicators, who can choose either rational arguments or more superficial means of gaining attention and assent by way of simple cues and positive images and associations. The model is summarized in Figure 19.2.

The model has wide application, but only limited predictive value. It helps to summarize and describe aspects of persuasion. It also distinguishes between strategies for change that are likely to lead to more or less enduring effects. It reminds that the potential for 'learning without involvement' (Krugman, 1965) may sometimes be greater than an active interaction between source and receiver.

A related, but different, aspect of processing incoming information is discussed by Cappella and Jamieson (1997). This is the distinction between 'online' and 'memory-based' approaches. The first of these assumes that the key information (e.g. in a news story) is all provided in the message itself as it is viewed or read. The second refers to the fact that any message (informational or persuasive) will tap into an existing store of information, impressions, beliefs, evaluations, and so on. It will activate predisposition rather than provide something entirely new. This is a complex matter and in reality both online input and memory are likely to be active during processing. However, it has implications for strategies and probabilities of influence. In general, the more that memory-based processing operates, the more 'peripheral' is the route and also the greater is the chance of effects such as framing and priming.

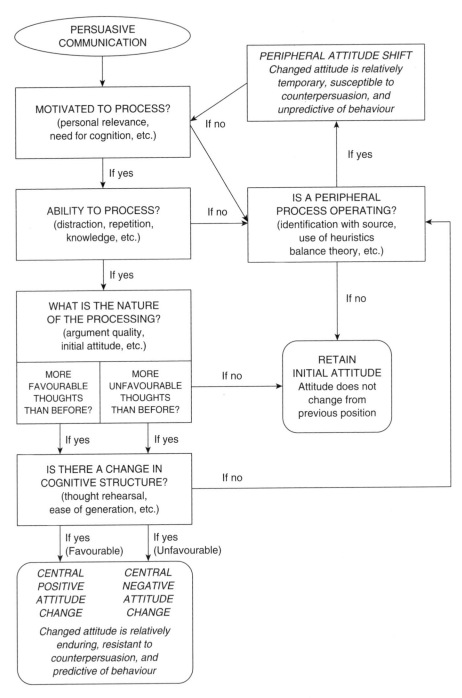

Figure 19.2 The elaboration-likelihood model of persuasion and information processing (Petty et al., 2002: 166)

The Spiral of Silence: the Formation of Climates of Opinion

The concept of the 'spiral of silence' derives from a larger body of theory of public opinion that was developed and tested by Noelle-Neumann (1974, 1984, 1991) over a number of years. The relevant theory concerns the interplay between four elements: mass media, interpersonal communication and social relations, individual expressions of opinion, and the perceptions which individuals have of the surrounding 'climate of opinion' in their own social environment. The main assumptions of the theory (Noelle-Neumann, 1991) are as follows:

- Society threatens deviant individuals with isolation.
- Individuals experience fear of isolation continuously.
- This fear of isolation causes individuals to try to assess the climate of opinion at all times.
- The results of this estimate affect their behaviour in public, especially their willingness or not to express opinions openly.

In brief, the theory proposes that, in order to avoid isolation on important public issues (such as political party support), many people are guided by what they think to be the dominant or declining opinions in their environment. People tend to conceal their views if they feel they are in a minority and are more willing to express them if they think they are dominant. The result is that those views that are perceived to be dominant gain even more ground and alternatives retreat still further. This is the *spiralling* effect referred to.

In the present context, the main point is that the mass media are the most readily accessible source for assessing the prevailing climate, and if a certain view predominates in the media it will tend to be magnified in the subsequent stages of personal opinion formation and expression. The theory was first formulated and tested to explain puzzling findings in German politics where opinion poll indications were inconsistent with other data concerning expectations of who would win an election and signally failed to predict the result. The explanation put forward was that the media were offering a misleading view of the opinion consensus. They were said to be leaning in a leftist direction, against the underlying opinion of the (silent) majority.

Two studies from Sweden reported in Rosengren (1981a) provided confirmation of an influence from the Swedish press on public opinion about the Middle East and on political opinion that seemed to support the standpoint of Noelle-Neumann and other proponents of 'powerful mass media' and the spiral of silence. A different test of the theory concerned the issue of nuclear energy. Noelle-Neumann (1991) found evidence of increasing press attention on the issue, accompanied by a steady increase in negative reporting. Over time, public support for nuclear energy also declined markedly, and the timing and sequence of changes suggested an interactive spiralling effect as predicted in the theory.

The spiral of silence theory is a close neighbour of mass society theory and involves a similar, somewhat pessimistic, view of the quality of social relations (Taylor,

1982). According to Katz (1983), its validity will depend on the extent to which alternative reference groups are still alive and well in social life. The more that is the case, the less scope there is for the process described to operate, since there will be support for minority or deviant views. Moscovici (1991) also suggests that, in general, we should pay less attention in public opinion formation to silent majorities and more to 'loud minorities', which often play a larger part in opinion change.

The spiral of silence theory is much more than a theory of media effect and involves several dimensions that need to be investigated in conjunction. It is not surprising that it remains in a hypothetical form or that evidence is weak and inconsistent from one context to another. For instance, Glynn et al. (1997) concluded from a recent meta-analysis of survey studies that there was little evidence that perception of support or not for one's own opinion is related to willingness to speak out. Even so, there is supportive evidence (e.g. Mutz and Soss, 1997; Gunther, 1998) for a simpler version of the theory that media coverage does shape individual perceptions of public sentiment on current issues (opinion about opinion).

There is also continuing support for the view that 'fear of isolation' is a key factor in affecting willingness to speak out on a controversial issue. Moy et al. (2001) looked at the case of a controversial and morally laden Washington state initiative to end positive discrimination in employment and education, against a strongly opposed public opinion. Fear of isolation did inhibit speaking out to support a perceived minority position. However, it was also found that the relevant 'climate' was really a micro-climate of immediate family and friends rather than the public as a whole.

Third-party effects

Related to the spiral of silence theory is the idea of third-party effects of media on public opinion, first proposed by Davison (1983). The key point is that many people seem to think (or say to pollsters) that other people are affected by various kinds of media content, but not they themselves. This perception goes with a tendency to support censorship (McLeod et al., 2001). There is much empirical support for the tendency to attribute effects to others, which helps to explain the widespread belief in the power of the media, even where not supported by evidence (Hoffner et al., 2001). The overestimate of media effects is also associated with the equally widespread tendency to believe that the news media are biased against the point of view of those engaged by a particular issue (Gunther and Christen, 2002), also with little or no support in evidence. Asking people to estimate the influence of media on themselves is clearly not a way to uncover the direction and scale of actual effects. An interesting corollary to the hypothesis of Third Party effect is that the theory of 'Second-Person Effect'. This refers to reactions of public actors to stories that enter into the news. Typically they respond as if the fact of publication ensures that an entire public is paying attention (an unlikely circumstance). The result is to amplify and diffuse the original publication and set in train a new chain of events and interjections, with potential effects on public opinion. This process gives journalists (as part of their agenda-setting role) a degree of power that they would not otherwise have and which they may need to account for (Glasser, 2009).

Structuring Reality and Unwitting Bias

Common to much theory in this area is the view that long-term media effects occur unintentionally, as a result of media organizational tendencies, occupational practices, technical limitations and the systematic application of certain news values, frames and formats. Thus Paletz and Entman (1981) attributed the propagation of a 'conservative myth' by US media during the 1970s mainly to 'pack journalism' – the tendency of journalists to work together, arrive at a consensus, cover the same stories and use the same news sources. In their coverage of the Balkan wars, the Gulf crisis of 1990–1 and subsequently, most western media have tended to frame the news that is both consensual and supportive of western actions, although the Gulf War showed up deep fissures (e.g. Tumber and Palmer, 2004).

A tendency for mainstream media to take the side of the government of the day under conditions of war or emergency has often been observed, with various explanations offered (if explanations are needed). A key theory in this matter has been provided by Bennett (1990), which proposes that journalists tend to reflect or 'index' the range of voices and viewpoints according to the range of views in the mainstream political debate. This tends to marginalize minority and critical voices and promotes an apparent consensus. Althaus (2003) provides some evidence for this thesis and it seems to have been reconfirmed by the case of Iraq.

The notion that media 'structure reality' in a way that is often shaped by their own needs and interests has been demonstrated. An early example was the study by Lang and Lang (1953) of the television coverage of the return of General McArthur from Korea after his recall. This showed how a relatively small-scale and muted occasion was turned (in its reporting) into something approaching a mass demonstration of welcome and support by the selective attention of cameras and commentary to points of most activity and interest. The reportage was seeking to reproduce from rather unsatisfactory materials a suitable version of what had been predicted as a major occasion.

The media coverage of a large demonstration in London against the Vietnam War in 1968 followed much the same pattern (Halloran et al., 1970). The coverage was planned for an event predefined (largely by the media themselves) as potentially violent and dramatic, and the actual coverage strained to match this predefinition, despite the scarcity of suitable reality material. The same research supported the conclusion that audiences perceived the event more in line with its framing on television than as it had actually transpired.

Evidence of an actual effect from such media practices on how people define reality is not easy to find. However, in their study of how children came to define the 'problem' of race and immigration, Hartman and Husband (1974) showed that dominant media definitions were picked up, especially where personal experience was lacking. A different kind of effect was documented by Gitlin (1980) in relation to media coverage of the radical US student movement in the late 1960s. Here the media played a major part in shaping the image of this movement for the North American public. The line of effect generally accorded with the media's own needs (such as those for dramatic action, celebrities, personalities and conflict), and caused the student movement itself to respond to this image and adapt and develop accordingly. A more recent study of the definition by the media of the women's movement in The Netherlands in its early days (van Zoonen, 1992) provides another example of a similar process at work. Lind and Salo (2002) examined the framing of feminists and feminism in US TV news and public affairs programmes during the 1990s. They found a consistent tendency to marginalize and demonize both, with feminists portrayed as unlike 'regular women'.

While the media are often acting without any deliberate bias, it is possible for their known tendencies to be made use of for purposes of news management, as shown in a study of the reporting of protests directed at the World Economic Forum in the years 2001–3 (Bennett et al., 2004). The essential details are given in Box 19.5.

19.5 Media management of the public sphere

Bennett et al.'s (2004) study of media reporting for the World Economic Forum (WEF) aimed to investigate the way in which mass media represented the two sides in the 'Great Globalization Debate' – on the one hand activists for change, and on the other elite participants and officials. The role of media in relation to the public sphere was theorized as 'giving access (who gets into the news?); recognition (who is formally identified?); and responsiveness (who responds to whom?)'. The study was of news coverage of the WEF in the years 2001, 2002 and 2003. A total of 88 articles and editorials in the *New York Times* were analysed and all activist themes were identified and expressed either as linked to WEF participants, protestors or other. The results were as follows. With regard to access, most activist themes were credited to the WEF participants (53%) and only 40% to the activists, giving an impression of official concern for these issues. With regard to recognition, WEF participants were identified much more than protestors (66% versus 23%), a sign of marginalization. And with regard to responsiveness, virtually no mutual responsiveness was found.

The main conclusions were that the WEF elite gained disproportionate and unearned credit for their concern and protestors were framed in ways that reduced their legitimacy and status: 'The news media actively constructed the grassroots critics as marginal, largely nameless scruffians who threatened civil order with violence' (Bennett et al., 2004: 482).

Most of the effects referred to here probably derive from 'unwitting bias' in the media, but the potential to define reality is often exploited knowingly. The term 'pseudo-event' has been used to refer to a category of event more or less manufactured to gain attention or create a particular impression (Boorstin, 1961; McGinnis, 1969). The staging of pseudo-events is now a familiar tactic in many election (and other) campaigns, but more significant is the possibility that a high percentage of media coverage of 'actuality' really consists of planned events which are intended to shape impressions in favour of one interest or another. Those most able to manipulate actuality coverage are those with most power; so the bias, if it exists, may be unwitting on the part of the media but is certainly not so for those trying to shape their own 'image' (Molotch and Lester, 1974).

The Communication of Risk

One of the functions attributed to mass media is that of providing a public warning of possible dangers and risks. This is one of the explanations (if not justifications) offered for the disproportionate attention in news (and fiction) to crime, violence, disaster, death and disease. At certain key moments, media reports of danger can lead to short-term panic responses, but the issue of media effects is usually posed in other forms. First, there is the established tendency of media to portray the world, implicitly at least, as more dangerous than it really is (statistically speaking). Attention is skewed away from the mundane causes of death, disease and disaster (road accidents, poor diet, poverty) and towards more dramatic but rarer calamities (terrorist outrage, air crash, earthquake, etc.). This can be said to mislead the public about the true nature of risks. A similar criticism applies to the links between crime reporting, real crime and public fear of crime (e.g. Lowry et al., 2003; Romer et al., 2003).

Secondly, there is the relative failure of the press, through lack of expertise and the intrinsic uncertainty of the case, to give advice to the public on many genuine risks connected with scientific innovation, environmental threats, biotechnology, genetics and similar matters (Priest, 2001). There is a third issue that relates to the tendency of the media to act as a conduit for all kinds of information and argument from all kinds of sources that can be alarming or reassuring, but for which no editorial responsibility is (or often can be) taken. The Internet opens new floodgates in this respect. In the end, it seems as if the media themselves are a source of uncertainty and danger that the public has to take at its own peril, or avoid.

Political Communication Effects in Democracies

There has always been an intimate connection between mass communication and the conduct of politics, in whatever kind of regime. In totalitarian or authoritarian societies, ruling elites use their control of the media to ensure conformity and compliance and to stifle dissent by one means or another. In democracies, the media have a complex relationship with sources of power and the political system. On the one hand, they usually find their *raison d'être* in their service to their audiences, to whom they provide information and views according to judgements of interest and need. In order to perform this service they need to be independent of the state and of powerful interests. On the other hand, they also provide channels by which the state and powerful interests address the people, as well as platforms for the views of political parties and other interest groups. They also promote the circulation of news and opinion within the politically interested public.

This general view of the neutral and mediating role of the media in politics has to be modified to take account of variant forms, especially one in which particular media choose to play a partisan role on behalf of a party or interest, or are closely allied with some powerful economic interest or ideological bloc. There is a third possibility where the state has considerable effective power over nominally free media and uses this power for its own advantage. Such a situation appears to pertain more and more in post-communist Russia, and other countries, such as Italy under Berlusconi, have approached a similar position. In global terms, the situation is not at all unusual.

Against this background we can identify and briefly characterize the main forms of political communication which can be considered under the heading of 'effects'. First, there are periodic campaigns for *election* in which the media are usually used intensively by competing candidates and parties. Secondly, there is the continuous flow of *news* which carries messages about events that reflect positively or negatively on governments and other actors in the political arena. This provides many opportunities for news management and PR intervention. Thirdly, there are, in varying degrees, opportunities for political *advertising* by the same actors, independent of elections. Specific attempts are also sometimes made to influence opinion on particular issues on behalf of various lobbies and pressure groups, by various means.

The most studied communication form is that of the election campaign, with research going back at least until 1940, when Lazarsfeld et al. (1944) made a detailed enquiry into the presidential election of that year. Since then, thousands of democratic elections have been an object of research (see Semetko, 2004), with some consistency in broad findings about effects. First, election campaigns are usually short and intensive and are not typically characterized by a great deal of net change from intention to vote. The media are intensively used by campaigners, but usually received with less interest by electors. It is rare to find clear support in evidence that media make a great deal of difference to the outcome of an election. They have little direct effect on voting (or not voting). Basic political attitudes are usually too deeply rooted to be susceptible to much change, although a growing detachment from firm allegiances opens the way for more influence. Opinions on particular issues may be influenced by media and there is evidence of a potential for learning about issues and policy stands, especially by the relatively ignorant and disinterested. To some extent this reflects the 'agenda-setting' process described above. Learning effects can be important when they lead to opinion change or, more likely, to perceptions of reality that favour one side or another. An unusual piece of experimental research by Norris et al. (1999) in a British general election showed that exposure to party positions contained within news broadcasts could significantly influence attitudes to the parties in the short term.

Election campaigns attract widely varying degrees and kinds of motivated audience attention (and much inattention) and the effects they do have depend more on the dispositions and motives of voters than on the intentions of campaigners. Blumler and McQuail (1968) found that an intensive general election campaign had larger effects where it reached sectors of a more or less captive audience that was previously uninformed and without firm allegiances. Schoenbach and Lauf (2002) call this a 'trap' effect. A strong claim has been made that, as a result of audience fragmentation, we have entered a 'new era of minimal effects' (Bennett and Iyengar, 2008). The key factor they point to is the 'demise of the inadvertent audience' (thus of the 'trap effect') and the rise of partisan selective exposure aided by a comination of social change and technology. There are some weaknesses in this proposition, since the actual evidence for any strong effect era is hard to come by and the idea that the new media have actually brought new news is open to challenge. In many parts of the world, partisan selectivity has been a long established feature of old media.

The relative lack of decisive effects from media campaigns can be attributed to several factors aside from selective attention and variable motivation. These include the lack of room for change on familiar issues, the cancelling effect of opposing messages, the part played by personal relations (see pp. 472–3) and the ritual character of much campaigning that offers little that is new of any substance. In many western democracies, where the media are not co-opted by the political parties, the amount and quality of attention given to the main contenders tends to be very similar (Norris et al., 1999; D'Alessio and Allen, 2000; Noin, 2001). Campaigns tend to maintain the status quo, but we could expect large effects if one side failed to campaign, and sometimes a single incident can upset the equilibrium dramatically. Often election campaigns are aimed at maintaining the status quo rather than creating change.

Campaigning parties and candidates usually choose from among a number of available communication strategies, depending on circumstances and resources, and often depending on whether they are incumbent or not. They can seek to associate themselves with particular issues on which they have a particular record or claim. This is where being able to frame issues and set news agendas matters. They may try to win on grounds of ideology or principle, which is harder and riskier. They can aim to acquire an attractive image by association, style or personality rather than policy. They can attack an opponent on whatever ground of weakness presents itself, although negativity can demotivate voters generally.

The question of which medium is more effective in achieving results in campaigns was a central focus of attention in early research, especially with the arrival of television, but in a multimedia environment it is less salient and also harder to investigate. Norris and Sanders (2003) conclude that what counts more is the message and the disposition of the audience. The consensus view is that no medium is inherently superior, although each has some advantages. Different media do have institutional features that affect their influence (e.g. newspapers are more partisan than television) and they draw different audiences with differing motivations. Druckman (2005) reviewed evidence comparing television with the press, finding either absence of proof or contradictory results. However, his own study of influence in one election found that newspapers and not TV news played a significant role in informing the electorate.

Political communication by way of general news reflects a continuous process of news management and competition to define events and issues. All significant actors employ professional news managers (spin doctors) to ensure access on favourable terms in normal daily news and to put the best gloss possible on a news story. Such influences are impossible to measure in terms of effectiveness, but there is good support in theory for the belief that the news provides a good environment for influential messages since it is usually characterized by independence of source, credibility and lack of propagandist associations. In practice, in most functioning democracies, more or less equal access to news is usually available to the main contenders for office, sufficient to prevent a single dominant shape being given to the news.

Political advertising, on the other hand, depends on having resources, but is also limited in its potential by its propagandist character. It may have unpredictable side-effects, and clear evidence of the value of political advertising is hard to come by (Goldstein and Freedman, 2002), although it may work as intended by simple attrition and repetition. The same applies to all campaigns with a political objective. They tend to lack a number of the attributes necessary for successful persuasion, as shown in Box 19.4. Advertising on television has tended to take negative forms, with the risks noted above.

Ever since the famous Kennedy–Nixon televised debate in 1960, this campaign form has been advocated as a means of enlivening politics and providing a decisive test of leader competence and persuasiveness. It has been tried out in various forms (Kraus and Davis, 1976). The fear of disaster testifies to the potency attributed to such events. However, the findings of research (e.g. Coleman, 2000) have reported little in the way of dramatic electoral consequences (true of the original debate), although they do lead to changed perceptions of candidates and some learning of policies. They seem to have reinforcement effects on voter choice. In fact, incumbent politicians have typically been very wary of debates, seeing no certain advantage and fearing uncontrolled effects.

This brief overview of the effects of mass communication in election campaigns may seem inconsistent with the reality of contemporary political campaigning in which communication strategies are planned in fine detail by a myriad of advisers and professional publicists and many ways are found to spend large sums of money, especially by those in media advertising. The fact is that even though the chances of decisively influencing the outcome of an election by means of communication are usually quite small, it would be easy to lose an election by not campaigning or campaigning badly. Mounting a glittering, clever and confident campaign is an essential part of the institutional ritual and the appeal for public support, and not to campaign to the utmost would mean not being taken seriously as a candidate.

Effects on the Political Institution and Process

The case of politics provides fairly clear evidence of the adaptation of a social institution to the rise of mass media, especially given the fact that the media have become a (if not *the*) main source of information and opinion for the public. The challenge to politics from the growing centrality of the mass media and the rise of 'media logic' have taken several forms. These include:

- the diversion of time from political participation to watching television (video malaise);
- the negative effects of political marketing on voter trust and goodwill;
- the increasing negativity of campaigning and campaign reporting;
- the rising costs and bureaucratization of campaigning;
- the loss by parties of their own channels for reaching a mass following and increased dependence on media channels and gatekeepers.

Ideas about the influence of 'media logic' on political institutions (see Mazzoleni, 1987b) include: the diversion of attention from the local and regional to the national stage; the reliance on personality and image more than on substance and policy; the decline of face-to-face political campaigning; the excessive reliance on and use of opinion polls. Mass media gatekeepers are thought, rightly or wrongly, to have increased their power over who gets access and over terms of access for politicians to the public. It is they who 'set the agenda' for political debate, so it is alleged. In addition to all this, 'trial by media' has become a fact of public life in most countries for any politician touched in any way by scandal (Thompson, 2000; Tumber and Waisbord, 2004).

The triumph of media logic over political logic also finds expression in the treatment of elections as more 'horse-races' than occasions for learning about issues and policies (Graber, 1976b). More recently, this has been described as a tendency to concentrate on 'strategic' news, in which the ups and downs of the campaign and electioneering strategies become the news, not the substance of policy proposals and the related arguments. This undoubted tendency has been interpreted as steadily increasing the cynicism of voters (Cappella and Jamieson, 1997) and reducing informativeness (Valentino et al., 2001).

The view that modern political campaigning is counterproductive in respect of the aim to mobilize citizens to participate has not gone unchallenged. Norris (2000) reviewed much evidence showing that engagement with democratic politics is persistently associated with much attention to mass media. More recently, Pasek et al. (2006) concluded that media use, whether for information or entertainment, facilitates civic engagement and political awareness. Moy et al. (2005) found much the same. The true significance of voter cynicism has also been questioned. De Vreese (2005) found that strategic reporting was not conducive to cynicism and in any case cynicism, is not linked to non-voting *per se* since it is a quality of the politically more sophisticated. It is also arguable that the triumph of media logic has been overemphasized. Bennett and Iyengar (2008) cite the Obama presidential campaign as evidence that there is plenty of life in the old institution. A detailed study of Belgian political reporting at a general election time comparing media logic with party logic showed no evidence of the former trumping the latter (Van Aelst et al., 2008). This is a reminder of how much always depends on time, place and circumstances where communication is concerned.

There is little doubt that election campaigns have been widely transformed into skilfully and professionally managed events more akin to advertising, public relations and marketing than traditional politics (Blumler and Gurevitch, 1995). It is widely thought that the trends described originated in the USA and have been globally diffused (Swanson and Mancini, 1996; Bennett and Entman, 2001; Sussman and Galizio, 2003). The rise of the 'spin doctor' has been interpreted as marking a new stage in the development of political communication, with journalism providing 'meta-communication' about media manipulation, defined as 'the news media's self-referential reflections on the nature of the interplay between PR and political journalism' (Esser et al., 2000).

As always, it is hard to separate out the effects of media change from broad changes in society working both on the media and on political institutions, and there is much room for dispute about the real cause of any given institutional effect.

Cappella (2002) advises against treating the media as a 'cause'. Rather, media propagate and replicate a certain prevailing view. There is also need for caution about the more sweeping complaints concerning the decay of political communication and the ravages of 'video malaise' (Schulz, 1997). There is no single condition and many of the traditional media supports for democracy still operate quite well (Norris, 2000).

The term 'mediatization' has been widely used to describe the adaptation of politicians to the media criteria of success and the growing importance of symbolic politics (Kepplinger, 2002). The main meanings of the concept have been extracted and summarized by Schulz (2004). The essence can be read in Box 19.6. What is mostly at issue here are those aspects of change that have an impact on the way the democratic political institution works. All four aspects are present by implication, but probably the most important are the second and the fourth.

19.6 The concept of mediatization: key quotation

Four processes of change represent different aspects of mediatization. First, the media extend the natural limits of human communication; second, the media substitute social activities and social institutions; third, media amalgamate with various non-media activities in social life; and fourth, the actors and organizations of all sectors of society accommodate to the media logic. (Schulz, 2004: 98)

Meyer (2002) describes the process as one of colonization of one societal domain (politics) by another (the media). He writes: 'politicians feel themselves increasingly under pressure to get access to the media. They hope that if they master the rules governing access they can thereby increase their leverage over the way media present themselves to the public' (2002: 71). This leads to surrender to the logic of the media system, including a submission to theatricalization and symbolization of self-presentation. Critics also see a rise in superficiality and loss of sincerity and spontaneity. Strömbäck (2008) argues that a process of this kind passes through four main stages, beginning with the simple mediation of political information and ideas by way of the press and broadcasting. In the second and third phases, the autonomy of media increases and so does dependence by political and social actors on the media. Mediated reality becomes more significant than actual reality. In the final stage, actors *internalize* the logic of the media and politics become permanent campaigning. The media become the dominant party in the media-politics relationship. In Strömbäck's view, the Internet has not yet made any real difference one way or another to the process.

Although the Internet has already become an essential element in election campaigning and has been anecdotally credited with a rejuvenating role (as in the US election of 2008), there is still little precise evidence of a distinctive and decisive communication effect. Several studies tend to stress the extent to which the Internet has been 'normalized' by the established institution (Schweitzer, 2005, 2008; Vaccari,

2008). However, the question remains open since real efforts to transform politics in a more participatory and balanced direction have scarcely begun (Coleman, 2005). Bentivegna (2006) argues that we will only be able to identify the contribution of new ICTs to politics if we reconceptualize the idea of politics and abandon the territory of traditional politics:

> To begin with, it may be held that they [new ICTs] enable the confirmation of the presence and achievement of political action that would be otherwise difficult to implement ... In some cases, as in that of the anti-globalization movement, ICTs have been used to create trans-national networks ... In other cases, as in that of the organization of demonstrations in Spain after the Islamic bombing attacks, ICTs have been used to mobilize people ... It may also be held that they enable the expression of an idea of citizenship along the lines of what Schudson (2004) has called a 'democracy of rights'. (2006: 340)

Media Influence on Event Outcomes

The case for studying the role of the media in the outcome of significant societal events has been persuasively put by Lang and Lang (1981), and they applied their own advice by studying the Watergate affair and the downfall of President Nixon (Lang and Lang, 1983). Other researchers (Kraus et al., 1975) have also recommended the study of what they term 'critical events', mainly elections but also other occasions of significance for society. The mass media may rarely initiate change independently, but they do provide the channels, the means and an arena for the playing out of events in which many actors and interests are involved, often in competition with each other. The primary object of influence may be not the general media public itself but other specific organized interest groups, elites, influential minorities, and so on.

The media provide horizontal channels (especially between elites) as well as vertical channels for communicating in either direction. Influence flows from the top down, but politicians often treat the media as a source of intelligence about the mood of the country. Lang and Lang (1983) noted that the media 'present political actors with a "looking-glass image" of how they appear to outsiders'. What they call the 'bystander public' (referring to the general media public) provides a significant reference group for political actors, and it is often for the benefit of a bystander public that they frame many of their actions. This is part of a process of 'coalition building'.

The kind of event in which the media play an active and significant part, as it unfolds, is likely to be characterized by having a public and collective character, a historic significance and a long time scale in which media and key actors interact with each other. Major international crises often meet these criteria, and there is steady growth in interest in the part played by the media in such events as the fall of the Berlin Wall, the crises in the Gulf and the former Yugoslavia, and the many aid missions to Third World countries.

The term 'CNN effect' has been given (somewhat ethnocentrically) to the general phenomenon of media exerting an influence on foreign policy, especially in regard to some foreign intervention (Robinson, 2001). A similar potential effect has been looked at with reference to the giving of foreign aid (Van Belle, 2003). The term derives from the myth that new global television channels can connect governments at home most directly and quickly to unfolding events abroad. The idea has much deeper roots, since the press has often played a role historically in decisions about war (for instance, the American–Spanish conflict in 1899). According to Gilboa (2002, 2005), global communication can play a number of different roles: displacing policy-makers; constraining actions in real time; promoting intervention; and being used as an instrument of diplomacy. There is little doubt that global communication in general has become a more important factor in foreign interventions and it is more difficult to manage than domestic media. So far, there is no definitive evidence that it has been a major precipitating factor in any recent international conflict (Mermin, 1999; Robinson, 2001). Livingstone and Bennett's (2003) study of CNN news content does show some tendency for foreign news to be more event-driven and less managed by officials at home, making such services more independent gatekeepers. Media, including global branches, still tend to reflect the debates within national governments and also the general balance of opinion without proposing new initiatives – a process described as 'indexing' (Bennett, 1990) (see pp. 242–3).

Media can influence the outcome of quite different kinds of events and in different ways. In the case of the contested Bush–Gore election result in 2000, Jamieson and Waldman (2003) attributed the outcome in part to the Republican success in framing the debate in a way favourable to themselves, coupled with the failure of the press to fulfil its investigative role at the time. Another kind of event deserves attention, even if it is not always very significant. This is the political scandal, in which the media usually play a key role (Tumber and Waisbord, 2004). Thompson (2000) characterizes political scandals as 'mediated events that bring private and public life together'. Such events serve political as well as media ends and their course is often determined by the mass media.

Virtually all planned public events of significance attract a great deal of lobbying and advocacy, especially where decisions taken will affect large groups. Although it has been argued that new media open the way for a breakthrough by the less well financed activist-led causes, the evidence so far suggests otherwise. The case of the protest movement against the WTO is reported in Box 19.5 above as one example of control of the public sphere by more official voices and mainstream media. Thrall (2006) studied the relative success of 242 different US interest groups and concluded that the largest and wealthiest groups systematically gained most favourable treatment and the poorest groups the most negative, whatever the means employed.

Propaganda and War

Jowett and O'Donnell (1999: 6) define propaganda as 'the deliberate, systematic attempt to shape perceptions, manipulate cognitions, and direct behavior to achieve a response that furthers the desired intent of the propagandist'. The connotations of the term have generally been negative. It is the 'enemy' that makes propaganda, while 'our side' provides information, evidence and argument. In our time, the primary association of propaganda is generally with conflict between states and currently the 'war on terror', but the term can be applied to almost any area where communication is planned to achieve some goal of influence. It differs in some respects from simple persuasion attempts. It can be coercive and aggressive in manner; it is not objective and it has little regard for truth, even if it is not necessarily false, since sometimes the truth can be good propaganda. It comes in a range of types from 'black' (deceptive, frightening and unscrupulous) to 'white' (soft and with a selective use of truth). Finally, it is always carried out to further some interest of the propagandist, not the target audience. Under conditions of information monopoly or severe ethnic conflicts, control of the media has often been used to foster hatred and mobilize populations to violence. The historic examples of the twentieth century are obvious enough. More recent cases, as in the Balkans (Price and Thompson, 2002) and Rwanda (Des Forges, 2002), show that the same potential still exists.

The mass media are now regarded as essential to successful war propaganda, since they are the only channels guaranteed to reach the whole public and have the advantage (in open societies) of being regarded as trustworthy. The possibilities for synergy between war-making and news-making are obvious. The public demand for news is high. War news satisfies all significant news values. A variety of sources press for access. However, there are some obstacles. Journalists generally have an aversion to what they perceive as attempts to use them for propaganda purposes. Mass media are also uncertain instruments of propaganda since their audience cannot be restricted, and one of the requirements of successful propaganda is that the right message reaches the right group. Especially since the Vietnam War, which has widely (but not very correctly) been regarded as a propaganda failure for the American authorities, every military action in the western sphere of influence has been conducted with great regard for effective propaganda. In the Falkland Islands expedition of 1982, the 1991 Persian Gulf War, the Arab–Israel conflict, Kosovo, Afghanistan, the Iraq War and many minor skirmishes, the allied (western) authorities have sought to control the flow of military information (see Morrison and Tumber, 1988; Kellner, 1992; Taylor, 1992; Iyengar and Simon, 1997; Smith, 1999; Thussu and Freedman, 2003; Tumber and Palmer, 2004). Reports suggest that Russia had learnt which lessons to apply in the Chechnya War of 1999. Before these hot wars there was extensive (mainly American) propaganda at home and abroad in pursuit of Cold War aims (Foerstal, 2001; Newman, 2003), despite the successful propagation of the view that it was the 'other side' that used propaganda.

In most of the war cases mentioned, the strategy of becoming the main or only source of useful news content was largely successful in achieving the primary propaganda aim of maintaining at least tolerant support from domestic and significant world public opinion. In the recent Iraq War, the tactic of 'embedding' correspondents within the military (a practice with a long previous history) ensured a one-sided (and more favourable) view of events (see above, p. 511–12) for the forces concerned. The main conditions in support of successful propaganda have thus been present: near monopoly of supply of information and images (for the home population) and a broad consensus on goals. In most of the recent instances, 'enemy' propaganda has been largely unable to reach its targets in the 'home' country or internationally. An important condition is to maintain in the public mind a distinction between 'deserving' and 'undeserving' civilian victims.

Nevertheless, there is increasing difficulty in managing international opinion, mainly because the world is more divided and with more independent national information resources. In the case of Iraq, as events unfolded, control of the flow of information diminished and the propaganda of the victors was open to unsettling reality checks. Shifts in public opinion against the war in participating countries suggested that propaganda was successful initially and later weakened. The media of most countries tended to follow the policy line of their governments, although the media in Spain were mainly antagonistic and the British media were divided in opinion and torn between patriotism and reason (Murray et al., 2008). In both countries, public and elite opinion exerted a strong counter-pull that was absent in the USA, where only one member of both Houses voted against the war powers requested by President Bush. Snow and Taylor (2006) characterized US propaganda efforts as a success at home and a failure abroad. They also see the whole event as serving to expose the journalistic myths of an adversarial relation with government and of objectivity of practice. The facts flowing from government and military inevitably tend to gain more attention and have more impact than alternative versions of events without a strong basis in evidence. Even so, there is a difference between successful news management and good PR, which the Bush administration did usually achieve in the short run and overall long-term success in shaping public opinion as predicted by the hegemonic tradition of media propaganda theory. But even successful propaganda does not endure for ever. Pfau et al. (2007) cite evidence to show that overall exposure to TV news was linked to reduced pride in the US presence in Iraq and less support for the continuation of the war.

In the case of the Kosovo conflict in 1999, many of these conditions were also present, but there was more need of active official propaganda efforts by Nato countries because of the moral and legal dubiousness of the air attack on civilian targets in Yugoslavia and divided public opinion (Goff, 1999). Familiar methods were used to demonize the Serb enemy (see p. 381) and media were open to manipulation by pressure groups eager to provoke that attack on Serbia, especially by Croatian and Kosovo activists. Foerstal (2001) describes propaganda efforts in relation to Serbia as similar to those used by Kuwaiti exiles in the lead-up to the first Gulf War. Wolfgram (2008) describes the way in which information was invented or manipulated by the German and American governments about alleged Serbian atrocities in order to legitimate bombing. Two illusions were fostered: that there were multiple sources of evidence and that there was independent confirmation of charges. A blacker side of western mass-mediated propaganda was revealed than had been the case for some time. A somewhat similar scenario has obtained in the Afghanistan and Iraq wars.

Historical and present-day examples of propaganda in action indicate that there is no single formula for success, since all depends on the contingent circumstances. The record also shows that free and independent media can almost as easily become effective vehicles for well-managed propaganda as the media in the hands of propagandists or autocratic states. The one certain thing is that for propaganda to work it has to reach people and be accepted (if not believed). Acceptance mainly depends on the reputation of the media source, the absence of alternative objective information, the inherent plausibility of the content in the light of information available, and the emotional and ideological climate of the time. It is difficult to sustain the blacker and more aggressive type of media coverage over the long term. Despite the special character of propaganda, all the normal rules for ensuring communication effectiveness still apply.

Internet News Effects

Much attention has been given to the arrival of the Internet as a new medium of news, although we are hardly past the point of formulating hypotheses about the possible effects of the innovation. These include the idea that we will have more diverse and personally relevant sources of news; that we will have access to global news; and that we can interrogate the news sources ourselves and learn more through interaction. In short, there is a potential for those who are so motivated to be better and more quickly informed. The evidence so far gathered leads to less optimism, although these and other advantages exist and benefit a minority of Internet devotees. First, use of the Internet for news is still fairly limited, even in circumstances where it might seem to have advantages. For instance, Greenberg's (2002) (small) survey of media use after the 9/11 attack in New York showed little immediate use of the Internet. In the month following, only 22% made any use of the Internet as a source.

It is still very uncertain what information needs are met by the Internet (Tewkesbury, 2003) and it suffers from uncertainty concerning reliability and lack of trust (Schweiger, 2000; Metzger et al., 2003). The presentation of news on the Internet may be less effective in communication terms than the typically ordered presentation in print and television news (Tewkesbury and Althaus, 2000).

Scheufele and Nisbet (2002) concluded that at the present stage of its development 'the role of the Internet in promoting active and informed citizenship is minimal'. Some critics even fear the success of the Internet, since it will fragment the public sphere and the common basis of public knowledge on which democracy depends (Sunstein, 2001). An indication of support for this view was found by Althaus and Tewkesbury (2002). They tested the possibility that newspaper readers and online news users might derive different agendas by comparing readers of *The New York Times* with readers of the online version of the same paper. They found that the former had a broader exposure to public affairs and came away with systematically different perceptions of the problems facing the country, especially in relation to international issues. Nevertheless, it remains the case that the Internet does bring new voices into the public arena (Stromer-Galley, 2002) and the established media have often acted to narrow the range of public debate.

Conclusion

Our discussion of media effects, starting in Chapter 17, has stressed the continuing uncertainty that exists about their nature and degree, especially when it comes to predicting outcomes or establishing causal responsibility for effects with any certainty.

Our exploration of the topic has proceeded mainly by way of dividing it up according to different types and conditions of effect. The reader will have come away with the view that there are rarely, if ever, any simple black and white answers about causality in the matter of media effect. However, it is likely that he or she will also be left in no doubt that it is highly plausible that effects do occur and occur with some regularity in important as well as trivial cases. These are not incompatible conclusions. There are quite a lot of occasions, especially in respect of learning and opinion-forming, when it is hard to see what else other than the mass media could have caused the effects that are at issue. The search for evidence will continue, based on improving theories, concepts and models, and it is hard to envisage a time when interest in the topic will fade.

Further Reading

Capella, J. and Jamieson, K.H. (1997) *The Spiral of Cynicism: the Press and the Public Good*. New York: Oxford University Press.
The title summarizes the central thesis of this study of political campaigning in America, according to which the typical negativity and superficiality of media reporting of politics is responsible for much of the democratic malaise of the times.

Druckman, J.M. (2005) 'Media matter: how newspapers and TV news cover the campaign and influence the voters', *Political Communication*, 22 (4): 463–82.
Emphasizes the qualitative differences between print and TV that matter more than the relative quantity of attention to different media.

Graber, D., McQuail, D. and Norris, P. (2007) *News of Politics: Politics of News*, 2nd edn. Washington, DC: CQ Press.
A set of original chapters on the main aspects of the interactive relationship between politics and news. This has to be understood in order to estimate or understand observed effects.

Iyengar, S. and Reeves, R. (eds) *Do the Media Govern?* Thousand Oaks, CA: Sage.
A compilation of essays on the many issues linked to the title question.

Online Readings

Curran, J., Iyengar, S., Lund, A.B. and Salovaara-Moring, I. (2009) 'Media system, public knowledge and democracy: a comparative study', *European Journal of Communication*, 24 (1): 5–26.
Iyengar, S., Hahn, K.S., Bonfadelli, H. and Marr, M. (2009) 'Dark areas of ignorance revisited: comparing international affairs knowledge in Switzerland and the United States', *Communication Research*, 31 (3): 341–58.

McQuail, D. (2006) 'The mediatization of war', *The International Communication Gazette*, 68 (2): 107–18.

Moy, P., Torres, M., Tanaka, K. and McClusky, R. (2005) 'Knowledge or trust? Investigating linkages between media reliance and participation', *Communication Research*, 32 (1): 59–86.

Pasek, J., Kensler, K., Romer, D. and Jamieson, K.H. (2006) 'America's media use and community engagement', *Communication Research*, 33 (3): 115–35.

Snow, N. and Taylor, P.M. (2006) 'The revival of the propaganda state', *The International Communication Gazette*, 68 (5/6): 389–407.

Van Aelst, P., Maddens, J., Noppe, J. and Fiers, S. (2008) 'Politicians in the news: media logic or party logic?', *European Journal of Communication*, 23 (2): 193–210.

Part 8
Epilogue

20   The future of mass communication

20
The Future of Mass Communication

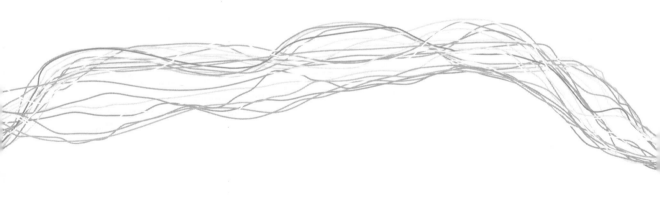

Origins of the Mass Communication Idea

The concept of mass communication was first coined during the 1920s or 1930s to apply to the new possibilities for public communication arising from the mass press, radio and film. These media enlarged the potential audience beyond the literate minority. Essentially new also was the industrial style and scale of the organization of production and dissemination. Large populations of nation states could be reached more or less simultaneously with much the same content, often content that carried the stamp of approval of those with political and social power. The then new mass media of press, film and radio, along with recorded music, also gave rise to a new variant of 'popular culture', in which political and social ideologies were often embedded.

The context for those developments was one of rapid change in the world of newly industrialized and centralized nation states. It was a time of growth and concentration of population in large cities, of the mechanization and bureaucratization of all aspects of life, and imperialist expansion by the great powers of the time, almost exclusively European or American. It was also a period of profound political change, of large social movements, unrest within states, and catastrophic warfare between states. Populations were mobilized towards national achievement or survival and the new mass media played their part in these events as well as providing the masses with the means of relaxation and entertainment. Against this background it is easy to understand why the concept of mass communication was forged and why it rose to a dominant status.

The early meaning of 'mass communication' and one that still lingers, derived much more from the notion of people as a 'mass' and from the perceived characteristics of the mass media than from any idea of communication. As explained in earlier chapters, the 'mass' was perceived primarily in terms of its size, anonymity, general ignorance, lack of stability and rationality, and as a result was vulnerable to persuasion or suggestion. It was seen to be in need of control and guidance by the superior classes and leaders, and the mass media provided the means for achieving this. When power was seized on behalf of the oppressed classes in the 1917 Russian revolution, the mass media were recruited to the task of re-indoctrination on much the same basic assumptions.

As 'communication science' developed, a more formal definition of the concept of mass communication emerged that was not based on untested impressions, the claims of publicists or social philosophy, but on objective characteristics of media that could be specified and put to the test. An abstract model of communication was developed with the following typical features:

- Centralized production of content by a few large channels, with a centre-peripheral network of dissemination – typically hierarchical and one-directional.
- An organization of production and distribution operated according to the logic of the market, or as a state-run institution of public communication.
- Message content in standardized forms open to all but also subjection to normative and political supervision or control.

- A mass public of receivers made up of many dispersed, anonymous and disconnected individuals.
- The attribution of great power to persuade and inform, arising from the prestige or popularity of sources, monopolistic control of channels, the near instantaneity of reception, the skill of practitioners and the supposedly high impact and appeal of the means employed.

The End of Mass Communication?

The mass communication idea was a compelling one that has proved very resilient because it is based on much that seems observable and plausible. It has a broad appeal to those who seek to benefit from it as senders, as well as to audiences. It is a convenient formulation for those who study it and, for those who are highly critical, it provides a useful summary of what is essentially wrong with the phenomenon. It is not easy to redefine or replace, even when many of the conditions of its origin have changed and many of its inbuilt assumptions have been disputed. For much of the twentieth century, the concept in this form has exerted an excessive influence on both popular and expert ideas about the influence of mass media. It has also shaped the direction of media research, despite recurrent evidence that has undermined the foundations on which it was based and cast doubt on the hypothesized effects. Even when it seemed close to rejection, it reappeared in a revised form, especially following Noelle-Neumann's (1973) rallying call under the title 'Return to the concept of powerful mass media'.

From one perspective, the general hypothesis of mass communication has played a fruitful role by the very fact of being comprehensively disputed and disproved. The research it generated led to a much firmer understanding of key principles underlying human communication, as recorded in this book. In this respect, we have been frequently reminded: that the conditions of effect (however defined) depend primarily on social structure and context, and on variable features of reception, rather than on the fact of transmission; that interpersonal communication is often a much more compelling or even competing form and source of influence; that the concept of an audience consisting of isolated individuals is largely an illusion; and that media content typically has no identifiable purpose for its transmitters and no fixed meaning for its receivers, thus largely without predictable effects attached. These and other lessons have been learned well enough, although there are still adherents to variants mass communication theory and there is no doubt that something like the predicted process of effect does occur in some circumstances. This applies especially to 'agenda-setting', news learning, and opinion formation, in crisis situations and at times of collective emotion and celebration. These are not minor exceptions. There is also no doubt that the theory in general outline is still dear to the heart of advertisers and propagandists. As noted earlier, much critical theory directed at mass media still depends on the essential validity of the original mass communication thesis.

Even so, it has by now become commonplace to pronounce the demise of mass communication on objective grounds. The trend in this direction dates back to the late 1960s, when it first became clear that the technological foundations for the concept were changing. A series of innovations, starting with the local cabling of television, the use of satellites for transmission and the wide availability of the means for personally recording and transmitting content began to undermine the massive edifice of highly centralized public transmission. These trends accelerated when the first precursors of the Internet appeared during the 1980s and even more so after the initiation of the Web in the mid-1990s. At the present time, the ever-expanding range and scope of the Internet seems to challenge virtually every element of the mass communication 'ideal type', as summarized above. The Internet allows and encourages communication that is not centre–peripheral in form, but networked; the new forms of communication are two-way and interactive, horizontal as much as vertical, connecting not isolating, no longer monopolized by professionals, highly diverse in content, subject to little social control, under-institutionalized and indeterminate in type and direction.

The many changes, still ongoing, that seem to have led to the implosion of the old paradigm were encapsulated at an early point in Bordewijk and van Kaam's (1986) sketch of the main patterns of information 'traffic', originally referring to telecommunications (see Chapter 6, pp. 147–8). Their version of the original mass communication pattern of direct address from one to many (allocution) was supplemented by three others: one of 'conversation' (the universal connectivity provided by the Internet); one of 'consultation' (the typical use of the Internet search engine and more); and one of 'registration' (the Internet as a central collector of data about uses and users of the system). This map of possible communication patterns is a reminder of the possibly subsidiary status of 'mass communication' functions in the total spectrum of mediated communication. It is also a reminder that patterns of communication do not coincide very closely with particular media or even their dominant forms. Older types of mass media (even television) have developed consultation and conversational possibilities and newer consultative online media are increasingly being used for 'broadcasting'. The telephone, once predominantly a medium of conversation, has joined in this expansion of potential. These processes are part of the larger process of convergence made possible by digitalization. What is not in doubt is that in some respects, the traditional mass media are in decline, even if they are also being transformed and still expanding in some respects.

There is a good deal of agreement that the physical newspaper has passed its high point in terms of circulation in the more economically developed world, as measured by circulation and readership, and probably in terms of share of advertising revenue. But there is still growth in developing countries, there are new forms of newspaper that are not so different and the institutional status of the newspaper ('the press') in relation to politics, economics and international relations does not seem noticeably different from that in the past. Television, most directly affected by an alternative new audiovisual medium (the Internet), has been diminished in some respects, especially in the loss of its very dominant position in audience terms of a small number of national channels. The Internet is gradually becoming a new form of broadcasting on demand and other media have been obliged to adapt to new possibilities of transmission. All the older media are having to adapt to new market conditions and business models.

The Survival of Mass Communication

These and other circumstances reflect not the end of mass media or of mass communication, but rather a significant and ongoing shift in the ways that purposes of public communication can be achieved. The means consisted primarily of reaching an entire national public with a restricted range of content. Transmission would be direct, rapid and very cost-effective. This 'industrial' vision of both ends and means has given way to a new version of mass communication. The overall goal of public communication is still to be able to know and give shape to the mediated experience of a target population, although not by the monopoly imposition of a suitable limited range of ideas, information, motives and stimuli. Now the chosen means is to provide a highly differentiated range of content targeted towards innumerable subgroups and segments in the public, taking account of the interests, tastes and circumstances of the receivers. The purposes are more varied and more opaque than ever in the past. The whole process is held together not by a rigid and uniform structure of provision and a stable pattern of mass reception, but by the voluntary engagement of the public in its own immersion in a rich and varied world of mediated experience. The personal networks and ties that were said to provide a barrier to the influence of older mass media are now playing a positive role in reinforcing demand and consumption on an endlessly changing and kaleidoscopic journey.

A somewhat similar conclusion about the replacement of the former mass communication by a new form has been reached by Castells (2007), to judge from the passage cited in Box 20.1.

Towards a new form of mass communication: Key quote 20.1

The growing interest of corporate media for Internet-based forms of communication is in fact the reflection of *the rise of a new form of socialized communication: mass self-communication*. It is mass communication because it reaches potentially a global audience through the p2p [person to person] networks and Internet connection. It is multimodal, as the digitalization of content and advanced social software, often based on open source that can be downloaded free, allows the reformatting of almost any content in almost any form, increasingly distributed via wireless networks. *And it is self-generated in content, self-directed in emission, and self-selected in reception by many that communicate with many.* We are indeed in a new communication realm, and ultimately in a new medium, whose backbone is made of computer networks, whose language is digital, and whose senders are globally distributed and globally interactive. (Castells, 2007: 248, original italics)

The survival of a condition or state of mass communication (as redefined), that can now scarcely be distinguished from other social processes, is primarily due to its high degree of functionality for key driving forces in society and its intimate connection with human aspirations. Many of the actors who benefit from the capacity to communicate to all in a measured and calculated way are visible and their motivations are transparent. They include big advertisers and global media firms (both bigger and more concentrated than ever before), the world financial system, rulers and national governments, states with imperial ambitions and concern or their image and the list goes on. It is inconceivable that these and others could dispense with the results of even 'smarter' and more effective communication to any chosen public constituency. The emerging, revived and reinforced form of mass communication is highly consistent with underlying trends towards convergence and the globalization and mediatization of everything.

Alongside the forces and trends mentioned there are other dynamics at work in changing the nature of mass communication. These stem from the potential of new media for open access and connectivity that is now widely becoming a reality. There are very many new voices making use of possibilities for open, interactive 'horizontal' communication. These individuals, movements and groups, with many different purposes, now have much more chance of being served by the means of communicating in and to the public, even if with no guarantee of being heard as intended. The wish to communicate does not stem only from political or economic necessity. People have always displayed an urge to combine, share and co-operate for personal and social ends that cannot be explained in material terms. This urge finds expression in the wish to share the pleasures and sorrows of life, to embody them in rituals and narratives of family, community, tribe or nation. In other words, there are strong, spontaneous tendencies that underlie the emergence of shared public culture and this applies no less to the apparently 'machine-made' culture delivered by the newly invented mass media of the twentieth century. The mass media of old could never have become mass media in the first place without a basis of this kind. The 'new media' are also tapping into the same fundamental human tendencies. The success of the new 'social media', like the success of many forms of 'reality television' as well as the apparent drawing power of 'media events', are evidence enough of a deep attraction towards the wider sharing of interests, emotions and experiences.

The Consequences of New Media for Mass Communication

The 'new media' that have arrived as a result of technological innovation have frequently been characterized in ways that set them apart from the 'old' mass media, but the 'medium theory' that has emerged is not yet a very good guide to media reality. It is still not clear how existing media will adapt to, or incorporate, the very diverse set of communication possibilities that continue to be developed on a trial-and-error basis in the media market. There may be no great logic in the outcome. However, there is a certain logic in the points of contrast they offer to the 'ideal type' summarized at the beginning of this chapter. They are multidirectional, not one-directional. They encourage, even require response. They have no 'audience', therefore no mass public. They are highly diverse in form and content, and of their essence multimedial and multimodal. They observe no clear line between private and public. They allow access to all and they seem to evade structures of control. They evade institutionalization but, as this implies, they offer no coherent model of a system of public communication, only endless possibilities.

These observations, all in varying degrees valid, have given rise to a rhetoric that is both optimistic and also oppositional. In the circumstances of under-determination, it turns out that the central propositions of mass theory can be applied or reversed for the new media conditions, without inventing any new theory. The potential consequences of digital media can also be expressed in terms that undermine central elements of mass communication theory:

- The power of the communicator to persuade or inform selectively is much reduced by the inability to reach large, captive audiences and by the ready availability of alternative sources of ideas and knowledge.
- Individuals are no longer restricted by their immediate social group and environment and by the physical availability of a few media channels, controlled by authorities and other agencies. They can enter and belong to new groups and communities across space.
- There is no longer any unitary 'message system' to which people are routinely and consistently exposed, leading to stereotypes and the adoption of consensual values.
- Individuals can 'answer back' to figures of authority or remove themselves from contact. They can also participate actively in informational and opinion exchanges in the context of important social and political issues.

These and similar propositions have become the basis for an increasing amount of research and new theory. They are more likely to refer to the potential benefits of escaping the constraints of mass media, thus, on balance, the outlook is optimistic. However, it is equally plausible to propose that much the same new features of media can be and are being used to modify and strengthen the process of mass communication as we have known it in the past. This happens when they are colonized by mass media and regarded simply as a new and more effective means of transmission. It happens when the interactive, participative and networking features of new media are incorporated in large projects of publicity and delivery of old-style media products under oligopolistic ownership. The 'new media' are particular effective in binding fans and followers to media sources and in feeding back information that can be applied to much more effective targeting of finely segmented subgroups in the relevant public Crogan (2008). They are reminiscent of the difference between the 'smart' bombs that supposedly hit single buildings and the randomly unloaded bombs of a century ago. It is still better not to be bombed at all. In practice, there are a number of different ways in which a process much the same as represented by the old 'industrial model', only much more effective, can be replicated by a combination of old and new media, bearing in mind the possibility of harnessing widely distributed human needs and the urge towards collective experience and enjoyment noted above.

The choice between these two rhetorics (leaving reality aside for the moment) is complicated by the fact that virtue is not all on the side of the new. There are quite a few discontents associated with new, as with old media, especially as represented by the Internet. The fact of lack of regulation and even of self-regulation is at the root of some fears, which seems to expose vulnerable groups and individuals to risks and exploitation. Even when used benignly, the Internet seems essentially individuating rather than participative, despite the promise of connectivity. The new media tend towards a reversal of the relatively equalizing trends of traditional media, especially television. They are not readily available for collective public or social purposes, where this might be wanted, and not accountable to society. The lack of professionalization may open access, but it also often means lower standards in information and culture. There is a persistent and insoluble problem of trust and reliability. The power of surveillance and registration of all communication uses and users greatly extends the central powers of the state and its agencies, without much chance of redress or possibility of complaint. As more and more everyday and necessary communication transactions are transferred to the Internet, whether wanted or not by the public, we are becoming increasingly in a very literal way dependent on access and appropriate skills. As a result, we are liable to new and serious forms of social exclusion, if we cannot or will not conform. If we do conform, as most will, we become more vulnerable to unwanted persuasion and manipulation.

As with mass communication in the past, we can choose a more optimistic or more pessimistic view of the consequences of 'new media'. We still lack clear support in evidence for either the benefits or harm from new communication and it is unlikely that any such general balance can be struck, much as with our experience of the true mass media of the twentieth century. A framework of analysis that depends on simplified beliefs about society and speculation about the potential consequences of technology will not take us very far.

Conclusion

We can now see more clearly that the era of mass communication, as the concept is featured in this book, is best viewed as a transitional phase of industrial mass public communication. It followed an early stage of development in which public communication and society-wide communication depended largely on the medium of the channels of social organization and the medium of print. The main content of public communication then originated in governmental and ecclesiastical authorities or in professional and cultural elites and was directed primarily towards an urban and literate minority of subjects/ citizens. The industrial model of mass communication that made its appearance early in the twentieth century represented a greatly expanded capacity for public communication, opening it also to a wider range of senders and varied new sources, and to new types of content. Its public was expanded to cover an entire population, reflecting more fundamental political and social changes rather than the capacity of the emerging media. By the end of the century this model had matured and was diffused globally. It has also gradually been changing, by way of supplementation and adaptation, into a new type whose form or forms cannot yet be determined, nor have we a name for it. We know only that it is multimedia and multimodal, highly flexible and even more effective for established purposes than its predecessor, and with new potentials that are still undeveloped.

But we can already recognize the continuity of mass communication as a society-wide process in new forms that is made up of a much finer and tightly woven network of lines and connections that has an organic character rather than being constructed and controlled by a few for their own ends. Mass communication in the original sense is still with us if we think of it in terms of single, central sources being received by large audiences and dedicated to maximum amplification and diffusion. It persists primarily because the organization of social life cannot dispense with roles, persons, institutions that are singled out as a focus of attention by a dispersed public, with an attribution of status, power, skill or other qualities. Similarly, key events, places, cultural works, and a variety of objects of attention come inevitably to be ranked according to interest and significance and sought in varying degrees by, or brought to the attention of, a wider public.

These features of social life were not created by mass media and will not go away even if mass media are replaced by less massive and centralized communication networks. There are some public functions that can only be served by dedicated professional and well-financed systems of communication. Apart from the needs of society for all things public – publication, public opinion, public order, shared norms and beliefs, political organization and so on – there are powerful economic and political forces that favour concentrations of media and 'Weapons of Mass Dissemination' for their own ends. In other words, institutionalization is inevitable and cannot be undone or escaped from. Digitalization in many respects has increased the effective deployment of mass communication, by refining reach, adding feedback and flexibility and multiplying channels for transmission of the same messages. It has also provided alternative channels that operate in a parallel fashion. This does not change or replace all that goes before.

It is clear that we need a much richer vocabulary to talk about the implications of the developments of communication that are taking place than is provided by a few terms such as 'mass communication', 'convergence', 'networks', 'connectivity' or 'interactivity'. It is also not helpful to think in dichotomies of mass versus non-mass or even in terms of degrees of 'massification'. There are many new communication situations that are emerging, based on network connections between participants that cannot be analysed in terms of apparent 'needs' of large-scale organized society or of characteristics of particular communications technologies. The literature of communication research is in fact full of examples of varied social bases for communication, supporting a great variety of relationships and purposes.

Digitalization has provided the impulse and possibility for many new initiatives to send, exchange, seek and express across the previously restricting social and physical boundaries. The key feature is a diversification of communication activity. One of the tasks of future theorizing will be to adequately map this enlarging field and to develop appropriate typologies that will allow us to escape from the limitations of a rather worn-out conceptual apparatus. At the least, we should realize that the range of communication technologies and their uses is now so large and variable that there is no longer any dominant technology or dominant model.

Glossary

Cross references to other glossary entries are in italics

Access. In a communication process or system, it can refer to the possibility either for a sender to reach a chosen audience or for an audience to receive certain messages or channels. In practice it mainly relates to the degree of openness of media channels to a wide range of voices, especially those with little power or limited resources. An example is a 'public access' channel provided in a cable system for community or non-profit purposes. As a general principle it is related to media *diversity*.

Active audience. The term arose in the context of revised ideas about the mass audience. Research established early on that media audiences are in varying degrees selective, motivated and resistant to influence. The kind and degree of audience activity is very relevant to the possibility of any effect from media. Audience activity has been studied in more detail within the tradition of *uses and gratifications* research as well as *reception analysis*. In the latter case, activity is mainly found to reside in differential interpretation.

Advertising. Paid publicity in media for goods or services directed at consumers. It has various aims including the creation of awareness, making brand images, forming positive associations and encouraging consumer behaviour. There are many different categories of advertising, which are linked to different media forms (classified, display, personal, etc.). For some major media, advertising provides the greater part of income. All advertising content shares the fact of being paid for by its source. Advertising has been controversial for several reasons, especially the following. It is not generally wanted by its receivers; it has a *propagandist* character and is suspected of deception and manipulation; it has a distorting effect on the relation between media and audience; its content is stereotyped and misleading; the presence of advertising influences other non-advertising content. The general effectiveness of advertising for its purposes is more or less accepted, but certain evidence of success or of reasons for success is hard to come by. Advertising is integrated into a very large industry of market research, *public relations, viral advertising* and *marketing*.

Agenda-setting. A process of media influence (intended or unintended) by which the relative importance of news events, issues or personages in the public mind are affected by the order of presentation (or relative salience) in news reports. It is assumed that the more the media attention given to a topic, the greater is the importance attributed to it by the news audience. The media influence is not on the direction of opinion but only on what people think about. The concept has been mainly applied to political communication and election campaigns especially. Despite the near certainty that the process does occur as hypothesized, it is not easy to prove, because media take their priorities from public opinion as well as from politicians. See also *framing*.

Attitude. An evaluative disposition of an individual towards an 'object' of whatever kind (person, idea, group, country, policy, etc.). For measurement purposes it is conceived as a mental set that can be elicited by verbal questioning about concepts related to the object of inquiry. Attitudes vary in direction (positive or negative) and in strength, and attitude scales have been developed to record these variations. In general an attitude is considered as a relatively deep and underlying tendency, linked to personality and resistant to change by mass media. A single attitude is generally connected with other related attitudes in a consistent way.

Audience. All those who are actually reached by particular media content or media 'channels'. The audience can also exist as an imagined 'target' or intended group of receivers. It may coincide with a real social group or *public*. Audiences can be defined according to the relevant media and content or in terms of their social composition, location or time of day. Media audiences are not fixed entities and may only be known after the event as statistical abstractions (e.g. 'the ratings'), with a known probability of recurrence. This is typically the view 'from the media', but there is an equally valid alternative perspective of the audience as a collective social-cultural entity.

Bias. Any tendency in a news report to deviate from an accurate, neutral, balanced and impartial representation of the 'reality' of events and social world according to stated criteria. A distinction is usually made between intended and unintended bias. The former stems mainly from partisanship, advocacy and the ideological standpoint of the medium or source. The latter is generally attributed to organizational and routine factors in selection and processing of news. See also *objectivity*.

Birmingham School. Name used to denote a number of authors associated with the Centre for Contemporary Cultural Studies (CCCS) at the University of Birmingham, England, established in the mid-1960s. Original founder was Richard Hoggart, in association with Stuart Hall. The work of the school was a major influence firstly in the study of popular culture and secondly in the development of critical cultural studies, including *reception analysis* and feminist media studies.

Blog. The word is a shortened version of weblog, which indicates its origin as a set of diary entries or related content posted on the Internet for a variety of reasons, mostly of a personal nature. Most interest centres on those blogs which are intended to play a public role of one kind of another, often a commentary on the news. Their relationship with *journalism* is ambiguous, especially as many journalists publish their own blogs, either on their own account or on behalf of the news organizaton. The chance for readers to leave comments in an interactive format is a novel feature of the blog compared to normal journalism. The influence of blogs is much disputed, since few have any large *audience* of their own, but they represent a significant opening of public access and a challenge to institutional control of public information. The word 'blogosphere' has been coined to refer to the whole alternative public communication space occupied by non-institutionalized voices.

Broadcasting. The transmission of radio and television signals over air from fixed terrestrial transmitters and with limited range, before the advent of cable and satellite systems from the 1970s onwards. Broadcasting was intended for open reception by all within the transmission range and was mainly financed either by advertising or by receiver sets or household licences. It was and remains governed by legal and regulatory regimes designed to allocate licences and supervise performance. It is virtually the only major medium in public or government ownership in non-socialist societies. See *public service broadcasting*.

Campaign. The planned attempt to influence public opinion, behaviour, attitudes and knowledge on behalf of some cause, person, institution or topic, using different media over a specific period of time. The main types of campaign are: advertising; political; public informational; fund-raising. Public campaigns are usually directed towards socially approved goals. They are often based on research and subject to evaluation of success.

Catharsis. A type of effect of tragic or violent fiction and drama that leaves the audience purged of emotion and released of any urge to be affected by the actions portrayed. Originally suggested by Aristotle and taken up by researchers into media violence to account for seeming lack of harmful behavioural effects. Although theoretically plausible, it does not seem to have been specifically demonstrated or measured.

Celebrity. A quality of being extremely well known by the majority, often an object of adulation and *fandom*. In normal circumstances, high, continuing and positive media attention is a necessary condition of celebrity. Celebrity status can be based on recognition of distinction in different spheres including sport, entertainment, the arts, science, politics and 'society'. Sometimes media prominence is a sufficient condition, as in the concept of 'being famous for being famous'. Persons who are celebrities are an object of *gossip* and their celebrity can be taken away as well as given by the media.

Censorship. Refers to the control by public authorities (usually church or state) of any form of publication or transmission, usually by some mechanism of examining all material before publication. Constitutional guarantees of press freedom typically outlaw advance or preventive censorship, although there may be legitimate grounds for suppression or even punishment of a publication after the event. The term is loosely applied to actions which impede expression, as in references to 'private censorship' by media editors or owners.

Civil society. The term has been widely used in recent social theory to refer to forms of social organization that offer alternatives to totalitarianism or excessive government control. The key aspect is the existence of an intermediate 'zone' between private life and the state, where independent voluntary collective associations and organizations can operate freely. A precondition for this is freedom of association and expression, including the necessary means, amongst which the media are very important. Free media can thus be regarded as an institution of civil society. See also *public sphere*.

Code. The most common meaning is of a set of laws, regulations or guidelines. When applied to mass media, it mainly refers to a set of standards applied in self-regulation of content and conduct, for instance in relation to *journalism*. Professional codes have been adopted by national and international associations of journalists. Codes have also been produced and applied in broadcasting and film exhibition, covering such matters as the display of violence, advertising, sexual matters, portrayal of crime, racism, blasphemy, etc. A new (but related) meaning of code has been introduced to describe the precise instructions written into computer programs that can be used to limit freedom of use and open up content to surveillance (Lessig, 1999).

Coding (or encoding) and decoding. Broad terms for the production and 'reading' of texts of all kinds. The reference is less to the use of specific language (verbal or visual) than to structures of meaning embedded in or extracted from texts. The terms were popularized by Stuart Hall and incorporated in a much cited model of the relationship between media and audience. An important feature of the associated theory is that meaning is 'decoded' according to the social and cultural position of the receiver. Most texts 'as sent' are also held to carry some 'preferred reading', that is essentially ideological, but we can usually expect alternative readings. In the case of news, Stuart Hall suggested that interpretations could either take up the preferred 'hegemonic' meanings, follow some more distanced 'negotiated' variant, or reverse the intended meaning in an 'oppositional' reading. See also *ideology*.

Cognitive dissonance. The term was coined by Leon Festinger to describe the situation of an individual faced with new *information* on a given topic that is inconsistent with existing information, attitudes and values. The underlying theory holds that an individual seeks balance and consistency of attitudes and values, and consequently avoids or misperceives incoming messages (e.g. from mass media) that challenge settled opinions and beliefs. In so far as cognitive consistency dominates, it will limit change effects from communication and encourage reinforcement of existing views. However, compelling new information from trustworthy sources may overcome the barriers indicated and lead to change, but this will require a reassessment of outlook over a wide range. Although the theory is sound enough, there is quite a lot of evidence that in matters of *public opinion* that are not deeply held, people can tolerate quite high levels of apparent discrepancy.

Commercialization. A process by which media structures and contents come to reflect the profit-seeking goals of media industries and are too much governed by market considerations. The main reference is usually to cultural consequences, and these always have a negative connotation. Commercialized media content is believed to be in varying degrees lacking in independence, 'inauthentic', standardized and stereotypical, given to *sensationalism* and personalization. It promotes materialism and consumerism. It is also thought to be less creative and trustworthy. Commercial media are suspected of lacking full independence from their owners and advertisers. In some contexts the process is also referred to as 'Americanization', on the grounds that imports of American content are involved, usually coupled with American production standards and values. See *advertising*, *tabloidization* and *commodification*.

Commodification. The word originates in Marxist theory, according to which all entities have a material cash value. In relation to media, two aspects stand out. One is the treatment of all media messages as 'product' to be bought or sold in the media market, without reference to other criteria of value. The other is that the audience can be treated as a commodity to be sold by media to advertisers at so much per head, according to ratings and other market criteria. See *Marxism*.

Communication. The term has many different meanings and definitions, but the central idea is of a process of increased commonality or sharing between participants, on the basis of sending and receiving 'messages'. Theoretical disagreement exists about whether we should count as communication the transmission or expression of some message, on its own, without evidence of reception or effect or completion of a sequence. The most important dimensions of communication concern two points: the degree of response or feedback (one-way versus interactive process); and the degree to which a communication relationship is also a social relationship. In general, modern technologies increase the possibility and likelihood of detaching communication (message transmission or exchange) from any social basis.

Community. An idealized form of human association in which the members share boundaries of space, identity and interaction. A community is typically a largish and enduring social group based on residence, but it can also be formed on the basis of some other significant identity. In its ideal form, community is characterized by a mutual liking and assistance and relative equality between members who put the common welfare ahead of individual wants.

Computer-mediated communication (CMC). Any communicative transaction that takes place by way of a computer, whether online or offline, but especially the former. Characteristics include: interactivity in situations where the participants are not physically together; and possibility for anonymity and concealment while communicating. CMC can transgress the social and physical boundaries that normally limit our potential for communicating with others. Not all CMC features are beneficial. We are more exposed to unwanted communication from others. Computer mediation reduces the personal character of the experience, and the commonality or community achieved in *cyberspace* may be illusory. Communication mediated by computers connected to networks is also more open to various forms of surveillance.

Connectivity. Essentially, the capacity of a network to link participants together in a common space of communication. As such, it is also an attribute of groups and communities that can vary according to the density of network links, the frequency of use and thus the strength and surability of ties. The Internet and other personal communication media can achieve much higher degrees of connectivity than traditional mass media.

Content analysis. A technique for the systematic, quantitative and objective description of media texts, that is useful for certain purposes of classifying output, looking for effects and making comparisons between media and over time or between content and 'reality'. Content analysis is not well suited to uncovering the underlying meaning of content, although it can provide certain indicators of 'quality' of media.

Constructionism. An approach to the study of meaning and media effect that rests on the assumption that there is no uniquely correct and fixed version of the 'real world'. Reality can only be apprehended and communicated about by way of selectively perceived versions that are dependent on the attitudes, interests, knowledge and experience of the perceiver. The effects of communication about some aspect of 'reality' will depend on a negotiation of meaning between the participants in the circumstances of the moment. It makes no sense to search for direct effects in the sense of transfer of meaning from a source to a receiver.

Convergence. The process of coming together or becoming more alike. It is usually applied to the convergence of media technologies as a result of *digitalization* (computerization). The distinctive physical characteristics of media cease to matter, at least for purposes of production, processing and transmission. The contemporary trend of convergence has been used as an argument for media deregulation, since most regulatory regimes are linked to specific technologies (e.g. printing, broadcasting, cable, projection, etc). Despite the potential at the reception 'end' for convergence on a single apparatus, diversification seems to increase.

Convergence culture. A new concept introduced to describe the cultural consequences of technological convergence. In its broadest terms, it refers to the new situation in which work, life and play are increasingly intermingled and overlapping, without separate compartments of time and space. Its most specific manifestation in relation to the mass media is the coming together of two trends: one from the media to encourage engagement and participation of audiences and users in new interactive forms of communication; the other is the trend on the part of the public to become media producers and communicators, as enabled by the new technology. The most striking result is the appearance of new forms of media in which production and consumption are blurred and the line between amateur and professional fades. The terms 'prosumer' and 'produser' have appeared to reflect a new role in the spectrum of media life. Wikipedia, the 'blogosphere', *Myspace* and *YouTube* are primary sites where the new trends can be observed, but there are many others.

Copyright. Means essentially the recognition of the ownership rights of authors in their own published works. This was achieved long after the invention of printing. The issue of copyright (more broadly, intellectual property rights) has been much complicated by the extension of copyright claims to new categories of 'author' and new forms of media and publication and republication, especially in electronic form. The *Internet* changes the nature of publishing and has opened up an extensive and disputed territory.

Critical theory. A general term for late Marxist versions of the part played by the mass media in maintaining a dominant *ideology* or *hegemony*. The origins are usually found in the work of the *Frankfurt School*, but there are several variants, especially the cultural and the political economy forms. The first of these has been associated with structuralist and semiological interpretations of texts (hermeneutics generally) and also with audience *reception analysis* and ethnography. The second has generally engaged with issues of structure and ownership and control of the media. Critical theory is often regarded as an alternative to empirical, behaviourist or 'scientific' approaches to the study of mass media. It is by definition normative, involving notions of an alternative and better form of society and media system.

Cultivation analysis. Term given to a particular type of media effect research, developed by George Gerbner. The underlying process is one of 'acculturation', meaning that people gradually come to accept the view of the world as portrayed on television (in particular) as a true representation of reality and adapt their hopes, fears and understandings accordingly. The main method of cultivation analysis is to chart the dominant 'television view of reality' in fiction and news and compare this with the views expressed by audience members, according to their degree of habitual exposure. The hypothesis is that the more people view television, the more their ideas correspond with the 'television view'.

Cultural imperialism. A general expression for the tendency of global media industry exporters (especially from the USA) to dominate the media consumption in other smaller and poorer countries and in so doing impose their own cultural and other values on audiences elsewhere. Not only content is exported, but also technology, production values, professional ideologies and ownership. The analogy is with historical imperialism where the means were military and economic power. Explicitly or implicitly, it is assumed that cultural imperialism leads to dependence, loss of autonomy and a decline in national or local cultures. Some latitude exists as to whether the process is deliberate and about the degree to which it is involuntary at the receiving end. The concept is a fairly crude one, but it has a strong resonance.

Cultural studies. A branch of theory and research that overlaps with the media and communication field but has a much wider reference to all forms of cultural experience and symbolic expression. It has been distinguished by a *critical* and humanistic orientation and also a strong focus on 'popular culture', especially of youth. It originated in Britain, but is now international in scope, very diverse and largely independent of media and communication studies. See *Birmingham School*.

Culture. In the present context it has a primary reference to the symbolic artefacts produced by media industries, but it also has a wider reference to customs, practices and meanings associated with the mass communication process (production and reception). It is sometimes used to refer to the wider framework of beliefs, ideology, and so on, of society (the 'superstructure') that provides the context of media operation.

Cyberspace. This term is now very widely used to refer to the metaphorical space occupied by the World Wide Web and the Internet. It was first coined by William Gibson in 1984 to describe the world of cybernetics. It has no very precise meaning but, in contemporary usage, cyberspace is imagined by its inhabitants to be free from many of the constraints of real space, besides laws and regulations. The reality of cyberspace is turning out to be somewhat different than dreamt of by its creators and is certainly not technically beyond the reach of regulation as was once assumed.

Denotation. A term from *semiology*, referring to the direct literal signification of the meaning of some referent by linguistic or visual symbols. It is contrasted with connotation.

Diffusion of innovations. The process of spreading any kind of new technical device, idea or useful information. It generally follows an S-shaped pattern, with a slow start, an acceleration of adoption and a long tail. The 'early adopters' tend to be untypical in terms of social composition and communication behaviour. The mass media have been found to play a secondary role in influencing diffusion, with personal communication, example and known authority sources being primary. The media themselves provide typical examples of innovations that fit the S-curve pattern of diffusion.

Diffusion of news. Process whereby awareness of 'events' is spread through a population either by mass media or via personal, word of mouth contact with or without media involvement. Key questions concern the degree and speed of public diffusion in relation to actual or types of events and also the relative weight of media and personal sources in achieving the outcome.

Digital divide. A term now widely used to apply to the various inequalities opened up by the development of computer-based digital means of communication. The new inequalities derive from the relatively large cost of equipment, dependence on advanced infrastructure and the higher skills needed to communicate. These inequalities arise between persons, social groups and national societies, for the most part following familiar fault lines. See also *knowledge gap.*

Digitalization. General word for the computerization of all data transmission, storage and processing employing the binary code, and as such the basis for *convergence* of media. It is currently best known in reference to the replacement of analogue by digital transmission of television signals, leading to a large increase in potential channel capacity and scope for interactivity.

Discourse analysis. Applies to all forms of language use and textual forms, but the essential idea is that communication occurs by way of forms of 'text and talk', adapted to particular social locations, topics and kinds of participant. These are sometimes known as 'interpretative communities'. 'Critical discourse analysis' investigates the dominance exerted and expressed through linguistic forms that are vehicles for carrying socially prevailing sentiments and ideologies.

Diversity. In simple terms, it is no more than the degree or range of difference on any chosen dimension: the more difference, the more diversity. When applied to mass media it can relate to structures of ownership and control, to content as produced and transmitted and to audience composition and content choices. Each of these can be empirically assessed in terms of diversity. Diversity is associated with access, freedom, choice, change and equality. It stands as a positive value in opposition to monopoly, uniformity, conformity and consensus.

Effects of media. The consequences or outcomes of the working of, or exposure to, mass media, whether or not intended. They can be sought at different levels of social analysis. There are many types of effect, but it is usual to distinguish at least between effects that are behavioural, attitudinal (or affective) and cognitive. Effects are distinct from 'effectiveness', which relates to the efficiency of achieving a given communicative objective.

Empathy. An attitude or orientation of sympathy and understanding towards others, especially with reference to casualties and victims of society and those who are stigmatized, marginalized and excluded. It is one of the informal roles adopted by the media, especially in *journalism*, documentary and realistic drama, to encourage public empathy. It can be achieved by reporting on its own, without conscious advocacy.

Entertainment. Describes a main branch of media production and consumption, covering a range of formats that generally share the qualities of attracting, amusing, diverting and 'taking people out of themselves'. It also refers to the process of diversion itself, and in this sense it can also relate to the genres that are not usually regarded as entertaining, such as news, advertising or education. It is often perceived as problematic when addiction to entertainment excludes informational uses of media or when the 'entertainment' mode invades the sphere of reality content – especially news, information and politics, as it seems increasingly to do. The term 'infotainment' has been coined to describe the result.

Fandom. The phenomenon stimulated in response to media *celebrities*, implying intense attachment to and involvement in the achievements and personal lives of star performers, especially in music and popular entertainment. It is often perceived as associated with irrationality and loss of touch with reality.

First Amendment. The First Amendment to the Constitution of the United States was enacted in 1791 and it outlawed Congressional (i.e. federal government) interference in or regulation of freedom of speech, religion and the press, etc. It has become a shorthand term to cover all matters of freedom of expression and opinion in the United States, often involving the mass media. Many other countries have equivalent constitutional provisions, although they are usually expressed in terms of the rights of citizens. The way the First Amendment is formulated has tended to identify government as the arch-enemy of freedom, strongly associating free media with the free market. See *freedom of the press*.

Fourth Estate. A term attributed by the historian Thomas Carlyle to the eighteenth-century polemicist Edmund Burke and applicable to the press gallery of the English House of Commons. Burke asserted that the power of the press was at least equal to that of the other three 'estates of the realm' – lords, commons and clergy. It became a conventional term for journalists in their role as reporters of and watchdogs on government.

Fragmentation. In respect of the media audience, refers to the general decline of the mass audience for newspapers and dominant television channels, brought about by multiplication of new media forms and television channels. There are many smaller and more temporary audiences. Fragmentation has been thought to reduce the power of mass media generally, although many smaller audiences does not necessarily mean greater true diversity.

Framing. A term with two main meanings. One refers to the way in which news content is typically shaped and contextualized by journalists within some familiar frame of reference and according to some latent structure of meaning. A second, related meaning concerns the effect of framing on the public. The audience is thought to adopt the frames of reference offered by journalists and to see the world in a similar way. This process is related to *priming* and *agenda-setting*.

Frankfurt School. The name applied to the group of scholars who originally worked in the Frankfurt Institute of Social Research and emigrated to the USA after the Nazis came to power. The central project of the group was the critical analysis of modern culture and society in the Marxist tradition. The main figures included Theodor Adorno, Max Horkheimer, Herbert Marcuse and Leo Lowenthal. They were all very influential in the development of critical theory in North America and Europe after the Second World War and especially in media and cultural studies. Their pessimistic view of 'mass culture' was, paradoxically, one stimulus to a later revalidation of popular cultural forms.

Freedom of information (or communication). Freedom of information has a broad meaning that covers all aspects of public expression and transmission of, and access to, all manner of content. It has been advanced as a human right that should be guaranteed internationally and not just within a society. In a narrow sense it usually refers to public rights of access to information of public interest or relevance held by various kinds of authority or official agency.

Freedom of the press. A fundamental principle of individual, political and human rights that guarantees in law the right of all citizens to publish without advance censorship or permission by authority, or fear of reprisal. It has to be exercised within the limits of law and to respect the rights of others. In practice, freedom of the press is often limited by (economic) barriers of access to the means of publication. The right is usually regarded as fundamental to political democracy. It is related to, but distinct from, freedom of expression, opinion or belief and also *freedom of information* and the *First Amendment*.

Functional analysis. In relation to mass communication, this mode of early-twentieth-century sociological theory treats the working of mass media as in some sense necessary to the 'normal' operation of any social system (society). The main 'function' attributed to the media is to contribute to social cohesion and integration. In this light, the effects of media can be treated as either functional (positive) or dysfunctional (negative) for individuals, groups or society. The theory has largely been discarded as offering no analytic purchase and being unable to deal adequately with social conflict and change, when 'normality' is itself problematic. Even so, it still provides a general orientation to some larger questions of social process, such as integration and interdependence.

Gatekeeping. General term for the role of initial selection and later editorial process-ing of event reports in news organizations. News media have to decide what 'events' to admit through the 'gates' of the media on grounds of their 'newsworthiness' and other criteria. Key questions concern the criteria applied and the systematic *bias* that has been discerned in the exercise of the role. See also *portal.*

Genre. Essentially just a word for any main type or category of media content. It can also apply to certain subcategories of theme or plot in fiction, film, drama, etc. It is useful for analysis because many genres embody certain 'rules of encoding' that can be manipulated by their producers and also certain 'rules for decoding' that allow audiences to develop appropriate expectations and 'read' texts as intended.

Globalization. The overall process whereby the location of production, transmission and reception of media content ceases to be geographically fixed, partly as a result of technology, but also through international media structure and organization. Many cul-tural consequences are predicted to follow, especially the delocalizing of content and undermining of local cultures. These may be regarded as positive when local cultures are enriched by new impulses and creative *hybridization* occurs. More often they are viewed as negative because of threats to cultural *identity*, autonomy and integrity. The new media are widely thought to be accelerating the process of globalization.

Gossip. A form of news characterized by its reference to personalities and its uncer-tain origin and reliability. Its main habitat is in personal conversation, but it provides the basis for a media genre found mainly in newspapers and magazines. Here the con-tent focuses on *celebrities* (mainly the rich and famous). Differs from *rumour,* which often deals with highly significant news and travels faster and more completely in the relevant population. See also *human interest.*

Governance. A general term to cover all forms of control, regulation and guidance applied to some institutional process, involving multiple agencies, formal and infor-mal, public and private. It has become common to use the term in relation to media structures that are typically organized in the form of networks open to many inputs and not fully hierarchical or autocratic, in keeping with the cultural and social roles fulfilled.

Hegemony. A term introduced by the early-twentieth-century Italian Marxist the-orist Antonio Gramsci to describe a certain kind of power that arises from the all-embracing ideological tendencies of mass media to support the established power system and exclude opposition and competing values. In brief it is a kind of dominant consensus that works in a concealed way without direct coercion.

Human interest. A type of news story or format that focuses on personal actions and consequences, employs dramatic, humorous or narrative styles, and usually deals with matters close to everyday emotions and experience. It is associated with *commercialization* and also with *tabloidization*.

Hybridization. The process whereby new cultural forms are forged out of disparate elements, especially a combination of alien or imported forms and local or traditional cultures. Associated with *globalization*.

Hype. A new term for an old news phenomenon. It describes a 'news wave' that occurs where a certain topic of the moment receives overwhelming and continuing news coverage from all media at the same time. It starts with a single news event of unusual clarity and audience appeal and is pursued beyond its objective significance or information value and beyond the normal life of such an event, with journalists seeking more and more marginal new information to keep it alive. The conditions of a hype to occur can include a relative shortage of other newsworthy items. A related phenomenon is that of 'pack journalism', where all media relentlessly pursue the same story in much the same way.

Icon. A type of sign that has a clear physical likeness to what it stands for. Different media can employ iconic signs, but usually they are depicted, reproduced or sculpted images of people, things or scenes. Early letter systems (hieroglyphs) made much use of icons. Photography has to rely almost entirely on icons to communicate meaning, since the first meaning of a photograph is the object photographed. More loosely, icon is sometimes used to refer to a person or piece of work so distinguished that it becomes the standard image.

Identity. Specific characterization of person, place, and so on by self or others, according to biographical, social, cultural or other features. Communication is a necessary condition for forming and maintaining identity. By the same token, it can weaken or undermine it. Mass communication is only one amongst several contributory factors.

Ideology. Generally refers to some organized belief system or set of values that is disseminated or reinforced by communication. While mass media do not typically set out deliberately to propagate ideology, in practice most media content (of all kinds) does so implicitly by selectively emphasizing certain values and norms. This is referred to as a 'preferred reading' in the theory of *coding and decoding*. Often these reflect the national culture that provides the context of the media system, but also the class position and the outlook of those who own, control and make media.

Information. In a broad sense, the content (messages) of all meaningful communication is information. More narrowly (but still loosely), information usually refers to verifiable and thus reliable factual data about the 'real world'. This includes opinions as well as reports about the facts of the world. Even more narrowly and precisely, information may be equated with communicated 'data' that do (or can) enable discriminations to be made in some domain of reality and thus 'reduce uncertainty' for the receiver.

Information society. A term widely used to describe contemporary society in terms of what is thought to be its most central driving force or source of productive power, namely information of all kinds. The justification for this assumption derives from the seeming dependence of much of modern life, materially as well as culturally, on the production, handling and application of information and on the operation of complex networks of communication. The information and communication technology sector appears to have become the chief source of wealth in more economically advanced societies.

Infotainment. A term coined to capture the intermingling of information and entertainment that characterized mass television in the later twentieth century. It seemed particularly applicable to the forms of news that were feared would result from the extensive privatization of broadcasting in Europe and increased competition for mass audiences. The term is generally used pejoratively, with the implication of 'dumbing-down' and the inevitable dilution and greater superficiality of news and information. It has analogies with the idea of *tabloidization* affecting newspapers. With reference to political communication, it is also related to the triumph of *media logic* over party logic.

Inscribed reader. Derives from the tendency of media communicators to shape their text according to an imagined or predefined audience, with certain characteristics of background, taste, interest, capacity, etc. To a certain extent the 'intended' audience can be read from the text. It is more typically a feature of mass communication than, say, artistic creation.

Interactivity. The capacity for reciprocal, two-way communication attributable to a communication medium or relationship. Interactivity allows for mutual adjustment, co-orientation, finer control and greater efficiency in most communication relationships and processes. The single most defining feature of 'new media' is their degree of interactivity, made increasingly possible by *digitalization*.

Internet. The worldwide system of interconnected networks, using the telecommunications infrastructure, that now supports a large number of types of computer-based communication exchanges, including consultation of databases, websites and homepages, conversational interactions, e-mail, many kinds of electronic commerce and financial transactions. The Internet is gradually taking over many functions of 'traditional' mass media (e.g. advertising, news and information). Access to the Internet is still restricted by costs to the user, plus barriers of language, culture and computer literacy.

Interpretative community. A term originating in linguistics that describes the set of users of a given language or cultural code, among whom there will be shared understanding of texts and symbols. When applied to a media *audience*, it usually relates to a particular group of fans or devotees formed around some performance, performer or work, among whom similarly there is a large measure of shared values, interests and meanings. Such communities usually arise spontaneously and are not exclusive. They are also encouraged to form for purposes of publicity.

Intertextuality. Refers to the tendency for different media texts to refer to each other at different levels and across genres, and also the process by which 'readers' make meaningful connections across formal boundaries of texts and genres. The connections extend from media texts to material objects of consumption by way of branding and merchandising. Advertising makes much deliberate use of intertextual connections. Conversational texts of media audiences extend the influence of the original texts into everyday life and language.

Journalism. Literally taken, this refers to the product or the work of professional 'news people'. As product it typically means informational reports of recent or current events of interest to the public. In this sense, journalism is another word for 'news', with its many typical and familiar features, especially the aim of being up to date, relevant, credible and interesting to a chosen audience. As a work process, journalism has mixed connotations, reflecting uncertainty about the status of the profession. There are several styles and schools of journalism differentiated by purpose and audience and also by national media cultures.

Knowledge gap. A term coined to refer to the structured differences in information levels between groups in society. The original promise of mass communication was that it would help to close the gaps between the 'information rich' and the 'information poor'. The concept has stimulated research to investigate how far this has happened and what types of media use and other conditions are associated with such an 'effect' (or its reversal). The dominant outcome has been that newspapers have been better at closing gaps than television. Current expectations are that new media are more likely to widen than to close gaps because of their differential availability to the already better informed.

Libel. Refers to the offence in law (as it usually is) of defaming another person in a published work by way of derogatory references that cause either damage to the person's reputation or material harm to their interests or both. The truth or otherwise of the defamatory reference is not directly relevant, although it does count for something legally, depending on the jurisdiction.

Lifestyle. The idea has a long history in commercial market research and has affinities with theories of taste and family background developed by Pierre Bourdieu. It refers to patterns of personal consumption and tastes of all kinds that are generally self-chosen but also shared with some others. They can be relatively independent of social class and material circumstances although they are likely to be shaped by a number of external factors, amongst which income is certainly one, along with age, education, social milieu and outlook. A lifestyle may be a way of expressing an individual identity, but for media it can also be a way of constructing and managing consumer markets. See also *taste culture*.

Marxism. Theory of society based on the work of Karl Marx, according to whom human progress takes place on the basis of conflict between succeeding 'classes', whose dominant power depends on ownership of the current main factor of production (e.g. land, raw material, capital or labour). The dominant class exploits other classes in order to maximize profit and output. The relevance for mass communication lies in the proposition that the media are an ideological asset that can be used to defend, or attack, a dominant class position. In Marx's own time and later, the mass media were owned and operated in the interests of the dominant class. This remains an issue to be determined.

Mass. The term describes a very large but amorphous set of individuals that engage in similar behaviour, under external influence, and are viewed by their would-be manipulators as having little or no separate identity, forms of organization or power, autonomy, integrity or self-determination. It represents one view of the media audience. It is used with the same negative connotations in a number of related expressions, including mass behaviour, mass opinion, mass consumption, *mass culture, mass society*, and so on, and of course 'mass communication' itself.

Mass culture. When current (approximately 1930–70), this term described the 'culture of the masses', generally meaning 'lower' forms of entertainment and fiction appealing to the uneducated and 'uncultured' majority, as opposed to the 'high culture' of the majority. Cultural change and new perceptions of popular culture have changed the meaning of the term and made it largely redundant or undesirable. When current it was more ideological (upholding elite cultural values) than empirically valid, since all but a small minority tended to participate in at least some aspects of 'mass culture'.

Mass society. A form of society theoretically identified as dominated by a small number of interconnected elites who control the conditions of life of the many, often by means of persuasion and manipulation. The term was first applied both to the post-war United States by radical critics (especially C. Wright Mills) and also by political theorists to the European societies that fell under the spell of fascism and communism. Large-scale and centralized forms of social organization are typical, accompanied by feelings of anomie and powerlessness. The mass media are necessary instruments for achieving and maintaining mass society.

Media accountability. A composite term for the idea, and the associated processes for realizing it, that media can and should be held to account for the quality, means and consequences of their publishing activities to society in general and/or to other interests that may be affected. This brings accountability into potential conflict with freedom. The idea of media accountability is sometimes, though not necessarily, associated with ideas of *social responsibility*. It does presuppose some mutual relationship between media senders and receivers. It is also closely linked to the idea of there being a *public interest* in the media.

Media concentration. The coming together of media organizations to form larger units either by vertical or by horizontal integration of firms. The former refers to joining of various sequences in the media process (e.g. paper production, printing, publishing and selling of books), the latter to conglomeration of firms at the same stage in the sequence. Both lead to greater monopoly and less *diversity*. Concentration can also take place within the same national market or transnationally. The usual main reference is to concentration of ownership, although it is possible for there to be varying levels of concentration of different work processes in a media conglomerate.

Media ethics. Principles of good conduct for media practitioners, bearing in mind the public role of the media in a given society, as well as the claims of individuals. The relevant conduct relates especially to the ways in which information is obtained and to decisions about what and how to publish, especially bearing in mind the consequences that might follow for all concerned. In non-informational content areas, there are also numerous ethical issues, although these are less likely to have been codified or play a part in decision-making. The claim of *journalism* to be a profession depends to some degree on the voluntary development and acceptance of ethical standards. See *media accountability*.

Media event. The specific idea was conceived by Dayan and Katz (1992), although the notion of 'pseudo-event' had already been used (Boorstin, 1961) to refer to events created by the media or minor events without substance that owed their apparent significance to media attention or '*hype*'. Dayan and Katz's concept identifies a particular media genre, one they say is unique to television. For a televised occasion to count as a 'media event', certain conditions have to be met: unusual events of great symbolic or historic importance, such as coronations or state visits; live coverage; extramedia sponsorship; a high degree of preplanning; reverence and ceremony in presentation; an emphasis on national sharing and celebration; and having an appeal to very large (often international) audiences.

Media logic. Usually refers to a set of interrelated values that are believed by producers to constitute good (i.e. successful) practice and professionalism for a given medium for given purposes, or believed by observers to be operating unconsciously. While different media (e.g. radio, film, newspapers) may have different logics, there are a few central recurring components, especially: personalization, sensationalism (appeal to senses and emotions), drama and action, conflict, spectacle, high tempo. These attributes are thought to widen appeal and increase attention and involvement. The term is usually used by critics with the implication that media logic exalts form over substance and conflicts with goals of being informative, or otherwise conveys deeper meaning or reflection. In relation to politics, it is held that media logic detracts from substance and conviction.

Mediatization. The process by which the mass media come to affect many other areas of society, especially institutions with a public role, such as politics, justice, health, education, religion. Observation suggests that many public activities are now undertaken with a high regard for how they can gain access to publicity on favourable terms and with maximum impact. The term implies that activity may often be distorted, with timing, priorities and meanings being adapted to the requirements of the media and to *media logic*.

Medium theory. The type of theory that attributes causal influence to the intrinsic character of a given medium of communication, distinctive by its technology and capability for carrying meaning. Although technological determinism along these lines is the most common form taken by medium theory, each medium has other attributes besides the technology that affect how it will be applied to communicative purpose and also how it will be perceived and actually experienced. Media develop within particular institutional settings and cultural settings that have effects independent of technology. Medium theory is most commonly identified with the *Toronto School*.

Moral panic. The term was first applied by the criminologist Jock Young to sudden expressions of often irrational mass anxiety and alarm directed at 'crime waves' or other supposed evidence of disorder and social breakdown (including promiscuity and immigration). The media are implicated through their tendency to amplify such 'panics'. They are also sometimes objects of moral panics, when alarm at their harmful effects suddenly gains currency (e.g. in the form of crime waves, suicides or rioting). New media, such as computer games and the Internet, tend to generate some degree of panic at alleged harm to their (young) users.

Network. Any interconnected set of points, which could be persons, places, organizations, machines, and so on. In communication, interest focuses on the flow of information through the 'lines' of a network, with particular reference to their carrying capacity and interactivity, and of course to whom or what one is connected more or less tightly and exclusively. Compared with other types of organized human association, networks are less hierarchical and more flexible and informal. The term 'network society' has been coined by theorists (e.g. Castells and van Dyke) as an alternative way of expressing the reality of the *information society*.

News. The main form in which current information about public events is carried by media of all kinds. There is a great diversity of types and formats as well as cross-cultural differences, but defining characteristics are generally held to be timeliness, relevance and reliability (truth value). See also *journalism*.

Newspaper. Traditionally this has referred to a print media form appearing regularly (usually not less than once a week), containing (at least) reliable reports of recent or ongoing events of general interest and offered for public sale. Associated characteristics are usually independence or transparency of ownership and editing and a geographical range of coverage and circulation. Variant forms have emerged, including the 'free newspaper' paid for by advertising, and more recently the 'electronic newspaper' that is offered online and lacks the limits of time and location of the traditional newspaper.

News values. The criteria applied by journalists and editors in news organizations to determine whether or not to carry particular items of *news*. In commercial media, the consensus 'value' is whether or not the item concerned is likely to interest a potential audience. However, there are other sources of value, including a judgement of intrinsic significance or the pull or pressure of influential interests other than the audience.

Non-verbal communication. The term refers primarily to non-verbal (vocal or non-vocal) communication between persons, rather than to media that use music or images, for instance. Non-verbal communication is sometimes called 'paralinguistic' or 'prelinguistic'. Non-verbal human communication often adds to or extends verbal communication. Although the lack of codification and rules for non-verbal communication make it less than a language, there are often agreed meanings in a particular culture attaching to noises, gestures, postures, and the like that are characteristic of much non-verbal communication.

Normative theory. Refers to theory about how media ought to operate, rather than theory seeking to describe and explain how they actually operate or to predict outcomes of the way media operate (especially effects). The latter kind of theory might be described as objective or scientific theory. Normative theory applies primarily to the relationship between media and society and deals with claims on the part of the media, especially in respect of their freedom, and also claims on the part of society. See *freedom of the press* and *social responsibility*.

Objectivity. A theoretically contested term applied to *news*, although in 'commonsense' terms it sums up a number of the qualities that make for trust and reliability on the part of the news audience. These include factual accuracy, lack of *bias*, separation of fact from comment, transparency about sources, and not taking sides. The reasons for controversy about the term stem mainly from the view that true objectivity is unattainable and it is misleading to pretend otherwise. In brief, all news is said to be ideological, and objectivity is held by critics to be another ideology. The requirements of objectivity make it possible for sources to manipulate the news and only serve to conceal bias, whether this is intended or unintended.

Opinion leader. A term introduced by Elihu Katz and Paul Lazarsfeld, in early research into the influence of mass media, to describe the social role of persons who influence the thinking or behaviour of others in informal social relationships. The identifying characteristics vary according to the 'topic' of influence and social setting, but the people concerned are generally better informed, make more use of mass media and other sources, are gregarious and are likely to be respected by those they influence. The failure of early research to find 'direct' effects from mass media was attributed in part to the variable and often invisible contribution of opinion leaders (known as 'personal influence').

Parasocial interaction. A term for the pseudo-interaction that can take place between individuals in audiences and fictional characters or media personalities. Some degree of loss of contact with reality is involved, and it may be the basis for influence on behaviour.

Phonogram. A convenient, though not very much used, term for all forms of recorded and personally replayed music, which were originally (almost) only available via the 'gramophone', previously 'phonograph', later 'record-player'. The word covers records, tapes and discs of all kinds.

Political economy. The original word for theoretical economics, but for some time used by critical theorists working in the neo-Marxist tradition to refer to a general view of media and society in which material (economic) factors play a determining role and in which politics is primarily about economic power.

Pornography. Used loosely to describe media content that involves description or display of explicit sexual themes and scenes that go beyond the normally accepted threshold for public acceptability with reference to offence or perceived harm (in particular to children or women, who are victimized in some forms of pornography). It is presumed that the main aim of media pornography (as shared with the audience) is sexual arousal. Publication of pornography is defined differently as an offence (or not) in different jurisdictions.

Portal. Can apply to any one of several different kinds of access point into 'cyberspace' (as when seeking to connect) or from it (as when searching for some information). In general a gateway to the Internet, with the main reference being to one or other of the following: a major media provider, such as Yahoo or Google; a particular *search engine*; a *social network site* such as *YouTube*; a specific website for certain kinds of content; a community or network. The Internet portal is qualitatively different from the gateways provided by former mass media, since they enable a two-way flow.

Postmodernism. A widely current (cultural) theory that underwrites the view that the 'age of ideology' is over along with the 'industrial society' and its massive forms of social organization and control and dedication to rationality. Instead we are living in an era of unstructured diversity, uncertainty, contradictions, open-ended creativity and individual freedom from imposed rules and social constraint. It has become fashionable to discern the exuberant growth of mass media forms as the essence of popular postmodern culture. Neither the material conditions of contemporary society nor forms of organization of mass media exhibit clear signs of postmodernism. Much as with earlier critical cultural theory, postmodern thinking can support divergent optimistic and pessimistic outlooks.

Power. A term open to many interpretations, but the basic idea is a reference to a capacity to gain the compliance of another, even against their will (as with police or military power). In this meaning it has no direct relevance for communication, since no effect can be compelled. However, we can speak of a probability of gaining compliance with some communicative purpose (in relation to information or opinion) and the term 'influence' is widely applicable to mass communication, with compliance gained by force of argument or certain psychological rewards.

Prejudice. A term applied either to attitudes on the part of the public, or to media publication that involves systematically negative views about or negative treatment of (usually) some social group or category. Frequent targets of prejudice have been ethnic minorities or outgroups such as homosexuals, foreign immigrants, the mentally ill, etc. The media have been accused of fomenting prejudice, sometimes unintentionally, and also credited with some capacity to counter prejudice.

Press Council. A widely used general term for a quasi-public body that adjudicates on complaints from the public about the conduct of the press, in societies where freedom of the press is guaranteed. Press councils usually represent media and public interests. They do not deal with criminal offences and have no power to punish. Their primary sanction is publicity and asking 'offenders' to apologize by way of publication. A press council is one important means of *media accountability*.

Priming. Refers to the activity of the media in proposing the values and standards by which objects of media attention can be judged. The origin of the term lies in social psychology (socialization theory) but it has latterly been more applied in political communication to the evaluation of political figures by public opinion. See also *framing* and *agenda-setting*.

Profession. Refers to members of a particular occupation that maintain certain standards of technical performance and of ethics by means of self-regulatory procedures. Professions involve recognized training, and control of entry to the profession is maintained by the responsible body of the profession. There is much debate about the status of *journalism* in particular as a profession. On some, but not all, criteria it can claim professional status.

Propaganda. The process and product of deliberate attempts to influence collective behaviour and opinion by the use of multiple means of communication in ways that are systematic and one-sided. Propaganda is carried out in the interest of the source or sender, not the recipient. It is almost certain to be in some respects misleading or not fully truthful and can be entirely untrue, as with certain kinds of disinformation. It can also be psychologically aggressive and distorted in its representation of reality. Its effectiveness is variable, depending on the context and dispositions of the target audience more than on 'message' characteristics. See *advertising, public diplomacy* and *campaign*.

Public. As a noun it refers to the general body of free citizens of a given society or some smaller geographical space. Its connotations are strongly influenced by democratic theory, since freedom and equality (of rights) are generally only available in a democracy. The members of a genuine public in a democracy are free to associate, converse, organize and express themselves on all subjects, and government is ultimately accountable to the will of the 'public as a whole' according to agreed procedures. This large notion of what constitutes the public is one reason why public communication has a certain claim to protection and to respect in a democracy. See also *public opinion, public interest* and *public sphere*.

Publication. The act of making public, thus crossing a line between private and public expression. Publication usually involves a clear decision to express ideas in a fixed or formal way via the press, public speech, poster, etc. Private expression is confined to a designated personal interlocutor or circle. The distinction has legal and practical significance, especially in connection with confidentiality, privacy, potential harm or offence. New media have blurred the distinction between what is actually and consciously public and what may be considered so because it can be accessed by others. Publication has also become much easier for individuals, if they choose it.

Public diplomacy. A general term to describe the efforts by nation states to win support and a favourable image among the general public of other countries, usually by way of news management and carefully planned initiatives designed to foster positive impressions. Public diplomacy has increased in significance as an adjunct of foreign policy in the more multi-polar world of the twenty-first century, especially when military actions affecting other countries are contemplated. It may be viewed as a softer form of *propaganda*.

Public interest. Expresses the idea that expectations from, and claims against, the mass media on grounds of the wider and longer-term good of society can be legitimately expressed and may lead to constraints on the structure or activity of media. The content of what is 'in the public interest' takes various forms. Its most minimal interpretation is that media should meet the needs of their audiences, but ethical, ideological, political and legal considerations may also lead to much stronger definitions. The expression of public interest also takes place in many ways, including via *public opinion*, politicians, critics and many interest groups affected by public communication. See also *media accountability*.

Public journalism. A movement from within the journalistic profession (especially in the USA) to counter criticisms of journalistic standards by advancing various practical public goals for the news. These goals would involve discovering and addressing the needs and interests of the immediate audience served by a given medium. Information of practical value would be stressed and journalists would engage actively in community affairs.

Public opinion. The collective views of a significant part of any *public*. This part is sometimes taken to mean a numerical majority as measured by polling, but this far overstates the capacity of the measuring instruments and misses the essential point that opinion is always diverse, dynamic and variable in strength. Historically and in certain contexts public opinion may be taken to refer to 'informed opinion', or the general view of the more educated and aware members of the society. No statement concerning public opinion is likely to be unambiguous or beyond dispute without some clear definition. See *spiral of silence*.

Public relations. Now a reference to all forms of influence carried out by professional paid communicators on behalf of some 'client' and designed primarily to project a favourable image and to counter negative views that might exist. The means are various, ranging from direct communication to providing gifts and hospitality. Public relations is often a source of supply for news media or seeks to influence news in other ways. See also *advertising* and *propaganda*.

Public service broadcasting (PSB). The (mainly European) system of broadcasting that is publicly funded and operated in a non-profit way in order to meet the various public communication needs of all citizens. These were originally virtually all needs (i.e. inclusive of entertainment), and the justification for PSB lay in the 'natural monopoly' character of broadcasting distribution. This justification is no longer valid, and PSB survives on grounds of general *public interest* and because it can meet certain communication needs that tend to be neglected in commercial systems because they are unprofitable. These include universal service, special needs of certain minorities, certain kinds of educational provision, and services to the democratic political system by giving some degree of open and diverse access, supporting general informational aims and meeting the specific needs of politicians in the electoral and government process.

Public sphere. The conceptual 'space' that exists in a society outside the immediate circle of private life and the walls of enclosed institutions and organizations pursuing their own (albeit sometimes public) goals. In this space, the possibility exists for public association and debate leading to the formation of public opinion and political movements and parties that can hold private interests accountable. The media are now probably the key institution of the public sphere, and its 'quality' will depend on the quality of media. Taken to extremes, certain structural tendencies of media, including concentration, commercialization and globalization, are harmful to the public sphere.

Reception analysis. An alternative to traditional audience research (concerned with counting and effect) that takes the perspective of the audience rather than the media sender and looks at the immediate contextual influences on media use and the interpretation and meaning of the whole experience as seen by the recipient. Ethnographic and qualitative methods are required.

Rhetoric. The art of public speaking with persuasive intention.

Rumour. Communication that takes place mainly by word of mouth in the absence of reliable or complete information about events of great concern to those involved. Mass media can feed rumour (e.g. early reports of some disaster) or replace rumour. Rumour develops where mass media are generally inadequate or unreliable (as in totalitarian societies or under conditions of war). Networks of personal relations facilitate rumour, but under extreme conditions are not necessary.

Schema. Refers to the preconceived frame or script which is typically available to journalists for reporting isolated cases or events. A schema is an aid to communication and understanding, because it provides some wider context and sense-making. However, schemata also introduce some closure, but applying an existing frame of meaning. Audiences also have their own schemata for making sense of incoming news information. See *framing*.

Search engine. The computerized information retrieval system developed by Internet service providers in order to give convenient access for users in search of information or specific content to the universe of material that has been digitized and is available in 'cyberspace'. The key component of the system is a powerful search program that 'crawls' through data on the World Wide Web, following links. The value added by search engine sites is to provide indices, based on key words, and ranking of search results as well as accessibility. In theory, searches are supposed to be neutral, but are inevitably skewed by various considerations, including commercial ones, since they are extremely popular and profitable. They are also very highly monopolized, with one firm, Google, having well over half the total search engine market. Another limiting factor is that only a relatively small part of the potential web universe is (or can be) searched.

Segmentation. The process of classifying a potential audience for purposes of production and delivering content according to relevant categories, usually either socio-demographic or psychographic (e.g. by lifestyle and taste). It plays a key role in the planning and costing of advertising in all media. Although sometimes regarded as a trend running counter to mass communication, it can be considered as a better controlled and more effective form of mass communication. See also *fragmentation*.

Semiology. The 'science of sign systems' or 'signification'. Originally founded on the study of general linguistics by Ferdinand de Saussure, it was developed into a method for the systematic analysis and interpretation of all symbolic texts. Systems of signs are organized within larger cultural and ideological systems that ultimately determine meaning. A key element of semiology is the idea that any (meaningful) sign (of any kind) has a conceptual element that carries meaning as well as a physical manifestation (word, image, etc.).

Sensationalism. At one level, an everyday word for all aspects of media content that are likely to attract attention, excite or inflame emotions. In this sense it is related to *commercialization* and *tabloidization*. It has also been deployed as a concept in content analysis, defined in terms of some 'indicators' for measuring the degree of sensationalism. The reason for doing so is a concern at the inconsistency between sensational and *objective* news reporting.

Soap opera. A conventional term for a very wide range of radio and television drama in (long-running and frequent) serial form. The term originates in early American commercial radio. Despite the variations, some typical features of soap operas are: contemporary realistic settings of the action; continuity of characters and plots, which link to issues of the moment; a focus on the intermixed personal relationships of the characters; a strong claim to audience identification and 'addiction'; and a particular appeal to women audiences in family settings.

Social network sites. Often known just as 'social media', these comprise a number of Internet websites that have been set up to enable and encourage users to create networks of acquaintances and also to share messages and audiovisual material, often available to a wider public. The current examples of internationally very popular social media are *Facebook*, *Myspace*, *YouTube*. They have become valuable commercial properties, especially for related advertising, cross-media publicity and generating content from users. See also *viral advertising*.

Socialization. The general process of social formation of the young under the influence of the so-called agencies of socialization – traditionally the family, neighbourhood, school and religion, and now mass media.

Social responsibility. Attributed to the mass media in certain normative theories of the press and based on propositions about the needs of (democratic) society. It involves the unwritten obligations towards society and its members that are implicit in freedom of publication as well, besides general moral principles relating to truth and justice.

Spin doctor. Contemporary expression to refer to all those who have the job of managing (or massaging) the public presentation of information or ideas (especially on behalf of politicians) to maximum advantage. Their work results in the manipulation of news and is related to *public relations* and *propaganda*.

Spiral of cynicism. A hypothetical process, similar to the *spiral of silence*, whereby persistently negative media coverage of a political campaign and politicians, especially where this emphasizes insincerity, corruption, dirty tricks, personal ambition and ignores substance and honest intention, is thought to create a climate in which trust and the wish to participate in the democratic process is diminished. In effect, the thesis holds that the more exposure to the media, the less there will be public trust and participation. The causes are held to lie especially in the process of *mediatization* and are also linked to *media logic*.

Spiral of silence. Concept that describes one version of the 'third-party' effect in opinion formation: the tendency for people to be influenced in what they think (or say they do) or by what they think other people think. The term was first applied by Elizabeth Noelle-Neumann to refer to the tendency for those who think they hold a minority or deviant view to refrain from expressing it in public, thus accelerating the dominance of the supposed consensus (the spiralling effect). The hypothesis is based on a presumed 'fear of isolation'. The main thrust of the theory is to attribute to the (leftist) media a powerful effect, since they are the main source of what people think is the dominant opinion of the moment. Also related to the better-known 'bandwagon effect', whereby apparent front runners pick up support on this basis alone.

Stereotyping. The process of using stock images of social groups, situations, events, countries, etc., in fiction or factual mass communication. A stereotype is an early graphic form of facsimile reproduction. Since the early years of communication research, the idea of a stereotype has been applied to media content that encourages prejudice or to the expression of prejudice in opinion and attitude. There is an almost inevitable element of stereotyping mass media production for reasons of simplification and efficiency as well as ill-will or ignorance. The idea is related to that of *framing* and *schema*.

Stimulus–response. A psychological process by which an experimental subject learns to perform some action in response to a message stimulus that has become associated with the action in question. It underlies a large body of learning theory that was applied in early research into the effects of communication and media. It has not proved a very good guide to reality.

Strategic communication. Designates the type of information in election campaigns and political news that refers to the strategies of candidates and the 'horse-race' aspects of politics rather than the political ideas of policies. See *spin doctor*.

Surveillance. This term has two meanings in media studies. One refers to the 'function' of news media for the audience in providing a view on the events of the world. The other refers to the capacity built into new online media allowing third-party access (by service providers, search engines, some authorities) to all communicative transactions. Use of these media is no longer guaranteed privacy.

Tabloidization. A term derived from the common tabloid format for sensationalist (i.e. gossip and scandal-mongering) newspapers, to refer to the alleged process of 'dumbing down' or going 'down market' of the more serious press in many countries. The main believed cause was commercialization and intense competition for readers. The process has also affected television news and 'actuality' formats in general, especially in the United States, and caused alarm at the decline of journalistic standards, the rise in public ignorance and the risk of confusion between fiction and reality (e.g. 'infotainment').

Taste culture. A more or less organized and semi-autonomous set of cultural preferences based on certain shared tastes, although independent of actual social organization. In this the concept differs from the earlier approaches to taste patterns that were mainly explained in terms of social background, class or milieu. Related to *lifestyle*.

Third-party effects. The perceived effects on others that many people believe to occur, even though they think they are not affected themselves. See *spiral of silence*.

Toronto School. Describes a body of work mainly derived from the theories of Marshall McLuhan, and in turn derived from an earlier scholar at the University of Toronto, the economic historian Harold Innis. At the core is a form of communication technology determinism that attributes distinctive social and cultural effects to the dominant form and vehicle of communication, independent of the actual content.

Uses and gratifications approach. A version of individualist functional theory and research that seeks to explain the uses of media and the satisfactions derived from them in terms of the motives and self-perceived needs of audience members. This is also one version of 'active audience' theory and has been applied in the study of media effects on the grounds that any effect has to be consistent with the needs of the audience.

Viral advertising. Planned publicity that spreads spontaneously and rapidly 'by word of mouth' (but also by e-mail) throughout a potential media consumer market, primarily by harnessing the resources of existing interpersonal networks (often existing fan groups). Strategic use of *social network sites* is considered a prime means of stimulating the process. There are limited applications, but large advantages, especially the speed and thoroughness of reach, low cost and the seeming absence of manipulation.

Virtual community. Describes the group or close personal associations formed online by participants in Internet exchanges and discussions. A virtual community is thought to have many of the features of a real community, including identification, bonding, shared norms and outlook, even without any physical contact or real personal knowledge of other members. See *community*.

References

Aday, S., Slivington, M. and Herbert, M. (2005) 'Embedding the truth: a cross-cultural analysis of objectivity and TV coverage of the Iraq war', *Harvard International Journal of Press/Politics*, 10 (1): 3–21.

Adorno, T. and Horkheimer, M. (1972) 'The culture industry: enlightenment as mass deception', in *The Dialectic of Enlightenment*. New York: Herder and Herder.

Aguado, G., Sanmartí, J.M. and Magallon, R. (2009) 'The effect of the state on the evolution of print media in European Mediterranean countries', *International Journal of Communication*, 3: 780–807.

Akdeniz, Y., Walker, C. and Wall, C. (2000) *The Internet, Law and Society*. London: Longman.

Alali, A.O. and Eke, K.K. (eds) (1991) *Media Coverage of Television*. Newbury Park, CA: Sage.

Alasuutari, P. (1992) '"I'm ashamed to admit it but I have watched *Dallas*": the moral hierarchy of television programmes', *Media, Culture and Society*, 14 (1): 561–82.

Alasuutari, P. (ed.) (1999) *Rethinking the Media Audience*. London: Sage.

Alberoni, F. (1972) 'The "powerless elite": theory and sociological research on the phenomenon of the stars', in D. McQuail (ed.), *Sociology of Mass Communication*, pp. 75–98. Harmondsworth: Penguin.

Allen, R.C. (ed.) (1987) *Channels of Discourse*. London: Allen and Unwin.

Allen, R.C. (1989) '"Soap opera", audiences and the limits of genre', in F. Seiter et al. (eds), *Remote Control*, pp. 4–55. London: Routledge.

Allor, M. (1988) 'Relocating the site of the audience', *Critical Studies in Mass Communication*, 5 (3): 217–33.

Althaus, S. (2003) 'When news norms collide, follow the lead: new evidence for press independence', *Political Communication*, 20 (4): 381–414.

Althaus, S.L. and Tewkesbury (2000) 'Patterns of Internet and traditional news media use in a networked community', *Political Communication*, 17 (1): 21–45.

Althaus, S.L. and Tewkesbury, D. (2002) 'Agenda-setting and the "New News": patterns of issue importance among readers of the paper and online versions of the *NYT*', *Communication Research*, 29 (2): 180–207.

Altheide, D.L. (1974) *Creating Reality*. Beverly Hills, CA: Sage.

Altheide, D.L. (1985) *Media Power*. Beverly Hills, CA: Sage.

Altheide, D.L. and Snow, R.P. (1979) *Media Logic*. Beverly Hills, CA: Sage.

Altheide, D.L. and Snow, R.P. (1991) *Media Worlds in the Postjournalism Era*. New York: Aldine de Gruyter.

Althusser, L. (1971) 'Ideology and ideological state apparatuses', in *Lenin and Philosophy and Other Essays*. London: New Left.

Altschull, J.H. (1984) *Agents of Power: the Role of the News Media in Human Affairs*. New York: Longman.

American Behavioral Scientist (2003) Special issue on media bias, 46 (12).

Anden-Papadopolous, K. (2008) 'The Abu-Ghraib torture photographs: news frames, visual culture and the power of images', *Journalism*, 9 (1): 5–30.

Anderson, A. (2003) 'Environmental activism and the news media' in S. Cottle (ed.), *News, Public Relations and Power*, pp. 117–32. London: Sage.

Anderson, B. (1983) *Imagined Communities*. London: Verso.

Anderson, J., Collins, P.A., Schmitt, R.S. and Jacobowitz, R.S. (1996) 'Stressful life events and television viewing', *Communication Research*, 23 (2): 243–60.

Andersson, M. and Jansson, A. (1998) 'Media use and the progressive cultural lifestyle', *Nordicom Review*, 19 (2): 63–77.

Andrew, D. (1984) *Concepts in Film Theory*. New York: Oxford University Press.

Ang, I. (1985) *Watching 'Dallas': Soap Opera and the Melodramatic Imagination*. London: Methuen.

Ang, I. (1991) *Desperately Seeking the Audience*. London: Routledge.

Ang, I. and Hermes, J. (1991) 'Gender and/in media consumption', in J. Curran and M. Gurevitch (eds), *Media and Society*, pp. 307–28. London: Arnold.

Arcetti, C. (2008) 'News coverage of 9/11 and the demise of the media flows, globalization and localization hypothesis', *International Communication Gazette*, 70 (6): 463–85.

Armstrong, C.L. (2004) 'The influence of reporter gender on source selection in newspaper stories', *Journalism and Mass Communication Quarterly*, 81 (2): 463–85.

Asp, K. (1981) 'Mass media as molders of opinion and suppliers of information', in C.G. Wilhoit and H. de Back (eds), *Mass Communication Review Yearbook*, vol. 2, pp. 332–54. Beverly Hills, CA: Sage.

Atkinson, D. and Raboy, M. (eds) (1997) *Public Service Broadcasting: the Challenges of the Twenty-First Century*. Paris: Unesco.

Austin, P.J. (1992) 'Television that talks back: an experimental validation of a PSI scale', *Journal of Broadcasting and Electronic Media*, 36 (1): 173–81.

Avery, R. (1979) 'Adolescents' use of the mass media', *American Behavioral Scientist*, 23: 53–70.

Babrow, A.S. (1988) 'Theory and method in research on audience motives', *Journal of Broadcasting and Electronic Media*, 32 (4): 471–87.

Baehr, H. (1996) *Women in Television*. London: University of Westminster Press.

Baerns, B. (1987) 'Journalism versus public relations in the Federal Republic of Germany', in D.L. Paletz (ed.), *Political Communication Research*, pp. 88–107. Norwood, NJ: Ablex.

Bagdikian, B. (1988) *The Media Monopoly*. Boston: Beacon.

Bailyn, L. (1959) 'Mass media and children: a study of exposure habits and cognitive effects', *Psychological Monographs*, 73: 1–48.

Baker, C.E. (1994) *Advertising and a Democratic Press*. Princeton, NJ: Princeton University Press.

Baker, C.E. (2007) *Media Concentraion and Democracy.* Cambridge: Cambridge University Press.

Baker, R.K. and Ball, S. (eds) (1969) *Violence and the Media*. Washington, DC: Government Printing Office.

Bakker, P. (2002) 'Free daily newspapers – business models and strategies', *International Journal on Media Management*, 4 (3): 180–7.

Ball-Rokeach, S.J. (1985) 'The origins of individual media-system dependency', *Communication Research*, 12 (4): 485–510.

Ball-Rokeach, S.J. (1998) 'A theory of media power and a theory of media use: different stories, questions and ways of thinking', *Mass Communication and Society*, 1 (2): 1–40.

Ball-Rokeach, S.J. (2001) 'The politics of studying media violence: reflections 30 years after the Violence Commission', *Mass Communication and Society*, 4 (1): 3–18.

Ball-Rokeach, S.J. and DeFleur, M.L. (1976) 'A dependency model of mass media effects', *Communication Research*, 3: 3–21.

Bandura, A. (1986) *Social Foundations of Thought and Actions: a Social Cognitive Theory.* Englewood Cliffs, NJ: Prentice-Hall.

Bandura, A. (2002) 'Social cognitive theory of mass communication', in J. Bryant and D. Zillman (eds), *Media Effects: Advances in Theory and Research*, 2nd edn, pp. 121–54. Hillsdale, NJ: Erlbaum.

Bantz, C.R. (1985) 'News organizations: conflict as crafted cultural norm', *Communication*, 8: 225–44.

Bantz, C.R., McCorkle, S. and Baade, R.C. (1980) 'The news factory', *Communication Research*, 7 (1): 45–68.

Bar, F. and Sandvig, C. (2008) 'US communication policy after convergence', *Media, Culture and Society*, 30 (4): 531–50.

Bardoel, J. (2002) 'The Internet, journalism and communication policies', *Gazette*, 65 (1): 501–11.

Bardoel, J. and d'Haenens, L. (2008) 'Reinventing public service broadcasting: promise and problems', *Media, Culture and Society*, 30 (3): 295–317.

Barker, M. (2003) 'Assessing the "quality" in qualitative research', *European Journal of Communication*, 18 (3): 315–35.

Barnes, B.E. and Thomson, L.M. (1994) 'Power to the people (meter): audience measurement technology and media specialization', in J.S. Ettema and D.C. Whitney (eds), *Audiencemaking: How the Media Create the Audience*, pp. 75–94. Thousand Oaks, CA: Sage.

Barthes, R. (1967) *Elements of Semiology*. London: Cape.

Barthes, R. (1972) *Mythologies*. London: Cape.

Barthes, R. (1977) *Image, Music, Text: Essays*, selected and translated by Stephen Heath. London: Fontana.

Barwise, T.P. and Ehrenberg, A.S.C. (1988) *Television and its Audience*. Newbury Park, CA: Sage.

Bass, A.Z. (1969) 'Refining the gatekeeper concept', *Journalism Quarterly*, 46: 69–72.

Baudrillard, J. (1983) *Simulations*. New York: Semiotext(e).

Bauer, R.A. (1958) 'The communicator and the audience', *Journal of Conflict Resolution*, 2 (1): 67–77. Also in L.A. Dexter and D.M. White (eds), *People, Society and Mass Communication*, pp. 125–39. New York: Free Press.

Bauer, R.A. (1964) 'The obstinate audience', *American Psychologist*, 19: 319–28.

Bauer, R.A. and Bauer, A. (1960) 'America, mass society and mass media', *Journal of Social Issues*, 10 (3): 366.

Bauman, Z. (1972) 'A note on mass culture: on infrastructure', in D. McQuail (ed.), *Sociology of Mass Communication*, pp. 61–74. Harmondsworth: Penguin.

Baym, N.K. (2002) 'Interpersonal life online', in L.A. Lievrouw and S. Livingstone (eds), *The Handbook of New Media*, pp. 62–76. London: Sage.

Becker, J. (2004) 'Lessons from Russia: a neo-authoritarian media system', *European Journal of Communication*, 19 (2): 139–64.

Becker, L. (1982) 'The mass media and citizen assessment of issue importance', in D.C. Whitney et al. (eds), *Mass Communication Review Yearbook*, vol. 3, pp. 521–36. Beverly Hills, CA: Sage.

Becker, L., Vlad, T. and Nusser, N. (2007) 'An evaluation of press freedom indicators', *International Communication Gazette*, 69 (2): 5–28.

Behr, R.L. and Iyengar, S. (1985) 'TV news, real world cues and changes in the public agenda', *Public Opinion Quarterly*, 49 (1): 38–57.

Bell, A. (1991) *The Language of News Media*. Oxford: Blackwell.

Bell, D. (1973) *The Coming of Post-Industrial Society*. New York: Basic Books.

Beniger, J.R. (1986) *The Control Revolution*. Cambridge, MA: Harvard University Press.

Beniger, J.R. (1987) 'Personalization of mass media and the growth of pseudo-community', *Communication Research*, 14 (3): 352–71.

Benjamin, W. (1977) 'The work of art in an age of mechanical reproduction', in J. Curran et al. (eds), *Mass Communication and Society*, pp. 384–408. London: Arnold.

Bennett, W.L. (1990) 'Towards a theory of press–state relations in the US', *Journal of Communication*, 40 (2): 103–25.

Bennett, W.L. (2003) 'The burglar alarm that just keeps ringing: a response to Zaller', *Political Communication*, 20 (2): 131–8.

Bennett, W.L. and Entman, R.M. (eds) (2000) *Mediated Politics*. Cambridge: Cambridge University Press.

Bennett, W.L. and Iyengar, S. (2008) 'A new era of minimal effects? Changing foundations of political communication', *Journal of Communication*, 58 (4): 707–31.

Bennett, W.L., Lawrence, R.G. and Livingstone, S. (2007) *When the Press Fails*. Chicago: Chicago University Press.

Bennett, W.L., Pickard, V.W., Iozzi, D.P., Schroeder, C.I., Lago, T. and Caswell, C.E. (2004) 'Managing the public sphere: journalistic constructions of the great globalization debate', *Journal of Communication*, 54 (3): 437–55.

Benson, R. and Neveu, E. (2005) *Bourdieu and the Journalistic Field*. Cambridge: Polity Press.

Benthall, J. (1993) *Disasters, Relief and the Media*. London: I.B. Taurus.

Bentivegna, S. (2002) 'Politics and the new media', in L.A. Lievrouw and S. Livingstone (eds), *The Handbook of New Media*, pp. 50–61. London: Sage.

Bentivegna, S. (2006) 'Rethinking politics in the world of ICTs', *European Journal of Communication*, 21 (3): 331–44.

Berelson, B. (1948) 'Communication and public opinion', in W. Schramm (ed.), *Communications in Modern Society*. Urbana, IL: University of Illinois Press.

Berelson, B. (1949) 'What missing the newspaper means', in P.F. Lazarsfeld and F.M. Stanton (eds), *Communication Research 1948–9*, pp. 111–29. New York: Duell, Sloan and Pearce.

Berelson, B. (1952) *Content Analysis in Communication Research*. Glencoe, IL: Free Press.

Berelson, B. (1959) 'The state of communication research', *Public Opinion Quarterly*, 23 (1): 16.

Berger, A.A. (1992) *Popular Genres*. Newbury Park, CA: Sage.

Berger, C.R. and Chaffee, S.H. (1987) 'The study of communication as a science', in C.R. Berger and S.H. Chaffee (eds), *Handbook of Communication Science*, pp. 15–19. Beverly Hills, CA: Sage.

Berger, P. and Luckmann, T. (1967) *The Social Construction of Reality*. Garden City, NJ: Anchor.

Berkowitz, D. (1990) 'Refining the gatekeeping concept for local television news', *Journal of Broadcasting and Electronic Media*, 34 (1): 55–68.

Berkowitz, D. (1992) 'Non-routine and news work', *Journal of Communication*, 42 (1): 82–94.

Berkowitz, L. (1984) 'Some effects of thoughts on anti- and prosocial influence of media events: a cognitive neoassociationistic analysis', *Psychological Bulletin*, 95 (3): 410–27.

Bermejo, F. (2009) 'Audience manufacture in historical perspective: from broadcasting to Google', *New Media and Society*, 11 (1/2): 133–54.

Bertrand, C-J. (2003) *An Arsenal for Democracy: Media Accountancy Systems*. Mahwah, NJ: Lawrence Erlbaum.

Biltereyst, D. (1991) 'Resisting American hegemony: a comparative analysis of the reception of domestic and US fiction', *European Journal of Communication*, 6 (4): 469–97.

Biltereyst, D. (1992) 'Language and culture as ultimate barriers?', *European Journal of Communication*, 7 (4): 517–40.

Biltereyst, D. (1995) 'Qualitative audience research and transnational media effects: a new paradigm?', *European Journal of Communication*, 10 (2): 245–70.

Biocca, F.A. (1988a) 'The breakdown of the canonical audience', in J. Anderson (ed.), *Communication Yearbook 11*, pp. 127–32. Newbury Park, CA: Sage.

Biocca, F.A. (1988b) 'Opposing conceptions of the audience', in J. Anderson (ed.), *Communication Yearbook 11*, pp. 51–80. Newbury Park, CA: Sage.

Bird, S.E. (1998) 'An audience perspective on the tabloidisation of news', *The Public*, 5 (3): 33–50.

Bird, S.E. and Dardenne, R.W. (2009) 'Rethinking news and myth as storytelling', in K. Wahl-Jorgensen and T. Hanitsch (eds), *The Handbook of Journalism Studies*, pp. 205–17. London: Routledge.

Blanchard, M.A. (1977) 'The Hutchins Commission, the press and the responsibility concept', *Journalism Monographs*, 49.

Blanchard, M.A. (1986) *Exporting the First Amendment: the Press–Government Crusade of 1945–1952*. New York: Longman.

Blau, P. and Scott, W. (1963) *Formal Organizations*. London: Routledge and Kegan Paul.

Blumer, H. (1933) *Movies and Conduct*. New York: Macmillan.

Blumer, H. (1939) 'The mass, the public and public opinion', in A.M. Lee (ed.), *New Outlines of the Principles of Sociology*. New York: Barnes and Noble.

Blumer, H. (1969) *Symbolic Interactionism*. New York: Prentice-Hall.

Blumer, H. and Hauser, P.M. (1933) *Movies, Delinquency and Crime*. New York: Macmillan.

Blumler, J.G. (1985) 'The social character of media gratifications', in K.E. Rosengren et al. (eds), *Media Gratification Research: Current Perspectives*, pp. 41–59. Beverly Hills, CA: Sage.

Blumler, J.G. (ed.) (1992) *Television and the Public Interest*. London: Sage.

Blumler, J.G. (1998) 'Wrestling with public interest in organized communications', in K. Brants, J. Hermes and L. van Zoonen (eds), *The Media in Question*, pp. 51–63. London: Sage.

Blumler, J.G. and Gurevitch, M. (1995) *The Crisis of Public Communication*. London: Routledge.

Blumler, J.G. and Katz, E. (eds) (1974) *The Uses of Mass Communications*. Beverly Hills, CA: Sage.

Blumler, J.G. and Kavanagh, D. (1999) 'The third age of political communication: influences and fears', *Political Communication*, 16 (3): 209–30.

Blumler, J.G. and McQuail, D. (1968) *Television in Politics: Its Uses and Influence*. London: Faber.

Boczkowski, P. (2004) *Digitizing the News*. Cambridge, MA: MIT Press.

Bogart, L. (1979) *Press and Public*. Hillsdale, NJ: Erlbaum.

Bogart, L. (1995) *Commercial Culture*. New York: Oxford University Press.

Bogart, L. (2004) 'Reflections on content quality in newspapers', *Newspaper Research Journal*, 25 (1): 40–53.

Boorstin, D. (1961) *The Image: a Guide to Pseudo-Events in America*. New York: Atheneum.

Bordewijk, J.L. and van Kaam, B. (1986) 'Towards a new classification of tele-information services', *Intermedia*, 14 (1): 1621. Originally published in *Allocutie*. Baarn: Bosch and Keuning, 1982.

Bourdieu, P. (1986) *Distinction: a Social Critique of the Judgement of Taste*. London: Routledge.

Boyd-Barrett, O. (1980) *The International News Agencies*. London: Constable.

Boyd-Barrett, O. (2001) 'National and international news agencies', *Gazette*, 62 (1): 5–18.

Boyd-Barrett, O. and Rantanen, T. (eds) (1998) *The Globalization of News*. London: Sage.

Braman, S. (2004) 'Technology', in J.D.H. Downing, D. McQuail, P. Schlesinger and E. Wartella (eds), *The Sage Handbook of Media Studies*, pp. 123–44. Thousand Oaks, CA: Sage.

Braman, S. and Roberts, S. (2003) 'Advantage ISP: terms of service as media law', *New Media and Society*, 5 (4): 522–48.

Bramson, L. (1961) *The Political Context of Sociology*. Princeton, NJ: Princeton University Press.

Brants, K. (1998) 'Who's afraid of infotainment?', *European Journal of Communication*, 13 (3): 315–36.

Brants, K. and Siune, K. (1998) 'Politicisation in decline', in D. McQuail and K. Siune (eds), *Media Policy*, pp. 128–43. London: Sage.

Breed, W. (1955) 'Social control in the newsroom: a functional analysis', *Social Forces*, 33: 326–55.

Breed, W. (1956) 'Analysing news: some questions for research', *Journalism Quarterly*, 33: 467–77.

Breen, M. (2007) 'Mass media and new media technologies', in E. Devereux (ed.), *Media Studies*, pp. 55–77. London: Sage.

Brodasson, T. (1994) 'The sacred side of professional journalism', *European Journal of Communication*, 9 (3): 227–48.

Brown, J.R. (ed.) (1976) *Children and Television*. London: Collier-Macmillan.

Brown, J.R. and Linné, O. (1976) 'The family as a mediator of television's effects', in J.R. Brown (ed.), *Children and Television*, pp. 184–98. London: Collier-Macmillan.

Brunsdon, C. (2000) *The Feminist, the Housewife and the Soap Opera*. Oxford: Oxford University Press.

Bryant, J. and Miron, D. (2002) 'Entertainment as media effect', in J. Bryant and D. Zillman (eds), *Media Effects: Advances in Theory and Research*, 2nd edn, pp. 549–82. Hillsdale, NJ: Erlbaum.

Bryant, J. and Zillmann, D. (eds) (1986) *Perspectives on Media Effects*. Hillsdale, NJ: Erlbaum.

Bryant, J. and Zillmann, D. (eds) (2002) *Media Effects: Advances in Theory and Research*, 2nd edn. Hillsdale, NJ: Erlbaum.

Buckingham, D. (2002) 'The electronic generation? Children and new media', in L. Lievrouw and S. Livingstone (eds), *The Handbook of New Media*, pp. 77–89. London: Sage.

Bucy, E.P. (2003) 'Media credibility between on-air and online news', *Journalism and Mass Communication Quarterly*, 80 (2): 274–84.

Burgelin, O. (1972) 'Structural analysis and mass communication', in D. McQuail (ed.), *Sociology of Mass Communications*, pp. 313–28. Harmondsworth: Penguin.

Burgelman, J.C. (2000) 'Regulating access in the information society: the need for rethinking public and universal service', *New Media and Society*, 2 (1): 51–66.

Burnett, R. (1990) *Concentration and Diversity in the International Phonogram Industry*. Gothenburg: University of Gothenburg.

Burnett, R. (1996) *The Global Jukebox*. London: Routledge.

Burns, T. (1969) 'Public service and private world', in P. Halmos (ed.), *The Sociology of Mass Media Communicators*, pp. 53–73. Keele: University of Keele.

Burns, T. (1977) *The BBC: Public Institution and Private World*. London: Macmillan.

Calvert, C. (1997) 'Free speech and its harms: a communication theory perspective', *Journal of Communication*, 47 (1): 1–19.

Cantor, M. (1971) *The Hollywood Television Producers*. New York: Basic Books.

Cantor, M. (1994) 'The role of the audience in the production of culture', in J.S. Ettema and D.C. Whitney (eds), *Audiencemaking*, pp. 159–70. Thousand Oaks, CA: Sage.

Cantor, J. (2002) 'Fright reactions to mass media', in J. Bryant and D. Zillmann (eds), *Media Effects*, pp. 287–306. Mahwah, NJ: Erlbaum.

Cantril, H., Gaudet, H. and Hertzog, H. (1940) *The Invasion from Mars*. Princeton, NJ: Princeton University Press.

Cappella, J.N. (2002) 'Cynicism and social trust in the new media environment', *Journal of Communication*, 52 (1): 229–41.

Cappella, J.N. and Jamieson, K.H. (1997) *The Spiral of Cynicism: the Press and the Public Good*. New York: Oxford University Press.

Carey, J.W. (1969) 'The communication revolution and the professional communicator', in P. Halmos (ed.), *The Sociology of Mass Media Communicators*, pp. 23–38. Keele: University of Keele.

Carey, J.W. (1975) 'A cultural approach to communication', *Communication*, 2: 1–22.

Carey, J.W. (1988) *Communication as Culture*. Boston: Unwin Hyman.

Carey, J.W. (1998) 'Marshall McLuhan: genealogy and legacy', *Canadian Journal of Communication*, 23: 293–306.

Carey, J.W. (2003) 'New media and TV viewing behaviour', *NHK Broadcasting Studies*, 2: 45–63.

Carlson, M. (2007) 'Order versus access: news search engines and the challenge to traditional journalistic roles, *Media, Culture and Society*, 29 (6): 1014–30.

Carlsson, U. (2003) 'The rise and fall of NWICO', *Nordicom Review*, 24 (2): 31–67.

Carlsson, U. and von Feilitzen, C. (eds) (1998) *Children, Media and Violence*. Paris: Unesco.

Carragee, K. and Roefs, W. (2004) 'The neglect of power in recent framing research', *Journal of Communication*, 54 (2): 214–33.

Cassidy, W.P. (2005) 'Variations on a theme: the professional role conceptions of print and online newspaper journalists', *Journalism and Mass Communication Quarterly*, 82 (2): 264–80.

Castello, E. (2007) 'The production of television fiction and nation-building', *European Journal of Communication*, 22 (1): 49–64.

Castells, M. (1996) *The Information Age*. Vol. I: *The Rise of the Network Society*. Oxford: Blackwell.

Castells, M. (2001) *The Internet Galaxy*. Oxford: Oxford University Press.

Castells, M. (2007) 'Communication power and counter power in the network society', *International Journal of Communication*, 1: 238–66.

Chadha, K. and Kavoori, A. (2005) 'Globalization and national media systems: mapping interactions in policies, markets and formats', in J. Curran and M. Gurevitch (eds), *Mass Media and Society*, 4th edn. pp. 84–103. London: Hodder Arnold.

Chaffee, S.H. (1975) 'The diffusion of political information', in S.H. Chaffee (ed.), *Political Communication*, pp. 85–128. Beverly Hills, CA: Sage.

Chaffee, S.H. (1981) 'Mass media effects: new research perspectives', in C.G. Wilhoit and H. de Back (eds), *Mass Communication Review Yearbook*, vol. 2, pp. 77–108. Beverly Hills, CA: Sage.

Chaffee, S.H. and Hochheimer, J.L. (1982) 'The beginnings of political communication research in the US: origins of the limited effects model', in E.M. Rogers and F. Balle (eds), *The Media Revolution in America and Europe*, pp. 263–83. Norwood, NJ: Ablex.

Chaffee, S.H. and Roser, C. (1986) 'Involvement and the consistency of knowledge, attitudes and behavior', *Communication Research*, 3: 373–99.

Chalaby, J. (2001) 'New media, new freedoms, new threats', *Gazette*, 62 (1): 19–29.

Chalaby, J. (2003) 'Television for a new global order', *Gazette*, 65 (6): 457–72.

Chang, T.-K., Himelboim, I., and Dong, D. (2009) 'Open global networks, closed international flows', *International Communication Gazette*, 71 (3): 137–59.

Chan-Olmstead, P. and Chang, B.-H. (2003) 'Diversification strategy of global media conglomerates', *Journal of Media Economics*, 16 (4): 213–33.

Chibnall, S. (1977) *Law and Order News*. London: Tavistock.

Christians, C. (1993) *Good News: Social Ethics and the Press*. New York: Oxford University Press.

Christians, C., Glasser, T., McQuail, D., Nordenstreng, K. and R. White (2009) *Normative Theory of the Press*. Urbana, IL: Illinois University Press.

Clark, T.N. (ed.) (1969) *On Communication and Social Influence: Collected Essays of Gabriel Tarde*. Chicago: Chicago University Press.

Clauson, R.A. and Trice, R. (2001) 'Poverty as we know it: media "portrayals" of the poor', *Public Opinion Quarterly*, 64: 53–64.

Clausse, R. (1968) 'The mass public at grips with mass communication', *International Social Science Journal*, 20 (4): 625–43.

Cohen, A. (2001) 'Between content and cognition: on the impossibility of television news', in K. Renckstorf, D. McQuail and N. Jankowski (eds), *Television News Research: Recent European Approaches and Findings*, pp. 185–98. Berlin: Quintessence.

Cohen, B. (1963) *The Press and Foreign Policy*. Princeton, NJ: Princeton University Press.

Cohen, E.L. (2002) 'Online journalism as market-driven journalism', *Journal of Broadcasting and Electronic Media*, 46 (4): 532–48.

Cohen, J. (2001) 'Defining identification: a theoretical look at the identification of audiences with media characters', *Mass Communication and Society*, 4 (3): 245–64.

Cohen, S. (1972) *Folk Devils and Moral Panics*. London: McGibbon and Kee.

Cohen, S. and Young, J. (eds) (1973) *The Manufacture of News*. London: Constable.

Coleman, S. (1999) 'The new media and democratic politics', *New Media and Society*, 1 (1): 67–74.

Coleman, S. (ed.) (2000) *Televised Election Debates: International Perspectives*. New York: St Martin's Press.

Coleman, S. (2001) 'The transformation of citizenship' in B. Axford and R. Huggins (eds), *New Media and Politics*, pp. 109–26. London: Sage.

Coleman, S. (2005) 'New mediation and direct representation: reconceptualizing representation in the digital age', *New Media and Society*, 7 (2): 177–98.

Collins, R. (2006) 'Internet governance in the UK', *Media, Culture and Society*, 28 (3): 337–58.

Collins, R. (2008) 'Hierarchy or homeostasis? Hierarchy, markets and networks in UK media and communications governance', *Media, Culture and Society*, 30 (3): 295–317.

Comstock, G. (ed.) (1988) *Public Communication and Behavior*. New York: Academic.

Comstock, G., Chaffee, S., Katzman, N., McCombs, M. and Roberts, D. (1978) *Television and Human Behavior*. New York: Columbia University Press.

Connell, I. (1998) 'Mistaken identities: tabloid and broadsheet news discourses', *The Public*, 5 (3): 11–31.

Conway, J.C. and Rubin, A.M. (1991) 'Psychological predictors of television viewing motivation', *Communication Research*, 18 (4): 443–63.

Cook, T.E. (2006) 'The news media as a political institution: looking backward and looking forward', *Political Communication*, 23 (2): 159–72.

Cooper, E. and Jahoda, M. (1947) 'The evasion of propaganda', *Journal of Psychology*, 23: 15–25.

Cottle, S. (ed.) (2003) *News, Public Relations and Power*. London: Sage.

Craft, J. and Wanta, W. (2004) 'Women in the newsroom: influences of female editors and news reporters on the news agenda', *Journalism and Mass Communication Quarterly*, 81 (1): 124–38.

Crogan, P. (2008) 'Targeting, television and networking', *Convergence*, 14 (4): 375–85.

Curran, J. (1990) 'The new revisionism in mass communication research: a reappraisal', *European Journal of Communication*, 5 (2/3): 135–64.

Curran, J., Douglas, A. and Whannel, G. (1981) 'The political economy of the human interest story', in A. Smith (ed.), *Newspapers and Democracy*, pp. 288–316. Cambridge, MA: MIT Press.

Curran, J., Iyengar, S., Lund, A.B. and Salovaara-Moring, I. (2009) 'Media system, public knowledge and democracy: a comparative study', *European Journal of Communication*, 24 (1): 5–26.

Curran, J. and Seaton, J. (1997) *Power without Responsibility*, 5th edn. London: Fontana.

Dahlberg, L. (2001) 'Democracy via cyberspace', *New Media and Society*, 3 (2): 157–77.

Dahlberg, L. (2004) 'Cyber-publics and corporate control of online communication', *Javnost*, 11 (2): 77–93.

Dahlgren, P. (1995) *Television and the Public Sphere*. London: Sage.

Dahlgren, P. (2001) 'The transformation of democracy' in B. Axford and R. Huggins (eds), *New Media and Politics*, pp. 64–88. London: Sage.

Dahlgren, P. (2005) 'The internet, public sphere and political communication', *Political Communication*, 22 (2): 147–62.

Dahlgren, P. and Sparks, C.S. (eds) (1992) *Journalism and Popular Culture*. London: Sage.

D'Alessio, D. (2003) 'An experimental examination of readers' perceptions of media bias', *Journalism and Mass Communication Quarterly*, 80 (2): 282–94.

D'Alessio, D. and Allen, M. (2000) 'Media bias in presidential elections: a meta-analysis', *Journal of Communication*, 50 (1): 133–56.

D'Angelo, P. (2002) 'News framing as a multiparadigmatic research programme: a response to Entman', *Journal of Communication*, 52 (4): 870–88.

Darnton, R. (1975) 'Writing news and telling stories', *Daedalus*, Spring: 175–94.

Davis, A. (2003) 'Public relations and news sources', in S. Cottle (ed.) *News, Public Relations and Power*, pp. 27–42. London: Sage.

Davis, D.K. (1999) 'Media as public arena' in R.C. Vincent and K. Nordenstreng (eds), *Towards Equity in Global Communication*. Cresskill, NJ: Hampton.

Davis, D.K. and Robinson, J.P. (1986) 'News story attributes and comprehension', in J.P. Robinson and M. Levy (eds), *The Main Source*, pp. 179–210. Beverly Hills, CA: Sage.

Davis, D.K. and Robinson, J.P. (1989) 'Newsflow and democratic society', in G. Comstock (ed.), *Public Communication and Behavior*, vol. 2. Orlando, FL: Academic.

Davison, W.P. (1983) 'The third person effect', *Public Opinion Quarterly*, 47 (1): 1–15.

Dayan, D. and Katz, E. (1992) *Media Events*. Cambridge, MA: Harvard University Press.

Deacon, D. (2007) 'Yesterdays news and todays technology', *European Journal of Communication*, 22 (1): 5–25.

Dearing, J.W. and Rogers, E.M. (1996) *Agenda-Setting*. Thousand Oaks, CA: Sage.

Dee, J.L. (1987) 'Media accountability for real-life violence: a case of negligence or free speech?', *Journal of Communication*, 38 (1): 106–32.

DeFleur, M.L. (1970) *Theories of Mass Communication*, 2nd edn. New York: McKay.

DeFleur, M.L. and Ball-Rokeach, S. (1989) *Theories of Mass Communication*, 5th edn. New York: Longman.

Delia, J.G. (1987) 'Communication research: a history', in S.H. Chaffee and C. Berger (eds), *Handbook of Communication Science*, pp. 20–98. Newbury Park, CA: Sage.

Deming, C.J. (1991) 'Hill Street Blues as narrative', in R. Avery and D. Eason (eds), *Critical Perspectives on Media and Society*, pp. 240–64. New York: Guilford Press.

de Mue, J. (1999) 'The informatization of the world view', *Information, Communication and Society*, 2 (1): 69–94.

Dennis, E., Gilmor, D. and Glasser, T. (eds) (1989) *Media Freedom and Accountability*. New York: Greenwood Press.

de Ridder, J. (1984) *Persconcentratie in Nederland*. Amsterdam: Uitgeverij.

de Saussure, F. (1915/1960) *Course in General Linguistics*. English trans. London: Owen.

Des Forges, A. (2002) 'Silencing the voices of hate in Rwanda', in M. Price and M. Thompson (eds), *Forging Peace*, pp. 236–58. Edinburgh: Edinburgh University Press.

de Smaele, H. (1999) 'The application of Western models to the Russian media system', *European Journal of Communication*, 14 (2): 173–89.

Deuze, M. (2002) 'National news cultures', *Journalism and Mass Communication Quarterly*, 79 (1): 134–49.

Deuze, M. (2003) 'The web and its journalisms', *New Media and Society*, 5 (4): 203–30.

Deuze, M. (2005) 'Popular journalism and professional ideology: tabloid reporters and editors speak out', *Media, Culture and Society*, 27 (6): 801–22.

Deuze, M. (2007) *Media Work*. Cambridge: Polity Press.

De Vreese, C. (2006) 'Media message flows and interpersonal communication', *Communication Research*, 33 (1): 19–37.

De Waal, E. and Schoenbach, K. (2008) 'Presentation style and beyond: how print newspapers and online news expand awareness of public affairs', *Mass Communication and Society*, 11 (2): 161–76.

Dimitrova, D.V., Kaid, L.L., Williams, A.P. and Trammell, K.D. (2005) 'War on the web: The immediate news framing of Gulf War II', *The Harvard International Journal of Press/Politics*, 10 (1): 22–44.

Dimmick, J. and Coit, P. (1982) 'Levels of analysis in mass media decision-making', *Communication Research*, 9 (1): 3–32.

Dimmick, J. and Rothenbuhler, E. (1984) 'The theory of the niche: quantifying competition among media industries', *Journal of Communication*, 34 (3): 103–19.

Docherty, T. (ed.) (1993) *Postmodernism*. New York: Harvester Wheatsheaf.

Domingo, D. and Heinonen, A. (2008) 'Weblogs and journalism: a typology to explore the blurring boundaries', *Nordicom Review*, 29 (1): 3–15.

Dominick, J.R., Wurtzel, A. and Lometti, G. (1975) 'TV journalism as show business: a content analysis of eyewitness news', *Journalism Quarterly*, 52: 213–18.

Donohew, L., Palmgreen, P. and Rayburn, J.D. (1987) 'Social and psychological origins of media use: a lifestyle analysis', *Journal of Broadcasting and Electronic Media*, 31 (3): 255–78.

Donohue, G.A., Tichenor, P. and Olien, C.N. (1975) 'Mass media and the knowledge gap', *Communication Research*, 2: 3–23.

Doob, A. and McDonald, G.E. (1979) 'Television viewing and the fear of victimization: is the relationship causal?', *Journal of Social Psychology and Personality*, 37: 170–9. Reprinted in G.C. Wilhoit and H. de Bock (eds), *Mass Communication Review Yearbook*, vol. 1, 1980, pp. 479–88. Beverly Hills, CA: Sage.

Dorfman, A. and Mattelart, A. (1975) *How to Read Donald Duck: Imperialist Ideology in the Disney Comic*. New York: International General.

Downes, F.J. and McMillan, S.J. (2000) 'Defining interactivity: a qualitative identification of key dimensions', *New Media and Society*, 2 (2): 157–79.

Downey, J. and Fenton, N. (2003) 'New media, counter publicity and the public sphere' *New Media and Society*, 5 (2): 185–202.

Downing, J. (2000) *Radical Media: Rebellious Communication and Social Movements*. Thousand Oaks, CA: Sage.

Downing, J.D. and Husband, C. (2005) *Ethnicity and Media*. London: Sage.

Dreier, P. (1982) 'The position of the press in the US power structure', *Social Problems*, 29 (3): 298–310.

Drotner, K. (1992) 'Modernity and media panics', in M. Skovmand and K. Schrøder (eds), *Media Cultures*, pp. 42–62. London: Routledge.

Drotner, K. (2000) 'Less is more: media ethnography and its limits', in I. Hagen and J. Wasko (eds), *Consuming Audiences?*, pp. 165–88. Cresskill, NJ: Hampton.

Druckman, J.M. (2005) 'Media matter: how newspapers and TV news cover the campaign and influence voters', *Political Communication*, 22 (4): 463–82.

Dupagne, M. and Waterman, D. (1998) 'Determinants of US TV fiction imports in West Europe', *Journal of Broadcasting and Electronic Media*, 42 (2): 208–20.

Dutton, W.H., Blumler, J.G. and Kraemar, K.L. (eds) (1986) *Wired Cities: Shaping the Future of Communications*. Boston: Chapman Hall.

Eastman, S.T. (1979) 'Uses of television and consumer lifestyles: a multivariate analysis', *Journal of Broadcasting*, 23 (3): 491–500.

Eastman, S.T. (1998) 'Programming theory under strain: the active industry and the active audience', in M.E. Roloff and G.D. Paulson (eds), *Communication Yearbook 21*, pp. 323–77. Thousand Oaks, CA: Sage.

Eco, U. (1977) *A Theory of Semiotics*. London: Macmillan.

Eco, U. (1979) *The Role of the Reader*. Bloomington, IN: University of Indiana Press.

Einsiedel, E. (1988) 'The British, Canadian and US pornography commissions and their use of social research', *Journal of Communication*, 38 (2): 108–21.

Eisenstein, E. (1978) *The Printing Press as an Agent of Change*, 2 vols. New York: Cambridge University Press.

Elliott, P. (1972) *The Making of a Television Series: a Case Study in the Production of Culture*. London: Constable.

Ellis, J. (1982) *Visible Fictions*. London: Routledge and Kegan Paul.

Elvestad, E. and Blekesaune, A. (2008) 'Newspaper readers in Europe: a multilevel study of individual and national differences', *European Journal of Communication*, 23 (4): 425–48.

Engwall, L. (1978) *Newspapers as Organizations*. Farnborough: Saxon House.

Enli, G. (2008) 'Redefining public service broadcasting', *Convergence*, 14 (1): 103–20.

Entman, R.M. (1989) *Democracy without Citizens: Media and the Decay of American Politics*. New York: Oxford University Press.

Entman, R.M. (1991) 'Framing US coverage of the international news: contrasts in narratives of the KAL and Iran air incidents', *Journal of Communication*, 41 (4): 6–27.

Entman, R.M. (1993) 'Framing: towards clarification of a fractured paradigm', *Journal of Communication*, 43 (4): 51–8.

Entman, R.M. (2005) 'Media and democracy without party competition', in J. Curran and M. Gurevitch (eds), *Mass Media and Society*, pp. 4th edn, 251–70. London: Hodder Arnold.

Entman, R.M. (2007) 'Framing bias: media in the distribution of power', *Journal of Communication*, 57 (1): 163–73.

Enzensberger, H.M. (1970) 'Constituents of a theory of the media', *New Left Review*, 64: 13–36. Also in D. McQuail (ed.), *Sociology of Mass Communications*, pp. 99–116. Harmondsworth: Penguin.

Ericson, R.V., Baranek, P.M. and Chan, J.B.L. (1987) *Visualizing Deviance*. Toronto: University of Toronto Press.

Esser, F., Reinemann, C. and Fan, D. (2000) 'Spin doctoring in British and German election campaigns', *European Journal of Communication*, 15 (2): 209–40.

Ettema, J. and Glasser, T. (1998) *Custodians of Conscience: Investigative Journalism and Public Virtue*. New York: Columbia.

Etzioni, A. (1961) *Complex Organizations*. Glencoe, IL: Free Press.

Eurobarometer No. 51 (1999). Brussels: The European Commission.

European Commission (1999) *Images of Women in the Media*. Luxembourg: European Commission.

European Journal of Communication (2007): (4). Special issue on the European Public Space.

Evans, J. (1999) 'Cultures of the visual', in J. Evans and S. Hall (eds), *Visual culture: a Reader*, pp. 11–19. London: Sage.

Fallows, J. (1996) *Breaking the News*. New York: Pantheon.

Febvre, L. and Martin, H.J. (1984) *The Coming of the Book*. London: Verso.

Feintuck, M. (1999) *Media Regulation, Public Interest and the Law*. Edinburgh: University of Edinburgh Press.

Fengler, S. (2003) 'Holding the news media accountable: a study of media reporters and media criticism in the US', *Journalism and Mass Communication Quarterly*, 80 (4): 818–32.

Fengler, S. and Russ-Mohl, S. (2008) 'Journalists and the information-attention markets: towards an economic theory of journalism', *Journalism*, 9 (6): 667–90.

Ferguson, M. (1983) *Forever Feminine: Women's Magazines and the Cult of Femininity*. London: Heinemann.

Ferguson, M. (1986) 'The challenge of neo-technological determinism for communication systems of industry and culture', in M. Ferguson (ed.), *New Communication Technologies and the Public Interest*, pp. 52–70. London: Sage.

Ferguson, M. (ed.) (1992) 'The mythology about globalization', *European Journal of Communication*, 7: 69–93.

Ferguson, M. and Golding, P. (eds) (1997) *Cultural Studies in Question*. London: Sage.

Ferguson, D.A. and Perse, E.M. (2000) 'The WWW as a functional alternative to television', *Journal of Broadcasting and Electronic Media*, 44 (2): 155–75.

Festinger, L.A. (1957) *A Theory of Cognitive Dissonance*. New York: Row Peterson.

Findahl, O. (2001) 'News in our minds', in K. Renckstorf, D. McQuail and N. Jankowski (eds), *Television News Research: Recent European Approaches and Findings*, pp. 111–28. Berlin: Quintessence.

Findahl, O. and Hoijer, B. (1981) 'Studies of news from the perspective of human comprehension', in G.C. Wilhoit and H. de Back (eds), *Mass Communication Review Yearbook*, vol. 2, pp. 393–403. Beverly Hills, CA: Sage.

Findahl, O. and Hoijer, B. (1985) 'Some characteristics of news memory and comprehension', *Journal of Broadcasting and Electronic Media*, 29 (4): 379–98.

Fink, E.J. and Gantz, W. (1996) 'A content analysis of three mass communication research traditions: social science; interpretive studies; and critical analysis', *Journalism and Mass Communication Quarterly*, 73 (1): 114–34.

Finn, S. (1997) 'Origins of media exposure: linking personality traits to TV, radio, print and film use', *Communication Research*, 24 (5): 507–29.

Fishman, J. (1980) *Manufacturing News*. Austin, TX: University of Texas Press.

Fishman, M. (1982) 'News and non-events: making the visible invisible', in J.S. Ettema and D.C. Whitney (eds), *Individuals in Mass Media Organizations*, pp. 219–40. Beverly Hills, CA: Sage.

Fiske, J. (1982) *Introduction to Communication Studies*. London: Methuen.

Fiske, J. (1987) *Television Culture*. London: Methuen.

Fiske, J. (1989) *Reading the Popular*. Boston: Unwin and Hyman.

Fiske, J. (1992) 'The cultural economy of fandom', in L. Lewis (ed.), *The Adoring Audience*, pp. 30–49. London: Routledge.

Fitzsimon, M. and McGill, L.T. (1995) 'The citizen as media critic', *Media Studies Journal*, Spring: 91–102.

Fjaestad, B. and Holmlov, P.G. (1976) 'The journalist's view', *Journal of Communication*, 2: 108–14.

Flanagan, A.J. and Metzger, M.J. (2000) 'Perceptions of Internet information credibility', *Journalism and Mass Communication Quarterly*, 77: 525–40.

Flanagan, A.J. and Metzger, M.J. (2007) 'Perceived credibility of web and web-based information', *New Media and Society*, 9 (2): 319–42.

Flegel, R.C. and Chaffee, S.H. (1971) 'Influences of editors, readers and personal opinion on reporters', *Journalism Quarterly*, 48: 645–51.

Foerstal, H.N. (2001) *From Watergate to Monicagate: Ten Controversies in Modern Journalism and Media*. Westport, CT: Greenwood Press.

Fortunati, L. (2005) 'Mediatizing the net and intermediatizing the media', *International Communication Gazette*, 67 (6): 29–44.

Frank, R.E. and Greenberg, B. (1980) *The Public's View of Television*. Beverly Hills, CA: Sage.

French, J.R.P. and Raven, B.H. (1953) 'The bases of social power', in D. Cartwright and A. Zander (eds), *Group Dynamics*, pp. 259–69. London: Tavistock.

Frick, F.C. (1959) 'Information theory', in S. Koch (ed.), *Psychology: a Study of a Science*, pp. 611–36. New York: McGraw-Hill.

Friedson, E. (1953) 'Communications research and the concept of the mass', *American Sociological Review*, 18 (3): 313–17.

Frissen, V. (1992) 'Trapped in electronic cages? Gender and new information technology', *Media, Culture and Society*, 14: 31–50.

Frith, S. (1981) *Sound Effects*. New York: Pantheon.

Fuchs, C. (2009) 'Information and communication technologies and society: a contribution to the critique of the political economy of the internet', *European Journal of Communication*, 24 (1): 69–87.

Gallagher, M. (1981) *Unequal Opportunities: the Case of Women and the Media*. Paris: Unesco.

Gallagher, M. (2003) 'Feminist media perspectives', in A.N. Valdivia (ed.), *A Companion to Media Studies*, pp. 19–39. Oxford: Blackwell.

Galtung, J. and Ruge, M. (1965) 'The structure of foreign news', *Journal of Peace Research*, 1: 64–90. Also in J. Tunstall (ed.), *Media Sociology*, pp. 259–98. London: Constable.

Gamble, A. and Watanabe, T. (2004) *A Public Betrayed*. Washington, DC: Regnery Publishing.

Gamson, W. and Modigliani, A. (1989) 'Media discourse and public opinion on nuclear power: a constructivist approach', *American Journal of Sociology*, 95: 1–37.

Gandy, O. (1982) *Beyond Agenda Setting*. Norwood, NJ: Ablex.

Gans, H.J. (1957) 'The creator–audience relationship in the mass media', in B. Rosenberg and D.M. White (eds), *Mass Culture*, pp. 315–24. New York: Free Press.

Gans, H.J. (1979) *Deciding What's News*. New York: Vintage.

Gasher, M. and Klein, R. (2007) 'Mapping the geography of on-line news', *Canadian Journal of Communication*, 33 (2): 193–211.

Gaziano, C. (1983) 'The "knowledge gap": an analytical review of media effects', *Communication Research*, 10 (4): 447–86.

Gaziano, C. (1989) 'Chain newspaper homogeneity and presidential endorsements 1971–1988', *Journalism Quarterly*, 66 (4): 836–45.

Gaziano, C. (1997) 'Forecast 2000: widening knowledge gaps', *Journalism and Mass Communication Quarterly*, 74 (2): 237–64.

Gaziano, C. and McGrath, K. (1987) 'Newspaper credibility and relationships of newspaper journalists to communities', *Journalism Quarterly*, 64 (2): 317–28.

Geiger, K. and Sokol, R. (1959) 'Social norms in watching television', *American Journal of Sociology*, 65 (3): 178–81.

Geraghty, C. (1991) *Women and Soap Operas*. Cambridge: Polity Press.

Gerbner, G. (1964) 'Ideological perspectives and political tendencies in news reporting', *Journalism Quarterly*, 41: 495–506.

Gerbner, G. (1969) 'Institutional pressures on mass communicators', in P. Halmos (ed.), *The Sociology of Mass Media Communicators*, pp. 205–48. Keele: University of Keele.

Gerbner, G. (1973) 'Cultural indicators: the third voice', in G. Gerbner, L. Gross and W. Melody (eds), *Communications Technology and Social Policy*, pp. 553–73. New York: Wiley.

Gerbner, G. and Gross, L. (1976) 'Living with television: the violence profile', *Journal of Communication*, 26 (2): 173–99.

Gerbner, G., Gross, L., Morgan, M. and Signorielli, N. (1984) 'The political correlates of TV viewing', *Public Opinion Quarterly*, 48: 283–300.

Gerbner, G., Gross, L., Morgan, M. and Signorielli, N. (2002) 'Growing up with television: cultivation processes' in J. Bryant and D. Zillmann (eds), *Media Effects*, pp. 19–42. Mahwah, NJ: Erlbaum.

Gerbner, G. and Marvanyi, G. (1977) 'The many worlds of the world's press', *Journal of Communication*, 27 (1): 52–66.

Giddens, A. (1991) *Modernity and Self-Identity*. Oxford: Polity Press.

Giddens, A. (1999) *Runaway World: How Globalisation is Shaping our Lives*. London: Profile Books.

Gieber, W. (1956) 'Across the desk: a study of 16 *Telegraph* editors', *Journalism Quarterly*, 33: 423–33.

Gieber, W. and Johnson, W. (1961) 'The City Hall beat: a study of reporter and source roles', *Journalism Quarterly*, 38: 289–97.

Giffard, C.A. (1989) *UNESCO and the Media*. White Plains, NY: Longman.

Gilboa, E. (2002) 'Global communication and foreign policy', *Journal of Communication*, 52 (4): 731–48.

Gilboa, E. (2005) 'The CNN effect: the search for a communication theory of international relations', *Political Communication*, 22 (1): 27–44.

Gitlin, T. (1978) 'Media sociology: the dominant paradigm', *Theory and Society*, 6: 205–53. Reprinted in G.C. Wilhoit and H. de Back (eds) (1981), *Mass Communication Review Yearbook*, vol. 2, pp. 73–122. Beverly Hills, CA: Sage.

Gitlin, T. (1980) *The Whole World Is Watching: Mass Media in the Making and Unmaking of the New Left*. Berkeley, CA: University of California Press.

Gitlin, T. (1989) 'Postmodernism: roots and politics', in I. Angus and S. Jhally (eds), *Cultural Politics in Contemporary America*, pp. 347–60. New York: Routledge.

Gitlin, T. (1997) 'The anti-political populism of cultural studies', in M. Ferguson and P. Golding (eds), *Cultural Studies in Question*, pp. 25–38. London: Sage.

Glasgow Media Group (1976) *Bad News*. London: Routledge and Kegan Paul.

Glasgow Media Group (1980) *More Bad News*. London: Routledge and Kegan Paul.

Glasgow Media Group (1985) *War and Peace News*. Milton Keynes: Open University Press.

Glasser, T.L. (1984) 'Competition among radio formats', *Journal of Broadcasting*, 28 (2): 127–42.

Glasser, T.L. (1986) 'Press responsibility and First Amendment values', in D. Eliott (ed.), *Responsible Journalism*, pp. 81–9. Newbury Park, CA: Sage.

Glasser, T.L. (ed.) (1999) *The Idea of Public Journalism*. New York: Guilford Press.

Glasser, T.L. (2009) 'Journalism and the second-order effect', *Journalism*, 2: 326–8.

Glasser, T.L. and Craft, S. (1997) 'Public journalism and the search for democratic ideals'. Stanford, CA: Stanford University Department of Communication.

Glasser, T.L., Awad, I. and Kim, J.W. (2009) 'The claims of multiculturalism and journalism's promise of diversity', *Journal of Communication*, 59 (1): 57–78.

Glenn, T.C., Sallot, L.M. and Curtin, P.A. (1997) 'Public relations and the production of news', in *Communication Yearbook 20*, pp. 111–15. Thousand Oaks, CA: Sage.

Glynn, C.J., Hayes, A.F. and Shanahan, J. (1997) 'Perceived support for one's opinion and willingness to speak out', *Public Opinion Quarterly*, 61 (3): 452–63.

Goff, P. (1999) *The Kosovo Wars and Propaganda*. Zurich: International Press Institute.

Goffman, E. (1974) *Frame Analysis: an Essay on the Organization of Experience*. New York: Harper and Row.

Goffman, E. (1976) *Gender Advertisements*. London: Macmillan.

Golding, P. (1977) 'Media professionalism in the Third World: the transfer of an ideology', in J. Curran, M. Gurevitch and J. Woollacott (eds), *Mass Communication and Society*, pp. 291–308. London: Arnold.

Golding, P. (1981) 'The missing dimensions: news media and the management of change', in E. Katz and T. Szecsk (eds), *Mass Media and Social Change*. London: Sage.

Golding, P. and Elliott, P. (1979) *Making the News*. London: Longman.

Golding, P. and Harris, P. (1998) *Beyond Cultural Imperialism*. London: Sage.

Golding, P. and Middleton, S. (1982) *Images of Welfare: Press and Public Attitudes to Poverty*. Oxford: Blackwell.

Golding, P. and Murdock, G. (1978) 'Theories of communication and theories of society', *Communication Research*, 5 (3): 339–56.

Golding, P. and van Snippenburg, L. (1995) 'Government communications and the media', in *Beliefs in Government*, vol. 30. London: Oxford University Press.

Goldstein, K. and Freedman, P. (2002) 'Lessons learned: campaign advertising in the 2000 elections', *Political Communication*, 19 (1): 5–28.

Goodhart, G.J., Ehrenberg, A.S.C. and Collins, M. (1975) *The Television Audience: Patterns of Viewing*. Westmead: Saxon House.

Gouldner, A. (1976) *The Dialectic of Ideology and Technology*. London: Macmillan.

Grabe, M.E., Karnhaus, R. and Yelyan, N. (2009) 'Informing citizens: how people with different levels of education process TV, newspaper and Web news', *Journal of Broadcasting and Electronic Media*, 53 (1): 90–111.

Grabe, M.E., Zhou, S., Lang, A. and Boll, P.D. (2000) 'Packaging TV news: the effects of tabloids on information processing and evaluative response', *Journal of Broadcasting and Electronic Media*, 44 (4): 581–98.

Grabe, M.E., Zhao, S. and Barnett, B. (2001) 'Explicating sensationalism in TV news: content and the bells and whistles of form', *Journal of Broadcasting and Electronic Media*, 45 (2): 635–55.

Graber, D. (1976a) 'Press and television as opinion resources in presidential campaigns', *Public Opinion Quarterly*, 40 (3): 285–303.

Graber, D. (1976b) *Verbal Behavior and Politics*. Urbana, IL: University of Illinois Press.

Graber, D. (1981) 'Political language', in D.D. Nimmo and D. Sanders (eds), *Handbook of Political Communication*, pp. 195–224. Beverly Hills, CA: Sage.

Graber, D. (1984) *Processing the News*. New York: Longman.

Graber, D. (1990) 'Seeing is remembering: how visuals contribute to TV news', *Journal of Communication*, 40 (3): 134–55.

Gramsci, A. (1971) *Selections from the Prison Notebooks*. London: Lawrence and Wishart.

Green, S. (1999) 'A plague on the panopticon: surveillance and power in the global information society', *Information, Communication and Society*, 2 (1): 26–44.

Greenberg, B.S. (1964) 'Person-to-person communication in the diffusion of a news event', *Journalism Quarterly*, 41: 489–94.

Greenberg, B.S. (ed.) (2002) *Communication and Terrorism: Public and Media Responses to 9/11*. Cresskill, NJ: Hampton.

Greenberg, B.S., Hofschire, L. and Lachlan, K. (2002) 'Diffusion, media use and interpersonal communication behavior', in B. Greenberg (ed.), *Communication and Terrorism: Public and Media Responses to 9/11*, pp. 3–16. Cresskill, NJ: Hampton.

Gringras, C. (1997) *The Laws of the Internet*. London: Butterworths.

Gripsrud, J. (1989) 'High culture revisited', *Cultural Studies*, 3 (2): 194–7.

Gripsrud, J. (2007) 'Television and the European public sphere', *European Journal of Communication*, 22 (4): 479–92.

Groebel, J. (1998) 'The UNESCO global study on media violence', in U. Carlsson and C. von Feilitzen (eds), *Children and Media Violence*, pp. 155–80. Göteborg: University of Göteborg.

Gronbeck, B.E. (2006) 'The USA Patriot Act: coming to terms with silenced voices', *Javnost*, 11 (2): 37–48.

Gross, L.P. (1977) 'Television as a Trojan horse', *School Media Quarterly*, Spring: 175–80.

Grossberg, L. (1989) 'MTV: swinging on the (postmodern) star', in I. Angus and S. Jhally (eds), *Cultural Politics in Contemporary Politics*, pp. 254–68. New York: Routledge.

Grossberg, L. (1991) 'Strategies of Marxist cultural interpretation in R. Avery and D. Easton (eds), *Critical Perspectives in Contemporary Politics*, pp. 254–68.

Grossberg, L., Wartella, E. and Whitney, D.C. (1998) *Media Making: Mass Media in a Popular Culture*. Thousand Oaks, CA: Sage.

Grossman, M.B. and Kumar, M.J. (1981) *Portraying the President*. Baltimore, MD: Johns Hopkins University Press.

Gumucio-Dagron, A. (2004) 'Alternative media', in J.D.H. Downing, D. McQuail, P. Schlesinger and E. Wartella (eds), *The Sage Handbook of Media Studies*, pp. 41–64. Thousand Oaks, CA: Sage.

Gunaratne, S.A. (2001) 'Paper, printing and the printing press', *Gazette*, 63 (6): 459–79.

Gunaratne, S.A. (2002) 'Freedom of the press: a world system perspective', *Gazette*, 64 (4): 342–69.

Gunaratne, S.A. (2005) *The Dao of the Press: a Humanocentric Theory*. Creskill, NJ: Hampton.

Gunter, B. (1987) *Poor Reception: Misunderstanding and Forgetting Broadcast News*. Hillsdale, NJ: Erlbaum.

Gunter, B. (1999) 'Television news and the audience in Europe', *The European Journal of Communication Research*, 24 (1): 5–38.

Gunter, B. and Winstone, P. (1993) *Public Attitudes to Television*. London: Libbey.

Gunther, A.C. (1998) 'The persuasive press inference: effects of the media on perceived public opinion', *Communication Research*, 25 (5): 486–504.

Gunther, A.C. and Christen, C.-T. (2002) 'Projection or persuasive press? Contrary effects of personal opinion and perceived news coverage on estimates of public opinion', *Journal of Communication*, 52 (1): 177–95.

Gunther, A.C. and Mugham, R. (2000) *Democracy and the Media*. Cambridge: Cambridge University Press.

Gurevitch, M., Bennet, T., Curran, J. and Woollacott, J. (eds) (1982) *Culture, Society and the Media*. London: Methuen.

Gurevitch, M. and Levy, M. (1986) 'Information and meaning: audience explanations of social issues', in J.P. Robinson and M. Levy (eds), *The Main Source*, pp. 159–75. Beverly Hills, CA: Sage.

Haas, T. and Steiner, L. (2006) 'Public journalism', *Journalism*, 7 (2): 238–54.

Habermas, J. (1962/1989) *The Structural Transformation of the Public Sphere*. Cambridge, MA: MIT Press.

Habermas, J. (2006) 'Political communication in media society: does democracy still enjoy an epistemic dimension? The impact of normative theory on empirical research', *Communication Theory*, 16 (4): 411–26.

Hachten, W.A. (1981) *The World News Prism: Changing Media, Changing Ideologies*. Ames, IA: Iowa State University Press.

Hackett, R.A. (1984) 'Decline of a paradigm? Bias and objectivity in news media studies', *Critical Studies in Mass Communication*, 1: 229–59.

Hafez, K. (2002) 'Journalism ethics revisited: a comparison of ethics codes in Europe, North Africa, the Middle East and Muslim Asia', *Political Communication*, 19 (3): 225–50.

Hagen, I. (1999) 'Slaves of the ratings tyranny? Media images of the audience', in P. Alasuutari (ed.), *Rethinking the Media Audience*, pp. 130–50. London: Sage.

Hagen, I. (2000) 'Modern dilemmas: TV audiences, time use and moral evaluation', in I. Hagen and J. Wasko (eds), *Consuming Audiences? Production and Reception in Media Research*, pp. 231–47. Cresskill, NJ: Hampton.

Halavais, A. (2000) 'National borders on the world wide web', *New Media and Society*, 2 (1): 7–28.

Halavais, A. (2009) *Search Engine Society*. Cambridge: Polity Press.

Hall, A. (2003) 'Reading realism: audiences' evaluations of the reality of media texts', *Journal of Communication*, 53 (4): 624–41.

Hall, S. (1974/1980) 'Coding and encoding in the television discourse', in S. Hall et al. (eds), *Culture, Media, Language*, pp. 197–208. London: Hutchinson.

Hall, S. (1977) 'Culture, the media and the ideological effect', in J. Curran et al. (eds), *Mass Communication and Society*, pp. 315–48. London: Arnold.

Hallin, D.C. (1992) 'Sound bite news: TV coverage of elections 1968–1988', *Journal of Communication*, 42 (2): 5–24.

Hallin, D.C. and Mancini, P. (1984) 'Political structure and representational form in US and Italian TV news', *Theory and Society*, 13 (40): 829–50.

Hallin, D.C. and Mancini, P. (2004) *Comparing Media Systems*. Cambridge: Cambridge University Press.

Halloran, J.D., Elliott, P. and Murdock, G. (1970) *Communications and Demonstrations*. Harmondsworth: Penguin.

Hamelink, C. (1983) *Cultural Autonomy in Global Communications*. Norwood, NJ: Ablex.

Hamelink, C. (1994) *The Politics of Global Communication*. London: Sage.

Hamelink, C. (1998) 'New realities in the politics of world communication', *The Public*, 5 (4): 71–4.

Hamelink, C. (2000) *The Ethics of Cyberspace*. London: Sage.

Handel, L. (1950) *Hollywood Looks at its Audience*. Urbana, IL: University of Illinois Press.

Hanitsch, T. (2007) 'Deconstructing journalism culture: toward a universal theory', *Communication Theory*, 17: 367–85.

Harcup, T. and O'Neill, D. (2001) 'What is news? Galtung and Ruge revisited', *Journalism Studies*, 2 (2): 261–79.

Hardt, H. (1979) *Social Theories of the Press: Early German and American Perspectives*. Beverly Hills, CA: Sage.

Hardt, H. (1991) *Critical Communication Studies*. London: Routledge.

Hardt, H. (2003) *Social Theories of the Press*, 2nd edn. Lanham, MD: Rowman and Littlefield.

Hargittai, E. (2004) 'Internet access and use in context', *New Media and Society*, 6 (1): 115–21.

Hargittai, E. and Hinnant, A. (2008) 'Digital inequality', *Communication Research*, 35 (5): 600–21.

Hargrave, A.M. and Livingstone, S. (2006) *Harm and Offence in Media Content*. Bristol: Intellect.

Hargrove, T. and Stempel, G.H. III (2002) 'Exploring reader interest in news', *Newspaper Research Journal*, 23 (4): 46–51.

Harris, N.G.E. (1992) 'Codes of conduct for journalists', in A. Belsey and R. Chadwick (eds), *Ethical Issues in Journalism*, pp. 62–76. London: Routledge.

Hartley, J. (1992) *The Politics of Pictures*. London: Routledge.

Hartman, P. and Husband, C. (1974) *Racism and Mass Media*. London: Davis Poynter.

Harvey, D. (1989) *The Condition of Postmodernity*. Oxford: Blackwell.

Hassan, R. (2008) *The Information Society*. Cambridge: Polity Press.

Hawkes, T. (1977) *Structuralism and Semiology*. London: Methuen.

Hawkins, R.P. and Pingree, S. (1983) 'TV's influence on social reality', in E. Wartella et al. (eds), *Mass Communication Review Yearbook*, vol. 4, pp. 53–76. Beverly Hills, CA: Sage.

Hebdige, D. (1978) *Subculture: the Meaning of Style*. London: Methuen.

Hedinsson, E. (1981) *Television, Family and Society: the Social Origins and Effects of Adolescent TV Use*. Stockholm: Almqvist and Wiksell.

Heeter, C. (1988) 'The choice process model', in C. Heeter and B.S. Greenberg (eds), *Cable Viewing*, pp. 11–32. Norwood, NJ: Ablex.

Heinderyckx, F. (1993) 'TV news programmes in West Europe: a comparative study', *European Journal of Communication*, 8 (4): 425–50.

Held, V. (1970) *The Public Interest and Individual Interests*. New York: Basic Books.

Hellman, H. (2001) 'Diversity: an end in itself?', *European Journal of Communication Research*, 16 (2): 281–308.

Hellsten, I., Leydesdorp, L. and Wouters, P. (2006) 'Multiple presents: how search engines rewrite the past', *New Media and Society*, 8 (6): 901–24.

Hemánus, P. (1976) 'Objectivity in news transmission', *Journal of Communication*, 26: 102–7.

Herman, E. (2000) 'The propaganda model: a retrospective', *Journalism Studies*, 1 (1): 101–11.

Herman, E. and Chomsky, N. (1988) *Manufacturing Consent: the Political Economy of Mass Media*. New York: Pantheon.

Hermes, J. (1995) *Reading Women's Magazines*. Cambridge: Polity Press.

Hermes, J. (1997) 'Gender and media studies: no woman, no cry', in J. Corner, P. Schlesinger and R. Silverstone (eds), *International Media Research*, pp. 65–95. London: Routledge.

Hermes, J. (1999) 'Media figures in identity construction', in P. Alasuutari (ed.), *Rethinking the Media Audience*, pp. 69–85. London: Sage.

Hermes, J. (2007) 'Media representations of social structure: gender', in E. Devereux (ed.), *Media Studies*, pp. 191–210. London: Sage.

Herrscher, R.A. (2002) 'A universal code of journalism ethics: problems, limitations and purposes', *Journal of Mass Media Ethics*, 17 (4): 277–89.

Herzog, H. (1944) 'What do we really know about daytime serial listeners?', in P.F. Lazarsfeld (ed.), *Radio Research 1942–3*, pp. 2–23. New York: Duell, Sloan and Pearce.

Hessler, R.C. and Stipp, H. (1985) 'The impact of fictional suicide stories on US fatalities: a replication', *American Journal of Sociology*, 90 (1): 151–67.

Hetherington, A. (1985) *News, Newspapers and Television*. London: Macmillan.

Hills, J. (2002) *The Struggle for the Control of Global Communication*. Urbana, IL: University of Illinois Press.

Himmelweit, H.T., Vince, P. and Oppenheim, A.N. (1958) *Television and the Child*. London: Oxford University Press.

Hindman, D.B. and Wiegand, K. (2008) 'The Big Three's prime time decline', *Journal of Broadcasting and Electronic Media*, 52 (1): 119–35.

Hirsch, P.M. (1977) 'Occupational, organizational and institutional models in mass communication', in P.M. Hirsch et al. (eds), *Strategies for Communication Research*, pp. 13–42. Beverly Hills, CA: Sage.

Hirsch, P.M. (1980) 'The "scary world" of the non-viewer and other anomalies: a reanalysis of Gerbner et al.'s findings in cultivation analysis, Part 1', *Communication Research*, 7 (4): 403–56.

Hirsch, P.M. (1981) 'On not learning from one's mistakes, Part II', *Communication Research*, 8 (1): 3–38.

Hjarvard, S. (2008) '"The mediatization of society": a study of media as agents of social and cultural change', *Nordicom Review*, 29 (1): 105–34.

Hobson, D. (1982) *Crossroads: the Drama of Soap Opera*. London: Methuen.

Hobson, D. (1989) 'Soap operas at work', in F. Seiter et al. (eds), *Remote Control*, pp. 130–49. London: Routledge.

Hocking, W.E. (1947) *Freedom of the Press: a Framework of Principle*. Chicago: University of Chicago Press.

Hodges, L.W. (1986) 'Defining press responsibility: a functional approach', in D. Elliot (ed.), *Responsible Journalism*, pp. 13–31. Beverly Hills, CA: Sage.

Hoffmann-Riem, W. (1996) *Regulating Media*. London: Guilford Press.

Hoffner, C.H., Plotkin, R.S. et al. (2001) 'The third-person effects in perceptions of the influence of TV violence', *Journal of Communication*, 51 (2): 383–99.

Hoijer, B. (2000) 'Audiences' expectations and interpretations of different TV genres', in I. Hagen and J. Wasko (eds), *Consuming Audiences? Production and Reception in Media Research*, pp. 189–208. Cresskill, NJ: Hampton.

Hoijer, B. (2008) 'Ontological assumptions and generalization in qualitative (audience) research', *European Journal of Communication*, 23 (3): 275–94.

Holden, R.T. (1986) 'The contagiousness of aircraft hijacking', *American Journal of Sociology*, 91 (4): 876–904.

Holub, R. (1984) *Reception Theory*. London: Methuen.

Horsti, K. (2003) 'Global mobility and the media: presenting asylum seekers as a threat', *Nordicom Review*, 24 (1): 41–54.

Horton, D. and Wohl, R.R. (1956) 'Mass communication and parasocial interaction', *Psychiatry*, 19: 215–29.

Horvath, C.W. (2004) 'Measuring TV addiction', *Journal of Broadcasting and Electronic Media*, 48 (3): 378–98.

Hoskins, C. and Mirus, R. (1988) 'Reasons for the US dominance of the international trade in television programmes', *Media, Culture and Society*, 10: 499–515.

Hovland, C.I., Lumsdaine, A.A. and Sheffield, F.D. (1949) *Experiments in Mass Communication*. Princeton, NJ: Princeton University Press.

Huaco, G.A. (1963) *The Sociology of Film Art*. New York: Basic Books.

Huesca, R. (2003) 'From modernization to participation: the past and future of development communication in media studies', in A.N. Valdivia (ed.), *A Companion to Media Studies*, pp. 50–71. Oxford: Blackwell.

Huesmann, L.R. (1986) 'Psychological processes prompting the relation between exposure to media violence and aggressive behavior by the viewer', *Journal of Social Issues*, 42 (3): 125–39.

Hughes, H.M. (1940) *News and the Human Interest Story*. Chicago: University of Chicago Press.

Hughes, M. (1980) 'The fruits of cultivation analysis: a re-examination of some effects of TV viewing', *Public Opinion Quarterly*, 44 (3): 287–302.

Hutchins, R. (1947) Commission on Freedom of the Press. *A Free and Responsible Press*. Chicago: University of Chicago Press.

Innis, H. (1950) *Empire and Communication*. Oxford: Clarendon Press.

Innis, H. (1951) *The Bias of Communication*. Toronto: University of Toronto Press.

Iosifides, P. (2002) 'Digital convergence: challenges for European regulation', *The Public*, 9 (3): 27–48.

Isfati, Y. and Cappella, J.N. (2003) 'Do people watch what they do not trust? Exploring the association between news media, skepticism and exposure', *Communication Research*, 30 (5): 504–29.

Ishikawa, S. (ed.) (1996) *Quality Assessment of Television*. Luton: Luton University Press.

Ito, Y. (1981) 'The "Johoka Shakai" approach to the study of communication in Japan', in G.C. Wilhoit and H. de Bock (eds), *Mass Communication Review Yearbook*, vol. 2. Beverly Hills, CA: Sage.

Ito & Kochevar, I.J. (1983) 'Factors accounting for the flow of international communications', *Keio Communication Review*, 4: 13–38.

Iyengar, S. (1991) *Is Anyone Responsible?* Chicago: University of Chicago Press.

Iyengar, S. and Kinder, D.R. (1987) *News That Matters: Television and American Opinion*. Chicago: University of Chicago Press.

Iyengar, S. and Simon, A. (1997) 'News coverage of the Gulf crisis and public opinion', in S. Iyengar and R. Reeves (eds), *Do the Media Govern?*, pp. 248–57. Thousand Oaks, CA: Sage.

Iyengar, S., Hahn, K.S., Bonfadelli, H. and Marr, M. (2009) '"Dark areas of ignorance" revisited: comparing international affairs knowledge in Switzerland and the United States', *Communication Research,* 36 (3): 341–58.

Jackson, C., Brown, J.D. and Parden, C.J. (2008) 'A TV in the bedroom: implications for viewing habits and risk behaviors', *Journal of Broadcasting and Electronic Media*, 52 (3): 349–67.

Jakubovicz, K. (2007) 'The Eastern European/post communist media model countries', in G. Terzis (ed.), *European Media Governance*, pp. 303–14. Bristol: Intellect.

Jameson, F. (1984) 'Postmodernism: the cultural logic of late capitalism', *New Left Review*, 146 (July–August): 53–92.

Jamieson, J.H. and Waldman, P. (2003) *The Press Effect*. New York: Basic Books.

Jamieson, P., Jamieson, K.H. and Romer, D. (2003) 'The responsible reporting of suicide in print journalism', *American Behavioral Scientist*, 46 (112): 1643–60.

Jankowski, N. (2002) 'Creating Community with media' in L. Lievrouw and S. Livingstone (eds), *The Handbook of New Media*, pp. 34–49. London: Sage.

Janowitz, M. (1952) *The Community Press in an Urban Setting*. Glencoe, IL: Free Press.

Janowitz, M. (1968) 'The study of mass communication', in *International Encyclopedia of the Social Sciences*, vol. 3, pp. 41–53. New York: Macmillan.

Janowitz, M. (1975) 'Professional models in journalism: the gatekeeper and advocate', *Journalism Quarterly*, 52 (4): 618–26.

Jansen, S.C. (1988) *Censorship*. New York: Oxford University Press.

Jay, M. (1973) *The Dialectical Imagination*. London: Heinemann.

Jenkins, H. (2004) *The Cultural Logic of Media Convergence.* New York: New York University Press.

Jenkins, H. and Deuze, M. (2008) 'Convergence culture', *Convergence*, 14 (1): 5–12.

Jensen, J. (1992) 'Fandom as pathology: the consequences of characterization', in L.A. Lewis (ed.), *The Adoring Audience*, pp. 9–23. London: Routledge.

Jensen, K.B. (1986) *Making Sense of the News*. Aarhus: Aarhus University Press.

Jensen, K.B. (1991) 'When is meaning? Communication theory, pragmatism and mass media reception', in J. Anderson (ed.), *Communication Yearbook 14*, pp. 3–32. Newbury Park, CA: Sage.

Jensen, K.B. (1998) 'Local empiricism, global theory: problems and potentials of comparative research on news reception', *The European Journal of Communication Research*, 23 (4): 427–45.

Jensen, K.B. (2001) 'Local empiricism, global theory: problems and potentials of comparative research on news reception', in K. Renckstorf, D. McQuail and N. Jankowski (eds), *Television News Research: Recent European Approaches and Findings*, pp. 129–47. Berlin: Quintessence.

Jensen, K.B. and Jankowski, N. (eds) (1991) *A Handbook of Qualitative Methodologies*. London: Routledge.

Jensen, K.B. and Rosengren, K.E. (1990) 'Five traditions in search of the audience', *European Journal of Communication*, 5 (2/3): 207–38.

Jhally, S. and Livant, B. (1986) 'Watching as working: the valorization of audience consciousness', *Journal of Communication*, 36 (2): 124–63.

Johansson, T. and Miegel, F. (1992) *Do the Right Thing*. Stockholm: Almqvist and Wiksell.

Johns, A. (1998) *The Nature of the Book*. Chicago: Chicago University Press.

Johnson, T.J. and Kaye, B.K. (2002) 'I heard it through the internet: examining factors that determine online credibility among politically motivated internet users', in A.V. Stavros (ed.), *Advances in Communications and Media Research*, vol. 1, pp. 181–202. Hauphage, NY: Nova.

Johnstone, J.W.L., Slawski, E.J. and Bowman, W.W. (1976) *The News People*. Urbana, IL: University of Illinois Press.

Jones, S.G. (ed.) (1997) *Virtual Culture: Identity and Communication in Cybersociety*. London: Sage.

Jones, S.G. (ed.) (1998) *Cybersociety 2.0: Revisiting Computer-Mediated Communication and Community*. London: Sage.

Jowett, G. and Linton, J.M. (1980) *Movies as Mass Communication*. Beverly Hills, CA: Sage.

Jowett, G. and O'Donnell, V. (1999) *Propaganda and Persuasion*, 3rd edn. Beverly Hills, CA: Sage.

Kahn, R. and Kellner, D. (2004) 'New media and Internet activism: from the battle of Seattle to Bloggery', *New Media and Society*, 6 (1): 87–95.

Kalyanaraman, S. and Sundar, S.S. (2008) 'Portrait of the portal as a metaphor: explicating web portals for communication research', *Journalism and Mass Communication Quarterly*, 65 (2): 239–56.

Kaminsky, S.M. (1974) *American Film Genres*. Dayton, OH: Pflaum.

Kaplan, E.A. (1987) *Rocking Around the Clock: Music Television, Postmodernism and Consumer Culture*. London: Methuen.

Kaplan, E.A. (1992) 'Feminist critiques and television', in R.C. Allen (ed.), *Channels of Discourse Reassembled*, pp. 247–83. London: Routledge.

Karppingen, K. (2007) 'Against naïve pluralism in media politics: on implications of radical-pluralist approach to the public sphere', *Media, Culture and Society*, 29 (3): 495–508.

Katz, D. (1960) 'The functional approach to the study of attitudes', *Public Opinion Quarterly*, 24: 163–204.

Katz, E. (1977) *Social Research and Broadcasting: Proposals for Further Development*. London: BBC.

Katz, E. (1983) 'Publicity and pluralistic ignorance: notes on the spiral of silence', in E. Wartella et al. (eds), *Mass Communication Review Yearbook*, vol. 4, pp. 89–99. Beverly Hills, CA: Sage.

Katz, E., Adoni, H. and Parness, P. (1977) 'Remembering the news: what the picture adds to the sound', *Journalism Quarterly*, 54: 231–9.

Katz, E., Blumler, J.G. and Gurevitch, M. (1974) 'Utilization of mass communication by the individual', in J.G. Blumler and E. Katz (eds), *The Uses of Mass Communication*, pp. 19–32. Beverly Hills, CA: Sage.

Katz, E., Gurevitch, M. and Haas, H. (1973) 'On the use of mass media for important things', *American Sociological Review*, 38: 164–81.

Katz, E. and Lazarsfeld, P.F. (1955) *Personal Influence*. Glencoe, IL: Free Press.

Katz, E., Lewin, M.L. and Hamilton, H. (1963) 'Traditions of research on the diffusion of innovations', *American Sociological Review*, 28: 237–52.

Katz, J.E. and Rice, R.E. (2002) *Social Consequences of Internet Use: Access, Involvement and Interaction*. Cambridge, MA: MIT Press.

Kaye, B.K. and Johnson, T.J. (2002) 'Online and in the know: uses and gratifications of the web for political information', *Journal of Broadcasting and Electronic Media*, 46 (1): 54–71.

Kellner, D. (1992) *The Persian Gulf War*. Boulder, CO: Westview.

Kelman, H. (1961) 'Processes of opinion change', *Public Opinion Quarterly*, 25: 57–78.

Kepplinger, H.M. (1983) 'Visual biases in TV Campaign coverage', in E. Wartella et al. (eds), *Mass Communication Review Yearbook*, vol. 4, pp. 391–405. Beverly Hills, CA: Sage.

Kepplinger, H.M. (1999) 'Non-verbal communication', in H.-B. Brosius and C. Holtz-Bacha (eds), *The German Communication Yearbook*. Cresskill, NJ: Hampton.

Kepplinger, H.M. (2002) 'Mediatization of politics: theory and data', *Journal of Communication*, 52 (4): 972–86.

Kepplinger, H.M. and Habermeier, J. (1995) 'The impact of key events on the presentation of reality', *European Journal of Communication*, 10 (3): 371–90.

Kepplinger, H.M. and Koecher, R. (1990) 'Professionalism in the media world?', *European Journal of Communication*, 5 (2/3): 285–311.

Kerner, O. et al. (1968) *Report of the National Advisory Committee on Civil Disorders*. Washington, DC: Government Printing Office.

Kingsbury, S.M. and Hart, M. (1937) *Newspapers and the News*. New York: Putnam.

Kiousis, S. (2001) 'Public trust or mistrust? Perceptions of media credibility in the information age', *Mass Communication and Society*, 4 (4): 381–403.

Kiousis, S. (2002) 'Interactivity: a concept explication', *New Media and Society*, 4 (3): 329–54.

Kitzinger, J. (2007) 'Framing and frame analysis' in E. Devereux, E. (ed) *Media Studies*, pp. 134–61.

Klaehn, J. (2002) 'A critical review and assessment of Herman and Chomsky's "Propaganda Model"', *European Journal of Communication*, 17 (2): 147–82.

Klapper, J. (1960) *The Effects of Mass Communication*. New York: Free Press.

Klotz, R.J. (2004) *The Politics of the Internet*. Lanham MD: Rowman and Littlefield.

Knight, A., Geuze, C. and Gerlis, A. (2008) 'Who is a journalist?', *Journalism Studies*, 9 (1): 117–31.

Knobloch, S. and Zillmann, D. (2002) 'Mood management via the digital juke box', *Journal of Communication*, 52 (2): 351–66.

Kracauer, S. (1949) 'National types as Hollywood represents them', *Public Opinion Quarterly*, 13: 53–72.

Kraus, S. and Davis, D.K. (1976) *The Effects of Mass Communication on Political Behavior*. University Park, PA: Pennsylvania State University Press.

Kraus, S., Davis, D.K., Lang, G.E. and Lang, K. (1975) 'Critical events analysis', in S.H. Chaffee (ed.), *Political Communication Research*, pp. 195–216. Beverly Hills, CA: Sage.

Kramar, M. (1996) 'Family communication patterns, discourse behavior and child TV viewing', *Human Communication Research*, 23 (2): 251–77.

Krcmar, M. and Vierig, E.V. (2005) 'Imitating life, imitating television', *Communication Research*, 32 (3): 267–94.

Krippendorf, K. (2004) *Content Analysis*, 2nd edn. Thousand Oaks, CA: Sage.

Krotz, F. and von Hasebrink, U. (1998) 'The analysis of people-meter data: individual patterns of viewing behavior and viewers' cultural background', *The European Journal of Communication Research*, 23 (2): 151–74.

Krugman, H.E. (1965) 'The impact of television advertising: learning without involvement', *Public Opinion Quarterly*, 29: 349–56.

Kubey, R.W. and Csikszentmihalyi, M. (1991) *Television and the Quality of Life*. Hillsdale, NJ: Erlbaum.

Kuhn, M. (2007) 'Interactivity and prioritizing the human: a code of blogging ethics', *Journal of Mass Media Ethics*, 22 (1): 18–36.

Kumar, C. (1975) 'Holding the middle ground', *Sociology*, 9 (3): 67–88. Reprinted in J. Curran et al. (eds), *Mass Communication and Society*, pp. 231–48. London: Arnold.

Küng, L., Picard, R.G. and Towse, R. (eds) (2008) *The Internet and the Mass Media*. London: Sage.

Lacy, S. and Martin, H.J. (2004) 'Competition, circulation and advertising', *Newspaper Research Journal*, 25 (1): 18–39.

Laitila, T. (1995) 'Journalistic codes of ethics in Europe', *European Journal of Communication*, 10 (4): 513–26.

Lang, G. and Lang, K. (1981) 'Mass communication and public opinion: strategies for research', in M. Rosenberg and R.H. Turner (eds), *Social Psychology: Sociological Perspectives*, pp. 653–82. New York: Basic Books.

Lang, G. and Lang, K. (1983) *The Battle for Public Opinion*. New York: Columbia University Press.

Lang, K. and Lang, G.E. (1953) 'The unique perspective of television and its effect', *American Sociological Review*, 18 (1): 103–12.

Langer, J. (2003) 'Tabloid television and news culture', in S. Cottle (ed.), *News, Public Relations and Power*, pp. 135–52. London: Sage.

Lanzen, M.M., Dozier, D.M. and Horan, N. (2008) 'Constructing gender stereotypes through social roles in prime time TV', *Journal of Broadcasting and Electronic Media*, 52 (2): 200–14.

LaRose, R. and Eastin, M.S. 'A social cognitive theory of internet uses and gratifications: towards a new model of media attendance', *Journal of Broadcasting and Electronic Media*, 48 (3): 358–77.

Lasswell, H. (1927) *Propaganda Techniques in the First World War*. New York: Knopf.

Lasswell, H. (1948) 'The structure and function of communication in society', in L. Bryson (ed.), *The Communication of Ideas*, pp. 32–51. New York: Harper & Row.

Lauristin, M. (2007) 'The European public sphere and the social imaginary of the "New Europe"', *European Journal of Communication*, 22 (4): 397–412.

Lazarsfeld, P.F. (1941) 'Remarks on administrative and critical communication research studies', *Philosophy and Social Science*, IX (2).

Lazarsfeld, P.F., Berelson, B. and Gaudet, H. (1944) *The People's Choice*. New York: Duell, Sloan and Pearce.

Lazarsfeld, P.F. and Stanton, F. (1944) *Radio Research 1942–3*. New York: Duell, Sloan and Pearce.

Lazarsfeld, P.F. and Stanton, F. (1949) *Communication Research 1948–9*. New York: Harper & Row.

Lehmann, I.A. (2005) 'Exploring the transatlantic divide over Iraq', *The Harvard International Journal of Press/Politics'*, 10 (1): 63–89.

Lehmann-Wilzig, S. and Cohen-Avigdor, N. (2004) 'The natural life cycle of new media evolution', *New Media and Society*, 6 (6): 707–30.

Leiss, W. (1989) 'The myth of the information society', in I. Angus and S. Jhally (eds), *Cultural Politics in Contemporary America*, pp. 282–98. New York: Routledge.

Lemert, J.B. (1989) *Criticizing the Media*. Newbury Park, CA: Sage.

Lerner, D. (1958) *The Passing of Traditional Society*. New York: Free Press.

Lessig, L. (1999) *Code and Other Laws of Cyberspace*. New York: Basic Books.

Levy, M.R. (1977) 'Experiencing television news', *Journal of Communication*, 27: 112–17.

Levy, M.R. (1978) 'The audience experience with television news', *Journalism Monographs*, 55.

Levy, M.R. and Windahl, S. (1985) 'The concept of audience activity', in K.E. Rosengren et al. (eds), *Media Gratification Research*, pp. 109–22. Beverly Hills, CA: Sage.

Lewis, G.H. (1981) 'Taste cultures and their composition: towards a new theoretical perspective', in E. Katz and T. Szecskö (eds), *Mass Media and Social Change*, pp. 201–17. Newbury Park, CA: Sage.

Lewis, G.H. (1992) 'Who do you love? The dimensions of musical taste', in J. Lull (ed.), *Popular Music and Communication*, 2nd edn, pp. 134–51. Newbury Park, CA: Sage.

Lichtenberg, J. (1991) 'In defense of objectivity', in J. Curran and M. Gurevitch (eds), *Mass Media and Society*, pp. 216–31. London: Arnold.

Lichter, S.R. and Rothman, S. (1986) *The Media Elite: America's New Power Brokers*. Bethesda, MD: Adler and Adler.

Liebes, T. and Katz, E. (1986) 'Patterns of involvement in television fiction: a comparative analysis', *European Journal of Communication*, 1 (2): 151–72.

Liebes, T. and Katz, E. (1990) *The Export of Meaning: Cross-Cultural Readings of 'Dallas'*. Oxford: Oxford University Press.

Liebes, T. and Livingstone, S. (1998) 'European soap operas', *European Journal of Communication*, 13 (2): 147–80.

Liebes, T. and Riback, R. (1994) 'In defense of negotiated readings: how moderates on each side of the conflict interpret Intifada news', *Journal of Communication*, 44 (2): 108–24.

Lievrouw, L.A. (2004) 'What's changed about new media?', *New Media and Society*, 6 (1): 9–15.

Lievrouw, L.A. and Livingstone, S. (eds) (2002) *The Handbook of New Media*. London: Sage.

Lievrouw, L.A. and Livingstone, S. (eds) (2006) *The Handbook of New Media*, 2nd edn. London: Sage.

Lind, R.A. and Salo, C. (2002) 'The framing of feminists and feminism in news and public affairs programs in US electronic media', *Journal of Communication*, 52 (1): 211–28.

Lindlof, T.R. (1988) 'Media audiences as interpretive communities', in J. Anderson (ed.), *Communication Yearbook 11*, pp. 81–107. Newbury Park, CA: Sage.

Lindlof, T.R. and Schatzer, J. (1998) 'Media ethnography in virtual space: strategies, limits and possibilities', *Journal of Broadcasting and Electronic Media*, 42 (2): 170–89.

Linné, O. (1998) 'What do we know about European research on violence in the media?', in U. Carlsson and C. von Feilitzen (eds), *Children and Media Violence*, pp. 139–54. Göteborg: University of Göteborg.

Lippmann, W. (1922) *Public Opinion*. New York: Harcourt Brace.

Livingstone, S. (1988) 'Why people watch soap opera: an analysis of the explanations of British viewers', *European Journal of Communication*, 31 (1): 55–80.

Livingstone, S. (1999) 'New media, new audiences?', *New Media and Society*, 1 (1): 59–66.

Livingstone, S. (2002) *Young People and New Media*. London: Sage.

Livingstone, S. (2003) 'The changing nature of audiences: from the mass audience to the interactive media user', in A.N. Valdivia (ed.), *A Companion to Media Studies*, pp. 337–59. Oxford: Blackwell.

Livingstone, S. (2007) 'From family television to bedroom culture: young people's media at home', in E. Devereux (ed.), *Media Culture*, pp. 302–21. London: Sage.

Livingstone, S. (2009) 'On the mediation of everything', *Journal of Communication*, 59 (1): 1–18.

Livingstone, S. and Bennett, W.L. (2003) 'Gatekeeping, indexing and live-event news: is technology altering the construction of news?', *Political Communication*, 20 (4): 363–80.

Livingstone, S. and Lunt, P. (1994) *Talk on Television: Audience Participation and Public Debate*. London: Routledge.

Long, E. (1991) 'Feminism and cultural studies', in R. Avery and D. Eason (eds), *Cultural Perspectives on Media and Society*, pp. 114–25. New York: Guilford Press.

Lowery, S.A. and DeFleur, M.L. (eds) (1995) *Milestones in Mass Communication Research*, 3rd edn. New York: Longman.

Lowry, D.J., Nio, T.C.J. and Leitner, D.W. (2003) 'Setting the public fear agenda', *Journal of Communication*, 53 (1): 61–7.

Lubbers, M., Scheeper, P. and Wester, F. (1998) 'Minorities in Dutch newspapers 1990–5', *Gazette*, 60 (5): 415–31.

Lüders, M. (2008) 'Conceptualizing personal media', *New Media and Society*, 10 (5): 683–702.

Luhmann, N. (2000) *The Reality of the Mass Media*. Cambridge: Polity Press.

Lull, J. (1982) 'The social uses of television', in D.C. Whitney et al. (eds), *Mass Communication Review Yearbook*, vol. 3, pp. 397–409. Beverly Hills, CA: Sage.

Lull, J. (ed.) (1992) *Popular Music and Communication*. Newbury Park, CA: Sage.

Lull, J. and Wallis, R. (1992) 'The beat of Vietnam', in J. Lull (ed.), *Popular Music and Communication*, pp. 207–36. Newbury Park, CA: Sage.

Lyotard, F. (1986) *The Postmodern Condition: a Report on Knowledge*. Manchester: Manchester University Press.

McBride, S. et al. (1980) *Many Voices, One World*. Report by the International Commission for the Study of Communication Problems. Paris: Unesco; London: Kogan Page.

McChesney, R. (2000) *Rich Media, Poor Democracy*. New York: New Press.

McCombs, M.E. and Shaw, D.L. (1972) 'The agenda-setting function of the press', *Public Opinion Quarterly*, 36: 176–87.

McCombs, M.E. and Shaw, D.L. (1993) 'The evolution of agenda-setting theory: 25 years in the marketplace of ideas', *Journal of Communication*, 43 (2): 58–66.

McCormack, T. (1961) 'Social theory and the mass media', *Canadian Journal of Economics and Political Science*, 4: 479–89.

McCoy, M.E. (2001) 'Dark alliance: news repair and institutional authority in the age of the Internet', *Journal of Communication*, 1 (1): 164–93.

McDevitt, M. (2003) 'In defence of autonomy: a critique of the public journalist critique', *Journalism of Communication*, 53 (1): 155–64.

McDonald, D.G. (1990) 'Media orientation and television news viewing', *Journalism Quarterly*, 67 (1): 11–20.

McDonald, D.G. and Dimmick, J. (2003) 'The conceptualization and measurement of diversity', *Communication Research*, 30 (1): 60–79.

McGinnis, J. (1969) *The Selling of the President*. New York: Trident.

McGranahan, D.V. and Wayne, L. (1948) 'German and American traits reflected in popular drama', *Human Relations*, 1 (4): 429–55.

McGuigan, J. (1992) *Cultural Populism*. London: Routledge.

McGuire, W.J. (1973) 'Persuasion, resistance and attitude change', in I. de Sola Pool et al. (eds), *Handbook of Communication*, pp. 216–52. Chicago: Rand McNally.

McGuire, W.J. (1974) 'Psychological motives and communication gratifications', in J.G. Blumler and E. Katz (eds), *The Uses of Mass Communications*, pp. 167–96. Beverly Hills, CA: Sage.

MacIntyre, J.S. (1981) *After Virtue*. Notre Dame, IN: Notre Dame University Press.

McLeod, D.M. and Detember, B.H. (1999) 'Framing effects of television news coverage of social protest', *Journal of Communication*, 49 (3): 3–23.

McLeod, D., Detember, B.H. and Eveland, W.P. (2001) 'Behind the third-person effect: differentiating perceptual process for self and other', *Journal of Communication*, 51 (4): 678–96.

McLeod, J.M. and McDonald, D.G. (1985) 'Beyond simple exposure: media orientations and their impact on political processes', *Communication Research*, 12 (1): 3–32.

McLeod, J.M., Daily, K., Guo, Z., Eveland, W.P., Bayer, J., Yang, S. and Wang, H. (1996) 'Community integration, local media use and democratic processes', *Communication Research*, 23 (2): 179–209.

McLeod, J.M., Kosicki, G.M. and Pan, Z. (1991) 'On understanding and not understanding media effects', in J. Curran and M. Gurevitch (eds), *Mass Media and Society*, pp. 235–66. London: Arnold.

McLuhan, M. (1962) *The Gutenberg Galaxy*. Toronto: Toronto University Press.

McLuhan, M. (1964) *Understanding Media*. London: Routledge and Kegan Paul.

McManus, J.H. (1994) *Market-Driven Journalism: Let the Citizen Beware*. Thousand Oaks, CA: Sage.

McMasters, P.K. (2000) 'Unease with excess', *Media Studies Journal*, Fall: 108–12.

McNair, B. (1988) *Images of the Enemy*. London: Routledge.

McQuail, D. (1977) *Analysis of Newspaper Content*. Royal Commission on the Press, Research Series 4. London: HMSO.

McQuail, D. (1983) *Mass Communication Theory: an Introduction*. London: Sage.

McQuail, D. (1984) 'With the benefit of hindsight: reflections on uses and gratifications research', *Critical Studies in Mass Communication*, 1: 177–93.

McQuail, D. (1992) *Media Performance: Mass Communication and the Public Interest*. London: Sage.

McQuail, D. (1997) *Audience Analysis*. Thousand Oaks, CA: Sage.

McQuail, D. (2003a) *Media Accountability and Freedom of Publication*. Oxford: Oxford University Press.

McQuail, D. (2003b) 'Making progress in a trackless, weightless and intangible space: a response to Keith Roe', *Communications*, 27: 275–84.

McQuail, D. (2006) 'The mediatization of war', *International Communication Gazette*, 68 (2): 107–118.

McQuail, D., Blumler, J.G. and Brown, J. (1972) 'The television audience: a revised perspective', in D. McQuail (ed.), *Sociology of Mass Communication*, pp. 135–65. Harmondsworth: Penguin.

McQuail, D. and Siune, K. (1998) *Media Policy: Convergence, Concentration and Commerce*. London: Sage.

McQuail, D. and Windahl, S. (1993) *Communication Models for the Study of Mass Communication*, 2nd edn. London: Longman.

McRobbie, A. (1996) '*More!* New sexualities in girls' and women's magazines', in J. Curran, D. Morley and V. Walkerdine (eds), *Cultural Studies and Communications*, pp. 172–94. London: Arnold.

Maccoby, E. (1954) 'Why do children watch TV?', *Public Opinion Quarterly*, 18: 239–44.

Machill, M., Beiler, M. and Zenker, M. (2008) 'Search-engine research: a European–American overview and systematization of an interdisciplinary and international research field', *Media, Culture and Society*, 30 (5): 591–608.

Machill, M., Kohler, S. and Waldhauser, M. (2007) 'The use of narrative structures in TV news', *European Journal of Communication*, 22 (2): 185–205.

Machlup, F. (1962) *The Production and Distribution of Knowledge in the United States*. Princeton, NJ: Princeton University Press.

Maisel, R. (1973) 'The decline of mass media', *Public Opinion Quarterly*, 37: 159–70.

Mancini, P. (1996) 'Do we need normative theories of journalism?' Paper, Joan Shorenstein Center on Press, Politics and Public Opinion, JFK School of Government, Harvard University.

Manheim, J.B. (1998) 'The news shapers: strategic communication as a third force in news-making', in D. Graber, D. McQuail and P. Norris (eds), *The Politics of News: the News of Politics*, pp. 94–109. Washington, DC: Congressional Quarterly Press.

Mansell, R. (2004) 'Political economy, power and the new media', *New Media and Society*, 6 (1): 96–105.

Marcuse, H. (1964) *One-Dimensional Man*. London: Routledge and Kegan Paul.

Martel, M.U. and McCall, G.J. (1964) 'Reality-orientation and the pleasure principle', in L.A. Dexter and D.M. White (eds), *People, Society and Mass Communication*, pp. 283–333. New York: Free Press.

Massey, B.L. and Haas, T. (2002) 'Does making journalism more public make a difference? A critical review of evaluative research on public journalism', *Journalism and Mass Communication Quarterly*, 79 (3): 559–86.

Matheson, D. (2004) 'Weblogs and the epistemology of the news: some trends in online journalism', *New Media and Society*, 6 (4): 443–68.

Mattelart, A. (2003) *The Information Society*. London: Sage.

Mazzoleni, G. (1987b) 'Media logic and party logic in campaign coverage: the Italian general election of 1983', *European Journal of Communication*, 2 (1): 55–80.

Media Studies Journal (1993) 'The media and women without apology', Special Issue, 7 (1/2).

Media Watch (1995) *Women's Participation in the News: Global Media Monitoring Project*. Toronto: Media Watch.

Melody, W.H. (1990) 'Communications policy in the global information economy', in M.F. Ferguson (ed.), *Public Communication: the New Imperatives*, pp. 16–39. London: Sage.

Mendelsohn, H. (1964) 'Listening to radio', in L.A. Dexter and D.M. White (eds), *People, Society and Mass Communication*, pp. 239–48. New York: Free Press.

Mendelsohn, H. (1966) *Mass Entertainment*. New Haven, CT: College and University Press.

Mermin, J. (1999) *Debating War and Peace: Media Coverage of US Interventions in the Post-Vietnam Era*. Princeton, NJ: Yale University Press.

Merton, R.K. (1949) 'Patterns of influence', in *Social Theory and Social Structure*, pp. 387–470. Glencoe, IL: Free Press.

Merton, R.K. (1957) *Social Theory and Social Structure*. Glencoe, IL: Free Press.

Messner, M. and Distow, M.W. (2008) 'The source cycle: how traditional media and weblogs use each other as sources', *Journalism Studies*, 9 (3): 447–63.

Metzger, M.J. et al. (2003) 'Credibility for the 21st century', in P.J. Kalbflesch (ed.), *Communication Yearbook 27*, pp. 292–335. Mahwah, NJ: Erlbaum.

Meyer, P. (1987) *Ethical Journalism*. New York: Longman.

Meyer, T. (2002) *Mediated Politics*. Cambridge: Polity Press.

Meyrowitz, J. (1985) *No Sense of Place*. New York: Oxford University Press.

Meyrowitz, J. (2008) 'Power, pleasure, patterns: intersecting narratives of media influence', *Journal of Communication*, 58 (4): 641–63.

Middleton, R. (ed.) (2000) *Reading Pop: Approaches to Textual Analysis in Popular Music*. Oxford: Oxford University Press.

Mill, J.S. (1991/1859) *On Liberty*. Oxford University Press.

Mills, C.W. (1951) *White Collar*. New York: Oxford University Press.

Mills, C.W. (1956) *The Power Elite*. New York: Oxford University Press.

Modleski, T. (1982) *Loving with a Vengeance: Mass-Produced Fantasies for Women*. London: Methuen.

Molotch, H.L. and Lester, M.J. (1974) 'News as purposive behavior', *American Sociological Review*, 39: 101–12.

Monaco, J. (1981) *How to Read a Film*. New York: Oxford University Press.

Montgomery, K.C. (1989) *Target: Prime-Time*. New York: Oxford University Press.

Moores, S. (1993) *Interpreting Audiences*. London: Sage.

Moorti, S. (2003) 'Out of India: Fashion culture and the marketing of ethnic style', in A.N. Valdivia (ed.), *A Companion to Media Studies*, pp. 293–310. Oxford: Blackwell.

Morgan, M. and Shanahan, J. (1997) 'Two decades of cultivation research: an appraisal and meta-analysis', *Communication Yearbook 20*, pp. 1–46.

Morley, D. (1980) *The 'Nationwide' Audience: Structure and Decoding*. BFI TV Monographs no. 11. London: British Film Institute.

Morley, D. (1986) *Family Television*. London: Comedia.

Morley, D. (1992) *Television, Audiences and Cultural Studies*. London: Routledge.

Morley, D. (1996) 'Postmodernism: the rough guide', in J. Curran, D. Morley and V. Walkerdine (eds), *Cultural Studies and Communication*, pp. 50–65. London: Arnold.

Morley, D. (1997) 'Theoretical orthodoxies: textualism, constructivism and the "new ethnography" in cultural studies', in M. Ferguson and P. Golding (eds), *Cultural Studies in Question*, pp. 121–37. London: Sage.

Morris, M. and Ogan, C. (1996) 'The internet as mass medium', *Journal of Communication*, 46 (1): 39–50.

Morrison, D. and Tumber, H. (1988) *Journalists at War*. London: Sage.

Morrison, D. and Svennevig, M. (2007) 'The defence of the public interest and the intrusion of privacy', *Journalism*, 8 (1): 44–65.

Moscovici, S. (1991) 'Silent majorities and loud minorities', in J. Anderson (ed.), *Communication Yearbook 14*, pp. 298–308. Newbury Park, CA: Sage.

Mowlana, H. (1985) *International Flows of Information*. Paris: Unesco.

Moy, P., Domke, D. and Stamm, K. (2001) 'The spiral of silence and public opinion on affirmative action', *Journalism and Mass Communication Quarterly*, 78 (1): 7–25.

Moy, P., Scheufele, D.A. and Holbert, R.L. (1999) 'TV use and social capital: testing Putnam's time displacement hypothesis', *Mass Communication and Society*, 2 (1/2): 27–46.

Moy, P., Torres, M., Tanaka, K. and McClusky, R. (2005) 'Knowledge or trust?' Investigating linkages between media reliance and participation', *Communication Research*, 32 (1): 59–86.

Munson, W. (1993) *All Talk: the Talkshow in Media Culture*. Philadelphia: University of Temple Press.

Murdock, G. (1990) 'Redrawing the map of the communication industries', in M. Ferguson (ed.), *Public Communication*, pp. 1–15. London: Sage.

Murdock, G. and Golding, P. (1977) 'Capitalism, communication and class relations', in J. Curran et al. (eds), *Mass Communication and Society*, pp. 12–43. London: Arnold.

Murdock, G. and Golding, P. (2005) 'Culture, communications and political economy', in J. Curran and M. Gurevitch (eds), *Mass Media and Society*, pp. 60–83. London: Hodder Arnold.

Murdock, G. and Phelps, P. (1973) *Mass Media and the Secondary School*. London: Macmillan.

Murphy, D. (1976) *The Silent Watchdog*. London: Constable.

Murray, C., Parry, K., Robinson, P. and Goddard, P. (2008) 'Reporting dissent in war-time', *European Journal of Communication*, 23 (1): 7–27.

Mutz, D.C. and Soss, J. (1997) 'Reading public opinion: the influence of news coverage on perceptions of public sentiment', *Public Opinion Quarterly*, 61 (3): 431–51.

Napoli, P.M. (2001) *Foundations of Communication Policy*. Creskill, NJ: Hampton.

Negus, K. (1992) *Producing Pop*. London: Arnold.

Nerone, J.C. (ed.) (1995) *Last Rights: Revisiting Four Theories of the Press*. Urbana, IL: University of Illinois Press.

Neuman, W.R. (1991) *The Future of the Mass Audience*. Cambridge: Cambridge University Press.

Neuman, W.R. and Pool, I. de Sola (1986) 'The flow of communication into the home', in S. Ball-Rokeach and M. Cantor (eds), *Media, Audience and Social Structure*, pp. 71–86. Newbury Park, CA: Sage.

Newbold, C. (2002) 'The moving image', in C. Newbold, O. Boyd-Barrett and H. van den Bulk (eds), *The Media Book*, pp. 101–62. London: Arnold.

Newcomb, H. (1991) 'On the dialogic aspects of mass communication', in R. Avery and D. Easton (eds), *Critical Perspectives on Media and Society*, pp. 69–87. New York: Guilford Press.

Newhagen, J.E. and Reeves, B. (1992) 'The evening's bad news', *Journal of Communication*, 42 (2): 25–41.

Newman, P. (2003) 'If only they knew what nice people we are', *Political Communication*, 20 (1): 79–85.

Nightingale, V. (2003) 'The cultural revolution in audience research', in A.N. Valdivia (ed.), *A Companion to Media Studies*, pp. 360–81. Oxford: Blackwell.

Noam, E. (1991) *Television in Europe*. New York: Oxford University Press.

Noble, G. (1975) *Children in Front of the Small Screen*. London: Constable.

Noelle-Neumann, E. (1973) 'Return to the concept of powerful mass media', *Studies of Broadcasting*, 9: 66–112.

Noelle-Neumann, E. (1974) 'The spiral of silence: a theory of public opinion', *Journal of Communication*, 24: 24–51.

Noelle-Neumann, E. (1984) *The Spiral of Silence*. Chicago: University of Chicago Press.

Noelle-Neumann, E. (1991) 'The theory of public opinion: the concept of the spiral of silence', in J. Anderson (ed.), *Communication Yearbook 14*, pp. 256–87. Newbury Park, CA: Sage.

Noin, D. (2001) 'Bias in the news: partisanship and negativity in media coverage of Presidents G. Bush and Bill Clinton', *Harvard Journal of Press/Politics*, (6) 3: 31–46.

Nordenstreng, K. (1974) *Informational Mass Communication*. Helsinki: Tammi.

Nordenstreng, K. (1997) 'Beyond the four theories of the press', in J. Servaes and R. Lie (eds), *Media and Politics in Transition*. Leuven: Acco.

Nordenstreng, K. (1998) 'Professional ethics: between fortress journalism and cosmopolitan democracy', in K. Brants, J. Hermes and L. van Zoonen (eds), *The Media in Question*, pp. 124–34. London: Sage.

Norris, P. (2000) *A Virtuous Circle*. New York: Cambridge University Press.

Norris, P. (2002) *Digital Divide*. New York: Cambridge University Press.

Norris, P. and Sanders, D. (2003) 'Message or medium? Campaign learning during the 2000 British General Election', *Political Communication*, 20 (3): 233–62.

Norris, P., Curtice, J., Sanders, D., Scammell, M. and Semetko, H. (1999) *On Message: Communicating the Campaign*. Thousand Oaks, CA: Sage.

Norstedt, S.A., Kaitatzi-Whitlock, S., Ottoson, R. and Riegert, K. (2000) 'From the Persian Gulf to Kosovo – war journalism and propaganda', *European Journal of Communication*, 15 (3): 383–404.

Ogden, C.K. and Richards, I.A. (1923) *The Meaning of Meaning* (reprinted 1985). London: Routledge and Kegan Paul.

Olen, J. (1988) *Ethics in Journalism*. Englewood Cliffs, NJ: Prentice-Hall.

Oliver, M.B. (2003) 'Race and crime in the media: research from a media effects perspective', in A.N. Valdivia (ed.), *A Companion to Media Studies*, pp. 421–36. Oxford: Blackwell.

Olson, S.R. (1999) *Hollywood Planet. Global Media: the Competitive Advantage of Narrative Transparency*. Mahwah, NJ: Erlbaum.

Oltean, O. (1993) 'Series and seriality in media culture', *European Journal of Communication*, 8 (1): 5–31.

Osgood, K., Suci, S. and Tannenbaum, P. (1957) *The Measurement of Meaning*. Urbana, IL: University of Illinois Press.

Ó Siochrú, S. and Girard, B., with Mahan, A. (2003) *Global Media Governance: a Beginner's Guide*. Lanham, NJ: Rowman and Littlefield.

Ostini, J. and Fung, A.Y. (2002) 'Beyond the four theories of the press: a new model of national media systems', *Mass Communication and Society*, 5 (1): 41–56.

Padioleau, J. (1985) *Le Monde et le Washington Post*. Paris: PUF.

Paek, H.-J., Lambe, J.L. and McLeod, D.M. (2008) 'Antecedents to support for content restriction', *Journalism and Mass Communication Quarterly*, 85 (2): 273–90.

Paletz, D.L. and Dunn, R. (1969) 'Press coverage of civil disorders: a case-study of Winston–Salem', *Public Opinion Quarterly*, 33: 328–45.

Paletz, D.L. and Entman, R. (1981) *Media, Power, Politics*. New York: Free Press.

Palmgreen, P. and Rayburn, J.D. (1985) 'An expectancy-value approach to media gratifications', in K.E. Rosengren et al. (eds), *Media Gratification Research*, pp. 61–72. Beverly Hills, CA: Sage.

Pan, Z. and Kosicki, G.M. (1997) 'Priming and media impact on the evaluation of the President's media performance', *Communication Research*, 24 (1): 3–30.

Papathanossopolous, S. (2002) *European Television in the Digital Age*. Cambridge: Polity Press.

Park, R. (1940/1967) 'News as a form of knowledge', in R.H. Turner (ed.), *On Social Control and Collective Behavior*, pp. 32–52. Chicago: Chicago University Press.

Pasek, J., Kensler, K., Romer, D. and Jamieson, K.H. (2006) 'America's media use and community engagement', *Communication Research*, 33 (3): 115–35.

Pasti, S. (2005) 'Two generations of Russian journalists', *European Journal of Communication*, 20 (1): 89–116.

Paterson, C. (1998) 'Global battlefields', in O. Boyd-Barrett and T. Rantanen (eds), *The Globalization of News*, pp. 79–103. London: Sage.

Patterson, T. (1994) *Out of Order*. New York: Vintage.

Patterson, T. (1998) 'Political roles of the journalist', in D. Graber, D. McQuail and P. Norris (eds), *The Politics of News: the News of Politics*, pp. 17–32. Washington, DC: Congressional Quarterly Press.

Pauwels, C. and Loisen, J. (2003) 'The WTO and the Audiovisial sector', *European Journal of Communication*, 18 (3): 291–314.

Peacock, A. (1986) *Report of the Committee on Financing the BBC*. Cmnd 9824. London: HMSO.

Peirce, C.S. (1931–5) *Collected Papers*, edited by C. Harteshorne and P. Weiss, vols II and V. Cambridge, MA: Harvard University Press.

Pekurny, R. (1982) 'Coping with television production', in J.S. Ettema and D.C. Whitney (eds), *Individuals in Mass Media Organizations*, pp. 131–43. Beverly Hills, CA: Sage.

Perkins, M. (2002) 'International law and the search for universal principles of media ethics', *Journal of Mass Media Ethics*, 17 (3): 193–208.

Perse, E.M. (1990) 'Audience selectivity and involvement in the newer media environment', *Communication Research*, 17: 675–97.

Perse, E.M. (1994) 'Uses of erotica', *Communication Research*, 20 (4): 488–515.

Perse, E.M. (2001) *Media Effects and Society*. Mahwah, NJ: Erlbaum.

Perse, E.M. and Courtright, J.A. (1992) 'Normative images of communication media: mass and interpersonal channels in the new media environment', *Human Communication Research*, 19: 485–503.

Perse, E.M. and Dunn, D.G. (1998) 'The utility of home computers and media use: implications of multimedia and connectivity', *Journal of Broadcasting and Electronic Media*, 42 (4): 435–56.

Peter, J. and Valkenberg, P.N. (2006) 'Individual differences in perception of internet communication', *European Journal of Communication*, 21 (2): 213–26.

Peters, A.K. and Cantor, M.G. (1982) 'Screen acting as work', in J.S. Ettema and D.C. Whitney (eds), *Individuals in Mass Media Organizations*, pp. 53–68. Beverly Hills, CA: Sage.

Peterson, R.C. and Thurstone, L.L. (1933) *Motion Pictures and Social Attitudes*. New York: Macmillan.

Petty, R.E. and Cacioppo, J.T. (1986) 'The elaboration likelihood model of persuasion', in L. Berkowitz (ed.), *Advances in Experimental Social Psychology*, pp. 132–205. San Diego: Academic.

Petty, R.E., Priester, J.R. and Briñol, P. (2002) 'Mass media attitude change: implications of the elaboration likelihood model of persuasion', in J. Bryant and D. Zillmann (eds), *Media Effects*, pp. 155–98. Mahwah, NJ: Erlbaum.

Pfau, M., Haigh, M., Gettle, M., Donnelly, M., Scott, G., Warr, D. and Wittenberg, E. (2004) 'Embedding journalists in military combat units: impact on story frames and tone', *Journalism and Mass Communication Quarterly*, 81 (1): 74–88.

Phillips, D.P. (1980) 'Airplane accidents, murder and the mass media', *Social Forces*, 58 (4): 1001–24.

Phillips, D.P. (1982) 'The impact of fictional TV stories in adult programming on adult fatalities', *American Journal of Sociology*, 87: 1346–59.

Picard, R.G. (1985) *The Press and the Decline of Democracy*. Westport, CT: Greenwood Press.

Picard, R.G. (1989) *Media Economics*. Newbury Park, CA: Sage.

Picard, R.G. (2004) 'Commercialism and newspaper quality', *Newspaper Research Journal*, 25 (1): 54–65.

Picard, R.G., McCombs, M., Winter, J.P. and Lacy, S. (eds) (1988) *Press Concentration and Monopoly*. Norwood, NJ: Ablex.

Plaisance, P.L. and Skewes, E.A. (2003) 'Personal and professional dimensions of news work: exploring links between journalists' values and roles', *Journalism and Mass Communication Quarterly*, 20 (4): 833–48.

Pool, I. de Sola (1974) *Direct Broadcasting and the Integrity of National Cultures*. New York: Aspen Institute.

Pool, I. de Sola (1983) *Technologies of Freedom*. Cambridge, MA: Belknap.

Pool, I. de Sola and Shulman, I. (1959) 'Newsmen's fantasies, audiences and newswriting', *Public Opinion Quarterly*, 23 (2): 145–58.

Porat, M. (1977) *The Information Economy: Definitions and Measurement*. Washington, DC: Department of Commerce.

Porto, M.P. (2007) 'Frame diversity and citizen competence: towards a critical approach to news quality', *Critical Studies in Mass Communication*, 24 (4): 303–21.

Poster, M. (1999) 'Underdetermination', *New Media and Society*, 1 (1): 12–17.

Poster, M. (2006) 'Culture and new media: a historical view', in L.A. Lievrow and S. Livingstone (eds), *The Handbook of New Media*, pp. 134–40. London: Sage.

Postman, N. (1993) *Technopoly: the Surrender of Culture to Technology*. New York: Vintage.

Postmes, T., Spears, R. and Lea, M. (1998) 'Breaching or building social boundaries? Side-effects of computer mediated communication', *Communication Research*, 25 (6): 689–715.

Potter, W.J., Cooper, R. and Dupagne, M. (1993) 'The three paradigms of mass media research in mass communication journals', *Communication Theory*, 3: 317–35.

Price, M. and Thompson, M. (2002) *Forging Peace*. Edinburgh: Edinburgh University Press.

Priest, S.H. (2001) *A Grain of Truth*. Lanham, MD: Rowman and Littlefield.

Pritchard, D. (2000) *Holding the Media Accountable*. Bloomington, IN: University of Indiana Press.

Propp, V. (1968) *The Morphology of Folk Tales*. Austin, TX: University of Texas Press.

Puppis, M. (2008) 'National media regulation in the era of free trade', *European Journal of Communication*, 23 (4): 405–24.

Putnam, D. (2000) *Bowling Alone*. New York: Simon and Schuster.

Quandt, T. and Singer, J.B. (2009) 'Convergence and cross-platform content production', in K. Wahl-Jorgenson and T. Hanitsch (eds), *The Handbook of Journalism Studies*, pp. 130–44. London: Routledge.

Quortrup, L. (2006) ' Understanding new digital media: medium theory or complexity theory', *European Journal of Communication*, 21 (3): 345–56.

Radway, J. (1984) *Reading the Romance*. Chapel Hill, NC: University of North Carolina Press.

Rainie, L. and Bell, P. (2004) 'The numbers that count', *New Media and Society*, 6 (1): 44–54.

Rakow, L. (1986) 'Rethinking gender research in communication', *Journal of Communication*, 36 (1): 11–26.

Rantanen, T. (2001) 'The old and the new: communications technology and globalization in Russia', *New Media and Society*, 3 (1): 85–105.

Rasmussen, T. (2000) *Social Theory and Communication Technology*. Aldershot: Ashgate.

Rasmussen, T. (2008) 'The internal differentiation of the political public sphere', *Nordicom Review*, 29 (1): 73–85.

Ravi, N. (2005) 'Looking beyond flawed journalism', *Harvard International Journal of Press/ Politics*, 10 (1): 45–62.

Ray, M.L. (1973) 'Marketing communication and the hierarchy of effects', in P. Clarke (ed.), *New Models for Communication Research*, pp. 147–76. Beverly Hills, CA: Sage.

Raymond, J. (ed.) (1999) *News, Newspapers and Society in Early Modern Britain*. London: Cass.

Real, M. (1989) *Supermedia*. Newbury Park, CA: Sage.

Reese, S.D. (1991) 'Setting the media's agenda: a power balance perspective', in J. Anderson (ed.), *Communication Yearbook 14*, pp. 309–40. Newbury Park, CA: Sage.

Reese, S.D. and Ballinger, J. (2001) 'The roots of a sociology of news: remembering Mr. Gates and social control in the newsroom', *Journalism and Mass Communication Quarterly*, 78 (4): 641–58.

Reese, S.D., Grant, A. and Danielian, L.H. (1994) 'The structure of news sources on television: a network analysis of "CBS News", "Nightline", "McNeil/Lehrer" and "This Week With David Brinkley"', *Journal of Communication*, 44 (2): 64–83.

Reese, S.D., Rutigliano, L., Hyun, K. and Jeong, J. (2007) 'Mapping the blogosphere', *Journalism*, 8 (3): 235–61.

Renckstorf, K. (1996) 'Media use as social action: a theoretical perspective', in K. Renckstorf, D. McQuail and N. Janknowski (eds), *Media Use as Social Action*, pp. 18–31. London: Libbey.

Rheingold, H. (1994) *The Virtual Community*. London: Secker and Warburg.

Rice, R.E. (1993) 'Media appropriateness: using social presence theory to compare traditional and new organizational media', *Human Communication Research*, 19: 451–84.

Rice, R.E. (1999) 'Artifacts and paradoxes in new media', *New Media and Society*, 1 (1): 24–32.

Rice, R.E. et al. (1983) *The New Media*. Beverly Hills, CA: Sage.

Rivers, W.L. and Nyhan, M.J. (1973) *Aspen Papers on Government and the Media*. New York: Praeger.

Robillard, S. (1995) *Television in Europe: Regulatory Bodies*. European Institute for the Media. London: Libbey.

Robinson, J.P. (1972) 'Mass communication and information diffusion', in F.G. Kline and P.J. Tichenor (eds), *Current Perspectives in Mass Communication Research*, pp. 71–93. Beverly Hills, CA: Sage.

Robinson, J.P. (1976) 'Interpersonal influence in election campaigns: 2-step flow hypotheses', *Public Opinion Quarterly*, 40: 304–19.

Robinson, J.P. and Davis, D.K. (1990) 'Television news and the informed public: an information processing approach', *Journal of Communication*, 40 (3): 106–19.

Robinson, J.P. and Levy, M. (1986) *The Main Source*. Beverly Hills, CA: Sage.

Robinson, P. (2001) 'Theorizing the influence of media on world politics', *European Journal of Communication*, 16 (4): 523–44.

Roe, K. (1992) 'Different destinies – different melodies: school achievement, anticipated status and adolescents' tastes in music', *European Journal of Communication*, 7 (3): 335–58.

Roe, K. and de Meyer, G. (2000) 'MTV: one music – many languages', in J. Wieten, G. Murdock and P. Dahlgren (eds), *Television Across Europe*, pp. 141–57. London: Sage.

Rogers, E.M. (1962) *The Diffusion of Innovations*. Glencoe, IL: Free Press.

Rogers, E.M. (1976) 'Communication and development: the passing of a dominant paradigm', *Communication Research*, 3: 213–40.

Rogers, E.M. (1986) *Communication Technology*. New York: Free Press.

Rogers, E.M. (1993) 'Looking back, looking forward: a century of communication research', in P. Gaunt (ed.), *Beyond Agendas: New Directions in Communication Research*, pp. 19–40. New Haven, CT: Greenwood Press.

Rogers, E.M. and Dearing, J.W. (1987) 'Agenda-setting research: Where has it been? Where is it going?', in J. Anderson (ed.), *Communication Yearbook 11*, pp. 555–94. Newbury Park, CA: Sage.

Rogers, E.M. and Kincaid, D.L. (1981) *Communication Networks: Towards a New Paradigm for Research*. New York: Free Press.

Rogers, E.M. and Shoemaker, F. (1973) *Communication of Innovations*. New York: Free Press.

Rogers, E.M. and Storey, D. (1987) 'Communication campaigns', in C.R. Berger and S.H. Chaffee (eds), *Handbook of Communication Science*, pp. 817–46. Beverly Hills, CA: Sage.

Rogers, E.M., Dearing, J.W. and Bergman, D. (1993) 'The anatomy of agenda-setting research', *Journal of Communication*, 43 (2): 68–84.

Romer, D., Jamieson, K.H. and Ady, S. (2003) 'TV news and the cultivation of fear of crime', *Journal of Communication*, 53 (1): 88–104.

Romer, D., Jamieson, P.F. and Jamieson, K.H. (2006) 'Are news reports of suicide contagious?', *Journal of Communication*, 56 (2): 253–70.

Rorty, R. (1989) *Contingency, Irony and Solidarity*. Glencoe, IL: Free Press.

Rosenberg, B. and White, D.M. (eds) (1957) *Mass Culture*. New York: Free Press.

Rosengren, K.E. (1973) 'News diffusion: an overview', *Journalism Quarterly*, 50: 83–91.

Rosengren, K.E. (1974) 'International news: methods, data, theory', *Journal of Peace Research*, II: 45–56.

Rosengren, K.E. (1976) 'The Barseback "panic"'. Unpublished research report, Lund University, Lund, Sweden.

Rosengren, K.E. (ed.) (1981a) *Advances in Content Analysis*. Beverly Hills, CA: Sage.

Rosengren, K.E. (1981b) 'Mass media and social change: some current approaches', in E. Katz and T. Szecskö (eds), *Mass Media and Social Change*, pp. 247–63. Beverly Hills, CA: Sage.

Rosengren, K.E. (1983) 'Communication research: one paradigm or four?', *Journal of Communication*, 33 (3): 185–207.

Rosengren, K.E. (1987) 'The comparative study of news diffusion', *European Journal of Communication*, 2 (2): 136–57.

Rosengren, K.E. (2000) *Communication: an Introduction*. London: Sage.

Rosengren, K.E. and Windahl, S. (1972) 'Mass media consumption as a functional alternative', in D. McQuail (ed.), *Sociology of Mass Communications*, pp. 166–94. Harmondsworth: Penguin.

Rosengren, K.E. and Windahl, S. (1989) *Media Matter*. Norwood, NJ: Ablex.

Rositi, F. (1976) 'The television news programme: fragmentation and recomposition of our image of society', in *News and Current Events on TV*. Rome: RAI.

Ross, S.M. (2008) *Beyond the Box: Television and the Internet*. Malden, MA: Blackwell.

Rössler, P. (2001) 'Between online heaven and cyberhell: the framing of "the internet" by traditional media coverage in Germany', *New Media and Society*, 3 (1): 49–66.

Rössler, P. and Brosius, H.-B. (2001) 'Talk show viewing in Germany', *Journal of Communication*, 51 (1): 143–63.

Rosten, L.C. (1937) *The Washington Correspondents*. New York: Harcourt Brace.

Rosten, L.C. (1941) *Hollywood: the Movie Colony, the Movie Makers*. New York: Harcourt Brace.

Rothenbuhler, E.W. (1987) 'The living room celebration of the Olympic Games', *Journal of Communication*, 38 (4): 61–8.

Rothenbuhler, E.W. (1998) *Ritual Communication*. Thousand Oaks, CA: Sage.

Rothenbuhler, E.W., Mullen, L.J., DeCarell, R. and Ryan, C.R. (1996) 'Community, community attachment and involvement', *Journalism and Mass Communication Quarterly*, 73 (2): 445–66.

Roudikova, N. (2008) 'Media political clientilism – a lesson from anthropology', *Media, Culture and Society*, 30 (1): 41–59.

Royal Commission on the Press (1977) *Report*. Cmnd 6810. London: HMSO.

Rubin, A.M. (1984) 'Ritualized and instrumental television viewing', *Journal of Communication*, 34 (3): 67–77.

Rubin, A.M., Perse, E.M. and Powell, E. (1990) 'Loneliness, parasocial interaction and local TV news viewing', *Communication Research*, 14 (2): 246–68.

Ryan, M. (2001) 'Journalistic ethics, objectivity, existential journalism, standpoint epistemology, and public journalism', *Journal of Mass Media Ethics*, 16 (1): 3–22.

Ryan, M. (2006) 'Mainstream news media, an objective approach and the march to war in Iraq', *Journal of Mass Media Ethics*, 21 (1): 4–29.

Ryan, J. and Peterson, R.A. (1982) 'The product image: the fate of creativity in country music song writing', in J.S. Ettema and D.C. Whitney (eds), *Individuals in Mass Media Organizations*, pp. 11–32. Beverly Hills, CA: Sage.

Sabal, R. (1992) 'Television executives speak about fan letters to the networks', in L.A. Lewis (ed.), *The Adoring Audience*, pp. 185–8. London: Routledge.

Saenz, M.K. (1994) 'Television viewing and cultural practice', in H. Newcomb (ed.), *Television: the Critical View*, 5th edn, pp. 573–86. New York: Oxford University Press.

Sandel, M. (1982) *Free Speech and the Limits of Justice*. Cambridge: Cambridge University Press.

Schement, J. and Curtis, T. (1995) *Tendencies and Tensions of the Information Age*. New Brunswick, NJ: Transaction.

Scheufele, D.A. (1999) 'Framing as a theory of media effects', *Journal of Communication*, 49 (1): 103–22.

Scheufele, D.A. and Nisbet, M.C. (2002) 'Being a citizen online: new opportunities and dead ends', *Harvard Journal of Press/Politics*, 7 (3): 55–75.

Scheufele, B. (2008) 'Discourse analysis', in W. Donsbach (ed.), *The International Encyclopedia of Communication*. Oxford: Blackwell.

Schiller, H. (1969) *Mass Communication and American Empire*. New York: Kelly.

Schlesinger, P. (1978) *Putting 'Reality' Together: BBC News*. London: Constable.

Schlesinger, P. (1987) 'On national identity', *Social Science Information*, 25 (2): 219–64.

Schlesinger, P., Murdock, G. and Elliott, P. (1983) *Televising Terrorism*. London: Comedia.

Schmid, A.P. and de Graaf, J. (1982) *Violence as Communication*. Beverly Hills, CA: Sage.

Schoenbach, K., de Waal, E. and Lauf, E. (2005) 'Online and print newspapers: their impact on the extent of the perceived public agenda', *European Journal of Communication*, 20 (1): 245–58.

Schoenbach, K. and Lauf, E. (2002) 'The "trap" effect of television and its competitors', *Communication Research*, 29 (6): 564–83.

Schramm, W. (1955) 'Information theory and mass communication', *Journalism Quarterly*, 32: 131–46.

Schramm, W., Lyle, J. and Parker, E. (1961) *Television in the Lives of Our Children*. Stanford, CA: Stanford University Press.

Schrøder, K.C. (1987) 'Convergence of antagonistic traditions?', *European Journal of Communication*, 2 (1): 7–31.

Schrøder, K.C. (1992) 'Cultural quality: search for a phantom?', in M. Skovmand and K.C. Schrøder (eds), *Media Cultures: Reappraising Transnational Media*, pp. 161–80. London: Routledge.

Schroeder, T. (2001) 'The origins of the German Press', in B. Dooley and S. Baran (eds), *The Politics of Information in Early Modern Europe*. London: Routledge.

Schudson, M. (1978) *Discovering the News*. New York: Basic Books.

Schudson, M. (1991) 'The new validation of popular culture', in R.K. Avery and D. Eason (eds), *Critical Perspectives on Media and Society*, pp. 49–68. New York: Guilford Press.

Schudson, M. (1998) 'The public journalism movement and its problems', in D. Graber, D. McQuail and P. Norris (eds), *The Politics of News; the News of Politics*, pp. 132–49. Washington, DC: Congressional Quarterly Press.

Schultz, J. (1998) *Reviving the Fourth Estate*. Cambridge: Cambridge University Press.

Schulz, W. (1988) 'Media and reality'. Unpublished paper for Sommatie Conference, Veldhoven, The Netherlands.

Schulz, W. (1997) 'Changes of the mass media and the public sphere', *The Public*, 4 (2): 57–70.

Schulz, W. (2004) 'Reconstructing mediatization as an analytic concept', *European Journal of Communication*, 19 (1): 87–102.

Schutz, A. (1972) *The Phenomenology of the Social World*. London: Heinemann.

Schwalber, C.B., Silcode, B.W. and Keith, S. (2008) 'Visual framing of the early weeks of the US led invasion of Iraq', *Journal of Broadcasting and Electronic Media*, 52 (3): 448–65.

Schweiger, W. (2000) 'Media credibility: experience or image?', *European Journal of Communication*, 15 (1): 37–60.

Schweitzer, E.J. (2005) 'Election campaigning online: German party websites in the 2002 National Election, *European Journal of Communication*, 20 (3): 327–51.

Schweitzer, E. (2008) 'Innovation or normalization in E-campaigning?', *European Journal of Communication*, 23 (4): 449–70.

Schwichtenberg, C. (1992) 'Music video', in J. Lull (ed.), *Popular Music and Communication*, pp. 116–33. Newbury Park, CA: Sage.

Segrin, C. and Nabi, R.L. (2002) 'Does TV viewing cultivate unrealistic expectations about marriage?', *Journal of Communication*, 52 (2): 247–63.

Seiter, E. (2000) *Television and New Media Audiences*. New York: Oxford University Press.

Seiter, F., Borchers, H. and Warth, E.-M. (eds) (1989) *Remote Control*. London: Routledge.

Selwyn, N. (2004) 'Reconsidering political and popular understanding of the digital divide', *New Media and Society*, 6 (3): 341–62.

Semetko, H.A. (2004) 'Political communication', in J.D.H. Downing, D. McQuail, P. Schlesinger and E. Wartella (eds), *The Sage Handbook of Media Studies*, pp. 351–74. Thousand Oaks, CA: Sage.

Sepstrup, P. (1989) 'Research into international TV flows', *European Journal of Communication*, 4 (4): 393–408.

Servaes, J. (1999) *Communication for Development*. Cresskill, NJ: Hampton.

Shannon, C. and Weaver, W. (eds) (1949) *The Mathematical Theory of Communication*. Urbana, IL: University of Illinois Press.

Shelton, P. and Gunaratne, S.A. (1998) 'Old wine in a new bottle: public journalism, developmental journalism and social responsibility', in M.E. Roloff and G.D. Paulson (eds), *Communication Yearbook 21*, pp. 277–321. Thousand Oaks, CA: Sage.

Shen, M.C.H. (1999) *Current-Affairs Talkshows: Public Communication Revitalized on Television*. Amsterdam: University of Amsterdam.

Shibutani, T. (1966) *Improvised News*. New York: Bobbs Merrill.

Shils, E. (1957) 'Daydreams and nightmares: reflections on the criticism of mass culture', *Sewanee Review*, 65 (4): 586–608.

Shoemaker, P.J. (1984) 'Media treatment of deviant political groups', *Journalism Quarterly*, 61 (1): 66–75, 82.

Shoemaker, P.J. (1991) *Gatekeeping*. Thousand Oaks, CA: Sage.

Shoemaker, P.J. and Reese, S.D. (1991) *Mediating the Message*. New York: Longman.

Shoemaker, P.J. et al. (2001) 'Individual and routine forces in gatekeeping', *Journalism and Mass Communication Quarterly*, 78 (2): 233–46.

Short, J., Williams, E. and Christie, B. (1976) *The Social Psychology of Telecommunications*. New York: Wiley.

Siebert, F., Peterson, T. and Schramm, W. (1956) *Four Theories of the Press*. Urbana, IL: University of Illinois Press.

Sigal, L.V. (1973) *Reporters and Officials*. Lexington, MA: Lexington.

Sigelman, L. (1973) 'Reporting the news: an organizational analysis', *American Journal of Sociology*, 79: 132–51.

Signorielli, N. and Morgan, M. (eds) (1990) *Cultivation Analysis*. Newbury Park, CA: Sage.

Singer, B.D. (1970) 'Mass media and communications processes in the Detroit riots of 1967', *Public Opinion Quarterly*, 34: 236–45.

Singer, J.B. (2005) 'The political J-Blogger', *Journalism*, 6 (2): 173–98.

Singer, J.B. (2007) 'Contested autonomy: professional and popular claims on journalism norms', *Journalism Studies*, 8 (1): 79–95.

Singh, S. (2001) 'Gender and the use of the Internet at home', *New Media and Society*, 3 (4): 395–416.

Slack, J.D. and Wise, J.M. (2002) 'Cultural studies and technology', in L. Lievrouw and S. Livingstone (eds), *The Handbook of New Media*, pp. 485–501. London: Sage.

Slater, M.D., Romer, D. and Long, M. (2006) 'TV dramas and support for controversial policies', *Journal of Communication*, 56 (2): 235–52.

Slevin, J. (2000) *The Internet and Society*. Cambridge: Polity Press.

Smith, A. (1973) *The Shadow in the Cave*. London: Allen and Unwin.

Smith, J.A. (1999) *War and Press Freedom*. New York: Oxford University Press.

Smith, P. and Bell, A. (2007) 'Unravelling the web of discourse analysis', in E. Devereux (ed.), *Media Studies*, pp. 78–100. London: Sage.

Smith, S.L., Nathanson, A.I. and Wilson, B.J. (2002) 'Prime-time television: assessing violence during the most popular viewing hours', *Journal of Communication*, 52 (1): 84–111.

Smith, S.W., Smith, S.L., Pieper, K.M., Yoo, J.H., Ferris, A.L., Downs, E. and Bowden, B. (2006) 'Altruism on American television', *Journal of Communication*, 56 (4): 707–27.

Smythe, D.W. (1977) 'Communications: blindspot of Western Marxism', *Canadian Journal of Political and Social Theory*, I: 120–7.

Sonninen, P. and Laitila, T. (1995) 'Press councils in Europe', in K. Nordenstreng (ed.), *Reports on Media Ethics*, pp. 3–22. Tampere: Department of Journalism and Mass Communication.

Snow, N. and Taylor, P.M. (2006) 'The revival of the propaganda state', *International Communication Gazette*, 68 (5/6): 389–407.

Sotirovic, M. (2001) 'Media use and perceptions of welfare', *Journal of Communication*, 51 (4): 750–74.

Sparks, C. and Campbell, M. (1987) 'The inscribed reader of the British quality press', *European Journal of Communication*, 2 (4): 455–72.

Spilerman, S. (1976) 'Structural characteristics and severity of racial disorders', *American Sociological Review*, 41: 771–92.

Squires, J.D. (1992) 'Plundering the newsroom', *Washington Journalism Review*, 14 (10): 18–24.

Sreberny-Mohammadi, A. (1996) 'The global and the local in international communication', in J. Curran and M. Gurevitch (eds), *Mass Media and Society*, pp. 177–203. London: Arnold.

Stamm, K.R. (1985) *Newspaper Use and Community Ties: Towards a Dynamic Theory*. Norwood, NJ: Ablex.

Stamm, K.R., Emig, A.G. and Heuse, M.B. (1997) 'The contribution of local media to community involvement', *Journalism and Mass Communication Quarterly*, 74 (1): 97–107.

Star, S.A. and Hughes, H.M. (1950) 'Report on an education campaign: the Cincinnati plan for the UN', *American Sociological Review*, 41: 771–92.

Steemers, J. (2001) 'In search of a third way: balancing public purpose and commerce in German and British public service broadcasting', *Canadian Journal of Communication*, 26 (1): 69–87.

Steiner, G. (1963) *The People Look at Television*. New York: Knopf.

Steiner, L. (2009) 'Gender in the newsroom', in K. Wahl-Jorgenson and T. Hanitsch (eds), *The Handbook of Journalism Studies*, pp. 116–29. London: Routledge.

Stober, R. (2004) 'What media evolution is: a theoretical approach to the history of new media', *European Journal of Communication*, 19 (4): 483–505.

Stone, G.C. (1987) *Examining Newspapers*. Beverly Hills, CA: Sage.

Strömbäck, J. (2008) 'Four phases of mediatization: an analysis of the mediatization of politics', *The International Journal of Press/Politics* 13 (4): 228–47.

Stromer-Galley, J. (2000) 'On-line interaction and why candidates avoid it', *Journal of Communication*, 50 (4): 111–32.

Stromer-Galley, J. (2002) 'New voices in the public sphere: a comparative analysis of inter-personal and online political talk', *Javnost*, 9 (2): 23–42.

Sundae, S.S. and Ness, C. (2001) 'Conceptualizing sources in online news', *Journal of Communication*, 51 (1): 52–72.

Sunstein, C. (2001) *republic.com*. Princeton, NJ: Princeton University Press.

Sunstein, C. (2006) *republic.com.2.0*. Princeton, NJ: Princeton University Press.

Sussman, G. (1997) *Communication, Technology and Politics in the Information Age*. Thousand Oaks, CA: Sage.

Sussman, G. and Galizio, L. (2003) 'The global reproduction of American politics', *Political Communication*, 20 (3): 309–28.

Swanson, D. and Mancini, P. (eds) (1996) *Politics, Media and Modern Democracy*. Westport, CT: Praeger.

Tai, Z. and Chang, T.-K. (2002) 'The globalness and the pictures in their heads: a comparative analysis of audience interest, editor perceptions and newspaper coverage', *Gazette*, 64 (3): 251–65.

Takahiro, S. (2004) 'Lessons from the Great Hanshin Earthquake', in NHK, *Disaster Reporting and the Public Nature of Broadcasting*, pp. 25–157. Tokyo: NHK Broadcasting Culture Research Institute.

Tannenbaum, P.H. and Lynch, M.D. (1960) 'Sensationalism: the concept and its measurement', *Journalism Quarterly*, 30: 381–93.

Taylor, C. (1989) *Sources of the Self: the Making of the Modern Identity*. Cambridge, MA: Harvard University Press.

Taylor, D.G. (1982) 'Pluralistic ignorance and the spiral of silence', *Public Opinion Quarterly*, 46: 311–55.

Taylor, P. (1992) *War and the Media*. Manchester: Manchester University Press.

Taylor, W.L. (1953) 'Cloze procedure: a new tool for measuring readability', *Journalism Quarterly*, 30: 415–33.

Tewkesbury, D. (2003) 'What do Americans really want to know? Tracking the behavior of news readers on the Internet', *Journal of Communication*, 53 (4): 694–710.

Tewkesbury, D. and Althaus, S.L. (2000) 'Differences in knowledge acquisition among readers of the paper and online versions of a national newspaper', *Journalism and Mass Communication Quarterly*, 77: 457–79.

Thompson, J. (2000) *Political Scandals*. Cambridge: Polity Press.

Thompson, J.B. (1993) 'Social theory and the media', in D. Crowley and D. Mitchell (eds), *Communication Theory Today*, pp. 27–49. Cambridge: Polity Press.

Thompson, J.B. (1995) *The Media and Modernity*. Cambridge: Polity Press.

Thoveron, G. (1986) 'European televised women', *European Journal of Communication*, 1 (3): 289–300.

Thrall, A.T. (2006) 'The myth of the outside strategy: mass media news coverage of interest groups', *Political Communication*, 23 (2): 407–20.

Thrift, R.R. (1977) 'How chain ownership affects editorial vigor of newspapers', *Journalism Quarterly*, 54: 327–31.

Thussu, D.K. (2000) 'Legitimizing "humanitarian intervention"? CNN, NATO And The Kosovo Crisis', *European Journal of Communication*, 15 (3): 345–62.

Thussu, D.K. (2009) *The News as Entertainment: the Rise of Global Infotainment*. London: Sage.

Thussu, D. and Freedman, J. (eds) (2003) *War and the Media*. London: Sage.

Tichenor, P.J., Donahue, G.A. and Olien, C.N. (1970) 'Mass media and the differential growth in knowledge', *Public Opinion Quarterly*, 34: 158–70.

Tomlinson, J. (1999) *The Globalisation of Culture*. Cambridge: Polity Press.

Traber, M. and Nordenstreng, K. (1993) *Few Voices, Many Worlds*. London: World Association for Christian Communication.

Trappel, J. (2008) 'Online media within the public service realm? Reasons to include online into the public service mission', *Convergence*, 14 (3): 313–22.

Trenaman, J.S.M. (1967) *Communication and Comprehension*. London: Longman.

Trenaman, J.S.M. and McQuail, D. (1961) *Television and the Political Image*. London: Methuen.

Tuchman, G. (1978) *Making News: a Study in the Construction of Reality*. New York: Free Press.

Tuchman, G., Daniels, A.K. and Benet, J. (eds) (1978) *Hearth and Home: Images of Women in Mass Media*. New York: Oxford University Press.

Tumber, H. (1982) *Television and the Riots*. London: British Film Institute.

Tumber, H. and Palmer, J. (2004) *Media at War: the Iraq Crisis*. London: Sage.

Tumber, H. and Waisbord, S. (2004) 'Political scandals and media across democracies', *American Behavioral Scientist*, 47 (8): 1031–9.

Tunstall, J. (1970) *The Westminster Lobby Correspondents*. London: Routledge and Kegan Paul.

Tunstall, J. (1971) *Journalists at Work*. London: Constable.

Tunstall, J. (1977) *The Media Are American*. London: Constable.

Tunstall, J. (1991) 'A media industry perspective', in J. Anderson (ed.), *Communication Yearbook 14*, pp. 163–86. Newbury Park, CA: Sage.

Tunstall, J. (1993) *Television Producers*. London: Routledge.

Tunstall, J. (2007) *The Media Were American*. Oxford: Oxford University Press.

Tunstall, J. and Machin, D. (1999) *The Anglo-American Media Connection*. Oxford: Oxford University Press.

Tunstall, J. and Palmer, M. (eds) (1991) *Media Moguls*. London: Routledge.

Turkle, S. (1988) 'Computational reticence: why women fear the intimate machine', in C. Kramarae (ed.), *Technology and Women's Voices: Keeping in Touch*, pp. 41–62. London: Routledge.

Turner, G. (2004) *Understanding Celebrity*. London: Sage.

Turner, J.W., Grube, J.A. and Myers, J. (2001) 'Developing an optimal match within online communities: an exploration of CMC support communities and traditional support', *Journal of Communication*, 51 (2): 231–51.

Turow, J. (1989) 'PR and newswork: a neglected relationship', *American Behavioral Scientist*, 33: 206–12.

Turow, J. (1994) 'Hidden conflicts and journalistic norms: the case of self-coverage', *Journal of Communication*, 44 (2): 29–46.

Turow, J. (2009) *Media Today: an Introduction to Mass Communication,* 3rd edn. New York and London: Routledge.

Twyman, T. (1994) 'Measuring audiences', in R. Kent (ed.), *Measuring Media Audiences*, pp. 88–104. London: Routledge.

Vaccari, C. (2008a) 'Italian parties' websites in the 2006 election', *European Journal of Communication*, 23 (1): 69–77.

Vaccari, C. (2008b) 'From the air to the ground: the internet in the 2004 US presidential election campaign', *New Media and Society*, 10 (4): 647–65.

Valentino, N.A., Buhr, T.A. and Beckmann, W.N. (2001) 'When the frame is the game: revisiting the impact of "strategic" campaign coverage in citizens' information retention', *Journalism and Mass Communication Quarterly*, 78 (1): 93–112.

Valkenberg, P., Cantor, J. and Peeters, A.L. (2000) 'Fright reactions to TV', *Communication Research*, 27 (1): 82–94.

van Aelst, P., Maddens, B., Noppe, J. and Fiers, S. (2008) 'Politicians in the news: media or party logic?', *European Journal of Communication*, 23 (2): 193–210.

Van Belle, D.A. (2003) 'Bureaucratic responsiveness to news media: comparing the influence of the *NYT* and network TV news coverage on US foreign and civil allocations', *Political Communication*, 20 (3): 263–85.

van Cuilenberg, J.J. (1987) 'The information society: some trends and implications', *European Journal of Communication*, 2 (1): 105–21.

van Cuilenburg, J.J., de Ridder, J. and Kleinnijenhuis, J. (1986) 'A theory of evaluative discourse', *European Journal of Communication*, 1 (1): 65–96.

van Cuilenburg, J.J. and McQuail, D. (2003) 'Media policy paradigm shifts', *European Journal of Communication*, 18 (2): 181–207.

van der Wurf, R. (2004) 'Supplying and viewing diversity: the role of competition and viewer choice in Dutch broadcasting', *European Journal of Communication*, 19 (2): 215–37.

Van Dijk, J.A.G.M. (1992) *De Netwerk Maatschappij*. Houten, NL: Bohm Staffen von Loghum.

van Dijk, J.A.G.M. (1996) 'Models of democracy: behind the design and use of new media in politics', *The Public*, 3 (1): 43–56.

van Dijk, J.A.G.M. (1999) *Network Society: Social Aspects of New Media*. London: Sage.

van Dijk, T. (1983) 'Discourse analysis: its development and application to the structure of news', *Journal of Communication*, 33 (3): 20–43.

van Dijk, T. (1985) *Discourse and Communication*. Berlin: de Gruyter.

van Dijk, T. (1991) *Racism and the Press*. London: Routledge.

Van Gorp (2005) 'What is the frame? Victims and intruders in the Belgian press coverage of the asylum issue', *European Journal of Communication*, 20 (4): 484–507.

van Zoonen, L. (1988) 'Rethinking women and the news', *European Journal of Communication*, 3 (1): 35–52.

van Zoonen, L. (1991) 'Feminist perspectives on the media', in J. Curran and M. Gurevitch (eds), *Mass Media and Society*, pp. 33–51. London: Arnold.

van Zoonen, L. (1992) 'The women's movement and the media: constructing a public identity', *European Journal of Communication*, 7 (4): 453–76.

van Zoonen, L. (1994) *Feminist Media Studies*. London: Sage.

van Zoonen, L. (2002) 'Gendering the Internet: claims, controversies and cultures', *European Journal of Communication*, 17 (1): 5–24.

van Zoonen, L. (2004) 'Imagining the fan democracy', *European Journal of Communication*, 19 (1): 39–52.

Vartanova, E. (2002) 'The digital divide and the changing political/media environment of post-socialist Russia', *Gazette*, 64 (5): 449–645.

Vasterman, P. (2005) 'MediaHype – self-reinforcing news waves', *European Journal of Communication*, 19 (4): 508–30.

Verhulst, S.G. (2002) 'About scarcities and intermediaries: the regulatory paradigm shift of digital content reviewed', in L.A. Lievrouw and S. Livingstone (eds), *The Handbook of New Media*, pp. 432–47. London: Sage.

Verhulst, P. (2006) 'The regulation of digital content', in L.A. Lievrow and S. Livingstone (eds), *The Handbook of New Media*, pp. 329–49. London: Sage.

Vidmar, N. and Rokeach, M. (1974) 'Archie Bunker's bigotry: a study of selective perception and exposure', *Journal of Communication*, 24: 36–47.

Vincent, R.C. (2000) 'A narrative analysis of the US press coverage of Slobodan Milosevic and the Serbs in Kosovo', *European Journal of Communication*, 15 (3): 321–44.

Visvanath, K. and Finnegan, J.R. (1996) 'The knowledge gap hypothesis 25 years later', in *Communication Yearbook 19*, pp. 187–227.

Voltmer, K. (2000) 'Constructing political reality in Russia. *Izvestya* – between old and new journalistic practices', *European Journal of Communication*, 15 (4): 469–500.

von Feilitzen, C. (1976) 'The functions served by the mass media', in J.W. Brown (ed.), *Children and Television*, pp. 90–115. London: Collier-Macmillan.

von Hasebrink, U. (1997) 'In search of patterns of individual media use', in U. Carlsson (ed.), *Beyond Media Uses and Effects*, pp. 99–112. Göteborg: University of Göteborg, Nordicom.

Vyncke, P. (2002) 'Lifestyle segmentation', *European Journal of Communication*, 17 (4): 445–64.

Wackwitz, L. (2002) 'Burger on Miller: obscene effects and the filth of the nation', *Journal of Communication*, 52 (1): 196–210.

Waisbord, S. (1998) 'When the cart of media is put before the horse of identity: a critique of technology-centered views on globalization', *Communication Research*, 25 (4): 377–98.

Waisbord, S. (2000) *Watchdog Journalism in South America*. New York: Columbia.

Walgrave, S. and van Aelst, P. (2006) 'The contingency effect of the mass media's agenda setting', *Journal of Communication*, 56 (1): 88–109.

Wall, M. (2005) 'Blogs of war', *Journalism*, 6 (2): 153–72.

Wallis, R. and Baran, S. (1990) *The World of Broadcast News*. London: Routledge.

Walzer, M. (1992) 'The civil society argument', in C. Mouffe (ed.), *Dimensions of Radical Democracy*. London: Verso.

Warner, W.L. and Henry, W.E. (1948) 'The radio day-time serial: a symbolic analysis', *Psychological Monographs*, 37 (1): 7–13, 55–64.

Wartella, E., Olivarez, A. and Jennings, N. (1998) 'Children and television violence in the United States', in U. Carlsson and C. von Feilitzen (eds), *Children and Media Violence*, pp. 55–62. Göteborg: University of Göteborg.

Wasko, J. (2004) 'The political economy of communication', in J.D.H. Downing, D. McQuail, P. Schlesinger and E. Wartella (eds), *The Sage Handbook of Media Studies*, pp. 309–30. Thousand Oaks, CA: Sage.

Wasserman, H. and Rao, S. (2008) 'The glocalization of journalism ethics', *Journalism*, 9 (2): 163–81.

Watson, N. (1997) 'Why we argue about virtual community: a case study of the Phish. Net fan community', in S.G. Jones (ed.), *Virtual Culture*, pp. 102–32. London: Sage.

Weaver, D. (1996) 'Journalists in comparative perspective', *The Public*, 3 (4): 83–91.

Weaver, D. (ed.) (1998) *The Global Journalist*. Cresskill, NJ: Hampton.

Weaver, D. and Wilhoit, C.G. (1986) *The American Journalist*. Bloomington, IN: University of Indiana Press.

Weaver, D. and Wilhoit, C.G. (1992) 'Journalists: who are they really?', *Media Studies Journal*, 6 (4): 63–80.

Weaver, D. and Wilhoit, C.G. (1996) *The American Journalist in the 1990s: US News People at the End of an Era*. Mahwah, NJ: Erlbaum.

Weber, M. (1948) 'Politics as a vocation', in H. Gerth and C.W. Mills (eds), *Max Weber: Essays*. London: Routledge and Kegan Paul.

Weber, M. (1964) *Theory of Social and Economic Organization*. Ed. T. Parsons. New York: Free Press.

Webster, F. (1995) *Images of the Information Society*. London: Routledge.

Webster, F. (2002) 'The information society revisited', in L.A. Lievrouw and S. Livingstone (eds), *The Handbook of New Media*, pp. 22–33. London: Sage.

Webster, J.G. (2005) 'Beneath the veneer of fragmentation – TV audience polarization in a multi-channel world', *Journal of Communication*, 55 (2): 366–82.

Webster, J.G. and Lin, S.-F. (2002) 'The internet audience: web use as mass behavior', *Journal of Broadcasting and Electronic Media*, 46 (1): 1–12.

Webster, J.G. and Phalen, P.F. (1997) *The Mass Audience: Rediscovering the Dominant Model*. Mahwah, NJ: Erlbaum.

Webster, J.G. and Wakshlag, J.J. (1983) 'A theory of TV program choice', *Communication Research*, 10 (4): 430–46.

Weibull, L. (1985) 'Structural factors in gratifications research', in K.E. Rosengren, P. Palmgreen and L. Wenner (eds), *Media Gratification Research: Current Perspectives*, pp. 123–47. Beverly Hills, CA: Sage.

Westerstahl, J. (1983) 'Objective news reporting', *Communication Research*, 10 (3): 403–24.

Westerstahl, J. and Johansson, F. (1994) 'Foreign news: values and ideologies', *European Journal of Communication*, 9 (1): 71–89.

Westley, B. and MacLean, M. (1957) 'A conceptual model for mass communication research', *Journalism Quarterly*, 34: 31–8.

White, D.M. (1950) 'The gatekeeper: a case-study in the selection of news', *Journalism Quarterly*, 27: 383–90.

Wildman, S.S. (1991) 'Explaining trade in films and programs', *Journal of Communication*, 41: 190–2.

Wilensky, H. (1964) 'Mass society and mass culture: interdependence or independence?' *American Sociological Review*, 29 (2): 173–97.

Wilke, J. (1995) 'Agenda-setting in a historical perspective: the coverage of the American revolution in the German press (1773–83)', *European Journal of Communication*, 10 (1): 63–86.

Williams, R. (1961) *Culture and Society*. Harmondsworth: Penguin.

Williams, R. (1975) *Television, Technology and Cultural Form*. London: Fontana.

Williamson, J. (1978) *Decoding Advertisements*. London: Boyars.

Wilson, B.J. and Smith, S. (2002) 'Violence in children's TV programming: assessing the risks', *Journal of Communication*, 52 (1): 5–35.

Windahl, S., Signitzer, B. and Olson, J. (2007) *Using Communication Theory*, 2nd edn. London: Sage.

Winseck, D. (2002) 'Wired cities and transnational communications', in L.A. Lievrouw and S. Livingstone (eds), *The Handbook of New Media*, pp. 393–409. London: Sage.

Winston, B. (1986) *Misunderstanding Media*. Cambridge, MA: Harvard University Press.

Wober, J.M. (1978) 'Televised violence and the paranoid perception: the view from Great Britain', *Public Opinion Quarterly*, 42: 315–21.

Wodack, R. and Meyer, M. (eds) (2001) *Methods of Critical Discourse Analysis*. London: Sage.

Wolfenstein, M. and Leites, N. (1947) 'An analysis of themes and plots in motion pictures', *Annals of the American Academy of Political and Social Sciences*, 254: 41–8.

Wolfgram, M.A. (2008) 'Democracy and propaganda: Nato's war in Kosovo', *European Journal of Communication*, 23 (2): 153–71.

Womack, B. (1981) 'Attention maps of ten major newspapers', *Journalism Quarterly*, 58 (2): 260–5.

Woodall, G. (1986) 'Information processing theory and television news', in J.P. Robinson and M. Levy (eds), *The Main Source*, pp. 133–58. Beverly Hills, CA: Sage.

Wright, C.R. (1960) 'Functional analysis and mass communication', *Public Opinion Quarterly*, 24: 606–20.

Wright, C.R. (1974) 'Functional analysis and mass communication revisited', in J.G. Blumler and E. Katz (eds), *The Uses of Mass Communications*, pp. 197–212. Beverly Hills, CA: Sage.

Wu, H.D. (2003) 'Homogeneity around the world? Comparing the systemic determinants of international news flow between developed and developing countries', *Gazette*, 65 (1): 9–24.

Wu, H.D. (2007) 'A brave new world for international news? Exploring the determinants of foreign news on US websites', *International Communication Gazette*, 69 (6): 539–52.

Wu, H.D., Sylvester, J. and Hamilton, J.M. (2002) 'Newspaper provides balance in Palestinian/Israeli reports', *Newspaper Research Journal*, 23 (2): 6–17.

Wu, W., Weaver, D., Owen, D. and Johnstone, J.W.L. (1996) 'Professional rules of Russian and US journalists: a comparative study', *Journalism and Mass Communication Quarterly*, 73 (3): 534–48.

Yang, J. (2003) 'Framing the Nato airstrikes on Kosovo across countries: comparison of Chinese and US newspaper coverage', *Gazette*, 63 (3): 231–49.

Yay, H., Ranasubranuanian, S. and Oliver, M.B. (2008) 'Cultivation effect on quality of life indicators', *Journal of Broadcasting and Electronic Media*, 52 (2): 247–67.

Yin, J. (2008) 'Beyond the four theories of the press: a new model of the Asian and the world press', *Journalism Communication Monographs*, 10 (1): 4–62.

Yoon, Y. (2005) 'Legitimacy, public relations and media access', *Communication Research*, 32 (6): 762–93.

Zaller, J.R. (1997) 'A model of communication effects at the outbreak of the Gulf War', in S. Iyengar and R. Reeves (eds), *Do the Media Govern?*, pp. 296–311. Thousand Oaks, CA: Sage.

Zeno-Zencovich, V. (2008) *Freedom of Expression*. London: Routledge.

Zillmann, D. (1980) 'Anatomy of suspense' in P.H. Tannenbaum (ed.). *The Entertainment Functions of the Media*. Hillsdale, NJ: Lawrence Erlbaum.

Zillmann, D. (2002) 'Exemplification theory of media influence' in J. Bryant and D. Zillmann (eds), *Media Effects*, 2nd edn, pp. 19–42. Hillsdale, NJ: Erlbaum.

Zillmann, D. and Brosius, H.B. (2000) *Exemplification in Communication*. Mahwah, NJ: Erlbaum.

Zillmann, D. and Bryant, J. (1994) 'Entertainment as media effect' in J. Bryant and D. Zillmann (eds), *Media Effects*, 1st edn, pp. 447–59. Hillsdale, NJ: Erlbaum.

Zoch, L.M. and van Slyke Turk, J. (1998) 'Women making news: gender as a variable in source selection and use', 75 (4): 776–88.

Name Index

Page numbers in *italics* refer to figures

Subject Index

Page numbers in *italics* refer to glossary definitions